SECOND EDITION

New Venture Creation

To Tom Moore
Friend, fisherman, and Dean

SECOND EDITION

New Venture Creation

An Innovator's Guide to Entrepreneurship

Marc H. Meyer | Frederick G. Crane

Northeastern University

Los Angeles | London | New Delhi
Singapore | Washington DC

Los Angeles | London | New Delhi
Singapore | Washington DC

FOR INFORMATION:

SAGE Publications, Inc.
2455 Teller Road
Thousand Oaks, California 91320
E-mail: order@sagepub.com

SAGE Publications Ltd.
1 Oliver's Yard
55 City Road
London EC1Y 1SP
United Kingdom

SAGE Publications India Pvt. Ltd.
B 1/I 1 Mohan Cooperative Industrial Area
Mathura Road, New Delhi 110 044
India

SAGE Publications Asia-Pacific Pte. Ltd.
3 Church Street
#10-04 Samsung Hub
Singapore 049483

Acquisitions Editor: Patricia Quinlin
Assistant Editor: Maggie Stanley
Editorial Assistant: Katie Guarino
Production Editor: Brittany Bauhaus
Copy Editor: Talia Greenberg
Typesetter: C&M Digitals (P) Ltd.
Proofreader: Lori Newhouse
Indexer: Kathy Paparchontis
Cover Designer: Gail Buschman
Marketing Manager: Liz Thornton
Permissions Editor: Adele Hutchinson

Copyright © 2014 by SAGE Publications, Inc.

All figures unless otherwise indicated are copyright © 2013 by Marc H. Meyer and Fredrick G. Crane.

Spotlight image used in *Spotlight on Innovation* feature © iStockphoto .com/Zentilia.

Image used in TIP feature © iStockphoto.com/hh5800.

Printed in the United States of America

Library of Congress Cataloging-in-Publication Data

A catalog record of this book is available from the Library of Congress.

9781452257211

This book is printed on acid-free paper.

13 14 15 16 17 10 9 8 7 6 5 4 3 2 1

Brief Contents

Detailed Contents

PART 2: WRITING THE BUSINESS PLAN AND MAKING THE PITCH   177

Chapter 8: Financial Sources for Startups and Corporate Ventures   181

Acknowledgments

This book is the product of many helping hands.

The examples and teaching cases used throughout the book would not have been possible without the contributions of our friends who are entrepreneurs, investors, and corporate innovators. Our deepest thanks go to Rich D'Amore, Harry Keegan, Al Lehnerd, Mel Litvin, Dan McCarthy, Jeff McCarthy, Alan McKim, Jeff Noce, Rob Seliger, and Bob Shillman—individuals upon whom we have relied for continuous advice and support. We also extend our thanks to teaching colleagues who have actively helped us test and refine various sections of the book. These include Gordon Adomzda, Mathew Allen, Dan Gregory, Tucker Marion, Susan Penta, and Dennis Shaughnessy. Other testers include all the students in the eClub and IDEA venture accelerator at Northeastern University who have been using the book to teach and coach their fellow student entrepreneurs. And we so much appreciate the work of Chris Wolfel in helping to develop complementary materials for this book. We are also indebted to Professor Jeffrey Sohl for his unique data set on angel financing. The commitment of all these individuals to entrepreneurship and innovation is an inspiration that goes well beyond the pages of this book. And we remain forever grateful to our spouses, Olga and Doreen, who put up with the shenanigans in writing a book such as this.

We dedicate this work to the lasting memory of Tom Moore, who was our Dean at Northeastern for a decade. Tom was passionate about entrepreneurship. He was a warm, good-hearted man, and for all around him, a constant source of support. To use his own favorite word, Tom was a *brick*—steadfast and loyal—for us, his family, and his many friends and colleagues. He was the best boss we ever had, and we know that many others feel the same way.

The SAGE Publications team has also been an outstanding partner. In particular, we would like to thank our editors, Patricia Quinlin and Lisa Cuevas Shaw. We also wish to thank our copy editor, Talia Greenberg, and production editor, Brittany Bauhaus. The authors and SAGE also gratefully acknowledge the contributions of the following reviewers:

Gordon Adomdza, *Northeastern University*

Jeffrey R. Alves, *Wilkes University*

Wasim Azhar, *University of California, Berkeley*

Vernon Bachor, *St. Cloud State University*

Michael Brizek, *South Carolina State University*

D. M. Thèrèse Byrne, *Boston College, Carroll School of Management*

Shawn M. Carraher, *Minot State University*

Todd Finkle, *The University of Akron*

Ralph Griffith, *Delta College*

Andrew Hardin, *University of Nevada, Las Vegas*

Dmitri Kuksov, *Washington University in St. Louis*

Phil Laplante, *Penn State*

Wally Meyer, *University of Kansas*

John E. Mulford, *Regent University*

Stephanie Newell, *Eastern Michigan University*

Jose Rocha, *Florida International University*

Michael J. Rubach, *University of Central Arkansas*

Gerald Smith, *Boston College*

Colleen Stiles, *University of Colorado, Colorado Springs*

Gregory N. Stock, *University of Colorado, Colorado Springs*

Whittington Vara, *University of Florida*

And we would like to thank the entrepreneurs at Catch a Piece of Maine, Pure Pest Management, Tuatara Corporation/Gilapad, and Akrivis Technologies for allowing us to use screen shots from their Websites for the front cover of this book. They, as many of our former students, represent the special creativity, energy, and determination of the next generation of entrepreneurs who are pioneering new solutions across products, services, software, and biotech.

Introduction

Welcome! This is a book for students of all ages who want to build great companies.

It is likely that you are a person with that entrepreneurial itch, just waiting to be scratched. Why else would you be taking a course on entrepreneurship? As an entrepreneur in the making, we are sure that you are not afraid to try something new, to challenge yourself to accomplish things that others might not, and to take a few calculated risks to realize your entrepreneurial dream. You are probably also someone who relishes the thought of greater independence and control over your work. And we suspect that you have a healthy desire to enjoy the rewards of successful entrepreneurship—that unshakable financial independence that should come after a number of years of hard, focused work.

These personal characteristics are important and good. However, to build a strong venture requires other qualities of mind and spirit. It takes understanding what is, and what is not, a good market in which to venture forth; it takes gaining true insight into those products and services customers really wish to buy and how to ensure that they take pleasure in what they buy; and it requires that you thoughtfully determine how your venture will make money in these pursuits. And no venture succeeds without a carefully considered team, one whose collective thinking cannot only produce a good startup, but weather the trials and tribulations of growth. Each is a skill—an understanding—that can be taught through a set of reasonable, pragmatic frameworks and methods. That is how we are going to proceed in this book. It is a hands-on guide into the thinking necessary for a successful startup.

The chapters that follow are designed to create a bridge between your venturesome nature and the plan required to launch a great company. It is packed with approaches and methods that we have used as entrepreneurs and have improved over the years by watching our friends and students venture forth. And while these methods apply generally to all types of entrepreneurship—corporate ventures as well as startups—our focus here is not on "lifestyle" businesses, such as a small specialty retail store or monthly industry newsletter. Rather, our lens is set on ventures that can make you and your investors a lot of money. The majority of these will be *equity financed* either before or fairly soon after startup, either by angel investors, venture capitalists (VCs), or larger corporations. While many will be "high-tech," on the surface, just as many will be more traditional in industry focus, providing products and services for consumers and industry that invariably use technology in one form or another. As examples in the book, for example, you will see a pet food startup, a medical software company, and a consulting service. All—and so many more—are wonderful businesses that can be planned and launched using the methods in this book.

Innovation is at the core of our design for this book. The innovative idea—refined and tested with target customers—is essential before writing a single page of a business plan. And the innovative idea itself must be accompanied by a robust business model—a way to make money. One need only look at a company such as Apple to see that sometimes the business model itself (iTunes) can be just as innovative and exciting as the technology itself (iPhone). Innovation, as a grounding concept, also applies just as strongly to traditional products and services as it does to categories such as software, biotech, or new types of energy. You can start a highly innovative popcorn company, an equally innovative student travel services company, or even a lobster business that is so creative in its distribution model that the student entrepreneur wins the Small Business Administration Entrepreneur of the Year Award! Just take a look at some of the cases on the Website for this book at SAGE Publications (www.sagepub.com/meyer2e).

Innovation—the application of science and technology to solve problems among individuals, corporations, and society—is the foundation of great startups. And we prefer that the science and technology already be largely proven and working so that the entrepreneur does not have to wait for five years to launch products or services to market. Moreover, to innovate in a traditional industry can be just as exciting and productive as to innovate in an emerging industry. Just take a look at the MyM&M'S case on the Website to see how a group of innovative corporate entrepreneurs figured out both a product and a service that allowed them to charge more than ten times the price per pound compared to a standard M&M Candy! That's innovative, wonderfully entrepreneurial, and inspirational for any large corporation.

So as you prepare to venture forward with this book, know that there are no limits to the bounds of your innovative energies: a high-tech business or a low-tech business; a product or a service; a startup or a venture within an established corporation; or a market in your current country or one in a region abroad. There are no limits other than your own creativity and a steadfast willingness to validate your ideas with the very target customers you expect to pay for and use your products and services.

For all these reasons, you can see why we chose our subtitle: *An Innovator's Guide to Entrepreneurship.* Innovation is at the core of successful entrepreneurship, a necessary first step before writing a business plan or developing a financial model in Excel.

Entrepreneurship as a Learning Experience

The beautiful thing about planning a new venture is that it is a time when you can experiment with very little cost of failure. And it is through these experiments that you come to that winning combination of products, services, branding, distribution, pricing, and operations that is the foundation of a truly lasting venture. Business planning is also where you can test out team members and learn about those sets of skills that you will need to launch and scale a high-growth company.

There is a process to entrepreneurial learning. It is a myth that successful entrepreneurs sit alone in their basements brilliantly coming up with new ideas in isolation from the real world: *at least, not the successful entrepreneurs we know.* The innovative entrepreneur is guided by a clear understanding of the target customer. The entrepreneur observes, meets, and talks with customers to generate concepts. His or her moment of insight comes from that interaction. A solution to the customers' problems emerges, sometimes suddenly, in a flash of time, but most often gradually, through constant refinement, with more talking, more trial and error, and more work to design something that is truly special. And once the entrepreneur's product or service is launched, and those friendly users become paying customers, the learning doesn't stop. In fact, the entrepreneur's learning intensifies. It usually takes a year or so of business operations for the entrepreneur to truly learn the best products, services, and business models needed to build a high-growth company. Seasoned investors *know* this. The initial business plan has to be good—in fact, *very* good—but still, investors know that it is really only the basis for learning what will really work. Today's investors are looking for four major elements in new ventures: (a) a customer-vetted concept aimed at a growing market, (b) a dynamic product or services strategy that will exploit that opportunity, (c) a powerful business model that can generate profit as well as revenue, and (d) a team who is both balanced and skilled, with industry experience that can figure out the winning combination of the first three elements and then *execute* on the plan. The investors' money is a commitment to the entrepreneur to get to market as quickly as possible so that the real learning can begin, and from there, build a world-class company. Great companies, and the people managing them, never stop learning, adapting, and improving.

This book is substantially different than those traditionally offered to most students in entrepreneurship courses. Most books put an "idea" at the very beginning of the process, where the entrepreneur has an "Aha!" moment, recognizes a promising business opportunity, and proceeds immediately to begin writing a business plan and make detailed financial projections. All this detail is supposed to flow from that flash of inspiration—an impossible burden for the entrepreneur and his or her team. But many young entrepreneurs think that this "Aha!" approach is the norm. They think they need to be smarter than everyone else and know all the answers from the start in order to raise a penny of venture capital and build a business. We have yet to meet anyone who is consistently and reliably *that smart*.

Few succeed with this approach. According to the U.S. Small Business Administration, 78% of new businesses fail. While the reasons for failure are many—inadequate financing, poor management skills, or product/technology problems among them—our experience is that the biggest culprit is the founder's inadequate attention to the marketplace. Sure, you are smart. But your target customers are the true source of wisdom. Be smart in the sense of listening to customers to understand the entire ecosystem of products, systems, and services around them, as well as the companies that provide them. Then you can apply the other side of your brain or bring others on board to cleverly create solutions that solve unsolved problems, those nuggets of penetrating insight that you have learned by listening carefully to customers. Your goal is to allow your users to do things that they could not do before, to bring them new levels of satisfaction and pleasure in their work or leisure, and with that, new levels of economy, sustainability, and social good. None of this can happen if you sit alone in a room and think alone. Learn from customers; vet your ideas with them; be brutally realistic about competitors; and then, empowered by your customer and competitor insights, take the steps necessary to build a great company.

Therefore, while it is tempting to rush immediately from an "Aha!" to a business plan, you are not going to do that if you follow the methods of this book. Even if you are the most strong-willed sort of person, one who readily falls in love with your own ideas, we are going to ask you to set the urge to quickly write the business plan aside and think about your target customers. We will also ask you to learn the needs and motivations of the retailers or salespeople who will sell your products and services, and to think just as carefully about competitors. Your chance of having a great business design will increase dramatically!

You are going to develop innovative ideas—we call them Venture Concepts—and test them with actual customers. Pass GO and then write the business plan that will stand above others that are less well informed. And in this learning stage, there is also a very low "cost of failure": you have taken no money yet, either from a customer or an investor. Why not take the opportunity to experiment? You will learn so much. Then, armed with what you have learned, you will be ready to pull the trigger, and your aim is far more likely to be spot-on. It will be the voice of the market calling the shots.

The Design of This Book

Figure I.1 provides the design of the entrepreneurial learning process of this book that flows from the discussion above. Our approach is first to help you get the innovative concept down pat. This is Part I of the book. Only then do we help you develop the pragmatic financial projections, the tight cohesive business plan, and the pitch needed to raise startup capital to get the venture up and running. This is Part II of the book.

- Part I—**Defining the Focus of Your Venture**—teaches you how to approach the learning needed to start a winning company. Successful ventures are *focused*. Therefore, it is our job to help you define a clear focus. Again, it is based on a process of learning how to:
- **Define your target industry** and the type of company—product, service, or pure distribution—that you wish to start in that industry. It is great if your industry or your piece of a larger

industry is already substantial in terms of sales or customer demand. It is even more important that it is *growing*. Market growth works to the entrepreneur's advantage. This is the first step to shaping a *venture's focus*.

- **Define your target customers** you wish to serve in that industry. As experienced entrepreneurs will tell you, some customers are better than others for launching a venture. It is your job to find out the *who* and the *why* for this all-important second step in creating a focus for a venture.

- **Define the needs and wants of your target customers.** This is an essential element of the secret sauce of any venture. Understanding the needs, fears, frustrations, and desires of users and buyers is so very important for any entrepreneur, because this allows you then to design solutions that are unique, compelling, and value-rich. We must also differentiate between *users* and *buyers*. They are often not the same. For example, we can create a great new food product that appeals to the needs of health-conscious consumers, but we also need to understand just as much the merchandising and financial needs of the different types of retailers who might sell our products.

- **Define your solutions for customers.** This is the design of your solutions, the basic functions, features, and formats of your products and/or services—an offering that brings clear performance, pleasure, and value to target customers in a way that is special in the industry. From a single product or service concept, we can then create a more fully featured product line or services strategy, offering choice and variety to customers. We think of this as defining the "good, better, best" for products and services, all enabled by common approaches and "platforms" that empower everything the venture offers.

- **Define the business model.** This is how your venture is going to make money. You must determine how you plan to charge customers, how much you will charge, and how you will make customers pay for your products or services. You must also decide how you plan to do R&D, production (manufacturing or service fulfillment or Web services hosting), as well as sales and distribution. These four decisions will have a profound impact on how your venture will make money.

- **Define the positioning for your solutions and your business model.** *Positioning* describes how your solutions stack up in terms of performance and price relative to specific competitors. From this positioning, we can then create a dynamic branding strategy. *Branding* contains the imagery, messaging, and communications that you will use to tell prospective customers that your company has the hottest stuff in town. Strong branding is essential for software, industrial products, and financial services just as much it is for consumer products or consumer services. The entrepreneur needs to communicate *an edge*.

Put all six elements together and you have a clearly focused, and for its intended target, a powerfully focused Venture Concept. And in the spirit of entrepreneurial learning, we need to make sure that this is the *right focus*. At this point, it is just a Venture Concept—an idea—that you hope will be the basis of a powerful company. To validate the Venture Concept, we will teach you how to conduct a quick, customer-based Reality Check where you test your solutions, business model, and positioning against a reasonably sized group of target customers—say, just 20 or so. It is the capstone deliverable of Part I. From this work you will have the insight and learning you need to write a great business plan.

If the result of your Reality Check is not as successful as you might wish, do what other entrepreneurs have always done: Reformulate or fine-tune specific elements of your Venture Concept and test it again with target customers. This is the essence of entrepreneurial learning, and you are doing it before real money is at stake. If you first *innovate* well—which means following the steps in Part I of the book—writing your business plan is going to be a snap. And it will be a business plan that is all the more likely to please your professor and catch the interest of investors.

Part II of the book—**Writing the Business Plan and Making the Pitch**—dives right into the mechanics of implementing a customer-vetted Venture Concept. We will guide you through the process of:

- *Creating realistic financial projections,* where time to first revenue, revenue growth over the first three to five years, and profit from operations are all equally important. If done well, numbers are far more than just numbers; *they tell a compelling story about the venture as a business.* That is a story we want to teach you how to craft and sell to investors. And to do this, you need first to understand the different types of investors involved in the venture game. These investors are "the customers" for this part of the process, and they can be as different as the various types of customers who exist in your target market. We have a particular eye on angel investors because in this day and age, that is where the majority of "seed" or startup capital comes for our students' and friends' ventures. Venture capitals tend to come in a little later, a year or more after the entrepreneur has learned *what will really work!*

- *Creating a concise but powerful business plan.* The good news is the vast majority of investors don't want to carry around and read a 50-page business plan. The bad news is that it takes some very good thinking to write a tight, clean, integrated 15- to 20-page plan. Your efforts in Part I will give you a huge advantage because you will have already done a lot of the hard thinking. It is a matter of connecting your financial projections with the rest of your strategies, and forming around these a solid team, both inside the company and advising it. In each section of the business planning guide in Chapter 11, we also do our best to tell you what investors are *actually thinking* and what they expect to find when they read a particular section of the plan. More than relying on our own experiences as entrepreneurs and angel investors, we ran part of the book by a group of friends who are angels, VCs, and corporate executives (for corporate ventures). Their comments are a little devilish and fun. It's important stuff to know for the entrepreneur writing a business plan.

- **Creating a compelling pitch.** You've written a great plan and have been asked to present it. It's your time in the sun, the 15 to 20 minutes that will be make or break you in the eyes of your professor, or even better, an investor. There are techniques that will increase your chances of success—and it is these that we will teach you in the last chapter of the book. It all comes down to telling four "stories": the story of your customers, the story of your solutions, the story of how you will make money—and, of course, the story of your team. Investors want to see individuals who are not only smart about their customers' needs—how best to serve them and how to make money in the process—but who also are passionate and committed to the venture idea. You cannot fake a passion for a business. It needs to run deep. And this type of enthusiasm for a new business is a natural outcome of engaging in the innovation and entrepreneurial learning process in Part I of the book. Investors will see this. Whether they put their money into your idea or not, you will have earned their respect, and from this, references to other investors. "This is not my cup of tea," they might say, "but I know someone who will really like this venture. I'm going to give them a call and set you up. Let me know what happens." Most entrepreneurs, regardless of age, visit several dozen or more potential investors before they strike gold. And each time, your pitch will get better and better—because just like solutions design, you will be learning each step of the way.

Pathways to Success _____

For many readers, graduation will hopefully see you launch an exciting new venture. As business professors, we've observed scores of students develop and test Venture Concepts while still in school. Quite a few of these students hit the ground running after graduation. Funded

<table>
<tr><th>Part I</th><th>Part II</th></tr>
</table>

Part I

Defining the Focus of Your Venture

- Define the industry, the specific segment in that industry, and the attractiveness of that segment.
- Define the target customer group in that segment, differentiating between users and buyers.
- Define the needs of customers and drive that into the design of interesting, innovative, and compelling solutions.
- Define the product/service strategy, its underlying platforms, product/service choices, and an IP strategy.
- Define the business model, for example, how the business makes money based on revenue, R&D, supply, and channel strategies.
- Define the competitive positioning and branding for the venture.
- Test and validate the venture concept and its business model with target customers.

Result: A customer-vetted venture concept.

Part II

Create Financial Writing the Business Plan and Making the Pitch

- Identify appropriate investors for your venture, for different stages of growth.
- Develop pragmatic financial projections.
- Develop a "tight," cohesive written business plan.
- Design the venture team needed to launch the venture, and then to drive the first stage of growth.
- Develop a compelling pitch for investors, learn to deliver it with confidence, and anticipate likely questions.

Result: A "powerful" business plan and pitch tuned to the right types of investors for your venture.

Figure I.1   The Structure and Flow of the Book

by family and friends, or by "angel" investors, many have succeeded. In fact, many of the case studies on this textbook's Website are based on those students. And, not surprisingly, we have taught a number of students who cannot wait for graduation. They, like one of your authors, have actually started companies while still in school *and still managed to complete their academic programs*. Yes, we know that the founders of some of our highest-growth technology companies—Microsoft, Apple, and Facebook—all dropped out of college. But if you are young and have a burning passion to start a company, *please think twice* before dropping out of school to start your company. Do both—work twice as hard and be the master of your own destiny. You will want that degree at some point in time. Based on our personal experience, with the right team and very careful time management, you should be able to do both. Most often, it is a matter of playing Dr. Jekyll and Mr. Hyde for only a year or so before you graduate. And if you are an MBA student or using this book as part of an alumni program, you already know how to work on many different fronts at the same time. Quietly, assuredly, prepare your venture for launch as you are about to complete your degree.

Many young entrepreneurs, however, do not make the leap until they gain three to five years of work experience upon graduation, have learned how to manage people and projects, and have saved enough money to self-fund the earliest stage of a venture. If that's your plan, here is our advice: Work first for a top-flight company—a market leader in your target industry; meet highly qualified and effective individuals who have different skill sets; and do everything you can to get to know customers, what they wish to buy, and how best to sell to them. Never stop thinking about various ventures that you might launch into the market to serve those customers. When the timing is right—and don't wait too long!—form your team with the people you have met either at work or at school, apply the methods in this book, and launch that venture with all the passion and fortitude that you can muster.

There is yet another venue in which the entrepreneurial spirit expresses itself: inside large corporations. We have designed this book to also be effective for corporate ventures. Corporate venturing—or "intrapreneurship"—has its own challenges. Corporate entrepreneurs, for example, must deal with the power of the status quo and must compete for the attention of senior management. Innovating within a mature corporation, however, can be incredibly exciting and a great way to cut through many layers of management to interface directly with top-level executives. Moreover, large corporations already have the distribution channels and other assets that startup entrepreneurs struggle to achieve. Being a successful corporate entrepreneur can serve as a fast path to the C-suite.

To help you apply the frameworks and methods of this book, we have developed Reader Exercises at the end of each chapter. We hope you take these seriously and apply them to your venture development. These exercises embody the frameworks and methods of the book, one or two key frameworks that are presented as templates, and visual representations of an approach for thinking about and solving a task or problem. We also hope that you work in a small team. Working in a team in a project-focused course not only fosters the shared learning that comes with discussion, but it also makes the work a lot more fun. Moreover, successful companies may have a visionary entrepreneur, but successful ventures invariably are created by strong, diverse teams whose members learn together and can trust one another's commitment and skill sets. Whether you do this alone or in a team, remember to be flexible at every step along the way. *Innovate, test, and improve* is a mantra of this book. *Integrating the different pieces of a venture*—industry, customers, solutions, business model, positioning, and branding—*into a cohesive whole* is another. Let these two central ideas, plus an unwavering enthusiasm for serving customers better than anyone else, guide your journey.

Marc H. Meyer and Fredrick G. Crane
Boston, MA

PART 1

Defining the Focus of Your Venture

Defining and Testing Your Venture (Before Writing the Business Plan!)

The process for creating a new venture is just that—creation. It involves ideation, refinement, testing, and more refinement. Unlike producing a work of art, however, creating a new business requires that you ideate not only what you will do as a business, but how you will make money doing what you do—for example, manufacturing and selling products, or producing and selling services.

Within the creation of a new business, there is a balance between discovery of new technologies and the application of proven technologies to solve people's problems. It is easy to get confused by the difference between "invention" and "innovation." As an entrepreneur, you must understand these differences because your path toward success will likely be very different if you are focused on one or the other.

Invention is the discovery of new science and technology. For example, one of our former students led the team who developed a new flexible solar film that can be layered on top of radios, backpacks, vehicles, and so forth. A technology-intensive university spin-off—which is a company originating from a university research lab—typically takes years to realize its first dollar of real product revenue because there is so much research and development to do to get useful commercial products ready for market. Despite the great promise of his flexible solar film technology, this student knew he was in for a long haul. Not only did the "product" have to be perfected for specific applications, but the company had to design and develop an entirely new, capital-intensive manufacturing process for producing the flexible solar film. And a long haul it was! (This company raised over $100 million over a decade to commercialize this "power plastic" film—developing tremendous intellectual property along the way. It was also a challenged business, however, because while its applications were myriad in number, each was small in terms of generated revenue.) "Invention" takes years. The front end of invention is typically best left to a well-funded university or to corporate research labs.

In most cases, however, neither the startup nor the corporate entrepreneur have the time to wait for what often turns out to be a decade or more to see if a disruptive technology actually works and can be scaled into commercial form. For the entrepreneur involved in an invention business that takes many years to fulfill, hopefully there's enough money left over at the end of the discovery process to get on with the business of actually making money with the technology.

Biotechnology startups are the classic "invention" venture. Most need to raise $10 million just to get started and another $50 million to get to animal trials—even before testing a single drug on humans! Not many people can raise that sort of money. Nonetheless, the rewards can be immense, with hundreds of millions, and sometimes billions, of dollars garnered by successful therapies.

Innovation, on the other hand, is the application of science and technology to solve problems for consumers, companies, governments, or society at large. Entrepreneurs, in particular, tend to apply their innovative thinking to find and address *new market applications* (e.g., new sets of emerging problems, new challenges, and new opportunities). For example, we see myriad mobile software development startups creating new applications—for mobile advertising, mobile health monitoring, or smartphone-based financial transactions—based on existing communications standards or protocols and published software development toolkits from Apple, Google (Android), or some other major company. Or it might be the application of known nutritional science to create a new product line of healthy, great-tasting snacks for people—or their pets! Or it might be applying known materials to create new energy-efficient or sustainable household goods.

Regardless, using an existing set of hardware and software tools, chemicals, or any type of elemental ingredients does more than just reduce an important element of risk for the entrepreneur: An innovation focus is a market-driven focus. The drive becomes to understand what customers need and to design products or services to satisfy that need. It also allows the entrepreneur to focus heavily on the go-to-market aspects of being a successful business—the branding, the distribution or selling, and the additional follow-on services that the business can provide to customers.

This holds equally true for corporate entrepreneurs reading this book. You want to be in the position of taking and deploying existing—or, if it's new, well-proven—technology out of your company's research labs to new market applications to create new streams of revenue for your corporation within a year, or perhaps two, and at the very most, three. Try to select technologies that are ready to hit the ground running.

Trust us: It is best *not* to rush blindly into the startup process. Better to do it step by step, answering one set of questions first, and then tackling the next, integrating the whole into a powerful plan. This will help make your entrepreneurial learning process much more efficient.

Successful entrepreneurs and investors want to know answers to a series of questions for any venture:

1. *What is your target industry, and more specifically, what is the segment or niche of that industry that you wish to target?* Entrepreneurs focus on specific parts of an industry for startup through a process generally called *market segmentation*. A segment is generally viewed as a large part of an even larger industry; a niche is a smaller part within a specific industry segment (for example, the electric car niche within the passenger auto segment of the automobile/transportation industry). Entrepreneurs generally first succeed by targeting their work in a specific niche. After becoming a market leader in that niche, they expand to adjacent niches, or for the most ambitious, perhaps entirely new industry segments. But to enjoy success, that initial industry target needs to show customer demand and growth. Is there the demand and future growth in your industry target—the sheer market power—to reward you for all your hard work? Is your target segment/niche a good place to start a new venture over the coming decade, a good place for you and your investors to make money? The process of selecting that industry target—creating a laser focus on a particular part of an industry—is the first important step in defining a venture focus. The best way to show a strong industry target is to gather *data*—as much as you need to prove to yourself that it is an excellent area in which to start a company. That data come from government sources, industry trade associations, trade shows, or articles in publications. Much of this information is also available with diligent searches on the Web.

2. *Who, specifically, is the target customer in your selected industry, and what market potential does that target customer represent?* Within an industry segment/niche, there is often more than one type of customer. For example, in healthcare, there are children, teenagers, college students, young professionals, Baby Boomers, and seniors—all with different healthcare needs and different preferences for services. A younger person with chronic medical problems will be more receptive to the use of computers and sensors for home healthcare monitoring than elderly customers typically will, particularly those with cognitive disabilities. You, as the entrepreneur, must be very specific about which type of customer you wish to serve first with the solutions you have in mind. In other types of businesses, this choice might be in which city to start a services company, and then over time, to expand to other cities. Moreover, the entrepreneur needs to be crystal-clear about whether there is a difference between who buys and who uses the product or service. Answering this set of questions typically involves field research, visiting different types of customers in their places of work, leisure, or care, and seeing which ones need new solutions most.

3. With a target customer within a target industry segment/niche in hand, *what are the needs, fears, frustrations, and buying preferences of the target customer? And how do these needs translate into the design of a distinct new product or service?* The key to

success here is to understand how customers themselves define their problems. This takes careful listening and meaningful conversation. We think of this as "getting into the hearts and minds of users." Then, as innovators, you and your team can then best determine how to satisfy these needs. Is your target customer the building owner who needs energy management systems to automatically power equipment on and off to save money, or the municipality that requires flexible mounting systems to place and control solar panels throughout city property and buildings? Is it the small-business owner who is lost and confused about how to publish information on a Website, track his or her own customers in some sort of CRM (customer relationship management) system, and anticipate what he or she might need next? All are examples of understanding the compelling needs or different types of target customers in a clear, simple way. *That is what you want for your venture.* Once again, field research with customers in their place of use (which means in their homes or offices, not yours) is the best way to gain these insights.

4. *Using your basic product or service idea as a foundation, how can you develop a powerful product line or services strategy that offers a range of choices for different specific types of buyers in your target customer group?* No enterprise makes a lot of money on a "onesie"—that is, a single product or even a single service. Rather, ventures require a fully featured product line or a range of services—based on a common core—that can be tailored to specific customers within your target customer group. This requires you to create a product line or services strategy that provides variety and choice. Moreover, your products and services must have an elegant design—simple, powerful, and visually or emotionally appealing for the user. This is just as true for a business service, a newly designed piece of medical equipment, or an industrial machine as it is for a consumer product sitting on a retail shelf. *Design matters.* The best way to develop a winning design is through trial and error. This means designing your product or service on paper or computer, figuring out the best and least expensive way to prototype it, showing the result to target customers, getting their feedback, and then improving it through perhaps two or three successive iterations. These days, getting money from professional investors requires the entrepreneur to show not only a great business plan but a customer-vetted prototype as well.

5. With a target customer and a product or service concept in hand, *how is the business going to make money?* This is defining the *business model* for a venture. Business models for a venture can be just as much a point of competitive advantage as any specific products or services. Investors want to see a business model that is both pragmatic and exciting. The definition of a business model requires that you think about the structure and type of revenue from selling your products or services, as well as how you will do R&D, manufacturing or fulfillment, and distribution/selling. Also, the process of defining a business model bounces back to impact the design of a product or service, or even the choice of a target customer. For example, you might find that your initial target customer doesn't want to spend a lot of money on new products or services, but another group does. Or you learn that it is a good opportunity to sell follow-on services in addition to a product—and adjust your product line/services strategy accordingly. Regardless, defining a business model is the foundation for projections of revenue, expenses, operating profit, and capital investment needed for business planning later on.

6. *How will the venture differentiate from other companies already serving your target customers?* You might think you don't have competitors, but 999 times out of 1,000, you do, even for the most unique venture idea. And sometimes the customer you seek could be your competitor. In short, they could make a decision to make/do it themselves. The key is to truly differentiate yourself—make yourself distinctive enough to create a separation between you and your competitors. From this, you can then define a branding strategy, for example, how the venture communicates the

special nature of its products or services, and hopefully, premium value. Just look at Apple. It is both the master of elegant design for its computers, phones, and services, and the premium positioning of these offerings. Its branding communicates performance, fun and ease of use, and social consciousness. Most young entrepreneurs are so optimistic about their commercial offerings and business models that they fail to adequately consider current competition and competitive responses. Indeed, a lack of competitive due diligence leaves you subject to nasty surprises right after launch. And well before that, potential investors will dig into your competitive analysis. It is amazing just how much information can be surmised about competitors by examining their own Websites. You also need to learn how to define both your competitive positioning and brand communications from three important perspectives shown so well by Apple: *functional branding* (objective price/performance), *emotional branding* (the personal bond and attachment the consumer has with the brand), and *social branding* (the demonstration of social principles and behavior toward society and the environment).

7. *How will we know that the venture idea—its proposed commercial offerings, its business model, its competitive positioning and branding—all make sense for the target customer?* These elements of the venture idea all need to be vetted with prospective customers in the context of current and emerging competitors. We call this *conducting a reality check* on your venture idea. This reality check must be performed as a field-based exercise with target end-users and buyers. Any seasoned investor is going to ask after hearing your pitch, "Those new products and services sound great, but how do we know that any of this is really going to fly with target customers?" or, "Your business model sounds unique and potentially a source of sustained competitive advantage, but has anyone else ever succeeded in making money this way? Is it really feasible?" Being able to anticipate these questions and answer them with some degree of certainty—which means having data—is where you need to be to launch your venture.

We will help you explore these questions and develop answers in the next seven chapters of this book. Each of the basic questions above has its own chapter. We want you to read these chapters and apply the exercises to your own projects before writing the formal business plan. In other words, we want you to perform all the in-market learning and thinking first before writing a single page of the business plan. There are no shortcuts. Sure, you might get lucky and write a quick plan, raise a little money, and launch some products or services in a month or two. However, unless you are extraordinarily brilliant or have tried a similar type of business before and failed but are going at it again with the benefit of your prior mistakes, the chances are that you will have to scrap most of what was in your short-and-quick business plan and reinvent your business on the fly.

In contrast, going through the first section of this book successfully will make the second part—writing the actual plan—relatively straightforward. It will also greatly increase the chances of success in terms of raising money and executing with that money. You will bring all the research, insight, and integration of ideas from Part I into your business-plan writing and money-raising efforts. In short, the time spent in the first section will pay handsome dividends later on.

Now, *we hope you are ready not only to work but also to have fun in doing that work.* Think of this as not just working for a grade but working for yourself, for your own future. Creating something from scratch—seeing a business launch and grow from simply an idea in your head—is one of the most rewarding, exciting, and energizing things that anyone can do in their lives. It doesn't always work, but when a venture succeeds, *there is nothing else quite like it* for the mind and spirit.

1

Defining Your Industry Focus and the Type of Business You Want to Start

The Purpose of the Chapter

The biggest mistake a would-be entrepreneur can make is to follow blindly his or her passion about a particular invention or technology without regard or knowledge about the industry and applications to which that invention or technology will be applied. To be successful as an entrepreneur, you must select that part of an industry—that industry segment, and most often, initially a specific niche within that segment for startup—that can reward your hard work with customers who need what you have to sell and will pay you for it. Select a strong industry target—one that is growing and hungry for innovation, new products, and services—and with proper execution, your innovative idea can be the basis of a wonderful company.

This is a market-driven approach to entrepreneurship as opposed to one where you simply create technology and pray that it finds a good market and application to serve over time. A lot of technical entrepreneurs, for example, try this approach—and very few of these succeed in building great companies. You need a clear industry focus that drives you all the way to specific solutions for specific types of customers. Successful entrepreneurship rarely happens by accident. Sure, timing is extremely important, but being in the position to take advantage of fortuitous circumstances is what entrepreneurship is all about. Though "hunches" or intuition may open your eyes to real commercial possibilities, they may also lead you into a trap, where even a great idea is pulled down the drain by the overwhelming forces of a declining industry.

Also, if you are going to raise money from professional investors—angels, VCs, or larger corporations—*you are going to have to prepare a bold defense for the attractiveness of your target industry segment/niche* with data—facts that prove size and growth.

This chapter describes provides methods for you to:

1. Assess whether your own personal characteristics are well suited for venturing

2. Define a target industry, understand its essential business dynamics, and select the market niche in that industry where opportunity beckons most

3. See if there is a match between your experience, education, family connections, and personal passion with that market niche

4. Determine the type of business (product, system, or service; a standard money-making company or a *social venture*) with the greatest potential for success

Your own background and personality are critically important factors in determining the venture you wish to start. This chapter discusses the dynamic between your own personal experiences and interests, and the market realities needed to support a prosperous business. Entrepreneurs have passion for their new Venture Concepts. However, just because you are wildly enthusiastic about a particular hobby, business, or technology does not mean that starting a company based just on that personal interest will be worth the effort. This chapter will help you think about these two sides of the entrepreneurial coin and, we hope, strike a balance.

Successful entrepreneurship requires you to be brutally honest and pragmatic about the facts on the ground. You must do your utmost to gather the best information available around any particular decision, and then take the information you gather seriously. You cannot pretend that a "weak" industry will suddenly turn around and become a fertile ground for a new venture. If you come up empty, you must check other segments of that industry—and perhaps new, emerging niches within those industry segments—for better hunting. If nothing else, entrepreneurship requires persistence and an ever-positive attitude. You can do it!

Learning Objectives

After reading this chapter, you should be able to:

- Assess your ability to "take it on the chin" and come up swinging! This is what we call "dispositional optimism"—an essential trait for entrepreneurs.

- Take stock of your personal background as a foundation for selecting an industry target.

- Gather information on the attractiveness of a particular industry and the segments and niches within that industry.

- Gather information on the startup, investment, mergers and acquisitions, and new product and technology action within an industry.

- Use industry analysis to define *the industry focus* for your venture.

Are You Suited for Entrepreneurship?

There are some fundamental personal characteristics that separate successful entrepreneurs from unsuccessful ones. Do you have what it takes to succeed in the rough and tumble world of entrepreneurship? Just as important: Do your teammates have the "right stuff" for venturing?

There is no single type of entrepreneur. Some are highly educated; others don't finish college. Some are technology oriented; others, not in the slightest. Some are men, and increasingly, many are women. While many of you are reading this book in an American or European country, by your e-mails we know that many others are sitting in places such as Bangalore, São Paulo, Shanghai, Istanbul, or elsewhere. And while many entrepreneurs start companies while still in or just out of college, others do so much later on as a second or new career after decades in a major corporation. Trying to define a single type of entrepreneur—by age, gender, country, ethnicity, or background—is a fool's errand. Don't ever let someone else tell you that you can't or shouldn't become an entrepreneur.

Research has shown that there are other certain personal characteristics associated with successful entrepreneurs. Entrepreneurs strive for independence and autonomy in their decision making. They have a burning desire to control their own destiny (even though successful entrepreneurs will tell you that the truth is that *customers* control the venture's destiny, and for others, *investors* have a pretty important say as well). Perhaps most important, while entrepreneurs certainly enjoy the financial benefits of success, most of the entrepreneurs that we know do not start companies with the primary objective of making lots of money—at least, not at first. Successful entrepreneurs define success beyond strictly financial terms. Rather, the burning desire is to solve important problems in society, at work, or in leisure. There is the also the thrill of creating something new, of building a team, of making one's mark on industry and society. We know this because in addition to being professors, both your authors have started and grown successful companies. Sure, the money is nice, but it comes well after the fact for most startups, and the thrill of starting and growing a company—despite the hard work and inevitable setbacks—is beyond compare.[1]

But the most important questions to ask yourself at this point are: Do I have the commitment, motivation, skills, and talents to start and build a venture? And can I locate individuals to join my management team who have the skills and talents to help me succeed?

We suggest that you start your personal assessment by honestly comparing yourself to successful entrepreneurs. Perhaps the most important personal skill comes under that elusive heading called "leadership." Even young entrepreneurs have a good sense if they have the makings of a strong team leader—which means building and motivating a team. You also have to be comfortable making decisions for and with the team in a world of imperfect information. Successful ventures invariably have a strong leader.

Beyond leadership characteristics, successful entrepreneurs possess the following personal characteristics:[2]

- *Have drive and energy.* Successful entrepreneurs have the ability to work long hours for extended periods of time and can still function at a high level.

- *Have self-confidence.* Successful entrepreneurs believe in themselves and their ability to achieve success.

- *Can set challenging and realistic objectives.* Successful entrepreneurs have the ability to set challenging and realistic objectives.

- *Have long-term involvement.* Successful entrepreneurs make a commitment to the business and fully dedicate themselves to the business for the long haul.

- *Use money as a scorecard.* Successful entrepreneurs use money as a scorecard or measure for how well the venture is doing as opposed to an end in itself.

- *Solve problems.* Successful entrepreneurs have an innate desire to solve problems and persist until they achieve positive outcomes.

- *Can tolerate uncertainty.* Entrepreneurs must feel comfortable making tough decisions without perfect information. This ability to thrive under conditions of high uncertainty differentiates the entrepreneur from, say, a scientist who needs to resolve ambiguity before proceeding forward.

---

[1]Roberts, E. B. (1997). *Entrepreneurs in High Technology: Lessons from MIT and Beyond.* New York: Oxford University Press.

[2]This section is based on Dingee, A., Haslett, B., & Smollen, L. (1997). Characteristics of a successful entrepreneurial management team. In *Pratt's Guide to Venture Capital Sources* (pp. 23–28, Venture Economics, NY.); and Crane, F., & Crane, E. Dispositional optimism and entrepreneurial success. *The Psychologist-Manager Journal* 10(1), 1–13.

- *Can quickly and readily learn from failure.* Successful entrepreneurs learn from failure and use those lessons to avoid future failures. They accept failure as part of the entrepreneurial journey, but they are not discouraged by it.
- *Use constructive criticism.* Successful entrepreneurs seek out constructive criticism from informed experts, and they act on it.
- *Take initiative.* Successful entrepreneurs take initiative when they see opportunities. They also seek out situations where personal initiative can pay off.
- *Make good use of resources.* Successful entrepreneurs readily identify and use appropriate expertise and assistance to achieve their objectives.
- *Compete against self-imposed standards.* Successful entrepreneurs establish their own benchmarks of performance and focus on competing with themselves to improve personal performance. They don't need someone else to set goals for them. Successful entrepreneurs drive themselves hard.

While this list may seem long, every point is worthwhile and important. You should rate yourself on each of these characteristics (strong, average, or weak). To give these ratings a dose of reality, compare yourself to other individuals you know who rate strongly on these characteristics. If you rate yourself average or weak on most of these characteristics, it's a warning sign that a career in a larger, more mature organization might be the best ticket for you—at least for the time being. We have found that business skills are simply not enough to succeed. The psychology of an entrepreneur is essential for success. Granted, no single entrepreneur possesses all these attributes, yet many are ones that you can begin to practice on a daily basis, such as setting clear and challenging objectives for yourself or using constructive criticism to the best-possible result.

Additionally, entrepreneurs want to work in small companies! Don't forget that when you encounter a seasoned professional who wants to join your venture but comes from a large corporate environment. He or she may want to be a VP in a venture capital–backed startup with a hunk of stock, but has that person ever scheduled his or her own appointments, made the pot of coffee for others first thing in the morning, cleaned up the conference area for visitors, worked on a steel desk purchased from Craigslist or a discount furniture store, slept in travel hotels, and more generally, understood that the company's money is his or her money? These are tough questions to ask—but they need asking!

We also want to emphasize that if you don't view yourself as a gambler—a wild risk-taker— that's okay. In fact, that's more than okay. Most successful entrepreneurs are calculated risk-takers who constantly think about how to manage and mitigate apparent risks with specific strategies across the entire spectrum of the business. For example, if you only have average abilities in organizing work and making optimum use of scarce resources, bringing on board a more experienced manager with proven operational skills might be just the ticket.

Persistence and Perseverance: The Importance of Dispositional Optimism

As important, if not more important than anything else, is that entrepreneurs have an unshakably positive outlook on life and believe that good things will happen, in spite of the present challenges. In essence, they are "glass-half-full" individuals—*even when times get tough!*

This constant personality trait—to be able to take it on the chin and come up swinging—is essential for success in entrepreneurship. For those readers not familiar with this Western slang, it simply means that you need to be able to look adversity directly in the eye and maintain a naturally optimistic outlook on life and your ability to create change, make a difference, and build a company. This is called *dispositional optimism.* Anyone can try to become an entrepreneur. The real question, we suggest, is whether you are well suited for the journey. Entrepreneurship by its nature involves many difficulties, uncertainties, barriers, setbacks, and failures. And thus it takes a particular type of individual to start and continue the entrepreneurial journey.

So now, take a deep breath. We want you to take a simple test that is shown in Figure 1.1. It is called the LOT-R test. It will measure your own dispositional optimism. Dispositional

Be as honest as possible in completing this instrument. There are no right or wrong answers, per se. Please place the appropriate number, either 1, 2, 3, 4, or 5, on the line next to each statement listed below to indicate the extent to which you agree or disagree with the statement. Please score each of the following statements as honestly as possible. The scoring is: 1 = Strongly Disagree, 2 = Disagree, 3 = You are neutral about the statement, 4 = Agree, and 5 = Strongly Agree.

Remember to place the number 1, 2, 3, 4, or 5 on the line next to each statement.

1. In uncertain times, I would expect the best.   _____

2. It's easy for me to relax.   _____

3. If something can go wrong with me, it will.   _____

4. I am always optimistic about my future.   _____

5. I enjoy my friends a lot.   _____

6. It's important for me to keep busy.   _____

7. I hardly ever expect things to go my way.   _____

8. I don't get upset too easily.   _____

9. I rarely count on good things happening to me.   _____

10. Overall, I expect more good things to happen to me than bad.   _____

Figure 1.1 The LOT-R Test: Assess Your Dispositional Optimism

optimism is defined as the global generalized tendency to believe that one will experience good versus bad outcomes in life. In other words, it is about one's positive expectation for the future.[3] When people are faced with difficulties, optimists continue their effort to achieve their goals whereas pessimists tend to give up. We are asking that you take this test because we have found it to be a defining characteristic of successful entrepreneurs and corporate innovators. It has been shown to be highly correlated with entrepreneurial intent—the desire to be entrepreneurial.

So now, *take this test and see how you score*. Take it right now. Think a moment or two about your answers. Then, in the Reader Exercises at the back of this chapter, we will tell you how to actually score your answers. Please don't read the scoring guide until after you have completed the questions because that might bias your answers! And if it turns out that your score is high, you have a valuable asset going for you. If your score is low, it does not mean you should give up on entrepreneurship, but you may have to practice changing your mindset and deal with adversity in a more optimistic, "I'm going to get through it" sort of way. Research has shown that you can learn to be more optimistic; it just takes time and even some self- or guided training to do so.[4]

---

[3]Scheier, M., Carver, C., & Bridges M. (1994). Distinguishing optimism from neuroticism (and trait anxiety, self-mastery, and self-esteem): A reevaluation of the life orientation test. *Journal of Personality and Social Psychology*, 67(6), 1063–1078; and Scheier, M., & Carver, C. (1992). Effects of optimism on psychological and physical well-being: Theoretical overview and empirical update. *Cognitive Therapy and Research*, (16), 201–228.

[4]Baron, R. (2000). Psychological perspectives on entrepreneurship: Cognitive and social factors in entrepreneurs' success. *Current Directions in Psychological Science*, 9(1), 15–18; Crane, F., and Crane, E. (2007). Dispositional optimism and entrepreneurial success. *The Psychologist-Manager Journal*, 10(1), 1–13; and Crane, F., & Meyer, M. (2006). The entrepreneurial climate in Canada: The entrepreneur's viewpoint. *Journal of Small Business & Entrepreneurship*, 19(3), 223–231.

Taking Further Stock of Your Personal Factors _____

A venture should begin on a solid foundation of industry knowledge and customer insight. This leads directly to a set of basic questions: What business experience do you possess that might be relevant to a new venture? What are the facets of your educational background that might come into play, either technical, or internship in a sales channel, or perhaps classmates who might fill certain key roles? What connections do you have among your family and friends that might be brought to bear in a venture, say, for raising startup capital? And at a deeper level, what are your personal interests and passions for business? In your heart of hearts, where might you want to commit yourself for a 24/7 effort for the next five years?! These factors are all fundamental components of the "you" who will be the soul of the company you wish to start.

Most people who aim to start a business get their initial ideas, inspiration, and resources from one or more of the following personal sources:

- *Work experience.* We watched as salesperson Cheryl moved up the ranks successfully selling medical instruments for a market leader in eye surgery, including cosmetic surgeries. She was determined to start her own business. Fashionable, engaging, and market focused, Cheryl saw the combination of increasing skin cancer rates and the spending of disposable income on cosmetic products and minor procedures (such as dermal abrasion and Botox injections) as creating an opportunity to start a chain of skin health centers focused on upscale professional women in urban areas.

- *Educational background.* Matt, a business school student, took various entrepreneurship courses and believed that there must be a better way to design customized business models and create financial statements than using his professor's spreadsheet templates or buying one of the popular off-the-shelf packaged software sold for creating business plans. He created a Web-based, software-as-a-service package for business modeling and financial planning for new entrepreneurship students—selling it to entrepreneurship professors. Matt convinced his old business school professors to be the first test users!

- *Family background and business experience.* Walter, an old friend from high school, saw his father create a company that provides de-icing services to major airlines at many airports across the United States and Europe. Walter worked in the business and became the CEO after his father retired. Walter developed great connections through the industry. One of his de-icing customers was Federal Express (having a large fleet of its own airplanes). Walter wanted to make his own mark on the industry. He envisioned raising additional capital to start a feeder airline to transport FedEx packages to small, local airports in the southeastern United States. And that is precisely what Walter has done—and that feeder airline is itself a major business.

We see a current fad among student entrepreneurs to propose one social networking idea after another, following in the footsteps of Twitter or Facebook. The vast majority of these fail to become viable businesses. While the idea is "cool," there is no clear recipe for monetizing the innovation. This is all the more true if the Website is geared toward fellow students who are well trained not to pay for anything on the Web. This is not to say that the social networking trend is a passing fad or that you can't make money creating a social networking service. But the service needs to be monetized. Relying only on advertising revenue probably isn't going to do the trick.

For example, Tom, a former student, developed a plan to combine LinkedIn–type social networking with Hoover's-style business information to put all sorts of information in the hands of high-priced salespersons calling on corporations, large or small. Tom's plan was to charge a healthy monthly subscription fee for this sales productivity tool. He ended up selling his company for more than $50 million on $10 million in profitable revenue within just four years of startup, and with his brother, still owned a majority of the stock! Banner advertisements had absolutely nothing to do with Tom's business model. If you want to see how he raised early capital for his venture, and videos of Tom and other entrepreneurs, check out the Generate case on this textbook's Website.

So even "cool" new technologies and social networks must be approached with good business sense. At the end the day, you need to monetize your innovations.

You also don't necessarily need to work only in new, emerging industry niches. Many an entrepreneur has succeeded by bring new technology and new services into what most people consider "mature" industries. Most mature industries are in a continuous process of business transformation—and they need help. Just look at the energy utility industry, once the most "boring" but today one of the most exciting areas for energy-related entrepreneurship—some of it driven by new types of energy generation and a lot of the rest on information technology and analytics. As another example, we have a friend, Jim, who is building a great company that outsourced employee assistance services for major corporations. One of his new industry niches is providing counseling services for none other than university professors, particularly those going up for tenure! He is creating a network of university employees and private counselors, with his company sitting squarely in the middle with a subscription-based service. Jim loves bringing innovation in the form of new services to mature industries. The same type of innovation can be found in healthcare, energy, and transportation. And the advantage is that cash is already flowing in these industries—money that could be yours for the taking.

None of these factors—work, education, family experience, or the current trend—function in isolation toward new venture creation. In fact, in many cases, these factors combine in a type of synergy that makes entrepreneurship its own special life form. Take the case of Alvin, who was born in China and immigrated with his parents to the United States at a young age. Over the years, he earned an undergraduate degree in electrical engineering, a master's degree in computer science, and an MBA. He had a series of great corporate jobs in the United States, but his family heritage was a strong pull. He also saw the opportunity for building new businesses in China. After earning his MBA, Alvin took a job with Intel and then got himself an assignment in Shanghai to explore mobile consumer applications and services for the domestic Chinese market. A few years later, Alvin left to start his own mobile search company. Today, one of his major customers is China Mobile, which itself has over 300 million subscribers!

We share these stories for a purpose. Each individual took stock of his or her personal work experience, education, and family history—as well as his or her own passion for work and technology. (And, if you know them as we do, their desire to help society.) Each one of these individuals is very different from the other by way of work experience, educational background, family history, and personal passions. But the way in which they are the same is that they carefully listen to customers and integrate potential technologies and business models together. And each is a very "regular" sort of person in a social sense—individuals with whom you would enjoy having lunch or grabbing a beer: a good listener as well as a careful thinker. Perhaps most important, each is highly determined. They have been told "No!" a hundred times on their pathways to success—be it by potential investors, early customers, employees they wanted to hire, and in some cases family and friends who preferred a safer, more traditional career path. That dispositional optimism—being able to take it on the chin and come up swinging—is the characteristic that unites them together.

Figure 1.2 is designed to help you weigh how your own personal internal factors might direct you toward a particular industry as well as the target segment or niche within that industry. Take a look at it now and begin to think about filling in the boxes on the left side of that figure and how the combination of your own work experience, education, family background, and personal business goals point to an industry focus where your history and interests provide the insight and understanding needed for the road ahead.

However, it is critically important to note that following any of these internal factors blindly down the path to a Venture Concept might just as easily lead you into a lot of hard work with little return. Internal factors are seldom sufficient in and of themselves for success. To capitalize on the value they do contain, the entrepreneur must integrate them with favorable "external" factors such as rising market demand, positive industry trends, unsatisfied customer needs, and so forth. The best approach to do this is to find an industry (and a segment or specific niche within that industry) with those positive characteristics and then build an enterprise that capitalizes on them and the entrepreneur's internal factors.

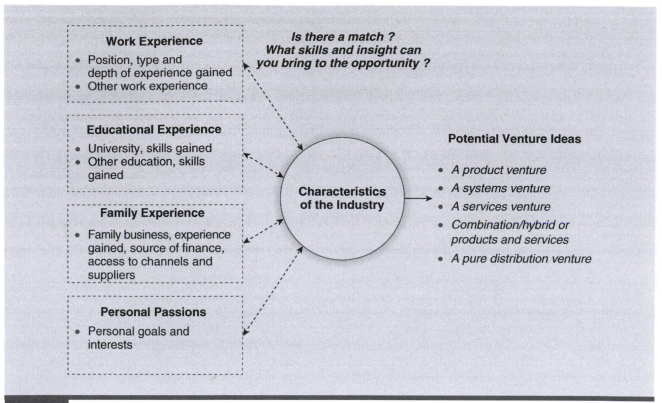

Figure 1.2   Balancing Internal and External Factors to Shape New Ventures

The importance of finding the "right" industry cannot be overemphasized. Being in the right industry is like bicycling with the wind at your back, making your journey easier. The key is to identify a source of powerful market demand and let that demand drive the design of your venture as well as the team who you build around the venture. And that market demand is itself an unfolding story. In doing your research, you might go after a particular segment within an industry, and in that research, find a more specific niche within that industry area that is most promising. Or you might find that an entirely different segment is even better.

Find an industry target with favorable supply/demand and competitive characteristics, *and* where one's internal strengths can be profitably applied. This is how we want you to approach your own venture.

The other important context-setting decision is whether you wish to start a new company from scratch or create a venture within an established corporation. Our examples and teaching cases in this book deliberately cover both types of situations, because each is a venture in its own right that can bring you satisfaction as well as considerable personal wealth. We have already provided you with lots of startup examples, so let's take a quick look at a classic corporate venture.

Steve, a gifted electrical engineer and MBA student in one our weekend classes for working professionals, was considering how to create a product line that would leverage his company's technology to an *adjacent* market application. The company made highly specialized chips that were used to process 3-D images in medical equipment—CT (computed tomography) and MRI (magnetic resonance imaging) in particular. Steve searched and searched for other medical applications but came up with nothing. Working with the professor, both came to the same conclusion: Think outside the medical field.

Several weeks later, while returning from a business trip, Steve noted the poor quality of the luggage scanning system deployed at the airport. He realized that the government would demand far better solutions—if there were any. Steve now had a venture target. He developed a plan for the course, which he took to the company's head of R&D. With the support of this executive, Steve received funding to lead a project to deliver improved scanning for airport security. September 11, 2001, had not yet happened, but it would soon rear its ugly head. Steve's project could not have been better timed. In the years since, his company has become a major supplier of imaging subsystems technology to manufacturers of explosive detections systems. For the entrepreneur, startup or corporate, having a market mandated by a federal government agency is perhaps as good as it gets.

Situations like Steve's are not usual. Ventures often emerge from the frustrations that people encounter. Thanks to their work experience and technical educations, midlevel corporate personnel like Steve often see problems or opportunities that their companies overlook, find too small to pursue, or might view as a new growth opportunity if only a well-considered plan is brought to management's attention. You can do the same by looking at the problems and frustrations you experience as potential opportunities.

Spotlight on Entrepreneurship: Starting From Ground Zero

Some students lack the industry or work experience that would help them recognize and pursue an entrepreneurial opportunity. Are you at a point in life where you have no real work experience? And you don't come from an enterprise-owning family that discusses business around the dinner table every night? And the idea of working for someone else leaves you cold? *Don't despair*. You are starting at ground zero, but your passion and a bit of good, old-fashioned luck might open the door to something special.

We once had several students who, frankly, were not stellar academic minds. School, books, and classrooms were not their thing. However, they had other admirable qualities of mind and spirit, and in particular, that magic ingredient called dispositional optimism. As graduation drew near and their need to find employment became more tangible, they approached their professor.

"Professor, can you help us find a job at a bank or something?"

"I don't think you fellows are cut out for banking," the professor said.

"Then what about consulting? That pays well, doesn't it?"

"Yes, it pays well, but consulting firms normally hire graduates with close to 4.0s," the professor responded.

"Then, what should we do?"

"Well, you'll soon have degrees from a fine university, and you seem to have plenty of energy and guts. Maybe you should start your own company. That way, you can control your own destiny."

"Great," they said, "what should we do?"

"Do something you really love, because you're going to have to work harder than you have ever worked in your life—and definitely harder than you've worked in my class!"

One of the young men laughed, "Well, we sure love beer. Maybe we should open a bar!"

"Have you ever worked in a bar?" the professor cautioned. "Do you have any idea how hard it is to run a bar? You never have a night off, and the employee problems are rampant."

They looked puzzled.

(Continued)

(Continued)

"My guess is that you guys are going out to a bar tonight; am I right?" the professor asked. (Nods all around.) "Well, instead of being customers as usual, keep your eyes on the bar owner. Watch everything that person does. And think about what it would be like to be that bar owner six nights a week. *Really* think about it. Then come back and talk to me."

The students were back the next day, this time with long faces. "Professor, we love beer, and we like hanging out in bars, but after watching that owner for hours, we would hate his job. But we think there is an opportunity to make really good beer."

The professor lit up. "Now you're talking. How about *making* a new line of specialty beers to sell to bars? I had some microbrewery beer the other day and it was great. Was very expensive, too. I bet there is room for another specialty beer label, as long as it's premium quality and has a good story crafted behind the product. Think about it and come back to me next week," the professor said.

Well, one of those students thought about it, a lot. After graduation he created a plan to enter the premium segment of the beer industry with a great Boston "story" behind the brand. This student had a passion for the craft and culture of brewing. He invested his time and money to learn about how the best beers are made and about the ingredients that go into them. Ten months after graduation, he and a new partner raised working capital from friends and family to start a specialty beer company. Within five years, the company passed $10 million in revenue and won the "Best of Boston" award in specialty beers. After another five years of continued growth, the partners sold the company to a large, national specialty brewer. Our "academically challenged" student made fistfuls of money!

Yes, passion and energy can take you a long way, if you follow it up with the hard work needed to become an expert in the various aspects of your industry.

Developing an Industry Focus: Investigating the Potential of an Industry _____

From this self-assessment, you should be forming an industry target for a venture in your mind. This is largely a "gut" call at this point. Where do your work experience, education, family experience, and personal interests point?

Now, from "the gut," we must move to "the head"—to make a decision based on detailed research on the industries where you might venture forth.

Industries, Segments, and Niches

An *industry* is a group of firms that produce products or services that are close substitutes for one another and that serve the same general set of customers. Industries are defined by the markets served by their competing participants.

Most industries can be subdivided into specific *segments* that include a set of competitors that address particular customer groups. For example, the financial services industry includes many segments: investment banking, commercial and retail banking, insurance, money management, and so forth.

Often, the segments of an industry also have subsegments, or *niches,* that include their own sets of customers, competitors, and commercial offerings. For example, in the insurance industry alone there are property and casualty, life, health, and long-term care niches.

Some segments/niches may have low growth, low profitability (over the past several years, for example, the property and casualty industry is suffering high claims due to natural catastrophes, storms, and the like), and little innovation; others, such as long-term care insurance or home healthcare, may exhibit dynamic growth and an abundance of opportunities to make money. The central idea here is for you, the entrepreneur, to do your research to focus not only on a promising industry, but to find the segment, and the niche within that segment, that offers you the best chances of starting a company and growing it to be a leader in that niche. Often, a niche that is emerging and seems small has a way of growing rapidly and becoming a major market in its own right.

Competition is very important as well. As an entrepreneur, you should not try to take on an entire industry and all of its established players, at least not in the beginning. Define your target market in a way that your venture is a rifle shot toward a specific opportunity, with just a handful of competitors—as opposed to a shotgun approach blasted at an entire market. This approach leads you to find a particular niche within the larger industry, to grow into the leading if not dominant player in that niche, and to expand from there. This lends focus to the new enterprise, and focus is all-important for everything else you will do: what to make, how to produce, how to sell and promote, and whom to hire.

It is all the better if your industry focus leads you to a segment/niche that exhibits a healthy rate of growth in terms of current or expected sales. We call this strong customer demand. It also good if there is a clear distribution channel to reach those customers, be it the Web, a major retailer, or an industrial partner. Otherwise, building an entirely new channel to market typically requires millions of dollars, if not tens of millions of dollars, every dime of which will come out of your own founders' stock.

Organizing Your Industry Learning

Therefore, you need to understand an industry both in broad strokes as well as what is happening in its various major segments and particularly interesting niches within those segments. At the end of the day, you are going to select one of those niches to start your venture—one that matches up your work experience, education, personal connections, and professional passions.

As you study a particular industry, its segments, and niches, look for positive indicators in the following areas:

- The current size and growth rates of customer demand, for example, sales
- Major trends sweeping across the industry
- The competition in the industry and evidence of successful business models
- The activity level of new companies, venture deals, and M&A transactions
- The technology life cycle stage of the industry overall, often reflected by new technologies, products, and services recently announced by players in the industry
- The channels of distribution within an industry
- Attractively priced suppliers for key components, technologies, or ingredients that you need for your products or services
- No existing barriers to entry that might make your life extremely difficult as an entrepreneur

The first step is to type in key words with descriptors for each of the eight bullet points above in your favorite search engine, including a label for your industry target, such "sales home healthcare," or "venture capital home healthcare," or "new trends technology home healthcare." Sit back and watch a wealth of information unfold before your eyes. Start browsing through the links. When an interesting company is mentioned, go to its Website, look at the management team, the Board (who will be investors if it is a startup), the products, and the customers. If it is publicly traded, take a look at the financial statements to see who is making money in the industry, and *how they are making it*. Also, look for industry reports from trade associations, articles that size a particular industry or emerging segment or niche, or a new product announcement by a company, large or small. You are looking for facts, figures, potential customers, channel partners, and competitors.

Create a set of folders on your computer desktop and store this information for later use. Most important, organize this information into overall industry information and more specific segment or niche information. You will be surprised just how much information exists, *for free,* on the Web for entrepreneurs willing to do a little homework.

Be thorough investigating these areas. The result should point the way to the robust business opportunity you need to start a successful company. In fact, if you have the passion, it will be hard to pull yourself away from the computer: There will be so much information! However, after a couple of hours at the keyboard, sit back and craft a story in your mind about the most attractive part of the industry you wish to enter. We refer to that story as an *industry analysis.* That analysis leads to the industry focus for your venture. And remember, professional investors want to know if you really know the industry and its underpinnings. Here are the major components of that story.

Conducting a Fast, Effective Industry Analysis

Industry Structure, Current Size, and Growth Rates

As noted above, industries tend to be comprised of multiple segments. Each segment contains different types of customers and different uses for products and services. Some of these segments might have low growth and low profitability; others might have dynamic growth and lots of opportunities to make money. This reasoning also extends to the niches within major industry segments. Understanding an industry structure is essential for developing an industry focus, and from that, a compelling plan.

Current size and growth rates for major segments/niches are critically important. Starting a new venture in a flat or declining segment is also usually a waste of time. Look for areas where robust growth is anticipated for years to come. "A rising tide," as the saying goes, "lifts all boats."

TIP: USING GOVERNMENT DATA SOURCES TO SIZE INDUSTRIES, SEGMENTS, AND NICHES

While it is often possible to find reports on the Web that present current industry size and projected growth rates—and from these, to create an industry structure—sometimes you need to go to the source data behind these reports. Certain regions in the world maintain excellent databases for sizing industries. For example, there are the North American Industry Classification System (NAICS) and U.S. Census Bureau data (www.census.gov/eos/www/naics and http://census.gov/econ/census07). NAICS provides common industry definitions for the United States, Canada, and Mexico, and groups the economic activities of specific companies into specific industries and their major segments. Similar classification systems exist in Europe, Japan, and the BRIC countries (Brazil, Russia, India, and China).

Let's say you want to start an organic, hydroponic vegetable growing business that would locate greenhouses on the rooftops of large, urban retail stores and reuse the heat and water from these stores for climate control in the greenhouses themselves. Using NAICS, you would find the "industry" defined as "Sector 11"—called

Agricultural, Forestry, Fishing, and Hunting. Then, you would drill down to Crop Production—"Subsector 111." In doing so, you have refined your industry space to a specific segment. Here, you can examine market size and growth across a range of crops. But, given that you intend to operate in the "greenhouse" space, you should define and identify your target more narrowly—a classic example of focusing in on a "niche." We do this by looking at "Subsector 1114"—labeled Greenhouse, Nursery, and Floriculture Production—that provides more specific insight regarding the size and growth of that niche. But wait! It is even possible to drill further, to Subsector 11141—Food Crops Grown Under Cover (exactly what you will be doing). It is possible to drill down to another level—Subsector 111419—and examine data on specific crops grown under cover. Using these data, you discover that organic tomatoes are in greater demand and selling at significantly higher margins than mushrooms! These industry data will help you to properly plan your product offerings.

Major Trends Sweeping Across an Industry

Most industries are in flux, driven by the combination of technological innovation and larger societal trends and challenges. This creates new possibilities for entrepreneurs and threatens existing incumbent firms competing with yesterday's products, services, and business models. In this part of your industry analysis, you need to understand the major trends affecting customers and competitors in your target industry.

Here are a few examples to consider.

- The security industry: September 11 created a new segment called homeland security. A host of startups and large defense contractors have been innovating with systems that feature smart software using new, tiny sensors to gather real-time information in the effort to stop terrorists. This continues to be a robust market.[5]

- The healthcare industry: The aging of the population, as well as new government regulations, have created growth opportunities in a range of segments: cost control in hospital-based care; new monitoring technologies for home healthcare; and new types of drugs based on technologies such as DNA sequencing, proteomics, and the like.

- The energy industry: The cost of fossil fuels is driving change across multiple industries, be it solar/wind power, materials for home construction, transportation, and the distribution of electricity itself—all the way down to our refrigerators!

- Government regulations for specific industries: Government regulation can drive entrepreneurial opportunities. For example, in financial services, fraudulent company accounting led to the Sarbanes-Oxley legislation put into effect in 2002 in the United States, and to a host of new software and service ventures to help companies become compliant.

There are often news stories on these major trends, new product announcements, and customer applications that can give you a sense of change and innovation. Each region of the world has its own information sources—so search them out on the Web and use them!

---

[5]Meyer, M. H., & Poza, H. (2009, May). Venturing adjacent to the core: From defense to homeland security. *Research Technology Management*, 31–48.

TIP: USING TRADE ASSOCIATION DATA TO GET A HANDLE ON INDUSTRY SIZE, SEGMENTS, AND GROWTH RATES

Trade associations and other related nonprofit groups often gather activity-related information from their respective members and make these data available to the public. This can be a great source of data on industry size, industry segments, growth rates, and major trends. These data are often updated on a regular basis, so the information is current.

There are literally thousands of different trade associations, not just in the United States but around the globe. You can see if there is a trade group for your target industry by simply doing a Web search for "trade association [industry name]." Or your university library might have a copy of the *Encyclopedia of Associations*, which contains information on more than 150,000 specific trade associations, both in the United States and abroad. From these searches, you can then go to the association's Website and search for freely available information.

Figure 1.3 shows an example. It comes from an industry trade group, the U.S. Travel Association (www.ustravel.org). After taking a look at the data in the figure, visit the association's Web site and look under the "Research" menu to see specific forecasts for domestic and international travel, as well as the number of trips for business and leisure travelers. Another Website maintained by the U.S. Travel Association, poweroftravel.org, provides more information, such as the fact sheet shown in Figure 1.3. You will also see that nearly all association Websites have reports both for the public and for members.

There are also many industry research consulting firms that gather similar types of data and pride themselves on being experts in predicting industry trends. Your business library just might have access to some of these research firms' publications. One of the best in this regard is Frost & Sullivan. Some business research libraries have Frost & Sullivan reports on their shelves. However, be prepared to see a price for such reports in the hundreds of dollars, if not more. This, or joining a trade association, might be an investment you have to make to gather the data you need to raise substantial amounts of capital from professional investors. For now, however, look for industry data on the Web or ask friends who might already have access to such data. Without the numbers, it will be hard to objectively assess industry attractiveness in terms of size, growth, and the most attractive segments for starting a new venture.

Data such as these will prove to be very useful later on when you are writing the Industry Analysis section of your business plan (not until Chapter 11!). So, whatever data you gather, remember to place them in an electronic or physical folder, clearly marked for later use.

Competition and the Existence of Successful Business Models

Some industries have one or two large leaders and half a dozen second-tier competitors, all jockeying for incremental gains in market share by introducing a new product or service and, just as often, lowering prices. It's very tough for a startup to compete in such an environment. A new corporate venture, on the other hand, stands a chance because it can often leverage the corporation's brands, distribution channels, manufacturing, and credibility to break into the market with a new solution.

U.S. TRAVEL ANSWER SHEET
FACTS ABOUT A LEADING AMERICAN INDUSTRY THAT'S MORE THAN JUST FUN

POWER of TRAVEL
www.PowerofTravel.org

LEISURE TRAVEL

- Direct spending on leisure travel by domestic and international travelers totaled **$564 billion** in 2011.
- Spending on leisure travel generated **$86 billion** in tax revenue.
- **3 out of 4** domestic trips taken are for leisure purposes (77%).
- U.S. residents logged **1.5 billion** person-trips* for leisure purposes in 2011.
- Top leisure travel activities for U.S. domestic travelers: (1) visiting relatives; (2) shopping; (3) visiting friends; (4) fine dining; and (5) beaches.

BUSINESS TRAVEL
(Including Meetings, Events and Incentive)

- Direct spending on business travel by domestic and international travelers, including expenditures on meetings, events and incentive programs (ME&I), totaled **$249 billion** in 2011.
- ME&I travel accounted for **$99 billion** of all business travel spending.
- U.S. residents logged **458 million** person-trips* for business purposes in 2011, with more than one-third (36%) for meetings and events.
- For every dollar invested in business travel, businesses benefit from an average of **$12.50** in increased revenue and **$3.80** in new profits *(Oxford Economics).*

* Person-trip defined as one person on a trip away from home overnight in paid accommodations or on a day or overnight trip to places 50 miles or more (one-way) away from home.

U.S. Travel Industry Impact

$1.9 TRILLION GENERATED

SPENDING	$813 Billion (Direct)	$1.1 Trillion (Indirect & Induced)

TAXES — **$124 BILLION IN TAXES (DIRECT)**

JOBS — 14.4 MILLION JOBS SUPPORTED
7.5 million (direct) 6.9 million (other industries)

BUSINESS TRAVEL (DIRECT)
SPENDING $248.8 B
TAXES $38.2 B
JOBS 2.2 million jobs

+

LEISURE TRAVEL (DIRECT)
SPENDING $564.1 B
TAXES $85.9 B
JOBS 5.3 million jobs

General Business Travel
SPENDING $150.2 B
TAXES $23.1 B
JOBS 1.4 million jobs

+

Meetings, Events & Incentive Travel
SPENDING $98.7 B
TAXES $15.0 B
JOBS 859,000 jobs

Each U.S. household would pay $1,000 more in taxes without the tax revenue generated by travel and tourism.

Source: U.S. Travel Association
Note: Direct spending totals do not include international passenger fares
= 1 million jobs

SOURCES OF TRAVEL SPENDING

FOODSERVICES	$192.0 B
PUBLIC TRANSPORTATION	$156.1 B
LODGING	$147.6 B
AUTO TRANSPORTATION	$147.2 B
RECREATION/AMUSEMENT	$85.4 B
RETAIL	$84.7 B

TOTAL: $813 billion Source: U.S. Travel Association

INTERNATIONAL TRAVEL

- In 2011, international traveler spending (export receipts) totaled **$153 billion** and travel spending abroad by Americans totaled **$110 billion** (travel import payments), creating a trade surplus of **$43 billion** in favor of the U.S.
- The U.S. received **62.3 million** international arrivals in 2011. Of those, approximately **27.9 million** were from overseas markets and **34.4 million** were from Canada and Mexico.
- The United States' share of total international arrivals is **6.4%** (down from **7.5%** in 2000).
- International travel spending directly supported about **1.2 million** U.S. jobs and wages of **$28.5 billion.**

Direct spending by resident and international travelers in the U.S. averaged $2.2 billion a day, $92.8 million an hour, $1.5 million a minute and $25,778 a second.

- Each overseas traveler spends approximately **$4,300** when they visit the U.S. and stay on average more than **17 nights.**
- Overseas arrivals represent **45%** of all international arrivals, yet account for **78%** of total international travel receipts.
- Greatest challenges facing international visitors: burdensome visa process; unwelcoming entry experience.
- Top leisure travel activities for overseas visitors: (1) shopping; (2) dining; (3) city sightseeing; (4) visiting historical places; and (5) amusement/theme parks.

TOP 5 INTERNATIONAL MARKETS TO USA (ARRIVALS)

ORIGIN OF VISITOR	2011
Canada	21.0 million
Mexico	13.4 million
United Kingdom	3.8 million
Japan	3.2 million
Germany	1.8 million

TOP 5 HIGH-GROWTH MARKETS THRU 2016 *(forecasted)*

ORIGIN OF VISITOR	ARRIVALS % CHANGE '16/'11
China	274%
Brazil	135%
Russia	131%
Australia	94%
Argentina	70%

Source: U.S. Department of Commerce–Office of Travel and Tourism Industries

The U.S. Travel Association is the national, non-profit organization representing all components of the travel industry that generates $1.9 trillion in economic output. It is the voice for the collective interests of the U.S. travel industry and the association's 1,400 member organizations. U.S. Travel's mission is to promote and facilitate increased travel to and within the United States. U.S. Travel is proud to be a partner in travel with American Express®. For more information, visit www.USTravel.org or www.PowerofTravel.org.

1100 New York Avenue, NW, Suite 450 • Washington, DC 20005-3934 • 1.202.408.8422 • email: feedback@USTravel.org • www.USTravel.org
Copyright 2012 by the U.S. Travel Association. All Rights Reserved.

U.S. TRAVEL ASSOCIATION

Figure 1.3 An Example of Trade Association Industry Information: The U.S. Travel Association

Source: Fortune Magazine, May 4, 2009; Copyright © 2011, US Travel Association.

Most entrepreneurs should avoid areas of concentration and intense competition and seek out *fragmented markets* in which there are many small competitors and no dominant leaders. In fragmented markets, anyone with an attractive value proposition, a strong work ethic, adequate capital, and imagination has a fair shot at success.

As you study an industry and its various segments, take note of companies that achieved success in your specific industry segment or niche. Look at the products or services they provided, how they sold these into market, how they charged for things, and their recipe for making money. Also—just as important—are there relatively new companies in your target industry that have not only developed good products or services, but designed a way to make money—a business model—that seems to be scaling to the point of achieving considerable success? These models of past success and emerging success are so very important to understand as you design your own business. They will also tell you which parts of your target industry are generating profits for participants. Take note of these companies and read all you can about them. Then begin to consider the best way for your venture to proceed and to make money.

For mature industries, you can also go to Yahoo! Finance, type in the name of an industry leader, and review the "competitors" section. If the company has a lengthy history, you'll find a wealth of information.

New Companies, Venture Deals, and M&A Transactions

Part of your industry analysis is to understand which segments/niches of your target industry are the subjects of venture investment activity. This is important because it greatly increases your chances of raising money in the likely event that you'll need startup capital.

The venture capital (VC) industry employs thousands of highly trained professional analysts to do exactly what you, an amateur, are trying to accomplish: identify areas of commercial growth and opportunity. When they find those areas, venture financing quickly follows. So let these professionals be your reconnaissance scouts and follow their money trail. Pricewaterhousecooper's *MoneyTree Report* (www.pwcmoneytree.com) tabulates recent quarter venture capital investments by technology industry. While most startups do *not* attract VC funding, VC behavior is a good indicator of where growth is anticipated and where other venture financiers, such as angel investors, are placing their bets. In the last quarter of 2011, for example, the top industries for venture capital investment were software, biotechnology, industrial/energy, medical devices, and IT services, according to the *MoneyTree Report,* a free source of information on the Web. You can also get regional breakdowns for investments. Specific news reports provide indicators of more niche-specific investments, such as Cloud computing plays in IT services. Yahoo! Finance and Hoovers are also excellent sources for M&A activity, another clear sign of hot industry areas.

Stage of Industry Life Cycle

Entrepreneurs also need to consider the stage of the industry life cycle. This life cycle has several stages: *emergent, growth, maturation,* and *decline,* driven by the rate of technological innovation and technology-driven change. This cycle is sometimes expressed as an S-curve[6] similar to that shown in Figure 1.4.

- The initial stage is a period of slow revenue growth, with few direct competitors. Many entrepreneurs in this stage are still working out their technology bugs and forming product/service concepts. A credible market may not yet exist. Nanotechnology (which is new material science working on the scale of a billionth of a meter!) has been in this emergent

---

[6]Utterback, J. M. (1994). *Mastering the Dynamics of Innovation.* Boston: Harvard Business School Press.

stage for years, but is finally breaking out of it with a range of applications, from non-iron clothes, to indestructible house paint, and soon, to better-targeted drug delivery.

- The next stage in the life cycle is characterized by rapid growth. This is when the product or service concept really clicks with customers. The cell phone segment of the telecom is blossoming in this stage. Every consumer, rich or poor, wants a cell phone.

- Eventually, growth markets become saturated, the rocketing growth curve tapers off, and competitors find themselves in the maturity stage of the cycle. The many companies now in the field resort to incremental changes, price discounts, and other mechanisms to generate revenues and poach customers from competitors. Gradually, weaker firms are forced out of the industry and only a handful of firms are left standing. The office productivity segment of the software industry is in the mature stage of its cycle, with just a few players holding the majority of the market share.

- Lastly, when a traditional industry paradigm stagnates, it goes into decline. This opens the door for an entirely new generation of technology and an entirely new S-curve. The new pioneers work to disrupt old products and business models. Simply think Apple, its iTunes/iPhone combination, and how its software, services, and hardware have disrupted both the media and cell phone industries.

The industry life cycle has important implications for technology-intensive ventures. At the front of the life cycle, a nanotechnology entrepreneur simply has to find an application that will show his or her technology not only working but also producing value for customers. At the back side of the life cycle, a brilliant engineer seeking to develop software, systems, or

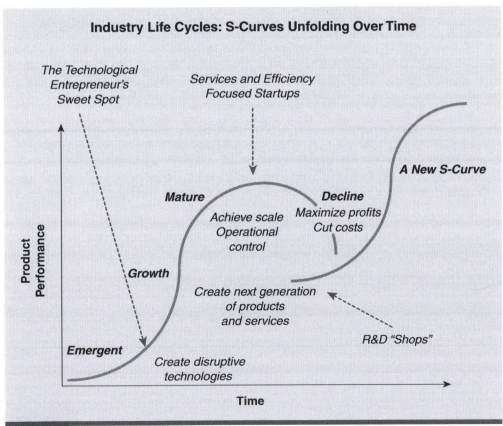

Figure 1.4   Industry Life Cycles

services for oil or gas producers surely is going to face several cost and pricing pressures, as will the entrepreneur targeting the automotive industry (original equipment manufacturers—OEMs). Costs are counted down to the pennies in mature industries.

Experience shows that technology-based ventures enjoy the greatest success when they enter the field *near the beginning* of the growth stage. This is the entrepreneur's sweet spot, shown in Figure 1.4. Customers are aware of the new technology, have money to spend, and are anxiously awaiting new solutions. Perfect. Too early in the game, and the entrepreneur has to wait for years for the technology to ripen. Too late, and you are up against well-established players. Jump to a next S-curve, and you are back in the research game again. Remember, there is a difference between invention of new science and technology, and innovation that uses proven science and technology to solve real-world problems. You want to be the latter.

News stories on company events, product announcements, and customer applications can give you a sense of change and innovation. Look to specialized industry publications such as *Computerworld* (for hardware and software innovations) or *New Scientist* (for chemistry and hard science breakthroughs). For environmental innovation, see Hot Topics on www.EarthPortal.com and online publications of the National Council for Science and the Environment. Or, once again, go to Yahoo! Finance and read the news stories on industry leaders. And, of course, a carefully constructed Google search may turn up incredibly valuable information on technology-driven industry dynamics.

Channels of Distribution Within an Industry

The entrepreneur seeks strong, clear channels of distribution that are receptive to new product or service innovations. For example, the third-party software business development programs of Microsoft, IBM, Oracle, and others provide a path to their respective customers. Or, if you are doing a consumer products venture, understanding the willingness of premium specialty retailers to try new products such as yours is very important. Whole Foods Market, Petco, and Target are all good examples. If you are doing a life sciences venture, today large pharmaceutical companies are desperate to fill their depleting pipelines with new potential drugs. Each one of these represents channels as well as development partners. New, small firms can prosper by aligning themselves with larger corporations that have access to large markets.

Suppliers

You need to make sure that the supply of necessary components, technologies, or ingredients needed for your types of products or services are readily available and reasonably priced. For a food company, that means recipe ingredients. If you are thinking of manufacturing solar energy panels, you should check the availability of key inputs, such as silicon. For a software company, these are the necessary software development tools. For a services company, that means reasonably priced labor that can be trained up to standard, and then low-cost yet powerful information technology to support the services.

On the same note, how eager are suppliers of key materials to deal with startups such as yours? You may find, for example, that a major competitor has "locked up" those suppliers. You have to be proactive and actually ask whether or not suppliers are open to cooperate with you. Suppliers will be honest if you ask, but it is your responsibility to determine this situation.

Barriers to Entry

A thorough investigation of a target industry must also consider the presence of barriers to entry and what, if anything, can be done to surmount them. A barrier to entry is any requirement—capital, technical know-how, and so on—that makes industry or market entry difficult or impossible. Of the many barriers faced by industry outsiders, three are particularly important for new venture entrepreneurs: capital and time, manufacturing, and marketing.

Capital and Time

Entry to some industry segments/niches requires huge amounts of capital—amounts that few entrepreneurs can raise. In others, years of R&D are needed to develop marketable products. As you can imagine, these two barriers usually go hand in hand. Consider, for example, the pharmaceutical industry, where more than ten years and close to a billion dollars are typically needed from start to launch for a single new drug! On the other hand, Web-based social networking presents minimal time and small amounts of investment capital to get started. Launching a new Web-based business can be fast and inexpensive.

Manufacturing

Certain manufacturing industries require particular types of machines to produce a given category of products. For building products, complex woodcutting, forming, and assembly machines are needed; for certain plastics and food products, specially built extrusion machines are required. And the list goes on. These machines can cost millions of dollars. An entrepreneur who insists on entering a capital-intensive industry needs to consider external manufacturing options—often called contract or co-manufacturers—to source his or her products. An increasing variety of these options exists both here and abroad.

Distribution

Marketing is the third major barrier to entry that an entrepreneur needs to consider. Gaining access to large retailers can be difficult and costly. For example, a new food venture faces a serious financial obstacle if it needs to pay "slotting fees" to national groceries in order to get its products on the shelves. Slotting fees can reach to several million dollars or more. Whole Foods Market, on the other hand, does not charge slotting fees; nor do "club" channels such as Costco. It is no surprise that food entrepreneurs go to specialty retailers and club stores to avoid this huge upfront expense. And while it can be difficult, working with larger resellers can be achieved even for the small firm. A small premium pet snack entrepreneur in Boston, for example, recently concluded an agreement with Target to create a branded "store in store" merchandizing area for his own products. And IBM has been gobbling up software products by the dozen from independent third parties to drive its own revenue. The lesson is that if you've got something good and you have the confidence to say it, the big boys may very well want your wares.

Defining the Type of Business You Might Want to Start

Figure 1.5 shows our progress so far in this chapter, and where we go next. On the left is your self-assessment of your personal factors; in the middle, your cogent industry analysis; and on the right, an initial definition of the type of business you want to start given your interests and the target industry segment or niche.

Figure 1.5 also shows the third and last step of defining the scope of a venture: deciding what type of business to be in terms of creating and providing products, systems, services, a hybrid combination thereof, or a pure distribution play. There are usually many ways to build a successful company in a given industry. In general, these types of businesses fall within these four categories—or some type of hybrid combination. It is also important to appreciate the differences between these types of businesses in terms of how they generate revenues. It is to the last step in determining the focus of a venture that we now turn our attention.

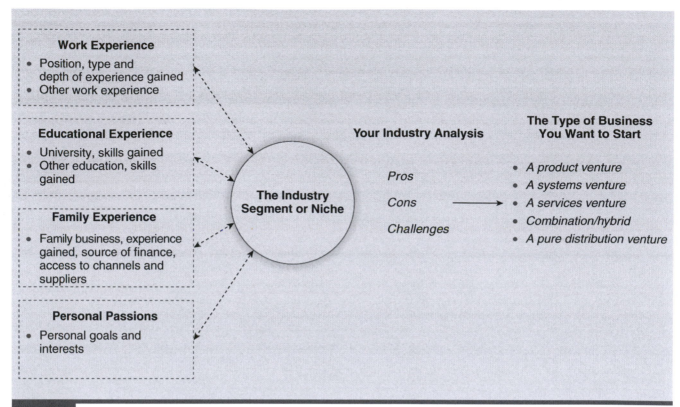

Figure 1.5 Defining Your Industry Focus and the Type of Business You Want to Start

Different Types of Business Opportunities in the Same Industry

It is not unusual to find customers in the same industry being served by different companies focusing on different things: some just on products, others on "systems," others just on services, and others largely as pure distribution companies selling other companies' products and services.

Suppose, for example, that we wanted to start a venture in the supply chain management industry, with a focus on mass-market retailers. Those retailers, led by Walmart, want to track every product they sell from suppliers' factories to their store shelves. Now, let's consider how different business "types" created by entrepreneurs could serve the needs of Walmart and others needing next-generation supply chain management solutions.

Products. We might create radio-frequency identification (RFID) sensors and readers capable of tracking products in transit by item and by pallet. The venture will obtain patents on its sensor technology and find third-party manufacturers to produce its sensors and readers. We would be selling RFID tags and tag readers.

Systems. We might create software-based systems to acquire data from the other vendors' RFID readers in real time, communicate those data to central servers armed with sophisticated workflow management software, and use software applications to inform customers of the status of products in production, in transit any place in the world, in the warehouse, or in the store. Customers will use these data to optimize inventory planning and distribution center operations. We are selling "systems" and support services for those systems.

Services. We take other companies' sensors, RFID readers, and server software, package it all together, and provide the implementation and customization services needed to tune these technologies for specific situations. We are selling our expertise and our bodies—in other words, a systems integration and consulting services firm.

Or we could try to be like IBM (which is hard to do for a startup venture) and provide a hybrid offering of several or more of these three types of businesses. Alternatively, we could propose to be a pure distribution player in a given industry sector. For example, one of our former students, Doug, took over, with his brother and cousins, the family's liquor distribution business. They developed a growth plan, and together have tripled the size of the business so that its sales are in excess of $500 million a year. Now *that's* a good distribution play. Many eCommerce ventures propose new distribution models as well. For example, pet food is now being custom ordered and drop shipped in the greater New York City area, using the Web as an ordering portal with a well-managed back-end fulfillment operation. The fact is that there are different creative ways to make money in an industry—and it is up to you to come up with different ideas, weigh the pros and cons of each, and take your best shot and begin to focus on a type of business. Once you delve into the field research with customers in the following chapters, you might learn new things that change your mind and shift the strategy of the venture into a different vector, say, from products to services. That's okay, but you need to put a stake in the ground in order to get started. It makes everything all the more tangible and real.

Making Money Is Different Based on the Type of Business

The three business types not only differ in how they create value for customers, but they also exhibit different revenue, cost, and margin profiles. Consider first a product-type business. For every $100 in product sales revenues, $30 to $40 is spent on manufacturing, and another $25 to $40 is spent on selling, marketing, R&D, and administration, leaving a net operating profit margin in the range of $15 to $25. The point of leverage in this business is to design a great set of products and manufacture thousands if not millions of them at a low cost per unit. Such businesses can require large capital outlays for production, although outsourcing can be a real advantage of "lean" startups. For example, one of the new battery manufacturers for electric cars raised $50 million for R&D from venture capital firms, but almost $500 million in debt and equity from various sources to build proprietary manufacturing capability.

Now consider the typical systems company. For every $100 of revenue, $20 to $30 might be spent on R&D, and another $10 to $20 might be spent on sales, marketing, and administration, leaving a net operating profit of $50 or more. At least, that is the goal! The point of leverage for a systems company is to hire the smartest programmers, have them create fantastic software, and then ship it electronically with virtually no cost of goods. The high profit margin enjoyed by this type of business explains why software continues to draw heavy venture capital investments.

Services companies aim to be product and systems *agnostic*. They are consulting firms, equipment service firms, transportation services providers, home healthcare providers, energy production and management firms, and so forth. Most are labor intensive. Thus, for every $100 of revenue, a typical services firm spends a third on labor; a third on technology, marketing, and administration; and then tries to walk away with $33 or more in operating profit. Its point of leverage is the design of the service, the people who deliver the service, and the technology that helps them deliver the service efficiently and effectively.

Pure distribution plays—such as the liquor distributor—tend to make about 5% to 8% operating profit on revenue. The key to success is logistics, and with that, information technology. Think of the UPS drivers in your area and their handheld devices. UPS's combination of people, trucks, and information technology is its secret for profitably delivering more than 20 million packages a day! Lately, entrepreneurs have been innovating on distribution models, including the Groupon model where it gets 50% of sales price of heavily discounted offerings, prices driven down by the grouping of individual consumers into larger purchasing bodies. Groupon shows that *business model innovation* can be every bit as exciting and rewarding as developing a new product or service.

In short, the four basic types of businesses—product-focused, systems-focused, services-focused, and pure distribution plays—are completely different in terms of what they do and how they make money. Their points of leverage are also entirely different. You can learn about the revenues, costs, and margin profiles of companies operating in your industry target through Yahoo! Finance and similar sources. Look up the industry leaders and examine their income statements.

Making the Choice of the Business Type for Your Venture

And so, having selected an industry and screened various possible segments and niches in that industry, you must now decide, "What type of business do I want to have?" Apple's decision in the mid-2000s to shift some of its energy to a distribution business—iTunes—demonstrates the power of type choice on earnings and company value.

Most entrepreneurs make the "type" decision by considering internal factors and the analysis they used in screening industries:

- For which type of business do I have the experience and education needed to succeed?

- What am I really good at? This is not only in terms of creating a product or system or service, but also in terms of *selling* the innovation.

- Do I want to create a new product or simply integrate different products together within a system or service? Am I most comfortable with the idea of providing a service?

- Which type of business in my chosen industry segment/niche do I perceive to be in greatest demand by customers?

- For which type of business is there the least direct competition? What type of business represents something truly new in the industry?

Time is another issue to consider in making the choice of business type. The longer it takes to generate revenues, the more difficult it will be to obtain financing—and the greater the risk for the entrepreneur.

As a general rule, product companies seem to take the longest time to move from business idea to first paying customer. A unique and appealing product must be designed, prototyped, customer tested, and manufactured. Even a simple product can take 18 months or longer to move to market. Medical products can take much, much longer! Systems companies tend to face a one- to two-year run-up to a workable product: lots of software development and iterative testing, a beta site with a few lead users, and then it's off to the races. Services companies, on the other hand, can start providing services right away if the team is capable. The time to first revenue for pure distribution is totally dependent on whether it is traditional warehouse or retail-type play, or a Web model such as Groupon.

Time to market is not the only consideration, of course; make a great product and there is far more leverage on time and effort and capital than all but the best of services businesses. Software can be even better.

In this chapter, you learned the importance of gathering information on the attractiveness of industries and the segments and niches within those industries. Successful entrepreneurs use information to drive their venture decisions. It is critical that you use objective information to determine if the innovative concept you have in mind also has the makings of becoming a good business. Do not let your passion for an idea interfere with applying common business sense to find those areas where your experience, your connections, and the industry dynamics can combine to create a great type of business.

Reader Exercises

Now it is your turn to apply these venture scoping ideas for how to establish a focus for your venture. The following exercises should be done sequentially.

Also, a few words about student project teams. This type of work is often performed in teams to emulate the venture team startup process. If you do recruit team members for a project, have a separate discussion offline in terms of roles and responsibilities. Do this early in the project so that everyone understands the amount of "skin in the game" that each team member is willing to contribute. Then, have a process for reviewing each other's work.

This commitment to getting the work done on time is so important. You don't want to have people join your team just because they think your idea is "cool." They must be willing to work because it is only through that work that your venture idea will continue to improve. As a fledgling entrepreneur, you don't have the time, nor should you have the patience, to carry noncontributors on your back.

Now on to the assignments for this chapter. It is time to define your industry and business focus!

Step 1: Score Your Individual LOT-R Test (see Figure 1.1)

- You should score only statements 1, 3, 4, 7, 9, and 10. The other statements are "fillers."
- Reverse score statements 3, 7, and 9. Reversing scoring means if you score a 5 make it 1, 4 make it 2, 3 make it 3, 2 make it 4, and 1 make it 5. For example, if for statement 3 you score a 5, add the score of 1 to your total.
- Sum your scores for statements 1, 4, and 10 and the reversed scores for statements 3, 7, and 9.

The scoring range is from 6 to 30. It should be pointed out that there are no true cut-offs for optimism and pessimism with this test since the constructs are a continuous dimension of variability. However, for the purposes of understanding your score, you should consider the midpoint score is 15. Therefore, any score below 15 would indicate that you tend to be pessimistic in your outlook. A score above 15 means you tend to be optimistic. That is, you tend to possess dispositional optimism. For the entrepreneurial journey, the higher the score the better. In fact, most of the successful entrepreneurs we have studied tend to score in the mid to high 20s. If your score is low, it does not mean you should give up on entrepreneurship. Don't get depressed! But you might have to practice changing your mindset. Use this course to begin that effort. The work you do in this course will provide plenty of opportunities to practice!

For those readers who score a 30, just make sure that your tremendous optimism does not blind you from accepting certain realities such as customers telling you that your idea is plain wrong for their needs. In other words, it doesn't work to be blindly optimistic and ignore the realities you may encounter as an entrepreneur. Instead, embrace "realistic optimism" and combine it with pragmatism—that makes a powerful combination!

Step 2: The Team Needs to Collectively Complete Figure 1.6

Put down your specific work and educational experience as well as family history as it pertains to business and entrepreneurship. After each team member does this for him or herself, you then need to assemble a composite list for the entire team. In a different color (such as red), make an equally important list of the skills, work experience, and connections that appear to be lacking for the venture you have in mind. If you have gaps, don't let that stop you; they can help direct your choice of new team members or the professors or advisers you seek out in the weeks and months ahead.

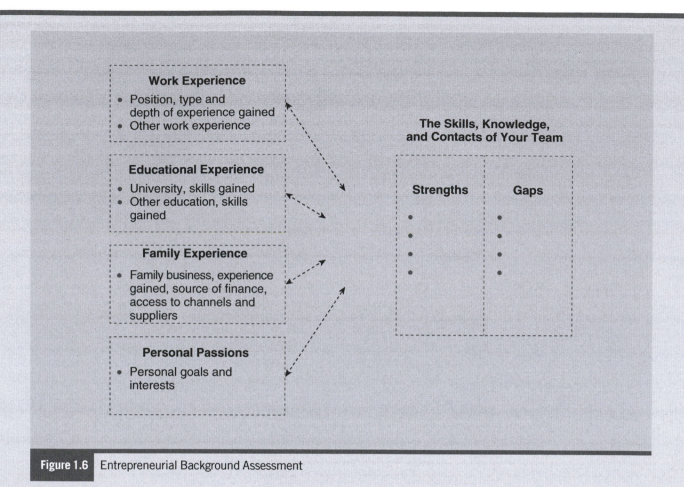

Figure 1.6   Entrepreneurial Background Assessment

Step 3: Conduct an Industry Analysis

This is a very important exercise. You need to search the Web and other data sources for information regarding your target industry. This includes hard numbers of the profitability of current market leaders and some intensive research on technology changes, channel changes, and competitors entering your industry. You also need to search sources such as *MoneyTree Report* (www.pwcmoneytree.com) to see the current flow of angel and venture financing into that sector. Examples of industries might be biotechnology, software, medical devices, energy, media and entertainment, networking and equipment, or healthcare services.

Then, once you have gathered these data, we want you to score the attractiveness of each dimension in Figure 1.7 for your industry target. We have provided nine important dimensions for you to consider. Then, make an honest assessment of these dimensions, using data where possible. Is the segment/niche a good place to start a venture? Does it have favorable industry dynamics or not?

The highest possible score is 100. An industry scoring over 75 in this template is very much worth consideration as a venue for a venture. Any industry scoring below 25 should probably be avoided. If your industry scores in the midrange on the scale—say, 50—then you must think about how you will overcome industry problems and obstacles.

If the assessment score is low, you might wish to consider looking at a different industry or a different segment of the industry. Otherwise, you need to have a serious discussion about how to overcome the negative dynamics you have uncovered. When it comes time to raise money from professional investors, assume that they know the potholes just as well as anyone else. Seasoned professionals are good at uncovering "show stoppers," defined as industry dynamics that make even a well-managed venture hard to grow.

	Facts/Data About Your Target Industry (Bullet points/facts)	Industry Score (1–10)
Current industry segment/niche size		
Industry segment/niche growth rate		
Favorable trends sweeping across industry		
Fragmented competition		
A feasible, money-making business model in the industry		
Activity in startups, financing, and deals in the segment/niche		
A favorable industry life cycle stage (not too early, not too late!)		
Existing channels of distribution in the industry		
Reasonably priced, widely available components, technologies, and ingredients		
No barriers to entry in terms of capital needed, production, and distribution		
	Total Score	

Scoring Key: 1 to 10, where:
1 is "a potential show-stopper for a new venture"; 3 is "a significant challenge"; 5 is "neither a barrier nor supporting success"; 7 is "conducive to a new venture"; and 10 is "an ideal setup for venture success".

Figure 1.7 The Industry Dynamics Scorecard

Step 4: Bring All of This Learning Together

Figure 1.8 integrates all of the prior work into a set of venture opportunities. Based on your personal work/education/family network and passions and your industry analysis, you should now be able to identify several venture ideas. At this point, you don't need to get too specific about the products or services in these venture ideas. Instead, focus on what they will do—the value they will bring to users—and how a business providing them can make money. Circle your favorite choice for type of business. Then prepare a crisp, concise rationale for your choice of target industry segment/niche and the type of business you prefer to start. This, dear readers, is the first important step—you will now have an industry focus! The following chapters in this book will help you refine and test that venture idea.

Great work! Now it's time to get feedback on your templates. Your professor may organize an in-class presentation session where you can share your ideas with the rest of your classmates and benefit from their experiences and insights. Don't be surprised if some people want to join your team, or if you want to join theirs. And the very best thing you can do next is try to meet an experienced business person or investor who has already worked in your target industry segment. It might be an alumnus of your university, a contact of your professor, or a family friend. Or it might be someone you know from work. Present your ideas and listen carefully to the feedback. Doing this early on in the game will give you an advantage beyond compare.

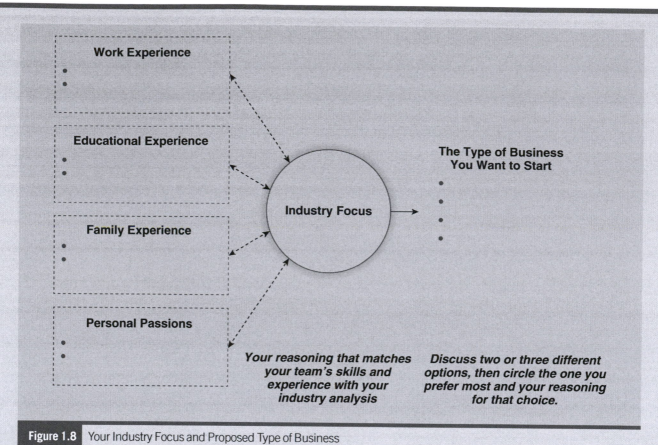

Figure 1.8   Your Industry Focus and Proposed Type of Business

Visit the Student Study Site at www.sagepub.com/meyer2e to access the following resources:

- Web Resources
- Video Resources
- General Resources in Entrepreneurship

2

Defining the Target Customer

Users and Buyers

The previous chapter helped you determine the focus for your venture: the industry—your target segment or niche—as well as the type of business you might launch: product, software/system, service, or pure distribution play. The next step toward a highly focused Venture Concept is to pinpoint your target customer. That is what you are going to learn in this chapter. In subsequent chapters, we will focus your ventures even further: clearly defining target customer needs; designing compelling solutions for those needs; defining a strong business model to make money; and effectively positioning the venture in a way to win against competitors and in a manner that truly excites potential customers.

Successful entrepreneurs typically find rapidly growing niches with a robust "parent" industry. The forward momentum of the larger market demand helps drive the potential of the niches within the industry. This is the story behind the hopes of so many social networking startups, seeking to leverage the industry segments dominated by Facebook (for the mass market) and LinkedIn (for the professional or business market). Generic social networking has been replaced by specific social networking "for what"—a precise purpose, such as researching biotechnology and healthcare, or gathering donations from long-lost alums at universities! The "find a hot niche" idea applies to many other industries as well. We see plans for new solar and wind energy collection systems, natural gas–powered machines, and all sorts of new building materials that are energy conscious. All of these are riding the wave of the expanding energy industries and its segments of energy generation, consumption, and conservation. Home healthcare is also an emerging segment in the larger, growing healthcare industry. For example, sensor-based monitoring for seniors is a hot niche. In the advertising space, the new play is in using data analytics and other technologies to drive mobile, location-specific messaging and promotions. In transportation, entrepreneurs are figuring out how to enable "smart cities." The bottom line is that successful entrepreneurs target niches within robust markets, and *so should you*.

As in our prior chapter, we will first learn through simple frameworks and examples. Then, at the end of the chapter, we will ask you to apply these ideas to your own ventures ideas.

> ### Learning Objectives
>
> After reading this chapter, you should be able to:
>
> - Segment target customers by thinking about different groups of users and different fundamental uses for products and services in that industry segment or niche
>
> - Determine which customer segment—that combination of user group and product or service use—that you wish to focus on first for your venture, which means conducting field research (to be covered in the next chapter!)

Creating a Customer Segmentation That Shows Users and Uses for the Types of Products or Services You Wish to Provide

Figure 2.1 shows the customer segmentation grids for a B2C venture within the snack foods industry sector. This customer segmentation was actually the basis for a wonderful corporate venture that is a case study on our textbook Website, called MyM&M'S. Go check it out! Or take a look at www.mymms.com. If you buy some, enjoy! There was a lot of careful

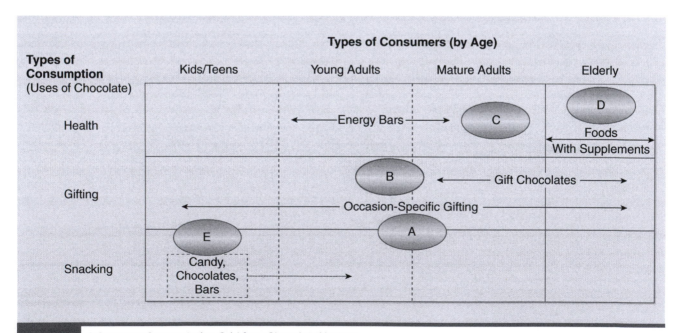

Figure 2.1   A Customer Segmentation Grid for a Chocolate Venture

thinking behind this venture to transform a commodity candy product into a premium-priced service based on printing personalized candy.

The axes for these customer segmentation grids need to be straightforward and meaningful. In the case of the snack food example in Figure 2.1, the horizontal axis shows different types of customers as measured by specific age groups. The reasoning behind using age as the basis for one of the axes is simply that people of different ages have different needs and preferences for snacking, be it for chocolate candies or anything else! The vertical axis in Figure 2.1 shows three major types of snack food consumption: *snacking* (or what we call "pigging out!" and which is an everyday sort of use for many consumers), *gifting* (as in giving chocolates to others for special occasions), and *healthy snacking* (which includes the energy bar segment). And each major use already has lots of current products in the marketplace, yet still offers considerable "white space" for innovation. The venture team used its own experience and judgment to define these three major uses and showed them to trusted colleagues for feedback and validation.

You can then overlay directly on top of a customer segmentation grid your own current products (if you are doing a new venture inside an existing corporation) or other major products already in the marketplace, and circle what you perceive to be open market spaces. You can even put in current segment/niche size and growth rates at the bottom or side of the grid. For example, for Figure 2.1, you could readily gather data on the current size and growth rate of the snack food segment, the gifting segment, and the healthy snacking segment, as well as the size and growth rates of the decennial age groups on the horizontal axis. The simple, single framework shown in Figure 2.1 then becomes a portal for all sorts of market, competitor, and opportunity pinpointing information. Any time you can present your team members or investors a simple, powerful picture rather than an entire memo or report, you are a winner!

Continuing with Figure 2.1 as a learning example, the competitive intensity facing a venture trying to start a new candy company aimed at kids and teens for regular snacking is intense. You will be fighting world-class brands such as M&M'S Candies® Hershey's, or Snickers. Similarly, trying to start a gift chocolate company that competes directly with Godiva for the attention of mature adults is going to be difficult, simply because of that company's formidable branding and distribution presence. And taking PowerBar head on in the mainstream energy bar market for young adults is going to be tough—no matter how good your chefs and their recipes. Entrepreneurs need to head for the "white space"—the adjacent areas in customer groups and basic product or service uses where there isn't much competition—or at least where the competition that exists is highly fragmented, for example, a bunch of other small companies that are also trying to figure things out and scale up their respective businesses.

The entrepreneur looks for open running room in a market. Continuing with Figure 2.1, there is lots of running room. For example, there are lots of entrepreneurs seeking to provide healthy drinks and snacks in the form of fortified water, bars, cookies, and dried vegetables for different types of consumers in the top row of our grid. In the second row of Figure 2.1, innovation in gifting is also pretty hot, with food and apparel companies like Vermont Teddy Bear bringing occasion-specific gifting ideas to market. And in the very first row of Figure 2.1, the traditional "pigging out" use, many food scientists working in companies large and small are trying to determine how to make more healthful yet still tasty snacks and treats. The obesity crisis is demanding change. Importantly, remember that an entrepreneur cannot focus on all three food uses as a startup. He or she needs to focus.

That same concept of focus also applies to customer groups. You can't make great tasty/healthy snacks for *everyone*—at least, not to start. Why not? Well, kids want different flavors and portion sizes than teens, and teens are different than the students reading this book; and you are very different than your parents. And the food itself is just one component. Positioning and branding are very different. Just consider the pictures and imagery shown for chocolates intended primarily for kids and teens, versus those for adults. And the distribution points are also often very different for different user/use combinations. Gift chocolates sell in one type of venue, energy bars in another, and regular candy in yet another (such as the checkout counter versus the healthy foods section of a grocer or convenience store).

In other words, *getting specific* about the customer group and the primary use for your intended products and services is fundamental for any venture—both for your venture planning and the execution of the plan once you start the company.

To complete our learning example in Figure 2.1, we show four distinct opportunities that the would-be food entrepreneur might target to start a venture:

- Circle A: Print customized, personalized printed candies for consumers of varying ages who are making purchases for different occasions. This was precisely the vision for the MyM&M'S team, which looked at little kids' birthday parties, bar mitzvahs, graduations, weddings, ongoing romance (Valentine's Day), sporting events, and business uses such as recruiting, corporate training, and retirements. The basis for this business is to print text messages and jpegs on little, round M&M'S Candies—ordered directly on the Web and shipped directly to a customers' house or place of business. And the venture charges at least ten times as much for these special candies as regular M&M'S Candies® sold at retail at checkout counters around the world.

- Circle B: Develop a venture around a more contemporary type of gifting chocolate that would be "cool" for young adults still in college or just out of it (e.g., a much more contemporary type of Godiva). This is reflected by the positioning of Circle B on the grid at a younger crowd than Godiva. If you want to see an example of an entrepreneur who selected this as his target, just go to www.mrchocolate.com, located, as you might suspect, in Manhattan, New York. Women consumers, particularly young professional women (or those who remain young at heart) *absolutely relish* his creations!

- Circle C: Develop a venture around health or energy bar products that have great taste, are less fattening for mature adults, and have functional supplements. For example, most energy bars have high caloric density—and don't taste all that great. A new, great-tasting energy bar product might be positioned for older, "aspirational" athletes, reflected by the positioning of Circle C.

- Circle D: A venture might also make functional bars for the region labeled Circle D, such as a great-tasting, portioned or tabbed chocolate bar loaded up with calcium and other ingredients designed to improve bone strength for mature women.

- Circle E: Or we might decide to fly right into the face of the established competition in the kids/teens snacking market, trying to add to or disrupt the established confectionary business. For example, we might try to make healthy snacks that are both really good for kids and that they love to eat! For example, there is a need for "fun fruit"—a whole serving of fruits, without heavy sugars, in different kid-friendly flavors and kids-designed packaging. Moms still have trouble getting their kids to eat fresh fruit, so this concept might be an answer for the lunch box. Unfortunately, there are multimillion-dollar slotting fees just to get on grocery shelves across the United States where most Moms shop. Most startup teams would have to look to other channels—specialty, premium retailers, club stores, or perhaps the Web—and hope that there was sufficient revenue until the point they could afford to go mainstream.

In this example, we see lots of opportunities that emerge from the process of customer segmentation. You can be an innovator even in what appear to be mature, stable, and rarely changing industries!

An entrepreneur needs to view and consider all the different possibilities in a target industry. From there, you can then focus on an area of the industry that represents an excellent business opportunity based on a number of factors: the size and growth rate of that segment/niche; the needs of users in various use types; and competition and other business realities, such as the cost of distribution.

For a business-to-business venture (B2B), entrepreneurs typically start segmenting customers by (a) industries or vertical markets, and (b) size of company. For example, a software company might segment its customers into financial services, retail, healthcare, and manufacturing companies, and then by size of company—small, medium, and large—within these vertical markets. The entrepreneur might then further focus by saying that he or she wishes to concentrate on providing CRM and analytics to small businesses doing eCommerce on the Web, and provide these analytics through the Cloud *as a service*.

Once you have a customer/use focus, you can then concentrate on the rest of the venture: the design of solutions for customers, the route to market, how to communicate value or otherwise brand products and services, how to charge for these solutions, and, ultimately, the revenue and profitability potential of the business.

A Customer Segmentation Example for Services

Many of you will be thinking about ventures that are services-related, as opposed to product-based. Customer segmentation works just as well for services as it does for products. Let's take a simple example.

Suppose that you want to start a travel services business. We have a group of former students who are travel entrepreneurs. Members of this team had worked or done internships for major travel agencies, had lived abroad for a bit, and were very enthusiastic about starting their own business. They had a clear need to focus on a niche within the enormous travel business. Going to www.ustravel.org, they quickly saw two major customer segments and major "uses": leisure travelers and business travelers, traveling either domestically or abroad.

For leisure travel in the United States alone, they found that the segment size was valued at over $560 billion in 2011; three-quarters of domestic trips were for leisure purposes, and that U.S. residents logged over 1.5 billion person-trips for leisure travel during that year, with primary "uses" being to visit relatives, to shop, to visit friends, and to do rural sightseeing and visit beaches. For business travel, the numbers were almost $250 billion in travel by U.S. residents during 2011, and 458 million person-trips. Then there is the "international" travel use occasion: In 2011, travel spending by Americans abroad totaled over $110 billion, and foreign visitors spent close to $153 billion visiting the United States. Overall, there was 9% growth of travel to Asia and the Pacific, 8% growth to Africa as well as the Middle East, 6% growth to Europe, and 4% growth for travel to the United States. For such a large existing industry, these were indeed impressive numbers.

With these and other data, the team looked to its own personal knowledge, its experience and desires, and decided to go after U.S. residents traveling abroad—at least a $110 billion a year market. For specific customer groups, the team then used an age/lifestyle approach for its segmentation: college students traveling (and studying) abroad, young professionals without children, young families, Baby Boomers, and seniors. They noted further that, while there are major players handling enormous chunks of business (through Web portals, the airlines, or the hotel companies), there is only highly fragmented competition focused on the adventure travel business. As they considered adventure travel further, they found some significant competitors serving mature adults and families, such as Thomson Safaris (Watertown, Massachusetts), *Outside* magazine's 2012 Active Travel Award & All-Time Favorite Trips Hall of Fame. But there didn't appear to be major players directly targeting younger U.S. travelers—college students or young professionals who don't have children yet, for example, Millennials—where adventure travel would seem to be a more natural fit.

Largely because the team was so familiar with the needs of the semester study abroad customer, it then focused first on college students and began its field research with students on their old college campuses and elsewhere. The team uncovered a niche opportunity to provide adventure travel—safe yet fun, and also educational—for college students studying abroad. Industry reports also showed this to be a booming niche within the leisure travel industry segment. The Travel Industry Association of America has estimated that about 10% of Americans have taken an adventure travel trip, and that this is growing by about 10% a year. Later, they would shift to young adults who had graduated from college and were holding their first or second professional jobs.

The rest of this team's story flows directly from its segmentation of the industry by travel customers and travel uses or types. First, several members of the team moved to Italy to arrange adventuresome weekends and week-long trips to interesting venues in Africa and eastern Europe, while others stayed in the United States to market directly to students and university administrators. Then sales began in earnest. Soon the team was selling to dozens of universities and providing hundreds of trips to Americans studying abroad in major European cities. If you would like to read more about this case, go to our textbook Website and read SnoworSand (www.sagepub.com/meyer2e). To grow, the team also decided to pursue the next age group, older Millennials and unmarried Gen Ys seeking adventure travel experiences. These latter niches were much larger than the college student niche leveraging its inventory of tours and partners for in-country travel, lodging, food, and sport/adventure activities.

Customer Segmentation Should Be Meaningful, Measureable, and Actionable

As this travel service and the prior chocolate examples show, it is also important to keep customer segmentation within your industry section simple, easy to explain to others, and still powerful in terms of providing clear vision into the different possible types of customers and their uses for your types of products or services. This will make your strategy easier to explain to partners, employees, and investors. It will also be easier to explain to your professor!

For these reasons, we try to limit customer segmentation grids to just *two, and at most three,* dimensions. It is fairly easy to explain phenomena that have two major dimensions. Once we get into three, it becomes a lot harder!

How do you know that your customer segmentation grid is a good one for planning a new venture? Here are some pointers:

- The axes and the boundary points in the axes must be *meaningful* to you and your team members. By meaningful, we mean that the axes are not obtuse or vague. For example, differences in consumer ages have impact in whatever you are proposing to do; differences in industry category have impact; differences in geography have impact. A customer segmentation grid must be able to speak for itself to the viewer.

- Your axes must be *measurable* and researchable: for example, age groups and genders. Industries, size of companies, and geographies are measurable in the sense that you can find data on the current size and growth rates of these segments. And the uses axis on your grid must be either current known uses for products or services in your type of business, or ones that industry observers regard as highly likely to exist in the future. Home medical monitoring, smart home energy management, and rooftop organic greenhouse vegetable growing are all examples of fundamental use cases whose time will come!

- Your customer segmentation grid must be *actionable*. This means it must show open running room, a clear path for innovation and venturing, such as we saw in Figure 2.1. If it is not actionable, then try a different design. Define your customer groups and uses in a more creative way where white space comes forth. The first design of a customer segmentation grid is rarely the last. This takes careful thought and usually a few iterations.

TIP: DETERMINING THE ADDRESSABLE MARKET _____

Professional investors such as venture capitalists often use the term *the addressable market* for a venture. The addressable market is a combination of the target industry segment/niche, the target customer with that industry area, and the amount of revenue that can be generated by serving those customers if all goes well. In other words, the addressable market is a revenue projection based on industry, customer, and the sales side of your business model. Venture capital firms (which are equity investors who pool much of their investment money from institutional investors such as investment banks, pension plans, and universities) often like to see a business plan that shows an addressable market of $1 billion over the coming five years, which if the venture takes 10%, leads to a $100 million plus revenue business. A $100 million business, generating profits, can be sold, depending on the type of business, for as much as four to five times revenue if not more! So, for example, if a group of VCs invests $25 million into your business over five years for 50% of the stock and then helps your company get acquired for $500 million, the VCs own $25 million grows to $250 million. (Moreover, their deal with you will typically be to get their $25 million paid back first before proceeds are divided among shareholders, which means they will get $25 million plus half of the remaining $475 million, leading to a total payout of $263.50 million.) Any time investors can get a return of 10X or more on their investment, well . . . they will be your friends for life and hope that you want to start yet another company soon thereafter!

HELPFUL TIPS

If you would like to see a clear example of defining an addressable market, take a look at the SilverRail Technologies case on the Website for this textbook. Aaron Gowell—the entrepreneur—started a business to aggregate open high-speed train travel seats across different countries in Europe, and present these as a single booking and financial transaction to consumers, typically through travel portals. He started with a $300 billion worldwide train travel market, of which $80 billion was in Europe. He then focused only on rail travel lasting between two and four hours, his "sweet spot." High-speed tracks were expanding rapidly across Europe and were taking majority share away from discount airlines for short- to medium-duration trips. Of these trips, only 13% were presently booked online due to a lack of a seat aggregator, and Aaron's goal was to get that number to 60% comparable to that of the United States. That opportunity gap represented an addressable market of initially $22 billion. He initially hoped to capture just 1% of that addressable market, growing to 10% over five years. At a 5% booking commission, his company would be about $150 million in revenue.

This is a strong example of narrowing down the addressable market, comprising a specific customer group and a specific use (high-speed intercity European travel not yet booked online). The entrepreneur raised $6 million in startup capital after a tough slog through dozens of potential investors. As stated by Aaron, the entrepreneur:

> When pitching VCs, it's very important not to talk about tackling the whole market, but to segment the market down into something more believable and achievable—it builds credibility with the VCs who are tired of companies pitching them on how they're going to "capture just 2% of the total market," which

(Continued)

(Continued)

is simply not a believable approach. If you talk about tackling the whole market, you're going to get kicked out of the room. The more detailed you are in your segmentation, the more credibility you gain.

Aaron ended up targeting a specific piece of the high-speed rail travel business in Europe—customers traveling four hours or less—and proposed to aggregate the complex financial transactions of purchasing tickets for trips across countries. By capturing 10% of that market, over five years, he could create a $100 million plus enterprise. It's a great case—SilverRail Technologies—check it out at www.sagepub .com/meyer2e.

Angel investors tend to be less demanding in their initial expectation—a $30 to $50 million revenue business that produces health profits will do just fine, as we shall learn in Chapter 8 of this book.

Established Versus Emerging Industry Niches

When we hear that an entrepreneur has "created an industry," what they have really done is to create a tiny new niche in an established industry that over time grows large. Fred Smith of Federal Express started with a couple of airplanes delivering mail overnight. Now expedited delivery is a global industry. People who have the vision and courage to create new niches within an industry are nothing short of business geniuses, such as Steve Jobs. Actually, many observers would say that Jobs created three industries: desktop publishing, with the Mac and PageMaker software; computer-generated animation for movies, with Pixar; and media convergence, with iTunes and iPod. The great thing about emerging industry niches is that competition is highly fragmented. The market is there for the taking. The bad thing is that customers are not yet spending lots of money for products or services in that niche—because there are few if any yet to be had! The entrepreneur has to be both an excellent innovator and business person to drive and service customer demand.

As these examples show, emerging industry niches have a habit of "taking off" to become major industry segments in their own right. Consider the example of eBay, now a multibillion-dollar business with operations in over 30 countries. It was founded by Pierre Omidvar, who had started a business called AuctionWeb in 1995. Omidvar discovered that there were collectors of all sorts of odd items scanning the world for things to purchase. He perceived the Web as a great way to connect buyers with sellers without having to go to antique stores, fairs, and the like. Now online auctioning is an important segment for consumer purchasing. It has also become widely used in certain types of industrial buying, known as Internet auctions. Corporations will put procurements for either products or services into an online auction, often forcing suppliers to bid down to the winning price.

As eBay shows, if the entrepreneur can successfully launch a product or service into an emerging niche, then learn and grow the business, he or she might have the opportunity to dominate that niche. At that point, the company has lots of options: It will probably become an acquisition for a corporation that is a lead player in the larger industry "segment"; or the venture might have the revenues and profitability needed to do an initial public offering, raising the cash needed to either do its own R&D or make acquisitions to grow into adjacent markets. This idea of finding a niche, learning as much as you can about it, innovating successfully, and developing excellence in go-to-market execution is a tried and true path to success in entrepreneurship—regardless of industry and technology.

An *emerging niche* is truly a small but growing slice of a large market characterized by customers and uses that no company quite understands or knows how to fully serve at the moment; it is therefore seen as either too small or too risky by most large, established competitors serving the larger market. For example, as we write this book now, it is obvious that the application of medical monitoring devices for home healthcare is a niche that is on the cusp of explosive growth. Such a solution can save society lots of money by reducing expensive hospital admissions, all for the cost of a few medical sensors, some wireless connectivity in the home, and a connection to some monitoring server software—just like ADT for home security. In contrast to this opportunity, monitoring devices in hospitals is the larger, established market, and it is already served by many major medical device manufacturers.

In contrast to pioneering emerging markets, many entrepreneurs decide to enter existing niches within established products and services and already sizable customer demand. The pathway to success in an established niche is that the entrepreneur must beat current competitors with better products or services, better marketing, and/or a new business model that hits the customer's sweet spot. Think iTunes, for example. The entrepreneurs working in an existing segment/niche bring so much quality, convenience, and branding to the category that they wrestle share from existing, slower-footed competitors. Clearly, the nice thing about innovating in an established niche is that there is already customer money flowing into the purchase of the products and services in that niche. However, if it is an existing niche, there will be strong competition that has already fought its way into the hearts and minds of customers. You have to be extra-differentiated in the design of your products and services, in your marketing, and in how you do business with customers, to win. And you might have to be price aggressive in order to convince existing resellers and end-customers to swap out other products for yours. That means smaller operating margins and the need to get more customers faster in order to have a successful business compared to new products and services for which there is less competition, and therefore less price sensitivity.

The Importance of Finding Innovative Customers

Whether it is an emerging niche or an existing one, it is also very important to find customers who have innovative attitudes and behaviors, who desire new solutions, and who appreciate the benefits of those solutions for improving their lives and businesses. To create a "hot" innovative company, find those customers who want to taste your hot sauce—even though your wares are not yet well-proven. These are customers who want to try the new—or at least to test the new.

For consumer products, this means finding retail customers who enjoy trying new products like yours in a store or online. Or, if you venture into services such as the energy segment, that means finding building owners who are convinced that the sensors and software for "smarter builds" can help them save energy expenses and maintenance costs, plus scratch their itch to help the environment. Or, if you are into healthcare, it could be the CIOs of large hospitals who are just dying (sorry for the pun!) to use interactive Web conference technology to keep patients on proper rehabilitation after leaving the hospital. This prevents hospital readmissions (which are expensive), and is good for patients. Indeed, there are many exciting places to start a company—*but you need to find and partner with actual customers who realize that as much as you, and who are willing to give their time to help design and test a solution.* These customers are sometimes called "lead users."[1]

Some niches are ripe with innovative customers. We have students who are starting an adventure travel company that uses the Web and social networking to link young travelers with their friends and families. Adventure travelers are, by definition, inclined to try new things, to experiment, and to share their experiences with others, including the entrepreneur. Other niches have a majority of conservative customers, especially in well-established niches. But still, if you look hard, you can find lead users. Building owners are a good example; there are an increasing number, particularly in areas such as hospitality, public buildings, and university

---

[1]Von Hippel, E. (1988). *The Sources of Innovation.* Oxford: Oxford University Press.

buildings, who are making "green" front and center in their designs and retrofitting of properties. If there are no lead users in a segment—customers naturally inclined to innovation—then you are most likely going to have a long, tough haul to building an exciting venture. Thus it would be best to find an adjacent niche where at least some customers will be receptive to your ideas.

Innovative customers actually like to try and even pay for brand-new products or services as part of their overall professional and personal makeup.[2] They are innovators, themselves. For the entrepreneur, such customers are very important, in many different ways. First, they will help you fine-tune your initial product or service to make it even better for the broader market. Second, any entrepreneur will tell you that the sales cycle for bringing new revenue in the door is one of the most painful realities facing new ventures. Shorten your sales cycle—particularly for a technology-intensive product—and you are well on your way to a successful business. Innovative customers buy quicker. Of course, this assumes that your product or service is more than a PowerPoint presentation and actually *works!* These customers are seeking to build a partnership with you, one based on trust and respect that goes both ways. They will not beat you down on price. They will look to you for your next set of solutions. And perhaps most important, they will serve as references to other prospective customers. You can put their names on your Website, for example. You can even have a few customers call them as part of a sale. They will also voluntarily spread the word about your company. All of this is gold for the entrepreneur. But again, *you must deliver.* Their respect must be earned.

So discover the lead users within your target industry segment/niche. Who are they? What do they need? How much will they spend? What other products or services might they want to use with yours? Think "partnership."[3] Find them and go talk to them. They are waiting to speak to you, but you just don't know one another yet. Don't be shy!

Defining Your Own Customer Groups

Now let's start building the customer segmentation grid for your venture. It is the next step after defining your target industry segment/niche. One axis is going to be major types or groups of customers; the other, major types of uses for your intended products or services.[4] Once you have these defined, you can then begin digging deeper into the needs and preferences of a specific set of customers needed to create the products, services, and business model for your venture.

Look at Figure 2.2. We want you to begin to complete this figure for your own venture.

You do not need to find a large number of different types of customers in a given target industry segment/niche. In most cases, you will find two or three distinct groups. And, if the buyers are not the end-users, you should create a second version of Figure 2.2 that focuses just on the different types of buyers within your market segment. For example, entrepreneurs will tell you that there is a big difference between a large retail chain and a specialty retailer, or between the purchasing departments of a for-profit hospital company and a nonprofit healthcare provider. It is important to understand the differences between buyers as well as users.

Figure 2.3 provides some helpful hints for completing Figure 2.2. We have included key words or data elements that you might find useful: one set for "B2C" ventures, where you are selling things to consumers; and another set for "B2B" ventures, where you are selling things to businesses or government organizations. Simply create a name for the specific customer group

---

[2]Moore, G. A. (1999). *Crossing the Chasm: Marketing and Selling High-Tech Products to Mainstream Customers.* New York: Harper Business Essentials.

[3]Von Hippel, E. (1988). *The Sources of Innovation.* Oxford: Oxford University Press; Von Hippel, E. (2005, September). "The best way to innovate? Let lead users do it for you" *Inc Magazine.*

[4]Derrick Abell, author of *Defining the Business* (Prentice-Hall, 1980), was a master at deploying this simple user and uses framework to develop strategies for business growth.

Customer Group	Description of Typical Customer Needs and Behaviors (Use bullet points)	Segment Size/Share (Use words or actual numbers)	Priority in Terms of Startup Focus

Figure 2.2 Identifying Different Types of Customers in an Industry Segment or Niche; Customer Segmentation Based on Common Core Behaviors and Needs

and then start to gather information for the various bullet points under the column that best represents your type of business. That will include the following:

- Indicate the specific end-user and buyer for your products or services
- Gather demographic or industry information
- Determine the decision-making level of the buyers: Who are they? What power or influence do they have in the purchase decision?
- Lastly, identify the primary needs and behaviors of end-users within the customer group

Once we have a handle on the major types of customers by virtue of their core needs and behaviors, we can then say with greater confidence and specificity which consumer we wish to serve first, and then drive everything in the business to better do so. There needs to be a good reason for your target customer selection. For example, let's say that you have chosen a specific customer group because it values high-quality products and services, appreciates good design, and is less likely to purchase just on price. Or, based on our prior discussion, that these customers you have chosen are lead users and are the only customers, at this point in time, willing to

	Business to Consumer	Business to Business
Customer Group Name	_____	_____
User Type	• Buying for self • Buying for others • Using what others have bought for me	• Buying for self • Buying for others • Using what others have bought for me
Demographics	• Age, income, gender, marital status • Health condition (for some categories) • Geography/Culture (for some categories)	• Industry—vertical market/segment • Size of organization • Status—profit/nonprofit
Decision-Making Level	• Head of household • Influencer • None of the above	• Business unit/department • Rank and authority • Role in buying decision
Needs & Behaviors	• Physical activities around product/service use • Used alone or with others • Attitudes and emotions, positive and negative • Only buys at certain occasions during the year	• Focused on revenue growth • Focused on reducing operating expenses • Risk-taking versus conservative • Only buys at certain times in the budget cycle

Figure 2.3 Factors to Consider When Describing Target Customers

experiment with your new products or services. Or that you have found industry data that show a particular customer group is the fastest-growing group in your target industry segment/niche. Or that there is a particular customer group that is so stuck with a specific problem that it is crying out for help. (This is probably the best reason!) All of these examples are good reasons for customer selection. In any case, you need to frame your justification based on insights gathered from industry data and your own field research with customers.

TIP: IDENTIFYING DIFFERENT CUSTOMERS FOR ENTERPRISE SOFTWARE

We worked with a highly dedicated, venture-capital-backed software team who was nonetheless stuck in its tracks. Its customer segmentation included financial services firms, telcos, and data service bureaus, all of whom used the company's device-independent "storage management" software. This software reconnoitered across the large computer networks of major corporations (using EMC, IBM, HP, Sun, and Hitachi for storage devices) to find where data were stored, how much data were stored, and how frequently the data were accessed. The software produced massive reports that created a graphic map of where big companies were storing all the various data around the world. Pretty impressive. But the software was only used by database administrators in IT departments, and *they* didn't have a lot of money to spend on anything.

We took a few of the lead engineers out into the field to visit key enterprise customers. As we poked around, we observed a fundamental use case that no one was solving at the time. This was to produce data that could be used to "chargeback" departments within a large company for their use of centralized computer storage and services. The CIO of a large enterprise could find out which departments were using centralized services, to meter that use and then charge the user-departments for their activity. This was the beginning of the shared services computing model—what today we call *Cloud computing*. Chargeback puts money back into the pockets of the CIOs.

Our client—a small software company—set about the work of creating a chargeback software product for CIOs. Fortunately, all the underlying data were already being gathered by this venture's software—and the new application required just a few more reports, a little more data to be gathered, and some accounting routines. The venture's programmers went to work, and a year later, this same venture—called Highground Systems—was purchased for more than 8X sales—over $400 million! Finding a new user within its current customers—the CIO who needed a chargeback application—was the key to success.

For enterprise software entrepreneurs reading this book, we encourage you to work "up" the customers' organization, find users with clout and money, and innovate *for them*.

Application of Customer Segmentation: Farming of the Future

These frameworks apply equally well to corporate ventures. Let's populate the Customer Segmentation Template from one such case. A few years ago, we came across a corporate venture team seeking to create software services for farm management. This was in the farm belt of the United States. The company had forever been in the "product business," and this team wanted to move into "services." Companies like John Deere had aggressively pursued this strategic path, and this venture team thought its company needed to get started down the same road.

The industry was the production of high-tech seeds for growing agricultural crops. Within this industry, the team then segmented the market according to the type of grain (corn, wheat, soy, and specialty crops) and the size of the farm based on the number of acres. The team's vision was to expand the business from just growing seeds to providing a comprehensive set of agronomic and analytical services to help farmers get the most out of their land, including using the correct type of seeds, fertilizers, and insecticides for each specific acre of land in the farm. This was all about developing computerized services that would match soil quality with agricultural inputs with harvested outputs.

The team thought it best to focus on the larger farms—those with more than 10,000 acres of land under management. The initial product idea was to create a software tool that would allow the farm owner to specify all grain farm inputs (seed types and quality, pesticides, herbicides, planting and harvesting machines, etc.) and agricultural outputs, and monitor profit and productivity to better plan the next growing season. This tool would be provided as a "hosted" service to farmers because the customer wasn't expected to have fancy computer systems.

Over the coming months, team members visited a dozen farming operations in their state. Those visits revealed four distinct types of grain farmers, shown in Figure 2.4. There were farmers who followed traditional methods, called "Steady Eddies." Then there were "performance optimizers," younger farmers who were comfortable with computers and who truly ran their farms as growing businesses. The team also visited weekend farmers as well as dairy farmers whose only interest was to grow corn to feed their livestock. The team took photographs of these customers and developed "personas" for each farmer type. A persona is a fancy way

Customer Group Label	Description/Persona	Segment Size/Share	Priority/Status
Steady Eddie	Wants to stay the same if possible, stay profitable, sell the farm in 5–10 years and move to someplace warm in the winter. Thinks intuitively. If he doesn't use a computer to run the business now, he is never likely to.	About 35% of U.S. acres for grain growing, and 160,000 farms\n\nDeclining share	May be large in market share but not a good target
Up & Comer	Thinker, Planner, Tester. A Performance Maximizer. Trained to use computers to manage business. Likely attended an agriculture college and may have an MBA. Trades commodities. Tracks inputs/outputs acre by acre.	20% of U.S. acres, about 70,000 farms\n\nGrowing share fast	No. 1 Top Target Customer
Sun Downer	Part-time farmers. Running the farm as a lifestyle choice, not to make money. May use computers in the city, but the farm is an escape from technology. Price focused in buying seed and equipment.	About 10% of U.S. acres, About 35,000 farms\n\nGrowing slowly	Not a target
Livestock Farmer	Looks for quality, but growing grains is not the top priority. Might be interested in a service to take the problem off his hands, but using his land.\n\nIncludes dairy, poultry, and pork farmers.	14% of U.S. acres, 89,000\n\n35%\n\nStable	No. 2 Priority\nFind third parties who grow grains on their land.

Figure 2.4   Farmer Customer Segmentation—The Major Groups in Grains Production, data circa 2010

Sources: Steady Eddie, Jupiterimages/Comstock/Thinkstock; Up & Comer, Digital Vision/Steve Bacon/Thinkstock; Sun Downer, Digital Vision/Thinkstock; Livestock Farmer, Digital Vision/Thinkstock.

of referring to a set of bullet points that describes the attitudes, behaviors, needs, and preferences of a particular type of end-user or buyer. The team then went to the Web and found federal government sources that provided data on size, growth rates, and trends in each customer group. Information from industry sources, such as trade associations and government agencies, is increasingly available on the Web. All this is shown in Figure 2.4. The team decided with good reason to target the innovative farmer—the performance maximizer—who already owned a significant percentage of grain production acreage and was buying up the land of the Steady Eddies.

Take a good look at the figure because this is what we believe you need to create for your venture! Major agricultural seed and equipment producers are now all getting into this future farming business with vigor! The market leader, Monsanto, has plans to make agricultural services just as large as its agricultural traditional seed and chemicals business.

This same approach of finding new, emerging customer groups can help your venture. It is insufficient for the entrepreneur to say that all customers within a given industry segment or niche are the same. There are likely to be distinctly different types of customers who want different things, act in different ways, and have preferences for buying products or services that are very different. And some of these customer groups just might contain the lead users you need to build an innovative venture, such as the performance maximizers in the example above.

With Customer Groups in Hand, Identify Different Basic Uses for Products and Services _____

Now we begin the process of learning what makes customers tick.

In general, the innovator—either as entrepreneur or corporate entrepreneur—wants to create powerful products or services that dramatically *improve the customer's experience*. Any experience is part of a use occasion. For example, Starbucks innovated the customer's experience of going to a coffee shop by adding a comfortable, den-like environment and wireless connectivity to excellent coffee products. MyM&M'S—the customer-printed candy case found on our textbook Website—transformed the chocolate gifting experience by allowing consumers to print messages and pictures directly onto M&M'S Candies.® The specific use occasions tend to be birthdays, graduations, weddings, romance, and retirements. Similarly, the GPS and social networking technology flooding into cars can dramatically improve the driver's experience for certain key use occasions—such as avoiding traffic jams or finding stores with certain types of products and promotions.

To get to this point of innovation—to improve the customer's experience with either products or services—you first need to identify specific uses (or use occasions), just as you identified different types of customers in the pages above. Once you have these key uses, it is fairly straightforward to make combinations of customers and uses, and then select those that you wish to study further for the purposes of innovating and building a business.

For example, consider Urban Outfitters. The very successful U.S. retailer has different brands to suit different user/use occasions: *Urban Outfitters* offers targets young, educated, urban-minded women and men in the 18- to 30-year-old range with clothes and indoor furnishings; *Anthropologie* brings a global, cultural artfulness to older professional female consumers looking for clothes and home furnishings; and *Terrain* provides outdoor furnishings for affluent, mature females. Urban Outfitters also created *BHLDN*, a retail concept that focuses on contemporary wedding dresses and accessories for women. Each one of these retail brands serves a different customer-use combination.

Or, for a business-to-business example, look to IBM. It divides its marketplace into more than a dozen major industries, each with specific segments. For example, IBM segments the financial services industry into retail and commercial banking, insurance, and investment banking. Then, across these segments, it has three major uses: running a big data center; using analytics to optimize business processes or workflows; and optimizing the utilization of physical assets with "smarter planet/smarter city" systems in which sensors feed data real-time into computers, and then initiate alerts, response, and ongoing maintenance. IBM then provides solutions for each major client, based on common core technologies. For example, it provides distinct data center solutions for the IT departments of insurers, retailers, and electronics manufacturers. Or IBM has specific analytic solutions for the marketing departments of banks and telecommunications companies trying to win new customers and up-sell current ones. Its smarter city solutions are targeting crime and safety, traffic management, and citizen services as specific integrated offerings. It is all about focusing on specific "users" and "use cases." This is a very powerful, focusing framework, be it for large companies or startups.

This "customers and uses" framework yields the framework shown in Figure 2.5. On the horizontal axis are distinct groups of customers as we have defined them above. Any information that you can gather—from the government databases, magazine articles, or trade associations—on the size and growth rate of these major customer groups is important because it can help you better focus on a particular customer group.

On the vertical axis of Figure 2.5 is a second term: *uses*. If it is easier for you, think about "use occasions" or "occasions of use." Different uses for a food company might be breakfast, lunch, dinner, and snacking; and then, "at home" or "on the go" (for customers of different ages and genders). For a software security company, uses include data center security, desktop security, and mobile security (for individuals, SME, and large corporate or government customers). For a healthcare venture, primary use occasions include hospital-based care, ambulatory care (e.g., walk-in clinics), and home care for customers varying by age and severity of disease (and, in the United States, type of insurance). Again, as the entrepreneur, this customers-uses segmentation allows you to pinpoint your innovations. For a food startup, these use cases might include breakfast, lunch, dinner, or snacking between meals, each arguably different for singles, married couples without children, or families.

Rarely can the entrepreneur identify all the current and new, emerging uses among a set of customers by just sitting behind his or her desk. You need to get out and enter the world of the customer. You already have your major customer groups from the work above. You need to determine where these representative customers exist and how best to visit them. Web browsing doesn't work here; it needs to be face to face. Then you need to go where these different types of customers actually use your types of products or services, and then, where they *buy* them.

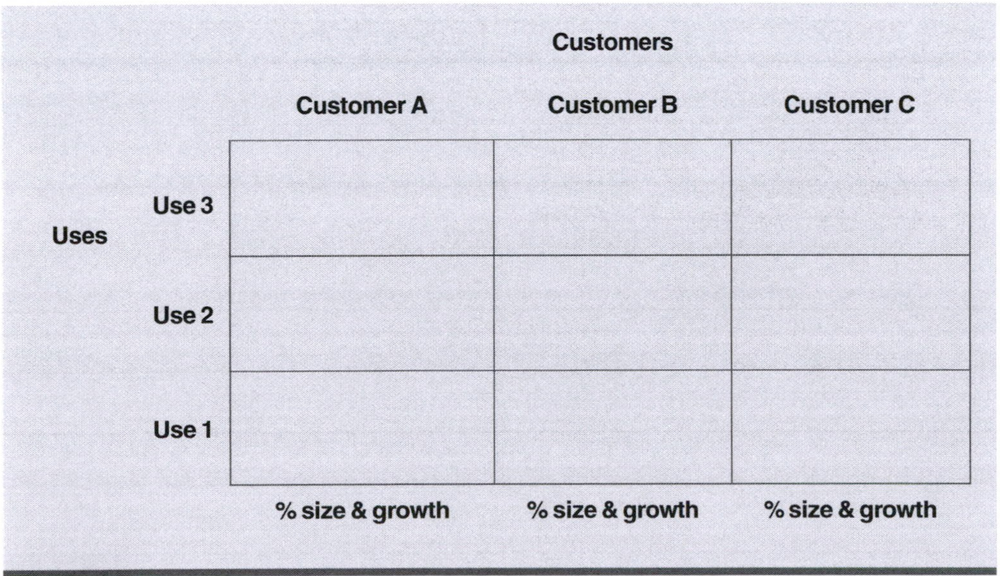

Figure 2.5 Customer Segmentation: Types of Customers and Types of Uses

Go to these places for an hour or two; watch, listen, and learn. Important use cases will come to light—we guarantee it. And from these, you will truly begin to innovate. That's another guarantee.

We recently wrapped an innovation session with a bunch of food innovators. Rather than dream new products up ourselves, we paired off to spend an evening shopping, cooking, and consuming with two groups of Millennials—one male and the other female. The differences between the two groups were stunning. Men are clearly from Mars, and Women from Venus! When it comes to food and attitudes toward food, they shop, cook, and consume in entirely different manners—and the only way one can truly learn this is by spending time intensively with each group. This is the truest source of innovation.

Or, for a B2B example, one of your author's very first company was a software venture that made real-time software for manufacturing process control for brewing beer. We actually became the market leader in this category. We had to visit large breweries, live and in-person, to learn the industrial environment, the variety of temperature and pressure sensors we needed to integrate, the types of specific information and automation plant operators needed for their jobs, and the daily and weekly information needed by plant managers on production runs. Only then, armed with these very specific use cases modeled with the "brewery process control" target, could we build the correct and necessary software. Another benefit, of course, was that we were also able to sample our customers' end-product, for example, their beer!

*** *** ***

In this chapter, we have shown you how to identify different types of customers within a target industry segment or niche, and then how to think about their different basic uses for your types of products or services. We want you to be just as specific about these uses as you are about different types of customers within your target segment or niche. By defining that intersection between customers and uses, you have a direct, immediate focus for your subsequent innovation. The next chapter examines how to understand how these target customers think, feel, and act in these occasions of use.

Reader Exercises

Step 1: Try Your Hand on Customer Segmentation by User and Uses for Flexible Solar Panels

Take a quick look on the Web for companies that are producing flexible solar films that can be wrapped around radios, backpacks, automobile rooftops, and so forth. It is very specialized technology relative to the fixed silicon solar panels that we see on homes and buildings. The flexible solar film market—or what ventures have called "plastic power"—is comprised of dozens if not hundreds of specific applications. Search the Web and use your imagination to segment this emerging market by "users" and "uses."

Step 2: Spend Time With Your Target Customers and Their Uses

Create the Customers and Their Uses Template for your own venture. Remember, you have already selected an industry focus and the type of business you want to create from Chapter 1. Now we begin to dig deeper into that target industry segment/niche to develop a further focus on the types of problems you want to solve, and for whom you wish to solve them.

a. Label the columns and rows for the Customers and Their Uses Template (Figure 2.6) for your venture. That means identifying the specific customer groups and their primary uses for products or services, such as the ones you might create.

b. Take a quick visit (if possible) to your different customer groups in their places of work or leisure. Spend an hour with each. Observe. See the primary use cases. Look for emerging use cases (such as virtual training versus face-to-face training for complex computer systems).

c. After constructing your customer segmentation grid, *circle your primary customer and use combination.* Start crafting the story behind why your customer target makes so much sense.

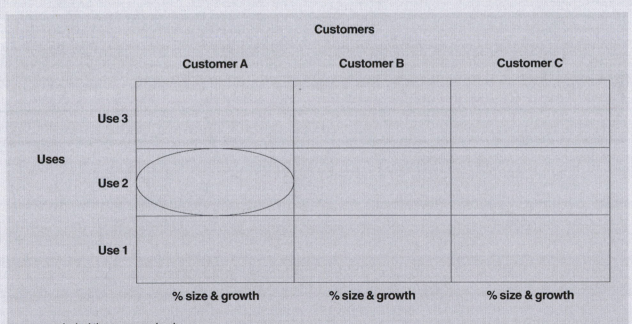

Figure 2.6 Customer Segmentation: Set Your Initial Target Customer and Use Case/Occasion

Step 3: Size Your Target Market

Next, hit the Web and try to find data for the relative size and spending for your target customer group and use occasion. Take another look at the travel industry fact sheet in the Tip Box provided in Chapter 1. (That was Figure 1.3.) Maybe you will be fortunate enough to find lots of data in a single, convenient source. Otherwise, keep digging and assemble the data yourself. Investors are definitely going to want to know the following:

1. The size of your target industry niche within the overall market

2. The market potential represented by your specific customer group in that industry niche and the use occasions you wish to serve

3. How you see your see that market size growing over the coming five years

Think about Aaron Gowell (the rail travel booking service) in the TIP box earlier in this chapter. He started with a very broad market (European train travel), got more specific (high-speed rail between two and four hours), and then got even more specific (another 50% or so that might be booked online) to size his "addressable market." He then estimated reasonable penetration rates and applied a standard 5% booking commission to get some revenue projections. Aaron did a "top-down" revenue projection. That's what we want you to get started on now. You cannot have a good business plan without a strong rationale for your revenue projections.

Later, in the Reality Check described in Chapter 7, we will teach you another method for revenue projection that is based on actually surveying prospective customers in your industry segment/niche. You will find their level of dissatisfaction with existing solutions, their "purchase intent" for your new solution, and how much they are willing to spend on your solution. We call this a "bottoms-up" approach to revenue projection. In reality, the entrepreneur needs to try to do both the top-down and bottoms-up approaches to market sizing and revenue projection, and then compare the results.

But for now, get started with the top-down approach. You need a healthy market to support all your hard work. This exercise is going to help you see if that is the case. If it doesn't feel sufficiently large, use your customer segmentation grid to explore adjacent segments/niches, or alternative or additional uses to enlarge the pie.

Visit the Student Study Site at **www.sagepub.com/meyer2e** to access the following resources:

- Web Resources
- Video Resources
- General Resources in Entrepreneurship

3

Defining the Needs of Target Customers

Getting Into Their Hearts and Minds

The Purpose of the Chapter

The previous chapter helped you segment your customers into different groups and their basic types of uses for your category of products or services. We then had you select your initial focus—the combination of customer group and occasion of use—as the basis for understanding customer needs. Now we move on to the business of how to quickly and effectively understand those needs. We call this getting into the hearts and minds of target users and target buyers. The two—users and buyers—are not always the same, but both are essential for getting a handle on "the customer" for any venture.

As in prior chapters, we will include a few basic frameworks and help illustrate them with examples. Then, in the Reader Exercises, we will ask you to apply these frameworks to your own venture—in this case, to do in-depth customer research.

Learning Objectives

- Refine your understanding of customer needs, with a clear distinction between users and buyers
- Develop the first design of your product or service based on those needs
- Take a first crack at defining the "value" customers will find in your solutions, be it functional, economic, emotional, or social

Getting Ready to Jump Into the Hearts and Minds of Your Customers

Many companies get started because the entrepreneur, in one way or another, has been "the user" and "the buyer" for the type of product or service he or she wants to create. As a representative user in the field, the entrepreneur recognizes the critical flaws in existing products and services, sees the gap in the marketplace for something better, and proceeds forward. Many of you reading this book may be such users already. You may be frustrated with what you have in your target industry segment/niche, and have already thought deeply about the design and performance of what you believe could be a much better solution. For example, one of our closest friends and mentors, Al Lehnerd, was a senior manager at Black & Decker. Al had six kids. His wife left for a church retreat for an entire weekend, leaving Al alone with all of their kids for two days straight. After 48 hours of nonstop cleaning, including plugging in the vacuum cleaner a dozen times, Al went to work with a pain in his back on Monday morning. In just a few days, he designed and prototyped a portable vacuum cleaner that didn't have to be plugged in!

However, even if you are like Al and have a brilliant personal insight as a frustrated user of current products and services in your target industry area, remember that you still need to validate your idea with other customers. You need to talk with a number of them to make sure that your pain is also *their pain*. As a fellow user and buyer, it should be pretty easy for you to start a conversation, commiserate, and learn more.

Even if you personally are not representative of the target customer in your industry and customer segmentation focus, no worries. We are going to learn how to observe, interview, and generally interact with target customers in a way that is highly productive for you and not threatening to them.

From the prior chapter, you have circled that combination of customer group and occasion of use that you will focus on for the work in this chapter. Now you simply need to find where these customers exist at work or leisure, observe them, and then, with certain methods, talk to them. We guarantee that you will uncover their fears, frustrations, and concerns. It is then up to you to create the product or service solutions that address these needs, and then the business model best suited for your solutions. Solving an important need or frustration in your customers makes your solutions a "must-buy" for them, as opposed to a "nice-to-buy"—and this is what you need for a great venture.

Also, in practice, many teams find themselves investigating several closely adjacent customer groups–use occasion combinations before deciding on the one best suited for their venture. In other words, they do the field research of this chapter on a couple of different targets, and let the research itself drive their final decision. It sounds like more work, but it can be well worth the effort if you are serious about starting a company.

For example, we had a team of female graduate students considering a social venture for selling jewelry crafted in South America; half of its operating profits would go back to villagers in the form of microloans to build up their jewelry production operations in a few selected rural areas. For customers, these students first targeted university students such as themselves as purchasers of the jewelry; but they also decided to extend their efforts to somewhat older professional women between the ages of 25 and 35. Their discussions with several dozen women in both segments showed two shared occasions of use—jewelry for everyday use and jewelry for special occasions. As a result of their research, they designed a fascinating concept for "modular jewelry," which could be repurposed from one occasion to the next. But they also found two entirely different distribution channels: "networked marketing," for example, college parties, for the younger crowd, and a boutique, retail channel for the older professional crowd. Their business plan first targeted the younger segment, but then leveraged the product design and supply/logistics strategy into a second offering for the older professional segment.

At this stage of the game, it is most important to experiment—to try a few different ideas and see which one is best. Many entrepreneurs start their field research with target customers already with a new product, service, or distribution idea in mind. That's okay, and it is highly motivating to think that you are inventing something new for the world. But you must be willing and open to being told that your initial idea is simply wrong or misguided; and, in that process, invariably you might learn *what* might indeed be a better idea. Entrepreneurs learn from trial and error—and the source of much of this wisdom lies directly with your target customers.

Doing the Field Research: Learning About the Attitudes, Behaviors, and Core Needs of Target Customers

Armed with some initial ideas for innovative solutions to customer needs, your key to success from this point forward is to identify and spend time with several or more target customers.

That experience tells the entrepreneur more about the intended customers' needs and wants and their willingness to pay rather than rely on opinions of any industry guru or consultant. Furthermore, this insight cannot be gained remotely. Communication over the telephone or through e-mail removes the intimacy of observation and the nonverbal expression that lies at the heart of identifying and understanding a customer's pain and frustrations. You are going to have to roll up your sleeves or otherwise get into the attire of your target customers and go "exist" with them for short but concentrated periods of time to get your true "Aha!" and march forward.

Understanding the customers' frustrations with current products or services in your chosen market niche is an essential element of a new business opportunity. Finding these frustrations, paying particular attention to knowledgeable, thoughtful customers, pays rich dividends.

If your field work does not unearth any clear customer frustrations, do not despair. Continue to look at the edges around your initial focus. Rarely are there no problems to solve.

Therefore, a mandatory requirement for successfully creating a new venture is to spend time with customers in a selected market niche. This is one of the most important parts of your teamwork in using this book. At the very least, spending time with customers helps you think more deeply about the business you could create and the products and services it might offer. More often, it will provide you with a direct indication of desirable products, services, pricing, and strategies for beating current competitors. Moreover, investors will know in a second if you are smart about your target customers.

Do not expect this customer research to be something that you can put off until two days before your class meeting when presentations are due. It is not easy, and it takes time to plan your attack, conduct the meetings, and synthesize the results. Reaching out to customers does not come naturally to some entrepreneurs, especially to those with strong technical backgrounds. Get over it. You and your team need to be deeply grounded in the world of your target customers—for products, services, and business model development.

Moreover, many users of consumer or business products or services will tell you that they "will definitely buy" or "are likely to buy" the products and services that already exist in the marketplace.[1] This is because the fierce, competitive nature of our economy has already driven most inferior products and services from the field. Truly bad choices have probably been purged from the marketplace. Therefore, your venture will have to supplant current products and services that have some good points. Your venture must be distinctive in some clear way. For many ventures, this distinctive edge comes in the design and functionality of the products or services. For others, the edge comes in the go-to-market aspect of the business—such as the best sales force or the coolest Website. And yet for a few others, the competitive advantage comes in the approach to pricing. An example might be creating a powerful software application that saves

---

[1]In traditional marketing science, this is called a "top two-box score," the percentage of customer voting for the two highest ratings in a range for a purchase intent question where the answers often goes from "will definitely buy" to "will likely buy" to "indifferent" to "probably won't buy" to "definitely will not buy."

customers demonstrable amounts of time and money. Instead of charging them a hefty licensing fee, the ventures request a percentage of the time and money saved. Whatever the method, your solutions must be distinctive for customers and differentiated from current competitors.

Some technologists believe that they can *think their way* to breakthrough business concepts from the comfort of their labs or offices. They are uneasy with the prospect of meeting with strangers and listening to people who have much less technical knowledge than they do. However, technologists cannot assume that they know what is best for customers. Personal brilliance works occasionally, but most of the time it leads to a "build it and they will come" mentality—which most often *does not work* for ventures. Instead, your mindset must be that the origins of winning Venture Concepts lie first and foremost with your target customers in their occasions of use.

TIP: UNIVERSITY SPIN-OFFS _____

Ventures can be based on technology that already exists in university research labs, waiting to be commercialized. University research labs are not only a hotbed for scientific and technological discovery, but places where faculty and graduate students are thinking about how to apply these breakthroughs to solve pressing customer and social problems. As but one example, MIT has seen numerous technology spin-offs that include Akamai (Cambridge, Massachusetts), which accelerates the delivery of Web pages for industry. Harvard and the Mayo Clinic have been the seeding grounds for dozens of health sciences ventures over the past decades, and both have active technology licensing operations and venture funds. At our own university, we have a number of graduate students who are doing their customer research on different potential application areas for their labs' technologies: detecting cancers of different forms with various chemistry, micro-fluidics and imaging technologies, non-invasive monitoring of blood chemistries, and nano-manufacturing. Or we see the same technological prowess in our visits to universities in other countries. For example, universities in the Netherlands have pioneered advanced technologies for areas such as water management, automated greenhouse production of vegetables, and green building materials and systems.

The trick, in all these cases, is for business-focused entrepreneurs to team up with brilliant technologists, to carefully and correctly license technologies from their universities, and then to do the careful customer research and business planning advocated in this book. From that work, prototypes get funded and tested, and serve as the basis for the venture funding needed to build world-class companies.

Further Appreciating the Differences Between End-Users and Buyers_____

The actual end-user and the buyer for a product or service are often not the same, and the entrepreneur needs to carefully consider the needs of both parties for his or her innovations and business models.

The buyer places the order and pays the bill; the user consumes or interacts with that purchase. Each is a "customer," and each must be listened to.

Consider the case of pet foods. For pet food makers, the buyers are pet owners; the end-users are dogs and cats. Buyers include both women and men; their attitudes are different and must be understood. Most women enjoy preparing meals for their pets, mixing kibble with sauce or leftovers; for them, pets are akin to children. Most men, according to trade experts, are convenience oriented when it comes to food—the simpler the better. On the user side, dogs and cats have different nutritional requirements, and many have taste preferences. Pet food developers must appreciate both human buyer attitudes and pet requirements and tastes. And for anyone actually in the pet food business, the actual "customer" is the retail store or chain that is its direct customer. Hence, there are three important sets of needs to be understood: the retailer, the pet owner, and the pet itself.

Similar examples can be found in B2B systems and services ventures. Workers in companies use software every day that has been purchased by decision makers somewhere else in the company. Innovators in the defense sector create complex electronic warfare systems for war fighters—who care about performance in life and death situations, regardless of cost—that are procured by desk-bound program managers for whom cost and maintenance are equally important. Energy management and telecommunications systems are sold to building owners, yet the users may often be tenants.

It is essential that you determine and keep track of the precise meaning of the "customer" as you advance your Venture Concept from idea to plan to reality.

TIP: CORPORATE SPIN-OFFS

Many ventures are started by employees of larger companies who find opportunity in niches that their corporate bosses deem too small to matter, or which they dismiss because they don't understand them: "This is a distraction for us. Perhaps you can make something of it. Good luck." The enterprising employee leaves and raises the capital needed to exploit the orphaned niche. In MBA classes for working professionals, it is not uncommon to find midlevel managers who develop business plans to spin-out an unwanted piece of their corporation's technology. The key to success here is to socialize your idea with executives, to appropriately license the technology, to give your company a financial incentive, and in general, to leave on good terms. In many cases, your old employer might even become your very first major customer, and if not that, an important channel partner.

If you want to see an example, check out the Sentillion case on the textbook Website (www.sagepub.com/meyer2e). Rob Seliger, the entrepreneur, spun out specific, unwanted healthcare software from the "old" Hewlett-Packard Medical Products Group as it was being acquired by Philips. Rob, a former top software manager at HP, focused on single sign-on by physicians and patient data synchronization as the two key use cases, both within large hospital customers. He built a great company over the next ten years, raising $30 million in venture capital. In 2010, Rob and his VCs sold the business for more than $150 million to a major IT company. Not only is Sentillion a classic corporate spin-off, but Rob will vouch for the deep customer research we advocate in this chapter.

Structuring Your Field Research

First, forget any preconceived notions of having a highly structured questionnaire that you learned how to create in a marketing class and might be expected to apply to hundreds of customers to get precise answers to well-known products or service features. (This comes later, in Chapter 7, when we do a "Reality Check.") It is far too early in your Venture Concept development *for that*. Instead, we are directing you to conduct exploratory field research to ferret out a new business idea in a series of in-depth conversations with a much smaller panel of target customers. The approach of this research is called *ethnography:* direct observation and depth interviewing in the customer's place or context of use.[2] For now, we want you to work directly with customers to get your "Aha!" from the perspective of their needs and frustrations.

From this point of view, there are a series of basic questions. First, how can you identify target end-users and buyers? Who are they, *precisely?*

The answer regarding with whom to speak comes from your Customers and Their Uses Template discussed in Chapter 2. Remember: Choice of industry segment and specific niche drive your customer segmentation—the customer groups and major uses by those customers for your type of products or services. So, for this step in the process, you are to find at least a half-dozen or so customers in each of your target customer groups that are involved in the major "uses" where you want to innovate. It's as simple as that.

What Is the Correct Number of Interviews for This Stage of the Process?

Students always worry about the number of customers to observe and converse with to get "reliable" results. Conventional marketing science tells us that a sample of a hundred or more is essential to do any serious statistics. Here, however, we are more concerned with deep insight than statistics. Deep insights rarely come from a one- or two-page survey. Instead, customer insights come from deep and thoughtful observation and conversation.

We studied a large number of "design firms"—companies that serve as innovation experts for large corporations. It showed that nearly 80% of those firms preferred in-depth interviewing with fewer than ten people for a specific design. The reason is two-fold: First, after a while, you don't learn anything new from talking to additional customers. In fact, when you stop gaining new insights is the best measure for saying "enough" rather than any hard and fast number. Second, time and money are short, particularly for the entrepreneur. Learn what you need to learn and get on with the process of building a company. Once you launch a business and its products or services to living, breathing customers, you will learn so much more and will have to adjust accordingly.[3]

So, ten or twelve in-depth conversations with customers are a reasonable goal for this activity. For some B2B ventures, the number may be less. For example, getting an hour with even six CIOs, or building managers, or large hospital administrators will be quite a challenge. Use your judgment, do your best, and always ask an interviewee if she or he has someone else that you should speak with about your venture idea. Six really good, in-depth interviews with target customers are worth their weight in gold at this point in the ball game.

Most Important: Work With Target Customers in Their Places of Use

Once you've identified target customers—end-users and buyers—how will you approach them for information and insights? We suggest the following: Do not ask them to visit you or meet in a neutral space. Instead, go to their place of activity—be it a place of leisure, of family activities, or

---

[2]There are some great supplemental readings on observing users in their context of use to design innovations. For example: Leonard-Barton, D., & Rayport, J. F. (1997). Spark innovation through empathic design. *Harvard Business Review*, 102–113; Norman, D. (2002). *The Design of Everyday Things*. New York: Doubleday; Atkinson, P., & Hammersley, M. (2007). *Ethnography Principles and Practice,* 3rd ed. New York: Routledge.

[3]Meyer, M. H., & Marion, T. (2010, Sep.–Oct.). Innovating for effectiveness: Lessons from design firms. *Research Technology Management,* 21–28.

of work, depending on your venture idea. Half of the insights you gain will probably come from simply observing customers in the appropriate setting and seeing them respond to certain situations, rather than sitting down with them for a formal talk.

For example, the WD-40 household lubricant was originally just an industrial degreasing and rust-preventing spray used in aerospace applications. The company, Rocket Chemical Company, had an early industrial customer named Convair, whose engineers used WD-40 to spray the outside of its military missiles. Norm Larsen, WD-40's inventor, learned that engineers were taking the lubricant home. His own in-depth interviewing with these engineers revealed a wide range of interesting household applications. So Norm developed a new aerosol can for household use! A world-class consumer product and brand were born. Today, the WD-40 company does about $250 million a year in revenue. And the company keeps coming up with innovations. Among them: all sorts of can sizes, and an aerosol straw that is built directly into the top!

Or, as another example, we worked with a corporate innovation team in a large baking business. We organized a baking party at our house, inviting a half-dozen young Moms (with young children, but not present at the party). We also had some company people—which included professional chefs, R&D staff, and marketers—come join in on the fun to watch, listen, and learn. In pairs, the "users" and "innovators" first went shopping, then baked together, and afterward ate each other's cakes and cupcakes. A little beer and wine helped accelerate the conversation. The Moms discussed their attitudes, behaviors, experiences, and frustrations baking cakes. What emerged was that the Moms cared most about the frosting on the cake (even more than the cake itself, as long as it was moist). They wanted a convenient way to personalize their frostings. A year later, the company brought to market *Frosting Creations*, a way to allow consumers to easily customize their frostings into a range of dozens of different flavors by sprinkling and mixing small flavor packets into one of three small tubs of base frosting mixes. *Easy customization* was the latent need, and it became the design driver for this corporate venture.

What do these examples mean for your projects? What sort of ethnographic experiences could you either directly participate in or construct in your dormitory or apartment? How might you do this for a pure software product or mobile application?

The Mindset and Approach for an Effective Conversation With Target Customers

If at all possible, we want you to observe users first and talk second. Simply observing the customer's activities for an hour or so may reveal a wealth of opportunities. Your authors never cease to be amazed at the inconvenience, poor quality, or simple nonperformance users across a rich array of industries and industry sectors put up with time and time again. Seeing that, with your own eyes, will be the source of your greatest opportunity. Look for frowns, sighs, and other signs of displeasure—as well as smiles, laughs, and other signs of the opposite. Are they sitting down or on the go? Are they alone or with other people? Look for what the user is doing *with other people* or *with other systems* in their places of use. There may well be opportunities to improve teamwork or multiperson collaboration within a product or service area. And, if you are in the B2B systems business, you will certainly have to know other systems with which your own system must work. Designing this type of interoperability up front into a solution makes life so much more convenient for the customer.

Then, it is time to talk. Once you begin a conversation, please try to listen more than you talk. You are not selling anything, yet. If you are selling anything to the customer, it is the importance of his or her needs and concerns *as a user or buyer* of what you want to do. And when a user tells you that something is important or a problem, always try to follow it up with, "Why is that important?" or "Why is that a problem?" This makes standard interviewing become "in-depth interviewing," a standard conversation much deeper, more meaningful, and useful for you as the entrepreneur. Then, after the person gives you an answer to your first *why*, ask *why* again, get an answer, and ask *why* perhaps one more time. This gets down to the deepest drivers for a need or frustration—and if you can uncover that need, you will be able to design a solution that is indeed very powerful or come up with a marketing message that hits a hot spot.

For example, if you turn to one of your teammates for this project, ask him or her why they he or she is getting his or her current degree. The first answer might be, "I want to learn new things." You might then ask, "Why is that important to you?" The response might be, "I feel that without this education, I won't be able to advance to the next level in my career." You might then ask, "Why has this been a problem?" And, if your teammate has a technical background and is getting an MBA, he or she might say, "Because I was pigeon-holed as an engineer that doesn't know and cannot manage business. What a drag." The result might be an innovation-focused MBA program design that combines lots of core business management courses with innovation courses where students help their companies grow. Or, if the student is relatively young, you might get answers that suggest that the individual really doesn't know what he or she wants to do and that the MBA is a vehicle for gaining exposure to different industries and making the contacts to get a first great job in a business career. Your *why's* should get different end-answers for different customer groups. In this case, all students want to learn, but the motivations of the technical student with substantial work experience versus the younger student with little work experience are markedly different.[4]

This technique of asking a successive series of *why's* in a customer interview is called *laddering*. In your field work associated with the chapter, please try to give laddering a try. It is simple yet so very revealing.

Also, even if you have some initial business ideas from your own prior experience, *please park your personal views and preferences outside the door!* Enter the world of users and buyers unencumbered by personal preferences and preconceived notions of their needs. Never assume that what excites you will excite *them* or that your problem is *their* problem. Be objective. Ask interesting questions. Learn. And then, think about the customer's own experience with products and services in your category and how to *improve that experience*. Your mission is to discover what customers like, what customers need, and what frustrates them.

Also, come prepared. You should have an idea of the types of information that you want—information that will help you focus your product and service development, how you price or charge, your marketing messages, and the route to market. Once again, knowing the types of information you need is different than coming into an interview thinking that you already know the answers.

TIP: CREATE AN "I DUNNO" FILE

Create a Word document or Excel spreadsheet containing any questions that emerge on this project for which you don't yet have an answer. You might even want to assign a name to find out an answer to that question if you are working in a team.

One of our closest, dearest mentors—Al Lehnerd, an executive with Black and Decker—taught us to keep an "I Dunno" file or folder for each new project. Often, people forget the questions they had earlier. Then an answer comes around, but they have already forgotten the question! Too bad, because usually those questions never die—they just disappear for a while and come back to haunt people later.

Keep an "I Dunno" file of some sort. Revisit it once a week as your venture project proceeds. It will also help organize your tasks moving forward. Entrepreneurship is all about learning—for customers, competitors, solutions design, and business models—and it never stops.

---

[4]This is a real example. At our university, this line of user research was pursued to design a High-Technology MBA program for the older, technical crowd and an internship-based co-op MBA program for younger, less-experienced students. Both provide great value to each specific student customer group.

Getting More Specific Insights From Your Field Research

Once you are done observing and then laddering a prospective customer to get fundamental insights, you can then pursue a more specific line of questioning to help get specific design points for your venture. Take a look at Figure 3.1. It contains a series of questions that will provide tremendous insight into the customer if you can gain his or her confidence to share this information with you.

Please read through these questions now. Imagine what these would be like for talking to users and buyers in your target customer groups and their primary occasions of use. The italicized sentences in parentheses after each question are the types of information you want to gather.

The combination of observation, laddering, and this more detailed questioning will make you very smart about your customers—and that, dear readers, is key to success for venturing. All it takes is some work, some open ears, and quiet time after these customer interactions to reflect on what you have learned. Sometimes this is best done with a partner, seeing and hearing customers with two sets of eyes and ears. Plus, two sets of hands for note-taking are always helpful, and shared learning is always exciting and fun. And it typically takes more than just a few minutes with a customer to gain this information; you should try to get at least an hour of intensive interaction with each individual.

Often, the best way to get this concentrated interaction is simply to ask the user if you can join him or her in your targeted occasion of use—such as when the user is shopping, exercising, cooking, working, using or fixing machines, or searching for certain types of information on the Web. You can ask the questions in Figure 3.1 as you join him or her in this activity.

1. How do you define the activity or problem? *(Teach me how I should think about the activity or problem area. It is probably bigger than how I define it now.)*

2. What do you now use in terms of products or services in this activity? *(Teach me the current competitive set.)*

3. Where or from whom do you buy products or services? What is good about that channel? What is not so good? *(Teach me the realities of the channels or the preferred routes to market.)*

4. How satisfied are you with your current products or services that you use in this activity? What is your greatest source of dissatisfaction or frustration with using these? *(Please tell me who you think is the best and the worst!)* What are your workarounds? *(I would love to see them!)*

5. Who is responsible for the buying decision? Is it you or someone else? *(Can you help me speak with them as well?)* How is the buying decision made? Who and what are the key influencers? *(You should be writing down notes because this is where most entrepreneurs slip up!)*

6. What are the criteria used when evaluating alternatives? Is there a clear set of metrics as part of those criteria? *(Can you teach me how you currently evaluate current products and services?)*

7. How much do you spend each month of year on products or services within this activity? *(Tell me if you think you are getting your money's worth, either by your facial expression or in words.)*

8. What would be the ideal solution for you? What would measure its value to you? *(Let me know what you think will be better than anything on the market today, and how customers would make their buying decisions.)*

9. What fears would you have in trying this solution? *(Would you ever buy something from a startup? Do you need to see a well-established brand name? Do I have to partner with a market leader in order to get you to try my wares?)*

10. Who would be the ideal supplier? What would be their approach, not just in terms of products, but in other things around the products? *(Teach me how to partner with you as opposed to just being a vendor.)*

Figure 3.1 A Discussion Guide for Conversations With Target Customers

When it comes to the detailed interview questions shown in Figure 3.1, it is very important for you to remember to:

- Position and conduct these discussions as *conversations,* not formal interviews. The customer is the teacher, and you are the student. This means detaching yourself from the solution for the moment—even if you are the smartest person in the room and think you know five times more than the person with whom you are speaking. Again, just park *that* outside the door.

- Use *open-ended* questions—that is, questions that cannot be answered with "yes" or "no." You can see that none of the questions in Figure 3.1 can be answered "yes" or "no."

- Apply the laddering technique—the *why's*—we learned above to these questions, too.

- Note that asking the customer about his or her ideal solution only comes later, in the specific questions. You need to establish the overall context of use and the competitive environment first. Only then will the customer's ideal solution make most sense.

- Always offer genuine thanks, both before and at the end of the conversation. If you meet ten target customers, chances are that three or four of those individuals may want to participate in trying your first prototypes of a new product or service. Or, if the "customer" is a store manager, he or she might actually become a launch channel partner. In fact, treat all of these people as partners. They may help you again. Be sure always to let them know how much you value their insights.

TIP: DEVELOP A PERSONA OF THE TARGET CUSTOMER_____

A "persona" is a profile of the target user, and also of the target buyer (if different). Included in that persona are the customer group's demographics, needs, attitudes, behaviors, and purchase preferences. We like to see innovation teams develop a persona for their target customers in a simple PowerPoint presentation. Following this up with a video of the customer in his or her occasion of use is even better. Bring along that video-recorder on your interviews, or better yet, just use your iPhone!

We define each of these terms as follows, and these categories serve as very good ways to organize the customer information you need to focus your innovation and marketing efforts:

Who they are, e.g., the consumer or industrial demographics of the target customer. This can be age, gender, and ethnicity, or industry niche, geography, size of a company, position, and level of responsibility of the person in the company.

Core needs. The customer's specific desires and frustrations as these relate to a specific occasion of use. These needs drive the features, performance, and price of a product or service. Uncovering core customer needs lies at the heart of entrepreneurial innovation. We like to think of these core needs as, in part, being derived from the attitudes and behaviors defined next.

Attitudes. These are the cognitive value or belief systems of customers. An example might be a young male's attitude toward driving versus Mom driving the kids to school versus professional commuters. In a corporate setting, "you can never get fired by selecting IBM" might be the attitude of mature IT managers, whereas younger ones might prefer to go with "open systems" and use smaller, independent service suppliers to get the job done.

Behaviors. These are the physical activities surrounding the use case. Using a car driving example, a young male wants to move lots of "stuff" and "party" with his buddies in his transportation; Moms and commuters display other behaviors, be it driving around with lots of kids or requiring an "office in the car" powered by communications technology. Purchasing behaviors are important here as well.

Purchase preferences. Customer behavior at the place of purchase provides essential insights for consumer-focused entrepreneurs. As a simple example, it is well known that males generally do not like to shop down the aisles of a grocery store. Rather, they prefer to shop the periphery, which includes the produce, deli, and chilled (not freezer) sections of the store. An entrepreneur trying to make tasty, convenient meals for husbands who need to cook for their families needs to know this, leading to perhaps new, easy-to-prepare meal formats for the chilled section of the store. If these products get stuck in the freezer aisle, most male shoppers will never see them, regardless of need.

Also, take a picture of someone you feel is highly representative of your target customer group, and stick it right in the middle of the text containing your persona. It brings the story of your customer to life!

Within Core Needs, Look for Latent Needs and Clear Customer Frustrations

When you do your observation, laddering, and specific interviewing of target customers, realize that not all customer needs are of the same priority for the entrepreneur. Some are more important—or more strategic—than others. Here is an important approach for prioritizing needs.

We had a friend who was interested in the pet industry, realizing that pet owners were tending more to treat their pets as family members. This was a hidden trend, one that was emerging but not yet mainstream. Pet owners increasingly wanted to care for their pets as if the pets were children. They also were frustrated that there were no credible health insurance programs to help cover the cost of premium pet care. Our friend thought to himself, "Valued family members have health insurance—what about pets?" From this insight, he test-marketed the service among affluent consumers and then proceeded to create a new, exciting business. Today, pet insurance has become mainstream in veterinarian clinics and pet food stores. Our friend had discovered a *latent need*, grounded in a growing trend (pet seen as a family member) within a target customer group (affluent pet owners) of a well-established industry (pet food and services).

A latent need is a fear or frustration that the targeted customer doesn't know how to solve. The need may be expressed with a quick phrase, some type of physical expression such as a sigh or clenched fist, or even a swear word. Part of that frustration is that the customer knows of this problem *but doesn't know how to solve it.*[5] Then later, when you present that same customer with a solution to the problem, he or she says, "Great! That's perfect!" You have put a smile on your customer's face, and hopefully, obtained a customer for a very long time.

---

[5]Meyer, M. H. (2007). *The Fast Path to Corporate Growth.* New York: Oxford University Press.

One of the secret weapons of successful entrepreneurs is that they work hard to find and validate latent needs in their target customer group for very specific uses or occasions of use. They have then built great businesses based on providing clear solutions for those latent needs, with a form, function, and price that screamed "value" to the user. This can be your recipe for success as well.

Latent needs stand in contrast to *perceived* needs. A perceived need is one that customers already recognize and, in many cases, have a fair idea of how it can be addressed: "I need it to drive faster!" "I need it to last longer!" "I need it to cost less!" Performance, quality, and price tend to be the "big three" perceived needs. All competitors in a target market can understand this with just a little customer research. As an entrepreneur, you must understand perceived needs as well as any competitor.

To truly differentiate yourself and your offerings, you must discover customers' latent needs and build solutions for them into your products or services—or how much you charge for these offerings. If you can find one or two latent needs and address them clearly and well, you will be on the path to success. At the same time, *you must also address perceived needs* that the customer expects in any product or service. For example, Tesla electric cars get tremendous acceleration, have great suspensions, and boast comfortable, luxurious interiors— all *in addition* to being electric vehicles with a 200-mile to 300-mile range on full charges. Teslas meet both sets of needs for the affluent but energy-conscious customer.

Latent needs are often found in the following areas:

- *Safety.* This latent need is driving entire industries, including border and facility security systems. Many of these ventures are spin-offs from large defense contractors. At the consumer level, the Spot Satellite Messenger (www.findmespot.com) is designed for outdoor adventurers, allowing them to send emergency locator beacons from any place in the world directly to emergency response teams and loved ones.

- *Reuse.* Reuse is a growing concern and source of frustration in industries. In software, it has become a major play of market leaders such as IBM (with its Services Oriented Architecture and associated software tools). In consumer products, it is transforming manufacturers' approaches to packaging volume and materials.

- *Sustainability.* This is a major latent need, particularly among younger customers and the industries that serve them. Once consumers have finished using a product, they are increasingly frustrated that they have to throw the product or packaging in a garbage bin. In many U.S. cities and towns, for example, one must pay a $20 fee to dispose of an old refrigerator, air conditioner, TV set, or computer monitor. Some ventures have flourished by recycling used equipment or replenishing equipment (e.g., ink-jet and laser printer cartridge refills). We have watched another student venture, Pure Pest Management, grow to provide environmentally safe, organic pesticides to residential and commercial properties. Sustainability is a powerful driver for entrepreneurship and innovation.

- *Personalization.* In a world of mass-produced products and services, many customers appreciate—and will pay extra for—items tailored to their specific needs. Few suppliers know how to address this need. Those that do can differentiate themselves. Dell rose from obscurity, in part, thanks to its ability to use flexible manufacturing to customize and quickly deliver PCs.

- *Convenience.* It seems that the Web is a particularly good venue for ventures that strive to make shopping and delivery convenient for consumers. Even without the Web, many service providers are now trying to provide their services any place, any time, and anywhere.

Any one of these types of latent needs can be a powerful driver for your own innovations. Also, products and services that address latent needs are less subject to price discounting—at least, during the early stages of market penetration. Apple iPod/iTunes addresses a common frustration: having to purchase an entire CD to get the one or two tracks one really wants. The price per song stayed at $1.29 for a number of years, and then lowered to $0.99 a song. In fact, Apple seems to be a master at sustaining premium pricing by striking a chord with customers in terms of combining powerful functionality, ease of use, and appealing design—in whatever it brings to market and in the appearance of its retail stores. Moreover, we have found that translating a frustration into a solution is one of the most exciting things that you can do as an entrepreneur or corporate innovator.

Example: Latent Needs in the Classroom

What are the latent needs among yourselves as users (e.g., students!)? Well, one of them must certainly be collaborative learning. You read from a book and write notes in your notepad or on your computer. You do the same for class lectures. The professor shares his or her PowerPoints with you on Blackboard or by e-mail. Then there are the supplemental readings. And you meet with classmates to share your notes either for project work or exams. When it comes time to study or advance a term project, you must gather all these different pieces, integrate them, and move forward. Everything is "point to point" rather than a seamless, integrated portfolio of knowledge, learning, and sharing. And it all "goes away" after the semester is finished.

There is a venture that has spun out of our own university that is seeking to integrate this entire classroom experience into a mobile, collaborative, lasting experience, erasing the boundaries between textbooks, notes, group work, and presentations, and replacing them with authorized sharing between teachers and students. This venture is determined to transform the educational publishing industry. There must be a dozen others like it across the country. This particular team has raised the money, hired the programmers, and lined up a number of large publishers to serve as test sites. It is a good example of designing a venture's solutions around clearly focused latent needs.

Make finding a latent need and solving it a litmus test for developing your venture idea. It is the best way to ensure that you won't have a "me-too" product or service.

Figure 3.2 provides examples of customer statements for perceived and latent needs. Before proceeding forward, take a moment to read these statements. Make sure you understand the difference between a perceived and latent need. Then jot down some notes on what you might expect to find for perceived and latent needs among your target customers.

	Perceived Needs	Latent Needs/Frustrations
For a product	• I want the best-tasting, smoothest chocolate that I can buy for $20 a box.	• I love chocolate, but I know that all the sugar makes me feel fat. I wish I had a great-tasting, indulgent chocolate that was also low-fat.
For a system	• I want my CAD software package to connect to the new generation of 3-D composite material printers so I can rapidly create prototypes.	• All my engineers make individual CAD drawings on their computers, but nothing allows them to make sure they have the same components. Because there isn't any reuse across our product lines, and we are losing a lot of profit.
For a service	• I want to get my MBA online because I don't have the time to sit in class.	• I took an online class, but I never got to know my professor or any of the students. I could have just read the books. I didn't learn anything from my classmates.

Figure 3.2 Examples of Perceived and Latent Needs

TIP: LEAD USER INNOVATION

Wouldn't it be great if one of your target customers has already designed the solution you want to sell?!

In fact, history has shown that the early forms of successful commercial innovations can sometimes be found right in the hands of customers in a target industry niche. With careful observation and good discussion, you might well find those lead users. They face a problem, but rather than sit on their hands waiting for a solution, they create their own solutions.[6] Yet they don't really want to leave their companies to commercialize their inventions. That's where you might engage.

A fine example comes in our friend Harry Keegan, a remarkably successful pharmaceutical entrepreneur. Harry has his own privately held pharmaceutical company that is now approaching a dozen new drug discoveries. (Current statistics put the cost of taking a drug from invention to market at more than a decade-long process, costing about $800 million per drug!) Harry tells the story of starting his company by providing medical research tools involving mice experiments to various medical schools. In that process, he became acquainted with various medical researchers. One of these was a brilliant physician whose daughters suffered from kidney disease and required frequent blood dialysis. Dialysis is a terrible thing for anyone, particularly the young. The process itself can strip the patient of needed blood chemistries, leading to greater sickness and even death. This physician was in a race against time to save the lives of his daughters. He had invented a "prep" that would retain electrolytes even after dialysis, but he needed help producing it. Harry recognized the genius of this solution and became the answer to this physician's urgent need. The two formed a partnership, formed a new company, and have since created a series of new therapies that leveraged this initial scientific discovery.

Look at the Before, During, and After of Each Use Case

A use case is simply the "use" or "occasion of use" that we have been describing—but a little more specific. To continue the chocolate example from Chapter 2, gifting of chocolate is a basic "use" or "occasion of use." Giving your girlfriend chocolate for Valentine's Day is a specific use case for which you might want specific flavors, colors, and even (for you guys) a "rush service" because you only remembered Valentine's Day a few days before! There might be a different use case for your wedding someday—where you want to buy hundreds of dollars of special, customized chocolates with your bride's picture on the packaging or on the chocolates themselves.

As another example— medical equipment—patient monitoring has different use cases for monitoring in the hospital, monitoring in the home, or monitoring "on the go," for example, an ambulance.

---

[6]Von Hippel, E. (1988). *The Sources of Innovation*. New York: Oxford University Press; Thomke, S., & Von Hippel, E. (2002). Customers as innovators: A new way to create value. *Harvard Business Review*, 80(4), 74–81.

Financial services planners love use cases: for example, saving money for your child's education is a different use case, featuring different approaches and financial products than saving for your own retirement.

Use cases involve the element of time. A use case almost always has *before the use, during the use,* and *after the use* time points. And though "during" might be the main event, you can uncover powerful latent needs in the *before* and *after* as well.

For example, an amateur astronomer takes his equipment to a backyard viewing location, aligns the telescope's mounting with the celestial pole, and sets out his star charts, red flashlight, and other accessories. He may also have to drag out a long electrical extension cord. This may take ten minutes, and it occurs *before* any stargazing activity can begin. The *during* phase involves finding the desired celestial objects in the sky, which may involve some calculations and searching, examining them under different magnifications and with different light filters, and perhaps some photography. The *after* part of this astronomer's use case involves bringing in and storing his equipment, logging his observations in a notebook, and possibly working with digital images created during viewing.

It's easy to be so fixated on the *during* part of a customer's use case that the *before* and *after* parts get overlooked—though each may be equally important for the customer and serve as the basis of a differentiated product or service solution. Using our backyard astronomer's experience as an example, equipment makers have been highly innovative in making the *during* activity easy and enjoyable. A new generation of computer-guided telescopes will point directly to a deep-sky object selected by the user from a handheld menu, eliminating the need to work with charts, make calculations, and fumble around in the dark. But customer needs in the *before* and *after* activities remain largely untapped. For example, we know of a venture that introduced a fiberglass shed with a roll-off roof and electrical connection that made telescope setup and breakdown unnecessary. We know of other ventures that provide software that allows amateur astronomers to record their progress surveying the stars.

Let's return to chocolate for a simple yet clever example. Take a look at Figure 3.3. This is the result of a team's field research with consumers of premium gift chocolate. Figure 3.3 also represents a template to guide your own work for the *before, during,* and *after* parts of a customer's use case. The figure shows two use cases: one of the male buying for his female partner and the other of the female buying for herself and her friends. (We could also create different use cases for different occasions, for example, Dads buying Halloween candy, or men buying chocolates on Valentine's Day, or women buying chocolate for a baby shower.) As you observe customers in their places of use, capture specific phrases that express their needs at each point in the use case. For perceived needs, use a regular font. For those needs that you feel are latent (unsolved frustrations), use an italic font to set them apart.

In the example shown in Figure 3.3, the team found the obvious: Men and women are completely different "animals" when it comes to chocolate! They have different motivations, different worries, and different needs in (a) buying chocolate, (b) eating it or watching it being eaten, and (c) disposing of the packaging.

The statements in Figure 3.3 are not only humorous but revealing. For the guys, *"I am so busy right now; I don't have time to go to the store"* suggests an occasion-specific eCommerce solution. Or for the women, *"I want chocolate that fits into my lifestyle"* might mean youthful, contemporary packaging with upbeat colors and candy combinations. For young professional women, recyclable packaging is getting more important, but for the guys, they don't really care—at least, not yet! All these insights, at different specific parts of the use case, give the entrepreneur clear design points for a new product or service. Think of developing a figure such as that in Figure 3.3 as a way to synthesize and apply your learning from observation, laddering, and the detailed questioning described earlier in this chapter.

In summary, whenever you go into the field and into the world of target customers, keep your eyes and ears open and look for specific needs in the *before, during,* and *after.*

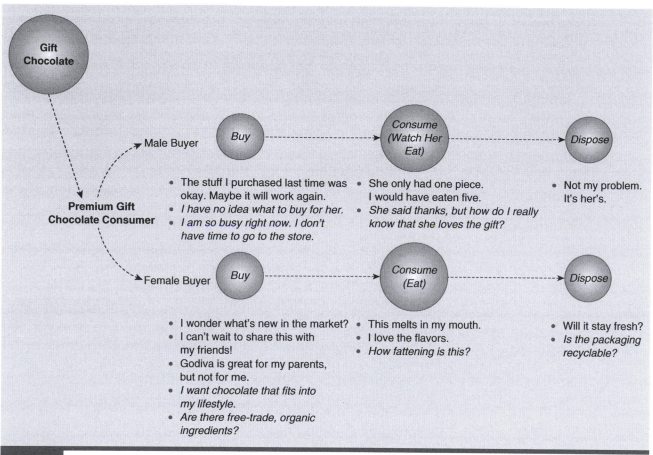

Figure 3.3 Use Cases: Perceived and Latent Needs for a Gift Chocolate Venture

TIP: ANOTHER SOURCE FOR NEW VENTURE IDEAS: TAKE AN IDEA THAT WORKS IN ONE GEOGRAPHY AND ADAPT IT TO ANOTHER

Some ventures originate in an entrepreneur's recognition of an opportunity to transfer a product, service, or technology from one regional context to another. Company folklore in Mars, Inc., has one of the Mars family members on vacation in Spain during the time of the Spanish Civil War. He observed peddlers selling pieces of chocolate coated in a hard shell of sugar. Villagers told him that the coating preserved the inside material. From this he got his "Aha!"—a chocolate core coated in a sugar shell that would melt in your mouth, not in your hand (M&M Candies®).

Or, for services, Zipcar is a membership club for car rentals by the hour and mile. This business idea was originally conceived and executed in European cities. An American team adopted the model and applied it first in Boston and is now expanding to other cities. Or, for the juggernaut we know as Starbucks, the immensely successful franchise emerged from a vacation Howard Schultz took in Italy where he enjoyed the coffee bistros. Schultz wondered if he could recreate a similar service and ambiance in America. That became the focus of his experienced-based service concept and the premium, retail business model behind it.

Create the Product or Service Concept _____

With target customer insights in hand—the problems and needs of a specific set of customers for a specific use case—the next step is to translate your idea into an initial product or service concept, or a combination of products and services.

This is the creative part of your entrepreneurial process. You have done a lot of thinking to get to this point. Remember, you want to be highly focused on a target customer and use. Also, when you create a product or service idea, you want it to be distinctive, not just a me-too idea like others already on the market. To make it distinctive at this point of the process, the best thing to do is to make your initial product or service idea directly address the "latent needs" you uncovered in your user research. Entrepreneurs score by leveraging latent needs into new solutions. At the same time, your product or service still has to meet the industry standard for satisfying the "perceived needs" of customers. For a food snack, that might mean meeting healthy nutritional standards, and at the same time, bringing unparalleled levels of taste and indulgence. Or, for a water purification reverse osmosis system, that might mean removing all unhealthful elements from the water, but doing so through a solar-powered system that might be used even in the most remote locations in Africa or Central America.

Figure 3.4 shows an approach for making sure that your product or service is distinctive from a user's perspective. It has four basic parts:

- The customer needs
- The design theme for your product or service that your think emerges from those customer needs
- The major components or parts of your product or service (some people would call this the high-level architecture or the major subsystems)
- The specific design points or features that you think you need in your new product or service

Then, as the figure shows, you first want to create design themes that address your customers' major needs, frustrations, and problems. For example, the design themes for the water purification systems above are (a) highly functional, (b) solar powered, and (c) BOP (base of pyramid) applications. Next, deconstruct your product or service into its major parts or components. For example, the water filtration system has (a) the water supply, (b) a water pump, (c) a filtration/separations system to clean deposits, (d) a reverse osmosis purification system to kill bacteria, (e) a solar panel energy system, and (f) a holding tank for the cleaned water. Then you innovate—matching specific design points to particular parts of the new product or service.

For the water purification system, our design points might be a set of low-cost yet reliable components, with a small footprint suited for shipping and use in poor, rural environments. Or, for the organic pest control venture mentioned earlier, it needs to use different types of all-natural organic fertilizers and herbicides for aspects of its service. Apple drives a simple user interface into its software operating system and a sleek, thin design into its physical hardware designs for the iPhone and the iPad. All of these are examples of how entrepreneurs systematically create innovative designs: They find compelling customer needs, create overall design themes, and

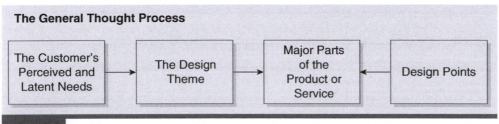

The General Thought Process

The Customer's Perceived and Latent Needs → The Design Theme → Major Parts of the Product or Service ← Design Points

Figure 3.4 Translate User Needs to Design Themes to Specific Design Points in Your Product or Service

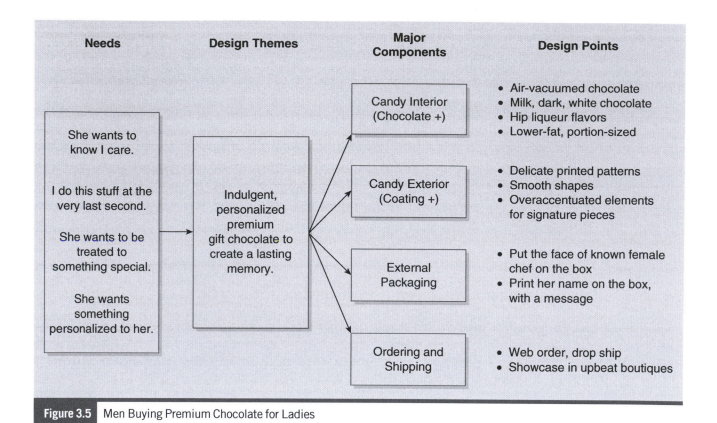

Figure 3.5 Men Buying Premium Chocolate for Ladies

then drive specific features as important design points within a product or service. As another example, the most successful premium window manufacturers have "lots of wood" built in to their window frames and sashes, not because the window functions better (it's the high *e* glass!) but because a prominent use of wood suggests a premium quality design in the eyes of the user.

Figure 3.5 shows a fun example of what we might design for an upscale gift chocolate venture aimed at young professional men buying candy for their ladies. All the classic emotion, convenience, and personalization needs are listed on the left. An indulgent personalized gift to create lasting memory is the design theme. Then we have the major parts of the product—the interior of the candy, the exterior shell, and the packaging—as well as the ordering and delivery service. Keep it very high level and simple at this stage of the process. Then we show a list of features that apply specifically to each part of the product. These include sucking all the air out of the chocolate so that it feels ultra-smooth and creamy in the mouth; buying high-quality chocolate of different basic types; and having "middles" that feature contemporary, hip liqueurs—such as Daiquiri or Tequila Sunrise—and lower-fat, smaller, more permissible candy sizes or portions. For the "signature" pieces, such as little chocolate fish or mice, we might want to overaccentuate the molding of the fish lips or mice ears—to make these items "pop." And we might want to figure out how to print the lady's name and a personalized message right on the box— to let her know that this is something special, just for her. And the Web ordering and drop-ship is for the last-second buyer, which is most certainly the vast majority of men for this type of gift!

Another way to think about latent needs is as "tensions" among target customers. A high-performance car that gets out-of-sight fuel economy solves a tension; a wonderfully casting fishing rod that is ultraportable solves another in the mind of a fisherman. Great-tasting but healthy food is a never-ending example, as are highly portable medical devices for monitoring that can save people's lives. "I want to use powerful medical technology, but I can't carry it on my belt or wear it on my wrist": Tensions such as these are gold for the entrepreneur if he or she can create a solution. Customers will say, "I can't believe they are doing that . . . all that work is for me! What a great product [or service]! What a great company!" When you can make something possible that, in the customer's eyes, had not been possible before, your venture is poised for success.

Example: This Approach Works Just as Well for Services Entrepreneurs

We warmly think of twin brothers Tom and Darr Aley. Both had held impressive corporate jobs, one at ZDNet (of Ziff Davis Publishing) and the other at Amazon, but they always knew that they wanted to start a company, together.

The two brothers had high-level business development and corporate selling jobs. Talking to each other during a vacation break, they reflected on their own experiences selling. They felt frustrated that it took so much time to prepare for each sales call. They would read dozens of industry-specific magazines, *The Wall Street Journal,* and local business journals; they would do searches on the Web for news stories about the companies and executives they were about to visit—and then have to boil all that information down into a call sheet. Good salespeople, particularly those engaged in large account enterprise selling, are often the most prepared. They know exactly what is happening in an account, at multiple levels, and they sell into those situations.

What if, the brothers reasoned, they could automate the entire process and filter down the most important tidbits of current information based on a salesperson's account's preferences and interests? The target user was any B2B salesperson. The design theme would be simple, automated access to just the most important information from thousands of streaming, real-time data sources. To execute on this theme, Tom and Darr then designed a premium information service that gathered the world's data; indexed and sorted the data on huge servers; and then provided a personalized graphical user interface for salespeople to indicate the accounts, types of events, and frequency with which they wanted everything delivered to their iPhones or PCs. Design points included the user interface, the search filters and algorithms, and the sheer range of databases' access for raw information and news stories.

After just three years, the brothers had built such an impressive business that Dow Jones acquired it for in excess of $60 million. And the brothers still owned most of the stock! (Check out the Generate, Inc., case on the textbook Website, as well as the short video of Tom Aley on our YouTube channel.)

Summarizing Your Product or Service Concept—On One Page! _____

Now we come to the home stretch. It is time to formalize your product or service *concept*. This builds on everything we have done in this chapter so far, so no worries.

First, we call this a *concept* because it is more detailed than just a general idea, and yet, as a *concept*, it needs to be validated with some target customers. To flesh out a product or service concept, you need:

- The target customer
- The specific use case or set of uses cases for which you are designing solutions
- A name and, if possible, picture/illustration/drawing of the product or service itself
- The problems you are solving
- The major design points and features of your product or service that solve these problems
- The major benefits for customers of your product or service solution

We try to put these all on one PowerPoint page. Take a look at Figure 3.6. It shows the product concept for our premium gift chocolate idea. Everything is nicely presented on a single page. This is important because you can easily show it to other team members, customers, and classmates.

Look at Figure 3.6. It has a picture of the target customer (a woman as the end-user and her husband as the buyer) and a textual description of the specific use case: gifting for romance on

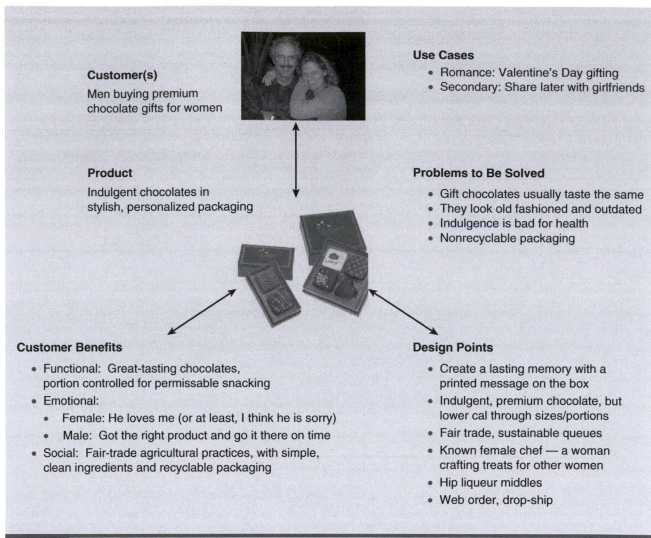

Customer(s)

Men buying premium
chocolate gifts for women

Use Cases

- Romance: Valentine's Day gifting
- Secondary: Share later with girlfriends

Product

Indulgent chocolates in
stylish, personalized packaging

Problems to Be Solved

- Gift chocolates usually taste the same
- They look old fashioned and outdated
- Indulgence is bad for health
- Nonrecyclable packaging

Customer Benefits

- Functional: Great-tasting chocolates,
  portion controlled for permissable snacking
- Emotional:
  - Female: He loves me (or at least, I think he is sorry)
  - Male: Got the right product and go it there on time
- Social: Fair-trade agricultural practices, with simple,
  clean ingredients and recyclable packaging

Design Points

- Create a lasting memory with a
  printed message on the box
- Indulgent, premium chocolate, but
  lower cal through sizes/portions
- Fair trade, sustainable queues
- Known female chef — a woman
  crafting treats for other women
- Hip liqueur middles
- Web order, drop-ship

Figure 3.6   The Product Concept for Contemporary Gift Chocolate

Sources: Image of author and wife, Rosa Meyer (photographer); Product image Copyright © Jacques Torres Chocolate. Visit www.mrchocolate.com to experience premium gift chocolate at its very best. Reproduced with permission from Jacques Torres Chocolate.

Valentine's Day. Underneath is a picture of an actual product concept developed into a contemporary gift chocolate business by a gifted pastry chef turned entrepreneur. At the right are major problem statements regarding taste, appearance, health, and environment. Then, below these problems are a range of different design points to solve these problems (each one focused at specific parts of the product we mapped in the prior figure). Finally, on the lower left side are the statements of customer benefits or value.

Anticipating and then validating customer benefits is important for an entrepreneur because it is the basis of competitive differentiation. In Figure 3.6, we introduce the idea of three distinct types of benefits:

- *Functional.* A functional benefit is when the product or service provides a clear, tangible benefit to the customer. These are often "hard benefits," measured on the basis of price and performance. "How good is the chocolate?" the customer might ask, or "How much am I paying for it?"

- *Emotional*. An emotional benefit is just that—we leave objective, measurable benefits and get into the "feeling" or belief of value: "How does this gift make me feel about not just my boyfriend, but about myself?" For B2B ventures, emotional benefits often come in the form of relieving untold frustrations on fixing broken equipment, networks, or computer systems. There is just as much emotion in a company as in a household—it's just a different type.

- *Social*. A social benefit is when the customer believes that he or she is helping others by using your product or service: "Does my consumption of this product in any way help cocoa growers in poor places?" "Is it hurting or helping the environment?" Do not underestimate the social component, particularly when targeting young consumers (such as many of you reading this book!).

Understanding these different benefits for your target customers becomes the basis of building a dynamic branding (see Chapter 6) and marketing communications program for your venture.

It still surprises us just how many bright, young entrepreneurs fail to look at their solutions from a clear customer-benefit perspective. Whether it's from arrogance or even just laziness, it can still be a fatal flaw. It is not what *you* think about your products or services that matters; it is what your *target customers* think. And that has been the point of this chapter. Now go apply the methods, and have some fun doing it!

Where We Go Next

In completing this chapter, you have come a long way on the road to creating a successful entrepreneurial venture. You now have much more than an "idea" for a business. You have a product or service concept, based on the needs, fears, and frustrations of your target customers and their occasions of use, where your innovations can make a big difference. You should be starting to get pretty excited.

In the next chapter, we will learn how to take a product or service concept and transform it into a full-fledged product line and suite of services. No entrepreneur makes money on a "onesie." You will make your money by offering some choice and variety to your customers, as well as giving them a path to buy more from you in the future. After you have completed this chapter's Reader Exercises, we will build a product/services strategy for your venture.

Reader Exercises

You have done a lot of industry analysis by this point in your project. You have also hopefully had that breakfast or lunch with a seasoned business person from your target industry sector. Now it is time to take your research to the next level. The only way to truly understand customer needs—and therefore the solutions you need to create and sell—is to enter the realm of the target customer.

Step 1: Hit the Streets: Develop Your Own Version of Figure 3.7 and Apply It

Your field work for this chapter is to observe and talk to target customers. That might be just two or three users at this stage, or it might be six or seven. No need at this point to talk to a lot more: We want quality more than quantity.

We also want you to spend some serious time observing and talking to target customers in their own *place of use* and *place of purchase*. If it's dog food, that means visiting their kitchen while they're feeding their dogs or accompanying them on a shopping trip to PetSmart, for example. If it's premium chocolate, that means visiting chocolate boutiques or coffee shops that sell premium chocolate, perhaps forming a small focus group with your friends. (Here, you might split up the men from the women so that each can talk freely!) If it's software, that means going into companies to spend time with the end-users of your type of software, or a few doctors or nurses for medical software, or a few architects and building owners at the buildings themselves for energy management software. Use Figure 3.7 as your discussion guide. And don't forget to "ladder" your interviewees!

1. How do you define the activity or problem? *(Teach me how I should think about the activity or problem area. It is probably bigger than how I define it now.)*

2. What do you use now in terms of products or services in this activity? *(Teach me the current competitive set.)*

3. Where or from whom do you buy products or services? What is good about that channel? What is not so good? *(Teach me the realities of the channels or the preferred routes to market.)*

4. How satisfied are you with your current products or services that you use in this activity? What is your greatest source of dissatisfaction or frustration with using these? *(Please tell me who you think is the best and the worst!)* What are your workarounds? *(I would love to see them!)*

5. Who is responsible for the buying decision? Is it you or someone else? *(Can you help me speak with them as well?)* How is the buying decision made? Who and what are the key influencers? *(You should be writing down notes because this is where most entrepreneurs slip up!)*

6. What are the criteria used when evaluating alternatives? Is there a clear set of metrics as part of those criteria? *(Can you teach me how you currently evaluate current products and services?)*

7. How much do you spend each month of the year on products or services within this activity? *(Tell me if you think you are getting your money's worth, either by your facial expression or in words.)*

8. What would be the ideal solution for you? How would you measure its value to you? *(Let me know what you think will be better than anything on the market today, and how customers would make their buying decisions.)*

9. What fears would you have in trying this solution? *(Would you ever buy something from a startup? Do you need to see a well-established brand name? Do I have to partner with a market leader in order to get you to try my wares?)*

10. Who would be the ideal supplier? What would be their approach, not just in terms of products, but in other things around the products? *(Teach me how to partner with you as opposed to just being a vendor.)*

Figure 3.7 Customer Interview Guide

Spending time in the field with customers is what the most successful *innovators* do—their inspiration comes from users. Remember, this is a difference between *invention* and *innovation*. Invention is a brilliant engineer or scientist sitting alone in a lab creating new technology or basic science. Very few inventors create category-leading companies. Innovation, on the other hand, is the application of known technology or science to solve consumer, industrial, or social problems. Innovators learn *what* to do from end-users and then work to figure out the *hows*. Successful entrepreneurs then take the matter one step further, transforming those users into paying customers.

The discussion should go well beyond product or service issues. The marketing and business model insights it seeks to gain from customers are the foundation of designing a powerful, dynamic venture strategy. We are confident that if you follow the discussion guide in your conversations with prospective customers, you will come back with new insights and inspiration. While this is "serious" work, it is also the most fun an innovative entrepreneur can have other than the joy of experiencing a multimillion-dollar "exit" seven or so years down the road.

Step 2: Create a Persona for the Target Customer: Apply Figure 3.8

How well do you really know your target customer? Prove it by developing a profile of that customer by completing the template shown in Figure 3.8. Surround a picture of the representative target customer with key phrases that pinpoint:

- Demographics, including income, gender, marital status, etc., for consumers; size, industry, etc., for B2B
- Core needs, latent as well as perceived
- Attitudes, cognitive values, and belief systems
- Behaviors in the important use cases for your product or service
- Purchase preferences in terms of information needed to make a purchase decision, channel, purchase frequency, and getting support (if needed)

The Customer Persona Template

Customer Demographics
- B2C: Income, gender, marital status, etc.
- B2B: Size, industry, location, etc.

Attitudes
- Values
- Cognitive belief systems

Customer Needs
- Perceived needs
- Latent needs

Picture or Sketch of the Target Customer

Behaviors
- For the important use cases for your product or service

Purchase Preferences
- Information needed
- Channel
- Purchase frequency
- Support preferences (if needed)

Figure 3.8 The Customer Persona Template

Step 3: Develop Use Cases: Apply Figure 3.9

You should come back from your field interviews with notes, perhaps videos, and fresh memories. The next step is to develop the primary use cases that will be the focus of your venture. We saw how this worked for the premium chocolate team. Now it is your turn to create this for your venture idea. To do this, use the template shown in Figure 3.9. Don't forget to try to incorporate the before, during, and after for your primary use case(s). And then try to distinguish between perceived and latent needs—for example, needs that customers expect all competitors to solve, and others that are pure, maddening frustrations that they aren't sure anyone can solve!

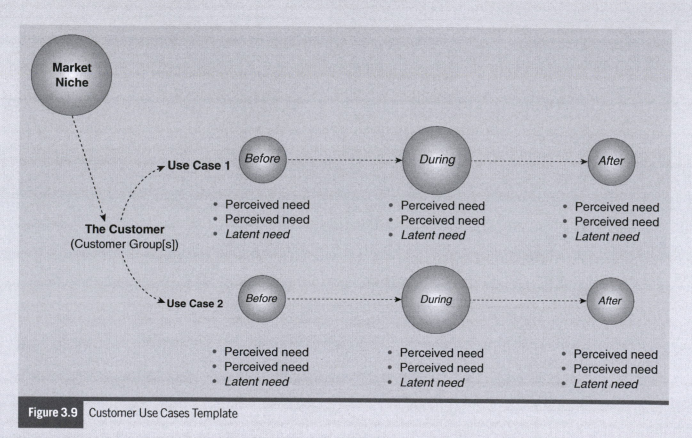

Figure 3.9   Customer Use Cases Template

Step 4: Create Design Themes From Customer Needs, and Then Design Points for Different Parts of Your Product or Service: Apply Figure 3.10

Apply the framework in Figure 3.10. Be creative!!!!! Design themes are essential for winning products and services. No "me-too" stuff here. And don't try to make it too complicated: *Powerful yet simple* are the operational words. Keep the major parts of your product or service as basic as possible. And each design point should have a home in one of those parts.

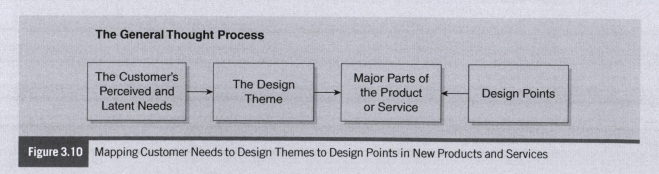

Figure 3.10   Mapping Customer Needs to Design Themes to Design Points in New Products and Services

Step 5: Develop the Product or Service Concept: Apply Figure 3.11

Lastly, construct your product or service concept. That's the template shown in Figure 3.11. Go to work! Make something truly special—something that you think your target customers will truly appreciate and enjoy. And think about those functional, emotional, and social benefits.

Put your findings into a short PowerPoint. This should be another major checkpoint with your teammates, professors, and classmates. Show everyone your product or service concept. Explain how it relates directly back to your target customers, their use cases, and their needs and problems within those use cases. Remember the importance of latent needs as well as perceived needs, and where you are focusing in terms of the before, during, and after within the use case.

Perhaps most important, bring your customer interviews into the conversation as the evidence for your choices. The insights from those conversations should make you confident about your work. But at the same time, *listen to the feedback* and *think*. And as you hear comments or criticisms, place yourself once again *into the hearts and minds of the target customers* to filter what you are hearing and how you respond.

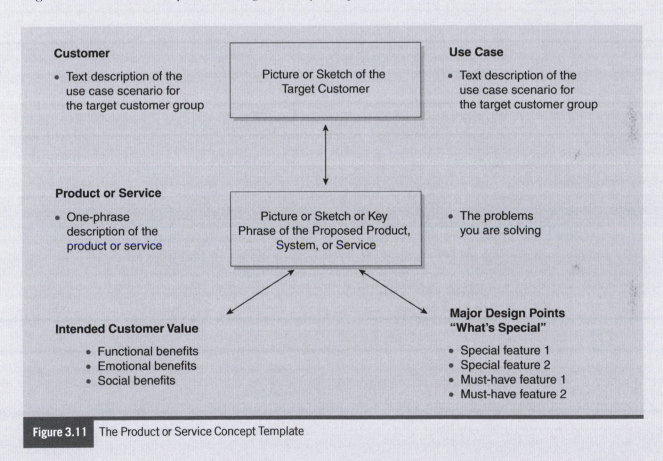

Figure 3.11   The Product or Service Concept Template

Visit the Student Study Site at **www.sagepub.com/meyer2e** to access the following resources:

- Web Resources
- Video Resources
- General Resources in Entrepreneurship

4

Defining Solutions for Customers

Developing a Product Line and Services Strategy

The Purpose of the Chapter

In this chapter, we take the product or service concept from the prior chapter and make it a more fully featured product line or suite of services. We will also see how to develop a technology and operations strategy for these products and services. Experience shows that offering choice and variety of products and/or services to the customer—while at the same time basing them on common, underlying platforms—are essential for high growth businesses.

Learning Objectives

After reading this chapter, you should be able to:

- Understand the importance of creating product lines or a suite of services
- Provide "good, better, best" in your solutions for customers
- Define technology strategies for new ventures
- Develop "lean" approaches to prototype product and service development

Defining a New Product or Services Strategy

No venture succeeds for long by selling just a "onesie." Rarely does a single product or service appeal to everyone in a target industry segment, or for most ventures, to every specific target niche in that segment. You need to have multiple arrows in your quiver, ready to aim and shoot for customers who believe that they have specific needs and uses beyond the standard, entry-level product or service. The old Henry Ford adage regarding the Model T—"you can have it in any color as long as it is black"—just doesn't apply anymore. Choice and variety are important for the target customer group, and it is up to you as the entrepreneur to define the nature and extent of that variety. If you are clever about it, this range of products or services can also be based on a common foundation of technologies and capabilities, so that you can make even more profit by leveraging these shared assets.

To do all this, you need a new product or services strategy. This is a plan for developing and launching specific products or services that meet different specific needs for certain customers and target uses. The result is a product or services *portfolio*. A product line or services strategy builds directly upon the new product or service concept you created in the prior chapter. All we are doing here is adding some flesh to the bones of that concept—to provide choice and variety to the target customer. It is also just as clear that the product or services strategy you create for a startup will most surely change over the first two or three years of the business. As you learn from in-market exposure with your first set of products or services, you will continue to refine your portfolio, bringing even better offerings to your customers.

Defining a Product Portfolio With "Good, Better, Best"

An entrepreneur can ill afford to have potential customers labor over their purchase decisions. Most buying, even for business products, has an important element of impulse—that is supported by good branding and marketing communications, or in some cases, a darn good salesperson. Whatever the means, you need to offer the customer some type of choice or variety. For some entrepreneurs, it might be a selection of three or four SKUs (stock-keeping units) on a retail shelf, such as four popular flavors of healthy snacks or drinks; for others, it might be a basic software program with a growing range of "plug-in" modules that tune the software for specific uses; and for yet other entrepreneurs, it might be a core service that is, by its nature, tuned for every single customer. Just think about a successful landscaping business in your neighborhood: basic services—landscape design and planting, mowing, fertilizing, spring and fall cleanup, tree pruning—each applied in a specific way to each customer. The same applies to a successful bank. Services customize a suite of general financial products to each individual or household. Either way, successful entrepreneurs do not try to force fit a single, standardized product into every customer or use occasion. A means to provide some variation, at low cost (either in the product itself or through service) makes the customer feel special and well-served.

At the same time, the entrepreneur needs to economize on his or her efforts, especially with limited financial resources. But even a great company such as Apple has a confined product portfolio—a dozen or so basic choices for hardware, as opposed to hundreds—and importantly, just one operating system so that users can connect all its different devices and computers together. The variety, bordering on mass customization, comes through one single, simple means: iTunes!

So, to provide choice but not go overboard with that choice, we recommend that venture teams consider just two or three different levels of functionality and price for their product or services portfolios. As we shall learn later in this chapter, if you can also create a modular architecture and some common platforms underneath your products or services, you can get to variety at little extra cost in terms of R&D and different types of manufacturing or fulfillment.

Those two or three levels of choice can be thought of simply as providing "good, better, best" alternatives.[1] If a customer thinks a particular offering is too expensive, you don't have to lose that customer. He or she can get something less costly with less functionality directly from you. On the other hand, if the customer needs more, he or she can get it by paying more. By adding choice and variety, a "good, better, best" product line or services strategy can definitely increase your sales.

What are some examples of "good, better, best" for different types of products and services? Consider the following, and then think about how these concepts can be applied to expand the underlying product or service concept you created in the prior chapter.

Products. Go to Dell's Website and browse its computer offerings. For its desktop computers, you will see three specific subbrands: the Inspiron, for standard usage; the XPS, for high-performance usage; and Alienware, with high-performance graphics for gamers. This is a good example of "good, better, best," or perhaps more accurately, "good, better, different." Then, within each subbrand, Dell has the customer define specific preferences for processors, memory, disk storage, displays, and so forth. This allows customers to create "personalized" products from common components, what some have called "mass customization."[2] And only then does Dell start the final assembly process. This is followed by direct-to-consumer delivery. Imagine the inventory carrying costs if Dell had to manufacture and ship every single possible version of its computers to retailers, or if it had to carry huge stocks of premade computers in its own warehouses. Dell's customization business model transformed the entire PC industry. It also allowed Dell to bring a huge price advantage to the marketplace by bypassing the traditional retailers and their 30% to 40% markups over wholesale prices. The company doesn't limit this product line strategy to its desktop computers; it also uses it for its laptops. All this variety is presented in a simple way to potential buyers—three basic choices suited for three different types of uses: basic computing, high-performance computing, and graphics-intensive gaming. Dell remains a great company, and Michael Dell one of our most brilliant entrepreneurs. Go study him and his company. Take inspiration from his product line strategy and the direct-to-consumer business model he created to execute it.

Software products. Many software firms offer "basic" and "premium" versions of their products. For example, one of our favorite software companies, Intuit, is a long and formidable survivor in the face of giants such as Microsoft, Oracle, or IBM. Most small businesses in North America today use Intuit's QuickBooks for their bookkeeping. At the time of this writing, Intuit provides two basic tiers of price-performance for QuickBooks. There is QuickBooks Pro for PCs or the Mac, for a one-time licensing fee of about $185 per company with general reports and financial management capability; and QuickBooks Premier, for about $320, which has reports tailored to specific industries and provides sales forecasting and expense planning modules. Next, Intuit expanded into truly medium-sized businesses with its Enterprise edition, which is based on an entirely different revenue model of about $500 per licensed user within a company. And Intuit also offers a software-as-a-service model for customers who don't want to run QuickBooks on their own computers. The pricing for this starts at about $13 a month, and continues upward. While this is easier for small businesses, many still don't want to keep their private financial data "on the cloud." Intuit is truly a great company, and it has thought hard about the product portfolio for QuickBooks, its flagship product. Go to its Website and study it!

Services. Computer support companies offer the equivalent of Bronze, Silver, and Platinum services featuring different levels of support. Car rental companies offer "preferred" customer plans that provide certain guarantees and expedited service. American Express's

---

[1]We have lots of additional examples in Meyer, M. H. (2007). *The Fast Path to Corporate Growth.* New York: Oxford University Press.

[2]Pine, J. (1999). *Mass Customization: The New Frontier of Business Competition.* Boston: Harvard Business School Press.

Platinum and Gold cards are associated with different levels of benefits. The idea is to provide a basic service for most customers and premium offerings for customers who are willing to pay for greater richness in services. Levels of warranty are also commonly used to differentiate levels of service and are priced accordingly. Or your variety of services might simply be tuned for specific applications or customer uses, where this is no "good, better, best," but just "different."

Let's look at an example. Figure 4.1 shows a simple framework recently put to good use by corporate entrepreneur friends working in a global business making heavy industrial equipment. They set out to define and build a set of IT-enabled services to accompany large pieces of equipment manufactured by their company, including tractors, trucks, and excavators. We think it is an interesting example because it represents the emerging category of "smarter planet" applications, where sensors are placed on people and machines, connected through wireless networks to computers, and a bunch of analytics constantly run to detect possible problems and otherwise help improve the productivity of the entire system, including people and machines. In this case, Figure 4.1 shows a "good, better, best" strategy for a new suite of services to help road construction companies, quarry owners, and mining companies—three big industry segments for equipment manufacturers such as Caterpillar, Komatsu, Volvo, or Deere.

The team was creating a new division based on monitoring and managing industrial equipment on large job sites (the basic service concept). The core of this was to put sensors on the engines, transmissions, and hydraulics on the equipment, and track and communicate all the streaming data through satellite networks needed for remote operations. From this, the team then thought about those features that should be tackled first and those that should be tackled next.

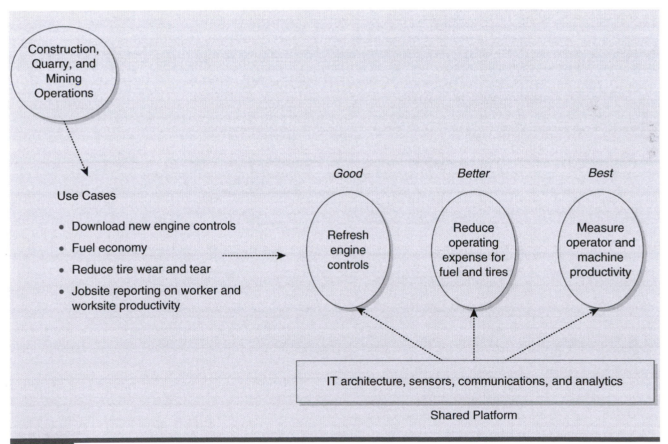

Figure 4.1   Defining a Product Portfolio for Monitoring Industrial Equipment

- Its "good" was to replace the tiresome and expensive manual process of installing new engine control "firmware" on literally millions of machines in the field. At present, service technicians drive around with new "cards" that they insert and test into individual machines. All this could be replaced through the airways, installing, testing, and provisioning each machine on a service plan from a central set of computers.
- For the "better," other sensors could be used to continuously monitor the health of the engines and pressure of the tires. Engine health is a very big deal for construction companies building highways, quarry operators, or mining companies. If a machine breaks down, hundreds of thousands of dollars of lost productivity result in a matter of just a day. And driving around on tires needing air results in lots of money wasted on fuel.
- Lastly, the "best" was seen as using clever analytics and several types of key sensors to actually measure operator productivity. This would include how many scoops are made with an excavator or payloads carried by a truck. With this information, the construction owners could actually reward operators for performance, something never possible before.

All of these features address "latent needs" on the part of equipment owners—problems for which there were only scattered, unsystematic solutions. The team is doing a global rollout of the "good" service offering—downloading the new engine control software—and developing software for the "better" and "best." These will be introduced to market over the next several years, one after the other, providing more functionality to customers and at the same time, a constant stream of new "news" for the marketplace. You can also see at the bottom of Figure 4.1 the technology that can be shared across these different product offerings—the IT infrastructure, the sensors, and the communications network. When you can define a shared backbone like this for different products and services, you can call it a *product* or *service platform*. Platforms can be very powerful for any company because they help all the individual products or services work better and be integrated more readily. And platforms can help drive down the costs of production.[3]

Defining a Services Portfolio

We can also apply the same thinking to define a services portfolio for a new venture. For example, we mentioned earlier the student venture called Pure Pest Management, which has developed a services portfolio based on what it considers to be "premium" pest control services for both residential and commercial applications. Its core mission is to use eco-friendly and pet-safe remedies to control mosquitoes, ticks (including deer ticks, which in New England often carry Lyme disease—a serious bacterial infection), indoor pests (rodents, ants, cockroaches, spiders, etc.), and deer themselves, which can chew up a flower or vegetable garden. All the products are plant extracts or natural oils.

Take a look at Figure 4.2. It shows that there are different service packages for residential customers versus commercial customers (restaurants, motels, etc.). There are also different treatments for different types of pests. The services portfolio therefore fits into a logical matrix of customers and uses, where customers can get precisely what they need for their property. But each of these services leverages to specific "platforms": the natural pesticides and inhibitors, and the procedures, systems, and staff used to administer these ingredients. The company also raised "angel" financing to create a franchise model for owner-operators across the United States and Canada. You can also see in the figure that this venture is packaging services for this franchising—targeting a new type of customer in the effort to rapidly expand the business. Its platforms apply here as well. Companies such as Pure Pest Management are simple, powerful examples of how to logically think about how to go from the general eco-friendly "pest control" concept to a distinct, fully featured suite of services that offers choice, variety, and *quality* to different types of customers.

---

[3]Meyer, M. H., & Lehnerd, A. P. (1997). *The Power of Product Platforms*. New York: The Free Press.

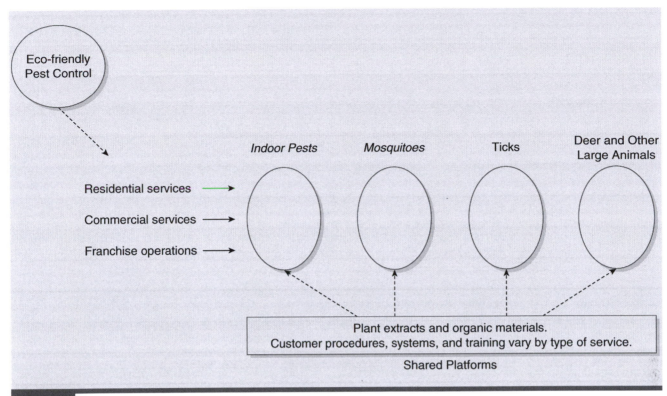

Figure 4.2   Defining a Services Portfolio for Pest Control Services

Make no mistake, services innovation can be just as important for entrepreneurs as product innovation.[4] So think about how the approach shown either in Figure 4.1 or 4.2 might apply to the basic product or service concept you created in the last chapter. Jot down some notes, because this will be a Reader Exercise at the end of the chapter.

As you do this, remember that a new venture doesn't have to have just products, or just services. You can use Figure 4.1 or 4.2 to show both products *and* services. There are many computer companies that get the majority of the revenues for selling hardware or software products, but still get a significant portion from selling complementary services as well—such as training and special customer support. For example, IBM sells even more services these days than either its hardware or software products. And within these services, IBM offers a variety of services that include technology programming and implementation, systems integration, data center outsourcing, and even business strategy consulting. And, for software, it has hundreds if not thousands of software "products," as well as dozens of different hardware products, for example computers and storage systems. The operating margins for each of these major groups of offerings in IBM's product and services portfolio are quite different as well. IBM's software business alone is providing operating margins close to 90%!

All this is in keeping with the "whole product" idea of Geoffrey Moore, who wrote the wonderful book *Crossing the Chasm*, intended primarily for technology-intensive businesses. Often, the first customers of new, disruptive technology are classic early adopters—people or companies who get a thrill out of trying new things. These early adopters are willing to play around with technology and creative new services. But later adopters will want more complete, mature solutions. The more your company's offerings hit that mark, the higher the growth potential of your business. Customers will be happier, and in most cases will pay more than if you just try to sell pieces or parts of solutions that they then have to assemble themselves. This means you

---

[4]Meyer, M. H., & DeTore, A. D. (1999). Product development for services. *Academy of Management Executive,* 10(3), 64–76.

have to provide services as well as products for enterprise-level systems, or well-engineered products that are plug-and-play for consumer markets. And sometimes, customers just might want you to outsource the whole solution for them and offer it on a *cloud*.

For example, suppose that we were part of a venture team who contained brilliant finance folks who were experts in risk management in banking for emerging markets—say, for credit cards or home mortgages in places such as India or Brazil. As we start selling, some early adopter banks are willing to buy just our software and figure out how to tune it and integrate it themselves. In fact, they help us fix and otherwise improve the software with new algorithms. The next wave of customers, however, want fully featured software that runs perfectly and comes with training. And the customer banks after these want to buy an entire fraud management system, including integration services for the data center. Some customers—we will call them *the laggards*—want us to run the entire fraud management system for them on a *cloud* and just give them back a "yes" or "no" for each new customer who wants to get a new credit card or mortgage. They want to pay by "the click," as opposed to buying software or integration services. Our venture then has become a new type of fraud bureau, with a different *business model* than if we were selling just software products, training, and integration services.

The bottom line here is you should really be thinking about the possibilities for both products and services, not just one or the other. Later on, we will show you how to actually test customer demand for both.

Offshore Markets Affect the Product or Services Portfolio

Speaking of emerging markets, ventures are increasingly turning their attention to these markets abroad. Twenty years ago, professors rarely saw this in student business plans. Now it is commonplace.

Many of our students—undergraduate and graduate—come from various countries around the world, and their heartfelt desire is to create a new business that will take them back to their home countries, where they believe commercial opportunity beckons. Take a look at the mInfo case on our textbook Website. The entrepreneur, Alvin Graylin, created one of China's first mobile (cell phone) search capabilities, based in Shanghai. One of his major customers, China Mobile, has over 300 million subscribers, a number that is growing by the day. In China, Alvin realized that if a user's initial mobile search did not find the desired result (such as a restaurant), it was cost effective to redirect the cell phone user to a call center for human operators to complete the search. You won't find this type of service integration behind a mobile search in the United States or in Europe. But for Alvin, adding these call center "services" to his software "products" was essential to win customers such as China Mobile. Moreover, the cost of doing so was not prohibitive in that part of the world.

In recent years, we have had students like Alvin starting companies in India, Indonesia, Southeast Asia, the Middle East, and Northern Africa—literally all around the world. They all have a similar story: They want to get back home and build their own successful businesses. Yet the products or services for their home markets are not always the same in terms of performance, features, and price as those that might do well in the United States. The same concepts we learned in Chapter 3 apply just as well here: Get into the hearts and minds of target customers, both the users and buyers, in these emerging markets; find out what makes them tick; and build that into your product or service concept. Then define the "good, better, best" you need for a strong product or services portfolio.

Growing interest in offshore markets by corporate entrepreneurs is also strong. Many large companies anticipate that a majority of their sales growth will come from emerging markets. This creates all sorts of corporate entrepreneurship opportunities for the willing and daring. Gillette, for example, has been selling its top-of-the-line, five-bladed razors for $3.00 or more a cartridge; its single-bladed, entry-level "shaving systems" for India are priced more than ten times less! The demand in India for shaving systems, with replaceable plastic cartridges as opposed to traditional double-edge safety razors, is expected to be enormous.

As this shaving example shows, the notion of the price-performance equation for "good, better, best" most often gets downshifted when focused on emerging markets. Consumers and companies simply have less money to spend on new products and services. There are always exceptions to the rule, however. Many Asian countries have urban areas where real estate, retail shopping, information technology, and financial services are on par in terms of price and performance with Boston, London, or Tokyo. New condominiums in Istanbul cost just as much if not more than in Boston; the affluent in Shanghai are on par with the affluent anywhere in the world. But the majority of buyers in emerging markets typically expect price levels that can be an order of magnitude less than the prices of products in the same category in developed markets.

Tata's Nano automobile is an Italian-designed four-seater that gets 52 miles per gallon. This sounds like a reasonable objective for any car manufacturer selling products in the United States or Europe. But for India, a car with all these features must still sell for incredibly low prices. The Nano, for example, retails for about $2,500!

There are other important differences in product line or services strategy when doing business abroad:

- *Product design.* "The best shave a man can get" in North America, with a five-blade, super-sharp shaving system, will actually cause skin burn, ingrown hairs, and blemishes on the skin of young African males due to different skin physiologies. Products that work well in certain countries do just the opposite in others. Gerber baby foods come in different varieties in different countries: vegetable with rabbit is a favorite in Poland, while freeze-dried sardines with rice are popular in Japan.

- *Packaging.* Japanese consumers value product packaging far more than Americans typically do—it must be as stylish and appealing as the product itself. As you think about designing packaging for your own products as an entrepreneur, consider the five senses: the impression made when you first see a product; then when you potentially hear it, touch it, or smell it; and finally, if it is food, when you taste it. Designing for the five senses is an incredibly powerful discipline—for any market.

- *Promotion.* L'Oreal, the cosmetics giant, sells the same product in many countries, but with different promotional messages. For example, its Golden Beauty brand of sun care products is promoted to northern Europeans as a dark tanning solution, to Latin Europeans as a skin protecting solution, and to Mediterranean Europeans as a beautiful skin solution—the same product, but different perceived uses and market positioning to suit different local markets.

As an entrepreneur, you must understand these differences in consumers and build that insight into your product or services portfolio. Even if your venture develops a so-called "global" product or service, it will have to vary it in terms of packaging and communication.

Intellectual property protection is an important consideration for entrepreneurs doing business abroad. A software venture that plans to do business in emerging markets must realize that most of the PC-type software used in countries such as China, Kenya, Russia, or Indonesia is pirated in one way or another.[5] For this, you need to design your products as a software-as-service model—running on a cloud or usable only with tight authorization codes issued for each user from a central server. And all this must be done at a price point that your new customers in developing countries can afford. Today's entrepreneurs cannot ignore these opportunities over the long term: There are simply too many potential customers—billions of them—in these markets entering B2C and B2B markets with newly found purchasing power.

---

[5]International Data Corporation. (2008, January). *The Economic Benefits of Reducing PC Software Piracy.* This report is available on the Web at http://www.bsa.org/idcstudy.aspx. The countries with the lowest piracy rates are the United States, Japan, New Zealand, and Luxembourg, all near 20%. Those with the highest piracy rates are Armenia, Bangladesh, Georgia, and Zimbabwe, all with more than 90%!

Thinking About Modularity as You Craft Your Product or Services Portfolio

A modular design underneath a set of products or a suite of services is like Lego: Different parts or components can be assembled together to make the final product or service for the customer. For example, a modular design for a food product might be if a manufacturer could replace sugar and other carbohydrates with lower-calorie ingredients to provide two types of snacks, regular and diet. Or in software, a company could provide a base-level product, such as Microsoft Word or Excel, for which users "plug in" various templates and macros to provide specialized functionality. Or, in services, a company could send out skilled service technicians, like Best Buy's Geek Squad, who apply specific rules and procedures for different appliances and media systems for installation or repair. The underlying training and customer service programs are the same: *a services platform*.

Why is modularity important for the entrepreneur from a business perspective? *Modularity helps you create new streams of revenue by easily serving closely related sets of customers*. The entrepreneur can conceive of all sorts of attachments, accessories, and other forms of complementary products and services to enrich the customer's experience—all marketed under the same, unifying brand.

Let's consider two simple, powerful examples from the world of coffee. For modular products, go to Green Mountain Coffee's Website and take a look at the various single-serve brewing systems and the types of coffees, teas, and chocolate drinks under the K-Cup and new Vue subbrands. Just like Gillette, Green Mountain provides brewing machines at a low-margin, affordable cost in order to get the recurring revenue of its single-serve beverage packs. Each coffee machine is a "money machine"! And for a modular services example, the obvious example is Starbucks. It is an international coffee company, based in Seattle, Washington, with over 20,000 stores in about 60 countries around the world. While it sells a standard line of premium espresso-based hot (espresso, cappuccino, latte, macchiato) and cold (frappuccino) drinks, as well as drip-brewed coffee and teas, Starbucks adjusts its portfolio for localities. In Japan, consumers prefer the "short" portion size, which is different than the "tall" or "grande" sizes (what we think of as small or medium) in the United States. Japanese customers also love teas, and Starbucks in Japan has a fantastic drink called "matcha frappe"—made from finely milled green tea, ice, and a little cream. And in terms of retail store layout, the sit-down store layout is different than an airport retail layout. Starbucks even has a partnership with cruise ship operators for Starbucks onboard.

If these two great companies can create modular designs for their products and services, *so can you*. It is one of the fundamental enablers of hyper-explosive venture growth. It just takes some careful thought in the design of your products and services.

One last example, just so that one of authors can include pictures of himself fishing in his book. It comes from Korkers Products, LLC, a Portland, Oregon–based company. In fact, both of your authors share a passion for fly-fishing, so bear with us. It is a great learning example.

We have fished in calm streams; in slippery, fast-moving rivers; and in the ocean. We have both hiked over mountains to reach remote streams and slogged through the night down beaches in search of ocean striped bass. Each is a different use case for the fly angler. And for reasons of safety and comfort, each has traditionally required a different type of wading shoe, be it to prevent slippage, to withstand salt water, or of late, to prevent the spread of water-borne parasites from one river to another. Each of these use cases requires at least a different sole: felt-soled for calm water, metal-studded for treacherous water, rubber-soled for saltwater beaches, and hiking boots for treks to remote fishing spots. Moreover, these soles are integral to the shoe. When the felt sole wears out after two or three seasons, the angler must purchase new boots. And because of some odd quirk of behavior, the avid angler never seems able to dispose of worn-out boots, a habit that leads to ever-growing piles of old, useless boots in "man-caves" or mudrooms across the country.

Along comes Korkers, a small, innovative company based on the West Coast. It designed a boot with interchangeable soles (see Figure 4.3). In that figure, you can observe on the left three

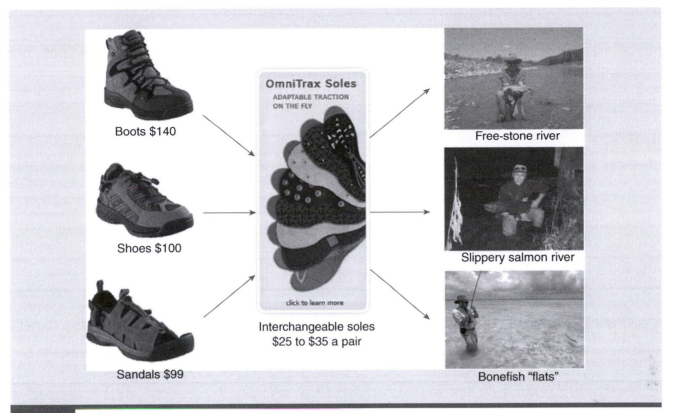

Figure 4.3   The Korkers Product Line Strategy: Variety Through Simple Means

Source: Parts provided courtesy of Korkers Products, LLC. Used with permission.

different assortments of fishing shoes: boots, sneakers, and sandals. The fishing boots are standard rugged fare; the sneakers are lighter and more contemporary; and the fishing sandals are great for surf-casting on the beach. Korkers actually has many more varieties of shoes than those shown here, and you are encouraged to visit its Website to see current offerings and prices. We have used all three and find them well suited for different fishing occasions.

The various soles for these three types of shoes are in the middle of Figure 4.3. These soles include two standard soles: felt and a rubber lug. In addition, you can see studded felt and studded rubber for slippery conditions. And to help solve the problem of anglers mistakenly transporting fish-killing parasites from one infected stream to another, Korkers has followed the industry trend by providing its own new sticky rubber-sole material called "Kling-On," as well as a new type of felt replacement called Svelte that has five times less material absorption than traditional felt. The little critters do not stick to these new materials. On the right side of Figure 4.3 specific use cases represent just a few of your authors' fishing experiences.

The beauty of this modular product line design is that the soles are interchangeable across any of the footwear products, making those footwear products multipurpose for different use cases. This eliminates the need to buy a different set of shoes or to make a mess in the hallway! It also means you can add or replace soles without buying new shoes. And you can throw on a pair of rubber soles to walk over mountains or through the woods to get to a stream and then in one minute change to a Kling-On sole that stores in your fishing pack for the wading into the river. The key to the Korkers solution is the interface between the front of the sole and the front of the boot, as well as the attachment mechanism on the backs of the soles. This interface architecture makes it easy for the customer to switch between different soles. That interface design creates the modularity that is the *design driver* for this line of fishing shoes.

Thinking About Intellectual Property as You Craft Your Product/Services Strategy

Intellectual property (IP) is legal protection for creations of the mind: inventions, literary and artistic works, and symbols, names, images, and designs used in commerce. IP can be divided into two major categories: (a) industrial property, which includes patents, trademarks, trade secrets, and industrial designs, and (b) copyright, which includes literary and artistic works such as novels, poems and plays, films, musical works, artistic works such as drawings, paintings, photographs, and sculptures, software, and architectural designs. Rights related to copyright include those of performing artists in their performances, producers of phonograms in their recordings, and those of broadcasters in their radio and television programs.

Developing IP can add greatly to the value of a venture. Using that IP to power a new generation of products or services that disrupt everything else in the market is of course even better. There are some companies that develop IP, choose or fail to deploy it, but nonetheless license or sell that IP to larger companies. This strategy, however, is not the focus of this book. And most new ventures do not develop some type of new IP. Instead, they build their value primarily by building a strong if not world-class brand based on products and services that utilize, integrate, and apply existing technology, either purchased or in the public domain.

Patents

When entrepreneurs think about IP, they think about patents. A patent, which in the United States must be be applied for through the U.S. Patent and Trademark Office, provides an exclusive right granted for an invention. This invention can be a product or a process that provides a new way of doing something, or that offers a new technical solution to a problem. To receive a patent your invention must meet certain requirements. For example, it must be of practical use; it must show an element of novelty (a new characteristic not previously known or discovered); and it must show an inventive step that would not normally be deduced by the average person (the latter step defined in U.S. law as being non-obvious). A patent provides protection for the invention to the owner of the patent, and this protection is granted for a limited period, generally 20 years from the date of filing the patent application.

In certain high-tech business, such as biotechnology, materials science, and various types of industrial and energy applications, professional investors may expect the venture already to hold patents, or to have exclusive access to IP through licensing arrangements with a university or corporation.

Patent applications need to be prepared by an attorney; this is not a do-it-yourself game. If you are pursuing this path, you must spend the time to find a patent attorney who has considerable experience working through the process with companies in your field of technology. Otherwise, you will find yourself wasting a lot of time and money. Effective patent applications take the hands of someone with deep familiarity with the area of science or technology involved in the patent. All good IP law firms have doctors, scientists, and technologists already on staff or at a moment's call to review the details of a potential patent application.

The classic patent application is either for a "utility patent" or "design patent." A utility patent is for a new, useful process, "article of manufacture," or, more generally, a new "composition of matter." If approved, the patent holder has 20 years of protection—a legal monopoly on the use of the invention—from the date of filing the patent application. A design patent covers the "ornamental" design or appearance of a new product. Once this type of patent is approved—a process that now typically takes several years—it is still up to the entrepreneur to enforce the patent against copycats. This type of patent protection in the United States lasts for 14 years from the date that the patent is issued. In the United States, there is also a third type of patent called a "plant patent," which covers asexually reproducing new types of plants; the term of this patent is 20 years from the date of issue.

Ventures with IP are also spending even more money to get patent protection in the European Union. In markets such as China and India, where IP has never been assured—patents or no—the entrepreneur must work with large international law firms with very specific expertise in emerging markets.

There are also patents that can be granted for the creation of a new business method in the most general sense. New workflows or methods for accomplishing a given task count here. Entrepreneurs often try to patent new business methods and models. For example, there are patents surrounding various aspects of online auctioning, or risk management in life insurance, or even the delivery of rich media content over mobile networks. Be cautious, though, as there is more prejudice against issuance and enforcement for these business methods, both in the U.S. Patent and Trademark Office and in the U.S. federal court system. Typically, such methods must be closely associated with software and a computing apparatus to have much chance of surviving the patent examination and patent enforcement stages.

Other Important Forms of IP

Another important type of IP is a trademark—a distinctive sign that identifies certain goods or services as produced or provided by a specific person or enterprise. The origins of trademarks date back to ancient times, when craftsmen reproduced their signatures, or "marks," on their creations or products. Trademarks may be one or a combination of words, letters, and numerals. They may consist of drawings, symbols, three-dimensional signs such as the shape and packaging of goods, audible signs such as music or vocal sounds, fragrances, or colors used as distinguishing features. Like patents, trademarks must be approved—and this process takes a number of months, so get started early! For U.S. trademarks, entrepreneurs can apply directly at www.ustpo.gov. All you need is some good artwork of your symbol and a small application fee. For other countries, consult your attorney or some other knowledgeable source.

A trademark protects your enterprise because it provides you with the exclusive right to use it to identify your products or services. The period of protection varies, but a trademark can be renewed indefinitely beyond the time limit on payment of additional fees. Trademark protection is enforced by the courts, which in most countries have the authority to block trademark infringement.

Today, many people use the term *trademark* interchangeably with the term *brand*. This is not correct. A brand should be much broader, and we will describe brand development in Chapter 6. For now, a brand includes both tangible and intangible components around new products and services, including trademarks, the design of the offering itself, your company's logo, and messaging and communications around the products or services. The entrepreneur cannot underestimate the value of developing a strong brand—it helps draw customers to your Website or to your products on the shelf; it can also help make them quickly receptive to someone selling a new service. A protected trademark is part of the foundation of building a strong brand.

Additionally, if you produce written materials, printed in hardcopy or published on your Website, add a copyright notice at the beginning of the material at the bottom of the page. For example: *Copyright © 2014, Marc H. Meyer and Fredrick G. Crane, Boston, MA. All rights reserved*. The copyright notice can be enforced in a court of law should a competitor try to take your material. This should also be done for every page of a PowerPoint show. Do it in a very small font so that it is not obtrusive—but do it!

The Scope of the IP Effort

The intensity with which an entrepreneur can pursue IP varies greatly. First, think about getting trademarks on your company and product names and logos. You will be investing lots of money into building awareness for these items. Make them your IP.

Second, religiously place copyright notices at the beginning of company publications, PowerPoints, and even business plans. You want the copyright there just in case a competitor "lifts" your material and you need to take legal action to stop it. Also, e-mail materials as PDFs. There are also ways in Adobe PDF Writer to preclude readers from cutting and pasting material from your files.

Third, decide the scope of your IP efforts in a way that fits your business. For some, particularly in advanced technology spaces, an important part of a venture strategy may be to pack a particular area of industry with a series of specific utility and design patents, creating a formidable barrier to entry for competitors who wish to enter your area of work in the years ahead. In fact, owning this IP may be the reason why a large company comes to you for a business partnership or outright acquisition.

For others, the IP strategy is less broad in scope. A single, powerful utility patent might support the venture's overall R&D strategy and reputation as a technology leader. Trademarks and design patents, on the other hand, will support a venture's branding strategy and provide a lasting set of "legs" for a compelling look and feel or design motif. And there are other firms that wish primarily to be in the business of creating new IP, patenting it, and then licensing it to other companies—living off the licensing revenue and never really commercializing a product or service. That is not the focus of our work in this textbook, but it is a model that a number of small R&D shops and universities pursue to generate revenue.

There is also what many observers think of as a poor man's patent application, called a provisional patent application. It can be used to quickly get one's foot in the door. Far less expensive and cumbersome than a full patent application, the provisional patent serves as a placeholder for one year from the time of filing. It can be used to possibly get some basic protection if someone needs to speak publicly about an invention (say, at a convention or tradeshow). However, a provisional patent can also convey false confidence. It's not worth anything unless it is enough to enable claims in a later patent application, and that later application has to be done within a year of the filing of the provisional patent application.

Perhaps most important, *know what you don't know*. There might be patent potential in the design of your products, or in the processes used within your new services. Or, using open source software can greatly affect IP rights for software ventures. You have to be very careful about combining your own proprietary software with open source software (such as the GPLv2 or GPLv3 licensed open source). The best protection is to find yourself an experienced patent attorney. Maybe that individual is an alum of your college or university and might get you started, at no charge, over lunch. But as much as entrepreneurs like to complain about expensive legal fees, a good attorney is worth his or her weight (quite literally) in gold for the long-term potential of a promising technology venture.

Finally, don't forget that the underlying ideas need to be protected as confidential in order to qualify for patent protection, or someone else may file for your inventions, or publication may bar you from getting protection if too much time has passed. As the United States morphs into a first-to-file system (like the rest of the world), it will be even more critical to protect your ideas from being lifted by others. A good attorney can outfit you with a Non-Disclosure Agreement (NDA) that you should have anyone sign before allowing them to learn about your invention. In general, it is a good idea not to engage in discussions with those outside of your company about nonpublic matters unless an NDA is in place. Moreover, one's ability to keep trade secrets, such as the formula for Coca-Cola, rely on good NDA practice. And, speaking of employees, make sure that each, as well as any consultants you may hire, agrees to assign rights in any inventions or copyright-protectable subject matter (such as software) to you or your company. Once again, an experienced attorney can provide you with a template for such an agreement.

The Last Step: Establish a Beachhead for Startup and Build a Roadmap for the Future

The last step in this chapter is to roadmap how your product line and services strategy will evolve over time. Investors will want to know where you will start and how you will grow. The start point is called the beachhead. The actual word *beachhead* comes from World War II, when the Allied forces landed on the beaches of Normandy. They first had to establish a secure beachhead before moving forward inland.

A beachhead is where you get started penetrating your target industry niche, the first unveiling of a larger product line or suite of services. These are the specific products or services offered within the first one or two years of business. It is an overlay of your "good, better, best" strategy—the product or services portfolio—on top of the customer grouping framework developed in Chapter 2.

Then, based on the initial market penetration—the first success—you show how your company will expand to other adjacent niches or to larger industry segments. It's that simple. This gives a trajectory for growth. Investors are always thinking about their next stage of investment. The first is for startup—for finishing the first products and selling to the first bunch of customers, either in a region of the country or to specific companies for B2B-type ventures. The next stage of investment is for expanding sales across the country or to all other similar companies in a B2B segment or niche. And then come product line or service expansion. That means new products or services for customers in adjacent niches, or your same customers who need a different set of products or services. For example, LinkedIn got into the job search and placement business, expanding from its core services of social networking for business professionals. And Starbucks expanded into different countries. Even though you will be raising money for the startup period, savvy investors will want to know your plans for growth.

So the beachhead comes first. The successive stages of growth come next. All we do is take your customer segmentation grid from Chapter 2 and place on top of it your product line or services strategy for, say, the first five to seven years of the business. Why five years? Well, that is what most professional investors think about in terms of the time it takes to start, improve, and scale a venture to the point where it can be acquired or go public. This is shown in Figure 4.4.

In that figure, you can see a representative beachhead in a target industry segment or niche, and then an expansion strategy denoted as one every two or three years. This is common for high-growth ventures. Tackle an industry niche, become a leader in that niche for your types of products or services, and then leverage your core technology and sales capability into nearby industry areas. Win that next target, and keep on moving forward, just like the unfolding events of World War II.

All the work that we did in prior chapters applies to assessing the attractiveness of those adjacent industry segments or niches that are the next targets of growth. The fastest growing segments or niches are typically the best. Or physical location might be a determining factor. We have a former student who grew his family's liquor distribution business by acquiring and growing other existing distributors in adjacent states in the United States, so that now he is sitting on a $500 million–plus business! All you need to have is a solid rationale behind your growth strategy and some facts or data to back it up.

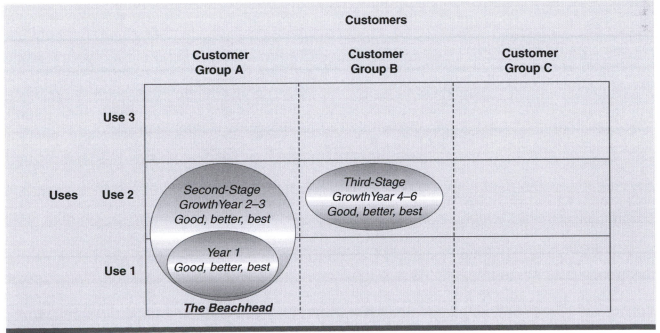

Figure 4.4   Defining Your Beachhead Strategy—and Then Next-Stage Growth

A great example of this beachhead strategy applied to technology-intensive services is Kinko's (now part of FedEx). It, too, was a student venture. Founded in 1970 by Paul Orfalea, he named the company after his own curly red hair (that's what entrepreneurs get to do!). Kinko's started next to the University of Southern California. With a $5,000 bank loan cosigned by his father, Orfalea set up a Xerox copier stand to make copies for other students. He also sold class materials. He then opened up similar student-focused stores on other campuses, forming partnerships with other students. He opened retail facilities near colleges and universities across the country. In the 1980s and 1990's, Orfalea then leveraged his idea to the small-business market. For example, he added Apple computers to his retail locations to allow small-business owners to generate their publications right in the store in addition to copying. He urged small-business owners to use Kinko's as "your branch office" and loaded them up with desktop publishing systems, sophisticated color copiers, laser printers, fax machines, and video-conference technology. Over time, these small businesses grew to be a majority of his business, providing more revenue than photocopying for college students. Orfalea had a thousand retail locations when, in 2004, FedEx acquired his company for $2.4 billion! The story of Kinko's shows how a highly customer-focused entrepreneur established a beachhead in one niche (college students in California), expanded to other adjacent niches (other college campuses in other states), and then hit a new segment (the small-business market) with a variety of new "good, better, best" products or services.

Recap: What We've Learned and Where We're Going

Let's recap. This is what we have learned to do over these past few chapters:

1. To identify an attractive industry segment based on actual market data, and within that, an interesting target segment or niche within that segment to focus our venture efforts. Most entrepreneurs focus on a specific niche and expand from there.

2. To identify the different types of customers and their occasions of use for your types of products or services within that niche, and then to focus on a specific customer and use occasion for your first product or services.

3. To really get into the thinking and behaviors of these target customers—to understand their hearts and minds—so that you can drive these needs into a truly interesting new product or service concept. Everything about your product or service innovation is highly focused on the needs and preferences of target users and/or buyers.

4. To then transform that basic product or service concept into a fully featured set of products and/or services. This might include specific offerings that represent "good, better, best" for your target customers, or simply different products or services that customers require at different points in time (think about the pest control venture), or combinations of products or services for a total or complete solution. We also learned about ways to protect your intellectual property. And we picked a beachhead—a focus for startup in terms of customers and their potential uses—on a customer segmentation grid, and then mapped where you might expand over a five- to seven-year time frame.

All this learning helps develop a clear focus for your venture, a focus that is based on market realities and customer needs rather than wishful thinking. To complete that venture focus, we need to clearly understand the business model that will accompany your products or services. As well as making for profitable businesses, strong, creative business models help drive and accelerate the penetration of product and service innovations into the market. And that is what we are going to learn next.

But first, a few very important Reader Exercises.

Reader Exercises

Now it is time for you to build your own product or services strategy. We have created some simple templates from the examples shown in this chapter. As in prior chapters, use these templates to think about your venture. Take out your Venture Concept Template and your Business Model Template. Bring all your customer and competitor research to the table. Then begin.

Step 1: Define "Good, Better, Best"

The first Reader Exercise is to apply the template shown in Figure 4.5 to define your product line or suite of services. All the customer and competitor research you have performed to date should guide your thinking here. You have segmented customers into groups, studied their use cases, and defined an interesting new product or service concept—now flex that concept into an initial handful of specific commercial offerings that will please different types of customers. Remember, some customers just want the basic product or service; others will want something more advanced, and will pay more for it. Yet others will want services in addition to products; and yet others who are buying primarily services will want you to include certain types of products with those services. This is about giving different types of customers what they need and want, all within your initial industry segment/niche and target customer group focus. Also, with some quick competitive research online, now is the time to begin to think about the pricing strategy that fits with your "good, better, best" portfolio design. Companies usually charge more for better and best.

After drawing your product line/services strategy, make a set of bullet points that contains the common features of your product or services portfolio. These might be a certain type of styling or packaging, a certain type of engine or microprocessor, a common user interface, or certain service guarantees. Later on, once you are building

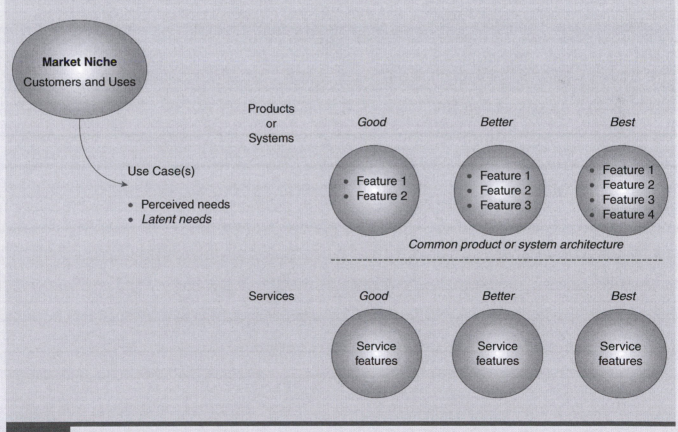

Figure 4.5 The "Good, Better, Best" Template

your company, these will turn into common platforms for your products or services—things that you can leverage across the entire portfolio.

Now step back. Take a look at the result with your team members. Does the combination of products and services set the foundation for an exciting, growing business? How can you make it even more exciting?

Step 2: Define Your Intellectual Property Strategy

This straightforward stuff is your company's name and logo, the trademark on your first product or service brand name, and copyrighting all company published material that is printed or placed on the Web. For logos, there are a number of online auction or bidding-type resources. For example, you can check out 12designers.com (be sure to set the language to English) or designcrowd.com to get access to all sorts of design capabilities.

Next come potential design and utility patents. Law firms with an established relationship with your university should be willing to have an initial conversation for free. Remember, you need to speak with not just a general business attorney, but one specialized in handling intellectual property. If you are doing a university spin-out of a technology developed in a research lab, now is a good time to pay a visit to the technology licensing office to get a taste of the terms and conditions. Look for the royalties, licensing maintenance fees, and any mention of stock ownership in "typical" licensing agreements. Whether your university or an attorney, don't promise stock to anyone. Too many entrepreneurs give up too much stock too early in the game, which only limits their ability to raise capital and control decision making later on. Remember, *everything is negotiable.*

Nor do you require patent applications (provisional or full) or completed technology licenses in order to write a business plan and get your company started. You just need to understand if these items are going to be required to build a successful company. Lots of software companies, for example, develop proprietary IP over the first two or three years of operation. They don't start with a patent. However, for certain types of ventures—particularly biotech—professionals typically expect some type of IP as part of the venture's assets. Having some type of IP, or access to someone else's IP, for your target application will greatly increase the valuation of your company.

Step 3: Define Your Beachhead and Growth Strategy

Figure 4.6 provides the template. Take your customer segmentation grid from Chapter 2 and overlay your product line or services strategy on top of it.

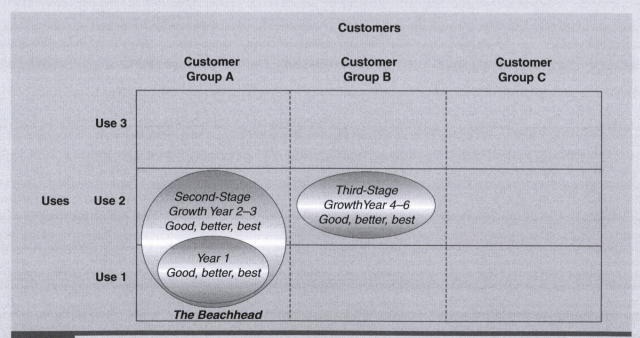

Figure 4.6   Define the Beachhead and Next-Stage Growth Template

If you wish to restructure your customer segmentation grid based on your continued learning over the past several chapters, now is the time to do it. Take the time to write down the clearly different customer groups that you encountered in your field research. We have used age, gender, size of company, type of pet, and other dimensions as customer grouping examples in this book. Also, what are the primary use cases? Think of the different types of fishing in our fishing boots example. Or for services, think about the industrial equipment example where downloading machine controls, monitoring tire pressure, and measuring worker productivity were three distinct use cases for large construction and mining companies. What is the analogy for your customers? For certain teams, expanding to a foreign country is by itself a new customer group by virtue of the huge differences in customer preferences and buying behaviors in those new markets.

For each cell on the template, try to identify your "good, better, best" within the template. How does Michael Dell's Inspiron, XP, and Alien strategy apply to your venture? And remember, whenever we say "good, better, best" it might just be "different," as in the case of the rodent, tick, and deer control for Pure Pest Management, or for various types of services that Kinko's brought to small-business owners, only one of which was photocopying.

After structuring your template, circle the region on the template that will be your unswerving focus for at least the first two years of your venture. This is your beachhead for startup. Then, where might you grow for the next stage of growth? What is your reasoning if someone—such as your professor or an investor—were to ask you?

Step 4: Huge Extra Credit: Begin to Make Prototypes of Your New Products or Services

This is where the rubber meets the road. Put your ideas to form. Start with a few sketches. For a product, this should be straightforward. Then start drawing some of the major parts of components with the product. Think about how this design matches up against the "persona" of the target customer—the type of user, be it a consumer or a person within a business, and their needs, frustrations, and behaviors. From the drawings, you might then try:

- If it is a food or drink product, go back to your kitchen, buy the ingredients, and prove your worth! Bring samples to class. If you are a software hacker, wear the badge proudly and go build a simple prototype of the user interface and some base-level functionality of the mobile app or software system you wish to create. Bring the product portfolio to life as simply and cleverly as you can.

- For other types of products, make cardboard or paper components or shapes for either the product or the packaging of the product.

- If appropriate for your types of products, go to the store and acquire similar types of products that have features and packaging that you think would work well for your proposed product. Also, try to get examples of "good, better, best" that have worked in your industry. You don't have to buy all these products; often, simply doing a Web search will provide you with all the images you require for a PowerPoint that can accompany your prototype.

- Use a software tool, such as Visio or even a CAD tool, to further design the product. If your university has a "3-D" printer, you can even create a small-scale prototype for your product.

Lean or "agile" development is clearly a significant factor in the startup world. In fact, there are now a wide range of services that allow a startup team to design, source, manufacture, and test new product concepts. Visit sites such as 12designers.com to get some concept sketches and quotes from professionals. Some entrepreneurs we know have found www.guru.com a useful source for finding just about any type of type of engineer, from software to mechanical engineering. Or, if you have a systems technology venture and need to find a microcontroller for a new device, take a look at DigiKey—a leading supplier of electronic components (www.digikey .com). If the venture needs manufacturing, contact a local co-manufacturer for a quote on low-volume production. Or you can upload your product designs on www.mfg.com. Coroflot (www.coroflot.com) or iFreelance (www .iFreelance.com) are also good sites to explore for design and manufacturing partners. Then there are services that use 3-D printers to quickly produce prototypes from CAD software models. Investigate your local area for such service providers, or you can take a look at 3Dsystems (www.3dproparts.com). These prototypes can be used for rapid feedback on design efficacy and from target customers. Another option, for small-scale, plastic-injected molded products, is Protomold (www.protomold.com).

And if it's a software product, software tools are so powerful and flexible now that in the hands of a skilled programmer, a basic prototype to show customers can be developed in a matter of several months or less. Hubspot (www.hubspot.com) has student versions of its Web development and analytics software that you just might be able to use for free to do a pilot launch and test for a Web venture. All these resources translate into not having to hire so many full-time employees or buy capital equipment at the very start of a business.

For services, prototyping simply means working with prospective customers directly to do what you would like your venture to do, for a vastly reduced price if not for free. In one way or another, this means providing assistance to target users to help solve a current problem or frustration. Your ability to address their needs and the learning you achieve in these initial attempts will directly shape the design of your new services. For many B2C services, and most B2B services, the thing you must often do is to help customers create workflows. Model the customer's use case as a structured workflow and seek ways to streamline it. In this way, you can make life or work more convenient and better within that use case. At the same time, you will see what type of information technology you require to provide and measure the results of that service. The bottom line is that to prototype services innovations, you need to roll up your sleeves, walk into the kitchen, and get your hands dirty—except that kitchen will be in the customer's place of work or leisure, depending on the focus of your venture.

Be it for products or services, prototyping means low cost, rapid, iterative, and fun! Don't go overboard. Is there a fellow student, a small design firm, or a customer engineering firm that, for little money, can help you create a prototype, be it a mobile app, a consumer product, or some new type of medical or electronic device? This is, of course, so venture- and location-specific that there are no universal answers. But do what you or your external partners can do quickly, and then show these prototypes as soon as possible to prospective customers. With prototypes in hand, we guarantee that the level of interest and interaction will go right through the roof! Arguably, it is as important as the business plan you will be creating from this book.[6]

Visit the Student Study Site at **www.sagepub.com/meyer2e** to access the following resources:

- Web Resources
- Video Resources
- General Resources in Entrepreneurship

---

[6]Rapid prototyping and testing is the central idea in the "lean startup" approach that has been popularized by Eric Ries. (Ries, E. [2011]. *The Lean Startup: How Today's Entrepreneurs Use Continuous Innovation to Create Radically Successful Businesses.* New York: Crown Business.) It refers primarily to rapid prototype development and testing. But we want to caution students not to rush out blindly to build prototypes without doing the customer segmentation, ethnography, and product/services strategy development described in earlier chapters—because otherwise, you just might waste a lot of time and money building prototypes for the wrong customers and serving unimportant needs!

5

Defining the Business Model for a Venture

A great product or services portfolio means little for an entrepreneur unless there is a clear way to make money by selling and servicing those offerings for customers.

In this chapter, you will learn how to design the *business model* for your venture. You will see how a strong business model can turn a good venture idea—the target industry niche, the target customer groups and their use cases, the product or service concept, and the product line or services strategy that fleshes out that concept—into an exciting, profitable new enterprise.

Dell, Southwest Airlines, and iTunes, for example, have excellent products or services, but so do most of their competitors. Other companies sell computers, provide air travel, or sell music. What has set these industry leaders apart and made them so spectacularly successful has been their innovative business models and the implementation of those business models. Dell bypassed traditional retailers to bring a new level of value to the PC industry; Southwest's lean, no-frills operating model made it a leader in terms of number of passengers carried by increasing the numbers of potential consumers who thought they could now afford to fly instead of drive; iTunes used the Web to provide single songs and other media to disrupt, and soon own, the mobile media distribution business.

As these examples show, while we all tend to think about "innovation" in terms of new technology for new products and services, innovating on the business model dimension can be equally if not more exciting and powerful than anything else. And to do it, you really need to *think*. So let's get started.

Defining a Business Model

For some of you, the term *business model* might suggest dry finance—for example, the financial projections for your business. But please try to think about a business model in another way. A business model is the economic and operational strategy for making money in a venture, and it generates financial outcomes. In other words, financial projections are the logical outcome of a well-designed business model. Simply put, a *business model* describes how a company plans to make money. It is not what you *do,* but how you will *make money* doing what you do. The actual financial results come from your company as a money-making machine.

Take a look at Figure 5.1. We show that a venture's strategy leads to its business model, and the business model leads to financial outcomes. The prior four chapters have all focused on developing the venture's strategy—the industry, the customers (and uses), and the product and services portfolio. Now we look at a venture's business model, which, remember, has both *economic* and *operational* dimensions. The economic dimension deals primarily with the revenue model. In terms of planning, there are four basic components to any revenue model:

1. The type of revenue (such as purchase or rent)

2. The frequency of that revenue (a one-time charge or recurring at certain intervals of time)

3. The price level of that revenue (typically per unit of product or service) relative to competitors

4. The number of distinct streams of revenue (such as different product lines or different services, or services that accompany products, such as paid support services for a computer). Each of these streams of revenue needs to be designed with the three dimensions above; the type of revenue, the frequency of purchase, and the price level relative to competitors.

The design of these four components should be driven by the needs of customers and the value proposition you are providing to them with your products and services, for example, all the good work you have done in the first four chapters of this book. Also, there is a fine balance between developing a revenue model that makes it easy for customers to begin doing business with you and giving away the store. We encourage you to try to generate a profit even on your first sales, despite all the craze for "free" or "freemium" revenue models. The idea is to create a healthy business, not just good products or services.

The *operational* components of a venture's business model are equally straightforward. The first of these is a company's approaches to R&D—its R&D model. If you are starting a company that does not require formal R&D, no problem. This might be a retailer or some other type of services company. You don't have to worry about that component of the business model.

Otherwise, you must because your investment in R&D has a direct impact on revenue (new products) and expenses (people and equipment). You can either make R&D an internal resource (do it in-house), outsource it, or have some combination of the two—such as a biotech firm sending its target drugs to contract research organizations for animal trials. Since technology is the magic sauce for most technology-intensive ventures, most R&D tends to be kept in-house.

The second operational component of a company's business model is its approach to production and fulfillment. You can use the terms manufacturing and logistics if your venture is in the physical products space, but production and fulfillment are more portable to services, be they financial, environmental, retail, and so forth. Ventures in each of these areas need to create and deliver efficient, effective services—often customized—to customers. The same internal versus external decision making that we saw for R&D applies here, too. If you are starting a restaurant, you will need to capitalize the development of a kitchen. The kitchen is an internal resource. On the other hand, if you are making food products to sell to restaurants, such as oven-ready pastries or chocolate desserts, there are both in-house and external options from which you can choose. Co-manufacturers will manufacture your products for you. You will perhaps sacrifice some margin, but you will save the capital required to build your own baking or food production process. Plus, these third-party manufacturers already know a lot about manufacturing, materials, and suppliers. Or you can start off with outside manufacturing and then move it in-house once your business grows. And you can have your own trucks to pick up and deliver finished goods or use a third-party distribution company. If you are starting a software or Web services company these days, most entrepreneurs outsource actual "production" or operations of their software to a large computer-farm or data center that can run such matters far more efficiently and effectively. If you are starting a services company or have services requirements as part of your product portfolio, most entrepreneurs hire and train their own service personnel (such as designers, consultants, systems integrators, customer support personnel, or more simply, waiters and waitresses). But once again, the external resource factor can also apply. For example, if you design a new consumer electronics device, you may want the Geek Squad to service it in consumers' homes.

Last but certainly no less important are a venture's decisions regarding channels and building awareness—or what we like to refer to more broadly as "go-to-market." There is clearly a make-buy decision here as well. For example, should you hire and train your own sales force, at a cost of at least $250,000 per person after everything is said and done, or work through distributors, sales representatives, or retailers? If you have a complex, technology-intensive product or service, you just might need a direct-to-customer sales force. Your draw from operating profit will be their base salary (which is often low), plus a 5% to 10% sales commission. In contrast, using a distributor or retailer provides you with the existing reach of that middleman into your marketplace, but you will often see 30% to 60% of the selling price go into their pockets. *Reach*, technical complexity, and the size of the sale (big computers, industrial equipment, and aircraft) often make your decision for you. An existing channel partner often already has substantial reach to target a set of customers that would otherwise take you years and vast sums of money to build.

These are all big decisions for the entrepreneur—as important as the product or service concept and the portfolio itself. Moreover, these decisions must go hand in hand with the product or service concept. *The entire stack of target customer and use occasion, product or services portfolio, and business model must fit tightly together into a powerful, cohesive whole.* Achieve this and you will have a tight, more readily understandable business plan and set of financial projections for investors to consider. And customers will intuitively know what you are doing and why you are doing it. Again, think Apple. The design and functionality of its products and stores embody its product and service concepts, with the specifics being its current product and services portfolio. Next comes its revenue model—premium pricing for one-time purchases and ongoing service agreements. And next, outsourced manufacturing to high-quality but low-cost suppliers. Then there is Apple's bold go-to-market model with its Apple stores, some of the best brand advertising the world has ever seen, and the Genius Bar in the stores themselves to help customers with training and problem resolution.

In summary, a venture's business model needs to consider these fundamental economic (the revenue model) and operational (R&D, manufacturing/production, and go-to-market) components. In the popular press, you will find many different definitions of business models and quite an amount of fuzziness around those definitions. Hopefully, the framework presented here makes common sense and will prove to be just as straightforward when you apply it to design the business model for your venture.

Now for the third part on the right side of Figure 5.1. Just as a business model is derived from a venture's strategy, a business model drives a venture's financial results. When a venture is just being planned—such as what we are doing here in this book—then these financial outcomes are really just financial projections.

For most ventures, the most important financial outcomes are the following:

- The size and growth rate of revenue
- The gross margins on that revenue
- The operating expenses in the business
- The capital required to grow the business
- The operating profits generated by the business
- Importantly, the time required to reach the first dollar of sales (as measured from the beginning of R&D)
- Just as importantly, the time required to reach operating profitability (positive cash flow from operations)
- For investors, even more importantly, the company valuation for potential "exit" five or more years down the road.[1]

Once a business is launched, the financial outcomes are real and investors will hold you accountable to your earlier projections. If the outcomes are not what you or your investors desire, then there is typically a reconsideration of the venture's strategy—its target niche, customers and their uses, and product or services portfolio—and with that reconsideration, rethinking about how to improve the venture's business model. Or even if things are going great, entrepreneurs use their financial outcomes to improve their venture strategies and business models. This is shown in the feedback loops in Figure 5.1.

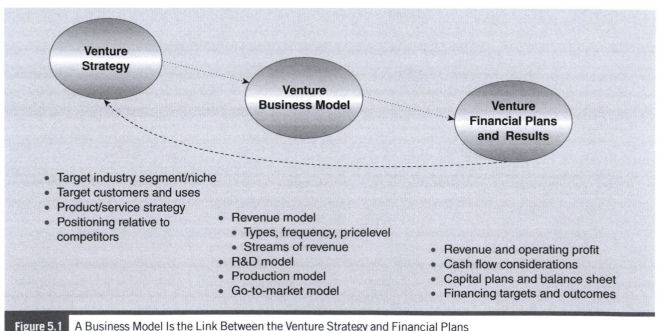

Figure 5.1   A Business Model Is the Link Between the Venture Strategy and Financial Plans

---

[1]Forget Facebook's $1 billion acquisition of Instagram. Only 18 months old, and with only 15 employees and no revenue—it's a bubble!

TIP: WHEN IT COMES TO BUSINESS MODELS, THERE IS OFTEN MORE THAN ONE WAY TO SKIN THE CAT FOR TYPE, FREQUENCY, PRICE LEVEL, AND STREAMS OF REVENUE_____

The same product or service concept can have two very different executions in terms of business model. Your job is to figure out the best way.

For example, there a number of art entrepreneurs who have entered into the business of renting paintings and sculptures to corporations for their waiting areas, conference rooms, and offices—as opposed to selling them works of art. This preserves the client's capital, turning a capital expense into an operating expense. It also allows the client to try new art from year to year. However, this business model also requires that the art renter either purchase or lease suitable works of art.

If we enter the world of software, Microsoft charges a hefty initial licensing fee ($400 at the time of this writing) for its standard Office suite. Google Apps is either free, or for the Google Apps for Business, $50 per user per year. There is no initial licensing fee, as in Microsoft Office. These are obviously very different revenue models. Or Red Hat offers its JBoss software development tools for $99 per year but charges thousands of dollars for its technical support service agreements. In contrast, IBM and Oracle charge tens of thousands of dollars for initial licensing fees for their own proprietary software development tools; they also have premium-priced support offerings.

So consider the different options as you design the business model for your venture, and let the voice of the target customer and an understanding of current competition point the way.

Understand the Winning Business Models in Your Industry _____

Take the time to search the Web and use data sources available at your university library to understand the entire "value chain" of your target industry and how companies are making money at different parts of that value chain. A value chain means the flow of raw materials to assembly to finished goods or services, to sale and customer service. In current times, the popular term is *ecosystem*. An ecosystem is simply the value chain for an industry, plus the various individuals, companies, and even universities that contribute elements along the way, such as specific technologies or logistics. Your goal is to map the ecosystem specifically for your target industry segment or niche. That means the major players along each step of the way.

Most of our students find it simplest to express an ecosystem as the following:

- A set of boxes with names and contributed technologies, products, or services inside the boxes
- Arrows connecting the boxes showing the flow of these items
- A major highlighted box showing where you would like your company to sit within the ecosystem/value chain
- A nice, big box or circle representing the customer

After completing this mapping, you can then identify a successful business model as it flows at each step of the way. How does each actor generate revenue? By actor, we simply mean an individual, company, university, or government agency. If appropriate, how would you characterize the actor's R&D, its production, and its go-to-market models? What you will probably find is that there are a number of different successful business models at each step along the value of a value chain, for example, for the raw materials or information suppliers, the assembly or production companies, the sellers, and the services or support companies. Sometimes these exist within a single large company—a vertically integrated business—but most often, different companies are focused on different parts of the value chain and have very specific business models that they have scaled to be leaders in their respective areas.

Having identified where you wish to play, try to find one or two companies that have developed a successful business model either directly in your line of work or adjacent to it. Try to understand how they make money and how they spend money, as well as each of the business model components that we described above. We are looking not only for guideposts for your own business model definition, but also feasibility. Does your business model have a long-standing tradition in your industry, or are you trying to introduce a new, disruptive business model to your industry?

For example, Cloud technology represents a disruptive business model for users: pay-as-you-go, on-demand IT and application services as opposed to spending capital to buy computers and lease software before use. But in the 1970s and 1980's, before wide-scale use of client-server computing and PCs, there was something called "time-sharing," a technology and business model where programs were provided in real time through networks to dumb terminals, and users paid to use the software as a service. So while Cloud might represent blazingly new technology, it implements a business model already well known to small businesses that cannot afford or manage their own computers and computer networks.

Therefore, while many entrepreneurs think that they might be creating an entirely new business model for a specific industry segment or niche, typically, there are analogies in other industries. For example, the Zipcar business model—hourly car rentals launched in Boston—was first pioneered in Europe. Try to find such precedents. It will make your business case much more tangible to prospective investors.

Also, you can often find important financial information for large companies working in your industry at Yahoo! Finance. This includes revenue growth, operating margin, operating profits, and links to annual reports and shareholder statements. In fact, a nice trick is to enter in the name of a market leader in your target industry, go to its financial information, and then hit the "Competitors" button. In a matter of seconds, Yahoo! Finance will show the size, growth rates, gross margins, and profitability of the major players in the industry. Read the news stories associated with the industry to learn more about current industry dynamics. Print out these summaries to show to your teammates. Highlight the key facts that pertain to your venture strategy and its business model.

The take-away: Don't build your business model until you familiarize yourself with those of other major players in your industry. This should only take an hour or two of work. And finding out how other companies make money is actually quite interesting.

Defining the Type of Revenue

Defining the type of revenue is as simple as identifying the type of transaction you wish to have with customers. Some of the obvious choices are:

- Is it a product (that is purchased or leased), or a service (that is paid for as used)? Or is it a product that can be repositioned as a service, such as software provisioned over a Cloud network?

- Is it an outright purchase, or is it a rental, license to use (as in software), or lease?

- For a Web service, is it free, an annual or monthly subscription, or some combination thereof (such as "freemium" on most mobile phone apps)?

- For consulting services, are you billing on a time and materials basis or establishing a project fee?

- For any of the above, are you requesting cash, or accepting credit purchases?

- If you are saving the customer a certain amount of money or enabling some type of financial gain or benefit, are you extracting a certain percentage of that saving or benefit? This is a contingency revenue model.

Contingency revenue models can be a powerful method for startups that need to prove themselves to customers. For example, the Mitchell Madison Group provided forensic accounting to help large corporations reduce operating expense by reducing costs in printing, temporary labor, purchasing PCs, and renting cars and hotel rooms. Instead of charging the usual consultant day rate, Mitchell Madison established a contingency fee, taking 20% to 30% of the amount of money found and saved. Fueled by this "win-win" business model, the company grew to 900 professionals and was eventually acquired for $500 million! A "win-win" business model can lessen the upfront risk for prospective customers and therefore shorten the sales cycle. Mitchell Madison Group could approach a CFO of a major corporation without asking for any money up front and, even better, payment only when the customer saved money.

Repositioning products as services is already important in many industries and will probably become even more so. The benefit of services is that customers generally subscribe to them, paying month after month, year after year. Products, on the other hand, are one-time purchases. Consider salesforce.com (www.salesforce.com), one of the first ventures to successfully deploy a product as a service revenue model. Its software services fall under the general category of customer relationship management: lead generation, pipeline management, sales forecasting, customer account management, and analytics-driven upselling. Traditional client-server software in this range used to be a $200,000 upfront investment by large corporations, plus 15% to 20% annual maintenance fees for bug fixes. Instead, salesforce.com asked for about $65 per user per month. If a company had 20 marketing personnel using the software, that might translate into about $15,000 a year. Salesforce.com offers different levels of "good, better, best" software services, with different subscription price levels. This revenue model, plus *really good software*, has helped drive the company past the $1 billion mark in a remarkably short amount of time. Plus, its Cloud model greatly reduces the threat of software piracy in uncontrolled offshore markets.

Speaking of government intervention, or the lack thereof, venturing in certain industries requires attention to government rules and regulations when establishing a revenue model. Healthcare practices, for example, can only bill for certain amounts when treating insured individuals, established by Medicare/Medicaid and private insurers. Other medical entrepreneurs are bypassing the insurance system altogether, offering longer visit times and home visits to patients who can afford to subscribe annually for this "concierge" primary care. The solar industry has relied heavily on government subsidies and tax credits for businesses and homeowners to make purchase cost effective. Now that the cost of solar panels is plummeting, by more than 50% over the past several years and with continued oversupply, these subsidies may not be as important in the future. Other solar ventures are leasing equipment to homeowners for 15-year time periods, guaranteeing a certain percentage of electricity savings each month during that time frame. In this case, the leasing company enjoys the tax credit. In both cases, the entrepreneur must understand the industry ecosystem and carefully work the numbers before deciding on the final design of his or her revenue model.

Last, the entrepreneur needs to think about how to convert a sale into hard cash for his or her business, as soon as possible. Credit cards or debit cards are one way of doing this. For consultants, setting terms for payment is another way, such as some percentage of a project fee in advance in order to start work, or net 30 days with interest penalties to encourage timely payment. If you are doing business with large corporations or nonprofits, do not underestimate the challenges of actually getting paid on large invoices. There has been many a technology entrepreneur (including one of your authors!) who has seen a 30 days receivable turn into 60 days, then into 90 days, and then some more. You may have to then resort to your own private credit to pay employees. When doing business with large corporations, try to negotiate prepayments for products delivered or services rendered.

Defining the Frequency of Revenue and Developing Recurring Revenue

Single, one-time purchases, such as that of a home, automobile, or boat, are obviously important parts of our economy. However, for the entrepreneur, the one-time purchase is hardly desirable because it requires either a very expensive single product purchase, or extensive reach into the market to get a large number of one-time purchases.

Instead, entrepreneurs try to design repeat purchases, otherwise known as recurring revenue. For products, think Gillette and the cartridges for its razors. And if a greater frequency of purchasing cannot be built in to the product itself, think services. When a company such as Caterpillar sells a large tractor, for example, it is selling three to four tractors' worth of replacement parts over the approximately 20-year life span of that tractor. Or frequency of purchase can be increased by selling services on top of single-purchased products. Think about how AppleCare has designed services to complement the purchase of a single computer or mobile device, its AppleCare with raining, hardware failure, and more general technical support.

Creating recurring revenue takes work. It involves producing follow-on products and services. It also includes specific marketing programs to maintain the customer's attention. These include developing customer loyalty programs, special pricing for product or service upgrades, and other types of special promotions. Some examples are worth considering:

- Motorcycle maker Harley-Davidson's target customers, typically Baby Boomer men with average incomes of over $80,000, spend more than $20,000 on their "Hogs." But that is not the end. Replacement parts and accessories comprise about 15% of Harley-Davidson's net revenues. Apparel and other "soft" accessories contribute another 5%. The vast majority of this private-label merchandise is sourced from third parties, which means that Harley-Davidson makes no investment in manufacturing.

- For a software company, such as MathWorks, the typical approach for achieving recurring revenue is first to sell the customer an initial customer license and then to develop special "plug-in" modules that provide specific functionality. Often, these plug-ins are made by third parties and sold back through the company's own channels. If you are a software entrepreneur, take a look at www.mathworks.com and then at all the various "toolboxes" listed under its Products and Services menu. Other software companies, such Symantec's Norton AntiVirus, work on an annual subscription basis, where the software automatically downloads virus definitions to customers' computers. Access to plug-ins is built into the subscription fee.

- One other important type of recurring revenue is the OEM agreement (which stands for original equipment manufacturer, or a supplier of components to a larger assembled product or system). For example, Ember is a Boston-based company with close to $100 million in private equity financing. It makes special chips for energy management applications, both in homes and industries, that are based on the ZigBee communications protocol. Ember gets recurring revenue when electronics manufacturers build its chips into their light switches, entertainment systems, appliances, or electricity meters. OEM agreements occur when a venture gets its technology designed into a larger manufacturer's systems, and gets paid a certain amount of money for each system shipped to end-users. "Design-ins" usually require a sales cycle of a year or more before the money starts flowing.

Every entrepreneur wants to achieve recurring revenue from customers. It usually takes a lot of work to win a new customer, so why not design a revenue model that keeps on getting more money from them? A repeat customer is a gift that keeps on giving. Investors look for recurring revenue in the financial planning of new ventures.

Defining Price Level of Revenue Relative to Competitors

Revenue models generally fall into one or another category:

1. Relative to current competitors with a similar revenue model, a *high-price, high-margin*, and *low-volume* business. Businesses that fit this description tend to have selective retail distribution or direct selling. They are selling expensive products and services to customers. High price is one distinct type of *competitive positioning* for a venture. We will have a lot more to say about competitive positioning in the next chapter.

2. Relative to current competition, a *low-price, low- or moderate-margin*, and *high-volume* business. *Low price* is another type of competitive positioning.

For products, simply consider the automobile industry. Honda, for example, sells about 400,000 Honda Accords in the United States each year versus about 40,000 Acura MDXs, its popular high-end SUV. Yet the margin on an Accord is smaller than the margin on an Acura. These are two distinct revenue model approaches: moderate price, smaller margin, and high unit volume on the one hand, versus premium price, higher margin, but lower volume on the other.

Services can also have the same price-differentiated revenue model. Consider a high-priced law firm. It may have perhaps 100 attorneys, some charging more than $500 per hour, and clients numbering in the low thousands. The legal work done by this type of law firm is customized for each client. Then consider Legal Zoom, a true services venture. It provides standardized legal services, low price but high volume, using software and the Web to automate document preparation. It will charge, for example, 10% to 20% of the price of the face-to-face premium firm, but providing the assurance of a human paralegal to review specific forms. Unlike a traditional law firm, Legal Zoom must draw tens of thousands of clients through its Web portal to generate substantial revenue.

As an entrepreneur, you must decide which type of business you wish to be—a high-price, relatively low-volume business, or a low-price, high-volume business. This decision will also drive your branding and the channels you select for distribution.

Sometimes, wonderfully successful companies such as Apple, IBM, or EMC, or companies that you don't often hear about, such as 3M, are able to get the best of both worlds: high prices relative to their competitors *together* with high volume. But this usually takes years of careful planning and operational excellence. The entrepreneur is best served by having a focus on one end of the spectrum or the other.

Our preference is to aim at better design, greater functionality, and higher prices relative to competitors, aiming at a smaller niche or part of a niche in an industry where customers are seeking these qualities in a product or service, and are willing to pay for it. The reasons for this preference are multiple: (a) you can apply the "good, better, best" thinking to your offerings to also reach mid-range buyers in your niche; (b) you are more likely to realize operating profits on each dollar of sales, and do it earlier upon first sales; and (c) there are simply too many large and often offshore competitors already working the low-price, high-volume areas of nearly all industries. Even areas that are considered "new" seem to quickly have fiercely competitive low-end commodity suppliers. When the price of solar cells drops by 50% in just a year or two, you either have got to invent a new disruptive-type solar collection device (such as Konarka) or get into the business of integrated systems and services (such as Sungevity).

Defining Distinct Streams of Revenue: Is a Single Stream Too Few or Five Streams Too Much?

IBM provides a great example. In the late 1990s and early 2000s, IBM had to transform itself from being primarily a computer hardware manufacturer with dwindling operating profit. In fact, IBM had about $40 billion in revenue at one point in the mid-1990s, yet managed to lose almost $8 billion in a single year! This near-death experience led to business model innovation in order to survive. The new strategy was to transform itself into a company that sells software and services as well as hardware.

As shown in Figure 5.2, IBM had developed five distinct streams of revenue. There is the hardware business, but also a range of new services: business consulting services, technology and infrastructure services—including outsourcing customers' data center operations—and systems integration/custom programming. Take a look at the operating margins: the profit after the cost of goods sold or services provided. You will see close to 90% for software, close to 50% for hardware, and 25% to 35% for various services. IBM also makes money financing customers' hardware and software purchases. Compared to the bad days of the mid-1990s, by 2012 IBM had more than doubled its revenue to over $106 billion. Ninety percent of its operating profit was coming from software, services, and financing, for example, all the "new stuff" that came with the business transformation.

How you count things into a stream of revenue is important. For example, IBM has hundreds of products and services, but it presents its business model as five distinct streams of revenue. Similarly, The MathWorks might be said to have five distinct streams of revenue: the MatLab and Simulink core products, its own toolkits for each, toolkits made by third parties, and "run-time" versions of MatLab that it sells for embedded systems. For the majority of entrepreneurs, however, five streams of revenue are too much to handle. Two or three make sense, especially to seasoned investors who want you to focus. You should also know that certain investors can try to steer you away from services, even though customers need them as part of a total solution. The logic concerns maximizing valuations for "exit" (e.g., achieving an initial public offering [IPO] or acquisition). Service company valuations tend to be substantially less than those of product-based ventures because of the nature of operating leverage in these two types of businesses—just as we saw in the case of IBM above, where its software margins were close to 90%, relative to various service margins in the 30% to 40% range. This leads to a fundamentally different profile for a product company versus a services company in terms of operating profit on each dollar of sale. For exit valuations for a privately held services company, the multiple ranges from one and a half to three times sales, depending on the industry. For a product company, the multiple has been running from four to five times revenue. Thus, a $25 million revenue software or medical diagnostics company might be acquired for more than $100 million. A $25 million services company might fetch between one and a half to two times revenue, or only about $40 million. A company with a balance of products and services might end up somewhere in the middle. Note that this company valuation issue upon exit is not without controversy. After all, investors should primarily be interested in helping to create great companies, and if a group of target customers requires services as much as products, then this should dictate your thinking. The vast majority of exits are based on revenue and operating profit (the Facebook $1 billion Instagram acquisition in 2012 notwithstanding!).

	Revenue in $ thousands	% of Total Revenue	Gross Profit
Global technology services	$40,879	38.23	35.0
Global business services	19,284	18.04	28.8
Software	24,944	23.33	88.5
Systems and technology	18,985	17.76	39.8
Global financing	2,102	2	49.8
Other (technology licensing, etc.)	722	.006	(54)
Total	106,916		

Figure 5.2 IBM's Revitalized Business Model: 2011 Revenue and Gross Profit

Source: IBM 2011 Annual Report, pp. 26–27.

Operational Components of the Business Model

Entrepreneurs need to *think lean,* which means working fast and effectively in all aspects of the business. Sometimes, this means not trying to do *everything yourself.* Focus on specific, value-added activities and partner with other companies, universities, or individuals for other activities. These third parties might help you get prototypes into the hands of customers more quickly or be key partners in ongoing production or distribution.

For most entrepreneurs, the work you are doing in the first part of this book—gaining the customer insight, creating the design of your product or service concept, developing the product/services strategy, and now here, generating a powerful business model—all comprise your "value added" for the venture. You as the founder of your company must do this work yourself, and keep doing it to adapt your venture to changing market situations. But to then proceed past the idea stage into actual implementation typically means first (a) developing prototyping of your products or services and quickly getting them into the hands of your target customers for rapid feedback, and then (b) actually producing those products and services in volume to generate revenue.

In each case—for the prototypes and the actual products or services to be provided to customers—you need to consider whether your own employees and equipment should be used to do the work, or to contract with other suppliers to do the work for your venture. Contracting others can also be referred to as *outsourcing.* Doing what you do best and working with other partners to capture what *they do best* can be considered a lean approach to startup operations.

The reason why this is so important to think about in the context of defining a business model is that it affects the upfront investment you need for people and machines, as well as ongoing operating expenses and margins based on whether your own staff performs a function, or others do it for you. Also, in-house versus outsourcing in R&D can easily affect your intellectual property position, which for technology ventures can be an important consideration for investors.

Defining Your R&D Model: How to Create the "Secret Sauce"

Not all ventures need original research and development. A restaurant, a residential services business, or the typical consulting firm does not have a line item in its Profit and Loss Statement for this activity. But if your venture needs to create or integrate new technology, managing R&D is going to be important for success. Often, there is at least one strong technologist as a cofounder in a technology-intensive venture, be it a software, systems, or biotech company.

You would think that a technology-intensive venture would conduct its research and development in-house. Traditionally, you would have been right! R&D was and largely remains an internally performed activity.

However, increasingly R&D is partitioned into specific chunks of activity, *some of* which are done in-house by building an R&D staff, and others outsourced to third parties. This can affect not only the overall quality of the final product or service, but also the time to market and the amount of money needed to start and grow a company.

The question is, Which aspects of R&D should be retained in the business and which can be outsourced?

To answer that question, ask yourself, "What are the things we want to do that will absolutely give us a competitive advantage and are essential in providing value to our customers?" Those activities are your "core competencies." Let us call them your company's "secret sauce"—the stuff that will make it special. In general, any part of the value-creating process that involves your "secret sauce"—whether it is R&D, production, or distribution—should be kept in-house.

If an activity does not involve a core competency, then carefully consider options for developing trusted external partners to whom you can outsource that work. Think "lean." Every single person in your company should be "high-value-added," contributing to some aspect of competitive advantage for your company. Of course, any time you outsource work, you need to develop an effective process for assessing the quality of what comes back. So, for example, if you are starting a Web company and you outsource the design and development of the Website to a third party, you still need to invest your time and that of key members of your team to review the work done by that outside firm. Your Website is the face of your company to the outside world!

In many industries, outsourcing some aspects of R&D may be mandatory because another company already owns a patent for a specific piece of your overall solution. If you develop technology that uses the same approach and materials, most likely you will be in violation of an existing patent. If the price is reasonable, you can license that patent and even buy actual product from the patent holder to use in your own products or services. This will impact your business model as an added expense, but it will also save you money hiring the R&D staff needed to recreate that technology. Then again, there are many companies that look at existing patents and decide to invent their way around them. This is a critical decision—for venture strategy, the business model, and actual day-to-day operations once the business is started.

For ventures creating complex systems with both hardware and software, it is not uncommon to see venture funds raised to pay for highly focused, external development of certain pieces of the overall system. We know of several well-funded new ventures that have forgone the traditional approach of doing all software R&D in-house and instead outsourced that work to other partner companies. The motivation for doing this is typically time to market. It takes at least six months to hire and integrate a first-rate software development team. The downside, of course, is that the crown jewels of the software company lie in a third-party developer, creating a dependency on that partner for ongoing improvements and bug fixes. It is more common these days to see a new venture keep its core software development in-house and, instead, farm out specific smaller developments, such as specialized reporting modules or hardware components to specialty R&D shops. Doing everything yourself in R&D for complex systems is no longer advisable or necessary, given the depth and breadth of talent in the industry. However, working with others requires strong relationships with managers in your external partners and strong legal contracts.

Outsourcing R&D is regularly done in the field of biotechnology. For example, ventures frequently contract with external research organizations to help "productize" new science. These outsourced activities include conducting analytical chemistry to identify and synthesize new compounds, setting up and conducting animal tests, and doing the same for human trials. Charles River Laboratories—a market leader in such services—provides the full gamut of services needed to turn discovery into therapy. In fact, some of our former students have created contract research organizations in Russia staffed by PhDs who will work at far lower rates than their North American counterparts. We have asked them, "How do you give your clients here in the United States the assurance that their intellectual property is safe on the other side of the world, in a country not known for the rule of law?" The only way, they answered, was to start small with their biotech clients and earn their trust.

Hiring someone else to do your discovery, design, or other important links in the value chain does have risks, however. By sharing important information with today's value chain partner, the entrepreneur may be creating tomorrow's competitor. For product companies, some part of the venture's "secret sauce" is often found at the junction of product design and manufacturing. A contract firm with access to that special knowledge may, despite intellectual property protections, become a competitor—or a partner of a competitor. One would think that the legal agreement between the venture and its third-party contractor would eliminate this risk, and the best contractors live by the terms of their agreements. However, take care. A startup seldom has the cash to sue anyone. So hire outside help if you require it—but at first, give that outside contractor a small piece of the work. See if they perform and are reliable. Only then expand the relationship. Moreover, if you wish to create a business of lasting and substantial value, keep the "secret sauce"—the knowledge of customers' needs and wants and the design of your product or services—inside the company and in the hands of loyal employees.

Perhaps more fundamentally, even if you do not do formal "R&D," every firm needs to build and sustain insight into its customers, current and future. Customer insight is the most important core competency for any venture. *Never outsource the development of your knowledge about customers.* Big companies do this all the time with their advertising agencies and consultants—and this can cause them to lose touch with the market. Not you! Keep doing your homework—read Chapters 2, 3, and 4 to gain keen insights into customer needs, problems, and frustrations and translate these into new products and services. That knowledge needs to be your defining wedge that drives everything else in your business. You can farm some of the development work and production work to others, but the customer insights are the crown jewels of your business. Learn these insights, refresh them, and be careful about disclosing them freely to anyone who comes for a visit.

Defining Your Production and Fulfillment Model

For business planning purposes, you need to have a fairly solid idea about how to approach production and logistics.

The use of third-party manufacturers has become commonplace. For startup ventures, this approach saves significant capital, as the cost of purchasing, installing, operating, and servicing production equipment is avoided. For corporate ventures, the benefit is that the team does not have to beg for time on existing manufacturing assets that may be running 24/7.

The drawback to outsourcing production, again, is that a third-party contractor with access to the intellectual capital of the venture, or its unique production process, may exploit it for its own benefit, legal agreements notwithstanding. This danger is particularly acute when ventures use overseas contractors, who may be difficult to observe or control.

Traditional product startups—food, beverage, and other consumer products—now regularly find contract manufacturers to produce finished goods and packaging. This is not always the case, however. Sometimes the manufacturing process is the secret sauce to the venture, and it must be kept in-house. For example, one of our students started a new popcorn venture that uses sorghum instead of corn for its base material, produced gluten free for people suffering from Celiac disease. The entrepreneur bought a large industrial popcorn cooker from a company going out of business, and then modified it to reduce the size of the mesh holes on the exterior so that the sorghum seeds would not fall out of the cooker when spun and shaked. That entrepreneur's products were soon sold in Whole Foods stores across the United States. He used a shipping company to get cases of his products to specific stores or distribution centers. More generally, Federal Express, UPS, or any of the other large shipping companies have the trucks, airplanes, and information systems needed to handle a first-rate logistics operation. Use them where you can!

Software does not involve much manufacturing, other than possibly printing CDs and documentation, which is easily outsourced. However, a number of software startups are turning to Amazon and other "on demand" computer services vendors to rent computer time for software development—such as mathematical modeling—or compiling large software programs. As they see it, why buy computers that will be obsolete in a few years when they can rent them at very low cost from Amazon? And when it comes time to put finished software into production for customers, most companies "host" their software on large servers run by third parties, with levels of security, systems backup, and scale that few startups can afford. We recently listened to a former student who started a venture to provide Cloud security services and analytics for enterprise users of Google applications. He described how he was able to start software development and marketing operations without buying a single "server" and literally had his fully up and running within a day after leasing space. All he needed was a good router to which everyone could connect their laptops and tablets. And with over thirty employees and over two million users (all just two years after startup), he still did all software R&D and customer provisioning of services through third-party infrastructure providers such as Amazon.[2] His was truly a "lean" operation.

Systems companies making some type of electronic devices—such as specialized computing, industrial, or medical equipment—typically do the assembly of the first set of customer systems on their own for testing purposes. But after that, many startups are now turning to large third-party manufacturers such as Flextronics International. Here, too, the use of contractors for assembly and testing saves time and capital for the new venture. The large contract manufacturers have achieved high levels of quality, low cost, and customer service. But you need to make sure that any contract manufacturer has a rock-solid reputation for timeliness of delivery and flexibility to make small configuration changes when a problem is found.

Services firms, by their nature, do nearly all "production" in-house. The service operation *is* the production plant. It is also the all-important "touch point" with customers, and as such is not a candidate for outsourcing. If we were to start an energy improvement service for residential homes, our own technicians would "produce" the service and directly interface with customers under a strict regimen that we would measure and control. Financial services and information products ventures are also services organizations that do most of their information "manufacturing" or data-mining in-house.

Defining Your Go-to-Market Model (Channel and Promotional Strategies) _____

In our experience, entrepreneurs consistently undervalue the importance of their "go-to-market" approach. By go-to-market, we refer to a venture's plan to engage and deliver products and services to customers. Inexperienced entrepreneurs tend to focus instead on their technology, the products or services themselves, and the financial projections for the venture. Your company's approach to marketing its commercial offerings must be as powerful and as much a source of competitive advantage as what it sells. In addition, that go-to-market approach has a direct impact on financial planning and outcomes. In creating a business model, the key go-to-market decision is going to be channel.

A business's distribution channel is its pipeline to customers and is often a key element in a successful business model. Staples, for example, innovated the first office supply "superstore." Dell famously bypassed the traditional retail channel, selling directly to PC buyers—first by phone and then online. When Apple opened the doors of its iTunes Music Store, it did so via the Internet. Now Apple's retail stores are so effective for its hardware and services that Best Buy—the leader in consumer electronics retailing—has seen its sales diminish in recent years.

There are a number of direct channels. The most obvious is a direct sales force—salespeople whom your company employs to sell its products, systems, or services to the customer. Ventures are well served having a good salesperson on the team from early on to help sell the first one or two customers. Nothing proves the merit of a venture like real customer money, and it typically takes great skill and persistence to achieve this for a company that is new and doesn't have any other customers! You also have to be very careful when bringing on salespeople. They need to have a track record of success in your target industry—with customers you can call to validate the salesperson's capabilities.

_____

[2]This venture is called CloudLock.

There are, of course, other direct channels. Your venture might have its own retail stores or its own eCommerce Website. Or you might find it best to propose a multichannel option in your business plan—combining a retail channel, for example, with a direct Web or mail order channel. For example, your authors sometimes purchase fishing gear from a company called Cabela's. It started off as a catalogue mail order business for outdoor sportsmen. It then opened its own retail stores, first in the Midwest, and is now expanding across the country. And now it has a robust Web order business. Thus Cabela's has three channels, all of which are "direct to consumer." L. L. Bean does the same, as does Apple.

Then there are many different types of indirect channels or selling intermediaries. These include:

- Retailers, who obviously sell directly to the end-users or consumers of products. Increasingly, they are selling services as well. For example, in the pet food industry, PetSmart now houses the Banfield veterinarian clinics as well, becoming a one-stop shop for the consumer. Dealers are typically synonymous with retailers, and your automotive dealer will try to sell you XM satellite radio and extended warranty services in addition to the vehicle itself. In the boating industry, for example, boat manufacturers reach the public through a network of boat dealers—who themselves tend to carry three or four different brands of boats. The business model implication here is that retailers or dealers expect to make a 30% to 50% margin on the end-user price of a product, and generally, less margin for add-on services.

- Distributors, who are the intermediaries that perform a variety of distribution functions, including holding inventory and marketing to and supplying retailers. Typically, a distributor buys your products at a price that provides it with 5% to 10% margin on the final customer price of the product. That's the business model implication of using a distributor. Distributors tend to cover an entire region or country for a certain class of product or service. Wholesalers are typically synonymous with distributors.

- Agents, who are the intermediaries that market a product/service for a fee. These are often referred to as manufacturers' agents or selling agents. You might retain an agent, for example, to find distributors or retailers in a foreign market or to get you into the front door of a large national retailer. Be sure to ask for evidence of the agent's effectiveness before signing an agreement! Many entrepreneurs have been promised "the moon," paid hefty monthly retainer fees for six months, and not seen a single penny in additional revenue. Don't be one of them!

- Brokers, who are the intermediaries that bring buyers and sellers together to negotiate purchases. They do not take title to anything but tend to work on some type of commission basis, often 5% or so. You will find numerous brokers across the various financial services industries, for example.

- OEMs, who are the manufacturers through which you sell products or systems where these are included as part of their own manufactured products. The term *OEM* stands for "original equipment manufacturer," and one tends to find it used in the computer and automobile industries. For example, one of your authors' companies sold its real-time operating system software on an OEM basis to the old Digital Equipment Corporation (DEC). That venture was the original component producer, for example, it made the software that DEC bundled onto its mini- and desktop computers. An OEM contract with a large corporation offers the promise of high volumes for the entrepreneur, but also often results in a substantial discount (sometimes up to 70%) of the "list price" for a product. OEM partners like IBM, HP, or any other large company also take a lot of upfront work because your component or software has to be engineered to work in their own systems.

- VARs, who are the "value-added resellers" that buy your products (typically computer hardware and software or devices of some sort) and then add their own software and services as part of the sale to the customer. VARs tend also to expect a significant discount off your list price, in the range of 30% to 40%. The great thing about VARs in certain high-tech industries is that they are focused on a specific vertical market or niche and have highly specialized direct sales forces that work directly with accounts in that niche. At the same time, VARs need support. You will have to assign an engineer to work with the VAR's own engineering staff to learn how to make your products or systems sing and integrate them with other technologies in their solution stack.

With indirect channels, you can also have a multichannel strategy—but here you must proceed with the utmost caution. Many software companies sell both through retailers and directly to consumers through the Web. Just think of Intuit or Symantec for examples of well-managed, multichannel strategies in software. Microsoft adds to this with a robust OEM strategy—with its software bundled by manufacturers onto their own computers.

Having more than one channel raises the specter of *channel conflict*—offering two ways to buy the same product—which can confuse customers. It can lead various channel partners to begin to discount your products in order to get the sale. As soon as this happens, even the best product can be blemished. Salespeople tend to say the best things about the products with which they make the highest commissions. Moreover, a channel partner is making an important commitment to your company by carrying your product. This involves training its own sales force and co-marketing your product or service. They will be upset if your own sales force or Website steal customers away. If you are going to use channel partners, your commitment must be to support *their sales* as best you can.

TIP: A MISTAKE OFTEN MADE BY YOUNG WEB ENTREPRENEURS

We see many business plans for new Web services that either underestimate or ignore what it takes to build and sustain a significant community of active users on the Web. Not everything takes off in an instant viral craze. Rather, search engine optimization, buying advertising placements on Google or LinkedIn or Facebook, and using the analytics to analyze incoming traffic from companies such as Hubspot cost money! In other words, you can't just make products and services available on the Web; you need to work the Web to develop and sustain interest.

You must think about the specific customer group (e.g., the "community") you wish to reach and how best to reach it, not just online but offline as well. You need to track not only how many people visit your Website, but also the intensity of their use. And measure the effect of new efforts to increase visits and use. Someone in your company must become highly proficient in search engine optimization so that your company pops up at the top of Google or Bing Web searches. In practice, Web startups need at least one person, if not more, who is going to worry about this challenge as a regular part of his or her job!

Becoming a channel for other companies that disintermediate current suppliers and channel members has become a valid venture strategy in its own right. *Disintermediation* means the removal or bypassing of established channel players to reach customers directly. In many ways, the Web has disintermediated many industries, allowing producers of products and services to develop direct relationships with customers. Zappos, for example, became a powerful online fashion merchandiser specializing in contemporary shoes and apparel, backed up with best-in-class delivery and customer service. It disintermediated traditional shoe retailers. Started only in 1999 outside of Las Vegas as an online retailer, Zappos was approaching a billion dollars in sales before Amazon acquired it in 2010! It was making retailer-type margins on its products sold.

There is also a long-established history of successful software companies adding incremental streams of revenue to their P&Ls by becoming a channel for third-party software developers—part of the recurring revenue model we described above. The software company markets its ability to provide access to customers to other independent software firms. These firms build applications on top of the venture's own software and are then marketed on the venture's Website as add-on applications. Not only does the venture receive a small sales commission, but it also presents a broader solutions portfolio to current and prospective customers. This is not disintermediation, per se, but it is becoming a channel in its own right—a "Pied Piper" for a community of like-minded software developers.

As an entrepreneur, your go-to-market questions are:

- Where do my target customers prefer to buy the type of products or services I aim to sell?

- How much information do they require to make the purchase? If it is a lot—as in buying enterprise software—then you will need a direct sales force that can speak to the advantages of your products. And even if you use a direct sales force, the more information you can put on a self-service Website, the better.

- How important is convenience to these customers? If it is a major factor in their decisions, an eCommerce Website backed by UPS fulfillment might be the way to go.

- How do I build visibility and awareness for my products or services and what are the realistic costs of achieving these ends, be they preferred placement or product sampling in a retailer, advertising in a magazine, search engine optimization, or even becoming a preferred merchant on Amazon? What are the best approaches for launching strongly into the market, and what are the financial implications of those approaches?

Putting yourself in the shoes of targeted customers and resellers will help you answer these questions. Build the answer into your go-to-market model.

Two Examples of Business Model Definitions: Low-Tech and High-Tech

To integrate and apply the concepts for business modeling in this chapter, let's look at two examples, one low-tech and the other high-tech. It is important to give several specific examples of how this all works for your learning. You will also need to define this type of detail for your own business model for any seasoned investor. So fasten your seatbelts for a bit and learn from the next two examples.

A Manufactured Product Line of Pet Snacks: HealthyWags

Over 40% of households in the United States have a pet! We have been friendly over the past decade with a venture building a business focused on the pet snack segment of the $30 billion North American pet food industry, with a particular eye on the premium, healthy snack niche where products are sold in specialty retailers and independent pet stores. Over recent decades, families have come to regard their pets more as four-footed children than as animals. This has resulted in greater spending on pet products such as food, accessories, pet grooming, and veterinary medicine. Pet specialty retailers, dominated by PetSmart and Petco, have risen to meet this growing demand for products and services. Demand for main meals has been addressed with increasingly nutritious, higher-protein foods. Snacks, on the other hand, have generally fallen into the "junk food" area—less than optimally nutritious. They are heavy on corn meal and meat flavorings, and are often shaped as cookies or bones. Snacks also include heavily processed raw hide "chews" and chicken strips—many of which are made in Asia in low-cost, poorly controlled facilities. Despite their lack of nutrition, pet snacks are highly profitable because a high price is charged for a small amount of food.

The venture team for this example—several dog enthusiasts—became highly knowledgeable in animal nutrition. They decided to create a venture that would bring health and nutrition to the pet snack category. One member of the venture team became well versed in dog nutrition, ingredient requirements, and safety issues. The other was the sales and marketing person.

They approached a small, upscale packaged snack bakery in the city where they had gone to school and offered the owners a partnership arrangement. The motivation was to partner with people who already understood how to bake snacks, handle food safety and quality issues, and package products in ways that appealed to upscale buyers. If things went well and they got along in terms of business and personality, the two parties would then merge into a single business entity in which the venture team would handle sales, branding, and finance, and the bakers would focus on product design and manufacturing.

The venture strategy is shown at the top of Figure 5.3: (a) the Target Market Niche (pet snacks); (b) the Target Customer (affluent pet owners); (c) the Products (whole, nutritious cookies and bars); and (d) the Competitive Positioning (snacks that are better for your pet, with a premium price positioning).

The financial planning of the team was very straightforward. They would invest $60,000 in high-volume baking and packaging equipment to be installed in the bakery. For their part, the bakery owners would design tasty and nutritious cookies and health bar pet snacks made from natural ingredients and few preservatives. The venture team would create a new brand and bring the products to market. The team planned the initial roll-out to focus on independent pet specialty stores, and later to the large high-end pet store chains such as PetSmart and Petco. Altogether, the team figured that it would need an additional $60,000 for an effective regional launch to the small retailers, plus another $5,000 or so in travel expenses to keep the team members on the road selling into the channel. When combined with the manufacturing investment, the total funds needed to start the business came to about $125,000. Between the founders' own assets and those of some close friends, that amount of capital was within reach.

In return for buying the baking/packaging equipment for the small pet bakery, the venture team planned to pay the bakers a royalty for new product designs and also to pay the bakery for finished, packaged goods.

You can see from the figure that the team's business model has a revenue model based on multiple items sold at retail. The goal was to create a high operating margin business (charge a lot per unit and preserve a 50% margin over cost of goods sold). As sales grew by geographic expansion, the margins would improve through economies of scale in purchasing raw materials. In addition, recurring revenue was built into that structure because most owners shop for snacks on a biweekly if not weekly basis. The actual "R&D" was handled jointly by the venture team and its baking partner. The venture's production model was to collaborate with the local pet snack bakery. And in terms of the go-to-market model, the independent pet store retail channel was chosen to gain market exposure, followed by the large specialty chains. One of the team members went out to independent pet store owners, one by one, and sold them on the taste and health benefits of the new snacks. The team also defined its marketing communications to include special in-store displays and checkout counter samples. These could be a good way to gain traction. The team's business partners—the pet snack bakers—would go to work developing a set of half a dozen new, healthy snacks as well as some preliminary packaging. These samples would be essential for selling storeowners. One of the entrepreneurs also envisioned a "store in store" within a large mass merchandiser as another distribution strategy—but that would come later.

Note how all four components of the business model "fit" well together for purposes of starting a venture at relatively low cost and in a short amount of time. Recognize further that the venture team could have pursued an entirely different model for the same venture strategy. For example, the venture team itself could have handled all production and product/package design in-house. However, that model would have required the hiring of at least three employees and entailed the risk of enlisting people with less experience in food design, safety, and packaging than the bakery owners. They wanted to achieve a short time to first dollar of sales, and with high prices, a quick path to profitability.

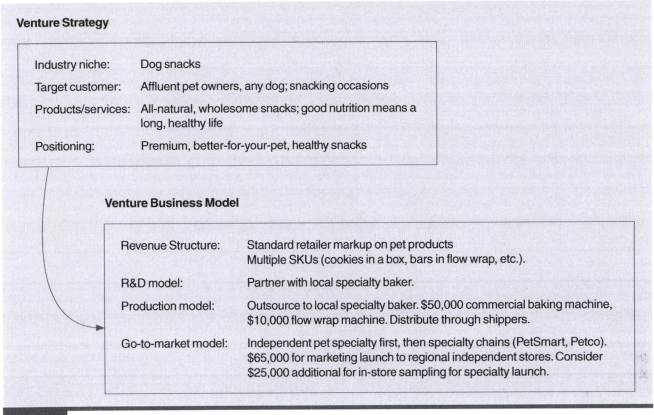

Venture Strategy

Industry niche:	Dog snacks
Target customer:	Affluent pet owners, any dog; snacking occasions
Products/services:	All-natural, wholesome snacks; good nutrition means a long, healthy life
Positioning:	Premium, better-for-your-pet, healthy snacks

Venture Business Model

Revenue Structure:	Standard retailer markup on pet products. Multiple SKUs (cookies in a box, bars in flow wrap, etc.).
R&D model:	Partner with local specialty baker.
Production model:	Outsource to local specialty baker. $50,000 commercial baking machine, $10,000 flow wrap machine. Distribute through shippers.
Go-to-market model:	Independent pet specialty first, then specialty chains (PetSmart, Petco). $65,000 for marketing launch to regional independent stores. Consider $25,000 additional for in-store sampling for specialty launch.

Figure 5.3 The Venture Strategy and Business Model for a Healthy Pet Snacks Venture

In the next section of this book, on venture financing and projecting financial performance, we see how a venture's business model not only drives financial projections but impacts potential exit strategy. In this case, the answers were clear: If the dog snack business could achieve $10 million to $15 million in sales after five years, and achieve industry average profitability, a valuation in excess of $30 million for being acquired was not out of the picture.

A High-Tech Example: Health Monitoring Systems

The second business model example comes from the emerging world of monitoring the elderly in homes and assisted living centers.

Figure 5.4 shows the venture strategy and the business model for one such health monitoring system venture. It aimed to provide basic blood testing and physiological monitoring for seniors using computer and medical technology.

The venture team in this case addressed a large opportunity. Forrester Research had described the remote personal health monitoring market as one of the most attractive technology markets and expected sales to reach $5 billion in 2010, exploding to $34 billion by 2015. This growth would be fueled by the aging of Baby Boomers and would accelerate over the next 20 years. Opportunity within the elder care technology market was validated by a GE and Intel announcement to invest more than $250 million over the next five years in the research and development of home-based health technologies for seniors. Earlier VC-funded ventures, as well as corporate ventures, had tried to penetrate this market but failed. The venture team would have to work smart to be successful.

Figure 5.4 shows the venture strategy and business model for this example.

The venture strategy targeted the elderly at home, providing basic physiological and related health monitoring systems in a minimally obtrusive way. Alerts would be sent to a centralized server to initiate responses by trained home healthcare workers. The competitive positioning

Venture Strategy

Industry niche:	Remote monitoring, in-home health segment
Target customer:	Seniors, cognitive capabilities okay
Products/services:	Continuous physiological monitoring and simple blood testing
Positioning:	Low cost, reliable, easy to use, continuous care

Venture Business Model

Revenue model:	Type: Subscription for monitoring, consumables for blood testing. Frequency: Monthly for monitoring, as needed (daily/weekly) for kits. Price-level: In line with ADT and do-it-yourself blood test kits. Streams: Monitoring, kits, and accessories (scales, breath measurement).
R&D model:	License sensors from university; outsource sensors to design firm; in-house development of software; purchase blood kits and accessories.
Production model:	Outsource manufacturing of sensors to FDA-approved contract manufacturer. Purchase blood kits and accessories.
Go-to-market model:	Partner with local home health agencies, visiting nurse associations, etc. Standard public relationships in healthcare magazines and conferences.

Figure 5.4 The Venture Strategy and Business Model for a Healthy Monitoring Venture

of the venture was one of low cost, reliability, and ease of use. The goal was to provide "smart" 24/7 care at an affordable cost to reduce emergency room admissions. The venture sought to give the elderly and their families greater assurance of care.

The team thought long and hard about its options in each of our four business model components described in the chapter: the revenue model and the three operational factors. A traditional approach would have been to charge customers for the "hardware" as well as a set-up fee. However, the team thought that the existing home security model was most attractive: to offer a reasonable, recurring monthly service fee as well as to install the sensors and communications system at a small charge, just like ADT.

For the R&D model, the team had exclusive access to a bed/chair sensor and a fall detector from a prestigious university. However, it would have to raise substantial capital to build the necessary alert and workflow software used for the patient monitoring. The software would be its "secret sauce." One of the team members was a skilled software architect and programmer. They all agreed that he would need a team of at least five additional programmers to get the job done and then tasked him to get started right away—with his own "sweat equity"—to build a prototype that could be shown with the business plan to venture investors.

For its production model, the venture planned to outsource that activity to FDA-approved, third-party contract manufacturers. This avoided the time and costs associated with having to set up its own manufacturing for sensors, blood kits, and accessories.

Perhaps the most important was the team go-to-market model. The team partnered with local home healthcare agencies and assisted-living centers, giving them a percentage of the subscription revenue. As one team member put it, "For a share of the monthly service fee, they would install our system, teach seniors how to use it, and replace sensors when necessary." Plus there would be highly trained, experienced people behind the ongoing use and maintenance of the system. These included nurses who would continue to visit the elderly in their homes or assisted living apartments. The team thought these nurses could provide feedback on the design of the system as well as a wealth of new product development opportunities over time.

As fortune would have it, one of the team members knew several executives in two large home healthcare agencies in two cities nearby who were seeking ways to automate their field operations as well as create a new stream of revenue. They collectively thought that $70 a month as a home monitoring fee was reasonable, given the rates charged by security companies. The executive also thought that a served population of 50,000 customers within the geographic region was also achievable if the system worked as promised. A half dozen home healthcare agencies working with several large health insurers could deliver that number, and he personally knew the key decision makers in each account. That usage would translate into $30 million in annual sales. Exit valuations for such technology-intensive ventures were currently four to five times revenue, which might make this a $150 million acquisition target in five years. With these objectives built in to a business plan, the team raised a first round of venture capital of $6 million, launched a test for three months on 100 elderly residents, proved the efficacy of the system, and began to scale its business regionally and later, nationally.

Note two very important things in both of these business models. First, as an entrepreneur, you do not have to exit unless, of course, you are one of those select few who actually bring in institutional venture capital to fund your startup. In that case, the venture capitalists will be working from Day 1 to get your company acquired or to reach an IPO, because *that is the only way they make money*.

Second, operating profits on the total business—after cost of goods or services sold, and after general administrative, selling, and R&D expenses—should be achieved as soon as possible in any business. In a consulting services business, you can do this in the first two months. For a product company, such as the pet snacks company, it might take a year. And in a technology-intensive company, such as the healthcare monitoring venture, it might take several years to turn a profit as a business. No matter what the business, if you can start generating small amounts of cash from your business within the first year of operation, a huge congratulations will be in order to you from your investors. It might sound old fashioned in this age of freemium Web services and open source software, but achieving paid, profit-generating sales early on is the surest way to both win the hearts and minds of early-stage investors as well as to build a solid, growing business.

Innovating on Current Business Models for a Corporate Venture: The Case of MyM&M'S _____

Business model innovation can be a powerful enabler for an entrepreneur or corporate innovator, as important as the new product or service itself. To learn this, we will dig into one last example—focused on business model innovation without a large, mature corporation. Custom-printed M&M'S Candies, called MyM&M'S, is our example. Take a quick look at www.mymms.com before reading on.

For decades, food scientists at Mars, Inc., had made incremental improvements to M&M'S Candies, changing the shell color, experimenting with new flavors (such peanut, crispy, or pretzel), and engineering a tremendously efficient manufacturing process. These little round candies were and remain phenomenally successful as a product line. Industry data from 2011 show that M&M'S Candies was the second most popular chocolate brand in the United States, surpassed only by SNICKERS, another Mars, Inc., brand. With nearly $450 million in sales during 2011, M&M'S Candies as a business represents a very specific business model: make tons of the candy on heavily capitalized internal manufacturing assets, ship it to large distribution centers, get it on the checkout shelves and vending machines around the world, and price it as a "value" product (which means low) but make a lot of money on the sheer volume of unit sales. The average selling price for a 16 ounce bag of M&M'S in 2011 was about $1, which means unit sales approaching 400 million bags. That is more bags of M&M'S sold each year than all the residents of the United States! It should be of no surprise that associates within Mars refer to the company's traditional business model as "Tons R Us."

In the early 2000s, a highly innovative process engineering manager and his team were roadmapping future R&D for the company's chocolate products. One of the dimensions that they thought would be important was personalization. An engineer went back to the lab, took a standard ink-jet printer, replaced the ink with food dyes, and was soon printing simple text messages on various chocolate products. Printing on a curved, round surface is hard, and the team figured out how to do it on a high-volume machine. Figure 5.5 provides an image of the product. Note the personalized images as well as text.

Figure 5.5   Business Model Innovation: Leveraging a Candy Snack Into a Premium Gifting Service

Images: Copyright © Mars, Inc. Reproduced with permission from Mars, Inc.

In fact, one of your authors worked with this team on its business planning. The venture idea was to have millions of dedicated M&M'S Candies lovers get onto a Website, order their own personalized custom-printed candies, print the candies right next to the main production line, and use a logistics leader such as UPS to ship finished product directly to consumers. And instead of the half-dozen standard M&M'S colors, Mars could provide access to the several dozen other colors of M&M'S. All together, the team thought that MyM&M'S might sell for as much as $30 a pound, plus shipping, which was more than ten times the price for traditional M&M'S Candies. The business model implications were profound:

- The revenue model. The big difference between MyM&M'S and M&M'S Candies is in the price-level per unit for each product line. For MyM&M'S, it started at $30 a pound versus $3 a pound, reflecting the "premium" versus "value" positioning. Moreover, the team expected the average order sizes to be somewhere between $70 and $120 (2–4 lb) for MyM&M'S versus $1 for a little bag of M&M'S. (As time passed, wedding and business event occasions were driving much larger order sizes.) The structure of revenue is also different: For MyM&M'S, a consumer pays extra for shipping the product to his or her home or place of business; for M&M'S Candies, logistics costs are built in to the price of each little bag of candy.[3]

- The R&D model. Part of the R&D was performed in-house, but key partners were contracted to develop highly specialized ink for printing, and the print-heads themselves. Those print-heads use specialized piezo-electric technology to spray the ink in perfect form on the candies. As a food manufacturer, Mars did not possess the chemistry and electronics skill sets needed for these two key components. And Mars

---

[3]Meyer, M. H., Willcocks, N., & Boushell, B. (2008, Jan.–Feb.). Corporate venturing: An expanded role for R&D. *Research Technology Management*, 34–42.

also used third parties to develop a dynamic consumer Website. Its own computer personnel were skilled at large-scale manufacturing IT, SAP, and the like; not eCommerce on the Web! In short, identifying and managing external resources for R&D became a very important part of this venture's success.

- The production and fulfillment model. MyM&M'S is drop-shipped directly to consumers, versus taken home from the store for M&M'S Candies. And MyM&M'S goes to consumers' homes or offices through UPS as the distribution partner, as opposed to M&M'S Candies rolling out to major distribution centers on a fleet of large trucks.

- The go-to-market model. This is perhaps the greatest difference of all. MyM&M'S features Website ordering versus the impulse, checkout counter buying for M&MS Candies, with associated (and substantial) slotting fees. Also, MyM&M'S advertising is very different, focused on media channels such as airline, food, and wedding magazines, and Web promotions on Amazon and Google.

Business model decisions can also be validated with market research. The MyM&M'S team conducted rapid market research to present consumers with different levels of price versus different levels of features. (This is called conjoint analysis, and a company called Sawtooth Software [www.sawtoothsoftware.com] has all the software you need to develop and run such a test.) When the results came in, the team was surprised! As you can see in Figure 5.6, the purchase behavior of men buying personalized candy is *very different* than that of women. For impulse gifts, price for men seemed to be of no concern. As a matter of fact, the more one charges, the more men seem to value the gift! Women, running a household budget, are much more price-sensitive. These insights helped the team plan the price level for MyM&M'S before launch.

With this work done, senior management stepped up to the plate with investment capital—just like a venture capitalist. It assigned a dedicated team to commercialize the idea. Today, MyM&M'S is a major business unit within Mars. With a lot of hard work, the business model proved to be a good one!

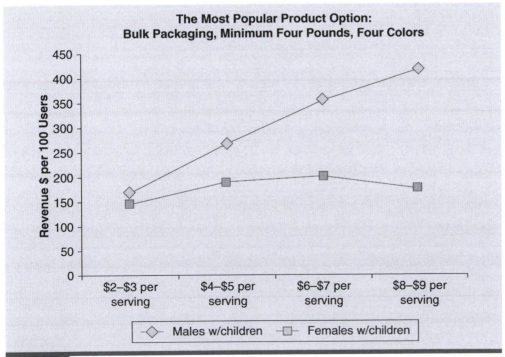

Figure 5.6 Market Research Performed Prior to Launch: Men Are Certainly Different Than Women!

Data reproduced with permission from Mars, Inc.

Beyond these four major dimensions of the business model for a new venture, corporate ventures have the advantage of leveraging existing assets within the corporation within new businesses. A corporate venture team should therefore consider platform reuse as part of its business model. For MyM&M'S, 99% of the product comes off existing M&M'S Candies production lines. Had MyM&M'S had to capitalize its own candy production lines (in addition to the customized printing lines), this business probably would not have been possible. And the cost of goods implications are equally profound; the team grabs tiny amounts of candy from the main lines at a cost of goods associated with literally tons and tons of candy. Truly, for MyM&M'S, M&M'S Candies itself was the ultimate *product platform*. And, if you think about it, M&M'S Candies was also a powerful branding platform. Who wouldn't want to try personalized M&M'S?!

TIP: SELLING BUSINESS MODEL INNOVATION TO CORPORATE EXECUTIVES

For corporate entrepreneurs using this book, even though business model innovation can be essential for market success, *it can also be hard to sell internally*. Getting senior management to understand and support business model innovation is often harder than selling customers on the products or services provided under a new business model. For every case like MyM&M'S that goes well, there are dozens that do not. Many mature companies find themselves desiring adjacent growth into new markets and new use occasions. Executives look toward corporate ventures as a means of developing and launching such ideas. The challenge, however, is that corporate entrepreneurs often have difficulty getting their more traditional corporate executives to fully understand the new business model required to build and scale such exciting new ventures. It takes careful thought, patience, and persistence to sell a senior executive on a business model that is different than the one ingrained in the current thinking of the corporation. Often, you must get them to "live the life" of target customers—to experience it themselves firsthand—so that they can see the compelling value proposition of your venture.

You can also read more about the development of this venture and the business model behind it by reading the MyM&M'S case on the Website for this book (www.sagepub.com/meyer2e). As you do that, watch a video of Dan Michaels, the R&D manager for the business. And as you watch, think about the business model innovation MyM&M'S truly represents relative to the traditional business model of large candy companies.

For ventures more generally, business model innovation may be the only way to break into entrenched markets to grab share from existing competitors. Everyone rightly thinks of Dell as a multibillion-dollar market leader in personal computing. However, at one point, it, too, was a startup venture based in a college student's dormitory room. Michael Dell assembled personal computers for fellow students by pulling together inexpensive components in his dorm room and selling them to customers at a lower price because the sale avoided the standard retailer markup. He then morphed this in the Web, challenging existing PC manufacturers whose business model was to manufacture and sell through distribution retail channels. By going directly to the consumer through the Web, Dell was able to bring a substantial price discontinuity to the PC market: excellent computers, less expensive than those on the shelf, customized to individual consumer preference through a Website, and shipped direct to the customer.

Some Final Words of Caution
on Popular Business Model Trends

Please, don't give value away for free! You might provide users with the ability to test a product or service at no cost for a little while, but soon the meter needs to start running.

Entrepreneurs often make the mistake of creating a next-generation product, system, or service that is a lot better than anything currently in the marketplace, and then charge less for it than those competitors offering inferior products. They think that this is the best way to ramp up sales. The problem is that a great product, system, or service is nothing if it does not also lead to a financially successful company. At some point, sooner rather than later, your venture will have to start generating cash from operations. If you train customers to get a lot and not pay a lot, it will be very difficult to get them to switch into a pay-more mode. It is also very difficult to support a flood of new customers in any new venture. We believe it better to get a solid yet constrained initial set of customers and serve them well. Learn what it takes to be a successful enterprise. Then raise the capital required to scale the business.

Consider EMC, started by the late Dick Egan and his partner, Roger Marino.[4] They started selling office furniture to generate cash to fund R&D for the product they really wanted to sell: a large-scale storage system to take on existing systems from IBM. EMC deployed a new architecture—called RAID—that permitted customers to hot-swap added storage arrays to their system. This allowed their systems to be more powerful yet have a lower cost of goods by using more common PC disks than other high-end systems on the market that used rarer 15-inch disks. Egan and Marino could have charged less than IBM, since their cost of goods was less. Instead, they priced their products at a 25% premium over IBM because EMC's RAID systems were 25% faster and more scalable. More than two decades later, EMC remains the market leader in storage. EMC has always worked hard to understand, deliver, *and price* to customer value.

Try to resist the allure of gaining mass numbers by giving products and services away completely for free. This relegates making operating profits from each new customer unlikely for a number of years. Sooner or later, the chickens will come home to roost. Your investors will want to see cash generated from each sale. In fact, a worthy goal is that a business model should seek profitability on the very first sale. Even if you have difficulty achieving this right away, it will provide the mindset and discipline needed for long-term success. It doesn't necessarily have to be cheaper—just better.

Of course, Facebook may end up being the great counter-example. We know that Facebook sounds attractive to young entrepreneurs—a founder who started developing the concept in college, gives his primary services away for free to get the "eyeballs" needed to support an advertising revenue model, and becomes a billionaire in the process! However, the fee for Web advertising at the beginning of 2008 was about $7 per 1,000 unique visitors per month, and at the time of this writing, hovered around $1 per 1,000 unique impressions. As the price per impression continues to drop, we suspect that this is going to be a tough revenue model to sustain unless Facebook builds and scales complementary streams of revenue with good margins. Indeed, Google is a fine example of an advertising-based Web venture that has developed an ever-expanding suite of value-added services that leverage its customers and various types of data. LinkedIn is another example. In addition to its social networking services, LinkedIn is now challenging Monster in the job placement arena—and charging a healthy price for the service to employers. *That is something to like!*

---

[4] Both Dick Egan and Roger Marino were alums of our university, Northeastern University. They were famous for hiring smart Israeli and Irish engineers while recruiting collegiate varsity athletes from local colleges as salespeople. The third key player in EMC was Moshe Yanai, the longtime head of R&D. Moshe served in the Israeli defense forces and brought intelligence, determination, and discipline to engineering. He would sometimes fly a helicopter to staff meetings held at Northeastern's off-campus conference center. EMC remains a very driven, entrepreneurial company, even though it is surging past the $20 billion mark in revenue.

Reader Exercises

Let's create a business model for your venture. Go to the template shown in Figure 5.7. It asks you to specify approaches in each of the major dimensions of the business model described in this chapter. Using the template makes this easy. Just follow these steps:

Business Model Dimensions	The Approach for Your Venture	Rationale for That Approach
Revenue Model Types of revenue Frequency of revenue Price level relative to competitors Multiple streams of revenue		
R&D Model Build technology or buy? What is the "focus" of internal versus external R&D?		
Production Model Manufacturing—internal or outsourced? Logistics—internal or outsourced?		
Go-To-Market Model Channel? Strategy for building awareness		
	Taken As A Whole, Do These All Fit Together? **How does this business model compare to other firms already in the market?**	

Figure 5.7   Define a Business Model Template

Think back to the venture focus and product/services strategy you developed in previous chapters. You should have (a) your target industry segment/niche, (b) the target customer(s) within that niche and their primary uses that you will be improving, (c) your products and/or services offerings, and (d) the positioning of those offerings relative to competitors. This is a great foundation from which to develop a business model.

Step 1: Define the Revenue Model

Begin at the top row—the revenue model. Write in a phrase or two to describe the four dimensions of your revenue model. If you are selling both products and services, you will need to specify the type, frequency, and price level relative to competition for each, respectively. More generally, how many streams of revenue are you shooting for? Will there be recurring revenue? (We hope so!) Can you achieve premium pricing?

As you answer these questions, think beyond the startup phase to a scaled-up version of your business three to five years down the road. Map this out on a whiteboard, and then fill in the worksheet. For your choices, state your rationale for anything that doesn't seem obvious. Are there analogies in the market that help show that your revenue model is in fact feasible? How is it the same, or different, than current players who operate in your chosen market niche?

Step 2: Define the Models for R&D, Production, and Go-to-Market

Do the same for your approach to R&D, manufacturing or production (fulfillment for services), and branding and distribution. Once again, always ask yourself why your approach for each area makes sense and if there are analogies in the marketplace. What is the reasoning behind these decisions? Also, we want you to anticipate the learning in Section II of this book by already thinking about the financial implications for the amount of startup capital needed to start your company and get to the moment of actual product or service launch. Be smart about this. If there are suppliers or channel partners with good reputations in your market niche, consider working with them. In the beginning of any venture, your goal should be to minimize fixed costs (lease office space; do not buy the building!), and instead, make them variable expenses. The less you have to raise, the less stock you have to give up as a founding team. Then, of course, the goal is to provide enough value in your products or services so you can charge a sufficient price to generate the operating profit needed to grow the business—and, potentially, bring some of these external activities *back into* the business as part of a scaled-up business model.

Step 3: Integrate

Take a step back. Consider your models for revenue, R&D, production, and go-to-market. How well do the four rows in Figure 5.7 for your venture integrate? Do they make for a single powerful, cohesive whole? If not, re-examine your reasoning for the dimensions that seem to be out of fit. You need to get this right!

At this point, we encourage you to organize a show-and-tell session for your business model with your professor and your classmates. Show your product or service concept, your proposed portfolio, and your business model as a package. *This is the time to use your business model to start bringing a full Venture Concept together.*

Visit the Student Study Site at www.sagepub.com/meyer2e to access the following resources:

- Web Resources
- Video Resources
- General Resources in Entrepreneurship

6

Positioning and Branding a Venture in the Marketplace

The Purpose of the Chapter

In reaching this point in the book, you have achieved a number of important milestones. You have:

- Determined your industry focus and the type of business you want to start
- Defined your target customer(s)
- Discovered the needs of your target customer(s)
- Defined your solutions to solve your customers' needs
- Developed the business model for your venture

This is powerful stuff that must be done *before* writing a single word of a formal business plan. *It is the thinking behind the plan*. This chapter will help you with two other critical pieces of Venture Concept fine-tuning: positioning and branding your venture in the marketplace. It will be impossible to do a better job of meeting customer needs than the competition without a thorough understanding of your competitors. In short, you need to determine who your competitors are and how you intend to compete against them. This involves the concept of positioning—and positioning to win! Once you determine that winning positioning strategy you need to focus on developing a powerful branding strategy.

Learning Objectives

After reading this chapter, you should be able to:

- Articulate your positioning on functional, emotional, and social dimensions so you can win against competitors
- Develop a positioning statement for your solution and venture
- Bring your intended positioning to life with a powerful and distinctive brand

The Importance of Positioning for New Ventures

Positioning a venture effectively is critical for success. Let's see why through a few examples.

We worked with a corporate venture team who wanted to use new types of proprietary materials to make energy-efficient windows. As its members surveyed all high-efficiency windows on the market, however, they realized that the market included many strong players, all of whom claimed to have the most energy-efficient windows. They had to say more than just being "highly energy efficient" to take business away from other major competitors. The answer came in two dimensions. First, the team planned to use an entirely new material, a composite of recycled wood and plastic, from which window frames and sashes could be extruded and assembled, as opposed to the traditional method of cutting, planing, and assembling wood components. Using recycled materials is a "sustainability" play that appeals to large numbers of consumers, particularly younger, first-time homebuyers. Second, the team focused on builders. Going onto construction sites, they observed that homebuilders always had to install windows from the exterior, which on multistory dwellings, means ascending ladders. And there were many steps to fit and shimmy windows into perfect place. The team designed a way to install windows from the inside of the house and to do so in a much simpler, less error-prone manner. This led to a second important element of differentiation: ease of installation. So while energy efficiency was the requirement to play, sustainability and ease of installation became true competitive differentiators for homeowners and builders. This innovative thinking has produced a winner. Some of you might live in a region where you see Andersen Renewal advertisements. That's the business.

This idea of innovating to important customer needs and positioning products and services accordingly works across all industries. It is a skill that entrepreneurs must learn. We have students who have developed solar-powered fruit dryers that will allow farmers in Africa to get their produce far more effectively to marketplace for sale. (Dried fruit lasts up to 20 times longer than fresh fruit before it spoils—see www.jolaventure.com.) Their positioning is nonelectrical, low-cost fruit drying, and much faster than drying fruit directly in the sun, where it is also subject to pests and spoilage. Or other students from Delft, the leading technical university in the Netherlands, developed an optimized direct current (DC) system that charges electric cars in only 30 minutes, compared to the 6–10 hour charging times for traditional alternating current (AC) systems. "Fast" is the positioning. (This was Epyon Power, now a business unit within ABB.)

Or, if life sciences is your field of venturing, a professor-student duo commercialized a new diagnostic technology that is 100 times more specific or sensitive in the detection of certain body chemistries than current immune-assay tests. It works at the "zepto" (10E-21) level, as opposed to the "nano" (10-E6) range! This allows physicians to find diseases at much earlier stages, for earlier and more effective treatment (www.akrivis.com). The functional positioning here is "ultrasensitive" detection of cancerous microlegions or tumors ("zepto" for those "in the know"). The technology also promises a lower cost of ownership (being reagent-only based and not needing expensive readers like current competition). The venture's functional positioning is therefore multibenefit: ultrasensitive, flexible, and low cost.

In all these cases, innovation drives distinctive positioning, which in turn drives powerful branding that is brought to customers through various forms of marketing communications.

Competitive Analysis

Positioning is done against competitors to help customers clearly understand how your venture is better and different. Developing a positioning for your venture first requires that you understand and assess the offerings and strengths of competitors.

Competitive analysis takes work. You must identify and monitor all competitors who target your intended customer base. This includes determining the number, size, strengths, weaknesses, and behaviors of those competitors.

You can also be smart about this work. You do not have the time or resources to conduct detailed analyses of every single possible competitor; you must find a way to identify the most relevant rivals—the most direct competitors. This is accomplished through gathering *competitive intelligence*—the process of legally and ethically collecting data on potential competitors, including their products, services, channels, pricing, positioning, branding, and market communications activities. There are plenty of quick and inexpensive ways to gather such information. Here are a few of your options:

1. *Competitors' Websites*. Most company Websites have substantial information about the management team and, product or service offerings, and how these companies are funded. Look for recent press releases and announcements.

2. *Websites that contain financial information and news stories*. These include Yahoo! Finance (for publicly traded companies), Hoover's (www.hoovers.com), and Morningstar Document Research.

3. *Competitors' customers and suppliers*. Your competitors' customers can speak with authority about the strengths and weaknesses of those competitors' products and services, the qualities of their sales forces, and the channels they use for distribution. In fact, this should also be part of the in-depth interviewing you do with customers as part of the work you do for the first half of this book. Ask customers and suppliers what the competition does well, what the competition does poorly, and what areas the customers think are unserved in the marketplace.

4. *Competitor's go-to-market strategies*. Go into the marketplace and see where and how your competitors' products are bought and sold. This can include visiting retail stores, competitors' Websites, and so forth.

5. *Asking competitors directly*. As crazy as it sounds, you can sometimes talk directly to your competitors. Tradeshows and conferences are two typical opportunities to "talk shop" with these rivals. If a tradeshow has an exhibit area, chances are that all major competitors and many customers will be there. Be bold—go into vendor booths, ask about what they do.

This competitive intelligence allows you to say back to investors *how you will compete*. You need to know competitors' revenues, profits, market share and/or customer focus, marketing expenditures, product or services portfolios, future product or technology direction, and other market-related and operating performance statistics.

Figure 6.1 contains an example of a competitive assessment for a particular venture. This is a company competing in the industrial systems space, specifically focused in healthcare technology. Note the elements of the analysis shown in the figure. These include:

- Revenue
- Sales growth (Compounded Annual Growth Rate, or CAGR)
- Market position (no. 1, or top 3, or top 5, or *not*)
- Number of employees and sales per employee

- Product and technology trends
- Market focus and expansion
- Sales force/channel reach and quality
- Quality and tenure of senior management
- Quality of investors (if not publicly traded already)

	Company A	Company B	Company C
Revenue	$75M	$20M	$8M
Sales growth	10%	12%	20%
Market position	#1	#2	Top 10
Operating profit	15%	12.50%	20%
Sales employee	$750k	500k	650k
Product/tech trends	High quality. Pursuing process automation	Positioned as price leader	New analytics software
Market focus/expansion trends	NAmerica/ Europe	Expanding to APAC	Primarily
Quality of sales force	Very strong, well trained	Bottom-feeders	Entrepreneurs doing the selling still. Opportunistic
Quality of senior management	Excellent, long-standing	New mgt team	Founders
Quality of financial position and investors	A VC startup, now owned by large corp.	VC firms	1 top-tier VC firm
Overall assessment	Potential partner	Trying to win on price	Trying to compete on software/ analytics. Very interesting play.

Figure 6.1 An Example of Competitive Analysis

We cannot overstate the importance of understanding competitors' channel strengths and promotion strategies. In addition to having innovative, best-of-breed products or services, we also want you to strive for excellence in channel. Great companies have both: Apple, IBM, Amazon, Google—they excel on both fronts.

TIP: EVERY VENTURE HAS COMPETITION! _____

One thing always to remember: *Never tell a potential investor that your venture has no competition!* Even if you think not, there is bound to be a current alternative to your Venture Concept, even if it is a home-grown, do-it-yourself type of solution made by customers themselves. In fact, sometimes the ultimate type of competition in the B2B space is the target customers themselves, where customers can decide to make their own solutions and bypass your products or services.

So you need to do a great job in properly identifying those competitors. If you tell professional investors that you have no competitors, they will do their very best to call friends and colleagues to find prove you wrong, and walk away from the deal. It is best to identify a set of competitors, and then show how you will be the best choice for customers based on substantial price/performance advantage relative to current competition.

Types of Positioning: Functional, Emotional, Social, Against Competitors, and for Customers____

With a broad competitive analysis in hand, the next step is to dig into specific positioning of competitors' products and services relative to the ones you wish to provide.

Traditionally, positioning a new venture was almost always based on winning through some type of new functionality at a given price. This meant building a better mousetrap in the figurative sense, either for a new product or a service. This was an objective assessment, typically some combination of performance and price. Entrepreneurs then sought to provide better value—more bang for the buck.

Now, however, things have changed. There are multiple dimensions for positioning a venture and its products or services. Three are most important: *functional* positioning, *emotional* positioning, and *social* positioning. Each of these can lead to important insights and actual communication plans for *branding* a new product line or suite of services.

Functional Positioning

Determining functional positioning starts by identifying the most direct, current competition. Then you analyze those competitors very carefully and systematically along key attributes of product or service features, performance, quality, and price. And perhaps at a higher level, you need first to understand their revenue model. For example, many software companies now functionally differentiate and position themselves as a "Cloud" company, like salesforce .com. Then you must also examine competitors' go-to-market capabilities as part of their business model. Who among your competitors has done the very best job in terms of channel or sales strategy? Have they done such a good job, in fact, that you are locked out of a particular channel?

To gather this specific type of information, go to competitors' Websites first. Also do a Web search for readily available materials that might include product brochures, technical whitepapers, articles, or customer reviews. Also search for industry tradeshows or association meetings coming up in your area. Try to attend. The entire ecosystem in your industry may be on display, and everyone will be trying to sell their wares. Tradeshows are often a great opportunity to get a snapshot on competitors, channel partners, and major customers.

You can also visit a store where your competitors' products are in full view of what is appropriate for your line of business. Talk to salespeople and ask them why they prefer selling one company's products or services over others. Find their preferred products or services, and then find out their reasons and motivations.

All along, take note of the specific features in your competitors' products or services. Begin to dimensionalize the major categories of features. Also look for pricing. The data that you want to gather at the product or service level include:

- Specific product/service features
- Product/service quality
- Price relative to competitors
- In some cases, revenue model (For example, a new revenue model—subscriptions or a win-win revenue share with gains achieved by customers—can also disrupt a marketplace and be a source of competitive advantage. You want to know if a competitor has successfully done something like this.)

For functional positioning, the fundamental question is, How do you plan to be different in terms of performance, features, quality, and price? For example, is it your intention to be a premium features/price player—a BMW, for example—or, a low-cost, few-features player, such as a Kia? Or do you plan to be somewhere in between—a Ford, for example? Each of these companies will proudly claim the value it provides to its customers—but note, each represents a distinctly different type of value formulation.

Don't expect your venture to have an advantage on every dimension identified above. Planning to be the best at everything—performance, all major features, quality, price—usually turns out to be unrealistic. If you do more, you should charge more. If you provide less, you might consider charging less. Unless, of course, you are bringing to market unparalleled levels of capability on the basis of an entirely different business model, such as a subscription model for powerful Cloud-delivered software instead of a heavy, upfront software license on a server-by-server basis. Then your strategy is to shift the performance-price equation onto a different playing field. That's okay, but be explicit about the strategy and understand its potential risks.[1]

Figure 6.2 provides a specific example applied to another venture coming out of a university research laboratory—a high tech example in the life sciences. We are seeing a number of technology-intensive ventures spinning out of university research laboratories these days. Some of these are security-software related, others, environmental; or new industrial materials, but many are in the field of new medical technology.

This venture developed proprietary imaging technology to detect certain types of skin disease. The main "competition" is the traditional resection of the questionable tissue—a biopsy and examination of different tissue layers under a microscope. The entrepreneurs—graduate students working in a lab—took a different approach to this problem. They designed a table-top imaging machine where finely scanned images were communicated back to a central server for image analysis using complex algorithms. The type and probability of disease is reported back to the caregiver. The team proposed to provide this diagnostic imaging as a service (e.g., not sell machines), charging a modest amount of money for each test performed. In short, a pay-as-you go model, and designed as consumable for each scanned use to enhance imaging. The team identified two other competitors, both also relatively new companies offering imaging technologies for ambulatory care settings. A representation of this team's functional positioning is shown in Figure 6.2.

The figure shows the positioning of the traditional biopsy procedure and the two new competitors. By visiting medical research facilities, the team was able to dimensionalize product performance along several key factors. The team saw its real-time diagnostics as a service as a major part of its competitive advantage. The traditional medical method—biopsies and microscope examinations—often take several days to complete. To complete its positioning as also "lower cost," the team compared its pay-as-you-go model to the cost of traditional biopsies.

Some entrepreneurs (as well as many professors) prefer to present comparison data in a chart that shows where a venture positions itself against competitors. Three or four dimensions are hard for anyone to grasp in a framework, so data are typically boiled down into a two-dimensional chart. Figure 6.3 shows this chart for the medical imaging venture. It is called a "perceptual map." For *functional positioning*, perceptual maps typically contrast *performance versus price*.

At the top right of Figure 6.3 is the biggest competitor, the traditional medical approach of biopsies and microscope examination: expensive, slow, but very flexible. Company A was the early entrant using imaging to replace biopsies. It had limited flexibility, however, and was selling an expensive machine. Company B was also coming to market with an expensive machine, but was using a new, more flexible imaging technology. And the venture is shown in the lower right. It features flexible imaging and diagnostic hardware and software, and with a service

---

[1]This also happens to be the fundamental business problem facing industry leaders such as IBM, HP, EMC, or Microsoft. A large software license allows these companies to recognize revenue right away, which is great for quarterly stock reports. Cloud computing, on the other hand, leans heavily toward a subscription revenue model—where customers pay much smaller amounts of money each and every month or year, typically for each user (as opposed to server). This means that once the meter is turned on, revenue is recognized bit by bit over extended periods of time. In the long term, a software vendor can work out a revenue model that shows even greater amounts of money *in aggregate*—say, over ten or more years—but in the short term, such as the next one or two years, the revenue is clearly less. The challenge for industry leaders with Cloud is not the technology, but the business model for their own CFOs and commissioned sales forces. *And that is the great advantage for software entrepreneurs who do not yet have to report quarterly sales and earnings to the public.*

	Traditional Approach	Company A	Company B	Venture Strategy
Performance				
Accuracy	Best	Good	Innovating on New Feature May be Best	Best
Types of Disease	Best	Good	Good	Better -> Best
Speed	Good	Better	Better	Best
Overall	The old, expensive "hands-on" method	First innovator, not selling well, however	A direct threat	Commodity hardware, best software, Cloud delivery model
Quality	Excellent	Moderate	TBD	TBD
Price	$$$	$$	$$	$
Revenue Model	Fee for Service	Selling complex machines	Selling complex machines	Table-top machines Fee for service Data mining revenue

Figure 6.2 A Functional Positioning Example

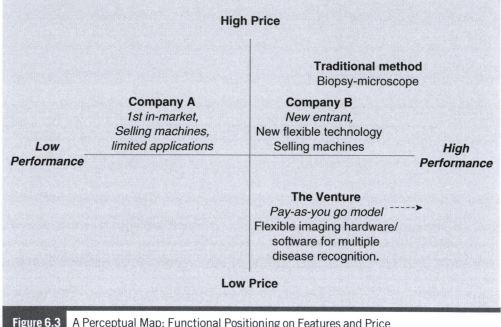

Figure 6.3 A Perceptual Map: Functional Positioning on Features and Price

model, promises to be much lower cost than "box" sellers. Not shown are the data-mining possibilities enabled by the Cloud delivery model—for example, the ability to quickly summarize and report skin disease trends across large populations if this new approach were to be adopted broadly by physicians. This would add a third dimension to the venture's functional positioning.

These types of competitive data give you the ammunition to think and strategize from a realistic, pragmatic perspective, fully aware of competitors. It allows you to think about how your own new offerings—either products or services— provide more value than those of competitors. You may decide to price your wares higher than anyone else, but also *do a lot more than anyone else*. In contrast, a venture can decide to be a price leader, based on the use of less expensive materials or supply chain efficiencies.

TIP: DON'T IGNORE COMPETING ALTERNATIVES _____

When we think about positioning, we naturally think about direct competitors and the concrete measures that customers could use to evaluate their products and services. However, direct competitors do not always represent the universe of possibilities available to customers; they may see alternative solutions outside that circle.

For example, Zipcar, the hourly car rental service, had to position itself against not only car rental companies but against personal car ownership and public transportation. Lower cost, convenience, and the concept of sharing came to bear as positioning statements. If you are in the enterprise B2B space, often the biggest competitor is when the customer simply decides to do it themselves instead of buying any outside product or service. You need to take this "source" of competition into account and position effectively against it.

Think broadly: What alternative solutions do targeted customers have to the offerings you propose in your product or service concept from Chapter 3? And how are those alternative solutions currently positioned in the marketplace?

Remember, as an entrepreneur, you must be superior in one or more of these dimensions in order to thrive. Most entrepreneurs try to achieve some clear advantage in product or service functionality—environmentally friendly pest control, more energy-efficient HVAC systems, a new type of algorithm that provides new insights into data, or a new type of snack food that is healthier for consumers. Other ventures might try to gain advantage on services provided, such the ability to personalize or customize a commodity product. Competing just on price has also worked as a functional branding for some noteworthy ventures: Amazon, eBay, Groupon, and Priceline are major examples. Note, however, that razor-thin margins make life difficult for any entrepreneur. You will always be short on cash and probably need considerable venture capital to scale the business.

For those ventures where distribution is the business—a Federal Express or Amazon—then the design, performance, and cost of the channel itself become a primary focus for functional positioning relative to competitors. In such cases, dimensions of distribution—such as variety, reach, and speed of service—comprise the elements of service performance. For example, we had students who created a rapidly growing chain of high-quality clothes and interior furnishing cleaning stores in affluent suburbs, with in-store or at-home service and delivery. It positioned itself in a premium functional position relative to typical Mom and Pop dry cleaners.

Emotional Positioning

Functional positioning to achieve competitive differentiation is important, but often not sufficient by itself. Enter emotional positioning, and the branding that comes with it.

A lot of guys just love their John Deere ride-on-top lawn mowers because they bring the personal feeling and emotional connection to the tradition and heritage of farming—even though it's just the homeowner's lawn. In the same manner, many women have an emotional, passionate connection with their favored brand of chocolate, making for a permissible form of self-indulgence and sharing with other female friends.

It's not that the tractor or the brand of chocolate is that much better than direct competitors in the market, but there is something about using that particular product itself that makes the customer feel better about themselves in some wonderful, subjective way. The same can be said about Apple's retail stores. Or, if you have the chance, wander into a Nespresso coffee retail store to see the magic of what retail design and packaging can do to create a feeling of personalization and indulgence to commodity coffee. This is "experience-based" design and merchandising—where consumers want to partake in that produced experience, as opposed to just considering features and price. *It's not just a computer, and it's not just coffee.* These products are transformed into distinct experiences that certain customers relish.

In short, the power of emotional positioning is that it can lead to equally powerful branding and buying experiences. And, of course, the product has to deliver. Apple's laptops, for example, are more than okay; they are quick, increasingly light, and the "Retina" display brought to market at the time of this writing is dazzling. To use another example, Nespresso's cappuccino tastes as if it came directly from a European café. In fact, serving customers their favorite coffee drink at a coffee bar has become part of the retail experience that the company has built in to its retail stores. Apple's "Genius" bars in its retail stores are also something special—staffed by upbeat, smart, and often young technical-savvy professionals. These examples support each firm's emotional positioning for its target customers.

Forming an emotional positioning for your venture requires a different mindset. Abandon the notion that customers base their purchase decisions solely on *features, functions,* and *price.* Yes, you have to win somehow on functionality—it is required, but it is not sufficient. Winning on functionality means winning over the customer from a rational perspective. Too few of the right features and functionality will cause customers to pass over your offer; too high a price will scare many away. But customers must also "feel good" about the products and services they buy. In other words, you have to win the customer over through emotion.

Never underestimate the role customer emotions can and do play in buying decisions—*even for high-tech products* and for B2B offerings. For example, a CIO in a large company perceives emotional security when buying from IBM instead of from a tiny startup ("No one around here ever got fired for choosing IBM!"). Or executives feel "assured" that they will get the best advice when bringing McKinsey on board for consulting. If the customer does not "feel good" about purchasing your product or service, he or she will not buy.

Your job is to find out the role emotion plays in making such decisions and how to appeal to customers based on those emotions. Again, perceptual mapping can be used here. Simply use dimensions other than objective performance and price relative to competitors.

A good example of creative emotional positioning is MyM&M'S. In Figure 6.4 you will see a perceptual map for MyM&M'S. The corporate venture team developed two axes for its emotional positioning of gift services. One of those axes represented volume: from "mass produced" to "personalized." The second axis represented the emotional connection to the offering, along a spectrum of "serious" to "fun." By characterizing the market with these two dimensions, the MyM&M'S team was able to create white space for itself, occupying the upper-right-hand quadrant—the intersection of personalized and fun. Note that Disney (in the lower-right quadrant) is fun but clearly mass produced, just as traditional M&M'S Candies at checkout counters around the world are both "fun" and "mass produced."[2] It doesn't hurt that MyM&M'S sells for more than ten times the price per pound relative to standard M&M'S Candies. That type of margin allows a low-volume venture to survive for the first several years until it achieves scale. Furthermore, many observers would argue that the premium price supports the unique nature of this particular chocolate gifting service.

It well worth your time to consider how your product or service connects emotionally with the target buyer, *even if that buyer is a B2B customer* or a professional such as physician. Never underestimate the importance of impulse purchasing, *for anyone.* The goal here is to understand "how customers feel" about your competitors' offerings and your proposed offerings, and then capture that insight into a positioning framework.

Talking deeply with representative customers can help here. They will help you to: (a) determine which emotional dimensions should be measured on the map; (b) place competitive products and services on that map; and (c) place yours to achieve competitive differentiation. Continue to sample customers until a clear picture emerges.

---

[2]See Chapter 10 in Meyer, M. H. (2007). *The Fast Path to Corporate Growth.* New York: Oxford University Press.

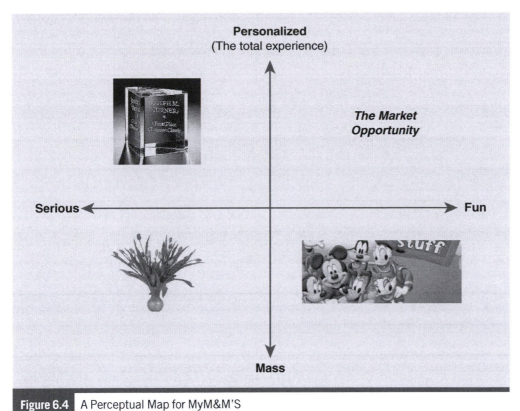

Figure 6.4   A Perceptual Map for MyM&M'S

Source: Tulip image, Ablestock.com /Thinkstock.

Social Positioning

The third dimension of positioning focuses on perceived social benefits for customers.

Social positioning and the branding that follows it are particularly important when targeting and selling to younger customers. Our experience is that purchase decisions by Millennials and Gen Ys are strongly affected by their perception of social factors. Younger people "care" about society—from living healthily and consuming responsibly, to protecting the environment, to improving social awareness of problems pertaining to the disadvantaged—and reflect this in their purchase decisions. Social positioning means paying attention to your target consumers' social principles toward society.

You still have to win somehow in functionality—all customers want "value." But it is insufficient to ensure victory. Just like the personal emotional positioning, a broader social positioning is another level to consider. It may be, like Pantagonia, that you contribute a small percentage of your profits to an environmental cause. Or, like Nespresso, that the packaging of your products uses materials that can be recycled (in this case aluminum), that the coffee is grown with sustainable practices, and that the machines are energy-efficient—all part of the company's "ecolaboration" initiative. Another example is TOMS shoes (www.toms.com). It has a unique social positioning component to its business model: "With every pair you purchase TOMS will give a pair of new shoes to a child in need. One for one."

Nearly all major industrial corporations also have a "sustainability" initiative across their operations; if you are planning a new venture selling into the B2B space, it might be very helpful to consider how environmentally friendly materials, processing, and logistics can help shape and position your enterprise. For example, an increasing number of consumers are buying wine from vineyards that are certified "green" or organic—in other words, it is not just the wine that counts (price, taste) but how the grapes are grown and how the wine is produced.

For an increasing number of entrepreneurs, social positioning is the most important part of their ventures, the very essence of their purpose and being. These are social enterprises. The aforementioned example of the solar-powered fruit drier is a social venture (see www.jolaventure.com). The target is rural farmers in Africa, and the system allows them to dry their products so that they can be transported to market without spoilage. Within months of launch, the team had orders for thousands of these systems, many of which came from nongovernmental organizations seeking to help the rural poor. Or another recent student venture partners with women in Kenya to hand-manufacture various types of apparel. These items are then sold through college dormitory parties, a new form of network marketing. The venture shares its operating profit back with its Kenyan producers, women who then expand into other microbusinesses. Already, the team has found substantial improvements in the standard of living of their African partners (see www.njabiniapparel.org).

Social positioning can place an extra plus in your marketing efforts. Customers want to feel good about the companies from which they purchase goods and services. This is particularly important for younger consumers, who, studies have shown, are less brand loyal in general compared to their parents. Younger consumers are much more willing to try new things—be it apparel, financial services, or leisure activities. If Millennials and Gen Ys are your target, you must try to create a powerful social and emotional connection to your brand—and the specific products and services within that brand. This takes careful thought and very disciplined execution. Your product or service has to deliver as promised or you are unlikely to see that same customer again. However, if you are about equal with competitors in terms of function and price, the tie-breaker will go to the company that has that emotional and social spark to its positioning and brand communication.

Building a Powerful and Distinctive Brand Based on Positioning

With a trio of functional, emotional, and social positioning formulated, the entrepreneur can then begin to design the branding for his or her venture.

You don't need to hire a fancy New York advertising agency to start an exciting, powerful brand. You are now mindful of your target customers. And as a consumer yourself, you already know about some of the great brands we have mentioned in this chapter. Or, if you live in the United States, take a quick trip to a Whole Foods store to see combined functional (fresh, organic food at premium prices), emotional (better health for myself and my family), and social positioning (fair trade and honest business practices). As a consumer yourself, you see and feel the benefits of companies that excel in positioning and branding. Now it is time to apply this insight to create a powerful brand for your venture. It is every bit as important as the technology or product or service designs for your company.

What Is a Brand?

A brand is much more than a company name or logo. A venture's brand is the total experience that you, as the entrepreneur, and your team create for customers, as well as for employees, suppliers or partners, and outside observers, such as the trade press. Think of all the various "touch points" though which a customer may interact with your company: learning about your products or services for the first time, the retail or shopping experience, seeing your product or service for the first time, using it, getting service for it, and so forth. Each one of these touch points is an opportunity to develop and deliver a powerful, consistent brand experience to target customers. It is definitely something to be planned beforehand, orchestrated and coordinated, and not left to chance.

Brands get *expressed* in company, product, and service names, signs, symbols, designs, or combinations of these elements.[3] That image conveys specific, important meaning for the

---

[3]Keller, K. (1998). *Strategic Brand Management.* Mahwah, NJ: Prentice-Hall.

customer. It provides something of "value" for the customer, be it functional, emotional, or social in nature.

Lots of things contribute to a brand beyond company name, specific products, and services. For example, your Website is an important part of communicating or expressing your venture's brand. Events or activities where you reach out directly to your customers—even if you are selling primarily through retailers or other channel partners—also strongly contribute to brand. And at a different level, sustainable or socially focused business practices contribute to overall brand, while at the same time helping to attract and recruit some of the best employees.

When it comes to a venture engaging for the first time in its chosen marketplace, the total brand experience must embody your offer of value—your promise—to the customer. Ultimately, that brand experience is a blend of what you say it is, what others say it is, and how well you deliver on your promise to the customers. You should also realize that some elements of the total brand experience can be spoken, while other elements contain certain symbols that are strictly visual, such as the rainbow-colored apple logo that Apple, Inc., puts on its products and in its advertisements.

For the entrepreneur, branding might as well start with the name of your company. At this point, as you are preparing to write and present a business plan, the plan itself is a "product" that you wish to "sell" to investors. The first thing that every reader of your business plan sees is the name of your company—on the cover page in a very large font. Your company name—and the branding that it represents—becomes a cornerstone of your branding strategy. And in many ways, the name and imagery of your company become integrative tools for the entire venture. Everything needs to connect for the external reader or customer.

A brand then quickly goes beyond just the company name. It comprises multiple elements, all of which fit within a "brand architecture."[4] In most instances, the entrepreneur will have a "brand umbrella," such as FedEx, which has FedEx Express, FedEx Ground, FedEx Freight, FedEx Custom Critical, FedEx Trade Networks, and so forth. The key elements that support that brand framework—the ones that matter most—are:

- *The logo and imagery that accompany your company name.* They will appear on your Website, business cards, letterhead, brochures, and other sorts of marketing material. In this early planning stage, it is not necessary to have a logo finished in hand. But you will need one once you start selling. Since most entrepreneurs are not graphic artists themselves, designing a logo is something you should probably outsource to professionals. Take a look at www.12designers.com for links to a broad community of graphic artists and Web designers who will provide samples and make a bid for your business.

- *Product or service names.* There is an art to naming products or services well. And it rarely comes after the first try. It involves intense discussions with your team, friends you trust, and prospective customers. (In the next chapter, you are going to perform another quick round of customer testing—and this would be a great opportunity to test a set of three or so brand names for your products or services. See which name has the greatest resonance with your target customers.) A great example is IBM's "Smarter Planet" initiative, which seeks to combine real-time sensors, communications, and highly intelligent analytics on back-end servers to drive better decision making and automate important processes. As IBM gets more into designing and selling complete solutions (as opposed to just selling hardware, software, and support services), you can see how "Smart" and "Smarter"

[4]Aaker, D., & Joachimsthaler, E. (2008). The brand relationship spectrum: The key to the brand architecture challenge. *California Management Review* 42(4), 8–23; Devlin, J. (2003). Brand architecture in services: The example of the retail financial services. *Journal of Marketing Management* 19, 1043–1065.

branding is being populated across different vertical market application areas. (For example, it has Smarter Cities, Smart Banking, Smarter Commerce, Smart Energy, Smarter Healthcare, Smarter Oil, Smarter Public Safety, Smarter Traffic, and Smarter World. These are all registered trademarks of IBM. You can study this for yourself by browsing IBM's trademark Web pages.) IBM wants to associate "Smarter" with its efforts across the board. It is a bold gambit—and given IBM's performance over recent years, one that seems to be working. This is the power and importance of branding—for B2B selling, and not just consumer marketing. Can you build a thematic name into your brands?

- *Product or service messaging.* This is often in the form of three to five words that are placed right under your company name. This tells new customers in a very short word burst the key benefits or purposes of the product or service. For example, we have former students working on new medical diagnostics venture developing ultra-sensitive technology for detecting certain types of cancers much earlier that existing tests. It's messaging is: "enabling zepto-sensitive, multi-immunoassay testing to provide rapid, cost-effective care" underneath the product name. While there is no magic recipe for product or service brand name messaging, we prefer that entrepreneurs go right back to their functional, emotional, and social positioning and try to carry this through here.

- *Special feature naming and messaging.* Think about short, powerful, meaningful word combinations that lend zip to the marketing of a new product or service. Our opinion is that at this more detailed feature or component level, it is all about superior functionality. Certain states and insurance companies in the United States offer a "Safe Driver Insurance Plan" that rewards accident-free drivers with discounts on car insurance premiums.

- *Websites and social media.* Websites are so ubiquitous now that we often forget that they are the primary portal for customers to learn about and interact with a company. The Website itself is a branding statement, and part of the brand architecture, not an afterthought. Also, for many categories of businesses, word-of-mouth selling has been supercharged with Web community building, customer reviews, and forums for uses of a new product or service to share their ideas and experiences. Facebook, LinkedIn, Twitter—these and other social media sites need to be factored into your branding strategy, particularly if yours is a B2C venture. While our purpose here is not to go through the do's and don'ts of Website development, we strongly recommend that you visit Websites of companies in and around your target industry niche and see which ones you like best and which you like least. Look for simple, powerful, and clear presentation; effective messaging; and great imagery. And learn what search engine optimization means, how it is accomplished, and what third-party service you might engage at the start of your venture to get things moving along quickly. If you have business partners, try to get them to highlight your venture's Website on theirs. All this must be planned, and none of it left to chance!

These elements should be tied together within a single, cohesive brand architecture. Figure 6.5 shows a simple example shared by the creators of the Whitepages.com branding platform.[5] Their goal was to create a distinct personality to the Website that would differentiate it from just being an online phone book, and rather, as the one place they could visit to find the information they needed on people, places, and things to power their own social networking. Note that there is a higher-level corporate brand, which is then followed and supported by specific product/service brands, subdomains (important for this type of business), and then branding for specific features within products and services themselves.

---

[5]Lusk, J. (2009, April 23). Brand Building: WhitePages Strategic Brand Platform. whitepages.com/blog.

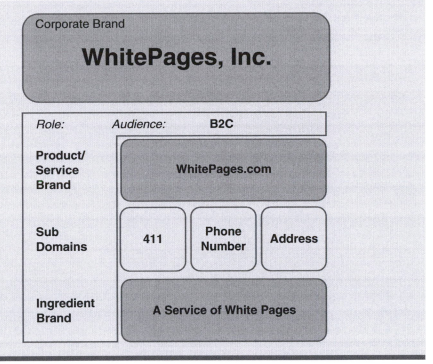

Figure 6.5 An Example of a Brand Architecture

Source: Copyright ©2012 John Lusk. Reproduced with permission.

Marketing professionals would call this a "corporate house of brands" strategy—as opposed to a dispersed set or hodgepodge of different brand names and messages. Brands are connected. For the entrepreneur, developing a brand architecture up front is part of being as focused and purposeful as possible.

TIP: ENTREPRENEURS SHOULD STUDY APPLE'S BRANDING STRATEGIES

Apple has obviously been a brand leader, and we can learn from it as an example.

First, it is perhaps ironic that Apple sourced its original name from Steve Jobs's involvement in a community farm in Oregon. It had nothing to do with the computer industry or computer users at that time. But from then on, brand names, images, and messaging were carefully crafted. In fact, even the notion of a community (emotional, social) and of simple health and wholeness (functional) flow from the Apple brand name and give it an easily accessible, user-friendly image.

The subbrands for products are extensions of the Apple company name. The Mac subbrands—MacBook, Mac Mini, and Mac Pro—all fit with the Apple superbrand. And the "I," initially created with the iMac product name in 1997, has been replicated into iPod, iPhone, iPad, and iMac—just like IBM's "Smarter" theme.[6] And what

(Continued)

---

[6]Actually, Steve Jobs wanted to call the first iMac something else—"MacMan" (yuck!). But, apparently, another company owned rights to MacMan and would not accept Jobs's buyout offer. He then had to go with his advertising agency's name, "iMac." (See Wikipedia for the full details of this story. And thank goodness for that turn of events! Which is cooler for you: iPhone or MacPhone?)

(Continued)

better name for soup-to-nuts customer service than "AppleCare"? It is worldwide; covers all products, with reservations booked online and delivered mostly through Apple's retail stores; and, of course, is an important source of recurring revenue. And the stores themselves: Wow! These are all part of the total brand experience.

Next, Apple brings certain components to the forefront and brands them with an emphasis on functionality. For example, Apple called its new high-resolution display for notebooks "Retina" and messaged it with, "It's a whole new vision for the notebook." Its charging connectors were named "MagSafe"—where the connector is held in place by a magnet. If suddenly grabbed, the connector pulls out of the socket safely without damaging either the computer or the connector. Very cool, and functionally described by the brand name. It's also patented. Or consider Apple's Thunderbolt communications port. It combines multiple interfaces into a single serial port and can support lots of individual devices or a hub off a single port. (Intel actually developed the technology, but Apple named it. Thunderbolt, MagSafe, and Retina—great names, and all a spin on super-functionality.) And AppleCare is delivered through "geniuses" working at the stores' "Genius Bar." With naming like that, they must be smart as well as social—just what the doctor ordered for the new or confused computer user.

Of course, Apple is not the be-all and end-all for branding, but it is certainly a fine example of how to bring all these elements together: functional, emotional, and social positioning; the company name and logo; product line and service names; carefully considered naming for specific product or technology features; and consistent, powerful messaging across the board. The functionality of Apple's products is strong: well designed, easy to use, and powerful. And AppleCare service is great. But we believe that the emotional and social connection that consumers often have with their Apple equipment is rather special—and quite different than with their Windows-based PCs. Could the promise of recurring revenue that brand loyalty provides be part of the reason why Apple's market capitalization has soared above all others? You bet it is.

Positioning and Branding Checklist_____

We have covered a lot of ground here with regard to positioning and branding your venture. The key now is to reflect, take stock, and answer these questions:

1. What functions are critical to the customer when buying particular products and services? Have you created the proverbial "better mousetrap"? Can your venture win on a purely functional dimension (e.g., better performance at a given price)?

2. What role does emotion play in the buying process? Can the venture win over the customer using an emotional positioning strategy, by making that customer feel "empowered" or in some way intimately "connected" to your product or service, or to what the product or service enables the customer to do?

3. Does the social behavior and awareness of the target customer impact the positioning of your own company's products or services? Do you need to be "green" or "sustainable" as part of your positioning? Can this be a tie-breaker when all other things are equal?

4. As you reflect on these three positioning dimensions, how does your venture stand apart from current competitors? What single dimension or combination of the three make for a strong, clear, distinctive positioning for your products and services in the hearts and minds of your target customers?

5. What are your ideas for carrying this positioning through into your company name, the brand names for your products and services, feature branding, and the messaging surrounding each of these elements? In other words, what is your brand architecture?

The bottom line for the entrepreneur is first to win on some dimension of functional performance, for example, the performance-price value equation. Then explore the emotional and social connections your target customers can form not only with your products and services, but with your company as a whole. And then drive these benefits home with clear, powerful branding across the continuum of the company's face to the outside world. Don't leave these things to chance, and don't leave them until later.

Clear positioning and powerful branding can make for a powerful launch. Recognizing your products or services by virtue of strong branding allows customers to be more efficient shoppers—and pick your offerings over others! Swatch knows this, or as service examples, so do great companies such as Starbucks or American Express. These are reliable, consistently value-rich, and distinctive brands, each with a certain élan or spirit that provides emotional and often social connections for a customer.

Over the long haul, strong branding also helps retain current customers—the essence of the recurring revenue that is so important for any venture. Brand loyalty eases the customer's decision-making anxiety about what to do next. Think of your favorite product—an automobile, your iPhone, your favorite running shoes, your favorite line of clothing, etc. When that product seems to be getting a little old and in need of replacement, your head and heart turn to that same brand. As an entrepreneur, that same reflex on the part of customers is *what you want and what you need*.

Reader Exercises

Step 1: Do Your Competitive Analysis

Complete the Functional Position Research Template.

Complete Figure 6.6. You will have to determine your major current competitors and hit the Web to find out information as best you can about them.

Also, try to talk with people who are actually selling and/or using competitors' products or services. They will know better than anyone else the strengths and weakness of these companies! Are there one or two people you can talk to over the coming week who truly know the activity within your target industry niche? Set up a time to visit them *now!*

	Company A	Company B	Etc .
Revenue			
Sales growth			
Market position			
Operating profit			
Sales employee			
Product/tech trends			
Market focus/expansion direction			
Quality of sales force			
Quality senior management			
Quality of financial position and investors			
Overall assessment of strengths and weaknesses			

Figure 6.6 Competitive Business Intelligence Template

Step 2: Do Your Functional Positioning

Refer to the methods described in this chapter for gathering specific information on competitors' products, services, business models, and distribution strategies. That means hitting the Web, perhaps a convenient tradeshow in your area, and talking to some target customers who are already using competitors' products or services.

Next, dimensionalize performance. Then develop tiers or levels of cost. For some of you, total cost of ownership over the life cycle of product or service use might be more meaningful and important than the single upfront purchase price. As you gather these data, begin to fill in the Functional Positioning Template shown in Figure 6.7.

Then create a draft perceptual map that shows the "white space in the market you wish to occupy." Refer to Figure 6.8.

	Company A	Company B	Company C	Your Venture Strategy
Performance				
Feature 1				
Feature 2				
Feature 3				
Feature 4				
Overall				
Quality				
Price				
Revenue Model				

Figure 6.7 Functional Positioning Template

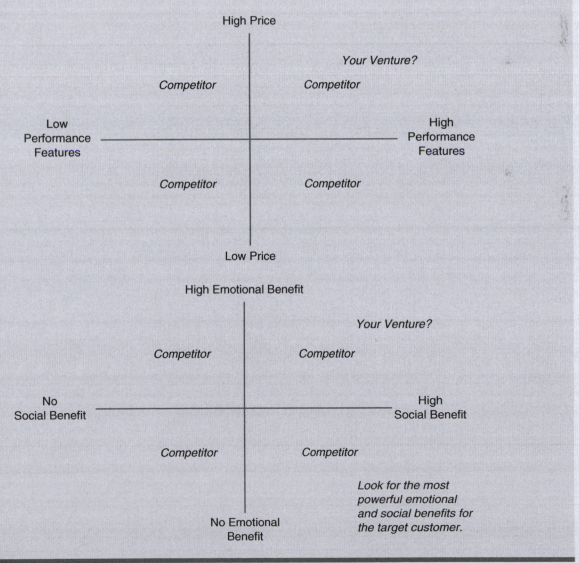

Figure 6.8 Perceptual Map Templates for Functional, Emotional, and Social Positioning

Step 3: Do Your Emotional and Social Positioning

We have emphasized that emotional and social branding are very powerful marketing levels for new ventures. Now try to do it for your venture.

- Think deeply about your target customers. For consumer-focused products or services, how do your proposed products or services help them feel better about themselves or of the jobs that they are doing? Going back to Chapter 3, how will your company help them escape a certain fear or frustration? To live better or healthier, to experience or enjoy or learn new things? In other words, how might you put a smile on the customer's face?

- If you are selling to businesses, what are the subjective "hot buttons" that you might hit for important decision makers or stakeholders in your target customers? For example, some former students are starting a virtual mobile computing company that separates and protects company versus personal workspaces on tablet computers or Smartphones. Functionally, it creates firewalls, VPNs, etc. But emotionally, this software will allow the CIO of any large company to sleep a lot better at night knowing that thousands of mobile devices are now protected, secured, and controlled. It's the same thing as above: How do you put a smile on the customer's face, and in doing so, take away the frown or worry?

Social positioning is in many ways more direct. You toned to tie the features of your products and services into a larger societal need. If it is for a developed, advanced societal context, think health, wellness, education, security/safety, environment, and we suspect in the future, water and infrastructure resource management. Make a connection to something bigger and larger than your own specific company and its specific focus. And for ventures going after underdeveloped or developing markets—social ventures or new product initiatives aimed at base of pyramid (BoP) applications—the connections are the same, and in some ways, even simpler and more direct. Think about those connections, determine your social positioning, and bring it into your branding. Also, try to draw a second perceptual map that contains a combination of your emotional and social positioning. Refer to Figure 6.8.

Step 4: Develop Names, Imagery, and Messaging Within Your Brand Architecture

Look at the Brand Architecture Template in Figure 6.8. Let's start to fill it in.

Take a moment to write down two or three company names, product or service names, and messaging for your company as a whole and for the specific products or services or features you want to provide. Then place them into the template in Figure 6.8. Keep improving your ideas on this template as you think about your branding over the coming weeks.

Some of you may have already begun designing the Website for your venture. If you have, that's great, and think about how your Website connects to the branding expressed in Figure 6.9. If you haven't started a Website yet, that's okay, but also think about how the design, imagery, content, and services might reinforce the branding in Figure 6.9. What will be your primary social media strategies for building awareness and hopefully a customer community on the Web? Most Websites are frankly flat, boring, and a one-way street for customers. How might yours cut through the clutter without being "cute" or "contrived"? How can you make your Website a place for customer learning, involvement, and engagement?

Target Customer: _____

Specific Messaging
functional, emotional, social queues

Company brand: (name) _____ Logo, color, imagery associated with company brand:	
Product/service brands • • •	
Feature/ingredients brands • • •	
Web – social media strategies • • •	

Figure 6.9   Brand Architecture Template

TIP: CREATING BRAND NAMES FOR COMPANIES, PRODUCTS, AND SERVICES _____

Picking names can be hard. Try for obvious choices, however, and then keep plugging away if names, trademarks, and URLs are already taken. (This can be quickly checked by typing the name into a Web search engine. For specific trademarks, you can also check with the U.S. Patent and Trademark Office, www.uspto.gov, or its equivalents in Europe and Asia.)

As a checklist, considering the following:

- The company name needs to be not "taken" by someone else. Also, investigate the URLs. With all sorts of new URL suffixes coming into play (.net, .biz, etc.) you might have more options than just .com. Having said this, we think you still need a .com URL to provide a sense of credibility and seriousness for investors.

(Continued)

(Continued)

- Product and service names should suggest key benefits, either functional, emotional, or social. "Bug-Be-Gone," or "Safe Driver Insurance Plan" are examples. Look at the Websites of creative companies in your industry and see the most powerful brand names for products and services.

- Names for companies, products, and services should be distinctive and convey a positive meaning. Names should fit the company or product image.

- Color choices should reinforce that meaning and messaging.

- The name should have no legal or regulatory restrictions (e.g., the trademark and URL consideration).

- The name should be easy to pronounce and remember (even if it is in the life sciences!).

- If possible, product and service names should connect to emotional and social positioning uncovered as the ground work for a branding strategy.

- Names should translate easily into foreign languages.

- The name should have enough "flex" so as not to constrain the growth and expansion of the venture.

Whatever you call your company— its products and services, and the messaging behind them—will soon have to survive in a crowded and brutally competitive marketing space. You will be spending lots of time and money trying to build these brands. Give yourself a chance. Start with something good, something that you, your teammates, your friends, and prospective customers all agree has "legs"!

As you develop your first set of branding names and messages, run your ideas through the following four-item checklist:

1. Each branding element must be "relevant" and "meaningful" to your target customer. Everything, individually and collectively, must "resonate" deeply with that customer on more than a superficial basis.

2. All elements in your brand architecture must be mutually reinforcing; they must build upon one another in a "natural," nonforced way that makes sense to the customer.

3. The overall brand and its various elements are easily understood by your customers and your employees. Nothing takes much of a further explanation.

4. Even better, can your proposed branding tie into a larger, sustained consumer, industrial, or social need? Safety, health and wellness, environment, optimizing the use of scarce resources, or learning and education for people of all ages, are but a few examples. This might give your branding some oomph! for the future—the possibility for a sustained presence in the marketplace. It might also inspire you and your teammates to know that you are doing more than just building a product or service. There could be something "larger" as a driving motivation.

Step 5: Review These Templates With a Few Select, Knowledgeable Target Customers and/or Resellers

Assemble your versions of these last three templates—Figures 6.6, 6.7, and 6.8—and show them to a few knowledgeable customers. Just a few smart ones will do. And be sure to bring your pencil and eraser along for the ride! We promise it won't feel like "work"!

To conclude this chapter and its exercises, strong, integrated branding that is based in well-considered positioning along functional, emotional, and social dimensions is *as important* as the products and services you have designed in the prior chapters of this book. Most entrepreneurs save positioning and branding as an afterthought. Not you and your venture!. Applying these methods early in venture development sets the edge, an edge that will truly help you with early investors and customers.

Visit the Student Study Site at www.sagepub.com/meyer2e to access the following resources:

- Web Resources
- Video Resources
- General Resources in Entrepreneurship

7

Conduct a Reality Check on the Venture Concept and Its Business Model

Every year, millions of individuals generate venture ideas that they believe could be the beginning of a great startup. While many of these concepts may seem to be outstanding from a 50,000-foot level, talk is cheap. You must transform your venture idea into a valuable business proposition for both you and your target customers.

Throughout the first six chapters of this book, you have worked to develop an increasingly level of focus and specificity for your venture. It started off with defining a target industry, getting down to a specific segment, and within that in most cases, a specific niche. Then you looked at different customer groups and their specific use case, the combination of which are truly your target market, or what some investors might call your addressable market. You then did "ethnography" with target customers to develop a specific product or service concept—one that is distinctive in its value for customers—and then created a fully fledged product or service line from that concept. You then formed a specific business model that complements your product/services strategy. That business model included both a detailed revenue model and your approaches for handling R&D, production, and distribution, with an eye toward using outside partners where appropriate, for example, a lean approach to startup operations. Then you learned how to position and brand your venture in a way that, with proper execution, stakes a claim to a special place in your market, for example, "the best," "the most innovative," "the most complete" or "full service," "the easiest to use," or conversely, "the greatest value" or "lowest cost."

Now it is time to put your work to a last, simple, powerful test before writing your business plan. We are going to learn how to do a field-based Reality Check for a Venture Concept that is fast and effective. This Reality Check is not only going to validate your venture strategy and its various components, but it will also provide context, richness, and ways to differentiate your solutions, business model, and branding.

This Reality Check will be your second pass at interviewing target customers. In Chapter 2, you performed ethnography with a dozen or fewer target customers to get your basic "Aha!" from understanding their needs, wants, and frustrations. Now it is time to go back out into the field once again to validate these ideas with a more structured questionnaire. Your goal here is to become even more expert about your target customers and their core needs than anyone else—*including your professors!*

In our experience, too few budding entrepreneurs spend enough time to properly conceptualize and test their ventures. Done correctly, this can save you a lot of headache and possible heartache down the road.

After this, you can start writing your business plan with confidence. And at that point, you should give yourself a big pat on the back for getting to this stage. You are already a winner.

Learning Objectives

After reading this chapter, you should be able to:

- Plan the "Reality Check"

- Understand the different elements of the Reality Check—the "stuff" you need to learn from this Reality Check

- Formulate a Venture Concept into a statement of its solutions and value for customers

- Define specific questions within the Venture Concept to test customers' levels of dissatisfaction with current products and services, their purchase intent for your solutions, their buying preferences, and how they see your solutions relative to those of current competitors

- Organize customer panels—the interviewees—with an eye toward getting this research done in one or two weeks

- Quickly conduct the field research itself—methods that work best for approaching end-users and buyers whom you don't already know

- Analyze the results of the field research to validate the Venture Concept—your solutions, business model, and positioning

- Use the Reality Check to take a first crack at sizing up the revenue potential for your venture

- Integrate the results of the Reality Check to improve your venture strategy and the business model. This is a platform for launching into the next section of this book: projecting financials, writing the business plan, and making the pitch

Developing the Field Research Instrument for the Reality Check _____

First, let's set the foundation for the Reality Check. Figure 7.1 shows a "dashboard" that summarizes all your learning in the prior six chapters: industry segment/niche, customer group and use, the fundamental customer purchase motivation, the customer benefits and needs (the voice of the customer), the product or service solutions, the business model, and the

Target Industry Segment/Niche

- Gift chocolate
- $18 billion U.S., growing 3% per year
- Premium price niche, 20% of gift chocolate segment, growing at 8%

Target Customers and Uses

- Romance: Married guys buying for women; young men buying for women
- Self-treat: Women buying for themselves
- Share: Women buying to share with their friends

The Customer Insight

- Buying for love.
- Buying as a treat.

The Voice of the Customer

- F: I love chocolate. I have a passion for it.
- M: A nicely packaged box of truffles always does the trick with my wife.
- F: I love to treat myself with chocolate.
- M: I work too much. I need a special present to get out of the doghouse with my girlfriend.
- F: When my girlfriends come over, chocolate is perfect with coffee and tea.

Solutions for Customers

- Boxed chocolates, with upscale contemporary packaging, sold in specialty or premium retail, and Web.
- Permissable portioning to meet health concerns.
- Organic chocolate SKUs

Business Model

- Average price of $35 per pound.
- Purchase for multiple, special occasions each year
- Internal choc development, internal choc production, selling through a flagship store, Web, "store-in-store" display in premium department stores.

Positioning and Branding

- Functional: Great taste and ingredients
- Emotional: Contemporary
- Social: Fair-trade chocolate, recycled packaging materials.

Figure 7.1   A Chocolate Team's Venture Concept Dashboard

positioning. Together, all of these constitute the *Venture Concept*. Just as we can test a new product or service idea, we can test a more complete Venture Concept. That is what we are going to do in this chapter.

Figure 7.1 shows a team's Venture Concept statement for the chocolate idea described earlier during our "customer hearts and minds" discussion in Chapter 3. You might remember that this is a contemporary gift chocolate business serving young, upscale professionals, where the buyer is often a male and the user is nearly always a female, and the overall purpose of which is create a lasting memory in the eyes of that special lady, and then hopefully, for her guy.

The dashboard shows the target industry niche size, its size and growth rates, and then the target customers and use occasions. In the middle are the customer insight, a persona, and the product/service portfolio. And on the right is the business model along economic and operations dimensions, followed by the positioning of the venture in terms of functional, emotional, and social branding.

All of this, with a few short bullet points, fits on a single page. All the elements should fit together nicely into a coherent, cohesive whole. If not, work certain elements of the dashboard again until you achieve that result. A simple, clear logic should flow from beginning to end.

The power of summarizing the entirety of your insights and information on a single page cannot be underestimated. You can show a friend, mentor, or colleague your Venture Concept in a single, clear statement, and then talk about how the different pieces connect with and support one another. Some of our students take the poster board approach. Go to Staples. Buy a large, fold-down poster board, and assemble the different pieces of the Venture

Concept on it. And do not forget the pictures of the customers! This brings your audience into the world of your customers. It will make your conversations and presentations all the more real and poignant by addressing the needs and concerns of actual people and organizations.

Creating a Statement of the Venture Concept to Show to Customers

While you might be able to show peers, professors, and mentors your Venture Concept dashboard, it's too much for customers. They won't have the time or knowledge to connect the dots together.

Instead, you need a simple, powerful paragraph. We call this the Venture Concept statement. It is something you can quickly show to customers with little explanation. This Venture Concept statement is something you can either say to customers or have them read in less than 30 seconds, have them understand it, and be ready to answer some questions about it. If you have done that special Reader Exercise at the end of Chapter 4—to sketch or actually build a prototype of your new product or service idea—you can show this to customers as well. It will make the Venture Concept all the more real.

A Venture Concept statement has a specific structure. We recommend that you apply the following format to your own venture idea that focuses on the target customer, the problem to be solved, the difference from competitive offerings, and the benefits that customers will expect:

> ABC is our business that [*solves what problem*] for [*whom—which target customers*]. It is different from the current competitors because of [*why customers buy*]. The benefits that we expect to provide [*name the major benefits*] will make ABC stand out from all competitors.

Now let's build some Venture Concept summaries to show to customers. To do this, we can use the three examples, two of which were used in earlier chapters.

For those of you wishing to create a manufactured products business, let's look at the pet snack idea. The following might be a reasonable Venture Concept summary to show to prospective customers:

> HealthyWags is a startup that will bring health and nutrition to pet snacks for those of you who feel that your pet is a special member of your family. Our special variety of tasty snacks will use all-natural ingredients, be nutritionally complete, and have the meaty flavors that dogs relish. We will also carry nonmeat snacks for those of you who prefer only grains and vegetables. Our packaging is also made from 100% recycled materials. Our goal is to keep your pet healthy for a long, happy life.

Next, for those of you building software or system-type ventures, let's build a Venture Concept summary for the home health monitoring company. Remember that this venture seeks to deploy a series of monitoring sensors in the homes of the elderly in partnership with home health agencies:

> Health Monitoring Systems keeps a 24/7 electronic monitoring for the elderly living at home or in assisted-living centers. Rather than rely on your elderly loved ones to make the emergency call on their own or a visiting nurse to detect a problem, our system constantly monitors basic heart rate, movement, and other key factors and uses advanced software when problems arise and alerts our partner home healthcare agencies as well as family members. And we do this monitoring without having to make your loved ones wear any special equipment or bracelets or install video cameras that invade their privacy. Our sensors are woven into bedding, seats, and other living spaces. In actual trials, our system significantly reduces stressful and costly hospital admissions, plus it gives loved ones that peace of mind that comes from 24/7 health monitoring.

Remember, the concept summary should state the what, how, and why in terms of customer value. In other words, it should clearly state the benefits of the Venture Concept from the perspective of the target customer.

Lastly, there are undoubtedly those of you reading this book who will wish to start some type of consulting or professional services firm. Let's use the example of a startup that builds mobile apps for large retailers seeking to use smartphones as a portal for their customer loyalty programs. We will call it "MobileAppSolutions":

> MobileAppSolutions is a consultancy to design, program, and deploy new mobile apps for supercharging your customer loyalty programs. We help shoppers register, get news on new promotions, and receive coupons as valued customers. We work with all major smartphone platforms and know how to tie our apps into major CRM applications and databases. We will also work closely with your marketing, merchandizing, and IT managers to design a mobile app that fits your current branding and products. Instead of trying to find your own mobile app developers—which is hard to do these days—come to us for a full-service, premium-quality design and building solution.

Now take a moment to write down a few sentences that you might show to prospective customers. This should be based on your Venture Concept diagram from Chapter 2. Later on, in the Reader Exercises, we will have you complete this task.

The Questions That follow a Venture Concept Statement

The next step is to develop specific questions that test different aspects of your Venture Concept, business model, product/services strategy, and positioning. The questions will also help you forecast the potential revenue for your venture.

Look at Figure 7.6. This figure contains questions to ask customers. You should provide your Venture Concept statement on a separate page that can be handed to customers so they can refer back to it as you work through the questions.

Please trust us that it takes a lot of careful thinking to write a powerful, clear concept summary in two or three sentences. The more abstract the venture—such as a software or information services business—the harder it is to be brief. Spend sufficient time with your team getting the ideas and words down correctly. A poorly worded statement destroys the efficacy of your Reality Check.

The questions shown in Figure 7.2 help customers assess the attractiveness of your Venture Concept as well as important aspects of the business model. Each question gathers information about an important aspect for the venture:

- The end-users and buyers
- The major problems addressed by the venture's offerings and the value of solving those problems for the customer
- Since innovation rarely happens in a vacuum, the degree to which customers like the solutions they already have now
- The competitive positioning and distinctiveness of the venture
- Purchase intent, as well as the frequency and amount of purchase
- The preferred point of purchase, be it a store, the Web, or face to face
- The preferred venues for learning about offerings such as yours
- Complementary products and services that customers might want in addition to those proposed here

(To be applied with different potential target customers. Provide your Venture Concept Statement for Customers on a Separate Page. Also, provide a simple description of your product or service, using a sketch or diagram if this helps customers understand your venture.)

First, can you tell us a little bit about yourself or your company? (Open ended, but look for key demographic descriptors to align with your market segmentation and customer groups.) Then:

1. This is what our product or service generally does (provide a quick description or a picture/sketch on a separate page). Do you view yourself as a potential customer of this offering? What would be the different ways that you would want to use the (product or service)?

2. How satisfied are you with the current products/services you use now?

Very dissatisfied   Dissatisfied   Neither Dis/Sat.   Satisfied   Very Satisfied

3. Do you see the proposed offering as distinctive from the competitors?

Not different   Somewhat different   Highly distinctive

4. How much would be willing to pay for this offering for this offering compared to the current products/services you use now?

Less   Same   More

5. How often do you buy similar products or services? (Open ended)

6. How much do you spend each time you make a purchase? (Open ended, but looking for a dollar amount. Also, try to validate the structure of revenue — e.g. does the customer want to purchase, license, subscribe, try before buy, etc.)

7. Where is the best place to buy products/services such as this? (Open ended, but look for a specific preferred channel and ways in which they test or try products/services)

8. Where do you get your information about products/services such as this? (Open ended. Look for preferred information sources.)

9. How likely is it that you would be willing to buy this offering?

Very unlikely   Unlikely   Neither   Likely   Very Likely

10. What additional features do you think are important in a (product or service) such as this? (Open ended)

Figure 7.2   The Field Research Instrument for the Reality Check

Now take a few minutes to work down the questions in Figure 7.2 with pencil in hand. You might wish to refine these questions to best suit your proposed venture (but not too much!). Don't leave any of the key points out, because you will need all of them not only to do a Reality Check but to create a foundation for building your business plan and financial models in the next section of this book.

Organizing Customer Panels_____

Many of you by now have one primary target customer group, and based on your field work, feel confident that you are on target. But we have worked with enough teams over the years to know that some of you might still be debating the best market fit for your idea. This Reality Check is the perfect opportunity to determine the correct focus. For example, a team of graduate students created a new modular jewelry concept that allowed women to personally customize their jewelry for day, evening, work, or social occasions, with color variations matching the clothes being worn. As students themselves, they initially targeted young women still in school. But in their ethnography and Reality Check, they also talked to young professional women out of school. The concept was tested against both customer groups. As one might expect, it was the somewhat older professional women who wanted modular, flexible fashion items even more. The Reality Check made this customer focus clear. Too often, student teams think that they themselves are the only or the best target customer. And just as often, *that is not the case!*

Therefore, we want you to structure customers into distinct groups (following your segmentation work in Chapter 2) and then ask representative members of each group for their thoughts on your Venture Concept and the business model for it. It might take a little more work to do more than one customer group, but the benefits can be tremendous. In this way, you can use the Reality Check to make sure you have targeted the best customer group for your products or services and that these offerings are positioned appropriately for their tastes and preferences. It will also help you appreciate how the different groups vary. And you might actually find a better set of customers for launching your venture (such as those who have more money to spend or have greater need of your solutions). Or you might learn what needs to be added to your product line or services to expand your business at the next stage of growth.

For example, if we were making a new type of tasty energy bar for young adults in their 20s, we would also want to find out reactions to that product concept by teenagers on one hand and adults in their 30s on the other. This information will help sharpen your focus. You might find that your tasty energy bar concept actually applies better to an older crowd, for example, or to a broader population that includes two or three distinct customer segments.

As a quick exercise, pretend that you are a pet owner and are answering the questions for the pet snack team. Pretend (or not!) that you are a young professional woman, single or married, and have a dog (Spot) with whom you have a special, almost mother-child relationship. You tend to shop at Whole Foods grocery store, buy the all-natural pet food brands there, and spend whatever time it takes at your veterinarian to keep Spot healthy. When it comes to snacks, you explicitly read labels and look for natural, healthy ingredients. Now switch your customer group by virtue of demographics, attitudes, and behaviors. Pretend to be a pet owner who has a more distant relationship with the pet. You shop at Walmart for inexpensive pet food in bulk. You have never been to the vet. You also make the animal sleep in the mudroom. And you feed your pet cheap cookies for snacks. Now switch one more time. Let's say that you are a single male (as many of you are), live in an urban area, and often eat "on the run." You go to PetSmart or Petco to buy what seems like really healthy pet food—but you don't bother reading any labels. When it comes to snacks, you want Spot to have fun and will buy things that look like chews or are colorful, even to the point of being silly. Besides, if it is in a premium retailer, the snack can't be all that bad.

In each role, you will come up with very different answers with respect to demographics, attitudes, behaviors, and core needs for pet snacks in key areas such as ingredient type and quality, price, and preferred place of purchase. *As an entrepreneur, this is the type of information you need to know for targeting and execution.*

We have seen the same approach work just as well for B2B ventures. A biomedical device team might have a series of potential applications for a new diagnostic technology coming out of the research lab—but it is only when team members talk to actual doctors that they find the one or two compelling applications on which physicians will actually spend time and money.

It is important to get feedback from members of each adjacent customer group on your Venture Concept. You might find, in fact, that your original idea appeals more strongly to a group of customers different from your original target. Or you might also find ways to expand or refine your core offering to adjacent customers in the target market. Beyond simple validation, the Reality Check for a venture is all about refining your targeting and fleshing out your product or services strategy. *Listen* to the customers and *learn*.

Conducting the Field Research _____

In Chapters 2 and 3, we had you observe and talk to target customers to gain the insights into your customers' needs required to define the solutions for your venture. Now we are seeking more specific responses—data—for more specific things. You will be generating these data by asking people questions and recording their responses. You have several options for doing this. You can collect the data by:

- Personal interviews (face to face) following a structured discussion guide
- Telephone interviews also following a structured discussion guide
- Mailed surveys that respondents complete and mail back to you
- Online surveys, using one of the popular survey tools offered on the Web. There a number of such tools that you can use at no initial cost with a simple Google search.

In choosing between these alternatives, you will have to make important trade-offs, such as the cost of gathering the information against the expected quality of information obtained. Figure 7.7 provides some of the pros and cons of each particular method.

Personal interviews (face to face) have the major advantage of enabling you to ask probing questions or see reactions of the respondents. But personal interviews can be time consuming and expensive to conduct, particularly if the people you want to talk to live in a different city or region. Yet, just as we learned in Chapters 2 and 3, any face-to-face time with a target customer is worth its weight in gold to the entrepreneur. You simply cannot get enough of it—and this is our preferred method for testing Venture Concepts—particularly if you only often need a dozen or so respondents to get good directional input from the target market. As we also learned, try to do this research *in situ*—in the customer's actual buying or usage environment, or even better, some of each! If this is not possible, do so in an environment that is most comfortable for the respondent. In other words, do this work on their home turf, not yours.

As for the other possible methods, collecting data by mail can be slow and response rates low. Also, in mailed surveys, there may be bias in the data because those likely to respond will typically have either strong positive or negative reactions to your Venture Concept. Additionally, a mailed survey does not give you the flexibility to explain to the customer what you mean by a particular question or idea. Often, customers misunderstand what you mean or simply get lost and therefore fail to complete a research instrument. Mail seems to be something of the past.

Basis of Comparison	Personal Interview	Telephone/Skype	Mail	Online
Cost of completed survey	Most expensive	Moderately expensive	Not very expensive	Very inexpensive
Ability to probe and ask complex questions	Much; this is a face-to-face conversation	Some; interviewer can probe and elaborate	Little to none	Depends; can go back and ask respondent to clarify responses; or make changes to the concept and re-test
Potential of interviewer bias on the results	Significant; voice, appearance, gender, and "know it all" attitude can easily bias the results	Also significant, although appearance is taken out of the picture	None	Little, if done correctly
Anonymity given to respondent	Little, because of face-to-face contact	Some, because of telephone contact	Complete, unless coded instrument is used	Some; e-mail/customer name may be known
Response rate	Good	Fair; refusal rates are increasing	Poor or fair	Very good, if done correctly
Speed of data collection	Moderate, depending on travel time to customers	Good	Poor	Very good

Figure 7.3 Comparing Field Research Methods of a Reality Check for a Venture Concept

Collecting data by telephone allows the flexibility to talk to customers and walk through a research instrument. For business-to-business (B2B) ventures, we have seen this method used to great effect, grabbing 15 minutes of a busy manager's time to run through a set of important questions. However, for business-to-consumer (B2C) ventures, the telephone method is becoming increasingly difficult because consumers are sick and tired of marketing calls. Also, with many unlisted telephone numbers, it is becoming harder and harder to obtain a good sample of respondents.

Using the Web to collect data, on the other hand, is becoming increasingly popular. In our MBA classes, we find that student teams have no trouble finding 30, 40, and sometimes well over 100 people to complete their online "concept tests." One of the nice things about the online survey route is that you can make changes to various aspects of the product or service offering and "re-test" to get customer or buyer reactions.

Importantly, the key driver you must consider when determining a data collection method is whether or not you wish to present a "prototype" or visual of your core offering. If it is important for the potential customer to actually see the prototype or visual, then you must use the personal interview or the online method. Remember, an online survey can include a picture of the proposed product or a strong description of the proposed service. Visuals bring a concept to life for target customers. We strongly encourage you to use pictures, sketches, or actual prototypes whenever possible.

Analyzing Your Data and Interpreting the Results

The Goal: Validate Your Customer Insights and Business Model Vision

So let's say that you have designed your key questions, identified target customers and buyers, and have reached them either face to face, through the phone, or through the Web. You have gathered data for these questions and are ready to start your analysis. The purpose now is to consolidate what you have learned about the demographics, attitudes, behaviors, and core needs of the potential target customer groups you have identified and then to validate your product/services strategy and its competitive positioning.

The next step is to consolidate all the data from your field research into a simple, single source of information. We recommend that you use the Field Research Discussion Guide as a template for doing this. Take a look at Figures 7.4A through 7.4D. We have used the HealthyWags case as an illustration for what a consolidated data set might look like as a result of the Reality Check field research. We have chunked up a single consolidated data set into four pieces to make it easier for you to read—but on the team's computer this is a single document (supported by a number of supplemental files). In the pages that follow, we are going to show you how to analyze various parts of these data to validate and improve your Venture Concept.

Validating the Core Needs, Attitudes, Behaviors, and Demographics of Your Target Market

Successful entrepreneurs become experts in their target customers and their uses for a product or service. While many of the insights shown in Figure 7.5 should emerge in the ethnography done earlier in Chapters 2 and 3, the Reality Check is the time to test these insights against a set of closely related customers.

Remember, in Chapter 2 we learned about identifying distinct customer groups—where "customers" might be customers and/or buyers. The Venture Concept dashboard (Figure 7.1)

Question 1. Can you tell us a little bit about yourself or your company? (Open ended, but look for key demographic descriptors to align with your market segmentation and customer groups)

Results (Combination of earlier ethnography and the reality check field research):

Mother Goose (attitude: dog as family member, but still a pet). Customers are health conscious when purchasing at the grocery store, and many are going to Whole Foods. They expect quality ingredients, but they are not label readers. They are explicitly focused on taste but value is also important because dog snacks are part of the overall household food budget. They will accept fortification of ingredients, as opposed to all-natural recipes. They take supplements themselves! Key motivation for feeding snacks: "I feed my dogs just for love." Key target customer. **50% of market**

Dog Mommy (attitude: dog as family member, dog as child and may be a surrogate child for some). Customers are very health conscious. These customers want quality ingredients and not at lot of fat and calories. All-natural is another key driver. They want all-natural ingredients, good taste, and minimally processed products. They are deliberate shoppers, including reading the ingredient list. Key motivation for feeding snacks: "I want my dog to be as healthy as I am." Key target customer. **40% of market**

Pet Buddy (attitude: dog as pet friend.) Predominantly male. They are focused on ingredients on a more scientific basis. All-natural is less of a concern. He does not mind using a dog snack as an indulgence. Milk Bones will do for this customer. Key motivation for feeding snacks: "If he is happy, I am happy." Looks at dog as exercise buddy. **10% of market**

Question 2: This is what our product or service generally does (provide a quick description or a picture/sketch on a separate page). Do you view yourself as a potential customer of this offering? What would be the different ways that you would want to use the (product or service)?

Mother Goose	100	Snack pet	$n=12$
Dog Mommy	100	Snack pet	$n=12$
Pet Buddy	50	Snack pet	$n=6$

Figure 7.4A   HealthyWags' Consolidated Field Research Data: Questions 1 and 2 ($N=30$)

Question 3: How satisfied are you with the current products/services you use now?

Very dissatisfied   *Dissatisfied*   *Neither Dis/Sat.*   *Satisfied*   *Very Satisfied*

Mother Goose: 30% Dissatisfied or Very Dissatisfied
Dog Mommy: 40% Dissatisfied or Very Dissatisfied
Pet Buddy: 5% Dissatisfied or Very Dissatisfied

Question 4: Do you see the proposed offering as distinctive from the competitors?

Not different   *Somewhat different*   *Highly distinctive*

Mother Goose: 20% Highly distinctive
Dog Mommy: 30% Highly distinctive
Pet Buddy: 10% Highly distinctive

Question 5: How much would be willing to pay for this offering compared to the current products/services you use now?

Less   *Same*   *More*

Mother Goose: 10% would pay more
Dog Mommy: 20% would pay more
Pet Buddy: 100% would pay the same

Figure 7.4B   HealthyWags' Consolidated Field Research Data: Product/Services Strategy and Positioning Questions

Question 6:   How often do you buy similar products or services? (Open ended)

Mother Goose:	Once a month
Dog Mommy:	Once a month
Pet Buddy:	Once every 2 months

Question 7:   How much do you spend each time you make a purchase? (Open ended, but looking for a dollar amount).

Mother Goose:	$5
Dog Mommy:	$7
Pet Buddy:	$3

Question 8:   Where is the best place to buy products/services such as this? (Open ended, but look for a specific preferred channel and ways in which they test or try products/services)

Mother Goose:	Supermarket, Pet specialty store
Dog Mommy:	Pet specialty store
Pet Buddy:	Supermarket

Question 9:   Where do you get your information about products/services such as this? (Open ended. Look for preferred information sources.)

Mother Goose:	Print, television, friends
Dog Mommy:	Internet, friends
Pet Buddy:	In-store

Figure 7.4C   HealthyWags' Consolidated Field Research Data: Go-to-Market Questions

---

Question 10:   How likely is it that you would be willing to buy this offering?

Very unlikely	*Unlikely*	*Neither*	*Likely*	*Very Likely*

Mother Goose:	25% likely/very likely
Dog Mommy:	50% likely/very likely
Pet Buddy:	10% likely/very likely

Question 11:   What additional features would make you more likely to buy this (product or service) ? (Open ended)

Mother Goose:	Bulk packaging to buy it for less money per lb. Want smaller portion treats for training purposes.
Dog Mommy:	A no-meat version because "I don't eat meat myself."
Pet Buddy :	"Can you make it look like a bone?"

Figure 7.4D   HealthyWags' Consolidated Field Research Data: Purchase Intent Questions

should list the specific end-users and buyers in a target market. It should also include a picture or sketch of your primary target customer together with simple needs statements based on your ethnography. Now we want to validate and improve those insights, to create even crisper "personas" of the various target customers in your target market. This helps focus everything else in the venture: your commercial offerings, your positioning, your go-to-market strategy, and the structure and nature of revenues.

Also to refresh, customers are often their own buyers. But just as often, they are not. In the B2C space, for example, many readers may have just purchased their first new automobile—and hopefully a lot of careful thinking as well as brand emotion went into that decision. When you were much younger, however—say, still in diapers—your mother made the Pampers,

Huggies, or store-brand purchase decision for you. Similarly, in the B2B space, self-employed home office entrepreneurs make their own decisions about the office productivity and other forms of software to be used; however, in any larger sort of corporation *someone else* makes that decision for us, and the process for that decision making is typically more complex based on volume discounts, support agreements, and so forth.

Let's stick with the pet snack case—it's fun, and we bet that quite a few of you come from households with a dog. Take a quick look at what might emerge from a Reality Check for HealthyWags. Our focus here is primarily on Questions 1 and 2 of the Field Research Discussion Guide. Look at the consolidated data set in Figure 7.4A:

Question 1: Can you tell us a little bit about yourself or your company? [Open ended, but look for key demographic descriptors to align with your market segmentation and customer groups.]

Question 2: This is what our product or service generally does [provide a quick description or a picture/sketch on a separate page]. Do you view yourself as a potential customer of this offering? What would be the different ways that you would want to use the product [or service]?

Figure 7.4A shows the consolidated data set for these two questions for HealthyWags. The team applied its discussion guide to 30 dog owners in all, speaking with dog owners in their neighborhoods or in dog-walking parks. There were three distinct customer groups that emerged from this research as distinguished by owners' attitudes and behaviors toward pets. Demographics also supported the customer grouping. In Figure 7.4A, you can see specific descriptions for each of these three groups: Mother Goose, Dog Mommy, and Pet Buddy. Those descriptions contain lots of useful information on attitudes and behaviors that drive needs for both products and services. You can also see that all the prospective customers in the first two groups saw themselves as potential customers for healthy dog snacks, while only half of the Pet Buddy customers saw themselves as customers (the other half were satisfied with their current relatively unhealthy snacks).

What is particularly interesting—and the type of insight you need to discover for your venture—is how different target customers perceive themselves as customers for your proposed product or service. In the case of HealthyWags, here are the results:

Question 2: This is what our product or service generally does [provide a quick description or a picture/sketch on a separate page]. Do you view yourself as a potential customer of this offering? What would be the different ways that you would want to use the product [or service]?

Mother Goose	100%	$N = 12$
Dog Mommy	100	$N = 12$
Pet Buddy	15	$N = 6$

The female customers have a much stronger identification with healthy dog snacks than do the male pet owners. For HealthyWags, the second part of the question is rather obvious: snacking for the pet. However, the venture team found other uses: snacks specifically for training (which might suggest a smaller portion size for each snack), and snacks for in the car (which might suggest resealable packages rather than boxes to avoid mess). In other types of business, the range of use cases that emerged as you talk with customers can be real eye-openers! For example, in our home monitoring case, the very same system is not only to identify and initiate responses for health problems in the elderly but also to provide loved ones with the ability to stay in closer touch with their parents' health and well-being.

Now we want you to make a simple chart—but one with a complex array of information. Do you remember the customer grouping of the farmers in Chapter 2—Figure 2.4—with the

"Steady Eddie," the "Up & Comer," the "Sun Downer," and the "Livestock Farmer"? This is what we want you to create with greater detail than before, capturing the full extent of core needs, attitudes, behaviors, and demographics.

Figure 7.5 is an example of applying this framework to HealthyWags. Mother Goose and Dog Mommy represent distinct female personas, one older, the other younger, with different attitudes and shopping behaviors. Mother Goose is the primary grocery shopper of the family and buys her pet food along with the rest of the family's food. That leads to supermarkets and mass merchandisers as preferred channels. And she is looking for a nutritious snack from a brand-name manufacturer.

Dog Mommy is a distinctly different customer. This became the team's primary target. Dog Mommy could be married or single, but she views her pet as her child. She is highly receptive to all-natural health, seeks minimally processed food, tries new products, and pays for better quality. Importantly, this customer is willing to experiment with new brand names; in fact, she sometimes has a distrust of "big-name" manufacturers. Smaller is better. The all-natural goodness that she seeks for herself is what she wants for her special family member—her pet. Knowledgeable salespeople in a store are important to her.

The last "customer" is a male for whom the pet is a friend and "buddy." This customer seeks convenient, "fun" snacks and does not expect a pet snack to be particularly healthy—just as he views his own snacks! This attitude and set of behaviors pretty much apply to both younger and older males.

These are the types of insights we want you to have for your various potential target customer groups. The chart is a nice way of summarizing all these insights into a simple, readily accessible form. Not every target customer will fit perfectly into one of your specific groups, but there should be strong alignment by virtue of shared needs, attitudes, behaviors, and perhaps demographics.

For those of you venturing into the software and systems business, Health Monitoring Systems is a good illustration of different customer groups emerging from the combination of ethnography and validation in a Reality Check. That venture found two types of elderly: those chronically ill and needing constant supervision in a controlled medical environment such as an assisted-living center or nursing home, and others who are still relatively healthy and live either in their own personal residence or a special elderly residence community. In its research, the team found that the typical cost of an emergency room readmission for an individual is over $12,000—and many of these are preventable by detecting problems before they become crises. The team decided to focus on elderly in assisted-living centers or still living at home—the customer group where automated monitoring could make the biggest impact and where the sheer number of customers made the best business case.

Lastly, for those of you venturing into services, the mobile app developer for retail business found the larger chains or big-box stores to be an entirely different type of customer than the small independents with a dozen stores or less, and these, completely different than "Mom and Pop" single store operations.

Validating Your Product or Services Strategy, Its Positioning and Branding

The next step is to validate the attractiveness of your product or service idea of your venture with the target customers. There are several aspects to this: (a) the extent to which the customers are dissatisfied with their current solutions; (b) the extent to which they find your solution distinctive (special and meaningful for their use case application); and (c) the extent to which customers value that differentiation with a willingness to pay more for it relative to existing solutions.

The stars align for your venture if target customers are highly dissatisfied with current solutions, your offerings are special, and customers appreciate that with a willingness to support premium pricing. The entrepreneur seeks a clearly differentiated position—one that stands out from the competition. And this may not just be in terms of a dramatically lower price for customers. Since it is typically the established, large-scale manufacturers or service providers that use economies of scale to drive prices down, often the most powerful points of differentiation for a new venture with limited volumes will come in an area other than price.

Target customers	Core needs	Attitudes (toward family or work or lifestyle)	Behaviors (include buying preferences)	"Hard" demographics including percentage of total market / survey
Mother Goose	Perceived: nutritional health. Latent: Snacks matched as part of a nutrition system that includes main meal.	• Caring to the pet, a member of the family • I feed my dogs just for love • Doesn't study ingredient list. • Dog walking is a another household to-do. • Looks for brand name manufacturers.	• Shops for pet food while shopping for the family. • Looks at big bag as way to economize. • Prefers grocery channel.	• Married with children. • Primary grocery shopper. • Mature (over 35 yrs).
Dog Mommy	Perceived: nutritional healthy snacks. Latent: all natural goodness, not over-processed, low fat.	• Views pet as surrogate child. • *I want my dog to be as healthy as I am.* • Dog walking is major enjoyment event. • Looks at ingredients. • Seeks simple, all natural goodness. • Some want grains and vegetables only.	• Shops for pet food separate from own food purchases. • Prefers premium specialty channels, combination of Petsmart, Petco, and independent retailers. • Receptive to food innovations for self and pet. • Likes to have a knowledgeable salesperson to speak with about product choices.	• Single or married without children. • "Professional" with disposable income.
Pet Buddy	Perceived: between meal snacking. Latent: a "fun" snack; an on-the-go convenient meal substitute.	• Views pet as a friend, a buddy. • If he is happy, I am happy. • Looks for brand name manufacturers. • Dog walking is personal fitness occasion.	• Rarely shops for pet food. • Like big bag bulk purchases. • Traditional cookies are good enough: "It's just a snack."	• Married or in steady relationship. • Not primary grocery shopper; "impulse" buyer.

Figure 7.5   HealthyWags' Customer Grouping

Conversely, customers might be very interested in your idea conceptually, but if they are already pleased with their current product or service, most customers will tend not to try your offerings due to switching costs and the uncertainty of working with a new firm. Or they might perceive your concept as special but not special enough to support healthy pricing. To test these things, our Field Research Guide has three questions:

Question 3: How satisfied are you with the current products/services you use now?

Very dissatisfied   Dissatisfied   Neither Dis./Sat.   Satisfied   Very satisfied

Question 4: Do you see the proposed offering as distinctive from the competitors?

Not different   Somewhat different   Highly distinctive

Question 5: How much would be willing to pay for this offering compared to the current products/services you use now?

Less   Same   More

Turning to the HealthyWags' consolidated data (Figure 7.4B), it is clear that certain target customers appreciate the premium, all-natural, healthy positioning. The Reality Check showed that premium features—all-natural nutrition—would command a price premium over current snacks. Some might say that a high price reinforces the premium perception in the hearts and minds of consumers. Let's take a look at the actual data:

Question 3: How satisfied are you with the current products/services you use now?

Very dissatisfied   Dissatisfied   Neither Dis./Sat.   Satisfied   Very satisfied

Mother Goose	20% Dissatisfied or Very dissatisfied
Dog Mommy	40% Dissatisfied or Very dissatisfied
Pet Buddy	5% Dissatisfied or Very dissatisfied

Those "Dog Mommy" customers—younger females who view their pet as their child—show the highest level of dissatisfaction with current pet snacks. This makes them a primary target customer for the venture. That's what you need to find for your venture. Conversely, those "Pet Buddy" guys don't seem to really care about quality of snacks (including for themselves!). Those are the type of customers who you need to know about ahead of time so that you don't waste your product development, distribution, and marketing money on them.

Question 4: Do you see the proposed offering as distinctive from the competitors?

Not different   Somewhat different   Highly distinctive

Mother Goose	20% Highly distinctive
Dog Mommy	30% Highly distinctive
Pet Buddy	10% Highly distinctive

Question 5: How much would you be willing to pay for this offering compared to the current products/services you use now?

Less   Same   More

Mother Goose	10% would pay more
Dog Mommy	20% would pay more
Pet Buddy	100% wouldn't pay more

Once again, the stars align for the team to target that younger female. She has the highest level of appreciation for the proposed product and will support it with her spending. Mother Goose comes in a strong second; Pet Buddy's a distant third.

The Reality Check should also provide support for your strategy regarding product line variety (often "good, better, best") and complementary products or services developed in Chapter 4. This is the purpose of the very last, open-ended question in the Field Research Discussion Guide, and it is presented as a way to increase the customers' perception of his or her likelihood of purchase if they would like to see additional features or offerings.

Question 11: What additional features would make you more likely to buy this [product or service]? [Open ended]

Mother Goose: Bulk packaging to buy it for less money per pound; smaller-portioned treats for training purposes

Dog Mommy: A no-meat version because "I don't eat meat myself"

Pet Buddy: "Can you make it look like a bone?"

The Mother Goose primary grocery shoppers are always thinking about the family budget; therefore, bulk packaging would make sense. Also, being experienced in training (children as well as pets), it makes sense that these customers might want a new type of healthier training snack in a "bite-size" portion. The Dog Mommy customer—that younger female typically not yet with children and who views her pet as her child—is very much focused on her own eating needs when she thinks about the pet. Eating less meat is a growing trend among such consumers, and therefore that preference is passed onto the pet (even though dogs clearly love to eat meat!). Lastly, the male Pet Buddy is thinking about play and enjoyment with his pet: "Since dogs love bones, why not make it look like a bone?" Any of these ideas might be introduced at startup or later on once the business picks up steam.

Spotlight: The Reality Check for the Health Monitoring and Mobile App Development Ventures

The same type of Reality Check validation process for new product or services strategy applies equally well to high-tech ventures. For example, the Health Monitoring Systems team described earlier found its offering of a noninvasive, 24/7 monitoring system to be distinctive and well valued over existing alternatives—which for many elderly was Philips Lifeline, a push-the-button alert system to a call center that the individual wears around his or her neck. The team found that a significant percentage of its primary target customer—elderly with health problems and already receiving health services within an assisted-living center or from a home health agency—would pay more for an automated service compared to the traditional push-button alert system, especially when informed that the system would continue to monitor individuals at night while sleeping. The cost of push-button systems currently on the market was about a dollar a day. The product line strategy was flexed to serve different types of customers. Loved ones wanted visibility into their parents' medical monitoring and health history through the Web. So did the nurses providing care. And assisted-living center and home health agency managers wanted the "transactions" on the system to be fed into a database to track incidents and response times. With a growing elderly population, anything that could help manage patient health quality and nursing staff productivity would be "worth its weight in gold."

However, the team also learned from its Reality Check that a significant percentage of elderly users did not want to be monitored at all, even though such monitoring could be proven beyond doubt to provide more rapid care in the event of a health emergency. For this type of customer, 24/7 monitoring was nothing short of an invasion of privacy! That percentage of rejecters was over 50% of the target customer group, cutting down its addressable market by half. Correctly, the team applied that percentage to its revenue projects (which we will see in Chapter 9 in Section II of this book). It was still able to raise a large chunk of Series A capital, perhaps in part because it had done its research well and had realistic numbers.

The pure services venture described earlier—mobile app development for retailers—also found its Reality Check very useful. The team found lots of competition from well-established IT vendors for the large consumer electronics big box retailers but little competition in grocery stores and small retailer chains. In fact, these stores simply didn't know to whom to turn to put customer loyalty programs on a smartphone. The Reality Check itself led to quality customer leads!

Validating Your Go-to-Market Strategy

Entrepreneurs in technology-intensive businesses often focus so hard on their products or services that they shortchange the go-to-market aspects of the business. This can be a fatal flaw. Go-to-market is the hidden genie of any successful new product or service development. A bad salesperson or low-quality retailer can make the best products appear inferior. Or, as we have seen so often in Web and software ventures, developing communities around a new product or service can create the buzz needed to create critical momentum in a marketplace that would ordinarily be out of the reach of an entrepreneur if he or she had to buy such market awareness through traditional media.

The Reality Check for your go-to-market strategy includes getting customer feedback on four key elements guiding such a strategy:

- Frequency of purchase
- Amount typically "spent" for each purchase
- Preferred place of purchase
- Preferred information channel for product or service information

In the next section of this book, we will also learn how to go back to customers to test the branding for a new product or service. For now, however, all we need to do is to validate and gain further insight into the four issues above.

Perhaps the most important aspect for entrepreneurs is to determine if target customers agree with the channel strategy. For example, do customers want to buy directly from you? Or would they prefer to purchase from an already established channel member, such as a retailer for B2C ventures or an original equipment manufacturer (OEM; a larger firm) or systems integrator for B2B ventures? Remember, a successful channel strategy will accelerate your time to market and break even, increasing the return on investment for your startup company. However, this channel strategy must balance the ideal design for market coverage and meeting customer preferences with the costs of implementing that channel—particularly for a startup. For example, many successful entrepreneurs started first with a regional or "top ten accounts" penetration strategy before expanding to national and then global reach.

We want to emphasize that it is important to get feedback on all of these issues early and make any necessary adjustments now before going to market, since making after-launch changes can be very expensive. The way we do so is by asking customers four simple questions in the Field Research Discussion Guide:

Question 6: How often do you buy similar products or services? [Open ended]

Question 7: How much do you spend each time you make a purchase? [Open ended but look for a dollar amount]

Question 8: Where is the best place to buy products/services such as this? [Open ended but look for a specific preferred channel and ways in which they test or try products/services]

Question 9: Where do you get your information about products/services such as this? [Open ended; look for preferred information sources]

To illustrate how consolidated data can validate or change a Venture Concept, let's turn to HealthyWags once again. Take a look at the data below:

Question 6: How often do you buy similar products or services? [Open ended]

Mother Goose	Once a month
Dog Mommy	Once a month
Pet Buddy	Once every two months

These data support the team's focus on the female buyers as a startup strategy because they are more diligent, frequent shoppers.

Question 7: How much do you spend each time you make a purchase? [Open ended but look for a dollar amount]

Mother Goose	$5
Dog Mommy	$7
Pet Buddy	$3

These data provide strong directional guidance that the younger female shoppers—those who view their pets as surrogate children—are less price sensitive than the older, primary grocery shopping Moms trying to manage a family budget. And those guys—well, the Reality Check reveals that they are simply "cheap" when it comes to pet snacks (and, we bet, their own snacks!).

Question 8: Where is the best place to buy products/services such as this? [Open ended but look for a specific preferred channel and ways in which they test or try products/services]

Mother Goose	Supermarket (34%), pet specialty store (33%), Walmart (33%)
Dog Mommy	Supermarket (20%), pet specialty store (50%) including independents, mass merchant (10%), club store (20%)
Pet Buddy	Supermarket (60%), pet specialty store (10%), mass merchant (30%)

One of the team members was skeptical about the strength of the specialty channel for younger women—the primary demographic source for Dog Mommy. He went to a pet specialty store and discretely observed who was purchasing off the snack aisle over the course of an hour at the end of the working day. Sure enough, women were doing the vast amount of the purchasing, more younger than older, and hardly any men other than himself! Both the data and the in-store observation supported the team's focus on the female buyers as a startup strategy because they prefer the pet specialty channel, such as Petco, PetSmart, or independent retailers. From a practical matter, given the costs of getting shelf space in a supermarket and the difficulty of breaking into mass merchants such as Walmart, the venture team found the pet specialty channel attractive for a venture—particularly the independent pet retailers that serve as a good test bed for new products. Then, the team reasoned, it would have the credibility to do national agreements with the large specialty chains. Dog Mommy continued to find support as a primary target customer.

Question 9: Where do you get your information about products/services such as this? [Open ended but look for preferred information sources]

Mother Goose	Print, television, friends
Dog Mommy	Internet, friends
Pet Buddy	In-store

These data show that Dog Mommy—as a younger consumer—prefers social networking channels of information for new products (as well as services, we find). The traditional Madison Avenue advertising approach (expensive print and broadcast/cable advertisements) for marketing to an older consumer is sometimes distrusted by this young consumer. The primary grocery shopping Mom, on the other hand, prefers these traditional information sources—costly for a fledgling company. And Pet Buddy—well, it seems that male pet owners in this Reality Check like to be sold right in the store through pamphlets, displays, or in-store samples. Taken together, the Reality Checks showed a clear alignment toward the Dog Mommy consumer for the premium, all-natural, and healthy pet snacks that HealthyWags aspired to bring to market.

The go-to-market field research for Health Monitoring Systems supported a different set of go-to-market strategies. For example, the preferred channel was assisted-living centers and home health agencies versus selling directly to the elderly themselves, simply because technology scares many of the elderly. It was also a lot less costly in terms of advertising to build awareness. The elderly wanted to learn about new services from trusted sources, for example, their doctors and care providers. The field work also helped validate the revenue model. The elderly made the most direct connection to home security systems to prevent burglary—such as ADT. Such services carry an installation fee in the range of $300 and a monthly monitoring fee of $50. Those numbers became important for the financial modeling that the team had to perform to prepare its business plan to raise venture capital.

Last, for a service example, the mobile app consultancy found quite clearly that its proposed consultancy required direct, highly experienced sales contact with customers, armed with customer references, examples, and a milestone-based design and development process.

TIP: TESTING BRAND NAMES

You might want to do a quick check on your company and product or service brand names. We recommend that you do this *after* you ask all the questions to respondents in the Reality Check. If they seem willing, tell them you would like to run a few product or service brand names by them to get their opinions. It is also a fun way to end the interview process! We usually do not do company names in these types of tests—just product and service branding—it's too much for most customers who are busy and on the go to handle. The company naming is something you and your partners are going to have to think long and deeply about, and craft a story around it for potential investors.

To do a brand name and messaging test:

- From your work in Chapter 6, and specifically your version of the Brand Architecture Template, come up with two or three possible brand names for your products or services, and the simple, short, powerful messaging behind these brand names.

- Go onto the Web and find brand names for leading, competing products or services. You might also want to browse the startups in your industry niche and see what they are calling their new products and services. Often, you will find creative new naming. Also look for messaging.

- Have the interviewees first look at what you think are the best competitor brand names. Then have them look at yours. Setting this up as a simple table might be the best approach, with the various competitors' names and messaging in the first column, your possible brand names and messaging in the second column, and the third column open for notes.

- The type of responses you are looking for are:

  1. Of all the names and messages in the table, which are the clearest and most powerful?

  2. If your own brand names and messages "pop," what are the reasons for this? What do they like about your branding?

  3. If your brand names and messages seem a little off, what don't they like, and what might they recommend?

  Please continue to note the type of customer the respondent represents. Different types of customers often react to the same branding in very different ways. Your goal is to develop and validate a brand name and messaging that truly resonate with *your* target customer.

Getting a Handle on Revenue for a Scaled-Up Business

You might have a great product or service idea, *but can it be the basis for a good business?* That, readers, is the $64 question (and for some of you, the $1 million to $3 million investment decision) that you and your potential investors must try to answer.

The Reality Check can begin to answer that question by providing a picture of the revenue potential for a scaled-up venture. By scaled-up venture, we mean a company that has started successfully, has its sea legs, and has expanded its customer base and product or service offerings. This is typically a firm that is two to three years old. In the next section of this book, we turn to an even more granular project of revenue and then projected expenses and profitability. However, for now, our focus is on *revenue—which for a venture is the source of all things good*. The failure to produce a consistent stream of growing revenue is difficult if not fatal.

The Reality Check goes a long way to making sure you are not walking down a dead-end alley. You need to determine the extent to which your target customers want and will demand your offering. *No demand means no venture.* Weak demand means a venture that will struggle along until such demand evolves and grows within your marketplace—and then an established firm might enter your market and steal that demand.

We want you to use our "voice of the customer" Reality Check to create a *customer-driven projection of scaled-up revenue*. All too often we see revenue projections for new ventures that are based on assumptions such as obtaining at first 5% then 10% then 20% share of a given total market. Many business planning guides reinforce this top-down aggregate market share approach or have revenues resulting from projections based on costs and break-even numbers relative to investments. These revenue projections rarely stand up to time.

It is important to understand that there can be a significant difference between target customers' receptivity to buying your products or services and, moreover, a difference in interest in the concept and actually purchasing. In some cases, the idea sounds or looks better than the reality. This might be due to the inability to reasonably demonstrate the idea by virtue of not having a good sketch or physical prototype. Or a concept tests well but then fails in the marketplace. Or it might perform better than in prelaunch tests. In consumer products, good packaging and in-store displays can truly make new products shine. Or, in software and services, an excellent sales force can make an unclearly differentiated product sell better than others.

With this caveat in mind, we still need to get a read from target customers on their likelihood of purchasing your product or service offerings—assuming that they are placed in a channel that they prefer and priced to match their perceived value. For this, we have two questions in the Field Research Guide:

Question 10: How likely is it that you would be willing to buy this offering?

Very unlikely   Unlikely   Neither likely or unlikely   Likely   Very likely

Question 3: How satisfied are you with the current products/services you use now?

Very dissatisfied   Dissatisfied   Neither Dis./Sat.   Satisfied   Very satisfied

Question 3 moderates Question 10. Trial is often induced by dissatisfaction with current products. The reasoning is that while customers can express a high level of purchase intent (i.e., really like a new product or service), unless they are unhappy with their current solutions, most are not likely to try something new unless "novelty" is an intrinsic part of their nature. The answers to this question are therefore used to put some hard-nosed reality into expressed purchase intent.

For both questions, customers within distinct customer groups are asked to respond along that five-point scale ranging from *Very unlikely* to *Very likely*. We are interested in the percentage of the prospective customers in your Reality Check that select either *Likely* or *Very likely*. This is classically called a *two-box score*.

We then combine the answers to these two questions with three more questions from the field research guide that assess the frequency of purchase and the typical "spend" for each purchase for different customer groups:

Question 6: How often do you buy similar products or services? [Open ended, but this translates into frequency in the revenue model]

Question 7: How much do you spend each time you make a purchase? [Open ended, but look for the type of revenue (purchase, rent, subscribe, etc.) and the dollar amount and the price-level relative to competition]

Question 8: Where is the best place to buy products/services such as this? [Open ended, but look for a specific, preferred channel and ways in which they test or try products/services]

When combined with some key external data on market size, we can then estimate revenue based on the following equation:

Revenue projection = sum (1 to *N* = customer groups):

   Customer group % of total market x

   Purchase intent % x

   Dissatisfaction % (with current products/services) x

   Channel penetration x

   "Spend" on each type of purchase $ x

   Purchase frequency (times per year)

Let's first focus on getting a reasonable sizing of the target market, and then the percentage of each customer group within that total market. For these elements of the equation, a simple question on the field research guide won't suffice. Instead, you have to go to the Web and dig into government reports or industry statistics. In Chapter 1, we reviewed methods for mining public data sources for market size and growth rates. It is that same type of work that you must do once again to get a handle on *market size* in the terms of the number of potential customers: consumers, companies, or government organizations. If you cannot find hard data on the total market size of the percentage of the market for your target customer groups, you are going to have to make a reasonable estimate—and then be able to back it up with some good old common sense and supporting information. In addition, many new ventures have a channel strategy that itself is restricted to a specific part of the broader target market. That channel strategy also needs to be factored into the revenue projection.

Next, in the second element of the equation—purchase intent—we need the percentage of the top "two-box" score for each customer group. You must add the *Likely* and *Very likely* respondents to get that top two-box percentage.

The channel penetration is also an important consideration. If a particular channel can ultimately reach 100% of the total market—no problem. However, if it only reaches a part of a market, then that percentage needs to be factored into the revenue projection. For example, in the pet snack case, pet specialty only reaches 30% of the total market, on average, and in the field research, the team gathered specific channel percentages for each customer to help guide its projections.

Next, if we know how much customers in the group, on average, spend on such types of purchases, we have another key part of the revenue projection equation. That would be Question 7. Here, you are looking for an approximate dollar amount for each purchase occasion—such as a visit to the store, a purchase on a Website, buying a new software license, and so forth.

Subsequently, we need to understand the purchase frequency—the number of times per year that individuals in each customer group purchase, license, or subscribe to your product or service.

Now let's see how all of this works out for the HealthyWags case. Let's break down the equation into HealthyWags speak:

Our scaled-up revenue projection =

sum (1 to *N* for Mother Goose, Dog Mommy, and Pet Buddy groups)

* Mother Goose, Dog Mommy, and Pet Buddy size (% of the total market)

* Purchase intent % (Question 10)

* Dissatisfaction % (Question 3)

* Channel penetration % (Question 8)

* Spend on each purchase $ (Question 7)

* Purchase frequency (times per year) (Question 6)

Now let's look at the data, remembering that *N* was 30 dog owners for this particular Reality Check.

Total Market Size

- A simple Web search shows that the 2009/2010 National Pet Owners Survey found 62% of all U.S. households have a pet, which equates to 71.4 million homes! This has increased from 56% in 1988. (We wonder what this trend means for the pet industry in developing economies coming into newfound wealth!)

- Of those pet owners, 45% have at least one dog.

- The company wants to start as a regional player, focusing on New England. The break-down of households, reflecting approximate numbers gathered from public data sources, for the six New England states is as follows:

State	Households
Massachusetts	2,000,000
Connecticut	1,400,000
New Hampshire	500,000
Maine	475,000
Rhode Island	400,000
Vermont	240,000

Customer Group Size: Industry data show that about 75% of all pet food buyers are female. That percentage is even higher for pet snacks. The HealthyWags team's ethnography and Reality Check research supported those general observations: Mother Goose represents 50% of all target customers, Dog Mommy 40%, and Pet Buddy (i.e., males) only 10%. Furthermore, the field research shows that while 100% of women interviewed considered themselves customers of a healthy pet snack product, only 50% of the males interviewed did the same, reducing the male participation in revenue generation by a further half.

Channel Penetration: From Question 8 above, we have the following:

Question 8: Where is the best place to buy products/services such as this? [Open ended, but look for a specific preferred channel and ways in which they test or try products/services]

Mother Goose	Supermarket (34%), pet specialty store (33%), Walmart (33%)
Dog Mommy	Supermarket (20%), pet specialty store (50%) including independents, mass merchant (10%), club store (20%)
Pet Buddy	Supermarket (60%), pet specialty (10%), mass merchant (30%)

Purchase Intent: From Question 10, we have:

Question 10: How likely is it that you would be willing to buy this offering?

Very unlikely   Unlikely   Neither likely or unlikely   Likely   Very likely

Mother Goose	25% Likely/Very likely
Dog Mommy	50% Likely/Very likely
Pet Buddy	10% Likely/Very likely

Dissatisfaction With Current Products/Services: From Question 3, we have:

Question 3: How satisfied are you with the current products/services you use now?

Very dissatisfied   Dissatisfied   Neither Dis./Sat.   Satisfied   Very satisfied

Mother Goose	20% Dissatisfied or Very dissatisfied
Dog Mommy	30% Dissatisfied or Very dissatisfied
Pet Buddy	5% Dissatisfied or Very dissatisfied

Spend on Each Purchase: And from Question 7 we have:

Question 7: How much do you spend each time you make a purchase? [Open ended, but look for a dollar amount]

Mother Goose	$5
Dog Mommy	$7
Pet Buddy	$3

Purchase Frequency: And from Question 6:

Question 6: How often do you buy similar products or services? [Open ended]

Mother Goose	Once a month
Dog Mommy	Once a month
Pet Buddy	Once every two months

With these elements in hand, we can construct the revenue projections. Let's start first with one state and then expand to the rest. In fact, it would be reasonable for this venture to launch first just in Massachusetts, the team's "home turf" and the largest of the New England states in terms of dog owners and potential revenue. For Massachusetts alone, the revenue projection equation would be:

Total market for Massachusetts = 45% of 2,000,000 households = 900,000 households.

Mother Goose (mature female, kids or empty nester, primary grocery shopper)

50% of dog households (900,000) = **450,000** customers x (Question 1)

25% purchase intent (likely/very likely) = **112,500** customers x (Question 10)

30% dissatisfaction = **33,750** customers x (Question 3)

33% channel penetration (pet specialty stores) = **11,137** customers x (Question 8)

$5 spend per month * 12 months = **$668,250 per year**

Dog Mommy (younger female, no kids, primary grocery shopper, pet is the kid)

40% of dog households (900,000) = 360,000 customers x

50% purchase intent (likely/very likely) = 180,000 customers x

40% dissatisfaction (dissatisfied) = 72,000 customers x

50% channel penetration = 36,000 customers x

$7 spend per month x 12 months = **$3,024,000 per year**

Pet Buddy (male, not a primary grocery shopper, pet is friend/pal, not focused on healthy snacks)

10% of dog households (900,000) = 90,000 customers x

10% purchase intent (likely/very likely) = 9,000 customers x

5% dissatisfaction = 450 customers x

10% channel penetration = 45 customers x

$3 spend per month x 6 (every other month) = **$810 per year!**

Indeed, it doesn't make any sense to focus on those male shoppers unless the team can figure out a clever way to *bring more males into market!* But that takes a lot of time and a lot of advertising money—not the stuff for a new venture.

The total revenue projection for Massachusetts alone is therefore **$3,693,060.** This also assumes that those consumers who make an initial purchase continue to be "repeat" purchasers—which is not always the case. In fact, in many cases, entrepreneurs make estimates for initial and repeat purchase, with repeat purchasing being a percentage of initial purchase or trial. But, given that such a high percentage of the Mother Goose and Dog Mommy groups saw the product as distinctive, were dissatisfied with their current snacks, and showed a high purchase intent, in this case repeat purchase can be assumed strong. Of course, once HealthyWags is in the market—and if its products fail to "perform"—all bets are off with respect to repeat purchases. Execution is so very important for any good idea.

Now we can extend this framework to all of the states to get a picture of the scaled-up revenue for all New England—a reasonable sales target for this venture over the course of its second year of business. Take a look at Figure 7.6. You can see the projections marching through Connecticut, New Hampshire, Maine, Rhode Island, and Vermont. The business comes to the range of $9 million per year in revenue, just in New England alone.

We are not quite done, however. The price points stated by the three customers in the field research were retail-shelf prices. As the manufacturer, HealthyWags is only going to enjoy 65% of that number. Therefore, the actual revenue projection is more in the range of $6 million a year.

If the business were to scale nationally, the revenue number is very attractive since the 5 million households in New England pale in comparison to more than 100 million households (well, really, it is not 100 million as not all households have a dog—only 45%). Now that's a business! And in the next chapter, we will learn how to project expenses and then operating profit from such a business.

Most important, in Figure 7.6 you can see the direct connection between the 50% top two-box score for Dog Mommy—those young females still without kids for whom their pet is the child, our target market—and the resulting revenue projections. That young female is the HealthyWags sweet spot, for sure. Mother Goose is No. 2; and any business from guys for all-natural healthy pet snacks is going to be incidental to the success of the business. And, most important, potential investors who know the pet industry are going to look at the bases for your revenue projections, couple these with the product concept, and see the sense in the numbers. *That is what you want for people reviewing your Venture Concept, your business model, and the revenue projections for a scaled-up business. The bottom line is that you have done your homework on the revenue projections. Investors will respect that.*

State	Households	Dog households	Customer Group	% of Dog Households	% Purchase Intent	% Dissatisfied	% Channel Penetration	$ Spend	Purchase Frequency	Amount
Massachusetts	2,000,000	900,000	Mother Goose	50%	25%	30%	33%	$5	12	$668,250
			Dog Mommy	40%	50%	40%	50%	$7	12	$3,024,000
			Pet Buddy	10%	10%	5%	10%	$3	6	$810
										$3,693,060
Connecticut	1,400,000	630,000	Mother Goose	50%	25%	30%	33%	$5	12	$467,775
			Dog Mommy	40%	50%	40%	50%	$7	12	$2,116,800
			Pet Buddy	10%	10%	5%	10%	$3	6	$567
										$2,585,142
New Hampshire	475,000	213,750	Mother Goose	50%	25%	30%	33%	$5	12	$158,709
			Dog Mommy	40%	50%	40%	50%	$7	12	$718,200
			Pet Buddy	10%	10%	5%	10%	$3	6	$192
										$877,102
Maine	500,000	225,000	Mother Goose	50%	25%	30%	33%	$5	12	$167,063
			Dog Mommy	40%	50%	40%	50%	$7	12	$756,000
			Pet Buddy	10%	10%	5%	10%	$3	6	$203
										$923,265
Rhode Island	400,000	180,000	Mother Goose	50%	25%	30%	33%	$5	12	$133,650
			Dog Mommy	40%	50%	40%	50%	$7	12	$604,800
			Pet Buddy	10%	10%	5%	10%	$3	6	$162
										$738,612
Vermont	240,000	108,000	Mother Goose	50%	25%	30%	33%	$5	12	$80,190
			Dog Mommy	40%	50%	40%	50%	$7	12	$362,880
			Pet Buddy	10%	10%	5%	10%	$3	6	$97
										$443,167
									Total	$9,260,348
									65%	$6,019,226

Figure 7.6 HealthyWags' Scaled-Up Revenue Projection

Spotlight: Revenue Estimations for High-Tech Ventures

The same process can be applied to high-tech ventures as well.

The Reality Check for Health Monitoring Systems also showed attractive revenue potential. The team identified several large home health agencies and assisted-living center chains for a series of discussions. From these talks, the team found the numbers of elderly managed by those target accounts, and received permission to visit with nursing staffs and talk to about 100 individuals. From these interviews, the team determined purchase intent, price levels, and the likely uptake for residents within a home health agency or assisted-living center year by year, which estimated 20% per year for 50% of residents who (as we mentioned earlier in the chapter) actually wanted to be monitored in the first place. That 50% came directly from the "top two-box score" in the purchase intent question for "Definitely buy" and "Likely to buy" on the survey.

From its calculations, the team quickly found that the venture represented a revenue opportunity approaching $100 million after five to seven years. The venture raised over $7 million in first-round (called Series A) venture capital. And just six months later, the team landed its first multimillion-dollar contract to install monitoring devices in the facilities of a large assisted-living provider.

Spotlight: Revenue Estimation for a B2B Venture

If you are having trouble getting to a sufficient number of prospective customers for a B2B venture, you can still estimate revenue. In this case, it is a combination of industry demographics, customer segmentation, and field research with potential customers to see what they are already paying for competitive products or services, and what they might be willing to pay for your new solutions.

We can use Sentillion, a case on the textbook Website (www.sagepub.com/meyer2e), as an example of estimating revenue for a B2B venture.

The company developed specialized security software that would allow a physician or nurse to sign-on once in the day, and be "provisioned" with access to all the clinical software systems to which he or she was authorized. Then a single patient's information was synchronized across all these software systems, and all transactions tracked and recorded on remote disks. This is called "patient context management." Together, these two features did a lot to eliminate medical errors in the hospital associated with ordering tests or drugs for the wrong patient. It also saved a lot of hassle for physicians who had been forced to remember up to a dozen different passwords. Certain federal regulations (HIPPA) were forcing hospitals to get a handle on these issues, and quickly.

The team first did a "top-down" sizing of the addressable market. There were 5,000 hospitals across the United States. While the entire market was "addressable"—every hospital would need to comply with the new patient information security standard—the team figured that only 20% were deemed sufficiently large—as measured by the number of beds in the hospital and the number of physicians—to be target customers in the first five years of the business. That gave an addressable market of 2,000 hospitals. Even though there was competition for security software in hospitals, there was as of yet no direct competition for "single sign-on" and "patient context management." The team thought that over time, it might get 25% if not more of those 2,000 hospitals as customers.

Field research showed two existing revenue models for software in healthcare: a rather large, upfront software license followed by annual maintenance fees or recurring subscription fees for each person using the software. Hospitals were already buying identity management products from vendors such as RSA on a per user license model. And many were spending millions on enterprise software for electronic medical records and clinical information systems. Based on all this, the team went into the field and talked to physicians, nursing staff, and hospital administrators. From this, the team decided on a two-fold revenue model: a per user fee for the physician access management, and a single enterprise license per year for patient context management across different software applications.

The revenue estimations were then determined as follows:

- 500 hospitals (25% of the addressable market of 2,000 hospitals out of 5,000 total hospitals, and this was just in the United States)

- An average of 500 physicians in each hospital (some large teaching hospitals had four times as many physicians)

- $100 per year as a subscription fee for single sign-on

- $25,000 per year for the hospital for patient context management

This led to a revenue estimation of $25 million for the subscription model (500 × 500 × $100) and another $13.75 million for enterprise licensing for patient context management for a scaled-up business, or a total of $37.5 million. Over the coming years, the company not only met but exceeded its projections. Microsoft acquired Sentillion for an undisclosed sum in 2010. At that time, multiples of revenue for acquisitions for healthcare IT were going at four to five times revenue.

Just as important in this discussion of revenue potential is how customers prefer to pay for a new product or service. This is different than price level relative to competition. For example, HealthyWags is a straightforward credit card or cash transaction. Health monitoring, on the hand, requires decisions about monthly subscription fees or an annual fee, the cost of additional or add-on services (such as aggregated medical reporting and trend tracking for compliance purposes), and implementation fees for healthcare agencies or assisted-living centers.

Validating business models for pure services ventures is equally important. One simple option is simply to charge for time and materials; another is a total project fee, some paid upfront and the rest at the completion of the project; another is a "retainer" for services that guarantees access and work for a certain period of time; and yet another is that if the service creates additional revenue or reduces operating expenses for the client, a percentage of the revenue or savings becomes the revenue type. This contingency fee is typically the most risk for an entrepreneur, but it can also be the quickest way to get to "yes" because it does not require upfront payment from the customer. And in some cases, it can generate far more money than time and materials charges. For example, the Reality Check for the MobileAppSolutions example might show customer preference for a contingency fee based on the number of people who actually use the new mobile app, or a contingency fee based on new sales enabled through couponing delivered through the app.

Learning customer preferences with respect to revenue type, frequency, and price level are your challenge in the Reality Check. Plus, finding out if customers are willing to buy more than just one type of product or service is precisely the type of finding that can make your financial projections sing in the next section of this book!

Reader Exercises

As in all our other chapters, we have exercises for you to perform. This set is perhaps the most important because it is a field-based validation of everything you have done so far: target customers and uses, product and service innovations, business model with all its different dimensions, and the positioning and branding of your products and services. It's time to do it!

Step 1: Create Your Venture Concept Dashboard

Prepare your dashboard, integrating your strategies and decisions from the successive chapters so far in this book. Use Figure 7.7 as a template. Keep it simple. Use bullet points and short statements. And include a picture or video to bring the target customer and the use case in the dashboard to life. If you have a sketch or a prototype of your new product or service, include that as well as a separate exhibit.

Step 2: Create Your Venture Concept Statement

Prepare your textual, one-paragraph statement of your Venture Concept. It should be two to three sentences. Use the examples in the chapter as a guide. You should be able to communicate the essence of your venture to potential customers in about 30 seconds. If you have a drawing or prototype of your product or service idea, include that as an attachment or "show and tell" with the survey. It will make your survey all the more meaningful for respondents. Practice on yourselves first and then on friends outside of your team. Did those friends understand the concept in 30 seconds? If not, keep reworking the text statement until outsiders can clearly understand it.

Target Industry Segment/ Niche

- Description
- Size and growth rate
- % of total industry
- Dynamics and disruptive changes

The Customer Insight

- Driving need and motivations for purchase

A Picture of the Target Customer

The Voice of the Customer

- Customer benefits & value
- Compelling quotes for customers that express their needs, frustrations, and primary attitudes that affect your solutions design.

Target Customers & Buyers

- Customer Groups
- Primary uses / occasion of use
- Resulting addressable market: % of target industry niche

Product / Service Strategy

- Products (Good, better, best)
- Services
- Other: 3rd party products & services

Business Model

- Revenue model: streams of revenue, and the type, frequency, and price-level for each stream
- R&D (if needed), production, and go-to-market models

Positioning & Branding

- Functional, performance play
- Emotional pitch
- Social connection

Figure 7.7   The Venture Concept Dashboard Template

Step 3: Create Your Discussion Guide/Survey

Using Figure 7.2 as a reference, prepare your own Field Research Discussion Guide. You should cover all the various bases that are shown in that figure. Once again, practice with teammates and friends outside your team.

Above all, try to keep your survey short and focused. Most customers won't give you much more than 10 minutes for the entire survey itself! But of course, if a consumer or manager in a company wants to talk your ear off about their issues and problems, set the survey aside for a while, listen hard, take notes, and then come back to the survey and wrap things up with a big thank you. Always say thank you to everyone. Let them know that their knowledge and insights are very important for your venture. If they want to stay involved with your project, take their contact information and be sure to follow up. These individuals will help you test your new products or services.

Step 4: Conduct the Field Research

Talk with at least 30 potential customers. Why that number? For the ethnography, we suggested between 5 and 10 for observation and in-depth interviewing. This survey has a different purpose. We are trying to validate hypotheses for all your prior customer research. It should be done faster with each customer, and you need more data to have confidence in the results. If you have distinctive customer groups, be sure to talk to people in each group (e.g., 3 customer groups, 10 each = 30). If you feel that you still have unanswered questions or a lack of clear insight on product/service requirements, positioning, channel, and price, find more prospective customers. The more, the better. We have had student teams talk to 80 or more prospective customers, and these usually produce the most solid, insightful Reality Checks.

If you are working a B2B market space, you must still try to talk to a sufficient number of managers and users in target corporate customers, perhaps six to eight companies and a couple dozen individuals across those companies. There is no substitute for customer feedback on a structured, systematic Reality Check at this point in time for developing your venture.

Step 5: Analyze and Report the Data

Now begin to analyze what you have discovered. Use Figure 7.4 (A–D) as a reference for organizing the data and interpreting the results. What do the data tell you? For example, are customers interested in the concept? Are they likely to buy? How much are they likely to spend on each purchase? Through which channel do they prefer to buy your product or service? If you gather a sufficient number of respondents, the data should really tell the strength of customers' preferences for these and other important areas.

Overall, do the Venture Concept you created in Chapter 3, the business model you designed in Chapter 4, the product/strategy you developed in Chapter 5, and the positioning approach you took in Chapter 6 collectively make sense given this direct feedback from prospective customers?

Step 6: Take a First Crack at Revenue Projections for a Scaled-Up Business

Now, using Figure 7.6 from our pet snack example as a guide, or the similar methods described in the Spotlight boxes for the high-tech ventures, develop an estimation of the total revenue possible for a scaled-up version of your venture that wins in the target industry niche, the specific customers and their uses, that together define your addressable market.

Remember, you are multiplying the percentage of customers who are "likely" and "very likely" to buy your products or services times their actual "spend" on those purchases. We have called this a "top two-box score," and using these top two levels as an indicator of purchase intent is a widely accepted practice in marketing.

Also, remember to factor all the dimensions of the revenue model: the type of revenue, the frequency of purchase, and the price level suggested by respondents. In addition to "purchase intent," you will need to consider the overall penetration into your target market for the channels that you are going to use. If you have 50% of a target market being top two-box-type customers, but your channels only reach half of them for particular geographic or industry considerations, then you must cut that 50% in half in order to have a reasonable ballpark estimate of revenue.

Also remember that these projections are for a scaled-up business of some reasonable size—and not the revenues that are likely to be achieved in the three to four years of the business.

Do those revenue projections look attractive to you? Is this the type of business in which you want to dedicate your time and effort over the coming five years? If a business shows the promise of strong revenue, you can usually figure out "all the rest" in terms of people, expenses, and capital. Without strong revenue potential, everything else is so *very, very hard*.

Step 7: Summarize and Report Your Reality Check

Use Figure 7.8 as a template to report your findings. Each part of that template might be a separate PowerPoint slide—but use your own judgment. You want to create a concise, focused presentation.

First, group the questions into their logical buckets and report percentages for the Likert-type scale questions, for example, the percentages in each of the 5-point or 3-point scales depending on the question in the Field Discussion Research Guide. Then use major bullet points for the open-ended questions.

Do you view yourself as a potential customer of this offering?	Validate primary and secondary customer groups.
What would be the different ways that you would want to use the (product or service)?	Identify primary and secondary uses/ occasions of use.
How satisfied are you with the current products/services you use now? Very dissatisfied Dissatisfied Neither Dis/Sat. Satisfied Very Satisfied	Report percentages. Look for top two box scores ; Very Dissatisfied, Dissatisfied.
Do you see the proposed offering as distinctive from the competitors? Not different Somewhat different Highly distinctive	Report percentages. Look for top box scores: Highly Distinctive
How much would you be willing to pay for this offering compared to current products/services you use now? A lot Less Less Same More A lot more	Report percentages. Look for top two box scores for More, A Lot more
How often do you buy similar products or services? (Open ended)	Report time frequency of purchase
How much do you spend each time you make a purchase? (Open ended, but looking for a dollar amount. Try to validate the structure of revenue—e.g. does the customer want to purchase, license, subscribe, try before buy.)	Report money spent range, with average Report preferred revenue type
Where is the best place to buy products/services such as this? (Open ended, but look for a specific preferred channel and ways in which they test or try products/ services)	List channels, with percentages Validates go-to-market model
Where do you get your information about products/services such as this? (Open ended. Look for preferred information sources.)	List sources, with percentages Validates build awareness model
How likely is it that you would be willing to buy this offering? Very unlikely Unlikely Neither Likely Very Likely	Report purchase intent, top two box score for Likely and Very Likely
What additional features do you think are important in a (product or service) such as this? (Open ended)	List this desired features, with most popular & percentages first
Add your estimation of revenues for a scaled up business (after 5-7 years, or the time cycle appropriate for your industry—biotech ventures will be much longer)	This should show your assumptions.
Final checklist on key aspects of your venture strategy and business model.	Check them off! Final slide.

Figure 7.8   Reporting the Results of the Reality Check

Next, include a single slide on your revenue estimate for a scaled-up business.

Last, step back and assess your findings. Make a short-hand list for yourself and put this all on a single summary slide. This should include:

- A target customer group that is frustrated with current solutions
- Strong purchase intent for your product or service idea and who find it different and distinctive
- Validation for your proposed revenue model
- Scaled-up revenue potential that is sufficiently large to justify your efforts
- Clear, existing channels to market (or if you plan on selling direct, evidence that this is what customers want and expect)
- Good ways to build awareness of your products and services for target customers

As in our other chapters, the completion of this work presents a fine opportunity for a checkpoint before proceeding forward. Accordingly, we encourage you to show your results to your trusted advisers, professors, and classmates. Have some fun with it! Nobody comes back from the field without a few surprises. Think of yourself as a highly adaptive, fleet-footed individual who can respond faster to new insights than any established competitor in the target market. And if you are not satisfied with your findings, do what many other entrepreneurs have done before you: Do a quick revision of your target customer and use, the product or services strategy, the business model, and the positioning—create a new Venture Concept statement and survey—and *go out in the field again for a new Reality Check*. We have seen teams turn tough situations completely around in a matter of weeks and go on to launch successful ventures. *You can do it, too*.

Well done! A market-tested venture strategy and business model are a lot more than most first-time entrepreneurs have in their arsenal before writing a business plan and making a pitch to investors. We hope you now realize the power of your industry and customer insights and how they set you apart from those many other would-be entrepreneurs who just "wing it" in writing a business plan. The results of all this hard work are going to pay off "big time" in Part II—which comes next. So take a deep breath. Give yourself a big pat on the back. Go celebrate for a bit with your teammates and your advisers. And then, get ready.

In Part II, we will learn how to translate your work to date into a set of realistic financial projections, a well-written business plan, and a compelling pitch for investors.

Visit the Student Study Site at **www.sagepub.com/meyer2e** to access the following resources:

- Web Resources
- Video Resources
- General Resources in Entrepreneurship

PART 2

Writing the Business Plan and Making the Pitch

Writing the Business Plan and Making the Pitch _____

Part II of this book is focused on translating the Venture Concept and business model into a professional, pragmatic set of financial projections; a business plan; and a winning pitch. Whereas Part I was about industry insight, customer insight, competitors, and creative solutions, Part II is focused on execution. Now is the time to drive to the goal of getting startup funding.

Before starting down this path, it is essential first to understand the types of investors who finance ventures, their preferences, and behaviors. Chapter 8 walks through the different types of investors, how they think, and how they act. The entrepreneur needs to decide which type of investment source is most appropriate for his or her venture. This increases the likelihood of success; it also helps spare you a lot of wasted time and energy. If you have a classic niche-focused software company that—if all goes according to plan—can reach $20 million in sales over five years, it makes no sense to go after venture capital firms that only touch companies where at least $50 million if not $100 million is the target for portfolio companies. Creating a $20 million a year, profitable business is a huge accomplishment; there are many other sources of startup and growth financing that will be interested in such ventures. Or, if you are not willing to give control over key management decisions to outside investors, then this too narrows down the field of suitable investors. The trick is to know who you are as an entrepreneur and as a venture, and then seek investors who fit you and your venture in terms of industry interest, the amount of money available to invest, and the degree of hands-on involvement required by the investor.

The bottom line is that raising money for a venture is a sales process. Like any sales process, being successful is that you know your customer (the investor), what you have to sell (your company), and that they are predisposed to buy (to invest in) what you have to sell (your company!). Every investor has experiences in certain industry segments and niches; you need to try to match these experiences with your own venture focus. *Your chances of not only raising money but also getting excellent operational advice along with the money will increase a hundredfold.*

With these insights, we then have you march forward to create four deliverables:

1. *A comprehensive set of financial projections for the revenues, expenses, cash flow, and assets of the proposed venture.* This is the focus of Chapter 9. We take financial projections seriously, and so should you. There is a lot of thinking that needs to go into modeling revenue and expenses for a venture. If you simply make up a bunch of numbers and use the power of spreadsheets to thoughtlessly replicate those numbers out into the future, investors will spot it in two seconds. Chapter 9 teaches the discipline of creating robust, pragmatic financial projections for new ventures. Fortunately, none of you are starting from scratch. Your work in Chapter 4 (Business Models) and Chapter 7 (The Reality Check) serves as the platform for creating a great set of financials.

2. *A team plan.* However, before writing the plan, you also need to consider the skills and balance of your venture team—not only for what needs to go into the team section of the business plan, *but to write the plan itself!* Chapter 10 addresses the organizational aspects of writing the business plan and launching a venture.

3. *A written business plan.* A focused business plan integrates market, customer, solution, sales, team, and finance all in a single, concise, and powerful document. Chapter 11 focuses on actually writing the business plan. Here, too, all of your work in Part I of the book is the platform for writing a powerful plan. That document needs to reflect a rifle-shot plan to hit your target market, creative yet pragmatic in its contents and appealing to investors. Throughout the chapter, we will provide the questions that are at the top of investors' minds as they read each particular part of the business plan.

4. An investor pitch. Chapter 12 teaches you how to develop a short, compelling pitch for investors. There is definitely an art to making a successful pitch. Part of it is to know who you are pitching to. But the other part is to tell the story of your target customer and your business in a way that is clear, convincing, and engaging. How do you take all the information you have gathered and learned about your industry sector, customer, competitors, products or services, and business model and present this in ten slides or less? How can you stand out among the dozens of entrepreneurs professional investors see each and every month? What questions are likely to be asked, and how can you best respond to them? These are the challenges tackled in this chapter, the last in our book.

So, while you have worked hard in the chapters leading up to this point, now it is time to redouble your efforts and work hard in a different way. You now have intimate knowledge of your industry, customers, and competitors. You talked with prospective customers and have direct feedback on your solutions for them as well as the key dimensions of your business model. Now is the time to shape all this knowledge into "the numbers, the team, the plan, and the pitch." This is the launchpad for your venture.

8

Financial Sources for Startups and Corporate Ventures

The Purpose of the Chapter

Family and friends, "angel" investors, and venture capital (VC) firms—these are the major sources of financiers for new ventures. Their investments tend to differ by the amount of the money provided, ranging from tens of thousands of dollars for family and friends, to hundreds of thousands of dollars for angel investors, to millions of dollars for venture capital firms and direct investments by existing corporations. And the structure of these investments—while primarily cash for equity in the venture—can vary by a range of specific criteria and financial instruments. This ranges from a startup loan from family members, to equity with warrants to buy more equity at a specified price, to debt with interest convertible to stock (under certain conditions) with full voting rights as if the debt amount were stock. But beyond these facts, there is a lot to learn about the style as well as the substance of venture finance. That is the purpose of this chapter.

It is also important that you keep venture finance in its proper context. Sure, most startup or corporate ventures need some startup capital to get up and running—and then to grow. However, don't let the importance of finding money distract you from the even greater importance of creating products and services that customers want to buy and from which you will develop a profitable business. As a venture capitalist said to us recently, "Entrepreneurs should worry more about their customers than me or my colleagues with the money. Find an initial set of customers, serve them well, and you will find that the venture money will come to you."

The Stages of Venture Development and the Relevant Funding Types _____

Whenever successful entrepreneurs raise a current round of investment capital, their thoughts are always on the need and timing for the next round of financing to support the next stage of growth.

It is useful to think of a new venture evolving through distinct stages of growth where the company raises investment capital to achieve milestones in a current or next stage of growth. Here are six pragmatic stages of growth for startup ventures:

Pre-Financing: To Develop Business Plans and Initial Prototypes

This is what happens before you actually launch your company, such as the activities you are performing in this very class.

To raise money from professional investors, you need a business plan and most often, a prototype, even if it is for a service. Investors want to "kick the tires," to see that the product or service innovation described in the plan has the strong likelihood of being real.

Developing your business plan might require certain expenditures to visit customers or tradeshows, or to get access to highly specific market research. And a convincing prototype is more than a sketch! If it is a new type food or consumer product, you need to develop recipes and samples. For a piece of software, you will need some screens and some basic operational functionality. And, as you recall from Chapter 4, you might have to spend some money filing a provisional patent for your innovation. While every company is different, that "nut" tends to come to $5,000 to $15,000.

We think of this amount as "gap funding." It is actually the pre–seed stage money you need to spend to get to the point where you can raise the $100,000 or more from angel or other investors in what is generally known as "seed funding," described next. For most students, gap funding is by no means a small amount of money. But more often than not, it is going to have to come out of your own pocket, or those of friends and family.[1]

_____

[1]Our own university offers a venture accelerator program run by the students themselves that provides "gap funding" and coaching to teams to get ready for angel and VC investment. Go to www .neu.edu/idea to learn more. The student leaders of that accelerator are helping students elsewhere to establish their own programs.

Seed Financing: To Develop Working Prototypes and Test With Live Customers

At this stage, the founding team already has its Venture Concept and is trying to build a prototype of its product, system, or service. The entrepreneur's innovation is under development—which includes doing the user research as well as any sort of initial technology implementation—but the venture is not fully operational. This is where you are now having successfully completed the first section of this book. The goal is to make your product or service function, package it correctly for marketing, and get it to market through appropriate channels.

Such "ventures" have usually been in the "concept" stage for a year or less, and the founders are seeking money to get to their first commercial launch. Most technology-focused firms try to get to an initial "alpha" test of their product or service in three to four months, to a more full-scale "beta" test in another two months, and then to complete all the technology and marketing collateral development in another three months. This makes it a full nine months to a year to bring an idea to market and start generating revenue.

Over the years, this early-stage financing has been called "zero-stage," "seed," or "startup." The most common term is "seed" financing.

This initial round of funding is usually limited to under $250,000 and is more typically under $100,000. When funds are less than $100,000, bootstrapping—using funds from the venture team itself, or from family or friends—is typical. Angel investors are also frequently involved. When the seed amount is over $250,000, entrepreneurs tend to search for angel investors who operate either individually or in "groups" in their local area. And there are some venture capital firms that invest in the seed stages of companies.

Why not venture capital firms as a primary source of money for this seed stage of financing? Over the years, venture capital and other forms of institutional money have drifted even further from the seed stage. Venture capital firms—which are formalized investments pools with general (or investing) partners and limited partners (institutional money)—have comprised only about 5% of seed investments in the United States! If you had a perception that it is venture capital firms that fund startups *at the beginning*, the data do not support that perception. Only a handful of companies get their first-round financing from venture capital firms. In the teaching cases on the textbook Website (www.sagepub.com/meyer2e), we do include cases of startups that raised significant capital from institutional venture capitalists (called institutional because their own money comes from large institutions such as pension plans, universities, and large corporations). But we also include others where the startup capital came from the entrepreneurs themselves, family and friends, and angel investors. Their path is most likely to be your path. VCs tend to enter the picture later, if at all.

TIP: RAISING EQUITY FINANCING IS A BALANCING ACT BETWEEN GROWTH CAPITAL AND FOUNDER CONTROL _____

Every startup has milestones with respect to developing, testing, formally launching, and expanding its products and services. These milestones take time, people, and most importantly, *money.* When the entrepreneur raises equity capital, he or she must typically provide stock (or the promise of future stock in an instrument known as convertible debt) to investors in return for their money, all based on the percentage of the total post-money valuation of the business at that point in time. A brand-new startup might have a valuation of $2 million; one with fully testing products or services ready for launch, $5 million; another, which has its first stream of revenue flowing from successful products or services, $10 million; and yet another, which already has $5 million in revenue and wants to expand its portfolio and grow geographically, $25 million.

(Continued)

(Continued)

The more milestones you can achieve with a specific round of investment, the less stock you have to forfeit to investors. Put another way, when you need to raise money for future milestones, it will be at a higher company valuation. Today, $1 million takes sacrifices of 20% of all equity; but that same $1 million six months down the road, if you created greater value for the company by completing products or generating more revenue from customers, might require only 10% of the equity, or even less. The less you have to give up, the more you, your cofounders, and your earliest investors get to keep.

On the other hand, if you need money to grow rapidly—or worse, just to survive—it is a mistake not to try to find the money and put it to productive use. Later on, when your business has reached a certain size, it would be a mistake not to also find a bank to provide you with a pool of working capital that is non-equity dilutive, particular if interest rates are low.

This makes the equity financing very much a balancing act between startup and successive stage growth requirements, founder equity, and retaining control over major decisions. You need to understand that balancing act, with all its implications. This is where trusted senior advisers can help guide your thinking. And we guarantee that each situation will be different. The one guiding rule is to accomplish as much as you can with every single dollar of invested capital, which means being focused in everything your company decides to do and working smart to get each and every task done.

Series A Financing: To Fully Develop Your Product, Develop a Channel, and Launch

Funding at this point in time is generally called "Series A" financing. At this stage, the product, system, or service has been tested with users and is in some form of pilot production. And in a significant percentage of cases, the product or service might be commercially available in some limited way. Usually, the venture has been in business for less than several years and, more typically, fewer than 12 months. These have been long, hard months where the founders have received minimal salaries, fought for an initial set of customers, and worked day and night to create a functional prototype. The venture may or may not be generating revenue. However, if you want to raise money from professional investors, even a little bit of revenue suggests that your Venture Concept is worth a customer's cash—always a good indicator to an outsider.

Today, the vast majority of Series A financing comes from angel investors—successful business people working alone or in groups who pony up between $250,000 and $1 million to turn teams and working prototypes into money-making machines. The typical scenario is that a venture will spend its first year to 18 months proving its Venture Concept with a first set of products or services with live paying customers, using money from the founders themselves as well as from family and friends. Then, if successful, the founders will raise $1 million or more from a group of four to six angel investors for about 15% to 30% of the equity. The time needed to raise such funds all depends on the company and the networking contacts of the founders. Our experience is that you need to count on at least three months to complete that round, with lots of meetings and countless phone calls, and all the while, keeping the operations of your fledgling venture on track.

Typically, angel investors not only want to make money but to build a self-sustaining business as well. They have a certain amount of patience for trying things, learning, and adjusting strategies for growth. This is a fundamental insight for working with angel investors: They want to provide mentor capital as well as investment capital. The importance of finding angel investors who have operating experience in your target industry cannot be understated. If at all possible, you need to find "smart money" as opposed to just anyone's money.

For that handful of ventures that receives Series A financing from venture capital firms or other institutional investors, the financing amount tends to be higher. Only about 15% to 20% of Series A financings in the United States come from venture capital firms. The Sentillion case on the textbook Website is fairly typical: The company received $2.7 million for its "A round." It took the better part of six months to secure this particular Series A financing. Moreover, this company was a corporate spin-off in which Hewlett-Packard had already funded the initial software development.

Series A financing from venture capital firms tends to be in the $2 million to $4 million range, and often the funding comes from multiple sources. Rather, the lead VC firm brings other firms into the round. This is called a "syndicated" investment. That means that you, as the entrepreneur, will have not just one partner of a VC firm on your Board of Directors, but two or three! Be prepared, because these are "active" investors and the clock is always ticking. Building a category-leading company is the clear motivation; but achieving "exit"—one way or another— is clearly another. If you think that different VCs in a syndicated round will always agree on every important matter, you are mistaken. They can argue and be disruptive to moving forward just like any other set of individuals. That is why it is also important to try to find a group of VCs who have worked successfully together in prior investments and made good money for all concerned.

In addition to allocating invested capital in R&D and market launch, Series A investors—be they angels or venture capital firm partners—focus on building out the management team of a fledgling company. It is typically assumed that the venture has the technology smarts needed to be an excellent company—that is one of the foundations for the investment. However, it just as typically is assumed that the founding team does not have the marketing or operations expertise needed to scale up a business in a competitive marketplace. Be prepared for "suggestions" to augment the capabilities of your management team with some experienced managers.

Series B Financing: To Expand Rapidly Into the Target Industry Niche

This is generally called "Series B" investment. Sometimes, a follow-on Series C investment is made as well—all by the same core group of institutional investors plus new investors.

By this point in time, the company is two to four years old, has had a successful launch of its products or services, has an excellent management team, and is ready to scale. By *scale*, we mean that the company is set to increase production, engage in serious branding activities, expand market reach both regionally and globally, and substantially beef up its customer services and support. For technology-intensive ventures, next-generation R&D for new products and services will also be on the table for investment consideration—as might be a select acquisition or two to buy new technology. Moreover, not only has the company expanded its revenue, but it has also achieved its first operating profit. In short, with proper investment, the company has the plan and team in place to become a leading global brand.

Series B financing is typically a multimillion-dollar affair. Early angel investors may participate in this next round by having clauses in their investment agreements that guarantee the right to purchase additional shares at an attractive price. However, the bulk of a Series B financing comes from venture capital firms. Sentillion, to continue the example from above, received $9 million in its Series B financing within three years of startup. The company channeled this money into all key parts of the business: It expanded the product portfolio through R&D, built a strong North American sales program, and beefed up its field integration services for customers.

Recent data show that about 40% of all venture capital firm investment is made at this stage of growth.

Series C Financing: To Consolidate Market Leadership and Make Selective Acquisitions

This is generally referred to as "Series C" financing. In past years, entrepreneurs often referred to this as "mezzanine" financing, the step that gets the company to an initial public offering. Forty percent of all venture capital firm investment is channeled to this stage as well.

These later-stage investments are by venture capital firms with large funds to invest (sometimes in excess of a billion dollars to put to work!) or private equity investment firms such as Bain Capital. These later-stage investments tend to start at $20 million and can reach far higher. The goal here is to become the market leader in a specific category. Sentillion, for example, received close to $20 million in a Series C investment about four years after startup. All told, the company raised approximately $30 million in investment capital before Microsoft acquired it for many times that amount in 2010. If these numbers seem large to the reader, know that they do so to anyone, including most investors! The founder of Sentillion started off as a senior-level programmer in Hewlett-Packard but quickly learned the affairs of business and venture investment. He also had the common sense to ask trusted advisers the hows and whys of writing a business plan, pitching to early investors, and avoiding the most restrictive and potentially penalizing "covenants" in typical VC deals. *He knew what he didn't know and quickly took steps to find people to help him learn the answers.* You can watch a video of Rob Seliger on the textbook Website to see how much he matured from technology to business person by the time he was about to sell his company about a decade after startup.

Series C investments can also come in the form of direct investment from major corporations. For example, one of your authors cofounded a software company (real-time development environments for process control applications). That company received a $10 million "strategic" investment from Microsoft in 2000, after having received its Series A and B financing from venture capital firms.[2]

Exit: Getting Acquired or Doing an IPO

Very few ventures achieve an initial public offering of company stock—the ultimate exit investors hope for because of the enormous (we have seen more than 100 times) returns enjoyed with such events. Far more frequent is that "exit" that is achieved by being acquired by a larger corporation. These acquisitions are called "mergers and acquisitions" because often the acquisition is structured as a merger so that the buying company can use its stock for the transaction and investors can take advantage of certain tax regulations to reduce tax liability.

Courtesy of Thomson Reuters and the National Venture Capital Association, Figure 8.1 shows the reality for entrepreneurs and investors seeking an initial public offering (IPO). These data are for United States–based startups. For a few years, the situation for IPOs was nothing short of brutal. The number of IPOs in the United States dropped from a high of 84 in 2004 to a mere 6 in 2008, and 12 in 2009. In 2010, things truly started looking up again. This is denoted by the circled numbers in Figure 8.1. There were 74 IPOs recorded that year, and 53 in 2011. While not shown on the chart, there were 19 IPOs recorded in the United States alone in the first quarter of 2012. (To see the latest data, go to www.nvca.org and then go into the For Policymakers menu area.)

This turnaround in the IPO situation is a very big deal for investors because company valuations for IPOs are typically much greater than for exits through the acquisition route. It's not

---

[2]Look up *Ardence* in Wikipedia. Ardence started off as VenturCom and received investment from Microsoft in July 2000, which also licensed the software—a real-time module for embedded applications software development. Ardence was later acquired by Citrix, and then parts of the technology were spun out again as a new company called IntervalZero.

easy building a company, but it has become a lot easier cashing in for investors once a market-leading company has been created.

In contrast, exits achieved through mergers and acquisitions—the big company buying a small company—have remained fairly constant at about 350 deals per year. Even in the difficult 2009 time frame, 271 such deals occurred. In 2010, activity heated up to 445 reported exits of this type, and to 467 in 2011.

Figure 8.1 also shows why investors would prefer an IPO if that type of exit can be achieved. Even if the average deal size for acquisitions and IPOs are roughly the same for any given year, the valuation of each type of company, and hence the value of investors' stock-holders, is entirely different. The reason is that the deal size for an IPO is only for that percentage of the total company stock represented by that placed into the public offering. That percentage is typically between 10% and 20% of the total company stock. See a deal size for an M&A deal of $100 million and that is the total company valuation. If you own 30% of that stock, your equity is worth $30 million. In contrast, in a deal size of $100 million for an IPO, your 30% of company stock is worth $300 million minus the dilution that the newly issued stock for the IPO represents.

For example, Facebook IPO'd by offering about 10% of its stock, or 180 million shares, at $38 a share on May 18, 2012, producing a market capitalization of $104 billion. The founder, Mark Zuckerberg, saw his net worth skyrocket to $19,136.9 billion by holding a 28.1% equity stake in the company. (That net worth comes by multiplying his 28.1% stake, which is 503.6 million shares, times the IPO price of $38 per share. The share price had dropped to $28 per share by the end of the month, and to under $20 per share a few months later.) He also offered 30 million of his own shares to cover his tax liability from the IPO, but he also retained the right to purchase an additional 120 million shares of the company at any point in the future. And, at the time of this writing, he still controls 57% of the voting power through his remaining stock and

		Mergers and Acquisitions Exits				IPO Exits	
Year	Total M&A Deals	M&A Deals With Disclosed Values	*Total Disclosed M&A Value ($M)	*Average M&A Deal Size ($M)	**Number of IPO's	Total Offer Amount ($M)	Average IPO Offer Amount ($M)
2004	349	188	16,043.8	85.3	94	10,481.6	111.5
2005	350	163	17,324.7	106.3	57	4,482.4	78.6
2006	377	164	19,034.8	116.1	57	5,117.1	89.8
2007	379	168	29,460.0	175.4	86	10,326.3	120.1
2008	351	119	13,775.4	115.8	6	470.2	78.4
2009	271	91	13,531.1	148.7	12	1,642.1	136.8
2010	445	129	18,404.5	148.7	74	7,432.5	180.4
2011	467	166	24,081.8	145.1	53	9,921.9	187.2

Figure 8.1   The Market for Acquisitions and IPOs in the United States From 2004 to 2011

Source: National Venture Capital Association 2009 Yearbook, Thomson Reuters, 2009.

*Only accounts for deals with disclosed values.

**Includes all companies with at least one U.S. VC investor that trades on U.S. exchanges, regardless of domicile.

other shares promised by current shareholders to vote along with his decisions.[3] All the promise that Facebook offered for the recovery of the IPO market for venture capitalists seems to have worked in the reverse.

If you return to Figure 8.1, you can see roughly comparable amounts for average M&A deal size and average IPO offer amount. However, the *total valuation of the IPO exit is about nine times greater than for the M&A exit, after factoring in the ballpark 10% dilution of pre-IPO shareholders for an IPO.* Not bad, and you can see why venture capitalists in particular are delighted that the IPO market seems to be bouncing back.

IPOs still remain about 10% of all exits achieved by startup companies. In contrast, industry leaders such as IBM, Oracle, Microsoft, GE, Google, and Facebook are regularly acquiring small technology ventures to add spice and breadth to their respective portfolios. Sometimes these acquisitions are just to gain access to a technology; at other times it is to gain access to new markets or a new customer group, or to enter into a new use or application space.

Now turn to Figure 8.2. It shows the financial performance of a venture that is often attractive to the corporate buyer. The figure comes from yet another one of the teaching cases on the textbook Website: Generate, Inc.

Here, the twin brothers, each with extensive industry experience, started an information services company. The venture targeted professional sales forces by gaining access to thousands of real-time news feeds and filtering them to present information and business contacts simply and effectively, customized for individual preferences. The brothers invested $200,000 of their own money as "seed" capital, hired a small team to build a prototype, and did a pilot launch with several large customers. These initial customers served as good reference accounts later on. For the Series A to grow the business, they then secured $3 million as a strategic investment from the venture's largest news source suppliers. As the case describes, this money came at a higher company valuation than two other VC deals that the founders were also able to bring to the table, and there were no restrictive covenants demanded by the corporate strategic investor. This left the founders with majority ownership of the company even after the Series A was completed, as well as more freedom to operate. After tremendous execution of their business plan, the brothers developed a marketing partnership with Dow Jones. From Figure 8.2, you can see that the company had reached $10 million in annual sales with attractive gross margins. And it had achieved a small operating profit, which in most situations is essential for any sort of exit. Three years after startup, Dow Jones acquired the business to expand its own information services portfolio for an amount in excess of $50 million.

These examples collectively show a model for success for any entrepreneur to consider as he or she considers professional or corporate investors:

1. Seed a distinctive Venture Concept with your own savings

2. Build the prototype and get your first customers

3. Raise a Series A at the best valuation you can achieve from angels, VCs, or strategic investors

4. Build a profit-generating company with strong sales growth over the course of three or four years, and if necessary, raise Series B and C capital to fund that growth

5. Achieve an exit for you and your investors, either by M&A or IPO

---

[3]One of Zuckerberg's early venture capitalists, James Breyer, will be offering about 38 million shares in the IPO, valued at more than $13 billion. These obviously are enormous numbers and made Facebook one of the largest IPOs in terms of market capitalization in history. There were a number of problems with the IPO, not the least of which was that the lead underwriter informed some favored clients before the IPO that it was cutting its revenue estimates for Facebook. All this led to confusion and a stock price drop in the weeks following the IPO.

	Beta - 2005	2006	2007	2008
New Customers	2	30	49	147
Recurring Customers		2	34	83
Total Customers	2	32	83	230
Average Revenue per Customer	$17,000	$50,000	$50,000	$50,000
Recurring bookings		28,900	1,066,831	3,020,568
New bookings	34,000	1,571,000	3,034,043	8,458,897
Total bookings	34,000	1,599,900	4,100,874	11,479,465
Revenue	$4,250	$1,001,844	$3,401,870	$10,102,559
COS	$59,250	$978,417	$1,185,000	$4,649,710
GM	(55,000)	23,427	2,216,870	5,452,849
%	−1294%	2%	65%	54%
OpEx	613,093	1,552,233	3,100,438	4,903,550
Op Inc +/−	(668,093)	(1,528,806)	(883,568)	549,299
Adjustments for working capital		(30,055)	(102,056)	(303,077)
Ending cash	$3,774,144	$2,215,283	$1,229,659	$1,475,881
Headcount	11	33	73	91
FTE	5	27	55	81

Figure 8.2 Generate, Inc.: Financial Performance on the Road to Exit: A B2B Information Services Venture

Data reproduced with permissions from Thomas Aley.

You don't have to plan to sell your company or do an IPO in all situations. We know many entrepreneurs who are self-funded and who have built considerable businesses that generate large amounts of cash, making the founders millionaires many times over. However, if you take on professional investors, they are going to require an exit of one form or another down the road. That's the reality. If you are not able to deliver a good exit in a reasonable amount of time, life will be anything but easy for all concerned. So beware: Raising money sounds "cool," but rarely does it come without high expectations, often restrictive terms, and a marriage between entrepreneur and investors that is not always made in heaven.

Equity Versus Debt Financing

There are many sources of capital available for your new venture. At the highest level, there are two types of financing: equity and debt financing.

Of course, there is also a third type of investment—your own "sweat equity." This means working for no money during the startup period. Nearly all ventures have their share of that!

Equity capital is the investment made by an individual, partnership, or corporation in return for some form of ownership, typically through the purchase of stock at a predetermined price per share based on the pre-money valuation of the company. When a company is formed, a certain numbers of shares, say a million, are created; some are issued to founders and investors, and others are held in abeyance for employee stock option plans or for future rounds of financing. The Board of Directors of a company can also decide to issue more shares for future rounds of financing, in which case current shareholders are diluted by the percentage that the new shares represent of the new total number of shares.

There are two classes of stock that concern investors: preferred and common. Preferred has special rights over common stock. When a company goes bankrupt and all assets are liquidated, debt holders get paid first, preferred shareholders next, and only then do common shareholders receive money—by which time is little or nothing. Or, if the company is going great guns and decides to issue dividends by choice or by the terms of the earlier funding deals, the preferred shareholders get paid before common shareholders. Most often, dividends for preferred shares are also structured as regular payments, whereas dividends for common stock are decided by the Board during its meetings. The preferred shares sit somewhere in between common stock and debt instruments in terms of rights in liquidation and dividend payments. And that is why most professional investors insist on preferred shares in early-stage companies.

It is also common in early-stage financings to have warrants issued to buy even more stock at a future date. The price of the stock for those warrants is set to be advantageous relative to what the stock should be worth if the business met its goals and were to raise another round of money. For example, a startup gets valued at $3 million with a stock price of $5 a share for a group of angel investors putting in $500,000. The team gets its product to market, generates $2 million in sales, and wishes to raise another $3 million to build R&D and a sales force. The valuation is set at $12 million, and the price per share for this next round increases to $20 a share. A venture capital firm is very interested in doing the deal. But factored into the valuation are warrants that allow the original angel investors to the equivalent of 10% more of the company at $10 a share, or an effective valuation of $10 million. The VCs push back for a lower valuation for themselves as well—and the negotiation begins!

Debt capital is money that an entrepreneur tries to borrow for working capital to pay for salaries and other operating expenses or to purchase equipment needed for operations. The startup must repay the principal with interest over a specific period of time. As a general rule, debt capital does not include any ownership interest in the venture unless you are dealing with particularly avaricious investors who try to structure your deal as debt with principle and interest payments that are also convertible to equity upon certain conditions—such as an exit event.

There are many types of debt instruments used by entrepreneurs to fund startups: personal credit card debt, a second mortgage, or in some rare instances, a working capital line of credit from a commercial bank. However, without collateral in a startup, or receivables, it is hard to secure a line of credit for a new company. Revenue and assets need to be accumulated to secure such a loan—*particularly these days, when credit for small business is tight*. Doing a seed financing on a personal credit card or a second mortgage on personal property is very common—and, obviously, carries considerable personal risk! The advantage of debt financing is that the entrepreneur keeps his or her precious stock. The disadvantage of debt, however, is that startups are always short of cash. With debt, you most often have to meet your payments whether or not the business is making money. Interest and principal payments are a cash drain on the business.

Also read about the convertible notes financing instrument in the Tip Box. Angel investors prefer these debt instruments for early-stage investments for a number of reasons: simplicity, cost, speed, and the ability to put off the valuation decision to a point in time when the company has products or services and some actual customers. It's something definitely to consider for your own seed investment, and we think it should also be used with friends and family as well as angel investors. It keeps things clean and clear.

TIP: TERM SHEETS

When you raise money for a venture, either you or your investors will have to prepare and then negotiate a term sheet. A term sheet spells out all the specifics of the deal. There are two standard term sheets on our textbook Website. One is for convertible debt, a preferred instrument for seed or early-stage investing by angels. The second is a classic Series A institutional venture capital term sheet, provided courtesy of the National Venture Capital Association.

A *convertible debt* term sheet is an instrument now commonly used for angel investments. Sometimes it is called a *bridge loan,* bridging the venture to the next round of financing. The investor is issued a note, at a certain interest rate, which is convertible into stock (common or preferred) based on certain events, such as a next round of financing or an exit. That conversion price is set at a discount—often 15% to 20%—to the price per share of the valuation of the company at the time of that next event. This effectively puts off the company valuation decision—the price per share—until a later point in time when the company has real products or services, and real revenue, which serves as the basis for a pragmatic valuation. Both the entrepreneur and the investor can feel more comfortable about company valuation. And if things don't work out and the venture fails, the debt holder gets first in line in terms of dissolving the company's assets. And with the debt instrument, there can also be Board participation rights, even though the investor does not yet formally own stock; and yet, unlike a lot of stock deals, the entrepreneur typically remains in control of the Board.

Perhaps just as important, convertible debt agreements tend to be three to six pages long, easy to follow, and cost between $5k to $10k to execute. This is compared to the stock investment term sheets of venture capitalists, which are lengthy documents, having all sorts of contentious terms and conditions, and cost upwards of $50k in legal fees. If you are raising under $250,000, that's a big chunk of cash to spend on attorneys! All this makes raising money from angels under a convertible note relatively fast—once you have found the right angel, of course.

Also included in the textbook Website is a term sheet for Series A financing that uses "preferred shares." Such deals are typically loaded with terms and conditions, otherwise known as "covenants." In addition to the "pre-money" valuation contained in the term sheet (the total value of the company before investment), there will also be covenants. These might include:

Participating preferred stock. The founders own common shares. VCs often want preferred stock. This type of security has numerous protections that a VC can use to limit its loss in the event of company failure or poor performance. The preferred stock usually has full voting rights in its pro-rata participation in all equity issued by the company. It also comes with liquidation preferences that are described next. It was also structured as "participating preferred stock," which means that upon any liquidation event, the preferred stock would convert immediately to common stock to participate pro-rata in the distribution of the company assets.

Liquidation preferences. These are common in VC term sheets, with a broad definition of "liquidation," which includes an acquisition, bankruptcy, and the sale of a company's assets. The purpose is that the VC wants to get its money *ahead* of

(Continued)

(Continued)

the founders. This is usually structured as a 1 times liquidation preference with terms attached, but sometimes you might see a 1.5 times liquidation preference. If the company is liquidated (is acquired or goes into bankruptcy), the VC gets all of its investment back first, and then gets its pro-rata share of the remaining proceeds. If this sounds something like "double dipping," it pretty much is.

Dividends. Investors will sometimes insist on dividends on their preferred stock in the amount of 5% or so on their investment. This can be a cash drain on the business, or if the company is not yet cash positive, the dividend amount is paid in additional preferred shares.

Reverse vesting. The VC can also insist that the founders put all their shares into the employee option pool, and then have their pro-rata amounts vest over a period of three years. This effectively causes the founders to immediately lose control of the company, even though a Series A investor might only own a minority percentage of all shares. The investor can then decide to replace the board, ask the founders to leave, and use the option pool to hire new management. You might think this never happens; well, but it does.

Reserved stock. Investors might also request that the employee stock option pool (often 10% of all outstanding shares) be set aside pre-money, which means that it comes from the founders' stock and therefore dilutes them only. This both dilutes the founders' stock and has implications for board control.

Preemptive rights and "take me along" clauses. These are clauses that include right of first refusal for current investors to buy more stock in any subsequent financing event (other than exit) in order to preserve current equity share. For example, if the founders wish to sell some of their stock to another party, they also have to sell the same percentage to the current investors unless approved otherwise. This prevents the founders from using their own stock to bring in new investors to challenge the strategy and control of current investors.

Ratchet clauses. If the price of the stock drops below the Series A price per share in any subsequent round of financing, the Series A investors are automatically issued additional participatory preferred shares in the amount that would preserve their current ownership. That means that the newly issued stock for a downround first comes out of the founders' collective hides. This is effectively an antidilution clause.

Approval over cash disbursements. Regardless of Board membership, the investor receives approval/veto rights on single expenditures over a fixed amount, often set at $100,000.

The covenants are obviously not to be taken lightly! You must enter the negotiation with experienced mentors and attorneys who have done such deals before. Otherwise, you will pay dearly down the road. And whatever you do, walk away from the reverse vesting clause. Do not let any investor make you reissue all your own stock back as stock options to be vested over three or so years. It's just not worth it, and it's not a good signal of intent. If the investor gets control of your Board of Directors, you and your team can be shown the door, and all your hard-earned stock—now not yet vested—will no longer be yours! These are some of the realities of working with institutional venture capital. If you need it, get it; but when you get it, know fully well the terms and conditions—for example, your new life—that come with the money.

Remember that at the end of the day, your fortune may well be made largely on the value of the company in the form of equity—not your salary. The value of this equity will be in the stock or cash received from an acquisition, in the residual value of your holdings in an IPO, or in the pro-rata share of profits (without corporate taxation) that you are entitled to receive from a Subchapter S Corporation or a Limited Liability Company. Whatever the method, *your venture's equity should be near and dear to your heart.* You want to keep as much as possible for the founding team, knowing in advance that you will not be able to keep all of it if you need to finance growth. And whether it is equity or debt financing, raising significant amounts of money is difficult to do. As the saying goes, there are only two ways to raise money: the hard way and the very hard way.

Sources of Venture Financing _____

While there are many different sources of financing for startups, the ones that are most common are:

- Your own savings, the most uncomplicated of all forms of seed financing!
- Family and friends, who typically also provide seed financing
- Angel investors, who invest their own money primarily for seed rounds and also often participate in legitimate Series A financings
- Venture capital firms, which invest other institutions' money primarily into Series A, B, and C rounds. Increasingly, VC firms are focused on Series B and C rounds—putting more money to work at lesser risk relative to a brand-new startup. We think of VC firms as "institutional" investors because they draw their funds from institutional sources: pension funds, large corporations, and other investment companies.
- Direct strategic investment from large corporations. These may be suppliers for your venture, channel owners, large customers, or technology leaders who see synergy and leverage in your venture. This is an often overlooked source of Series A, B, and C financing. Experience suggests that valuations tend to be higher and covenants in the term sheets less restrictive in direct strategic investment than in traditional venture capital deals.

There are a number of other sources of financing for ventures as well. These include commercial banks, government programs that either provide direct research grants to technology companies or back commercial loans for any type of company, leasing companies, and direct investments by pension funds. Universities are also getting into the seed financing game, often giving up to $100,000 entirely as a grant to technology-intensive ventures as well as rent-free or near-rent-free space at adjacent incubators.

The most significant source of seed or early-stage financing for all new ventures, regardless of category, is a founder's personal savings. That means *your own money, as opposed to someone else's money.* Seventy percent of entrepreneurs had used personal savings as a main source of funding for their first businesses, more than four times the number for any other form of startup financing. Friends and family and bank loans were a source of funding for around 13% to 16% of startups. While very popular in the entrepreneurial press as a source of startup capital, the fact remains that angel investments played a small role in the seed stage funding: Just 9% of startups received early capital from angel sources. The same holds for venture capital firms: Just 11% of startups received venture capital. [4]

_____

[4]Thomson Reuters. (2012). National Venture Capital Association, MoneyTree Report.

As you might expect, the picture is a little different for serial entrepreneurs and their subsequent startups. More than half of the entrepreneurs still relied on their personal savings. But the proportion of entrepreneurs who obtain angel and venture funding increases with each subsequent business launch by the entrepreneur. A study of serial entrepreneurs found that 22% received private/angel financing and 26% received venture capital for their latest startup. Friends and family provided funding for 16%, and banks provided funding for 16% of the respondents' most recent startups. Direct strategic corporate investments comprised 7% of early-stage financing. Keep these statistics in mind as we discuss the various sources and types of venture funding.

Let's dig a little deeper into these investor types—their mindsets, motivations, and expectations for venture investing.

Founder Self-Financing

A common rule of thumb is to have enough cash saved to cover at least six months of basic personal living expenses before starting a business. It takes time for any business to reach breakeven and then to be able to provide consistent cash flow to pay the founding entrepreneurs and their initial staff. Entrepreneurs learn quickly that it takes some money to make money. Sadly, many entrepreneurs are forced to give up a new business because they simply run out of cash for basic operating expenses.

When self-financing, the entrepreneur may draw upon any number of potential sources of personal funds, including the following:

Personal cash. Entrepreneurs who have personal net worth often worth draw on personal assets to support a new venture. These funds are in invested directly into the business and comprise the startup capital or equity for the venture. Apart from the considerable "sweat equity" that you are investing in doing the work for Parts I and II of this book—do not undervalue the importance of this work for any venture!—you might also have the ability to invest the $10,000 to$15,000 needed to build your first prototype, or get some business cards, stationary, and marketing collateral needed to start providing your first professional services. Of course, not all businesses are amenable to low capital "alpha" and "beta" tests, and you've got to pay rent or the mortgage, and eat once in a while as well. Other common uses of personal cash invested in the business include buying equipment, inventory, and other startup expenses. Personal cash may also be used as a backup source of cash for personal needs for those times when a business is not able to pay the entrepreneur a salary.

Other personal assets. Often a business grows out of a part-time endeavor, personal interest, or hobby. In such cases, the entrepreneur already will have purchased tools and other equipment to support this interest or hobby. This equipment became an asset of the business and was treated as part of their equity contribution as shareholders of the business. Other common assets that are brought into a business include computers, cell phones, and office furniture.

Unsecured personal credit. A new venture is not likely to be able to secure credit financing. Many entrepreneurs will use personal credit cards or unsecured personal lines of credit to help finance a business startup. When personal credit is used for the business, it is essential to track personal versus business transactions very carefully to ensure clean record keeping. If an entrepreneur plans to use a personal credit card for the startup, it is preferable to get a separate credit card for the business transactions. Some credit card companies explicitly prohibit the use of personal credit cards for business purposes.[5]

---

[5]Wadhwa, V., Aggarwal, R., Holly, K., & Salkever, A. (2009, November). *The Anatomy of an Entrepreneur.* Kansas City, MO: Ewing Marion Kauffman Foundation. Entrepreneurs should carefully read the terms of use in the credit card contract for any personal credit card being considered for use in the business.

TIP: CASH FLOW AND THE NEW COLLEGE GRADUATE AS ENTREPRENEUR

Let's say that you have an excellent business plan and have received some initial funding from your school's business plan competition. Moreover, in your senior year, you have developed the first version of the product or service and have launched your company to gain initial paying customers. It is all very exciting.

Now it is time to graduate. You and your partners are on your own. Your parents are "done" supporting you. And there is not enough cash flow for you and your partners to live. So what do you do? This is the type of situation that countless undergraduate entrepreneurs face each and every year.

First, you need to anticipate the cash flow crisis six months before it happens. This is the time that you will need to find angel investors and get the working capital you need.

Second, you also need to think about how to cut down your living expenses. Living rich while in college—well, those days are over for a while. Look for the cheapest rent; use Skype; get rid of that car if you are living in the city. Minimize all of your personal and business operating expenses. Negotiate for favorable payment terms from suppliers. Think about everything you do from a cash flow basis—as opposed to the glorious P&L that won you a business plan competition.

Third, give it your best shot for a year of hard work and tight living. Then step back and reassess. If the business is not generating the cash you need to continue forward and you have not been able to raise angel investment using the methods in this chapter and the ones to follow, then the business may not be viable. It might be time to call it a wonderful learning experiment. Talk to your business mentors. Get their thoughts. If you decide to call it a day, don't give up on your dreams. Instead, work just as hard to get a job with an industry leader in your target industry. Learn the ropes, and if possible, get a customer-facing or product/service development job as opposed to an administrative job. Save every penny you can. And with great determination, set the goal to relaunch a better version of your venture three or four years down the road, but this time with a lot more experience and a bigger cash cushion under your belt. Many, if not most, entrepreneurs do not succeed the first time they start a business; but with that dispositional optimism we described in the first chapter of this book, they pick themselves up off the floor and determine a personal plan to move forward.

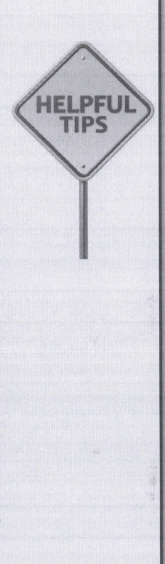

Second mortgage on property. For entrepreneurs who have built up equity in real estate, securing a second mortgage on a home or other property may be a way to fund a business startup through a bank loan. It is important to understand that this will be treated as a personal loan by the bank. The entrepreneur will be personally liable for the repayment of the loan independently of the success or failure of the business.

Pledging other personal assets. The entrepreneur also may be able to obtain a loan for the business by pledging personal assets that are easily liquidated and have verifiable market value, such as publicly traded stock or government bonds. Again, this loan will likely be considered a personal loan by the bank and not a direct loan to the business.

Working a second job. During the startup of a new business, many entrepreneurs continue to work their "day jobs" to support their personal expenses. If the new venture requires the entrepreneur to work during the daytime hours, the entrepreneur may pick up an evening job. If the business hours of the new venture are flexible, the entrepreneur may be able to keep a daytime job to make ends meet. A significant challenge is deciding when to phase out of the second job and rely fully on the proceeds of the transition. However, in reality the entrepreneur often faces a difficult, potentially risky decision of when to leap into a full-time, exclusive commitment to the new business.

There are also some other novel ways that you can employ to self-fund your new venture. For those students who are older (quite a bit older!), one source of capital can include your 401(k) retirement plan. Typically, early withdrawals of 401(k) funds face tax penalties. However, there are two ways entrepreneurs can use a 401(k) from a prior employer to fund their startup. First, entrepreneurs can convert those funds to stock in their company. This type of conversion requires a specialist to help establish what is called a Rollover as Business Startup (ROBS) by the IRS. Alternatively, entrepreneurs can take their 401(k) from their existing employer, move the funds to a 401(k) in their new firm, and then take out a traditional loan against that new plan. Such loans are limited to $50,000 and must be repaid within five years. Either approach can be risky, because failure means the loss of retirement money. However, in tough times, the access to these funds to start a business can be critical.[6]

You would be surprised at how many individuals become entrepreneurs as a second career upon retiring from a major corporation. This group of "older entrepreneurs" has been chomping at the bit for 20 years to start their own businesses, but with kids in college and mortgages to pay, they put up with the corporate politics, got the paycheck, and lived up to their responsibilities. An early buy-out/retirement plan is just the excuse needed to do what they have always wanted to do. Armed with industry contacts and personal financial resources, these seasoned professionals can be powerful entrepreneurs. And we have seen many younger entrepreneurs team up with older individuals on certain types of businesses for great effect—particularly businesses that require B2B or industrial selling.

Some forms of self-financing can be problematic. Another form of sweat equity in startups goes under the label of "deferred compensation." Without cash from customers, entrepreneurs can choose to pay themselves little or nothing but enter what they consider a fair salary as a deferred liability on the Balance Sheet. They then expect to get that deferred salary redeemed upon successful financing. Unfortunately, most angels and venture capitalists will insist on removing that liability as a precondition for funding. They simply do not want to see their money invested in yesterday's decisions.

Friends and Family

Another classic, important source of startup capital is friends and family. These are often gathered from the entrepreneur's individual and professional support network. It is useful to remember that friends and family have consistently been the most important source of startup capital for most types of entrepreneurial ventures, even technology-intensive ones. Walt Disney, for example, got started with funds from friends and family. This funding is secured most often at the "gap" or seed funding stage. You are known to the funding source, a trusted entity, and they wish you well. On the upside, it is unlikely that there will be any sort of battle over the pre-money valuation. Set a fair value. For a well-reasoned idea—complemented by some type of Reality Check, as described in Chapter 7, a well-executed business plan and perhaps a prototype of some sort—that valuation will typically be in the range of $1 million to $2 million. If you raise $100,000, the private investors get between 5% to 10% of your company. That is fair, particularly if your venture is grounded without the money.

Or better yet, use the convertible debt instrument that is described in the Tip Box above and that you can download and modify from the textbook Website.

---

[6]Cornwall, J. R., Vang, D. O., & Hartman, J. M. (2009). *Entrepreneurial Financial Management: An Applied Approach* (2nd ed.), pp. 165–167. Upper Saddle River, NJ: Prentice Hall.

There are downsides to taking money from friends and family—or, more specifically, family!

Let's say that your parents are physicians who know nothing about the software company that you are starting. You have two other partners. One partner's father sells farming equipment, and the other's family is involved in the newspaper business. You each borrow $25,000 from these family units. The parent-child relationship, while great for weekend visits, can prove difficult when real money in a real venture is involved. You cannot take calls every day in the middle of the day, even if their purpose is only to wish you well. In addition, a Board of Directors position for family members is awkward, at best. This venture is your time to stand up, be your own boss, and show leadership to people you bring into the business. The baggage of historical family relationships can easily distort the objective reasoning that you must have to grow your business.

Therefore, if you take family money to start your venture—and yes, it is often the only source and thus the best source—you need to set clear ground rules. Give your family members the stock they deserve at a fair valuation. Or structure it as convertible debt so you don't have to argue about valuations at such an early stage.

Angel Investors

Angels are an increasingly important component of entrepreneurship because they are professional investors who have a taste for seed and Series A financing. An angel investor is a wealthy individual who invests in startups—whether alone or in groups of like-minded individuals. Truly, these angel investors have become the financial engines for startups in our economy.

If you are going to raise money from an angel investor, you must understand his or her thinking and motivations. The majority of angel investors made their money by starting and/or building successful companies. The typical angel has already made the mistakes in his or her business career that you are about to make in the year or two ahead. Their desire is not only to put their money to work but also to put their experience to work to help make the investments worthwhile. While angels tend to have a lot of free time on their hands, they do not want to waste it. They want to find a younger entrepreneur who is serious about building a great company, one that is a good business as well as has or uses good technology, and who will listen to and appreciate the angel's advice as much as his or her money. If you enter into conversations with prospective angel investors with this attitude—and a great business plan and PowerPoint presentation—you have a reasonable chance of success. If you appear arrogant, immature, or are a poor listener, you have no chance. An angel investor does not need to invest in you to feel fulfilled or become successful as a business person. He or she already is.

Therefore, angel investing is an individual decision on the part of private investors. In other words, they are investing a portion of their net worth. Even when angel groups put money into a company, shares are issued to the members of the investment group individually. Usually angels or angel groups invest less than $1 million per startup, and the more typical investment is in the range of $250,000 to $500,000. Of course, there are "super angels" who invest $1 million to $2 million in a new firm—but these are rare.

As an entrepreneur, there are certain rules or restrictions for angel-type investment. Figure 8.3 shows the U.S. Security and Exchange Commission's current definition of an "accredited investor" for the purpose of private equity investing. The idea is that you only want those individuals or organizations that can afford to lose all the money they are investing in you. Ventures are inherently risky.

Traditionally, the process of working with angel investors is that you will typically try to convince a single angel investor on the merits of your plan, and then he or she will contact a group of friends who each throw in $25,000 or more to get you where you need to be in terms of seed or Series A financing. Ventures often put together a "private placement memorandum" that contains key elements of the business plan. It also contains the specific terms and conditions of the investment, be it a convertible debt instrument or the number of shares offered and the offering price of those shares. Governance mechanisms are also included (such as the structure of the Board of Directors), as well as other controls.

If it is an equity investment as opposed to convertible debt, some angels may want *preferred* stock rather than common stock because that provides a mechanism for preferential treatment in event of exit. Try to resist this. Angels are sometimes issued "warrants" to buy more stock at an attractive price per share relative to what the next round might be for new investors. Warrants are a sweetener in the deal.

Increasingly, individual angels work through angel groups. For example, the eCoast Angel Network is a highly regarded collection of angels working out of New Hampshire and Northern Massachusetts that has placed more than $20 million into a number of startups and supported these investments with deep operating experience among the members. And we have several others operating in the authors' Boston region such as the Launchpad Venture Group, Common Angels, or Walnut Ventures. On the West Coast, there are also dozens of angel groups providing funding for budding entrepreneurs.

If you work with an angel group, the typical process is that the entrepreneur is invited to make a "pitch" at an angel group meeting. Expect to get grilled—often by individuals who are not particularly expert in your specific area of business or technology. If there is sufficient interest by angels in attendance, one of the members of the group will take the lead on investigating you, your team, and your business plan. This is called "due diligence." If you are fortunate enough to get a seasoned professional at this stage, visiting prospective customers or suppliers with him or her will be valuable for the customers and incredibly educational for you. The lead angel will also structure and negotiate a term sheet for a possible investment in your company. This term sheet with his or her recommendations will then be presented back to the other angel group members for investment. Your job is to make the lead angel your champion to his or her peers.

Angel investors play an increasingly important role in the funding of new ventures. Professor Jeff Sohl, who runs the Center for Venture Research, has done a remarkable job over

Under the Securities Act of 1933, a company that offers or sells its securities must register the securities with the SEC or find an exemption from the registration requirements. The Act provides companies with a number of exemptions. For some of the exemptions, such as rules 505 and 506 of Regulation D, a company may sell its securities to what are known as "accredited investors."

The federal securities laws define the term accredited investor in Rule 501 of Regulation D as:

- A bank, insurance company, registered investment company, business development company, or small business investment company;
- An employee benefit plan, within the meaning of the Employee Retirement Income Security Act, if a bank, insurance company, or registered investment adviser makes the investment decisions, or if the plan has total assets in excess of $5 million;
- A charitable organization, corporation, or partnership with assets exceeding $5 million;
- A director, executive officer, or general partner of the company selling the securities;
- A business in which all the equity owners are accredited investors;
- A natural person who has individual net worth, or joint net worth with the person's spouse, that exceeds $1 million at the time of the purchase;
- A natural person with income exceeding $200,000 in each of the two most recent years or joint income with a spouse exceeding $300,000 for those years and a reasonable expectation of the same income level in the current year; or
- A trust with assets in excess of $5 million, not formed to acquire the securities offered, whose purchases a sophisticated person makes.

Figure 8.3   Accredited Investors According to the Securities and Exchange Commission

Source: Securities and Exchange Commission.

the years tracking the growth of the angel investment sector.[7] Jeff found the total value of angel investment in 2011 was $22.5 billion, funding a total of 66,230 entrepreneurial ventures in the United States alone. During that same time period of 2011, the number of active investors was approximated to be 318,480 individuals, a 20% increase over 2010. Overall, the data indicate that angels have significantly increased their investment activity, and are committing more dollars resulting from higher valuations.

For many entrepreneurs, their local angel communities are *the most feasible avenue for raising startup capital*—with the caveat that the amount of funding is in the $250,000 to $1 million range for any given company. At that level, angels are a strong source of seed and startup capital. In Jeff Sohl's most recent survey, 42% of all angel investments were for seed and startup financing. Angels also actively participated in later rounds of financing with 55% of their angel investments occurring at early and expansion stages.

As an entrepreneur who seeks funding from angels should know, angels tend to focus on specific industry sectors where they have operating as well as investment experience. That way, they give you hands-on advice in addition to money. Jeff Sohl's 2011 report indicates that software received 23% of total angel investments, followed by Healthcare Services/Medical Devices and Equipment (19%), Industrial/Energy (13%), Biotech (13%), IT Services (7%), and Media (7%). The report indicates that Industrial/Energy investing has remained a significant sector for angels for the last few years, reflecting a continued appetite for clean tech. In fact, we have an old college classmate who has a small angel fund that focuses exclusively on "green" startups (www.cevg.com).

There are also an increasing number of women's angel groups (e.g., Golden Seeds). In 2011, women angels represented 12% of the angel market. Women-owned ventures accounted for 12% of the entrepreneurs who were seeking angel capital, and 21% of these women entrepreneurs received angel investment in 2011. Minority angels accounted for 4% of the angel population, and minority-owned firms represented 7% of the entrepreneurs who presented their business concept to angels. The yield rate for these minority-owned firms was 15%. Overall, angel investments continue to be a significant contributor to startups in the United States, which by Jeff Sohl's estimates, have led to the creation of 165,600 new jobs during 2011 alone, or 2.5 jobs per angel investment.

There are many attractive aspects to angel investors generally. First, the angel investors we know have had management positions in operating companies. As noted earlier, they tend to have the time and interest to roll up their sleeves and help you succeed. If you find an angel investor who has extensive experience in your target industry, he or she will know what it takes to start a company, make those tough early sales, and build a team. In addition, when things get tough with customer payments or suppliers, many angels help add some of that toughness back into your own thinking. This type of "mentor" capital is just as important as the actual money they provide. See the Spotlight Box on one of your author's own angel experiences as a young man.

Angel investors as a group tend to have reasonable performance objectives for a venture. Having been operating executives, they understand how hard it is to crack that first $1 million of revenue, the next $5 million, the next $10 million, and so forth. Our experience is that an angel investor will want to make three to five times his or her money over five years, have far fewer investments, and focus more on each one—compared to the typical venture firm that is driven hard, for a number of reasons that we will address momentarily—to make at least twice that return.

Not all angels or angel groups are the same. It is essential that you try to find other entrepreneurs who have worked with a particular investor or an angel group to understand the dynamics of getting funding and working together to build a company. One useful site is www.thefunded.com. It contains the opinions of entrepreneurs who have worked with VC firms

---

[7]Sohl, J. (2012, April 3). *The Angel Investor Market in 2011: The Recovery Continues.* Durham, NH: Center for Venture Research. The Center for Venture Research (CVR) is presently based at the Whittemore School of Business and Economics at the University of New Hampshire.

TIP: ANGELS ARE MORE THAN MONEY: THE CAPTAIN TO THE RESCUE!

In one of your author's second company—another software firm started by a founding group in its early 30s—we had one of the largest systems integrators in North America as the first key "reference" account. That company owed us several million dollars for some special software that powered the integrator's own next-generation solutions for major government and private-sector organizations. When we won the project, we saw that money as sparing us the need to raise outside capital to scale up our R&D efforts and marketing. Moreover, up until that time, we had been self-funding our venture to the tune of about $100,000.

That one receivable from the large reference company was killing the business. It stretched from 30 days to 60 days to 90 days, and there was no certainty that it would not go to 180 days. Meanwhile, the customer's programming staff was using our software and expecting bug fixes as well as new features—right away. The venture was in a true pickle: stuck with one large account that was eating up our resources, with someone in the treasurer's office of that company treating us like all other small companies (e.g., like dirt).

Enter Mel, known among his friends as "The Captain," a serial entrepreneur who had launched half a dozen companies. In his youth, he had piloted . . . had piloted planes in the Pacific during the Second World War. (Originally one of the first high-tech entrepreneurs in New England who had achieved a good exit, Mel is now past the age of 90. He still goes to work every day in what he calls his "new" $30 million a year "low-tech, cash business" that he helped start in his late 70s.)

It occurred to us that perhaps if anyone could get us our money, it would be The Captain. Mel drove over for lunch. We told him our problem. After he called us "stupid young guys," the next thing we knew he was on a plane down to the client. The Captain had three conditions for his efforts. First, we had to pick up his plane ticket and his drinks at the airport. Second, we couldn't go with him: "You would only get in the way." And third, "If I give you the money, you're going to have to give me some of it for my trouble; not that I need your money, but how else are you guys ever going to learn?" We swallowed our pride and prayed for Mel's success.

Through other contacts, The Captain got 30 minutes with the general manager of the division that was our customer. And as the story is told, The Captain wasted little time pulling out "the nuclear option"—unless the general manager personally called up accounts receivable and authorized a wire transfer that very day, no one in "Mel's" company would answer calls from the client's R&D group, starting as of 9 a.m. the next morning. The Captain explained how the software was mission critical to the client's future sales. He also assured the general manager that as a former pilot, he could easily enforce the no-call rule with any of those "young fellas" working up in Cambridge.

Of course, we had thought about doing this earlier but had feared losing our No. 1 key reference customer. The Captain had no such trepidations. "Not going to happen," he said later. "They need your software too much, whatever the heck it does." In fact, he said later that the discussion with the general manager of the division lasted 15 minutes and was not particularly unpleasant. He had offered the manager a discount on the invoice if payment was executed the next day. The general

> manager responded, "Three days." Sure enough, in three days the customer wired to our bank account the money owed minus the discount. That money—which we still think of as "The Captain's money"—saved our company.
>
> Seasoned angel investors—those with true operating experience—do such things for younger entrepreneurs. In fact, *they relish every second of it*. Find a great angel who will also be your mentor—his or her value is a lot more than his or her money.

across the country. Use the various filters to narrow the search down to your location, type of investor (angel or VC), and size of investment desired.

Venture Capitalists

Venture capital is a fundamentally important segment of the private equity industry. In fact, many would contend that it has been the primary engine of technology-intensive entrepreneurship in the U.S. economy over the past 40 years. That success has brought a tremendous amount of money into the hands of venture capitalists—money that must be put to work in ventures that need and deserve that money. In 2012, for example, venture capital under management in the United States was estimated at $29 billion spread across over 3,750 deals. Those, we contend, are very big numbers fueling the next generation of the U.S. economy.[8]

Over the long term, the National Venture Capital Association reports that venture capital funds have paid out a net 15% to 20% internal rate of return (IRR) to their investors. At one point, before the tech bubble in 2001, those returns were considerably higher—in the 30% to 40% range for the most successful firms.

Not only do venture capitalists have a *lot more money* to invest than angel investors, but in some ways, they also face greater challenges than a private investor. Venture capital firms are professional, institutional managers of risk capital who enable and support the most innovative and promising companies. When an investment is made in a company, it is an equity investment in a company whose stock is essentially illiquid and worthless until a company matures six to nine years down the road. Unless a company is acquired or goes public, there is little actual value.

The venture capital firm itself has partners. There may be upwards of a half-dozen partners in a typical VC firm. The firm then creates "funds" (typically with ten-year terms over which proceeds are distributed to fund investors) and raises hundreds of millions of dollars for those funds. A venture capital firm will create a limited partnership with the investors as limited partners and the firm itself as the general partner. Each fund or portfolio is a separate partnership. A new fund is established when the venture capital firm obtains necessary commitments from its investors, which these days is between $400 million and $800 million for well-regarded venture capital firms. The money is taken from investors as successive investments are made. Typically, an initial funding of a new venture will cause the venture fund to reserve three or four times that first investment for follow-on financing. Over the next three to eight years or so, the venture firm works with the founding entrepreneur to grow the venture. The payoff comes after the venture is acquired or goes public. While there is a management fee in the range of 3% for invested capital, the VCs make their money on "the override" or "carry" on the invested capital.

This is how it works: Typically, most of the invested capital in the fund is committed over the first two or three years. That means just not the "A" rounds but the expected follow-on

---

[8]Thomson Reuters. (2012). National Venture Capital Association, MoneyTree Report.

investments in a venture over successive rounds on the journey to exit. Let's say that a venture fund has $400 million of invested capital and five individuals in the VC firm as the managing partners. A single partner can only manage at best five or six ventures (as an investor and Board member, and they need to be Board members to make sure that their money is being put to good use). That means that the portfolio of ventures in the fund will be in the range of about 20 to 25 companies. So let's take 20 venture investments, run by four individuals—the managing partners of the fund.

In terms of deal size, if you divide $400 million by 20, you end up with about $20 million that a single VC firm will invest over successive periods of financing in any given portfolio company. Plus, it is typically syndicating these rounds with other VC firms. Therefore, VCs tend to invest in ventures that need a lot of money—striving to become leaders in their respective industry niches, and therefore prime candidates for a large buyout or an IPO. If one thinks about an acquisition, most VCs will tell you that they want to get ten times their money back out of a company over the course of five to seven years. But let's say that they will be satisfied with five times their money back. That means that if a VC owns 50% of the stock of the venture and it has invested $20 million in that venture, the target valuation for this type of exit has to be in the $200 million dollar range ($5 \times \$20$ million = $100 million, which at 50% of the stock, requires a $200 million exit). And in a portfolio of 20 or so venture investments, more will fail than will succeed. This is the reason why VCs need to get a 10 times return or more on some of their ventures, and why a healthy IPO market is music to their ears. *Without healthy returns, VCs have no business.*

In fact, the typical situation (if there is a typical situation in the VC world) is that in a portfolio of 20 startups, 6 or more will be complete failures, and 10 or more perfectly viable businesses that nonetheless cannot provide even a five-times return on an exit. That means that within any given portfolio, there need to be those three or four stars that truly hit pay-dirt. That means a $500 million type acquisition or a multibillion-dollar type IPO. With a few "big hits," even in a portfolio saddled by moderately valued ventures as well as a good number of abject failures, a venture capitalist is going to gain a large personal benefit from the carry on the performance of the total fund.

The rewards can be substantial, for both the VC and entrepreneur. Over the fund time period—typically ten years—the fund returns the invested capital back to its institutional investors, and then divides the gains above that amount in the form of 80% for the institutional investors and 20% for the VC firm, for example, the general partners.

In "the good old days" of the technology bubble, we knew of several $400 million funds that grew to over $800 million. In those instances, the investors first received their original $400 million. Then the remaining $400 million is split 80/20 between the limited partners and the general partners of the fund, for example, the VCs. First, $320 million goes to the institutional investors, and $80 million to the VC firm. The four or five partners in the VC firm each get their share of the $80 million! That is serious money by any standard. And there are a number of funds where the venture capitalists did even better with even larger pools of money.

That is why the successful venture capitalist is so driven, demanding, and particular about his or her investments. Finding the jewel among the hundreds or more ventures that come across the table is very hard—and yet *it must be done*. And achieving strong returns is the only way the venture capitalist can go back to institutional sources to raise the hundreds of millions of dollars of risk capital to initiate another fund. While there are early-stage VC funds in the sub $100 million range, most today are in the $500 million plus territory. VC firms tend to raise new funds of this magnitude every three to four years, just enough time to put a current fund to work and free up time to put new money to work. It is an incredibly tough, demanding business—and this past recession has whittled down the ranks of those who call themselves venture capitalists.

Therefore, the fundamental insight for any entrepreneur visiting a top-level VC is that the person on the other side of table is *under a tremendous amount of pressure.* He or she has to put a lot of money to work in a very short period of time. Because ventures are risky on so many fronts, there have to be two or three really big hits to make the math work. And you never know which one of the 20 portfolio companies will become that hit. Hits, in the form of IPOs or high-priced acquisitions, are exceedingly rare.

For all these reasons, it is also exceedingly difficult to raise money from a venture capitalist as a startup. And since VCs manage their own risk by syndicating with their associates in other VC firms, you typically have to sell two or three VC firms for an initial investment. It can be done, however. The SilverRail Technologies case on the textbook Website raised $6 million from VCs as seed funding right in the heart of the 2008–2009 recession. The founder of Sentillion, also a case on the Website, raised about $30 million from a group of VCs over the course of three years. But to have success with VCs, you need four things:

1. A large, addressable market (our target customer group and their target uses)

2. A truly distinctive, unique solution (our product/services strategy)

3. A pragmatic, scalable business model

4. A first-rate management team

As a young entrepreneur, your greatest hurdle will be the last criterion, no matter how good your idea. However, if the VC loves your Venture Concept, he or she will help you build the management team you need to be successful. That will mean teaming you with an experienced venture CEO-type who has made money for the VC in a prior venture.

The bottom line is this: If you have a company that over the first three rounds of financing needs to take in $20 million or more to generate at least a $100 million revenue per year enterprise—which, upon exit, can bring in hundreds of millions of dollars in an acquisition or reach a billion-dollar market cap in a public stock offering—then venture capital may be your ticket. But you will have a lot of competition. For every 100 business plans that come to a venture capital firm for funding, usually only ten or so get a serious look, and only one ends up getting funded.

While it is nice to dream, most startups don't fit that mold; nor do they need that much money! And if you do, the VC is going to analyze your projected financials closely to see just how much money is really needed over five years to build a scalable, category-leading enterprise. For example, you may ask for $2 million and expect to give up 30% of your stock in a Series A financing. You thought you might keep controlling interest, at least until the second round. But the VC, based on very legitimate past experience, believes that you really need $4 million. Same valuation. That means 60% of the stock goes to the VC, and you no longer control the company. You might argue otherwise, but the choice may be $4 million for 60% of the company stock—or *no deal.*

That is why entrepreneurs try to shop their ventures for the best possible deal both in terms of dilution and terms. Unfortunately, however, VCs tend to share the same valuation insights and benchmarking services and structure their deals in similar ways as we described in a prior Tip Box. That means preferred stock, seats on the Board of Directors, participation rights in future offerings, preferential rights on exits, and various restrictive covenants that provide control and oversight on management decisions. Sure, these terms and conditions might be negotiable. But make no mistake, the "Golden Rule" is in effect with VCs: "It is our money, so we are going to play by our own set of rules!"

The VCs are also focused on certain key industries. They have to have expertise in the industry sector targeted by the venture team to provide value beyond money. If you want to call on a VC firm, visit that firm's Website. Look at its portfolio; read the backgrounds of the general partners. Do further research through the Web on the partner who invests in companies such as the one you wish to start or grow. *And then try to find a referral to that partner through a friend, a fellow entrepreneur, or an alumnus of your university.* The least preferred method for reaching out to a venture capitalist is a blind mailing. It is the last item on his or her queue—and that queue is indeed already very long. To get a meeting with a well-regarded venture capital firm, you need to give a personal reference to a general partner of that firm. *Someone will need to make a phone call or send an e-mail on your behalf.*

Many VCs also want the firm to be in the local geographical region simply because the lead partner on the deal is going to be an active board member. That means visiting the company every week or two in the beginning, calling on the telephone every day or two. Some VC deals are structured so that any significant financial expenditure must first be approved by the VC assigned to the Board of Directors. The VC is therefore a "hands-on" investor. Few inexperienced entrepreneurs approaching venture capital firms realize that they are essentially asking for one-sixth of a person! And the VC is asking, "Can I actually work with this person? Will they listen to me?" Ask any venture capitalist who has had successful investments and he or she will tell you that ventures that break through the gravity of the early-stage growth evolved from the original business plan concept with the careful input of experienced board members and advisers.

Figure 8.4 shows the top industry targets for VC investments in the United States during 2011. For example, the top four industry sectors receiving venture capital investment represent over 61% of total venture capital investment (software, biotech, industrial/energy, medical devices, media and entertainment). Also, note that a single state—California—accounted for 47% of total companies receiving venture capital in the last quarter of 2011! Massachusetts came in next at 9%, and New York at 8%. But if you don't live in one of these states, do not be discouraged. Our friends who are managing partners in these firms still say that they have a lot more money than good ventures in which to invest that money. It is a matter of gaining access, and for that, as noted earlier, you will need a personal reference into a specific firm that invests in your area of work.

By Industry Category	% of Total VC Investments
Software	17
Biotechnology	16
Industrial/energy	16
Medical devices and equipment	12
Media/entertainment	7
IT services	7
Semiconductors	6

By State	No. of Companies	% of Total	Investment (millions)	% of Total
CA	695	47	5,917.30	55.20
MA	138	9	898.2	8.40
NY	125	8	768	7.20
TX	56	4	510.2	4.80
WA	69	5	405.2	3.80
VA	37	3	291.3	2.70
IL	23	2	229.5	2.10
MD	32	2	220.6	2.00
NJ	33	2	182	1.70
PA	51	3	168	1.60
All other states	223	15	1,123.70	10.50

Figure 8.4 Venture Capital Investments in the United States (2011)

Source: *National Venture Capital Association 2011 Yearbook,* Thomson Reuters, 2011.

The pressures driving VCs to make handsome returns on their portfolio companies have led to the nickname of "vulture capitalists." It is true that in their capacity as Board members, venture capitalists have driven out many founding teams deemed inept or incapable of growing a business. But as a general rule, VCs simply want to grow extraordinary companies. If they do that, everyone usually wins: the entrepreneur, the institutional investor, and yes, the VC itself.

VCs are also notorious for playing hardball on valuations, including "down round" valuations that are less than prior rounds, which serve to further dilute early shareholders. But there are always two sides to any story: Many technical founders do not have the capability to manage and integrate all the functions of a business, and poor performance can well deserve a lower valuation in a subsequent round. But the most important thing to remember is that the entrepreneur's success is the VC's success. Most venture capitalists have done this enough times to know what it takes to grow successful businesses. This doesn't make the medicine any easier to swallow for the entrepreneur.

Receiving financing from a venture capital firm is a second form of marriage. You cannot expect to receive $2 to $4 million or more of someone else's money in an A round and not have him or her actively involved, particularly when his or her own investors want to see that money worth ten times as much six to nine years down the road. Their entire, unswerving focus is to make your venture successful to the point that it achieves an exit that benefits all involved. And we have found that the connections that a good VC can provide throughout the industry for next-stage investments, channel partners, and technology add-ins are unparalleled.

As with angel investors, you want to search out entrepreneurs who have worked with a particular VC firm before you get too deeply involved. Again, you can check out www.thefunded.com, a Website that contains the opinions of entrepreneurs who have worked with VC firms across the country. Use the various filters to narrow the search down to your location and the size of the investment desired.

On the other side of the equation—your side—the objective of the entrepreneur is to raise as much capital as needed to grow a business that can achieve an exit or become self-reliant from operational cash flows—*and to do this without giving up majority control of the company to outside investors for as long as possible.* Once majority control of equity is relinquished, the founding team is truly subject to the Board of Directors' decisions because the founders can no longer control Board membership. As such, the Board can choose to remove the founding team from senior management. No entrepreneur wants to see that happen. So the objective for the entrepreneur is to try to keep majority control. If not, construct a Board that is highly experienced and knowledgeable, and where egos are checked at the door. *Bon chance!*

TIP: SOCIAL VENTURE CAPITAL

There is also venture capital for social entrepreneurship, ventures that focus on social good, the environment, or tackling mature industries with new sustainable business models. For example, the Acumen Fund is a well-funded organization that makes investments (as opposed to grants) in healthcare, water, environmental, agriculture, and other types of social ventures in emerging economies. Its portfolio of projects is impressive. We encourage you to look at its Website (www.acumenfund.org) and consider for a moment how this type of work might fit at some point in your own career. Groups such as the Good Fund (San Francisco), Investors Circle (San Francisco and Durham, North Carolina), the Underdog Ventures (Vermont), or the Massachusetts Green Energy Fund work in various segments of social entrepreneurship in the United States. Some social enterprise groups make "grants" for community projects as opposed to equity investments in new types of companies. Seek social investors who nonetheless have strong business acumen. Any organization, profit or nonprofit, requires good management discipline and practices.

Strategic Corporate Investors

Working with large, mature corporations is an often underlooked source of venture finance. Clearly not appropriate for all situations, corporate money can still be the perfect complement to follow your own early-stage seed funding for a Series A or B, particularly given the long odds of raising money from venture capitalists. There are a number of forms of this type of investment. The three that we will describe here are direct strategic investment, corporate venture capital funds, and special innovation programs.

Direct corporate investment—often called strategic investment by entrepreneurs—takes personal contacts to get air-time with senior executives in a large corporation. If the entrepreneur can use these connections to raise capital, the money is only part of the benefit if the corporation is also a large reference customer. For example, the founder of Apropos, a call center software solution that identifies preferred customers and routes their calls to the front of the queue, was able to convince Allstate Insurance Company to participate in Apropos' $2 million early-stage financing. Since Allstate had one of the largest call center operations in the United States and became the venture's largest and best early reference site, the benefits were substantial. The founder, Kevin Kerns, made the poignant observation: "If some venture-capital firm uses our product, we can't say, 'They use our product at X venture-capital firm.' That means nothing. But Allstate is a name people recognize."[9]

Sometimes corporate investments are made directly from the C-Suite. More typically, the corporation forms its own venture capital fund to invest in early-stage companies. This "corporate venture capital" (CVC) is running between 6% and 8% of total venture capital investment, or $1.2 billion to $2.0 billion in the United States.[10] Corporate money is known to be more patient than traditional venture capital, and some entrepreneurs have found that higher valuations are possible from corporate sources. There are significant investment programs in large corporations such as Intel, GE, Motorola, or IBM that make investments in entrepreneurial companies. If your venture is in the technology field, Intel Capital's Website is worth examining (www.intel.com/capital). Similarly, Google Ventures (www.google.com/ventures), through which Google made a commitment to invest $100 million a year in start-ups, is another Website to investigate to get a feel about the foci and processes of corporate venture capital.

CVC programs in established corporations aim to learn about technology and business directions of strategic interest and then make investments that create new strategic opportunities for the corporation. By interacting with the firm's R&D and business operating units, CVC programs identify the operating units' interests and priorities. CVCs support the corporation's existing businesses by introducing new technologies and partnerships to its operating groups. At the same time, CVCs help identify technologies and opportunities that fall between or beyond the corporation's existing businesses, which could then form the basis for new business directions.

GE shows the synergies sought in corporate venture capital. For example, in 2008, GE started a $250 million fund to invest in new healthcare technology companies. Typically, a CVC makes a financial investment—just as an independent venture capitalist does—and receives a minority equity stake in the entrepreneurial company. CVCs will also frequently syndicate with or work through traditional venture capital firms. Perhaps more important, large corporations look for synergies between their own parent company and the new venture. In the case of GE, for example, its medical divisions are already market leaders in diagnostic and imaging

---

[9]Popper, M. (1999, October 4). Hunting for venture capital? Don't ignore the corporate crowd. *BusinessWeek*. Apropos was later acquired by Syntellect.

[10]MacMillan, I., Roberts, E., Livada, V., & Wang, A. (2008, June). *Corporate Venture Capital (CVC): Seeking Innovation and Strategic Growth*. Gaithersburg, MD: National Institute of Standards and Technology.

segments. The focus of the new fund is to advance solutions for disease prevention—that is, to move earlier in the healthcare continuum. GE has made a number of significant investments in the new energy sector as well.

Most if not all CVCs work hand in hand with traditional VCs, either syndicating with VCs on specific deals or making investments as limited partners in VC funds. By doing so, a CVC develops experience in venture investing, builds relationships in the venture capital community, and gains a view on the "deal flow" of technologies and companies seeking venture capital funding.

There are two important differences between most CVCs and traditional VCs. First, a CVC may make investments largely for strategic benefits and not just financial returns. A corporation may be interested in gaining a foothold on early-stage breakthrough technology that it knows will take ten years or more to ripen for wide-scale commercialization. A VC just doesn't have the luxury of waiting that long. Second, in many corporate venture capital groups, the partners are paid differently. Yes, there are bonus incentives for strong performance. However, typically these individuals do not participate directly in the override or carry on capital gains of investments. Remember, this is a powerful driver for the partners in a traditional venture capital firm, and it leads to certain tough-fisted behaviors. CVCs, on the other hand, do not have that same financial incentive. Many entrepreneurs feel that leads to higher valuations for their ventures and an involvement that is more patient than that of the typical VC. With that said, professionals working in a CVC are working to find good deals in great new companies, just like everyone else.

How Investors Make Money From Ventures

Before you take a single penny of investor money, it is important that you understand the mechanics of how an investment in your venture appreciates in value through stages of growth.

In very general terms, the basic formula is simple: If you need to raise $5 million and an investor believes the venture is worth $15 million, you will have to give that investor 33% of your venture in return for the investment. All prior shareholders will see their holdings diluted by 33%.

Working through a specific example will help you understand how investors expect to make money from your venture. This is very important for you to understand, so take it slow and make sure you follow each step along the way.

Take a look at Figure 8.5, which shows four rounds of investment, "Seed," "Series A," "Series B," and "Series C," followed by an exit event, in this case, an acquisition.

Let's say that you and two friends are starting a company. You have developed the prototype of a system that allows the owners of large truck fleets to have their drivers do a vehicle inspection check, record payloads, and integrate real-time GPS information for trip logistics, speed, fuel consumption, and so forth. This is a mobile application that rivals what UPS has developed for its own drivers. Your solution also has back-end analytics and a flexible reporting system. One of you knows mobile apps development, another the trucking industry, and the other, how to run a customer support operation. To start the company, you have each committed $10,000 from your own personal savings to pay for startup legal costs, a Website, and a small office. This is your pre–seed stage money, or gap funding.

To build the prototype, you need and get $100,000 from friends and family structured as a 5% interest convertible note that flips to 10% of the company stock upon Series A financing at a certain discount to the price of the stock at the Series A. On paper, this is a $1 million valuation at the seed stage.

Your team works day and night to build a prototype. You also gain the interest of a national food distributor with several thousand trucks on the road. It has been struggling with this problem for years. Truck maintenance, keeping track of shipments in progress, and mobile communications with drivers were just some of the problems described by a logistics

	Seed	Series A	Series B	Series C	Exit	Times Return
Post-money valuation	1,000,000	3,000,000	12,000,000	50,000,000	150,000,000	
Founders						
Investment	30,000 + Sweat					
%	90%	60%	35%	27%	27%	
Value	900,000	1,800,000	4,200,000	13,300,000	35,378,000 ***	1,179
Family and Friends						
Investment	100,000					
% Equity	10%	7%	4%	3%	3%	
Value	100,000	200,000	466,667	1,477,778	3,930,889 ***	39
Angels						
Investment		1,000,000				
% Equity		33%	19% *	15%	15%	
Value		1,000,000	2,333,333	7,388,889	19,654,444 ***	20
VCs						
Investment			5,000,000	12,000,000		
% Equity			42%	32% **	56%	
				24%	74,036,667 ***	4.36
					17,000,000	
Value			5,000,000	15,833,333	91,036,667 ***	

*   Early-stage investors, such as the angels, are often provided the right to participate for fixed number of share in the next round of financing, at a substantial discount on the price per share. In this case, they could buy more stock at say, 80% the price per share of the Series B, or a $12 million valuation. This is an incentive for them to invest early. This is not included in the example above. Angels, do not invest more money in Series B.

** Founders, family & friends, and angels' money upon exit is based on their % holdings times the exit price minus repayment of all invested capital by the VCs. There is no take-me-along anti-dilution rights for the VCs Series B investment shown here; otherwise, the VCs would have received about $10 million more.

*** The VC's equity at exit is the sum of getting their invested capital returned first, and then their 56% holdings multiplied by the balance of the proceeds.

Figure 8.5   Making Money on Equity in a Venture: A General Scenario

manager. And he told you that if he could get his drivers to stay under 70 miles per hour on the highway across the United States and Canada, at the current cost of diesel fuel it would drop $10 million down to his company's operating profits. He wants to do a pilot because he thinks your system might help accomplish all these things. If the pilot is successful on 20 trucks, his company will pay a certain amount of money per truck per year for the final solution.

Now it is time to get a Series A round into the company to finish the product and get the first two or three customers up and running with the new system. You've worked the numbers carefully, and all told, it will take $1 million to get to do the pilot, deploy the system, and do the same for two or three additional companies. You also learn that startups raising money in the intelligent fleet and logistics management space have received valuations as high as $5 million post-money.[11] Sounds good, but since your team is relatively young and inexperienced, you suspect your valuation will be less, perhaps considerably so.

After visiting a dozen venture capital firms, all you get is, "No, you are too early for us. But come back to us when you have three or four paying customers and want to expand to twenty." You think to yourself, getting to four paying customers is exactly what you need the money for *now*, not after. But that's just the way it is. VC is probably not going to work for your first $1 million investment.

You turn to the angel community. You find an alumnus of your university who is a highly successful entrepreneur and is known for doing startup deals. You have lunch and find him highly knowledgeable in the logistics area. And he has friends who know IT and mobile apps. You could see him potentially as a valued mentor as well as an investor.

A million dollars is beyond this alumnus's own personal limit, but he knows of four other friends who might also be convinced to pony up $200,000 each. But this angel investor says a week later that he has thought about the deal and isn't going to go above $3 million for a post-money valuation. It's 33% of the stock or nothing else. If he and his friends invest, he wants specific monthly milestones focused on turning your prototype into a fully functional system, getting it into a "beta" test site with the large distributor, and then fully deployed. He also wants to help develop a sales plan to get two or three more customers as soon as possible. He has a Rolodex of fleet owners in the food and beverage industry that should help.

If we turn back to Figure 8.5, the *pre-money* valuation for this Series A financing is $2 million; the *post-money* valuation is $3 million. The simple math is that for their $1 million investment, the angel investors receive a third or 33% of the equity.

With this Series A investment from the angel investors, the founding team and its family members are diluted by 33%. Collectively, the existing shareholders hold "only" 66% of the stock. However, from Figure 8.5, you can see that the founders' equity is worth $1.8 million (based on the $30,000 initial investment plus sweat equity) and that friends and family stock has doubled to $200,000 in value, at least on paper. That is the power of equity.

Eighteen months down the road, your team has successfully finished its pilot and installed the system not just at the first reference account, but also in four other fleet owners, two being distributors and the other two manufacturer-owned running trips from a few plants to warehouses across the United States and Canada. You have learned that $250,000 to $500,000 per customer, depending on the size of the fleet, might be a good target for this type of software as a service. The services contracts from these five accounts suggest about $2 million in recurring revenue. The business, and its business model, seem viable.

You need more money to scale the business. You rework your numbers, looking at R&D, the purchase of sensors and various "telematics" devices and bandwidth from several key vendors, and the cost of hosting computer operations at a large provider. There are several hundred trucking companies in the United States and Canada that you have identified as prime targets for the system. And you identify other logistics management services that you can also provide using your system as a platform. All told, you believe that the company can scale to $100 million business over the course of seven or eight years. Your planning points to another $5 million for growth capital. This is beyond your angel investors.

The lead angel, who has been your only outside Board member up to this point, invites you to lunch with a highly regarded venture capitalist in the region. After talking strategy, you spend a lot of time discussing customer acquisition, deployment, and customer service. The venture

---

[11]VentureSource, part of Dow Jones, is one of the popular private equity information portals that provides benchmarks on valuations at different stages (www.dowjones.com/privatemarkets/venture-source.asp), as is Thomson Reuters' SDC VenturXpert data service. BIZCOMPS is another interesting, paid data service with all sorts of granular details about private company transactions (www.biz-comps.com/).

capitalist wants to visit your initial reference customer and see the system in action. He also wants to visit an upcoming telematics show, together, to get a sense of the intense competition in this space.

After doing all this, over the course of several months, he agrees to the $5 million, but his firm will only do $3 million, and two of his friends at other VC firms will do $1 million each. And all three will replace two of your cofounders on the Board. You and the angel can stay on the Board, but three additional seats will belong to the new investors. The pre-money evaluation will be set at $7 million, more than three times your current revenue, in line with other current "B" round valuations in the industrial telematics space. There are lots of covenants in the deal as well, but fortunately, your angel investor is well versed in these matters and keeps you clear of the worst of them, such as take-me-along and antidilution ratchet clauses. But the investment will be in the form of participating preferred shares. Also, half of your shares will be converted back into options to be earned with good performance. Your new investors "insist."

Even though you don't want to give up control of the Board, you need the money. The term sheet is executed. All current shareholders are diluted by 42%. That means the founders' share goes from 60% to 35%; friends and family from 7% to 4%; and the angels, from 33% to 19%. But everyone's stock is worth a lot more—on paper. In fact, your founders' shares are now valued at $4.2 million! And since you consider your angel investor a good ally, the non-VC investors collectively still retain majority control of the stock.

The $5 million in growth capital sure makes a difference. You build a sales team, hire a bunch of programmers, and develop a dedicated customer implementation crew that travels across the United States and Canada to do rapid installations and training. Over the next three years, you shoot up to 30 customers, add new services, and achieve recurring revenue in the $15 million dollar range. But that's a far cry from the original business plan that showed $100 million after seven years.

The Board (which you no longer control—the three VCs now do) decides to double down on a Series C round to help grow the company to $100 million in sales. It wants to raise $12 million at a pre-money valuation of $38 million, which is not quite three times sales, but close. The three current VCs will put up $8 million of that and will find another $4 million from other VCs. All current shareholders will get diluted by 24%. Then again, on paper, everyone's stock is worth a lot more. You as founders, for example, are collectively worth over $13 million on paper!

The $12 million investment is secured quickly, in less than two months, because the VCs are raising the money from fellow VCs. Your company secures a partnership with IBM and Qualcomm, opens a UK field office, and starts looking at Mexico and South America. With IBM's help, computer operations are scaled. Your R&D team develops a new suite of IT-enabled services and provisions them as Web services to customers. You are also receiving calls from other industry segments with mobile fleets. Highway construction outfits seem particularly promising. And after three more years, you have doubled the number of customers and are seen as a market leader of sorts. But you have to explain to the Board that in this business, new customers are not proving any easier to sell than prior customers. Each one is run by tough, traditional fleet logistics and maintenance managers. They all need a test, a business case, and well-supported deployment.

It's now Year 7, going onto Year 8. Your recurring revenue will come in at $30 million for the year, with a nice 20% operating profit before taxes. Next year, sales might hit $40 million with the geographic expansion. Your angel investors are pleased that you have built a solid business with $30 million in recurring revenue and healthy profits. And, given the nature of the business, it will be hard for a newcomer to displace your systems in current customers. The IBM and Qualcomm relationships are also helping to expand the business beyond the United States and Canada.

The VCs seem fairly pleased at the Board meetings, too. But among themselves, you suspect that they realize it will take a long time to hit the $100 million mark. The possibility of an IPO is remote; the company is just not big enough.

A few months later, at the next Board meeting, the three VCs seem in an usually good mood and want take you to lunch. One of them received a call from the head of M&A at one of your strategic partners. They like your solutions so much that they want to acquire your company. The VC and strategic partner talked about a deal that will be four to five times next year's projected revenue. You and your partners are going to be wealthy individuals. But it will probably take at least six months to conclude the deal, so you've got to be pushing sales as hard as you can. There are also some strings attached. The acquiring company has written further provisions that the acquisition is contingent on the founders spending 18 months working within the new division. Salary and further stock incentives are structured based on achieving certain objectives. The entire package is presented as a *fait accompli*. No one has to mention that the VCs now own 56% of the stock.

As you can see in Figure 8.5, this is the Exit. The deal is pegged at $150 million, a multiple of about four times next year's projected sales of $40 million. This has been a fairly normal multiple for software acquisitions.

The VCs with participating preferred shares get their money out first. That's $17 million off the top. Then everyone splits off the remainder based on their pro-rata share. The VCs get a 4.5 times return on their $17 million investment. Not great, but certainly a lot better than most of their other investments.

On the other hand, the angel investors are absolutely delighted. They receive a 20 times return on their $200,000 investment made eight years earlier. Your lead angel has stuck by your side the entire way, remained a Board member, and in some ways, become like family. And his stock is worth $4 million alone, as is that of his friends, the other angel investors.

Your first investors, friends, and family, are beyond words. They are going to split up another $4 million. They had originally hoped to perhaps double their money, but $4 million on a $100,000 investment is beyond their imagination.

And for your team, after eight incredibly grueling but exciting years, your financial picture is forever changed. You have all survived VC governance to retain your senior management jobs. No one was forced out of the company or lost their stock. Yes, you all have to play the corporate game for another 18 months, but already, any thoughts of fighting the VCs to keep your company independent are long gone. You are already thinking about starting yet another company.

You have a separate lunch with your lead angel about joining his crew of private investors. His response: Forget all that and stay focused on selling more customers and keeping existing ones happy. The acquisition is by no means a done deal. Many fall through. You can talk about angel investing, *later*. We have described a rather ideal scenario. Nonetheless, as the National Venture Capital Association data showed earlier, something akin to the scenario described above has happened for hundreds of entrepreneurs *every year*. It is a win-win for all involved. In most cases, the founders end up with far less stock. And most often, if there is a team of three founders, one or two do not survive Board decisions. Boards of high-flying ventures always seek better, more experienced management to take a company to the next level.

How Corporations Evaluate and Make Money From Internal Corporate Ventures _____

Since we are equally concerned in this book with internal corporate ventures, the "investor" in this case is the sponsoring executive. These projects tend to be new product lines, systems, or types of services relative to the company's core business.

The executive team in the corporation will have well-developed measures for return that are based on the cash flows generated by the venture and the return on invested capital—either for operating expenses or in new plans and equipment.

You must structure your financial statements to produce these measures of success, and hopefully, your projections will meet corporate requirements, often called "hurdle rates," for return on investment.

There are three common metrics that we see used regularly within large corporations assessing the business plans for new internal ventures:

- Net present value (NPV). This is the value of cash flows from the venture discounted into current dollars, where the cash flows include ongoing investments into growing the business, operating profits, and adjustments to working capital. The discount rate is typically the corporation's own weighted cost of capital, with additional points if the venture is in an offshore, risky geography. While any NPV of cash flow greater than 0 should warrant investment, in practice, projected NPVs for new ventures should be substantial, in the millions if not tens of millions of dollars. The reason why NPV "works" better for internal corporate ventures than for independent startups is that the projected stream of cash flows from the venture are far more certain if the venture is working within an existing market and product or service category that is already familiar to the corporation. The uncertainty of the venture is further reduced if it can employ the corporation's existing sales channels—which is often the case. Team leaders are often well-known and proven entities. For all these and other reasons, the size and ramp-up of revenues for a new internal venture can be matched to the corporation's prior experience.

- Internal rate of return (IRR). The IRR of an investment is the discount rate at which the net present value of all the costs of a venture equal the positive cash flows of the venture. Since most of the costs are in the first year or two, and most of the benefits in outlying years, one would need a really high discount rate to minimize the impact of those positive cash flows and make them equal to the first one or two year costs. Companies then set hurdle rates on the IRRs on financial projections to consider a yes/no on the project. These hurdle rates tend to be the company's weighted average cost of capital plus a risk premium determined by senior management. You will often find hurdle rates in the range of 15%, but find your own company's hurdle rate and factor it into your sales pitch. Or your company may no longer use IRR and prefer NPV instead for new business proposals.

- Return on assets (ROA). In large corporations, the numerator is net income divided by total assets. For a new venture, teams often use EBITDA (earnings before interest, taxes, depreciation, and amortization) since so many "games" are played on the way to net income. This is divided then by the ongoing accumulated investment in fixed assets for the venture itself—such as newly installed manufacturing machines. Again, for most mature industries, the ROA sought by executives will be between 5% and 15% depending on the specific industry.

Whatever measures your company uses to prioritize investments and evaluate financial performance, learn the measures and include them in your financial projections and presentations.

How Investors Value Your Business _____

The real estate market is a good analogy for thinking about how to value new companies.

When you decide to sell a house, there is a fairly straightforward way of determining a fair market value. You find "comps." Comps is slang for comparable sales. This method involves finding homes sold within a recent period of time that compare in size, type of construction, age, amenities, and neighborhood. The values are reduced to price per square foot in order to compare apples to apples.

For seed and Series A investments, a "comp" approach is most often used by investors to determine the value of a startup business. The venture has little if any revenue and no profits. As indicated earlier, the investors subscribe to data services to get current comparables by stage of financing for your target industry sector. SDC/VenturXpert (Thomson Reuters), VentureSource (Dow Jones), and BIZCOMPZ are all popular services in this regard. If 20 biotech startups received first-round funding for new drug research in the United States in the past quarter, an investor might take the average of the valuations for these deals as a benchmark for the new investment. The data sources that venture investors use to establish valuations for companies at different stages of growth are updated regularly and maintained data by (a) industry sector or type; (b) geographic region; and (c) stage of growth, for example, early stage, growth, expansion, and exit.

In this day and age, when it is so difficult to get startup money from institutional sources (e.g., VC firms), entrepreneurs tend to have to settle for less than they think their business is worth. As one passionate entrepreneur complained the other day, "I asked for $500,000 seed and they only gave me a $1.5 million pre-money valuation. That's 25% of my company for not a lot of money!" If you don't have any other alternatives, no customer revenue, and no finished product, you may have no other choice!

Once a business is actually producing revenue, however, valuations are a different matter. You have a real business with real products or services that customers want to buy. Professional investors will subscribe to large-scale data sources mentioned earlier to find comparables by industry sector and stage of growth. In addition to these data sources, the primary driver of valuation is your own company's performance. There are fairly consistent multiples of the actual revenue and profit achieved by a venture in a specific industry sector. For mature industries, that might be two to three times revenues. For "hot," high-growth industries, the multiple might be as high as five or six times revenue. And the entrepreneur can often argue for *next year's projected revenues* based on the current year's performance. Achieve some type of operating profit on current revenues and your valuation at any given stage increases substantially.

Now take a quick look at www.pwcmoneytree.com. It provides lots of information— but in aggregate. To get the specific information you need, which is the typical valuation by stage of growth for ventures in your specific industry sector, do what other entrepreneurs seeking external financing have done: Go to venture networking events. Talk to investors, professionals, and other entrepreneurs at the event. Arrange a private lunch with those who are not trying to sell you their services, but rather are actually in the field either starting a company, growing a company, or investing in companies at different stages. Also, see if the professors in the Finance Department in your business school have a subscription to Thomson Reuters SDC (Securities Data Company) VenturXpert for their own research. This will provide you with the comparables you require for your industry and stage of growth.

If you do a quick search on the Web for "venture valuation methods," we are certain that you will find valuation methods other than adjusted comparables for startups, and multiples of revenue and profits for later-stage ventures. These include calculating the net present value of projected cash flows over a five- to seven-year time period as a basis for determining what a company might be worth at exit years down the road. This is sometimes referred to as "the terminal value" of a venture. In the next chapter, we will teach you how to project revenues and expenses and make adjustments to cash flow for your planning purposes. And you can use the Web to find multiples on sales and profit for your industry sector to determine what the business *might be worth* in the future.

However, your sales and profit projections will not be used by angels or VCs for a seed round or Series A valuation. The reason why is simple: Any projections beyond two or three years are usually complete speculation on the part of the entrepreneur, so working back from later points in time to the present doesn't add a whole lot of value. No, investors are going to look at "comps" and adjust from there based on your team, your Venture Concept, and your business model.

Ways to Improve the Valuation for an Early-Stage Venture

First, let's create a scenario in which you have a great business plan and have developed an initial prototype. Then you have asked friends and family to a small seed round to build the first working version of your product or service. You've completed a market or customer test successfully and even had some initial sales. Now it is time to do an "A" round from professional investors, either angels or early-stage VCs.

You've worked with an experienced angel group, have received a proposed pre-money valuation of $2 million, and are asking for $500,000. The angels have derived that value by doing "comparables" in your industry sector and lowered the valuation based on the fact that your team is young and inexperienced. By agreeing to this valuation, you will be giving 20% of your stock to the angels ($500,000 of a $2.5 million post-money valuation equals 20%).

You know that to build a national sales force you will need to raise another $2 to $3 million in 18 months in a "B" round. By then, you hope the company will have tripled in value, achieving a $6 million pre-money valuation or a $8 million to $9 million post-money valuation. By taking in the $2 million, the new investors get about 25% of your stock in the "B" round. If you play your cards right, you and your partners will still win majority control after Series B financing. You have 55%, and the investors have 45%. But you still expect to have to raise additional capital in order to scale up the business internationally—say, another $5 million at a pre-money valuation of $20 million, or 20% of the equity at a $25 million post-money valuation. It is likely that you will own perhaps 25% to 30% of the stock after the "C" round.

Wouldn't it be great to increase these valuations at each stage of growth? What if you could get a pre-money valuation of $5 million for the first round as you have heard other successful entrepreneurs achieve, $20 million for the next, and $50 million for the next? If you were able to do this, you would own a lot more of the equity as the company grows.

How might you improve your valuations at each stage of growth? For Series A financing (or even seed investments from professional investors), there are specific steps that you can take to increase the valuation. These steps include:

- If you are young (which means under 30), find yourself an experienced business person who understands the venturing process and knows your industry, and convince that individual to work with you—contingent upon financing. This person's role might be VP of Sales, VP of Finance, or who knows, maybe CEO of the company! If it is the right person, he or she will also know investors from prior ventures. That network of friendly investors may generate millions of dollars in added valuation at the startup stage. Of course, you will also have to provide that individual with stock based on performance. Just make sure that he or she is willing to work as hard as you in terms of building a company. Adding "brand-name," credible individuals to your Advisory Board can also have a beneficial impact on valuation for new companies.

- Hustle on finishing your prototype to get a first beta customer or channel partner who will testify that your product or service is indeed a worthy offering. Putting a few dollars of customer revenue on the table will do wonders for your valuation. It removes a great deal of risk from the venture: You have made a product, someone actually wants to buy it, and he or she will testify to the innovation's benefits relative to competitors' offerings.

- While not directly addressing the valuation level, you can also seek to reduce operating expenses so that you don't need as much capital, and therefore do not have to sacrifice as much cash. In the example above, instead of $500,000, let's say that you find a way to get the work done for $200,000. You get that amount from investors—granted at the low valuation—but once completed and successfully tested with customers, and with some actual customer revenue, your *next* round can jump to that $12 million Series B level for high-performing ventures in your category. In other words, you can "parse" your financing and raise only the $200,000 necessary to commercialize an initial product, give up less equity, and then jump to a higher valuation and raise greater amounts of capital at a far more attractive price.

- And perhaps most important, try to bring in that first dollar of real customer revenue as soon as humanly possible, and keep on selling. *Revenue* is the very best way to increase the valuation of the vast majority of ventures. Yes, there are a few ventures where the technology itself—the IP—drives valuation more than revenue, but these are rare cases, confined mostly to biotech (and Instagram, with millions of users but no reported revenue, acquired by Facebook for $1 billion in 2012).

We want to emphasize that the best way to win the valuation battle is to get paying customers signed up with your venture. You should worry more about customers with money, rather than angels and venture capitalists with money. If you are able to gain some customers with money, then funding your venture will be much more feasible. Being in the land of real paying customers instantly adds value to your venture. The value of a venture with real revenue is far greater than one with just speculated revenue.

In successive stages of financing, revenues and profits drive valuations above or below the comparable valuations in your industry sector. A multiplier of four to five times revenues is often used for successive rounds of valuation. Achieve $3 million in revenue from a Series A financing, and your Series B might reach $15 million. Achieve $10 million in revenues from the Series B financing—with operating profit—and your Series C might reach $50 million. It has for many other entrepreneurs. Remember, *drive to revenue, and then drive to operating profit*. This proves the merit of your products and services, and then proves the merit your business model. With each step, your business rises exponentially in value. Neither happens by accident. Once beyond startup, you require outstanding people who think smart, work hard, and act brave.

The Do's and Don'ts of Raising Capital _____

Through our own experience and that of our students and friends who played the startup capital game, there are some clear do's and several don'ts for raising capital. Here are the top ones to keep in mind:

Do's

Sharpen Your Focus

Sharpening your focus has two dimensions: making sure your venture is clearly focused and focusing your attention on the right investor. If you followed the guidance provided in this book, you have that focus. Investors want to know *what you are making and selling, who is buying it,* and *why they are buying it.* Then they need to see how you plan *to monetize* the opportunity. You need to present a laser focus on these issues, with a clear view on the target customer and uses, a distinctive solution, a strong product strategy, a robust business model, clear positioning, and a vision for a strong branding approach.

Know Who You Are Pitching To

It is essential that you do your homework on the angels, VCs, or strategic corporate investors you plan to pitch. This is not so that you can flatter them on their past successes, but rather to understand their industry interests and focus points. It makes no sense trying to raise money from VC firms that have never done a deal in your industry sector. They are unlikely to invest, and if they do, the chances of them adding real value to the business in addition to money are small. Also, if your financial projections (see the next chapter) don't show the opportunity to create a $100 million plus business, forget pitching to top-tier venture capital firms. Instead, look toward angels, strategic investors, or niche-type VC firms. These investors are perfectly happy with a $15 million plus business that generates healthy amounts of cash and that can be sold at exit for $50 million or more, depending on the size of their investment.

Try to Get a Referral Into the Angel Investor or VC Firm

A trusted referral is worth its weight in gold for the investor, removing a significant element of risk. It might not get you the money, but it will certainly get you the meeting. Raising funds for a venture depends as much on personal relationships as it does the soundness of the business plan and business deal. The referral can be another entrepreneur, an investee of the investor, a lawyer, or an executive with a major corporation—or another investor. Or it can be an alumnus of your university or a professor connected into the investment community. Once you identify a list of potential investors, you want to do some groundwork trying to find someone who can make a personal introduction for you. *Do not* contact the potential investor before trying to secure this introduction. This is where picking the right Advisory Board and other professionals (e.g., accountants, attorneys, etc.) proves invaluable. Sending a business plan "over the wall" to a VC firm is most likely a complete waste of time and paper.

Have a Good Advisory Board

The right Advisory Board carries with it many, benefits. A good strategy is to have a Board that has some "brand-name" experts from the particular industry in which you will compete. Also, make sure your Advisory Board is participatory—that is, the Advisory Board members provide wise counsel and guidance. Moreover, do not be afraid to ask them for help in raising funds for the venture, including having them make referrals and introductions. If you want a helpful and active Advisory Board, offer them an incentive (a fee) for attending Board meetings.

Have Good Legal Counsel

You should hire a good attorney from the onset, and you should look for one who has good connections and a network within the investor segment. You should also meet with several attorneys before making your selection. Find out if any will forego their fees until the venture is cash positive or until investment funds are raised. Securities law can be very complicated, and you will need a seasoned attorney who can and will protect your interests. Plus, for any sort of institutional investment (e.g., a VC investment) you are going to be paying them $20,000 or more in legal fees—so you might as well get a top-flight firm for the money.

Make Sure You Have a Handle on Your Secret Sauce

This is usually technology embedded in your product, system, or service, but for some companies, the secret sauce can also exist in a channel strategy, a product positioning, or some combination thereof. Investors can be brutal with their questions, and one of the toughest is when they ask why your venture is different from the others. Make sure you describe this secret sauce in clear, easy-to-understand language that will resonate with the investor.

Have a Great Business Plan With a Great Executive Summary

We will teach you how to do this in Chapter 11. The executive summary of the plan is the entrance card for getting the chance to pitch to a professional investor. A great executive summary is the "bait," and your clear value proposition—how you plan to monetize the opportunity—is the "hook." In many cases, an investor might simply request an executive summary of your business plan. If he or she likes what they see, you may get a request for the whole plan. A poor executive summary will ensure that you will not get a follow-up request from the investor. And remember, an investor is looking for a reason to say *no*, not to say *yes*. If your business plan is flawed and/or you lack a great executive summary, you are going to get a *no*.

Line Up Your References, Particularly Early Customer References

Make sure the references you use are relevant to your industry sector and to the potential investor, and let them know that you are using them in your pitch. Also, make certain these references will really support you and advocate for you. The best thing you can do is to get an investor to make a customer visit. It builds a shared interest in the solution and will get the investor thinking on your behalf.

Be Specific About Your Funding Requirements

Any investor is going to ask how much you want and how you are going to spend the money. Therefore, you must be clear and specific about "the ask." This includes at least a year-by-year expenditure detail, and in some cases, the investor may request a month-to-month detail to assess your burn rate. You must also be sure to align your financial needs with timing objectives and valuation expectations. Investors who know your business sector will often have experience with what it really costs in terms of business execution, and if your funding requirements are off (e.g., asking for too little or asking for too much), the investor will call you on it.[12]

Help the Investor Envision the Value of an Exit

You need to do your homework on recent "transactions" in your industry. That means equity investments, mergers and acquisitions, and IPOs. You need to paint the picture that other ventures like yours have realized exits of a certain level as multiple sales and/or profits. If the investor received, for example, 30% of your company stock for his or her money, they can then quickly do the math themselves. They will know full well the effect of dilution in successive stages of investing, for example, that their 30% will likely be reduced by another third to a half over time before exit occurs.

Don'ts

There are also some major "don'ts" in raising capital. These can be deal killers, so be mindful of each one.

Financial Projections With Unrealistic, Unfounded Assumptions

We often see business plans with financial projections that are flawed because they are based on poor assumptions, are unrealistically optimistic, or woefully lack validation. There are three potential problem spots:

1. *Crazy, wildly optimistic revenue numbers.* "I am calling on a VC that is expected to see a $100 million revenue number in Year 7, so that is what I am going to show." The VC will pick you apart in two seconds. Another common flaw is that

---

[12]Evanson, D., & Beroff, A. (1999, August). Ready or not? *Entrepreneur*, 56–69; Link, W. (2006). Pursuing venture capital. *Entrepreneurship* (5th ed.). New York: McGraw-Hill, pp. 90–92; Worrell, D. (2004, May). All in the delivery. *Entrepreneur*; and Jorgensen, B. (2001, May). The do's and don'ts of fund raising. *Electronic Business*, 29.

first-time entrepreneurs think that they will close every customer that is visited and that all customers will become repeat customers. Think again. Entrepreneurs also often have fantasies about ramp-up. "I have $1 million in revenue for the first year, $10 million the next, $40 million the next, and $70 million the next. We are another Google." Prove it.

2. *Unrealistic expenses.* You are calling on an experienced angel investor with a plan to build a national direct sales force for an enterprise selling at $150,000 per person. The "ask" needs to be for considerably more, yet you know that doubling the sales expense will kill the profitability of the venture for two more years. Guess what? Put in the correct numbers and figure out more products and more revenue for each salesperson to sell!

3. *Underestimating the total size of investment to achieve scale.* This means that over the course of three or four years and two or three rounds of capital, the total cost for the investor to build a viable, profit-generating enterprise is substantially underestimated by the entrepreneur. We are continually surprised by the number of business plans that don't even come close to the amount of money needed for sales and marketing. Or to build a powerhouse, you might need to create a national customer service of systems integration capability. Or you might need to spend as much money launching a brand in Europe as you did in the United States, and then that same amount again penetrating Asia. Or you might have a manufacturing business and a $20 million capital outlay needs to occur in Year 3, and it is unlikely that any bank is going to pony up debt for a company of your size and maturity.

Investors tend to have a lot of money because they are smart business people. They can rarely be fooled. As we discussed in Chapter 7, one way to develop realistic numbers for revenue is to gain user input directly for your Venture Concept: the Reality Check. If you do not have this validation, any investor will immediately discount your numbers. At the same time, experienced investors can help you think through the activities and cost needed to build a great company. We will build on these themes in the next chapter, on developing realistic financial projections.

Talking About Large, Generic Markets Instead of Specific Niches with Specific Needs

All too often entrepreneurs focus their argument about the validity of the venture opportunity by talking about large, generic markets that amount to "billions of dollars." Remember, you need to focus on a specific market niche, and then specific customer groups within that niche. It needs to be clearly defined and on its own, sufficient to support the revenue you plan to generate. In the parlance of VCs, this is the *addressable market* for your venture.

Focusing Only on Proprietary Technology at the Expense of Solutions for Users

Great technology companies are also great at finding, selling, and supporting users. While today's investors very much want to hear about your secret sauce, they know that successful companies are also strong on the market side of the business. And never start with the technology first. That is a *big mistake.* Start off with target customers, your solutions, and why these are compelling for the users. Then you can get into the weeds.

Asking for NDAs

Too many entrepreneurs believe what they are doing is so groundbreaking that they want to keep it a secret for fear someone else will steal their concept. They then make the mistake of asking potential investors to sign nondisclosure agreements (NDAs). This request puts off or insults the potential investor. The relationship between the entrepreneur and the investor is based on trust and mutual benefit. Asking a potential investor to sign an NDA negates this possibility.

Focusing Too Much on the Future at the Expense of the Next-12-Months Milestones

Another fatal mistake the entrepreneur makes is focusing too much on what "will happen" to the venture in the far-off future. First, projecting future performance is very difficult. Doing so beyond one to two years is tenuous at best. And yet, for most angels and all VCs, you must show the upside revenue potential of the business, say, in five or six years. Do so with caution, and try to find benchmark analogous companies against which to compare your own upside potential. Second, investors want to know what steps are needed to get to your first commercial launch. That typically means some type of "alpha" and "beta" test milestones, followed by a series of steps to successfully launch your new product or service. Get tangible, and let investors know what specifically is going to occur over the coming months.

Avoiding a Discussion of Your Competition or Actually Claiming Your Venture "Has No Competition"

Please, never pretend that there are no competitors. There is always some form of competition, even if it is competition for the customers' total budget or "spend" in your area. Moreover, a larger competitor can easily decide to get into your target application through an acquisition or commercializing its own R&D. Pretending that your venture is "the only one" will seriously undermine your credibility with seasoned investors who have heard this all too often. Besides, a market with successful competitors may be positive from an investor's perspective since it indicates that customers are already spending money for current, albeit inferior, solutions. We find that the weakest part of many business plans and presentations is the competitive analysis section.[13]

Closing Thoughts: Getting Funded Is Not for the Faint of Heart

Ultimately, you must keep in mind that getting venture funding is very difficult. For example, the entrepreneur described in the SilverRail Technologies case on the Website visited three dozen venture capitalists before he found the 37th, who gave him a whopping $6 million in Series A financing. The entrepreneur behind Sentillion, another case on the Website, visited two dozen VCs in his search for a Series A of approximately $3 million. Their experience is the norm in this day and age of tight venture funding for startups. And both had strong work experience as well as excellent venture strategies, business models, and founding teams.

If your business plan is going to call for greater than $250,000 in initial financing—which tends to take you beyond family and friends and angels—be prepared to work just as hard selling investors as you are trying to sell first customers. The odds are longer than you probably ever imaged. Some experts suggest, for example, that for every 1,000 plans that a VC sees on his or her desk, only two or three will get financing. So do your homework and focus your efforts on investors who are interested in your industry sector and who have a history of investing in your type of business; be sure to get a personal introduction, have solid references, and of course, a great business plan.

---

[13]Jorgensen, B. (2001, May). The do's and don'ts of fund raising. *Electronic Business*, 29.

Remember that if you are not passionate about your idea, then no one else will be, either. You are the messenger, the venture's chief salesperson. If you fail to be a passionate seller, you won't raise a penny. Investors not only want to see you put "skin in the game" (your own finances), but they also want you to be emotionally involved and passionate about the venture. An entrepreneur is going to have to live a 24/7 existence for of the duration of the business, making incredible sacrifices for a marginal salary at the start. Be it late nights working with engineers in the office, endless road trips to customers, or countless lunches courting new employees and investors, your work day will rarely end. But for most of you, it will be the most fun you will ever have. There will be challenges, and your passion and conviction will carry you through along the path to profitability. Seasoned investors know all this. If you appear unconvinced, uncommitted, or in any way, shape, or form passive about the venture, the game is over. "Committed" is different than "wild-eyed." Be professional as well as passionate about your Venture Concept and the business model you have created for it.

With that said, you need a thick skin on the hunt for investment capital. Do not take anything personally, because professional investors will be merciless with their questions! In fact, our experience in presenting to VCs is that they can have a feeding frenzy on who can ask the most difficult question. All the work we have had you do in the first section of this book should arm you well during the onslaught. Nonetheless, don a thick skin! You are likely to talk to dozens of investors before finding the right one for your business.

Reader Exercises

Raising capital has a lot to do with networking, getting the referral in to an investor, or leveraging university connections. These reader exercises are designed to help you discover these connections. This is also another opportunity for a check point with your trusted advisers, professor, and fellow classmates! You might be surprised at just how many angels, VCs, and corporate executives are networking into your university.

Step 1: Get a Feel for Deals in Your Industry Sector

Go to www.pwcmoneytree.com. This is PricewaterhouseCoopers' *MoneyTree* site, where you will find comprehensive reports on VC investment activities by industry, region, and stage of development. Navigate the site and study what activities are happening that are relevant to your Venture Concept. What kinds of conclusions can you draw as a result of your search?

Step 2: Learn About Local Angels

Go to www.angelcapitaleducation.org. This is the Angel Capital Education Foundation, and it provides education, information, and research about angel investing. Under "Resources" you can find a listing of angel groups by region. Check out angels in your region and try to learn about whom they are, what they do, and their investment strategies. Also, under "Research," check out the latest statistics on angel investment in the United States.

Step 3: Find Actual Angel Investors

Find out—any way you can—two or three angel investors who are alumni of your university. Determine further if you know anyone else who has contact with these investors on a personal basis. It might well be your professor. See if there is a way to meet them for breakfast or lunch. Extra credit: Have that meeting with them!

Step 4: Learn About the Venture Capital Industry

Go to www.nvca.org. This is the National Venture Capital Association Website. Under "Research," study the latest venture capital industry statistics. Also, under the "About NVCA" tab, look at the Members page and the hundreds of members of the association. Clicking on the member firms' names takes you directly to their Websites. There you can study their portfolios.

Step 5: Learn About Local VC Firms

Next, select three VC firms with companies in their portfolios that are in the same industry sector as your idea. Learn what you can from the Websites of those portfolio companies. Do they seem to be successful? Identify the partners of the VC firms who are the lead investors in those companies. Look at their educational and work backgrounds. See if there is some type of personal connection for you. Do the same with the backgrounds of their investees in your industry sector. The goal here is to determine if there is an individual who can make a call on your behalf to a partner in that VC firm.

Step 6: Learn About Potential Corporate Investors in Your Industry

Find a large corporation in your industry that has its own internal venture fund or direct investing activities. Intel and Google, for example, are well known for their corporate venture capital activities, but you would be surprised at how many corporations in industrial and consumer marketspaces view direct investments as part of their own long-term growth strategy. Once again, research the backgrounds of the executives—see if there is a connection for you, as alumni of your university or in some other way. Many executives in large corporations look for opportunities to help students or recent graduates of their alma maters.

Step 7: Develop a Strategy to Raise Funds

Develop a draft strategy for raising capital for your venture, including whom you might visit, the rough amount of funds you think you need for Series A financing, and how much of the stock you would be willing to provide for that capital.

Visit the Student Study Site at **www.sagepub.com/meyer2e** to access the following resources:

- Web Resources
- Video Resources
- General Resources in Entrepreneurship

9

Projecting the Financial Performance and Requirements for the Venture

The Purpose of the Chapter

Planning how your business will make money is as fascinating and important a process as designing the new product, system, or service that the venture will sell to customers. The work you did in Chapter 5 on defining your business model is the essential foundation for projecting financials. Think of this chapter as the execution and refinement of that business model into a crisp set of financial projections that are necessary both for you and your prospective investors. Teaching you how to do this is the purpose of this chapter.

In the process of translating your business model into actual numbers, you need to focus on projecting revenues, expenses, operating profit, the differences between "income" and "expenses" and actual cash flows, capital investments, and startup costs. And all the while, you need to make sure that these projections integrate your R&D, production, and go-to-market strategies.

For that reason, we recommend that you develop the financial projections for your venture first before writing the full business plan. Besides, from Part I of this book, you already have your strategies for R&D, production, and go-to-market developed and tested with actual customers. These provide the insight required for effective financial planning. Then, with a first set of financial projections in hand, you can revisit various aspects of the business model and improve them to enhance revenue, increase profitability, or reduce startup costs.

For example, let's consider the implications of all three major financial statements, the P&L, the Cash Flow Statement, and the Balance Sheet for the business strategies of startups and internal corporate ventures.

- *P&L.* If you present a stream of revenues without recurring revenue, it may be best to rethink the product section of your business plan to include add-on products or services to create that recurring revenue. This directly affects your product and services strategies as well as your business model.

- *Cash Flow Statement.* Similarly, if your cash flow projections show huge lags between when sales are booked and when revenue is collected, you might reconsider the nature and structure of how you price your products and services (as in some upfront payments for services provided).

- *Balance Sheet.* If you are starting a manufacturing firm or adding a new manufactured product line as an internal corporate venture, your Balance Sheet projections might show large fixed assets relative to sales and profits generated from those investments. This would be seen as a poor return on assets (ROA). You might want to seriously consider finding external subcontract manufacturers to shift your fixed costs into variable costs. Once again, this directly affects the operational aspects of your business model.

All of these are examples of how financial planning for a venture can reshape the strategies of the venture, and therefore make anything you write in the business plan obsolete. Put otherwise, a venture is in the business to make money.

Learning Objectives

After reading this chapter, you should be able to:

- Develop meaningful financial projections for a startup or corporate venture, and within this, different approaches for thinking about revenues and expenses

- Evaluate how these approaches work for a product startup, a systems venture, a services venture, and an internal corporate venture

The Whiteboard Approach

Remember when we suggested for the various chapters in Part I that the best way to design your Venture Concept and the business model was with team members working together on a whiteboard, and even perhaps with a beer or two in hand? Well, the same applies for designing the financial statements for your business. Except for this one, forget the beer. Creativity and the free spirit need to be replaced with pragmatism and discipline.

Using the whiteboard or pen and pencil may seem unusual in this day of the ubiquitous spreadsheet. However, we find that turning to the computer too quickly often leads to mindless financials. It is simply too easy to put some numbers into a worksheet, develop some standard percentage growth equations, and replicate everything into a rosy future scenario—that simply will never be real. In other words, beautiful financials, perfectly formatted . . . might mean absolutely *nothing*.

So instead, use the spreadsheets *after* you have figured out the assumptions and reasoning behind your revenues, expenses, operating profit, and capital infusions. Do your financial prototyping on the whiteboard—at least for the first year or two of the P&L, and particularly for the revenue part of the P&L. *Revenue drives everything in a venture.* Remember from Chapter 5: For each major stream of revenue, define the type of revenue, the frequency of purchase, the price point per unit for whatever is purchased. As the number of customers scales up over time, these specific variables can be adjusted and simply multiplied to produce revenue numbers.

Once you feel comfortable with the number of customers and the streams of revenue they are likely to produce, you can then develop a more complex spreadsheet to keep track of various expenses and how that leads to operating profit.

The textbook Website has various examples of integrated financial statements for various types of ventures. Do not use these blindly. Instead, think of them as accelerators in the development of your own, personalized financial projections.

The Financial Projections Necessary for a Business Plan

If you are uncomfortable with the structure and integration of any of the financial statements described below, get someone to join you who possesses that knowledge. And don't be sloppy with your spreadsheets. Investors will eventually find and dismiss numbers that do not add up or fail to integrate across financial statements. There are four key deliverables in the financial planning for most ventures: (a) a five-year detailed projection revenue, (b) a five-year Pro Forma P&L, (c) a five-year Pro Forma Cash Flow Statement, and (d) a five-year Pro Forma Balance Sheet.

The Five-Year, Detailed Projection of Revenues

- This projection is often based on the number of new customers, repeat customers, and price per unit for products or services to produce "top-line revenue." The default format for startups seeking angel and venture capital financing is to show monthly projections and the growth rate of changes to these components for the first two years and annually for outlying years. The reason for the monthlies is that they show specifically when you plan to realize your first revenue, and then, how that revenue ramps up over the coming 12 or 18 months. Your professor may require a different format, such as just annual projections for all five years. Or he or she may request a quarterly revenue projection for the first two years. However, to get to quarterly estimates, you typically have to do monthly projections anyway, and then sum them up in an appropriate manner. Startup investors are most likely going to want to see the details of the first two years of revenue, with the number of customers or units sold scaling up month by month upon product or service launch. We suggest that you use a separate worksheet for this purpose, complete with the assumptions driving the numbers.
- If you find that a particular investor or professor only wants to see annual projections, then the "hide" feature in spreadsheets is a simple way of covering up the monthly detail and showing just the summed annual amounts for the first two years. Moreover, PowerPoint presentations of business plans tend to show only annual amounts, and even those are in summary form. No one wants to look at figures in 8 or 10 font size on the projection screen!

Interestingly, for internal corporate ventures, most successful proposals that we have seen—such as the MyM&M'S teaching case included in this book—only use annual projections for the first years or more, depending on the nature of the business. Perhaps that is because most internal ventures go through existing channels so that there is far less uncertainty about sales volumes during the startup period. "Make a great product and we are pretty sure we can sell it through our channels at reasonably predictable volumes," is the school of thought. This may also be the case if you are constructing a venture proposal for within your present company.

The Five-Year Projected P&L

- Formerly known as the Pro Forma Profit & Loss Statement or Income Statement for the venture, this is typically structured in monthly periods for the first two years, and annually for the third, fourth, and fifth years. The revenue line(s) for the P&L are fed by the revenue projections above.

Once again, formats can vary based on the demands of your professor or the nature of your venture. As we will see in the next chapter on writing the business plan, we recommend that you include a summary of number of customers, revenue, and operating profit (EBITDA—earnings before income taxes, depreciation, and amortization) in a simple table showing annual amounts over five years. Then, for some investors (or professors), you will need a more detailed P&L showing various expense items that is still based on annual amounts. Lastly, for those investors and professors who want to dig into the details, you need a P&L projecting revenues, specific operating expenses, and operating profit both before and after tax that is monthly for the first two years of the business, and then annually for Years 3, 4, and 5. It is therefore our strong recommendation that you first generate this more detailed monthly P&L and then summarize it as needed for the particular audience and use.

Do not underestimate the importance of showing monthly figures for the first two years of the business for proving to investors that you have considered the specific needs and goals of the business. Monthly projections show investors the level of cash burn in the business before sales commence, and then, the timing when operating profit is achieved. The monthly numbers also show when key managers, R&D staff, or sales staff are brought on board as the business ramps up during the first several years.

More generally, most investors know that any numbers beyond the first two to three years in a projected P&L are largely speculation. However, the fifth-year estimation remains important because it gives some sense of potential exit value as a multiple of revenue and profit.

The Five-Year Projection of Cash Flow

Otherwise known as the Pro Forma Cash Flow Statement, this varies from the P&L based on delays in collecting on sales, paying creditors, "capital" expenditures (such as equipment or computers), and infusions of money in the form of venture or debt financing. These projections should follow the monthly and annual format of your revenue and P&L projections.

Revenue recognition and cash conversion are critical issues for most startups. Startup investors tend to want to see a monthly cash flow analysis—to gauge the amount of invested capital needed by the business at least to reach operating profit. Corporate ventures tend to stick to annual projections throughout. In addition, executives funding internal corporate ventures will probably want to see the net present value of the discounted cash flow produced by the venture.

The Five-Year Projected Balance Sheet

- Formerly called the Pro Forma Balance Sheet, this is only for startups and not generally associated with internal corporate ventures. Unlike the P&L and Cash Flow Statement, the Balance Sheet can be kept to year-end annual figures. As noted, internal corporate ventures do not require any Balance Sheet, but rather, a capital plan for projects requiring an investment in new plant and equipment. Executives will probably want to see annual projections of Sales to Invested Assets and then, Return on Invested Assets, where the return is the annual operating profits.

From these financial statements, you will also be able to produce what we think of as the financial "goalposts" for the venture. These goalposts include:

- *Startup costs.* These come directly from your Cash Flow Statement, specifically from the month-by-month breakdown of operating expenses and capital investments in plant and equipment. You need to focus on the cash requirements until you launch your first products or services to market. Remember that if you have included seed- or Series A–type infusions of cash as part of the cash flow projections, subtract these first before summing up your various cash needs for the business. Investors are typically interested in your plans for:

- *The time to first dollar.* When the business becomes "real." This information comes directly from monthly projections of revenue.

- *The time to first profit.* When the business achieves true investor value. This, too, can be found in the projected P&L.

- *First-round and anticipated second-round financing amount.* (e.g., seed funding and Series A, or Series A and Series B, depending on the point at which you request capital.) This is typically shown in the Pro Forma Cash Flow Statement.

- *Potential valuation for exit.* For example, the value of the company as an acquisition by a larger concern, and then, the money the investors might make based on their equity holdings and exit preferences. VCs are shooting for a ten-times return (often called a "10X" return) on their invested capital, and that is after all the money that they have invested into your company is *first* paid off. While angel investors might hope for a 10X return, our experience is that they will be perfectly happy with a three-times (3X) to five-times (5X) return over a five-year period. In one of the financial statement examples that we will show you in a moment, there is a specific row placed at the bottom of a projected P&L that shows possible exit valuations at Year 5 at an industry standard multiple of sales and EBITDA.

Do not minimize the importance of understanding the time to first dollar and the time to first profit. These will be primary questions of any professional investor—even after they have read an outstanding business plan: "How long do I have to wait before seeing proof that it is a viable, money-making business?" That should be your question, too.

TIP: BIOTECH VENTURES HAVE A DIFFERENT SET OF RULES!

Biotech financial plans rewrite the rules of the game because the average cycle time for starting R&D to getting a product to market is ten years or more. If your venture is to commercialize a scientific discovery of the biotech sort, your financial planning spans at least the 17 years that represents the protection period of a U.S. patent. For the biotech entrepreneur, there tends to be plenty of comparables in terms of revenues per year for certain classes of drugs, as well as benchmarks for the costs of R&D and clinical trial in the years running up to commercialization. Biotech entrepreneurs need to present and justify these long-tailed projections for investors to make an assessment of the considerable financial risk and reward.

Increasingly, investors are turning to "orphan drugs," which target disease populations of 100,000 persons or fewer—for example, rare diseases. The Orphan Drug Act (ODA) was passed by Congress in 1983 to provide incentives to spend the time and money needed to address small-population rare diseases. One of these incentives is seven years of market exclusivity once a drug-in-the-making is awarded orphan drug status by the Food and Drug Administration (FDA). In 2009, there were 150 drugs given this special status. The FDA also tends to give an expedited review to orphan drug applications, helping to shorten the development process. As a result, more ventures are pursuing these niche diseases. During the 2000s, orphan products comprised 22% of all new molecular entities (NMEs) and 31% of all significant biologics (SBs) receiving marketing approval by the FDA.

Projecting Revenue: Creating Realistic, Granular Projections_____

You are going to have to spend quality time developing your financial projections—and it all starts with projecting revenues.

The *very first two years of revenue projections* matter most for professional investors and corporate executives. We have attended investment meetings where prospective investors and executives have dug into those first two top-line numbers in a way analogous to a new root canal for the entrepreneur! Whatever numbers you present, you need to back them up with as much detail as possible. Think of this as a separate worksheet that feeds into the top revenue rows of your projected P&L.

Let's look at a few examples of how to develop granular—or what we like to think of as "bottoms-up"—revenue projections that can withstand investor challenges.

The most important aspect of projecting revenues is the assumptions behind the numbers. These will vary for every different type of business. You also took a first stab at projecting revenues in Chapter 7 (the "Reality Check"), where you developed a rough estimate of the annual revenue potential for your venture. Grab those assumptions now and use them as a starting point.

A few examples are helpful. In Chapter 5, on business models, we used an example of a "low-tech" venture making healthy dog snacks and a high-tech example of a healthcare monitoring venture. We will use these again to illustrate the structure and content of two very different types of businesses.

In the *pet snack business,* there are a number of critical assumptions, each one of which requires that you do the type of homework we described in the first section of this book. The financial projections for this teaching example are available on the textbook Website (www .sagepub.com/meyer2e). It's a good idea to open that spreadsheet and scroll along as we describe this example. It's a lot easier than reading the following exhibits!

The assumptions that drive the revenue model shown in the pet snack spreadsheet are as follows:

- The number of *stock keeping units* (SKUs)—the items on the shelf—and how that number of SKUs expands over time

- The on-shelf or *list price* of each SKU

- The *margins provided to retailers* (35% for the pet specialty channel), margins for distributors (10%)

- The *spin rate* for each SKU, or the number of units sold on average each month per store. This rate is usually category specific and can be learned from retailers when you ask them about best selling products.

- The *number of stores* for its major channels to market, in this case PetSmart (about 1,000 in 2009), Petco (about 900), Pet Supplies Plus (about 200), and the independent pet specialty stores (about 15,000). Remember, the focus of this venture was premium products and pricing; it therefore avoided the grocery and mass-merchandiser channels.

- The *launch strategy* of hitting local New England pet specialty stores for the first two years, expanding nationally, and also securing PetSmart in Year 2, Petco in Year 3, and Pet Supplies Plus in Year 4

- The team also learned that the independent pet retailers did not want their products also sold in PetSmart or Petco. Therefore, four new SKUs with somewhat different ingredients and very different packaging and branding would be introduced in Year 3 to hit the major retail chains.

If you turn to the spreadsheet (also shown in Figure 9.1) you can see how these assumptions translate into a simple projection of revenue, and from that, an estimation of gross profit.

The estimates from raw materials, conversion, packaging, and shipping were all developed with the owners of the Pet Bakery, with whom the MBA student team partnered on this venture. Also note when the venture gets to "first dollar." By necessity, discussions about the assumptions and numbers in a financial projection are highly detailed. If a professional investor starts digging into your financials, superficial, sloppy reasoning isn't going to get you very far!

If you have a venture where you can map actual customer numbers over time, specify the frequency of purchase, and see different levels of pricing for different streams of revenue, you can then build these details into a granular projection of revenue. That spreadsheet will directly address one of the major questions of investors: "What's really in your revenue numbers?"

The Top-Down, Share of Market Approach

While we are advocates of the "bottoms-up" approach to projecting revenue, in some cases the nature of the business does not lend itself to counting customers. The industry niche is so large, and so many customers are needed within the target niche, that a "market share" approach is used.

One case might be the sale of a service through a Web channel to reach a broad target market. In fact, SilverRail Technologies—one of the teaching cases featured on the textbook Website—is precisely such a case. We used it as an example in Chapter 2. Let's turn back to it for the financial projections and as an example of a "top-down" revenue projection.

Take a look at Figure 9.2. This is a generously adapted version of the financial projections of business founder Aaron Gowell. His actual projections were far more complex, but we have boiled everything down for teaching purposes into a projection of revenue, a summarized P&L, and an exit valuation. This is all in a single, easy-to-follow spreadsheet. Professional investors relish this conciseness in an initial presentation; they will then want to dig into the more detailed financials later on.

If you recall, Aaron's venture aggregated open seats on trains from different national railway systems so that the consumer could have a single view of a trip from one city to another across Europe, pay once, and have a back-end engine seamlessly make all the connections and split out the payments to the various railway systems. Dozens of specific individual steps in the workflow were consolidated into just a couple of steps for the end-user; the back-end software would do all the rest. Gathering all the open seats was no small technical feat, and if achieved, would be a major part of the venture's competitive advantage. Aaron would then make this inventory of open seats accessible to online travel sites as well as traditional travel agents.

Let's follow the logic on the financials that we have summarized from the founder's more detailed analyses. First, hearkening back to Chapter 2, Aaron determined his target customers and uses. The larger market of high-speed train travel in Europe was already over $80 billion and mandated to grow by the European Union to reduce carbon emissions. New, high-speed track would be installed in many countries, linking all the major cities of Europe.

Aaron then selected as target customers train travelers—both business and leisure—with target uses being trips between two and four hours in duration. Published studies showed that when high-speed rail was introduced in Europe, enabling trips between major cities, train travel quickly took over 80% of all travel, largely from air travel, discount or otherwise. The speed and convenience of train stations directly with urban centers made high-speed rail a consuming proposition for travelers, as long as the trip did not exceed four hours. This led to a $48 billion target market.

Next, Aaron had to make a critical assumption about the percentage of rail travel that would be booked online. He looked at the percentage of rail travel booked online in the United States, which was already over 70%, as well as online bookings for all types of travel in Europe (air, all rail, rental car, etc.), which were running at about 50%. Splitting the difference, he picked a target of 60% for online bookings of high-speed train travel in Europe. Might be more, might less—but it was an assumption that Aaron felt comfortable justifying with the data. The combination of the two- to four-hour window and the 60% online booking share produced the venture's "addressable market" in Europe: $22 billion. Published studies indicated that this would grow by 8% a year.

Four SKUs	On-Shelf Price	Retailer Margin	Wholesale	Trade Allowance (Samples, etc.)	Net Sale Price	Spin-Rate per Month per Store (Units sold per month)				
1 Meat and Oats (300 g–small)	$7.00	35%	$4.55	8%	$4.19	24				
2 Meat and Oats (1 kg–bulk)	$24.00	35%	$15.60	8%	$14.35	8				
3 Oats only (300 g)	$7.00	35%	$4.55	8%	$4.19	16				
4 Oats only (1 kg)	$24.00	35%	$15.60	8%	$14.35	4				

	Development	Test	Launch				Expand Independent Pet Specialty						
	Jan	Feb	Mar	Apr	May	Jun	Jul	Aug	Sep	Oct	Nov	Dec	Year 1
Revenue Projections													
Independent Pet Specialty Stores (15,000)	0	1	15	25	35	45	70	95	120	145	170	195	195
PetSmart (1,000) (new versions of 4 SKUs)	0	0	0	0	0	0	0	0	0	0	0	0	0
Petco (900) (new versions of 4 SKUs)	0	0	0	0	0	0	0	0	0	0	0	0	0
Pet Supplies Plus (200) (new versions of 4 SKUs)	0	0	0	0	0	0	0	0	0	0	0	0	0
Total stores selling products	0	1	15	25	35	45	70	95	120	145	170	195	195
SKU 1 revenue		100	1,507	2,512	3,516	4,521	7,032	9,544	12,056	14,567	17,079	19,590	92,025
SKU 2 revenue		115	1,722	2,870	4,019	5,167	8,037	10,908	13,778	16,648	19,519	22,389	105,171
SKU 3 revenue		67	1,005	1,674	2,344	3,014	4,688	6,363	8,037	9,712	11,386	13,060	61,350
SKU 4 revenue		57	861	1,435	2,009	2,583	4,019	5,454	6,889	8,324	9,759	11,195	52,586
Total revenue		340	5,095	8,492	11,888	15,285	23,776	32,268	40,760	49,251	57,743	66,234	311,132
Total units solds		52	780	1,300	1,820	2,340	3,640	4,940	6,240	7,540	8,840	10,140	10,140
P&L Projections													
Gross Sales		340	5,095	8,492	11,888	15,285	23,776	32,268	40,760	49,251	57,743	66,234	311,132
35% Raw materials (35% 1st year, declining next years)		119	1,783	2,972	4,161	5,350	8,322	11,294	14,266	17,238	20,210	23,182	108,896
10% Conversion to finished product (10%)		34	509	849	1,189	1,528	2,378	3,227	4,076	4,925	5,774	6,623	31,113
5% Packaging (5%)		17	255	425	594	764	1,189	1,613	2,038	2,463	2,887	3,312	15,557
3% Shipping/logistics (3%)		10	153	255	357	459	713	968	1,223	1,478	1,732	1,987	9,334
Gross profit		160	2,395	3,991	5,587	7,184	11,175	15,166	19,157	23,148	27,139	31,130	146,232
Gross margin		47%	47%	47%	47%	47%	47%	47%	47%	47%	47%	47%	47%
Sales and marketing		1,000	5,000	5,000	5,000	5,000	7,500	7,500	7,500	7,500	7,500	7,500	66,000
R&D (not full time in 1st year)	2,500	2,500	2,500	1,000	1,000	1,000	1,000	1,000	1,000	1,000	1,000	1,000	14,000
Manufacturing engineering/extra materials	5,000	5,000	1,000	1,000	1,000	1,000	1,000	1,000	1,000	1,000	1,000	1,000	15,000
Other G&A		5,000	5,000	5,000	5,000	5,000	5,000	5,000	5,000	5,000	5,000	5,000	55,000
Operating profit/loss to LLC Members	(7,500)	(13,340)	(11,105)	(8,009)	(6,413)	(4,816)	(3,325)	666	4,657	8,648	12,639	16,630	(3,768)
Net profit margin before tax													−1%

Figure 9.1   Projected Revenue and P&L for a Healthy Pet Snack Venture

													Add Petco Channel	Add Pet Supplies Plus	
Add PetSmart and expand Independent Pet Specialty															
Jan	Feb	Mar	Apr	May	Jun	Jul	Aug	Sep	Oct	Nov	Dec	Year 2	Year 3	Year 4	Year 5
245	245	295	295	345	345	395	395	445	445	495	495	495	600	800	1,000
200	200	200	200	200	200	1,000	1,000	1,000	1,000	1,000	1,000	1,000	1,200	1,400	1,600
0	0	0	0	0	0	0	0	0	0	0	0	0	500	900	1,100
0	0	0	0	0	0	0	0	0	0	0	0	0	0	200	250
445	445	495	495	545	545	1,395	1,395	1,445	1,445	1,495	1,495	1,495	2,300	3,300	3,950
44,706	44,706	49,730	49,730	54,753	54,753	140,147	140,147	145,170	145,170	150,194	150,194	1,169,401	2,772,806	3,978,374	4,761,994
51,093	51,093	56,834	56,834	62,575	62,575	160,168	160,168	165,909	165,909	171,650	171,650	1,336,458	3,168,922	4,546,714	5,442,278
29,804	29,804	33,153	33,153	36,502	36,502	93,432	93,432	96,780	96,780	100,129	100,129	779,601	1,848,538	2,652,250	3,174,662
25,547	25,547	28,417	28,417	31,287	31,287	80,084	80,084	82,955	82,955	85,825	85,825	668,229	1,584,461	2,273,357	2,721,139
151,150	151,150	168,134	168,134	185,117	185,117	473,831	473,831	490,814	490,814	507,798	507,798	3,953,689	9,374,726	13,450,694	16,100,074
12,740	12,740	15,340	15,340	17,940	17,940	20,540	20,540	23,140	23,140	25,740	25,740	25,740	31,200	41,600	52,000
151,150	151,150	168,134	168,134	185,117	185,117	473,831	473,831	490,814	490,814	507,798	507,798	3,953,689	9,374,726	13,450,694	16,100,074
52,903	52,903	58,847	58,847	64,791	64,791	165,841	165,841	171,785	171,785	177,729	177,729	1,383,791	2,812,418	3,900,701	4,508,021
15,115	15,115	16,813	16,813	18,512	18,512	47,383	47,383	49,081	49,081	50,780	50,780	395,369	937,473	1,345,069	1,610,007
7,558	7,558	8,407	8,407	9,256	9,256	23,692	23,692	24,541	24,541	25,390	25,390	197,684	468,736	672,535	805,004
4,535	4,535	5,044	5,044	5,554	5,554	14,215	14,215	14,724	14,724	15,234	15,234	118,611	281,242	403,521	483,002
71,041	71,041	79,023	79,023	87,005	87,005	222,701	222,701	230,683	230,683	238,665	238,665	1,858,234	4,874,858	7,128,868	8,694,040
47%	47%	47%	47%	47%	47%	47%	47%	47%	47%	47%	47%	47%	52%	53%	54%
15,000	15,000	15,000	20,000	20,000	20,000	25,000	25,000	25,000	30,000	30,000	30,000	270,000	843,725	1,210,562	1,449,007
6,000	6,000	6,000	6,000	6,000	6,000	6,000	6,000	6,000	6,000	6,000	6,000	72,000	468,736	515,610	567,171
2,000	2,000	2,000	2,000	2,000	2,000	2,000	2,000	2,000	2,000	2,000	2,000	24,000	46,874	67,253	80,500
15,000	15,000	15,000	20,000	20,000	20,000	25,000	25,000	25,000	30,000	30,000	30,000	270,000	656,231	941,549	1,127,005
33,041	33,041	41,023	31,023	39,005	39,005	164,701	164,701	172,683	162,683	170,665	170,665	1,222,234	2,859,292	4,393,894	5,470,357
												31%	31%	33%	34%

Next, given the volumes of transactions involved, Aaron found it impractical to forecast specific passenger counts within each national railway system. So he put forward a goal of capturing 10% of his addressable market over the course of five years. Why 10%? He felt it the "norm" in terms of percentage of a well-defined addressable or target market for VCs at the time. They wouldn't buy 2% of total market, or 5% of a specific industry niche. So Aaron took the 10% after five years and worked his back from there with market share projections: 7% in Year 4, 4% in Year 3, 1% in Year 2, and Year 1 essentially a proof of concept. This is shown in the second row of the spreadsheet.

Lastly, the venture's business model was to take a 5% transaction fee for online bookings conducted through its engine. That is shown on the fourth line of Figure 9.2. And since Aaron's company was actually passing through the transactions to its railway partners, he would be controlling the money and therefore not have to worry about accounts receivables.

Taken altogether, these assumptions produce a revenue projection of about $150 million by the end of Year 5. Then, in contrast to the top-down revenue projection, Aaron put together highly detailed expense spreadsheets that included headcounts for different types of positions, office costs, and technology operations, year by year. Plus, he developed specific startup costs, shown in the separate box on the bottom right of Figure 9.2, and integrated back into the main

	Year 1 *(3 months)*	Year 2	Year 3	Year 4	Year 5
Total market size	22,000,000,000	23,760,000,000	25,660,800,000	27,713,664,000	29,930,757,120
% of total market captured	0.25%	1.00%	4.00%	7.00%	10.00%
Gross revenue	55,000,000	297,000,000	1,026,432,000	1,939,956,480	2,993,075,712
Revenue (5%)	2,750,000	14,850,000	51,321,600	96,997,824	149,653,786
Expenses					
GS&A expenses	2,148,000	5,184,000	5,836,000	5,848,000	5,941,000
Systems operating costs	283,000	7,053,000	22,323,000	30,913,000	40,374,000
Fixed set-up costs	700,000	–	–	–	–
Total expenses	3,131,000	12,237,000	28,159,000	36,761,000	46,315,000
Operating profit	–381,000	2,613,000	23,162,600	60,236,824	103,338,786
Exit valuation	$826,710,285				

Assumptions		**Year 1 Costs (Taken Out of 1st Year Revenue)**		
Commission on bookings	5%	*Legal*		200,000
Growth rate	8%	*Travel*		80,000
EBITDA multiple	8	*Recruiting*		120,000
		Computers		200,000
		UK office set-up		100,000
		Total		700,000

Figure 9.2   A Top-Down Revenue Projection, P&L, and Exit Valuation

spreadsheet under expenses. If an investor wanted to know the specific use of funds for the first million dollars, Aaron had the specific answers.

Operating profit before interest, depreciation, and amortization is shown below. (Taxes are a complex affair since the business is operating across many countries, some of which have tax-free or advantaged zones for startup companies.) The exit valuation is based simply on an industry standard multiple of the EBITDA in the fifth year. You can see that Aaron planned to make a lot of money for his investors. He also had the experience, drive, and industry studies to make his projections credible (although he had to pitch to dozens of VCs first before he found the right one who believed in the venture strategy and the numbers for it). Plus, there was no rail travel aggregator yet in Europe. If he could launch quickly, the market could be his. All of these factors—the published market studies, applicable work experience that included business development in the travel sector, and a jump on any competition—are arguably necessary for an entrepreneur seeking to put forth a "top-down" market share argument for raising capital. Aaron pulled it off, largely because of the credibility he had due to his considerable experience in the travel industry. In our experience, few entrepreneurs can. Nonetheless, some of your professors might also think it best to run both sets of financial projections: bottoms-up and top-down to see how well these two very different approaches come to the same approximate revenue forecast, and by doing so, validate the other.

Biotechnology ventures also tend to use top-down revenue projections. Each venture focuses on a specific disease (or set of related diseases). The entrepreneur finds the number of individuals both in the United States and abroad who suffer from that disease. A benchmark pricing is established with analogous therapies and multiplied against the patient population to get an annual revenue number. These products are so very long in the making (ten or more years!) that any sort of granular revenue projection that far ahead in the future makes little sense. If the drug cures a disease, it is a safe assumption that those patients who can afford it or who have the insurance that covers the therapy will receive the drug. These revenue projections also tend to show how new therapies move across international borders to build revenue.

Being Specific About Key Assumptions Driving Revenue

Let's assume that most of you can do a bottoms-up revenue model. Whether your business is selling products, systems, or services, you will have to provide your reasoning for the assumptions that affect your revenue projections. These are based directly on the revenue model that you formulated in Chapter 5 and validated in the Reality Check for Chapter 7. This is what we suggest you consider for key assumptions, which are then brought not only into the financial projections but written in the financial section of your business plan:

- *Streams of revenue: What are the elements within your product line or services that produce revenue?* Think of these as specific rows, each with its own specific revenue stream. Product manufacturers think of these as SKUs; systems developers think of these as base-level licensing or subscription, then add-ons for more features and services; and services companies tend to "productize" their offerings into different capabilities at different fee structures—just as we saw above in the engineering services firm. Your new product/services strategy from Chapter 5 is the input needed for this key assumption.

- *Market penetration: How many points of exposure do you plan to have over time to prospective customers?* This could be the number of stores, inquiries from or visits to a Website or "infomercial," customer calls by a direct sales force, or any other lead generation and customer contact mechanism that suits your business.

- *Sales or customer capture rate: What is your "close" rate for first-time use—what some might call "trial" or initial adoption? How is the closing rate different for the various products or services that you plan to offer?* Even Steve Jobs could not close every customer Apple encountered—and indeed, for many years, his close rate was about 5% of PC users. As your company grows and improves, your close rate should improve.

- *Sales cycle: How long does it take to close each customer? Is it an impulse purchase or a long, drawn-out decision process by multiple committees?* For expensive goods, specialty goods, enterprise software or services, and industrial goods, the decision process may be many months; buyer committees are often involved. Technology products, for example, are very complex and their sales cycles can extend over many months. The sales cycle is only one of the good reasons to have a person with sales experience on the team—if only on a part-time basis.

- *Frequency of purchase: What is the "repeat" or continued purchase rate by customers who have started using your offerings?* This is the frequency of purchase in the revenue model for your venture. The subscription model for software ventures, for example, has a different (and we think preferable) frequency of purchase dynamic compared to traditional upfront licensed software.

- *Price level (also relative to competition): How much do you plan to charge for your products or services?* This is a "list" or another form of end-user pricing for your offerings (including those for "good, better, best" items). The Reality Check in Chapter 7 is critically important here. In many instances, the current market will suggest a suitable pricing structure. McKinsey, the prominent consulting firm, suggests: "Companies consistently undercharge for products despite spending millions or even billions of dollars to develop or acquire them. The incremental approach often underestimates the value of new products for customers."[1] We can't tell you how many times we have seen business plans in which entrepreneurs are essentially giving away fantastic new products just to achieve "market share." The problem with this approach is that low prices or free prices tarnish any appearance of a premium product or service—and they kill any hope of achieving an operating profit.

- *Growth rate: What is the growth rate, year to year, of the market size, customer acquisition, and ultimately revenue ramp?* Most ventures start off slow in the first year of selling and then ramp up over subsequent years. What are reasonable initial penetration rates for contact, close, and repeat customers? How will these improve over time? If new customers are flooding into your industry niche, all the better because this should increase your revenue.

Also, keep a careful eye on the timing to achieve first revenue. For "products," there tends to be a lag between company startup and product launch. That's okay, but try not to make it too long! For traditional services, revenue should start flowing in the door during the very first month of operations.

Use the revenue factors above as a checklist to guide your own revenue projections. And don't forget the whiteboard approach. Think through your assumptions and quickly rough out a set of revenue projections. Then turn to the spreadsheet. Put in a set of rows stretching out month by month for the first two years, and annually for Years 3, 4, and 5 that contain your key assumptions behind the revenue streams for your venture. Try to be as realistic as possible about your revenue goals in the first couple of years—including when you can actually start selling a commercial product, system, or service.

Revenue Recognition

Revenue recognition is one of those difficult and sometimes nasty issues that can ensnare the inexperienced entrepreneur. And not all accounting classes spend sufficient time helping students appreciate the important subtleties of revenue recognition.

If you are selling a consumer product—such as the healthy pet snacks venture described earlier in this chapter—then it is relatively straightforward. Let's say that the pet entrepreneurs sign a contract with PetSmart to supply stores with what is expected to be $3 million worth of product (at the price that PetSmart pays) in a given year. Those sales cannot be placed onto

---

[1]McKinsey & Co. (2004, June 15). Pricing new products. *The McKinsey Quarterly.*

the P&L all at once. Rather, you book or "recognize" the revenue when product is shipped to PetSmart's distribution centers or directly to its stores. Invoices are generated for shipped product, which then convert to cash typically in 30 to 45 days, when PetSmart pays its invoices.

If you sell to wholesalers—in the pet venture this means selling to distributors who are selling to independent specialty pet store retailers in a geographical region—that cash conversion can often occur within two weeks upon invoicing. And if you are selling through a Web store, the credit card merchant agreement dictates terms, where sales typically convert to cash within several days to a week.

Let's say that you have a software venture. You sell a site license to use the software to a major corporation with 50,000 users. The contract is for $250,000 that begins on March 1. The corporation plans to make the software instantly available to all of its employees. And its payment period to small firms such as yours is 60 days—that tends to stretch to 90 days—no matter how much you beg, scream, or holler. That would be a two- to three-month delay in that $250,000 or booked revenue hitting the all-important Cash Flow Statement.

But it can become much more complicated. Let's say that you are providing your software as a service, with a subscription model under a Cloud deployment. That means a monthly service fee for those 50,000 employees, which might come to $250,000 a year, but which cannot be recognized all on March 1. Rather, the revenue can only be recognized month by month, and the structure of the revenue is typically the number of users "provisioned" or given access to the software times the subscription fee per user negotiated with the corporation. Bottom line: The revenue recognition is stretched out over time. This is one of the aspects of Cloud computing that is causing the financial types working in large software vendors such as Microsoft, IBM, and SAP to lose sleep at night!

Similarly, let's say that your venture makes a new breed of environmental sensors. You sell a major contract with IBM for one of it's "Smarter City" public sector customers, valued at $10 million for the calendar year. Unfortunately, IBM only wants to take shipment of these sensors when it needs them for each new Smarter City implementation. Your accountants will not let you book the revenue until actual sensors are shipped to IBM at the price per unit as agreed to by IBM.[2]

When you prepare your financial statements, you must walk through these scenarios and generate numbers that reflect the reality of your proposed business model in terms of recognizing the revenue.

Shortening the Sales Cycle

This is what every entrepreneur would like to achieve, of course. But for complex products, systems, and services, this is easier said than done. Here are some tricks of the trade that might prove useful for your planning:

- *Mitigate the risk by starting small.* Many business-to-business (B2B) ventures create systems and other related technology that can be used across the entire organization. But the same positioning as a new, innovative company also scares executives in mature corporations. They want innovation but are also concerned about risk. We suggest that you consider first selling and implementing a test-site within enterprise customers. Let them try your solution and get comfortable with it. In this way, the system can prove its worth and win internal champions as a prelude to widespread adoption. And it is not necessary to give the test away for free. Rather, hold firm on your prices, but simply restrict the scope of the application. Also, these first-phase uses need to be constrained to specific periods of time. Two to three months is a reasonable number for both parties.

---

[2]Go to www.ibm.com to search for Smarter City solutions offered by IBM. These include public safety and crime prevention, intelligent traffic management, citizen services, and water management. There is a never-ending set of possibilities for entrepreneurs and corporate innovations to develop both sensors and analytic software to help cities become more efficient and handle risks through the use of computers.

- *Allow easy entry with a "good, better, best" upgrade strategy.* This is another version of risk mitigation. Depending on your product or service, consider offering a no-frills version at a moderate relative price—and then allow easy upgrade options for customers once they have become comfortable with your solution. Of course, a certain percentage of your target customer market will want "the best" right from the start. Just make sure you have them pay adequately for that privilege!

- *Create a "win-win" proposition for the customer.* One of your authors' current ventures is a software company selling error detection systems to hospitals. This company has some pretty fancy data-mining software that identifies missing medical charges by physicians and other care providers. The company adopted a strategy to sell its capabilities as a service, as opposed to selling complex enterprise software. By selling a revenue-finding service, the company could sell to the CFOs of client physician groups and hospitals, individuals known for quick, objective decision making. The venture asks for 20% of the missing medical charges once the client collects its money from the health insurers, making this a risk-free proposition for the CFO. This new selling approach has reduced the sales cycle from the typical nine months for selling enterprise software to committees comprising IT professionals and doctors to, on average, 60 days. In its first year of business, the company signed up several dozen major accounts—due primarily to this "win-win" selling proposition for customers.

- *Sell to higher levels in the customer's organization.* Information technology companies selling enterprise software find that the higher up the organization they go in terms of selling, the more rapid the decision-making process. An example is a storage management software company that was experiencing a very long sales cycle selling software that reported on all the files stored over enterprise storage networks. Part of the delay was because the team was selling to information technology managers with constrained budgets and who labored over price/performance analyses for procurements. The team decided to build an add-on module that produced all the data needed for "chargeback" to end-user departments for space used on central storage machines. This allowed a sale directly to the CIO of target companies who could now "make money" with the system. This dramatically shortened the sales cycle.

- *Manage stakeholders in the decision-making process.* What might seem to be a 60-day sales cycle can turn into many more months because other individuals inside a corporate customer in a B2B play are part of the sign-off process for a significant purchase. The entrepreneur must know who these individuals are and take specific steps to inform them about the products or services to be sold. You are going to have to do it sooner or later—so best sooner, to avoid any nasty surprises in trying to close a corporate sale. Make a list of all the key stakeholders in your customer's decision-making process. Establish a "call list" for having a conversation with these individuals and note any follow-on steps required. These individual meetings before "the big meeting" go a long way toward ensuring your success with a large client. B2B ventures need internal champions in enterprise customers. Getting access to senior-level managers in an enterprise customer takes networking and diligence.

You should know the nature of the sales cycle facing your venture from your Reality Check. If you feel that this is going to be a problem, don't hide it in your revenue projections. Rather, adjust your product/service and pricing strategy to shorten the cycle, and reflect these approaches in your revenue projections. Rest assured that your investors are going to be asking detailed questions about the sales cycle!

Identify and Show the Recurring Revenue

Achieving recurring revenue seems to be one of those "truisms" for successful ventures. Want to please a prospective investor? Show recurring revenue in your projections, and then have the customer input to back it up.

Experienced entrepreneurs will tell you that it is a lot of harder to win each new customer than originally expected. Rarely does a new venture enter into a clean market space. There are existing competitors, each with their own sales pitch and incentives to keep current customers. For software types of ventures, enterprise customers have often developed so many customer interfaces between all their various computer systems that switching to a newer, better alternative represents a huge leap of faith and substantial cost. Or consumer products entrepreneurs underestimate the difficulty of stealing shelf space from existing competitors or the cost needed to establish a brand presence in the market. That is why once you get a customer, investors want to see an aggressive plan for extracting additional revenue from each customer. That means add-on products or value-added services.

For many types of ventures, recurring revenue is a natural part of the business. For example, most services companies have recurring revenue; try it once, and use the services forever. A software company providing energy analytics probably won't have to work too hard convincing clients to buy a subscription model for information flows that are continuous and never ending. Or a third-party logistics venture can well expect to receive a continuing stream of business from corporate customers—if it proves that it does an effective job arranging the shipment of goods and materials around the world. Health sciences entrepreneurs naturally get recurring revenue by creating diagnostic kits, therapies for disease treatment, and various regimens for ongoing disease management. Prove it once and well for customers and you win a continuous stream of business—at least until the point where the quality of your service deteriorates or a competitor re-enters the market with a major price disruption. (Think "open-source" software or generic drugs.)

However, most ventures have to work hard to think through the meaning and nature of add-on products and services. You can be like Microsoft or Intuit and try to convince your installed base to upgrade to a new version of the software once every two to three years or so. Or you can mirror Symantec with annual renewal subscriptions (for its daily antivirus updates). We like this model! Or your recurring revenue might be professional consulting or integration services on top of a piece of software or third-party plug-ins. Or it could be a line of accessories for a consumer electronics product. Harley-Davidson, for example, realizes that about 8% of its revenue comes from selling Harley-Davidson–branded general merchandise made by third-party suppliers. And Apple achieved about $4 billion of its $43 billion of revenue in 2009 from the sale of music and other digital content through the iTunes store, iPod services, and Apple-branded and third-party iPod accessories. That is a remarkable number for a business that was launched just six years before!

Your investors will want to see a similar eye for the potential of recurring revenue in your business. This should appear as a separate line item or two in your revenue model.

Generating the P&L

Now we move on to generating the complete P&L projection. While we already took a look at a projected P&L in the SilverRail example above, there is actually quite a bit more detail that is typically required by professional investors. These were the "detailed" expense projections behind Aaron's summarized expense numbers.

Now let's do a more detailed P&L, using the high-tech healthcare monitoring case. We present this as the type of thinking you need to do for your financial projections if you wish to raise money from professional investors.

Figure 9.3 is the projected P&L for this teaching example. Like the other examples discussed in this book, the case is based on an actual company and was funded for more than $7 million in a Series A and B financing. It is also available on the textbook Website (www.sagepub.com/meyer2e), so grab it and follow along.

The online spreadsheet has very detailed financial projections for the health monitoring venture. These include the revenue projections, the P&L, departmental budgets and headcounts behind the expenses in the P&L, a statement of cash flows, and a Balance Sheet. Scan through these worksheets and have them at your fingertips as we read on. You will see that they show an initial capital raise of $2.5 million in the Cash Flow Statement, and a second capital raise of $5 million in Year 2. And yes, we know that these spreadsheets are highly detailed—but it is with such detail that most ventures are successfully planned and funded.

Before we get to the projected P&L, we need to discuss the revenue model for this case. There are a number of important assumptions driving revenue. The two channels selected by this venture team were assisted-living centers and home health agencies. Each channel partner was in many ways its own market niche, because each organization controlled a fixed amount of patients who were target customers for this new technology. Within these two channels, there are further assumptions, based on market research:

- *The "service" offerings.* Based on its customer research, the team identified two services: monitoring and alerts for the elderly, and a portal for medical staff caring for the elderly that would show statistics, trend-lines, and other types of patient information.

- *Subscription fees for the elderly: the type, frequency, and pricing of services.* The team had benchmarks for other nascent health monitoring ventures—plus the benchmark of ADT in home security. A fee of $79 per month per patient seemed very reasonable for 24/7 health monitoring and alerting—even if this would limit the market to middle-class individuals and above, up until the time that private and public insurers saw the wisdom of proactive alerting and initiated reimbursement. The assisted-living center and home healthcare partners would be provided 20% of this revenue—a "revenue share"—as an incentive to bring new residents/patients on board.

- *Charging for installation.* This could be a contentious issue for similar service–type businesses where the idea might be to install at no cost, and make up the money throughout recurring service revenue. However, the team decided to charge $249 for installation because the elderly residents being monitored might not be around long enough to make the no-charge install feasible. One visit to an assisted-living center revealed an average length of stay to be about three years! No charge for installation was made to the assisted-living facilities.

- *Subscription fees for assisted-living centers.* After discussions with several assisted-living center companies, the team decided to license its server software—the software that aggregated all the wireless communication, signal processing, alerting, metrics, and user identification—at a fee of $1,000 per month per facility. These chains each had tens of thousands of facilities and were adding new ones every month to meet demand. Certain portions of the software would reside locally on a computer residing in the facility itself that would be linked to the venture's own centralized servers for partner-wide reporting, medical record access, software downloads, and backups.

- *Subscription fees for home health agencies.* Again, based on customer research, the team set this price at a single fee per agency of $100,000 per year. This would cover access to the analytics and workflow management software for tens of thousands of residents in one single annual subscription fee.

- *Penetration rates in each channel.* You can see from the detailed numbers in the figure that one needs to be brutally realistic about the penetration rates of new technology. In just about any market, there are lead adopters who make up a very small percentage of the market (say 5%), and the later-stage adopters. The team hoped to get that 5% in each channel partner over the first six months, and then expand to 12% to 15% or more of elderly residents in the coming years.

- *Staging of the roll-out.* The team targeted sales and deployment into assisted-living centers because of the more controlled environment within the residences themselves. These multidwelling units tended to be "cookie-cutter" in spatial design: one bedroom, one bathroom, one toilet, one kitchen/dining area, and one living room. This made placement and test of the various sensors much easier to accomplish in a specific building. These sensors were fitted onto beds and reading chairs (for pulse, breathing, and activity monitoring), as well as hallways and bathroom floors (for fall detection). It also made response by skilled nurses faster and more reliable because skilled nurses were usually already on site. Penetrating the home health agencies come in the third year of the revenue model. This was an important assumption. (Several home health agencies approached the team for a partnership during the startup period!)

Again, go to the textbook Website to see the detailed projections of revenue based on these assumptions.

Next, we get to the projected P&L for this venture, Figure 9.3. It contains all the standard line items that one expects to find for a startup. In this particular venture, revenues do not start until the ninth month after startup. Note also the 20% revenue share with channel partners, for example, the assisted-living centers and the home health agencies. The monthly breakdown of expenses is useful to show the cash burn and the ramp-up of expenses in successive months. Moreover, the most powerful driver for spending in this type of technology startup is the spending on various types of employees—not just management, but salespeople, programming and quality-assurance staff, and customer support personnel.

Also, take a look at the staffing and headcount projections contained in the spreadsheet for this health monitoring venture on the textbook Website. This is very detailed. You should strongly consider building a staffing projection showing the types of people you wish to hire, how much you will pay them, and when you wish to do the hiring. This makes your business all the more real. It will also show that the venture is judicious regarding when to hire certain types of people. For example, it doesn't make sense to bring on an expensive VP of Sales until the development of the software and sensors that the company needs is nearing completion. Conversely, the venture needs to hire technical managers and staff in the very first month. Similarly, hiring technical support staff for installing systems and training channel partners only begins in earnest in Year 2.

All these headcounts in the spreadsheet then feed into the departmental budgeting, which is also included under a separate tab in the spreadsheet on the textbook Website. This is where computers, telecommunications, and other types of expenses are added to the labor cost on a person-by-person basis. Once you are running an actual business, you will be even more focused on each hire and the costs associated with that hire. Think of it this way: Each employee consumes your hard-earned sales dollars (or hard-won investments)—and therefore, each person must produce at a high level according to his or her role and responsibilities.

Perhaps most important, we hope that you have had some practice showing how certain elements of these financial statements flow from one statement to the other. This might be how net income from the P&L flows into the Cash Flow Statement and as earnings for the Balance Sheet. Alternatively, it might be how sales in the income statement drive accounts receivables in the Balance Sheet as adjustments to working capital in the Cash Flow Statement. Inventory flows across financial statements as well. The materials used to produce sales hit the Balance Sheet and your timeliness of paying suppliers affect working capital in the Cash Flow Statement. If this is all unfamiliar to you, we can recommend, as supplemental reading, *Financial Intelligence for Entrepreneurs: What You Really Need to Know About the Numbers,* by Karen Berman and Joe Knight.[3]

What most accounting books don't teach, however, are the basic considerations for the entrepreneur behind the various expense items in the P&L. Just as we dug into the details of modeling revenue, we need to do the same for projecting expenses. Whether you call it "Op Ex" or "cash burn," managing these expenses carefully is an essential part of getting a company to operating profit. Entrepreneurs need to be very careful about conserving the cash raised in a

---

[3]Berman, K., & Knight, J. (2008). *Financial Intelligence for Entrepreneurs: What You Really Need to Know About the Numbers.* Boston: Harvard Business School Press.

Revenue		Mar	Apr	May	Jun	Jul	Aug	Sep	Oct	Nov	Dec	Year 1	Jan
Recurring Service Revenue													
	Assisted-living monitoring	0	0	0	0	0	0	0	84,500	106,750	129,000	320,250	235,750
	Home health agencies monitoring												
	Total revenue	0	0	0	0	0	0	0	84,500	106,750	129,000	**320,250**	235,750
20%	**Less revenue share with channel partners**	0	0	0	0	0	0	0	16,900	21,350	25,800	64,050	47,150
	Net sales	0	0	0	0	0	0	0	67,600	85,400	103,200	**256,200**	188,600
Cost of Goods													
75	Installation in residencies ($100)	0	0	0	0	0	0	0	18,750	18,750	18,750	56,250	37,500
600	Sensors, PC, wireless modems ($500)	0	0	0	0	0	0	0	150,000	150,000	150,000	450,000	300,000
5%	Application hosting (5% of revenue)	0	0	0	0	0	0	0	4,225	5,338	6,450	16,013	11,788
	Total cost of goods	**0**	**0**	**0**	**0**	**0**	**0**	**0**	172,975	174,088	175,200	**522,263**	349,288
	COGS as % of revenue											163%	
GS&A													
	Executives and support staff	23,933	22,333	34,933	33,333	33,333	33,333	33,333	33,333	33,333	33,333	314,533	45,235
	Sales	0	0	0	0	0	0	0	32,333	41,033	55,533	128,900	62,633
	R&D	62,617	64,917	63,500	63,500	76,067	76,067	76,067	80,900	80,900	80,900	725,433	83,349
	Technical support	0	0	0	0	21,167	20,367	35,017	33,417	33,417	33,417	176,800	44,398
50	Subcontract field support for residences												
	System field test for new channel partners			200,000								200,000	
	Accounting service fees	350	350	350	350	350	350	350	350	350	350	3,500	350
	Legal fees (including patent)	24,000	12,000	2,000	2,000	2,000	2,000	10,000	2,000	2,000	2,000	60,000	3,000
	Insurance (product/commercial)	0	0	0	0	0	0	0	10,000	10,000	10,000	30,000	10,000
25,000	Public relations/media (25k/yr)	0	0	0	0	0	0	0	0	0	0	0	2,083
50,000	Direct marketing ($50k per partner/yr)	0	0	0	0	0	0	0	4,167	4,167	4,167	12,500	4,167
20	Rent and utilities ($20k/ft)	5,833	6,667	8,333	8,333	10,833	10,833	12,500	14,167	15,000	15,833	108,333	18,333
	Postage	100	100	100	100	100	100	100	100	100	100	1,000	100
	Trade shows ($60k/show)	0	0	0	0	0	0	60,000	0	0	0	60,000	0
24,000	Misc. office expenses (supplies, etc.)	2,000	2,000	2,000	2,000	2,000	2,000	2,000	2,000	2,000	2,000	20,000	2,000
	Operating expense (burn rate)	118,833	108,367	311,217	109,617	145,850	145,050	229,367	212,767	222,300	237,633	**1,841,000**	275,648
Operating Income		(118,833)	(108,367)	(311,217)	(109,617)	(145,850)	(145,050)	(229,367)	(318,142)	(310,988)	(309,633)	**(2,107,063)**	(436,335)
	Operating margin												
	Depreciation (see cap budget)	5,103	5,103	5,103	5,103	5,103	5,103	5,103	5,103	5,103	5,103	51,033	6,938
	Interest Income											23,943	508
Provision for Taxes (33%)												0	
	Net income	(123,937)	(113,470)	(316,320)	(114,720)	(150,953)	(150,153)	(234,470)	(323,245)	(316,091)	(314,737)	**(2,134,153)**	(442,765)
	Profitability on sales												

Figure 9.3 Pro Forma P&L for a Health Monitoring Venture

Feb	Mar	Apr	May	Jun	Jul	Aug	Sep	Oct	Nov	Dec	Year 2	Year 3	Year 4	Year 5
280,250	324,750	369,250	413,750	458,250	502,750	547,250	591,750	636,250	680,750	725,250	5,766,000	19,385,550	44,746,200	60,589,800
												3,691,000	12,620,000	28,683,000
280,250	324,750	369,250	413,750	458,250	502,750	547,250	591,750	636,250	680,750	725,250	5,766,000	23,076,550	57,366,200	89,272,800
56,050	64,950	73,850	82,750	91,650	100,550	109,450	118,350	127,250	136,150	145,050	1,153,200	4,615,310	11,473,240	17,854,560
224,200	259,800	295,400	331,000	366,600	402,200	437,800	473,400	509,000	544,600	580,200	4,612,800	18,461,240	45,892,960	71,418,240
37,500	37,500	37,500	37,500	37,500	37,500	37,500	37,500	37,500	37,500	37,500	450,000	0	0	0
300,000	300,000	300,000	300,000	300,000	300,000	300,000	300,000	300,000	300,000	300,000	3,600,000	7,650,000	15,240,000	23,850,000
14,013	16,238	18,463	20,688	22,913	25,138	27,363	29,588	31,813	34,038	36,263	288,300	1,153,828	2,868,310	4,463,640
351,513	353,738	355,963	358,188	360,413	362,638	364,863	367,088	369,313	371,538	373,763	4,338,300	8,803,828	18,108,310	28,313,640
											75%	38%	32%	32%
44,435	44,435	44,435	44,435	44,435	57,985	57,185	61,069	60,269	60,269	60,269	624,455	845,481	885,346	915,717
61,833	61,833	61,833	61,833	61,833	69,616	68,816	84,333	83,533	83,533	83,533	845,159	990,820	1,359,473	1,412,795
83,349	83,349	83,349	83,349	83,349	93,190	91,690	91,732	101,532	109,832	108,332	1,096,401	1,352,871	1,433,039	1,486,541
43,598	43,598	50,198	49,398	49,398	51,590	51,590	60,381	59,581	66,181	65,381	635,291	1,104,698	1,434,918	1,851,518
												150,000	550,000	1,300,000
											100,000	100,000	100,000	100,000
350	350	350	350	350	350	350	350	350	350	350	4,200	4,620	5,082	5,590
3,000	3,000	3,000	3,000	3,000	3,000	3,000	3,000	3,000	3,000	3,000	36,000	39,600	43,560	47,916
10,000	10,000	10,000	10,000	10,000	10,000	10,000	10,000	10,000	10,000	10,000	120,000	132,000	145,200	159,720
2,083	2,083	2,083	2,083	2,083	2,083	2,083	2,083	2,083	2,083	2,083	25,000	26,250	27,563	28,941
4,167	4,167	4,167	4,167	4,167	4,167	4,167	4,167	4,167	4,167	4,167	50,000	150,000	250,000	350,000
18,333	18,333	19,167	19,167	19,167	21,667	21,667	24,167	25,000	26,667	26,667	258,333	30,000	30,000	30,000
100	100	100	100	100	100	100	100	100	100	100	1,200	1,320	1,452	1,597
0	0	0	60,000	0	0	0	0	60,000	0	0	120,000	120,000	120,000	120,000
2,000	2,000	2,000	2,000	2,000	2,000	2,000	2,000	2,000	2,000	2,000	24,000	60,000	70,000	80,000
273,248	273,248	280,681	339,881	279,881	315,748	312,648	343,381	411,614	368,181	365,881	3,840,039	5,107,659	6,455,633	7,890,336
(400,560)	(367,185)	(341,244)	(367,069)	(273,694)	(276,185)	(239,710)	(237,069)	(271,927)	(195,119)	(159,444)	(3,565,539)	4,549,753	21,329,017	35,214,264
											-77%	20%	37%	39%
6,938	6,938	6,938	6,938	6,938	6,938	6,938	6,938	6,938	6,938	6,938	83,250	117,267	91,433	87,750
508	508	508	508	508	508	508	508	508	508	508	6,096	29,078	83,626	344,915
											0	1,511,014	7,066,172	11,734,529
(406,990)	(373,615)	(347,673)	(373,498)	(280,123)	(282,615)	(246,140)	(243,498)	(278,356)	(201,548)	(165,873)	(3,642,693)	2,950,550	14,255,038	23,736,900
												13%	25%	27%
											Exit at 8X EBITDA		170,632,138	281,714,115

seed or Series A financing because one never really knows just how long that cash will need to last before revenues start to roll in from your first products or services.

The bottom line is that the entrepreneur must be tight-fisted on operating expenses—both in the planning of the venture and in the actual execution of the plan. Investors will try to gauge your maturity and frugality. Below are some of the key areas that will be front and center.

Management Salaries (Including Your Own Paycheck!)

Continuing with our medical monitoring example, the staffing and headcount projections that we described above feed into the departmental budgets, and then those departmental budgets feed into the expense line items in the P&L (Figure 9.3). The online spreadsheet as detailed worksheets for each of these areas feed into the higher-level P&L. Now let's talk about your salary and those of fellow team members.

If you are an MBA student developing a plan to start a new company with $100,000 to $250,000 of angel money, you should be able to live with a salary in the $50,000 to $75,000 range for the first year or two until the venture becomes cash positive. This is probably a pay cut for many of you. However, remember that you are working for the value of your equity, and few if any will own as much of that equity as you in your new venture. Later on, once the business becomes cash positive, you can bring your salary up to market par.

The salaries of CEOs and VPs of Sales and Engineering of ventures raising $1 million to $3 million or more for Series A financing are generally in the $120,000 to $150,000 range. It is easy to see, however, that with those three or four senior managers, half a million dollars of that precious cash is consumed before any of the R&D salaries, manufacturing expenses, or sales commissions are paid to people doing the more detailed work of the company. Once sales begin to accrue, these salaries tend to bump up by $30,000 to $50,000 in outlying years. Ventures backed with $3 million or more in Series A financing tend to have senior management salaries in the $150,000 to $175,000 range.

If you have gone to our textbook companion Website and looked carefully at the staffing and headcount projections for the healthcare venture case, you can see how the management salaries quickly add up. In addition, you can see why a monthly breakdown of expenses is useful because it allows you to more accurately reflect the hiring of personnel to when you truly need them. This, in turn, has a direct impact on the projected P&L, month by month. Most entrepreneurs have highly detailed breakdowns of how many positions are filled over the first two years of the business, position by position, as shown in the departmental budgets. It is a good idea to create a separate worksheet on the timing and amount of personnel costs if these are among the major expense components of your business.

Spending Money on Office Space and Furniture

The moment you move out of a home office, rents tend to be the second biggest expense for new ventures after salaries. Most nonretail startups will have two or three cofounders, and over the course of the first year, perhaps ten other employees. That's three offices, a dozen cubicles, a conference room for meetings and selling, storage areas for supplies, and a small kitchen area. Add all of these up and it is no surprise that many startups look for between 2,500 and 5,000 square feet of space to lease in the first year of operations, hopefully with some adjacent options to expand. The simple table below shows the tremendous impact on operating expenses on the price per square foot.

Cost per Square Foot ($)	Space Needed	Lease per Year	Cost per Month
8	5,000	40,000	3,333
13	5,000	62,500	5,208
22	5,000	110,000	9,167

A price of $8 per square foot might represent some converted warehouse space ideal for software development; $15, a well-accommodated space in an office building with certain amenities, located outside a major city; and $25, the same within the city. Look at the immense differences in cash outlays on a yearly basis. This is, of course, a balance. You have to be where young, hardworking employees will want to come to work; and, for the "adults" helping to manage the business, you might have to spend more for parking spaces near your office. The bottom line is that you have to hunt for a good deal for your office space—and if you can, work out of your home office until you begin to hire employees.

Incubators are another option for entrepreneurs. An incubator is shared office space where angel groups or venture capital firms essentially subsidize rent for startups. Once you need to hire additional employees beyond the founders, then it's time to move out and find your own office space. If you use an incubator, however, be careful about giving up your equity in return just for office space, basic services, and supplies. There has to be a lot more value added to the business to warrant dilution for such commodities.

Talk to your friends, also starting ventures, who are in a similar position. For example, in one of your authors' first companies, our group of cofounders checked around our university community regarding office space. We heard about an alumnus who was leasing office space in the attic of his commercial building to students wishing to start new companies at the whopping price of $2 a square foot! There were certain conditions: no walls, a willingness to share computers, and not minding when the chemists from downstairs ran up to the attic to ask us to quickly open all of our windows (chemistry experiments were running on the lower floors). All of this sounded just fine to us. This alumnus had his hand in dozens of startups during his informal yet highly effective incubator.

Every office needs desks, couches, kitchen appliances, and other accessories to make it an effective place to work. That does not mean that the furniture has to be purchased new. Read the classified advertisements in your local paper, find the bankruptcy auctions of office equipment, or visit your local low-cost office furniture and supplies discounter to get bargain-basement prices for used items. The only places where you need to impress visitors are the reception area and the conference room—and even there, you can typically buy used items that are still very attractive. Another option is to look at leasing plans for new equipment. However, you can't really beat used office furniture at a "fire sale." Countless entrepreneurs have done this, and so can you.

Hiring Engineers

Entrepreneurs sometimes turn to "search firms"—otherwise known as recruiters—to fill marketing and technical positions. Since these firms are paid 20% to 30% of the first year's salary for successful placements, this can be a highly expensive way to find new employees. Instead, use your network, investors, classmates, and professors to spread the word that you have certain positions to fill. Moreover, rather than just posting on Web services such as LinkedIn, you want to get some sort of reference for each person you hire. Even one B player in a 15-person company can cause terrible harm, be it with the customers, the suppliers, or in the technology itself. As an entrepreneur, you must be committed to hiring A players from the very start.

You can also be creative in your search for new employees. Throw a few office parties, invite everyone in your network, and spread the word among your local university community. Let other people do the drinking while you talk to everyone attending, learning their interests and seeing if they are good listeners and collaborative in nature. If so, you can float the idea of working with your company—first on a trial basis to get to know one another, and then ongoing. Your authors have hired dozens of new technical employees in their various startups in years past, all without paying a single recruiter fee.[4]

---

[4]This "hiring technique" is what one of your authors and his partners did in their first software company: VenturCom. Fortunately, some of our early customers were large breweries. We received a keg of beer every month from large customers in return for the best customer service in the world! This arrangement sure helped hire a lot of great programmers.

In terms of financial projections for technical salaries, there are standard levels of pay for certain disciplines that you can determine by networking with other entrepreneurs or referring to the various templates on our own textbook Website. And be sure to include a small bonus pool at the end of each year for your technical people. Five percent goes a long way at Christmas time as a gesture of appreciation and will help retain your best engineers. Be assured that if they are talented and achieve success in your company, these same individuals will be receiving calls from other companies for employment. There is no doubt that the human dimension of a business also drives financial projections.

Many entrepreneurs feel that what you need to find and hire is a strong project manager who can organize a combination of engineering employees and external subcontractors found to augment the team in certain important areas. These include the exterior design of the product, packaging, or user interface.

Hiring and Compensating Salespeople

Hiring salespeople is an entirely different matter. This cannot be so easily subcontracted to independent sales representatives or other companies. Revenue is the lifeblood of any venture, and sales are something that you must not only control but excel at. Therefore, a few select sales or business development people are essential for the success of nearly all new ventures. A small firm needs *A* players especially in this area. And if they make more take-home pay than the founders based on sales commissions—well, that's a good thing because their success is making your equity worth millions. However, it is hard to know if any given sales candidate will prove successful selling your products or services *until they are actually doing it*. Some salespeople are very good at selling entrepreneurs on large, rich pipelines of customers *that never materialize into actual sales*. And, by the time you know it in six months, it may be too late for your fledgling company. Your author speaks from painful experience on this matter in one of his other startup companies:

There once was a guy named Dan,

who every day sold us a big pipeline, "man to man,"

but good old Dan never put a penny of real revenue into our can.

The Dan in this rhyme was all too real. Relying on him to generate sales led to a tough startup year and almost proved fatal to the fledgling business! Unfortunately, most entrepreneurs make this mistake at one time or another in their ventures. The only way to be sure about avoiding a similar mistake is to do your due diligence on every salesperson you hire. Find out their performance to sales quota over the past three years. If someone doesn't work out, you have lost three months between firing that individual, finding someone new, training, him or her, and turning him or her loose onto customers. Ventures can ill afford three months of lost time.

In terms of how these ideas hit the financial statements, if you have the choice between a $100,000 base and a 3% commission, versus a $50,000 base and a 5% commission, choose the latter. In fact, tier the commission level higher for more sales. For example, if it's software, 5% for the first $500,000; 6% for the next $250,000; 7% for the next $250,000; and 8% for anything beyond. The message is the more business closed, the more money made on each additional sale. A good salesperson will jump all over this and work tirelessly to succeed.

Spending Money on Attorneys

Retaining good legal counsel is money well spent in a new venture. Unfortunately, it is going to cost you a lot of money. In the health monitoring venture's projected P&L, you can see that we have budgeted $60,000 in the first year, which for that case, included incorporation, an employee stock option plan, a patent, and helping to structure agreements with initial customers. In writing this book, we once again asked former students and friends who have had ventures funded by angels, VCs, and corporate investors to share with us their startup financial projections. We observed attorneys' fees ranged from $20,000 at the low end to $100,000 at the high end for high-roller, technology-intensive ventures. Expect some significant upfront fees for incorporation, shareholder or partners' agreements, and employee stock options plans. You will also incur further upfront fees for "private placement memorandums" (which include the guts of your business plan) for angel-type investments. Or, if you are doing substantial venture capital fund-raising, be prepared for attorneys' fees that are in excess of $30,000! Insist that the legal fees for venture capital fund-raising are taken out of the post-raise piggybank—that is, to be shared with the investors, and not borne by you alone.

However, after these initial expenses, with careful management, your attorneys' fees can come back down to Earth. In our health monitoring venture, for example, the second-year fees come to $3,000 a month, or $36,000 for the year. For most technology ventures, that is not an unreasonable number—although we have seen many with expenditures twice that amount, and much more if patent work is involved.

At the same time, a good attorney is worth his or her weight in gold. As in so many other areas of entrepreneurship, the best way to find a good attorney is to network with other entrepreneurs in the area. See who your *successful* peers recommend. While the brand name on the firm is important, remember that you are hiring an individual. You want to try to get the name of an attorney who is highly experienced doing work in your specific industry sector.

In addition to keeping you out of trouble in matters of standard business practice, attorneys from well-established firms will introduce you to investors, angels as well as venture capitalists. Those from the largest firms may also have colleagues who represent other organizations that just might be your first set of hard-to-win customers. The types of advice that you will receive include how best to distribute founders' shares, to establish employee stock incentive programs, and where and how to incorporate or structure the business to serve the interests of both investor types and liability protection. For example, angel investors will have no problem with a Limited Liability Company because the losses of the startup are passed on through to the unit holders on a pro-rata basis. Venture capitalists, on the other hand, want preferred stock, which takes you into the C Corporation status. If your attorney cannot show insight into these fundamental matters, he or she is not the correct attorney for you. The attorney you want will also have access to seasoned intellectual property (IP) staff that can help protect the "secret sauce" of your company.

You want to try to get a "special deal" on first-year attorneys' fees—or at least until you are well funded. Good attorneys have a nose for high-potential ventures and will cut you a very good deal on fees up until the point you are generating solid revenue as a business. Their time with you is an investment on their part into helping grow a long-term client.

Also, be forewarned that using a good attorney can be addictive. And the meter is always running. To reduce legal expenses, your attorneys should be able to provide you with standard boilerplate-type contracts for customer and employee agreements. It should then be okay for you to fill in the blanks or modestly amend them without final review for each agreement. Entrepreneurs who send everything to their attorneys will find themselves with twice the bill for which they had planned.

For patents, you need to work with the very best IP attorneys in your city or area because the implications of a successful patent application can be enormous for the ultimate value of a venture. This is especially true for a life sciences venture. Do not shortcut your work on intellectual property!

First, entrepreneurs who think they have developed some type of "secret sauce" should first file a provisional patent through their attorneys—and this typically costs less than $5,000. Then there is the formal patent application for a technological process or method. This work can run the entrepreneur upwards of $50,000. No two patents are the same, and each one takes thoughtful preparation.

We have also observed ways to reduce this expense. We encountered a startup that spent "only" $12,000 for a first-rate patent application (at least the founding team hoped!). By their attorney's own estimation, this patent would have ordinarily cost the venture about $40,000 to prepare. The reason for the difference was the document that the team handed to the attorney was highly detailed and well prepared. The founding team had already done its homework with friends and associates, several of whom had extensive legal backgrounds.

Spending Money on Accountants

We strongly recommend that you find a reasonably priced, well-regarded accounting firm. This is not just to do your company tax returns but to provide advice and assistance on your book-keeping system and your own personal tax situation. If you spend $2,500 a year for various filings prepared by professionals, it is money well spent. You will also find yourself asking your accountant about how to handle difficult issues about revenue recognition, how to manage tax issues in doing business abroad, and how to participate in bank negotiations for working capital loans and the like. And, while QuickBooks might be the best tool for small business ever invented, you as the entrepreneur do not want to spend your time entering data and producing reports. Either hire a co-op student from your local university, or ask your accounting firm if it can provide some "in-sourced" talent during the startup months of your business. Later on, you can bring in a controller to manage the books—but until then, you and your founding team want to spend every waking second either selling customers, developing products, or raising the next round of capital from investors.

Spending Money on PR Firms

Many an entrepreneur will tell you that being the focus of an article in a local newspaper or trade publication led to critical sales in the early years. This type of publicity makes a small firm look larger and better established. The focus of these articles tends to be an exciting new product announcement or a major customer "win." Or sometimes articles are written on a new emerging market or technology trend, and the entrepreneur is interviewed as a subject matter expert.

We have worked with some entrepreneurs who are natural PR machines, fearless about reaching out to business reporters or trade journal editors. But most simply do not know how to do this and are shy about engaging with the press. That is where a good PR firm comes into play. Its job is to get your firm visibility. PR firms often work on a monthly fee for a pre-specified set of activities with tangible milestones. As with any supplier, you should create a trial period in which the PR firm can prove its capabilities before entering into a longer-term contract. Here, too, network with fellow entrepreneurs to find out the local PR firm that delivers best for firms like yours. PR firms tend to have contacts with media types in specific sectors.

Closing Comments on the P&L

Among all your various projections, investors will turn to your projected P&L first—and then come back to it repeatedly as they read a section of your business plan and then see how it translates back into a particular area of revenue, expense, or profitability. They will then most likely turn to your revenue model to dig further into the top revenue line(s) in the P&L, and then to the Cash Flow Statement to gauge the need for the amount and timing of investment capital. And, for most startups, it is not the Balance Sheet that is used to assess company value over time (e.g., a book value of the business), but rather some combination of a multiple of sales and operating profit in the outlying years—where the multiple itself is based on current deals in your target industry sector. Either way, the P&L becomes a central communication and selling tool in your business plan. It needs to be done carefully and well. This includes a complete set of reasonable assumptions that guide the numbers.

In most cases, you will need a summary version (say, just annual numbers) for an initial discussion, and then a detailed version (monthlies for the first two years) for deeper discussions. Once again, if you do take the more granular approach to projecting revenues and expenses, you can always do a "hide" columns command in your spreadsheet to produce the summary versions as needed.

Digging Into the Cash Flow of a Venture

Projected or booked revenue does not necessarily mean cash in your hand. Every new entrepreneur needs to learn that *revenue is not necessarily cash.* Thus, an important yet subtle point in business model design is to factor in when revenue gets translated into cash.

An example of the importance of understanding cash flow is a recent startup that finds missing charges in the billing records of large physician groups and hospitals. Studies have shown that upwards of 3% of all medical charges for healthcare in the United States are actually missing—which means procedures were performed but not billed to health insurers—due to human and computer error. For example, there are surgery charges without associated anesthesia charges, or anesthesia charges without surgery charges, and so forth. This company developed data-mining software to find these inconsistencies.

After trying without much success to sell software for $200,000 per license to the IT departments of large healthcare customers, the venture team realized that a better approach would be just to find the missed charges, collect the money, and look to take 20% of that cash. The sale was to CFOs or revenue managers of large physician groups. This new strategy turned out to be highly effective. Within a year, they have over 20 customers using "the service" with a contingency fee on tens of millions of dollars.

But the new business model imposed considerable need for working capital. Whereas a software license or subscription fee gets paid typically right way by a customer, a contingency fee can stretch conversion of sales into hard cash months down the road. In this case, the software first has to find the missing charge; next, the potential missing charge has to be communicated to the healthcare provider and validated. Only then can it be billed, and health insurers pay on a 30- to 60-day cycle. All told, the new business model imposed a four-month cash conversion cycle on the venture. Meanwhile, it had to pay employees to run the software on specific data sets, talk with hospital staff about each specific charge, and only then, assist in the billing of the charge. Then everyone had to sit back and wait for the insurer to pay the claim. The venture team had to raise more than a million dollars from angel investors to cover the first six months of operating expenses before cash began rolling into the business.

As an entrepreneur, you must anticipate a cash conversion issue and build it into your business plan. Angel investors and VCs are going to pay careful attention to your cash flow projections.

There are also other factors beyond accounts receivables that affect cash flow. These include:

- Accounts payables (which increase your cash on hand and also increase as your production or unit volumes increase over time)
- Interest income (which is the interest paid by banks on the cash balances or CDs in your commercial accounts—such as when you raise $2 million in venture capital and it is sitting in a bank while you are spending down the money)
- Interest expense (which is what you must pay to commercial banks or angel investors on a convertible note) for any sort of debt that you have in the business
- Depreciation expense (which adds to your cash flow because it is deducted directly from operating profit before taxes are paid)
- "Capital" investments such as purchasing computers, vehicles, industrial equipment, buildings, and other physical assets
- Line items for infusions of cash coming either from new equity or debt investments

	Mar	Apr	May	Jun	Jul	Aug	Sep	Oct	Nov	Dec	Year 1	Jan
Beginning cash	0	2,365,857	2,246,123	1,923,340	1,801,619	1,643,462	1,485,841	1,243,640	1,000,736	654,969	0	309,980
Net income	(123,937)	(113,470)	(316,320)	(114,720)	(150,953)	(150,153)	(234,470)	(323,245)	(316,091)	(314,737)	(2,158,096)	(442,765)
Less adjustment for A/R (30 days)	0	0	0	0	0	0	0	(84,500)	(22,250)	(22,250)	(129,000)	(106,750)
Add adjustment for A/P (30 days)	0	0	0	0	0	0	0	172,975	1,113	1,113	175,200	174,088
Add interest income 2%	0	3,943	3,744	3,206	3,003	2,739	2,476	2,073	1,668	1,092	23,943	517
Subtract interest payment 12%	0	0	0	0	0	0	0	0	0	0	0	0
Add depreciation	5,103	5,103	5,103	5,103	5,103	5,103	5,103	5,103	5,103	5,103	51,033	6,938
Less capital expense	(15,310)	(15,310)	(15,310)	(15,310)	(15,310)	(15,310)	(15,310)	(15,310)	(15,310)	(15,310)	(153,100)	(8,054)
Free cash flow	(134,143)	(119,734)	(322,783)	(121,721)	(158,157)	(157,621)	(242,200)	(242,904)	(345,767)	(344,989)	(2,190,020)	(376,027)
Net change in cash	(134,143)	2,246,123	1,923,340	1,801,619	1,643,462	1,485,841	1,243,640	1,000,736	654,969	309,980	(2,190,020)	(66,047)
Equity financing	2,500,000	0	0	0	0	0	0	0	0	0	2,500,000	5,000,000
Debt financing	0	0	0	0	0	0	0	0	0	0	0	0
Ending cash	2,365,857	2,246,123	1,923,340	1,801,619	1,643,462	1,485,841	1,243,640	1,000,736	654,969	309,980	309,980	4,933,953

Figure 9.4 Pro Forma Cash Flow Statement for a Health Monitoring Venture

Figure 9.4 shows an example of a cash flow projection for the health monitoring venture. On the textbook Website, there are a number of examples of Cash Flow Statements for various types of ventures. Find the template for the type of venture that works for you and study it. And never rely on these templates alone. Get someone on your team who knows how to run the numbers!

For completeness, Figure 9.5 also shows a simple, cleanly formatted Balance Sheet for the healthcare monitoring venture. Most professional investors doing equity deals will expect to see this as well, although the vast majority of their attention will be focused on the revenue projection, P&L, and Cash Flow Statement. Debt financing, however, will require just as much attention to the Balance Sheet as to any other statement because lenders are very focused on the amount of leverage and collateral in the business. But unless it is convertible debt for an angel investor, debt financing is largely for later-stage growth.

Revenue Rich, Cash Poor

"Cash is king" has been the long-standing mantra of entrepreneurs. There are many reasons for this. Perhaps foremost is the proverbial "cash crunch" that most entrepreneurs confront at one time or another. And this goes well beyond being short on cash for startup.

There are times in the ramp-up period for ventures when sales grow beyond expectations and, *at the same time,* it becomes difficult to meet the biweekly payroll. When this happens once, you can live with it. When it happens month after month, it means that while you have focused on managing the revenue dimension of the P&L, you have failed to adequately plan for cash needs. There tend to be two causes to the problem.

First, to meet increased levels of sales, you have to pay contract manufacturers and materials suppliers (for product companies), or application hosting suppliers (for software firms), or contract labor (for services firms) in advance of when revenue can be collected from customers,

Feb	Mar	Apr	May	Jun	Jul	Aug	Sep	Oct	Nov	Dec	Year 2	Year 3	Year 4	Year 5
4,933,953	4,491,795	4,040,000	3,655,669	3,202,597	2,983,420	2,619,111	2,332,945	2,006,668	1,687,265	1,401,862	309,980	1,143,921	3,037,372	14,208,378
(406,990)	(373,615)	(347,673)	(373,498)	(280,123)	(282,615)	(246,140)	(243,498)	(278,356)	(201,548)	(165,873)	(3,642,693)	2,950,550	14,255,038	23,736,900
(44,500)	(89,000)	(44,500)	(89,000)	(44,500)	(89,000)	(44,500)	(89,000)	(44,500)	(89,000)	(44,500)	(818,750)	(1,923,046)	(4,780,517)	(7,439,400)
2,225	4,450	2,225	4,450	2,225	4,450	2,225	4,450	2,225	4,450	2,225	209,688	733,652	1,509,026	2,359,470
8,223	7,486	6,733	6,093	5,338	4,972	4,365	3,888	3,344	2,812	2,336	6,096	29,078	83,626	344,915
0	0	0	0	(1,000)	(1,000)	(1,000)	(1,000)	(1,000)	(1,000)	(1,000)	(7,000)	(12,000)	(12,000)	(12,000)
6,938	6,938	6,938	6,938	6,938	6,938	6,938	6,938	6,938	6,938	6,938	83,250	117,267	91,433	87,750
(8,054)	(8,054)	(8,054)	(8,054)	(8,054)	(8,054)	(8,054)	(8,054)	(8,054)	(8,054)	(8,054)	(96,650)	(102,050)	(75,600)	(85,600)
(442,158)	(451,795)	(384,331)	(453,072)	(319,177)	(364,309)	(286,166)	(326,276)	(319,404)	(285,403)	(207,928)	(4,266,059)	1,793,451	11,071,006	18,992,035
4,491,795	4,040,000	3,655,669	3,202,597	2,883,420	2,619,111	2,332,945	2,006,668	1,687,265	1,401,862	1,193,934	(3,956,079)	2,937,372	14,108,378	33,200,414
0	0	0	0	0	0	0	0	0	0	0	5,000,000	0	0	0
0	0	0	0	100,000							100,000	100,000	100,000	100,000
4,491,795	4,040,000	3,655,669	3,202,597	2,983,420	2,619,111	2,332,945	2,006,668	1,687,265	1,401,862	1,193,934	1,143,921	3,037,372	14,208,378	33,300,414

	Year 1	Year 2	Year 3	Year 4	Year 5
Assets					
Cash	309,980	1,143,921	3,037,372	14,208,378	33,300,414
Accounts receivable	129,000	725,250	1,923,046	4,780,517	7,439,400
Equipment (net of depreciation)	102,067	115,467	100,250	84,417	82,267
Total assets	**541,047**	**1,984,638**	**5,060,668**	**19,073,312**	**40,822,080**
Liabilities					
Accounts payable	175,200	373,763	733,652	1,509,026	2,359,470
Debt					
Short-term debt	0	100,000	100,000	100,000	100,000
Long-term debt					
Total liabilities	**175,200**	**473,763**	**833,652**	**1,609,026**	**2,459,470**
Equity					
Invested capital	365,847	1,510,875	3,500,000	3,500,000	3,500,000
Retained earnings			727,016	13,964,286	34,862,610
Total equity	**365,847**	**1,510,875**	**4,227,016**	**17,464,286**	**38,362,610**

Figure 9.5 Pro Forma Balance Sheet for a Health Monitoring Venture

particularly large ones. In other words, your COGS (cost of goods sold) are eating up the cash in the business that you need to pay yourself and your full-time employees.

- Second, even with increased levels of sales, it often becomes harder and harder to actually collect money from customers. You simply have that many more customers to chase down, or a greater number of customers are lagging behind in payment. Sales are great, but because of the accounts receivable collection problem, the cash situation is poor. You, as an entrepreneur, find yourself spending morning after morning calling up corporate customers for payment!

Entrepreneurs then go to their commercial bank seeking a working capital loan—typically structured as a line of credit secured on collateral in the company—against which the company can borrow funds for short-term needs. Before the economic worries of 2009, most entrepreneurs could walk into their bank with proof of a strong and growing P&L and a strong Balance Sheet (where Total Assets exceeded Total Liabilities by a factor of 2:1) and walk out with that line of credit. However, these days, that visit to the bank has become more difficult. Many entrepreneurs have been forced to turn to other measures both to conserve and raise short-term cash—second mortgages on their personal property, reduced credit terms to their own customers, squeezing suppliers, and yes, reducing headcount. *The hardest time to raise additional money—short term from banks or longer term from investors—is when you really need it.*

Investors and serial entrepreneurs want to see that you fully understand the cash conversion cycle in your business. For a product type of venture, that means the time period between (a) when you have to pay for materials and the conversion of those materials into finished products in inventory; then (b) when the products are sold into channels to generate sales from customers; and then (c) when these sales from customers convert into cash as checks or electronic funds transfers deposited and cleared in your company's bank account. For a software or services venture, the cash conversion cycle typically boils down to how to get customers to pay you in a timely manner. Either way, that cash conversion cycle is crucial to how investors will think of you and your venture!

Needless to say, the shorter the cash cycle, the better. The question is, What can you, the entrepreneur, do to shorten it? For example, a homebuilder will ask customers for a down payment before construction begins. Should consulting ventures try to do the same? Otherwise, the consultant will do the work, invoice for time and expenses at the end of the month, and then wait 30 to 60 days for payment. Meanwhile, the consultant has had to pay his or her credit card company for expenses incurred. Better to estimate the project fee and immediately invoice for 25% of that amount with a two-week "rush" on payment so that the work can commence right away.

Similarly, most contracts have interest penalties for late payment beyond 30 days from receipt of invoice. Moreover, in some businesses, one finds incentives for early payment—such as a 2% discount for payment within 15 days.

On the other side of the equation, you need to manage your own suppliers carefully. You need to find suppliers who will give you terms of credit as well—and then treat those suppliers with respect and timely payment. The last thing an entrepreneur needs is to be the last in line to receive essential materials or components for a finished product or service that a large customer is expecting to receive at the end of the month!

How Financial Projections Impact Investor Valuations of New Firms

If we step back for a moment, the larger purpose of these financial projections is to show investors that your good product, system, or service concept can be turned into *a good business*. That means a business that produces a growing revenue stream, and from that stream, cash. Just as you might think of an "architecture" for a product or service, your financial statements reveal the "architecture" for making money in a venture.

These are just projections. For most of you, *there is no business yet*. As we described in the prior chapter, seed or Series A financing will be based largely on two things: (a) comparables for similar types of ventures at given stages of growth in the same target industry and market space; and (b) the experience of your management team. Investors have a number of online sources they can turn to for private equity deals—Dow Jones VentureSource is perhaps the leading service. If ventures in your "space" with just prototypes or early services—and little if any actual customer revenue—are getting valued at $5 million post-money for Series A financing, then that is going to be the starting point for you as well. *This is regardless of the fact that your financial projections might show $100 million in annual revenue down the road!* But you still need to show a robust set of revenue and profit projections just to get a seat at the table.

The quality of your management team should get you a bump on valuations at any stage of the business. In some cases, we have seen younger entrepreneurs who have recruited a serial, successful entrepreneur as the CEO and seen their financing valuations *double*. Plus, that CEO brings in his or her prior VCs into the deal. However, this is not a viable option for most entrepreneurs simply because experienced entrepreneurs will only join you after you have productized your technology or service idea and actually sold products to live customers. And for most of you, that will take some seed funding to get to the point of proving your Venture Concept in the marketplace.

Once your business starts generating revenue, however, your financial statements become a foundation for company valuation, either to raise the next round of financing or for acquisition valuation by a larger firm. Obviously, you need to update your monthly financials with company results—both for revenues and expenses—and revisit the outlying annual numbers with each passing month. And there is no single way that investors or acquiring corporations set a value on a business. Some simply do an industry-segment multiple on the mix of current year and next year's projected sales. Others do a mix of an industry segment multiple of EBITDA. And others do a blend of a multiple of sales and earnings. However, for most small firms, profits are scarce and the driving force for valuation is the current revenue and the growth of that revenue.

Determining Venture Investment Amounts _____

The P&L and Cash Flow Statements provide insight into the amount of startup money needed by the business. The simplest way is to look at the negative operating profit for the first several years of the business, adjust it for cash flow considerations before equity investment—and that is the investment required. Sure, it might be chopped up into a seed, Series A, and Series B, but overall, your own projections set a foundation for the capital raise.

Seasoned investors also know how to ask the questions that determine whether you are asking for enough money. For example, most Web social network–type entrepreneurs underestimate the cost of acquiring visitors to the Website, inducing purchase, and translating this into repeat purchases or recurring revenue. If you ask for $150,000 to start a venture, an angel might think that you really need $250,000. Or if you are developing a new type of analytics software, and have budgeted $500,000 to hire three salespeople to cover the United States, the VC might well see the need for eight salespeople, plus an experienced VP of Sales who already knows the effort and processes needed for enterprise selling. That translates into $2.5 million!

Whatever the total number, investors will go back to the rounds of financing described at the very beginning of Chapter 8, and parse total capital requirement into three stages:

1. How much money is needed to get the product or service to the point of an "alpha" or proof of concept test with a live, kicking customer? (If you can do this right away—which is often the case for a service—all the more power to you!) To use the terms from the prior chapter, this can be considered "seed financing."

2. How much money is needed to complete the product or service, and if necessary to manufacture an initial amount, to sell to the first wave of customers? This can be seen as Series A financing.

3. How much money is needed to scale up the business to achieve first operating profit? We think of this as the next round, or Series B financing.

Thereafter, if you get to a Series C or later-stage financing, it is likely to be in the tens of millions of dollars for major geographic expansion or to get into the business of acquiring smaller companies to create a consolidated play within an industry niche.

Different types of businesses represent different amounts of time and money for these major stages of financing and the specific milestones within them.

We have also worked with ventures where operating profits were achieved so quickly after first revenue that only a small amount of working capital or "bridge" financing was needed to pay employees and a few key suppliers. On the other hand, most ventures are not so fortunate.

A Closing Thought: Realistic Revenue, Please!

Perhaps most important, try not to be so enamored with your own Venture Concept that your revenue projections become wildly optimistic. Listen to your own Reality Check! Remember, a team will have to defend its numbers "six ways from Sunday" in front of investors. Putting silly numbers on a spreadsheet isn't going to fool anyone.

Several years ago, one of your authors was invited to observe a team's presentation to senior management for a new, exciting corporate venture. The team had prepared a detailed set of financial statements and was ready to make its business case by explaining them page by page. That didn't happen. Instead, one executive grilled team members for over an hour on the set of revenue numbers of just Year 1 and Year 2. I asked him later, Why the intense focus? The executive replied: "Revenue drives everything. Get it right, and we have a fairly good handle on cash flow and capital asset requirements. Get it wrong, however, and everything else is wrong. We've lost a lot of money in the past on revenue projections that were completely off base."

This executive wanted to know the sources of those revenues, their lower and upper ranges, and which sources were greatest. Who would be their best customers? This executive showed little interest in market share expectations in outlying years. Instead, he drilled down on the details of the early years: "How many units do you expect to sell through each channel month by month?" he asked. "How does that compare to competitors' sales in the same category? How can we establish a beachhead with the best customers in your target market, make them reference accounts, and leverage out from there?" He understood that not all customers are equal. He also wanted to know about the team members' proposed channel partners: "How will these partners give us more unit sales than those of current market leaders?" The executive was also curious about the impact of a higher price on sales projections: "A higher price might improve the profit margin, but it's bound to reduce unit sales," he told them. "So how many unit sales will a 10% price rise cost us, and how does that net out? Conversely, how will competitors respond when they learn that we are trying to take their business? Will they drop the floor on price? What will that do to your own profit projections?" The team didn't have an answer to this last question, and he asked them to work up a contingency plan.

This executive's approach was "bottoms-up" and fine-grained. Will you encounter investors or corporate executives with the same level of detailed curiosity? The only safe way to proceed is to be prepared to answer questions that go to the heart of a team's projections—the assumptions, the key customers, the most important drivers of both revenues and costs, and how the projections will change if those assumptions and drivers are altered.

A team preparing to defend its financial projections must be realistic. Most investors have had their fill of unreasonable, unachievable sales projections. Most entrepreneurs are naive about competitors' responses.

Remember, all startups and most new corporate ventures start small. It is okay for you to do the same. The investors and executives doing the grilling have been around long enough to recall the modest beginnings of today's 10X exits or corporate cash cows. Investors and executives expect and appreciate realistic numbers.

Besides, should you get your funding, you will be held accountable *to those same numbers!* So don't oversell. Don't create unachievable expectations that will get everyone in hot water a year or two down the road.

Reader Exercises

Now it is your turn to develop your own financial projections. To guide you through this process, you can find financial templates for various types of companies on our textbook Website.

Step 1: Develop a Granular Projection of Revenue

- Determine the format desired by your professor. We recommend monthlies for the first two years, or until you become cash flow positive. Afterward, annual projections are fine. Your professor may just want annual projections for all five years. Be sure to ask.

- Run through various scenarios on the number of customers, the products and services you are selling, and the unit prices for those commercial offerings. Don't forget to start on a whiteboard first before becoming too heavily engaged on a spreadsheet. Spreadsheets sometimes lead individuals into blind replication of numbers. Investors will challenge you on all your numbers; they do not appreciate thoughtless financial projections. Be realistic about customer ramp-up. Think hard about concrete objectives that lead to the "scaled-up" revenue potential that you determined in the Reality Check. (We think of that as a revenue target for the fifth year of operations.)

- Also think about recurring revenue from existing customers, as well as new revenue from new customers. Build these into your projections as well.

- If you are a products company, think about any services that you might offer with your products (if that is the case), the pricing for those services, and how these ramp up over time. Show these as separate line items. Some professors may ask you to double-check your granular revenue projections against a "top-down" projected share of market approach. In other words, what percentage of the target market do your revenue projections represent, particularly in Year 5? Is that in any way realistic? Is it insufficiently ambitious? If you think your venture's financial requirements put you into the league of institutional venture capital, then these are questions you will be asked and for which you will need reasonable answers.

Step 2: Develop a Pro Forma P&L

Summarize your revenue projections into the top portion of the projected P&L. Then think through your cost of goods. Try to do a "bottoms-up" estimate of the materials and conversion or assembly cost on those materials. For benchmarks, the COGS of manufactured products often come in at 30% to 40% of revenue; for software-based businesses, COGS are far less, from 2% to 15% of revenue; and for labor-intensive services, often at 35% of revenue. Then apply the guidance in this chapter to carefully consider your various operating expenses.

More generally, most investors know that any numbers beyond the first two or three years in a projected P&L are largely speculation. However, the fifth-year estimation remains important because it gives some sense of potential exit value as a multiple of revenue and profit. Once again, internal corporate ventures can satisfy with annual P&L projections. Take your best shot, remembering the "scaled-up" revenue projection you determined in the Reality Check.

Step 3: Develop a Cash Flow Projection

Cash flow is important to entrepreneurs and investors—where every dollar often means the difference between paying yourself a modest salary, or not, during the startup period. This is where you take your learning from accounting classes and apply it to your venture. These are the key questions to consider:

- What are the adjustments to working capital? The big items here are to adjust working capital for accounts receivable (increase working capital), inventory (increase working capital), accounts payable (decrease working capital), taxes (decrease working capital), and any prepaid expenses (decrease working capital).

- Are there adjustments due to fixed capital expenditures, such as spending money on machines of some sort?

- Are the increases to cash due to any short-term borrowing, such as amounts taken from a line of credit with a commercial bank or longer-term commercial notes?

- Are there any infusions of capital from investors?

The last point might lead some to question the extent to which to include seed, Series A, and successive rounds of financing in the cash flow projections. Figure out how much you need to cover cash shortfalls and to meet required investments in people, plant, and equipment. We suggest that you include those rounds of financing needed to (a) get your product to market, and (b) get your company to a cash flow positive footing. That might be $200,000 right in the beginning to complete development, $2 million in six months to build a sales force, and $4 million in two years to scale nationally. Often, services can be cash flow positive from the start, so the amount of money required is to hire the people and buy or lease the computers and office space needed to start delivering those services. Once again, your business model should be driving these projections.

Step 4: Develop a Balance Sheet (Optional)

Balance sheets are a snapshot of performance, year by year. Venture investors expect to see a Balance Sheet as part of a complete set of financial statements. However, unless you are planning on debt financing during the first year or two of operations, it is unusual to see an equity investor focus on the Balance Sheet.

Step 5: Establish Financial Goalposts

- *Startup costs.* These come directly from your Cash Flow Statement, specifically from the month-by-month breakdown of operating expenses and capital investments in plant and equipment. An investor will dig in to the cash flow projections to ask a million questions, one of which will be to pinpoint "startup costs" over the first six months to get to "alpha" or "beta" tests and the "launch" costs of successfully introducing a new product, system, or service to market. Remember, if you have included seed- or Series A–type infusions of cash as part of the cash flow projects, you should subtract these first before summing up your various cash needs to achieve specific milestones. Obviously, the purpose of those funding rounds is to cover the cash shortfalls on the path to profitability.

- *The time to first dollar.* When the business becomes "real", this information comes right from monthly projections of revenue.

- *The time to first profit.* When the business achieves true investor value, this, too, can be found in the projected P&L.

- *First-round and anticipated second-round financing amount.* (That is, seed funding and Series A.) If you are a corporate entrepreneur, do this for the startup capital and then the growth capital to scale your internal venture. As mentioned earlier, these rounds of financing are typically shown in the projected Cash Flow Statement and carried on to the Balance Sheet.

- *Potential valuation for exit.* (For example, the value of the company as an acquisition by a larger concern.) Use an industry standard multiple for your project valuation—say, after five years. If you cannot find a standard multiple, use the following until you do: for products, 2X revenue and 4X EBITDA; for software, 4-5X revenue and 8-10X EBITDA; for pure services, 1.5X revenue and 3X operating profit.

It is hard to develop a comprehensive set of financial projections alone. And rarely can they be done quickly. Set aside two or three solid working days to accomplish the steps outlined above. And take the opportunity to share your results with your advisers—including your professors. You need to be challenged on the numbers by trusted, friendly parties before running the gauntlet with professional investors.

For when it comes to the numbers associated with a business plan, the term *root canal* is a fair description of the type of probing that VCs and others will perform on your projections. The three questions that will run continuously through their minds will be:

1. Are the sales projected for the business both sufficient and based on a realistic revenue model?

2. How much will it really cost to get this business to scale? For example, is it really a million dollars, as the entrepreneur suggests, or is it really two or three million?

3. And if this business works as planned, what is the possible exit valuation based on performance in Year 5? More specifically, a million invested today will be worth how many millions down the road?

Your financial projections must answer these questions. While many investors get excited about new Venture Concepts, business model innovations, and the passions and experience of a venture team, *all investors* drop their smiles and become all too serious when it comes to the numbers. Prepare to defend your numbers, not just once, *but again, again, and again.*

Visit the Student Study Site at **www.sagepub.com/meyer2e** to access the following resources:

- Web Resources
- Video Resources
- General Resources in Entrepreneurship

10

Organizing the Venture Team

The Purpose of the Chapter

Venture capitalist Arthur Rock once said, "Good ideas and good products are a dime a dozen. Good execution and good management—in a word, good people—are rare."

The purpose of this chapter is to introduce you to the importance of organizing the right venture team. This includes first thinking about the legal organization of your venture, assessing yourself as founder of the venture (both in terms of personal characteristics and business skills), understanding the two types of venture teams—the one responsible for writing the venture business plan and the one who will execute the venture business plan, your Advisory Board, official Board of Directors members, and other stakeholders such as a customer Advisory Board. Organizing the right team is critically important for venture success.

Learning Objectives

After reading this chapter, you should be able to:

- Describe the differences between the team who writes the business plan and the team who implements the plan to build a venture
- Understand how to make the venture team work effectively
- Evaluate the importance of constructing a solid external Advisory Board
- List the roles, talents, and responsibilities for official Board members
- Describe the role other stakeholders can play in the venture, including a customer Advisory Board
- Understand the legal organizational options for the venture and the implications for liability protection and taxes
- Develop rewards and incentives for the venture team

For the Team Who Writes the Business Plan: Guard Your Founder's Stock Carefully _____

Let's start off with one of the more difficult questions facing young entrepreneurs. You are starting a venture in class with a group of people and everyone has the best of intentions. Should everyone receive the same amount of stock? Should you even be giving anyone stock at this point?

There is often a difference between those individuals who help write a business plan—such as the entrepreneurship class you are taking now—and the actual founding team for a funded venture. Usually one or two people from the class march forward and do all the work it takes to raise money and build a business. Everyone who helps work on a plan gets bragging rights years down the road when the venture is successful; but realistically, only those few who lay their careers on the line deserve founder's stock. It is a hard lesson for student teams but an essential one when term projects transform into startup enterprises.

Do not promise stock to anyone other than a rock-solid core team member. Contributors during the startup phase come and go. You will find that most people don't have the stomach for the risk, anxiety, and beyond-normal commitment required for new ventures. Giving stock away early on to people who may or may not stay with the venture—or on student teams who may not even be part of the venture—can take millions of dollars out of your own retirement.

For example, let's say that you are one of those rare entrepreneurs who sell his or her company for $100 million and realize a 100-times return on the value of founder's stock at that price. At the very beginning, you sold a certain number of shares of stock for $10,000 to a classmate who helped write the business plan. Other than giving you a little bit of money, the classmate didn't do much else thereafter. Ten years down the road, after the acquisition, that passive participant's $10,000 is worth $1 million. And you, having raised many millions in venture capital, have been taken down to about 9% of the company stock—typical in cases of successive rounds of financing. You walk away with $9 million. But it could have been $10 million. That hurts, particularly after paying taxes. In hindsight, it would have been far better to offer individuals such as this classmate some "friends and family shares" for, say, $100. At exit, that would be a $10,000 thank you, not a $1 million one. Remember, every share of stock you give to people outside the core team dilutes your own shares; investors will insist on this with their Series A and follow-on financing. Guard your stock carefully; it is the primary asset that you will be working for over the next several years—not salary, bonuses, or paid vacations.

Moreover, every mature person that you encounter in the process of a startup knows that working hard for a new venture and contributing in a meaningful way lead to stock. Professional investors have clear expectations for the percentage allocation of stock to key managers in a venture. If an individual becomes part of your management team funded by professionals, stock will come because investors know that stock ownership (or options to own stock) is a major part of incentivizing employees to work 24/7.

Now, let's consider the skill sets required for writing a business plan. Writing a business plan helps teams think through their strategy and then integrate all the different functions in a business toward a cohesive whole. In business school, we learn a lot about how to do an industry or market analysis. We also learn a lot about the basic mechanics of putting together a set of Pro Forma financial statements.

However, when it comes to an R&D and product strategy, and a sales or channel strategy, there is no substitute for experience. If your plan includes developing a technology-intensive product or service, it is best to have someone who has worked intensively with technology before, preferably on a product or service that actually made it to market. That person needs to understand that products are different than services and that both require underlying technology platforms, rapid prototyping to get to "alpha," quick fixes to get to "beta," and then the sheer amount of detail and effort needed to finish a commercial product or service.

Experience in the target industry sector is another great asset for a business plan writing team. If you are mapping out a channel strategy, it would be good to have someone on your team who has actually sold products or services before in a similar market space. It's easy enough to say, "We are going to sell through Whole Foods to reach premium consumers" or "IBM is going to be our channel partner into the healthcare space," but the complexities of actually getting into these or any other powerful channel require as careful a staging as any R&D effort.

Therefore, before you start working on the business plan, ask yourself who are the "right" types of people to have on your team and what it will take to get them to participate.

Some might be direct team members, others advisers to the team. Particularly helpful advisers might include someone already working in your channel—such as a store or regional manager for a consumer product, an industry sales executive in a large computer company for a software venture, or a manager of business development in a pharmaceutical company for a life sciences venture. Similarly, for your financial statements, you or one of your team members should be able to put together a set of coherent projections. We find, however, that the assumptions behind those projections always require bullet-proofing before the show-and-tell with investors. Find any tough, experienced business person who has had to "carry a bag" (i.e., sell) and collect cash from customers—and ask them to play the devil's advocate for your projections.

Every team needs to find a devil's advocate who tries to poke holes into an emerging business plan. Like anything else, if you are too close to a project it is hard to be sufficiently critical of it. As professors, we take the greatest pleasure from teams who approach us every several weeks for selective advice and counsel. This is far better than receiving a plan, sight unseen, on the last day of the semester. This allows your professor to also play the devil's advocate—as well as cheerleader.

Many universities have established mentor networks of individuals like these who want to help new entrepreneurs like you. Even before you start writing your plan, find out if such a network exists and plug in to it. You want to try to schedule meetings with your assigned mentor as soon as possible. Obviously, try to get a mentor who has worked in the industry that you wish to pursue. This will bring the benefit of decades of experience into your business planning.

For the corporate entrepreneur, all these ideas apply as well. You need to bring people with a diverse set of skills onto your venture planning team. It would be foolhardy to fall so much in love with your own idea that you fail to see the landmines both in the market and within the corporation. A strong devil's advocate helps avoid these traps by asking the tough questions and being somewhat skeptical *for your own good.*

The Team Who Actually Builds the Venture _____

Strive for a Balanced Management Team

Clearly, the success of a new venture is partly based on you, the founder. The irony is that while you want to hire people who are equally entrepreneurial, you do not want to hire people just like yourself in terms of competencies. The venture's performance relies far beyond the skills of any single founder and the founder's skill set. Scholarly research shows that the management team, working together, explains much in terms of what we know about venture success.[1] Successful ventures have strong, diversely skilled teams at the core. This typically means someone who excels at sales and marketing, another person who excels at technology (depending on the nature of your business), and another person who is highly competent in finance and/or operations. "One-person" shows rarely succeed because no single founder is good at everything, and the founder's skill limitations will soon limit the growth of the venture. This has actually been called "founder's disease."[2] Ventures constrained by the limited skill sets of their

---

[1]Roberts, E. B. (1991). *Entrepreneurs in High Technology: Lessons from MIT and Beyond.* New York: Oxford University Press; Hambrick, D. C. (1998). Corporate coherence and the top management team. In D. C. Hambrick, D. A. Nadler, & M. L. Tushman (Eds.), *Senior Leadership and Corporate Transformation: CEOs, Boards, and Top Management Teams in Turbulent Times* (pp. 24–30). Boston: Harvard Business School Press.

[2]Roberts, E. B. (1991). *Entrepreneurs in High Technology: Lessons from MIT and Beyond.* New York: Oxford University Press.

founders typically suffer the fate of "the living dead"—little companies that reach a million dollars in sales and never a penny more.

Accordingly, investors look very carefully at the venture team before determining whether or not to invest. This is not the plan-writing team, per se, but the company building team. Once again, the "bullet points on two sides of the page" method works well. Let's consider the necessary business skills required on a startup or corporate venture team:

- *Sales and marketing.* Someone on the team must have solid skills in the marketing and sales area, including marketing research, strategic sales, sales management and merchandising, direct sales, customer service, distribution management, marketing communications, branding, product management, and pricing. For Sales Directors, it is essential that they walk in the door to your company with specific customer leads *already,* and can then prove their ability by translating those leads into revenue. To do this, they have to know the industry, key customers, and how to sell. It is the ultimate litmus test for hiring a VP of Sales for both startups and corporate ventures. If your company is going to spend a year developing its first product or service, then it is not clear that you should spend the time, money, and stock recruiting a VP of Sales until you get closer to launch.

- *R&D, with a big emphasis on the D.* Someone on the team must have specialized skills and expertise in R&D, including leading and managing the R&D process and management of engineering. The person you hire needs to have brought a product or service such as yours to market as a successful commercial offering. Anything less and you are playing a game of Russian roulette.

- *Running a business or operation.* Sometimes called "general management," this is a key skill that must be on the venture team. Some might think of this as an individual with a few gray hairs in spirit (if not in the hair) who has helped build an organization of a significant size. This person must take charge of personnel, project management, planning, and overall administrative matters. In some cases, for young entrepreneurs, you might think of this person as a co-CEO of the company.

Depending on the business, you might also need a team member who knows how to run a manufacturing operation and how to manage suppliers. Similarly, usually after the first round of financing (Series A), ventures bring on a professional CFO-type who is experienced in finance and accounting processes. This individual helps structure subsequent financings; manages cash flow, credit, and collections; and puts in the systems needed to maintain and produce financial information.

Ultimately, your job as founder is to put together a management team who is skilled, highly motivated, and cohesive. In fact, management team cohesion has been found to be positively related to new venture growth.[3] So choose your team wisely. If you fail to build the right team—a team who will stick together in good times and bad—the future of your new venture is likely to be truncated. And every single person you bring on board in the startup phase needs to be highly competent in his or her own particular area. Competition is generally so fierce across an industry that you can ill afford to do otherwise.

This means that you must also assess your business skills. This is a simple personal audit of your strengths and weakness with regard to the basic functional areas of business that are necessary to start and grow a business. Consider the key areas of sales and marketing, R&D, general or operations management, finance and accounting, customer service, and supplier/manufacturing management. Rate yourself as strong (high skills and abilities), average (limited skills and abilities), and weak (low skills and abilities).

No professional investor expects a single individual to be strong in all of these areas. In Microsoft, for example, even the great Bill Gates (the product person and technologist of the business) hired Steve Balmer to run sales and operations. Therefore, discern your business

---

[3]Ensley, M., Pearson, A., & Amason, A. (2002). Understanding the dynamics of new venture top management teams: Cohesion, conflict and new venture performance. *Journal of Business Venturing,* 17(4), 365–385.

strengths and weaknesses. Let this be the driver of composing the startup team, *not just people you like or who are your friends or acquaintances.* Ventures that are just another type of social club among friends rarely become dynamic businesses. A venture requires disciplined activity across the major functions of the business, where key managers are held directly accountable for their respective activities and outcomes. If a founding team has two or three key members, count on the fact that one of these will not survive the first two or three years of the business due to skill and/or performance issues. Your goal is to find the necessary skills and abilities in others that complement your own to serve the needs of the business.

Spotlight on Innovation: A Mentor Provides a Lifelong Lesson

One of your author's mentors shared an approach to team formation that has served well across dozens of startups and corporate ventures. I was all of 23 years old at the time, and my partners were not much older. Mel, our mentor, didn't beat around the bush.

"You guys, for all those brains between those ears, don't know how to hire people, do you? And what's with these fancy headhunters, anyway? They cost *way* too much for a little outfit like yours."

So we listened.

"Take a blank piece of paper and write all the things that you and your partners are good at on the left side of the page. Then write down all the things on the right side of the page where you have no proven abilities—dreams, perhaps, but nothing real. By the way, you have four cofounders and that is way too many chiefs to run the show, but we will deal with that later."

So we wrote down the skills in which we excelled: Technology and face-to-face direct selling appeared on the left side of the page. But we had no one who had ever run a significant business operation, knew how to put together a real budget, or managed a nationwide sales force. These gaps were on the right side of the page. Our weakness as a team stood out like a sore thumb. The needs were fairly obvious. Yet, in our interviewing, all of us were still fixated on hiring brilliant software architects and programmers, and the few of us who could sell were spending more and more time on the road pulling in enterprise sales.

Our mentor stated the obvious. "All you guys want to do is meet other techies, go out and have a great lunch, talk code, and write it off on the business. That is because you feel comfortable meeting other programmers, and meeting people who aren't like you—the people you really need for the business—isn't so much fun. Well, it's time to grow up. Tear that piece of paper in half. Throw out the left side (the things you are good at) and keep the right side (the things you stink at), and only have lunch with people who can fill those gaps. Got it? Can I make it any simpler for you?"

Let his powerful method serve you as well as it has served us over dozens of startups and corporate ventures.

The Importance of Building a High-Performance Culture of *A* Players

An entrepreneur needs *A* players on the team. Any weak team member can cause damage—more in a small firm than in a larger corporation. There is simply no margin for error in a startup. That means that you cannot give up looking for an *A* player just because you are tired and have someone willing to take the job who is a *B* player. Experience dictates that the suboptimal choice never works. Rather, keep on looking for the *A* player and convince that person to take the job even though the salary is less than those of corporate positions. He or she will do that with a reasonable and appropriate amount of stock and for the sheer excitement of working on a dynamic venture team *with other* A *players.* That's the secret; A *players sell themselves on joining ventures.* Introduce an *A* player to weak members on your team or unimpressive Board of Directors or Advisory Board members, and the party is over.

To assess an individual's motivation and capabilities, look to his or her past behavior. Past behavior is a reliable predictor of future behavior. Try to discover the individual's record of achievement and self-motivation. As you interview a candidate, not only ask for key decisions that he or she had to make in the past, but the "why" behind those decisions. You might also want to ask individuals about concrete examples of situations they have been in and how they dealt with those situations. For example, you might ask, "Have you had a setback, and if so, how did you deal with it?" You could also ask a follow-up question: "Why did you choose that course of action?" The answer to this question reveals further insight about the individual's motivation.[4]

As noted earlier, when it comes to hiring sales and marketing professionals, a track record of success in your own specific industry sector is essential. Every entrepreneur has made the mistake of doing otherwise at some point in time, with deep regret. The sales and marketing hire has to be not just an *A* player but an *A* player within your industry. For R&D, software skills are wonderfully portable. The same reasoning applies to finance and accounting skills. Same with general and operations management. But sales and marketing is a different animal. You just don't have enough time for someone to learn who the customers are and how to sell to them in your target market. On the very first day he or she has to be running hard and producing results.

Every hire is critical. The customer support staff needs to wear smiles on their faces and at least not show the frustration they might feel for defective product or bad code; the financial controller must be tight-fisted on operating expenses and contract terms with suppliers, and be a great presenter to your investors and Board of Directors. Even the receptionist is a critical hire. This person will be the face of the company, literally or on the phone, day in and day out. In other words, in their own way, receptionists can be *A* players, too.

The goal of all this is to have a high-performance culture driven by a team of *A* players. Surround yourself with people better than you in certain key areas. Let them know what you expect and reward them for being overachievers. At the end of your first year in business, you want to sit back and say, "I have the best darn team around. They work hard, they are great people, and they are totally dedicated to the company. They are family to me. And I will do anything and everything to help them be successful." That success is your gain.

TIP: BE EXTRA CAREFUL HIRING YOUR FIRST SALESPEOPLE

Entrepreneurs in B2B ventures probably make more mistakes hiring their first one or two salespeople than in any other area. The entrepreneur gets sold a "pipeline" by the salesperson that simply never materializes. Month after month, the only thing that gets done is that your precious cash disappears on travel expenses and base salary. We have found that the only way to hire correctly is to have one experienced salesperson hire other salespeople. That means having such a person as a team member—or, as second best, a senior salesperson acting as a trusted adviser who will help do the interviewing with due diligence. Also, good salespeople will walk in the door *already having customers needing what you have to sell*, and therefore prove their worth by quickly closing on a few deals. You can never be too careful about who you hire to represent your company in the field, and you will depend on these people to produce the lifeblood of your company—customer revenue.

---

[4]Slaughter, M. (2004). *Seven Keys to Shaping the Entrepreneurial Organization*. Kansas City, MO: Kauffman Center for Entrepreneurial Leadership.

Create a Shared Vision and Culture of Teamwork and Success

Your job as a founder is to communicate your vision and values to everyone who joins your team. There are two sides of the vision and values deal for a startup:

1. *Your vision and values for the customer.* Ventures that are highly customer focused seem to excel time and time again. The goal is to bring the best possible experience and benefit to the customers. It is more than just throwing a new product at a customer, or even a new service. The total customer experience incorporates how they are sold, what they use, and how they are serviced in that use. This is a virtuous, reinforcing cycle that has the practical benefit of leading to recurring revenue and word-of-mouth referrals—where your customers become some of your best salespeople, advocates, and spokespersons.

2. *Your vision and values for your employees.* The words *teamwork, personal growth,* and *financial gain* are often used without substance. In your company, make them have real meaning by the actions you take with how you approach problem solving, career advancement, and financial incentives. It is all about finding the best people to work in your company and doing things that deserve their respect and loyalty. A company is worth nothing without its people, working hard and working together to serve customers. Here, too, there is a practical benefit. Employees will work hard to improve your company's business processes. They will cover for one another in an environment of constrained resources. And experienced staff will take pride in teaching newly hired staff the culture, discipline, and focus of your company.

As the founder, you must communicate a binding, forceful vision for these two areas. You, as leader, must get each team member to buy in to your customer and internal company visions. Ultimately, you are trying to create a unity of purpose that energizes everyone in the venture to work together. Your statement of purpose must be clear and consistent.

For example, McDonald's customer vision is to be the best at providing good-tasting, low-priced, quality fast-food in clean restaurants for people pressed for time. The vision can be written as a statement and shared with everyone, and it can also be vividly expressed verbally as a compelling story. It sets the tone and culture within your company. Set a target to be the very best in your target industry *at something,* and then articulate to your team what it takes to be *the best.* This helps everyone understand the importance of each and every function inside the company. You want your team to rally around this vision, be it the engineers who are working to make the most easy-to-use software that is still powerful and bug-free, the salesperson who represents your company with pride and purpose, or the front-office receptionist who greets visitors as a committed representative of your company. If all members of your company understand and believe in your customer vision, you will have a high-functioning team who shares a common purpose and goals. These are simple yet fundamentally important concepts that have served entrepreneurs well time and time again.

The employee vision is no less important. Starbucks values its employees, for example, by providing its part-time employees with health and other benefits. This translates into the spirit and high level of customer service that pervades the Starbucks stores around the world. It is equally important to provide clarity with regard to the roles, responsibilities, and accountabilities of every team member. This is often hard to do in a startup where everyone enthusiastically wants to do everything: a little bit of R&D, a little bit of selling, a little bit of customer service. But this simply doesn't work. Each team member needs to have a clear focus that aligns with his or her skills. The entrepreneur as manager has to provide clarity with regard to such questions as, "Who's going to do what?", "What part of the job is mine and what is yours?", "Whose responsibility is it?", and "How are we going to be held accountable?"[5]

---

[5]Slaughter, M. (2004). *Seven Keys to Shaping the Entrepreneurial Organization.* Kansas City, MO: Kauffman Center for Entrepreneurial Leadership.

It is so important that you understand the basic principles of retaining good, loyal venture team members:

1. Preach what you practice. Communicate the values, vision, and objectives of the venture. Practicing what you preach is also imperative.

2. Be selective in hiring. Hire people with values consistent with the venture.

3. Make use of small, talented teams for most tasks and give them the authority to act. Assign new marketing, product, or sales challenges to small teams of people empowered to give you a straight answer.

4. Supply excellent rewards for excellent performance. This means setting aside a portion of the operating budget—say, 5%—to selectively reward excellent work. Some entrepreneurs make a portion of individual performance compensation based on "team performance" measured against certain goals, such as total sales, meeting an R&D milestone, or overall customer satisfaction.

5. Listen hard, talk straight. Honest, two-way communication is required to build trust.[6]

Finally, it is extremely important for team morale to celebrate your victories. Everyone wants to be associated with a winner. So it is imperative that each victory (e.g., attracting a new client) be celebrated. This provides needed motivational fuel to keep the venture team working at optimal levels.

Boards in a Venture

Create an Advisory Board from the Get-Go

We believe that building an Advisory Board should precede the formation of a formal Board of Directors. Your Advisory Board is a group of individuals who you will invite to provide you with advice, counsel, and guidance as you attempt to build and grow your venture. But, unlike your official Board of Directors, your Advisory Board has no legal status and is not subject to the same regulations as the Board of Directors, including possible legal liability. The entrepreneur can begin building an Advisory Board from Day 1 of the venture.

An Advisory Board should consist of experienced individuals across the spectrum of functions: sales, technology, venture finance, and so forth. They are there to help you on a phone call, to help you, the entrepreneur, make tough decisions. And the Advisory Board members give quasi-officialdom to their contribution, coupled selectively with financial rewards. This might be a small amount of stock (options) for participating on the Advisory Board, additional stock for making the introduction to major accounts that result in revenue, an annual retainer to provide monthly reviews of technology plans and choices, and reimbursement for travel to the meetings you wish to conduct. For the most part, however, Advisory Board members are engaged individually by the entrepreneur and his or her key team members.

Our experience is that entrepreneurs form such Boards but, in the heat of battle, fail to use them as regularly and effectively as originally intended. Don't make the same mistake. These individuals can really help you with that outside, independent opinion. The types of calls entrepreneurs might make to Advisory Board members include:

- "I need to hire a new VP of Sales. Our current guy is good at managing current accounts but not at busting into new ones. And he isn't a closer. I would like you to meet him and give me your opinion. If you can't have lunch, can you take a phone call?"

---

[6]Reichheld, F. (2001, July). Lead for loyalty. *Harvard Business Review*, 76–84.

- "We are trying to crack into Company X. Do you know anyone who is an executive with that company? We need a referral into the account."

- "We need to start raising our next round of capital. It would be great if we could get the next round from angel investors. What do you think about that approach versus VCs? Would you be interested in participating? Do you have others in your network that we can talk to?"

- "My technology lead wants to shift to open-source tools. I am concerned that we might be sacrificing power or support of some sort. What do you think? Do you know someone I can talk to about this?"

- "This new product we have been talking about is ready to go live. I need help finding a beta test site. Where do you think we should go? Can you go in there with me to talk with the customer?"

Advisory Board members are valuable for their personal networks. Most entrepreneurs look at initial Advisory Board members as individuals who can help produce revenue for the venture through their personal contacts. But beyond this, the entrepreneur should look for people with a range of expertise to expand his or her knowledge base. Some companies, particularly in the biotech space, have both a business Advisory Board and a technical Advisory Board (with distinguished scientists). Importantly, you should seek out people who will be candid and honest with you and willing to bounce ideas around. The typical Advisory Board will consist of highly experienced individuals from sales and marketing, investment, and technical backgrounds. You might even find a few professors sitting on those Boards!

On the other hand, not every person working with your company deserves an Advisory Board position. For example, it is not uncommon to find entrepreneurs who place their professional services providers on the Advisory Board, with some stock included. But be careful here. You are paying these professional services providers for their services anyway. For a technology-intensive venture, figure at least $25,000 for a major financing and an ongoing amount of at least $5,000 a month. You are getting their advice anyway, and paying handsomely for it! On the other hand, if you are fortunate enough to have an attorney who can network you into your region's angel investment and venture capital community, then he or she truly deserves a taste of stock in your company that comes with Advisory Board membership. In other words, the value-add has to be beyond the specific professional service contracted.

The same reasoning applies to the accounting firm you retain for the business. These days you will be paying market rate for its services. (In a difficult economy, professional service providers have little desire to take equity in lieu of cash.) With that payment, you have the right to ask for additional advice. If, on the other hand, you feel that your accountant has operating experience and can spend time in your company helping to set up control systems and coach people hired to run operations, then an Advisory Board position makes very good sense.

The Board of Directors: Proceed With Care (If You Are Given a Choice)

The notion of having an official Board of Directors is largely driven by the form of organization you select to develop. (We will explore this issue in greater detail later in this chapter.)

If the entrepreneur decides to formally incorporate the business, a formal Board of Directors is required by law. The Board of Directors serves to protect the interest of the shareholders in a way that is independent of the managers of the business. It provides oversight and governance on key decisions and the managers making those decisions. But beyond this, you will find startups recruiting prominent members of the business community to serve on the Board of Directors to lend credibility to the venture. In addition, members of the Board play an active hand in raising subsequent rounds of funding.

The Board of Directors is typically composed of several key officers of the company (such as the CEO and the CFO) and then three or more outside members responsible for the oversight of the affairs of the venture. Boards that are greater than seven individuals prove unwieldy and incapable of making fast decisions. The more typical number is five individuals, keeping to an odd number to avoid deadlock in certain critical issues such as basic strategy, senior management changes, financings, and exits.

The Board of Directors is elected by shareholders based on a slate of Directors put forth by the management team. In reality, if your venture is financed by angels or venture capitalists, you can expect them to request a seat on the Board so they can closely watch how their money is being spent. Most investments are "syndicated," which means that the Board will consist of you, perhaps one other cofounder, and two or three professional investors. They will outnumber you and, if you are not the right person to build the company, your days at the helm will be numbered. That's the price of taking outside money from professional investors. In ventures just getting going, one will often find even smaller Boards of Directors, say two founders and one key angel investor. This is often more comfortable for the entrepreneur, although not necessarily better. It is a business and everyone, even the founder, needs to be held accountable for his or her decisions and actions.

Taking professional money is analogous to getting married. The Board of Directors' role is ultimately the investor's "stick" to demand a divorce, to keep the house, and to proceed forward without you. That is why when you convince an investor that he or she should invest in your company, have a serious heart-to-heart with your partners to determine whether you can see having that particular angel, VC, or corporate strategic investor sitting on your Board holding the Sword of Damocles over your head. And yes, you need to try to talk to a few other entrepreneurs who have lived under the sword of that same individual. In many if not most cases, it is a wonderful, productive relationship where the investor adds incalculable value to the business—value well beyond the money itself. But in other cases, the relationship becomes "a pain in the neck" and distracts the entrepreneur from building the business he or she wants to build. You obviously want to try to avoid this latter situation, and it all comes down to a matter of individual personalities. Do your homework on investors because they will most often be sitting on your Board.

The Board is expected to meet on a regular basis (typically monthly for startups). It will take a major role in setting strategic direction, appointing the officers of the firm, declaring dividends, approving major purchases, and reviewing the performance of management. The Board will also be involved in reviewing operating and capital budgets, assisting with your business plan and its execution, providing support for daily operations, overseeing proper use of resources, and resolving conflicts among owners and/or shareholders. That means that you, as the entrepreneur, must allocate several days (hopefully over the weekend before Board meetings) working with your management team to prepare the presentation to the Board as well as necessary financial statements. These need to be short, focused presentations and an accurate set of current month, past month, and quarterly financial statements. The details matter on revenue creation, cash on hand, and monthly burn. Revenue is the cure for many sins in a venture, and your Board members will want to dig into the revenue situation of the company. Expect Board members to want to see a breakdown of customers in the pipeline, customers closed, and the revenue expected or realized from each type of customer. They will want to help you build the pipeline but also hold your feet to the fire on closing sales.

As noted above, if you take outside professional money, your investors will hold the "outside" Board seats—and they will most often outnumber the "inside" Board seats of you and your founders. In fact, the composition of the Board will be a specific condition of the financing itself. The investor will already have his or her stock by virtue of the investment, and while the company remains privately held, there are no additional director's fees or payments expected or required. These investors/Directors are working to achieve an exit—just like you.

It is also possible to not have just investors sitting on your Board of Directors. These can be executives working in major corporations or the CEOs of other successful startups. In some cases, there might even be a professor with business experience sitting on the Board! The advantage of this type of noninvestor, outside Board member is that this individual can provide the external perspective on strategy and tactics that is not totally driven by "exit." For example, some venture capitalists have little or no true operating experience building and running a company; they are strictly "financial" types. If that is the case in your company, you can argue for finding an outside Board member who has already created the $100 million company that you wish to create. Prudent investors will want this as well.

For outside Board members who are not direct investors in your company, it is customary to provide between 1% and 2% of the stock in the business. This is compared to the 0.1% to 0.2% stock provided to Advisory Board members. That is ten times as much stock for at least ten times as much work. When giving this amount of stock, there is no need to pay Board members a monthly retainer—even though many entrepreneurs have found themselves agreeing to a retainer of some sort just to get the experienced, senior business person to attend meetings. Moreover, in some cases, we find outside noninvestors getting upward of 5% of the stock—but this is indeed rare. That Board member has to do a lot for the venture beyond the Board meetings deserve that amount of stock—help write the business plan, raise the seed or Series A financing, or help recruit and hire the management team. Of course, for the young entrepreneur, 5% does not seem like a big number. Trust us, it is. You can easily make the mistake of giving up a lot of stock to a senior individual who promises to do a lot and doesn't contribute much of anything over the course of time. Get an attorney experienced in startup deals to structure Board of Directors and Advisory Board shares as options that vest over time based on continued participation.

It is also extremely important that you set expectations and requirements for each Board member who is of the outside, noninvestor variety. For example, Board members must be able to devote 12 days a year to attend monthly meetings. In reality, that is closer to 20 days because Board members will meet with key managers outside of Board meetings. Their advice is both needed and important. Board members often communicate with management on a regular if not daily basis by phone or e-mail. Getting this involvement won't be a problem if an individual has money at stake in your business. Otherwise, it needs to be part of the deal for Board participation.

Of course, if you do not go the incorporation route, and instead elect for a sole proprietorship, partnership, or limited liability corporation, a formal Board of Directors is not required by law. Deep, experienced counsel can be rewarded through the Advisory Board described earlier. However, if you have outside investors with "member interests" (sometimes called "units" or "shares") in a limited liability corporation, they will insist on some form of oversight and governance. This includes periodic meetings. It is also achieved by preparing quarterly written "member consents" where investors approve certain major business decisions and actions undertaken over that time period, including additional financings, financial performance, and changes in corporate structure. But there is no structure through which you can be "fired" as the CEO. Poor performance simply means that you will not get additional investment simply because any future investor will want to talk and rely on the experience of current investors—handcuffs of a different sort than steel.

Form a Customer Advisory Board

Another important stakeholder group that entrepreneurs tend to overlook in terms of seeking counsel and advice is the venture's own customers. An important emerging trend that we are seeing and recommending to new ventures is the establishment of a Customer Advisory Board. This is also known as a Customer Advisory Council. It is a representative group of existing customers who meet with your team on a regular basis (two to four times per year) to offer advice to your venture and its future direction. A Customer Board offers feedback on customer satisfaction with the venture and its products and services; provides early warnings on shifts in customer needs and emerging opportunities; offers input on new product development; makes referrals to other customers; and provides intelligence on competitors' tactics and strategies. You may also be able to use a Customer Advisory Board to discover how customers are actually using your product and learn about future technologies your customers are currently evaluating.

Entrepreneurs who build deep relationships with their best customers create a great advantage over larger, stodgier competitors. It's well known that your top 20% of clients typically generate 80% of a typical firm's revenue. Therefore, engaging key customers on a Customer Advisory Board is essential for the entrepreneur (once products are launched to market).

Membership typically consists of 10 to 20 customers (again, representative of that 20% of customers that generate 80% of your revenue). Participation is voluntary. Customers love the feeling of influencing product or service direction. Advanced training on product features, for example, is a nice "throw-in" to these meetings.

Ideally, meetings should be held either at your company facility or at a nearby hotel so that as many employees can attend as is appropriate. Some groups meet in field offices for maximum regional participation. We believe it is important that you, as founder of the venture, make an appearance at these meetings. The entrepreneur must be willing to act on customer advice; otherwise, customers will soon quickly learn that attendance is a waste of time.

Invitations should go out well in advance, a couple months if possible, to allow customers to schedule the meeting appropriately. In most cases, a good member of a Customer Advisory Board will pay his or her own expenses to come to your office. Supply the meals, however. This is money well spent given the insights you will gather.

Once at the meetings, be sure everyone is introduced, company and customer participants. Take the time to discuss the challenges your customers face when dealing with your company and its products or services. Then discuss strategic initiatives and/or new products/services to get customer reactions and input. Leave lots of time for open discussion. You might also consider breakout sessions to get feedback from small groups that represent different customer types. Finally, find the time to do a recap of the meeting so participants receive confirmation that their voices have been heard.

A more recent trend with Customer Advisory Boards is to run them entirely online. Going online allows for scalability and global reach at reduced cost. One firm that went from ten Customer Advisory Board members attending an in-person meeting to over 40 members participating from multiple sites around the globe. Another advantage of an online Customer Advisory Board is you can increase the frequency of contact and obtain more insight and feedback.[7]

The Legal Organization of a Venture

Standing apart but related to team issues is the legal form of business, or "entity type," that a founding team should adopt to begin operations and raise capital. There are a number of options open to the entrepreneur—and each has important considerations for liability protection, taxes, and the classes of stock that certain types of investors prefer.

While there are many options, we will concentrate on the five major types used by entrepreneurs for different reasons:

- A sole proprietorship
- A partnership
- A Limited Liability Company (LLC)
- An S Corporation
- A C Corporation

Let's learn the differences.

With a *sole proprietorship,* you are the single owner and have full responsibility for the venture's operations. You retain total control. A significant benefit of a sole proprietorship is that there is only one level of income tax on the business income, which the owner pays

---

[7]Carter, T. (2003). *Customer Advisory Boards: A Strategic Tool for Customer Relationship Building.* New York: Routledge. If you wish to learn more, visit www.customeradvisoryboard.org/.

directly on his or her personal income tax return. The income is only taxed once, unlike a corporation where there are business income taxes and then personal taxes on profits paid out to shareholders in the form of dividends. In the sole proprietorship, all revenue, expenses, and depreciated assets are reported directly on the Schedule C as part of your personal tax return. Losses (under certain conditions) are also passed through onto your personal income tax returns. The downside to a sole proprietorship is that your personal assets—your bank accounts, personal investments, and personal property—are exposed to liability claims from customers, employees, or anyone else for that matter who interacts with your business. Thus, creditors could seize any assets you own outside the business to satisfy any outstanding debt the business has incurred. You are also legally liable in the case of any lawsuit made against the business. To help mitigate this risk, you can purchase insurance against commercial damages (typically up to a million dollars) on a sole proprietorship that can be attached to your personal homeowner's policy. The cost of such policies typically runs less than $1,000 a year. However, if you have full-time employees or a large number of customers, a sole proprietorship makes no sense whatsoever given the liability risks involved. Anything can happen at any time. It is just not worth the risk.

With a *partnership*, two or more individuals pool their resources to start the venture. And there can be some general partners and some limited partnership owners. As with a sole proprietorship, the partners share personal liability. The only legal protection for partners is to purchase insurance against liability suits and placing partner assets in someone else's name. There are rather complex "partnership agreements" that must be executed that stipulate the various rules of engagement in such entities, including the distribution of profits, decision-making rights, and ownership rights upon the exit or death of a particular partner. The partners in a partnership also enjoy the benefit of "single taxation" as well as participating in operating losses under certain conditions. Profits or losses are reported on the Schedule K-1 of the tax return. At the same time, however, partnerships operate "naked" in terms of potential liability. Traditionally, law firms were formed as partnerships because no one had the courage to sue a law firm! That's changed, however, and entrepreneurs and professional service firms alike have shifted to our next major form of company structure.

We believe one of the great business innovations for entrepreneurs is the *Limited Liability Company* (LLC), which offers almost complete liability protection to the business owners ("members" in the LLC form and "partners" in the LLP form). At the same time, the taxation is similar to that of a partnership or sole proprietorship. Profits and losses flow through to the "members" of the LLC based on the allocations set forth in the LLC agreement. Members own "units" of the pool of total outstanding "units" ("units" being the LLC equivalent of corporate "stock" or "shares"). Investors may purchase these units in successive rounds of financing, just as in a stock equity corporation. LLCs also file federal income tax returns, but only to report the business income and to which members that income is allocated. Members receive Federal Schedules K-1 showing their flow-through income from the LLC that must be included on the member's personal income tax return. As an added plus for angel investors, the early startup losses may be eligible for tax deductions against the angel's other investment gains. While LLCs have the full flexibility of determining income allocations, agreements are often written to be like a traditional corporate structure in terms of voting rights, board members, meetings, and so forth.

The next form of corporate structure for the entrepreneur is an *S Corporation*. This is what many entrepreneurs preferred as a corporate structure before the emergence of the LLC as an alternative. The S Corporation is a special type of corporation where profits and losses are distributed to stockholders and taxed as personal income. A formal Board of Directors must be established for an S Corporation—not a small matter for the entrepreneur. Like the LLC, an S Corporation also combines the tax advantages of a partnership and the liability protection of a traditional corporation. And like the LCC, the S Corporation has only one class of stock, in this case common stock. Unlike the LLC, tax returns for the business must be filed quarterly as well as annually. Shareholders report their income or losses on the Schedule K in the personal income tax return. In addition, the limit on the number of shareholders is set at 100 persons—and they must all be U.S. citizens. (These restrictions do not exist for an LLC.) That means that an entrepreneur cannot take an S Corporation public. Nor can a strategic corporate investor put money into an S Corporation entity. But the entrepreneur can also convert later from an S Corporation to a traditional C Corporation, described next.

The *C Corporation* is the gold standard of liability protection and flexibility in the number of shareholders, their citizenship, and the classes of stock. Venture capitalists tend to insist on this form of incorporation because it offers multiple classes of stock, in this case preferred shares (which is what the VCs will insist on owning) and common shares (for the entrepreneurs and employees). Should bankruptcy occur, or an exit in the way of acquisition, the preferred shareholders move to the head of the line before the common shareholders. A C Corporation has other benefits for investors: Shareholders can include individuals, other corporations, trusts, partnerships, and LLCs. The downside is that the C Corporation carries double taxation for shareholders—first corporate and then personal. Moreover, the losses incurred in the early years cannot be passed on to investors—a major detriment to certain types of early-stage investors, namely the angels. Tax filings are also more complex and quarterly as well as annual. In short, entrepreneurs tend to save the C Corporation for a much later point in time.

In general, it is advantageous for most entrepreneurs to start out with a simple flow-through (in terms of business income) entity type. This is due primarily to the tax benefits for early-stage angel investors. If partners or investors are not needed, and legal liability is limited, a sole proprietorship may work fine and you can purchase liability insurance if you have any concerns. When partners or early-stage investors are important, an LLC may be the right choice. The LLC provides solid liability protection for the entrepreneur's and investor's personal assets. Others might find that an S Corporation may be best when a more corporate legal structure is desired while still retaining the benefits of flow-through of business income and losses. However, the S Corporation has been overtaken in popularity by LLCs as a startup entity form. This is due to the wide flexibility of LLCs in terms of forming rules and governance structures while still preferring the flow-through tax benefit of the sole proprietorship, partnerships, or S Corporations.

Bottom line: You'd best do your homework first and then talk to a business accountant who advises startups. And if the accountant doesn't mention (unsolicited) an LLC or S Corporation in the first two minutes of serious discussion, say "thanks" and run the other way!

Providing Rewards and Incentives for the Venture Team

A common question from entrepreneurs is the best way to reward and incentivize a team. This invariably leads to a discussion on "how to slice up the pie." Our two overriding principles are to share the wealth equitably with those who helped you start and grow the venture, and grow the pie as big as possible.

This is a tough question to answer. On the one hand, you want to be stingy with your stock for advisers or employees who talk a lot but don't do a lot and disappear over the hill within six months or so. That happens frequently in new ventures. The faces seem to come and go. On the other hand, you want to recruit *A* players onto the team, and that takes stock. Those faces seem to stick and become the bedrock of your company. Therefore, guard your equity well. But do not forget that 51% of nothing is still nothing. Thus, you have to be prepared to share the pie and focus on the growth of the pie.

It is important to first test people before giving stock. Find the *A* players, set certain rules by convention or personal design for granting stock options based on performance, and then stick to the plan. For example, in a venture capital–funded startup, after several rounds of financing, the management team and employees might own as much (or as little depending on your perspective!) as 30%. That might mean 10% for the CEO; 3% to 5% for the VPs of Sales, R&D, and Finance, respectively; and about 10% for the rest of the various employees. Directors and advisers other than investors might account for another several percentage points of the total. Stock is not unlimited. Other rules of thumb are:

- Grant stock as options based on level or position that vest over time. (This applies to everyone except the founding team: *Do not* let the investors force you to convert all of your shares to options, then take control of your Board, and throw you out on your ear without any stock!) Your Advisory Board and attorney should be able to provide guidelines for ventures in your industry sector. If not, find an additional adviser and/or a new attorney!

- Reserve additional stock option incentives for stellar performance, be it in sales; delivering a new product out of R&D; or installing a complex system in a large, corporate customer.

- Make sure that every employee, even that front-office receptionist, gets a taste or more of stock. You want to create a "rugby team" atmosphere in the venture—and stock is an important element to achieving this.

- Review the stock option plan every year. Create (which may mean having the Board of Directors approve) additional stock incentive pools to provide to top performers across the company every year in addition to their current holdings. The goal is to have all employees be winners. Seasoned professional investors will require a future stock option pool (often 10% of the fully diluted company) set aside for attracting future talent and rewarding current employees.

There are a variety of compensation and reward plans available to stakeholders of a new venture. These include director stock option plans, cash bonus plans, future performance plans, stock option plans, stock purchase plans, and 401(k) retirement plans. Your Advisory Board and attorney are there to help you navigate through these waters. Proper plans take considerable forethought and reflection.

Always remember the type of contribution made by core team members, advisers, employees, and yes, classmates. It is our sincere advice not to let "stock" get in the way of lifelong friendships that are created in entrepreneurship classes. In a team of three or four persons working on a group project, chances are that only one or two has the taste for the risk and incredibly hard work required to actually raise money and launch a venture. Setting expectations ahead of time in terms of stock ownership is begging for disaster.

Our recommendation: Agree to not talk about stock until the team is formed to raise capital. To do this, you will have to assign roles and responsibilities—positions—in the company. One of you will have to be the CEO; another, run sales; another, R&D; and so forth. If you all get along famously and have the desire to "do a company," then the stock will take care of itself once investment money is in the offing. But some team members are likely to move on to other careers. Or others simply will not have the experience to take a certain position in a competitive market context. They need to work for such a person first, even if it is in a venture that they helped create!

Setting expectations up front—making commitments—will only lead to hard feelings down the road when a silent partner owns as much stock as several hardworking entrepreneurs. Leave the equity decision until after the class is over and you have made your first investor pitch and been thoroughly and completely grilled, and then see *who has the stomach for more.* Those team members who politely drop out of the venture can be fairly and warmly rewarded as the first and well-deserving members of the Advisory Board.

Sound good? Stay friends, first and foremost, and use fairness as the guide for dishing out the founder's equity in your venture.

Reader Exercises

Step 1: Conduct an Aggregated Skills Audit for Your Team

Use Figure 10.1 to audit the skills of your team. Simply write down the names of individuals who are focused in one or more areas of the venture, and candidly rate their skills. Then write down any comments about skills that need to be added at startup, or within the first year of operations.

Be sure to play the *devil's advocate*. Five to seven years of work experience with a proven record of accomplishment in an industry sector aligned with the venture might qualify as "strong." Remember: The focus of this is not just for writing the business plan but for implementing the plan—that is, to start and grow the company.

Core Skills	Team Members	Collective Team Skills			Implications for Recruiting
		Strong	Average	Weak	
Sales and marketing					
Product or Web design					
Finance and accounting					
General and operations management					

Figure 10.1   Team Skills Assessment Template

Step 2: Begin Building an Advisory Board

Start thinking about who might be available to you to serve on your Advisory Board. Consider the trusted advisers you might have already gathered in the process of doing the work for this book. Think about mentors who might be available to you through your university's network, or the different types of investors you might have encountered in your research on the types and sources of venture finance in Chapter 8. Begin to write down a few names.

Step 3: Take a First Pass at Structuring Your Organization

Try to complete the template shown in Figure 10.2. If there are gaps, simply put in "TBD" (to be determined) and form in your mind the brief bio of the type of person you would like to recruit into that position. Rest assured, your investors will ask!

One name you should probably *not write down* is that of the professor teaching this class! Save that for when the class is over. Otherwise, your dear professor will have to think of you as a student to be mentored and graded on one hand, and a ticket to early retirement on the other! That's hard to do. Neither one of you needs the complication. Soon, school will be over and you can both decide the best relationship moving forward.

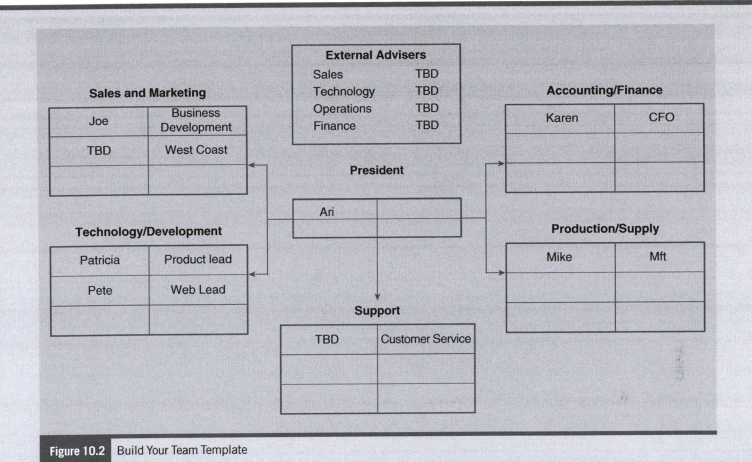

Figure 10.2 Build Your Team Template

Visit the Student Study Site at www.sagepub.com/meyer2e to access the following resources:

- Web Resources
- Video Resources
- General Resources in Entrepreneurship

11

Writing the Business Plan!

We will take the perspective in this chapter that a business plan is a sales document. Sure, writing a business plan can help you organize your business, sharpen your thinking, and consolidate all the market research, solutions design, go-to-market, and financial planning that you must do to start a venture—but at the end of the day, your purpose in putting together a business plan is to get someone else to invest their own hard-earned capital into your company.

In prior chapters, we have described how your venture might be valued for the purposes of providing investors with a certain percentage of the company equity for their investment. We have also considered the different types of investors that invest in new companies as equity participants. And we have worked through the details of projecting financial requirements for growth, as well as the financial outcomes of successful execution of a venture strategy. Now we are going to take all these pieces of the puzzle and put them together into an actionable, sellable plan for investors—leveraging all the insights you developed in Part I of this book.

To do this, we will work through the particulars of writing a business plan, step by step, providing instruction in terms of the information needed for each section of the plan—and perhaps most important, the most essential questions that will be top of mind for investors as they read each section. These questions come from our own experience working with teams to raise funds from various types of investors. We have also helped corporate venture teams apply this to their own projects. Following this chapter will help you produce a concise document no more than 20 to 25 pages in length, with 3 or 4 pages of financial statements added at the end. With all the research and thinking you have done up to this point, writing a great business plan should be the icing on the cake!

Unlike prior chapters, there are no specific exercises at the end of the chapter. Just go write your plan, mindful of all the Reader Exercises you have completed in preparation for this moment. These, and your Reality Check, are powerful ammunition for writing your plan and raising capital. Be sparse with your words. Keep your writing concise and full of the facts you have gathered from your industry, customer, and competitor research.

This chapter provides an outline for a business plan and practical advice on what investors are generally looking for in each section. It will also highlight where you might integrate templates from the first part of this book—either to help write the text or as outright exhibits. The deliverable is the first draft of a comprehensive business plan to which you will attach the financial projections created in Chapter 9.

Learning Objectives

After reading this chapter, you should be able to:

- Write a plan to raise startup or growth capital
- Develop an outline for a business plan
- Draft a comprehensive business plan

The Outline of the Business Plan and Where Your Prior Work Fits

The major sections of the business plan are:

1. Executive Summary
2. The Business Model and Financial Goals
3. Market Analysis: Industry, Customers, and Competitors
4. Solutions: Technology/Intellectual Property, Products, and Services
5. Go-to-Market: Channels, Pricing, Promotion, and Sales Plan
6. Operations, Production, and Supply
7. Organization
8. Major Milestones With Funding
9. Financial Projections and Exit Potential

In addition to key questions to answer for each section, we will provide a task organizer for each section so that you and your team can take responsibility for doing the research and writing of the text.

A quick note: For those of you who have seen other business planning structures, note that we do not include a special section stating the key risks and strategies to contend with these risks. While such a section is traditionally found in other business planning guides, we have reasons for excluding it. First, as stated earlier, a business plan is primarily a sales tool for raising capital for a startup. The risks will come up in the Q&A with your prospective investors. No need making them gun-shy right from the start. You want investors to fall in love with your venture idea, and then have your venture strategy, business model, and projected financial outcomes win their minds. And if you are honest about it, there are so many risks in any new venture that a thorough review of how to mitigate these risks could easily consume two or three pages in your business plan—precious pages that you do not have to spare. Professional investors know the risks—and if you get the right ones, they will know how to better manage those risks than you. That is why investment capital is called mentor capital.

Figure 11.1 shows where the thinking and work from prior chapters fit within the business plan outline. At this point, we would like you to create nine temporary folders on your computer or shared drive labeled for each of the sections shown in Figure 11.1. Begin to place

Business Plan Section	Reference Templates From Earlier Parts of the Book	
Executive Summary	• All of the chapters. Use the Venture Concept Statement in Chapter 7 to get started. Then summarize Industry, Customer, Product/Service Solutions, Team, and Funding Request.	
Business Model and Financial Goals	• Chapter 5, Business model summary. • Chapter 9, Revenue, profitability, exit potential: a summary over five years	
Market Analysis	• Industry attractiveness	Chapter 1
	• Target customer	Chapter 2
	• Customer needs	Chapter 3
	• Competitors	Chapter 6
Solutions (Products and Services)	• Product/service concept	Chapter 3
	• Product line/service strategy	Chapter 4
	• Platform strategy (if any)	Chapter 4
	• IP strategy (if any)	Chapter 4
Go-to-Market	• Channel strategy	Chapter 5
	• Brand development strategy	Chapter 6
Operations, Production, Supply	• Startup and scale-up operations	To be discussed in this chapter
Organization	• Team members	Chapter 10
	• Key positions to be filled	Chapter 10
	• Board and advisers	Chapter 10
Major Milestones	• Milestone template	To be discussed in this chapter
Financial Projections and Exit Potential	• Revenue projections	Chapter 9
	• Projected P&L	
	• Projected Cash flow	
	• Projected Balance Sheet	
	• Startup costs and financing request	
	• Exit potential	

Figure 11.1   Mapping Chapters to the Business Plan

copies of all your template work in the appropriate folders. If you have downloaded important articles from industry trade journals or other market studies as part of defining your industry focus, place these in the Market Analysis folder. The Organization section will require paragraphs on venture team members and key advisers. You can start gathering brief biographies and résumés right away. Place them in the Organization folder. In all of this assembling of materials, keep your eye open for graphs, illustrations, or digital photographs that will liven up your written document.

Appreciating Your Reader: The Professional Venture Investor

Venture investors put their time and money into good people with good ideas focused on clearly targeted and growing markets. You must be prepared to prove and defend your ideas and your team time and time again—until you launch your products or services and get checks. Then the market begins to do the talking.

So your business plan must speak to the prudent investor with confidence: "We have a great idea for a growth market, a solid strategy for executing on that idea, and a great team."

The business plan is a product in its own right. In the development of any product, you need to put yourself into the shoes of the customer—in this case, the investor. It is part of your responsibility to do some homework on the investors you approach: Where have they succeeded? Where have they failed? What do other entrepreneurs think about these individuals as investors? Are they antagonistic and disruptive or truly helpful and work to open doors into major customer accounts and raise additional capital? If you try to approach investors who have no interest or experience in your industry, or prefer second- or third-stage company investments as opposed to startups, you are wasting both their time and yours.

Beyond this, there are certain facts "on the ground" that you need to consider that should influence the style and the content of your written plan.

Fact 1: You will be one of many teams trying to get that investor's money. Raising capital for new ventures is a highly competitive situation. Friends of ours who are venture capitalists in the Boston and Silicon Valley areas throw around formidable percentages: For every 1,000 business plans that come across their desk, they will be seriously interested in ten and will invest in one or two of those ten. Those are not very good odds. That means that you have to have a very thick skin. You will be told "no" time and time again; but if you believe in your venture, and it needs investment capital beyond the $50,000 or $100,000 that you might be able to get from your family and friends, there is no choice but to suck it up and keep tackling investors.

TIP: STANFORD'S ENTREPRENEURSHIP CORNER

We recommend that you go to the Stanford University Entrepreneurship Corner (http://ecorner.stanford.edu/). Search for the entrepreneurship video called "Attrition Rates for Potential Investors," where two seasoned angel investors talk about the factors that lead them to actually listen to pitches from just a very few of the plans coming before them. The investors (very active "angels") talk about receiving 5 new plans a day, coming to about 150 a month, of which just 1 will receive investment. Deals are initially triaged based on the source or reference of the deal. If it is referred by a trusted source, the plan is going to get a look; otherwise, it is doubtful.

Fact 2: Your business plan is your bona-fide instrument for getting a face-to-face meeting—or, most often, a return telephone call before the meeting—with an investor. So obviously, it must be very well written. That means concise, clean, and error-free. If you don't take the time to clean up the language, and write carefully and meaningfully, the investor is probably going to discard your plan. If you are not a particularly good writer, get someone on your team who is! The business plan must also be engaging in certain ways. We find a few choice graphs and charts helpful.

Fact 3: It is a fairly safe assumption that a professional investor will not read your plan from the first page to the last in the very first sitting. Rather, he or she will read your Executive Summary, then your Business Model section, fast forward to your Team/

Organization section, and hit your Pro Forma P&L. If they don't like what they see in these first four sections of your plan, they won't read the rest, and you will certainly not get the meeting.

Jeff McCarthy, an alumnus of our university and partner in a very successful venture capital firm, shared his thoughts on what he looks for first before reading the entire business plan:

> Before I read a single page, I first look for a trusted referral. If we know the person who referred the entrepreneur, it makes a huge difference. Then, I go straight to the Executive Summary. If I understand what they are going to make, who they are going to sell it to, and why those customers are going to buy this product over any other product in the market, then I'm interested in reading more.
>
> I next go to the Team section. Has anyone on the team done a successful startup before? Do they have an established track record of success? Is there operating experience present? Do they have a good understanding of the market they will be attacking? The team is always the most important ingredient to us. If the team looks solid, then I read on.
>
> I next need to see how they plan to make money—not just get customers interested in the company's products or services, but to get them to actually buy and deploy the product. And then as I read the Financial section, what I am really looking for is two things: What is going to be the true capital required to finance the company and get it to scale? Second, is the revenue opportunity sufficient to make it worthwhile? For my firm, if it doesn't represent a $100 million plus revenue opportunity, we are not really interested.

Of course, there are other types of investors—ones who do not have hundreds of millions of dollars to put to work as do Jeff and other high-end venture capitalists—who will be interested in that $20 million, $30 million, or $50 million revenue opportunity. But for all the other elements, professional investors are *just like* Jeff McCarthy. Here is what they need to see:

- The Executive Summary has to shine—to give the vision and promise of the market, the compelling solution, the technology within the solution, and the team—all in a page or so.

- The Team section must show that even if you don't have all the key players, you are taking steps to find them. Professional investors want to see a member of the founding team who has successfully started and grown companies before. That experience also brings with it a network of other key team members who need to be recruited to supplement the founders in the first critical years of the business.

- The Business Model section also has to shine—to show that your approach to monetizing on the vision and opportunity is pragmatic and reasonable. As we emphasized in the Business Model chapter, investors want to see a structure of revenues that clearly features some type of recurring revenue. Even if you are selling an airplane, there should be line items for replacement parts, add-on systems, and ongoing services in your financials.

- The Financial section must show projections that are both exciting yet reasonable. Investors will also want to see a path to profitability (a positive operating profit) occurring over 18 to 24 months, unless of course you are proposing a biotechnology or similar type of deep, R&D-intensive venture. Investors will look at the assumptions behind the revenue projections carefully, as well as those behind the operating margins once revenue is generated. If the assumptions behind the financials seem unreasonable or random, you won't get the meeting.

Fact 4: Most people who have a lot of money and who wish to invest it in a new venture are of a certain age and tenure. Their tolerance for examining financial statements that go on page after page in font size 8 is nonexistent. (One of our particular beefs with the popular "question and answer" business-planning software packages is that you answer a bunch of questions and it produces a dozen pages of incredibly detailed financial statements—minutiae.) Think of it this way—you must be prepared to defend any and every number that you put in the back of your business plan. So like the plan itself, remember to keep your financials concise, powerful, and integrated. Spend just as much time on stating the assumptions behind your revenue, expense, and cash flow projections as on the numbers themselves. These assumptions tell an investor how you think about your venture *as a business*—and it is that thinking that he or she wants to understand, assess, and hopefully, improve.

Fact 5: Investors live by the "golden rule." He or she who has the money rules! Professional investors—serious angels, VCs, and strategic investors—believe that they know best how to build a profitable, money-making enterprise (whether this is true or not) and expect you to show a willingness to listen to what they have to say. So even if you have put together the greatest business plan of the last decade, unless you are Steve Jobs or Bill Gates, if your investor likes your idea, he or she is still going to want to make inputs and changes to certain elements of it. And it is unlikely to come in the areas of target market or product strategy—rather, it will be in the finer aspects of the business model—how to convert your idea into money. *Be prepared to listen and adjust.* The ability to try something, learn from it, and quickly integrate that learning into a scalable business is how the best investors view new ventures. The same goes for executives sponsoring internal corporate ventures. It is exceedingly rare that a venture hits a home run right in the first inning; rather, it's in the second or third where the pitching becomes familiar and the team begins to pick up its full stride. Harry Keegan, a successful entrepreneur and alumnus of our university (who started and runs his own pharmaceutical company), is also an active angel investor. Harry views managing the trials and tribulations of new ventures this way:

> Setting up a communication avenue with investors and using it both to inform and to solicit guidance is not a sign of weakness. Rather, it is utilizing resources who want to help and expect to contribute more than money. The vast majority of angel investors earned their wealth in the school of blood, sweat, and tears. Not to tap that wellspring in favor of learning the hard way by yourself is surely folly. Everyone makes mistakes. More can be learned from those that are honestly shared than from the war stories of victories long past. Nothing warms the heart of a mentor better than a pixel of contribution where the student avoids calamity or expands the scope of a success.

Fact 6: Investors hate being caught unawares. They invest in a plan and ordinarily expect you to stick to it. However, any business needs to adjust to conditions on the field. Just don't veer from the plan without first talking to your investors. That might be a competitive announcement that you should have known about and they learned before you. Or it might be a serious delay in a sale to an initial important customer that you promised would occur by a certain date. Bad news doesn't necessary get an entrepreneur in trouble with his or her investors; surprises will. As noted once again by our friend Harry Keegan:

> Entrepreneurs have an obligation to adhere to the business plan upon which the investment is solicited and not to run naked into the woods as soon as the checks clear. If course corrections are needed based on real-time feedback, angels need to know, as surprises are not welcome.

Fact 7: Every investor has been badly burned by what he or she had once felt was a highly promising venture at some point in time. There are many reasons why a venture can go sour—the biggest ones tend to be market related (the market wasn't ready yet or competition was not fully understood) or team related (individuals who were poor managers, inexperienced in the industry, or difficult personalities). As the investor reads your plan and gets to know you, he or she is going to be on guard for those subtle and not so subtle warning signs that you might be one of those horrible disasters who had cost the investor endless time, aggravation, and considerable money. If you set off a risk trigger—which can happen in the most unexpected ways because you have no way of really knowing how that investor got so badly burned in the past unless he or she tells you—then it is likely that *there is nothing you can do to turn things around.* You've got to be prepared to pack your bags and move on. Most entrepreneurs talk to literally dozens of potential investors before they find that particular individual who is willing to commit and bring other investors along.

Fact 8: Even if an investor loves your idea, he or she is still going to worry about how best to mitigate all the attending risks associated with any new venture. One way to mitigate these risks is to seek funds and go-to-market partnerships with major, well-established corporations. These partnerships may represent a technology or R&D "shortcut." Or even more powerfully, a corporate partnership may provide a go-to-market channel that is typically the hardest nut to crack for new ventures. A partnership with a major corporation will also help establish your credibility as an important player in the industry.

At the same time, if you have major channel partners, it is most often advisable that you try to "own" your customers—at least in the beginning. This means having direct contact with those customers. This allows you to directly learn from them. Second, direct contact with customers allows you to introduce and test new products and services quickly rather than have a channel partner control that decision. So sell with and through established players, but be part of the marketing and selling process. Tom Aley, the founder of the Generate case on the textbook Website, put it this way:

> Institutional investors, such as VC firms, are always looking for ways to reduce the risk in a new venture. One of the best ways for a startup to reduce risk for investors is to convince a large, industry player to be one of the investors. This gives immediate industry credibility for the VC. Someone with domain experience has agreed to invest. The VC will talk with the industry partner to learn as much as he or she can, as quickly as possible, to convince other VCs to invest.

The bottom line for writing a business plan comes to this: Above all else, clear writing is essential. Brevity is a must. Investors (and sponsoring executives for a corporate venture) want to see evidence of:

- A robust, growing *Market Opportunity* (and, more specifically, the industry niche, the target customers and their uses that will be the focus of your efforts and comprise your "addressable market")

- Distinctive product or service *Solutions* that target what customers need and want to buy

- A balanced, experienced *Team*

- A sensible, powerful *Business Model* that features recurring revenue and that generates cash with each sale and operating profit within a reasonable period of time

Perhaps most important, investors want to see a *clear, driving focus* in everything that you propose to do.

Lastly, if you get told "not interested" by the first 15 investors that you meet, *welcome to the club of entrepreneurs trying to raise money!* Only the most successful entrepreneurs, with a track record of making money for investors in the past—often multiple times through a series of successful ventures—can pick up the phone, call a former investor, and get commitments for a new venture over the course of several weeks.

Appreciating the Reader: For Corporate Entrepreneurs

For those of you who are starting corporate ventures—businesses within existing corporations—the reasoning above also applies for potential executive sponsors. There are many people vying for their attention. In the vast majority of cases, the executives who can fund your venture are also busy operating executives responsible for core businesses or functions in major corporations. Their time is short; their patience for poorly conceived or written business plans is even shorter. There are also a few additional "got to haves" when doing an internal corporate venture. The venture must (a) leverage company technology, (b) add necessary ingredients to the corporation's portfolio to address market opportunities or challenges, and (c) leverage the corporation's brand and channels to accelerate the creation of value.

Some executive suite members prefer to see just a PowerPoint containing the details of a venture rather than a fully written plan itself. However, we believe that a short written plan must still accompany the PowerPoint presentation. Moreover, unlike going to most VCs, our experience is that corporate executives will want an informal meeting before the meeting to provide their input into your plan and your milestones.

In addition, while the startup entrepreneur typically needs to manage one or several investors for the Series A financing, the corporate entrepreneur needs to manage a broader number of stakeholders within the corporation. These might include the CEO and his or her executive committee. These might comprise the general managers of adjacent lines of business, the CFO, the chief legal counsel, and the senior vice president of marketing and R&D. Again, this means a lot of meetings before the official meeting if you want to have any realistic chance of getting sponsorship and financial support from within a major corporation. And all of these stakeholders will be thinking about the risks inherent in "rocking the boat" with a new corporate venture. "Risk mitigation" strategies and customer or sales force migration plans will be even more important to corporate executives. While most will seek venturing that leverages core technology as a good path for growth, taking venture-type risks will not appear in any of their job definitions!

Before Writing, "Storyboard the Plan"

You can save yourself a lot of time and have a much more effective result if you first bullet-point the major elements of each section of the business plan before writing anything. We call this story boarding the business plan. It means walking through the plan from front to back, outlining the major ideas in each section, and seeing how they align and integrate to your core strategy—that is, the Venture Concept and Business Model.

Figure 11.2 shows a storyboarding template. Each section of the business plan is shown in that figure, with the major bullet points that you should think about with each section. The one section that isn't shown is the Executive Summary. The other sections feed into it. We have put a graphic icon to illustrate the seminal framework for most of the sections,

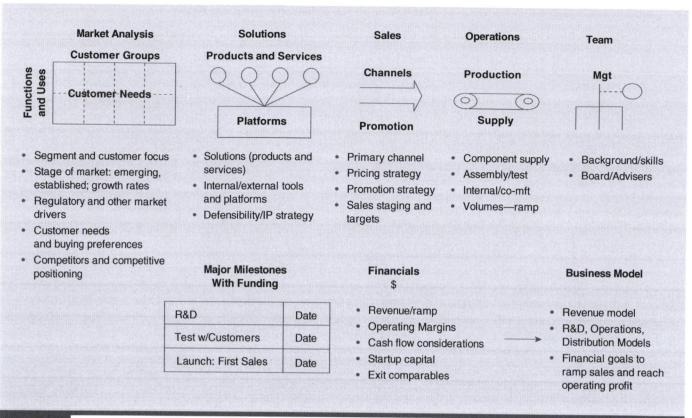

Figure 11.2   Storyboard the Business Plan

followed by the major bullet points for which you should have clarity and a strategy as you write your plan:

- The *Market* section shows a segmentation grid—the framework used to identify different types of customers, different types of use cases by customers, and customer needs within those use cases. By working through the first part of this book, you should be able to easily storyboard the major points about your target market, market size and growth rates, customer focus and customer needs, positioning, and any sort of regulatory events or trends that make your target market particularly advantageous—or less so. Without a clear focus for this section, nothing else in the plan will really work as needed.

- The *Solutions* section shows a graphic representation of an underlying platform and the products or services that utilize the platform. The idea here is that successful companies provide a range of products and services over time. Platforms are underlying parts, systems, or processes shared across multiple products or services that allow a company to achieve greater levels of profitability by virtue of increasing volumes of shared parts and systems. This section also contains your intellectual property (IP) strategy (patents, branding, etc.) if your venture is based on a new core technology.

- The *Go-to-Market* section is represented graphically by a straight arrow—reflecting the channel by which your products or services reach the customer. Entrepreneurs often underestimate the importance and cost of creating effective channels. Put another way, the greatest products or technology in the world will *not* meet their commercial promise without an equally powerful channel strategy. This section also contains a bullet point for your pricing strategy, which is a combination of your positioning and your decisions regarding the structure and nature of revenues in the business model chapter (Chapter 4). Promotion and branding is another essential part of a Sales Plan. The last bullet point is the sales staging and rollout after launch. This might be going from a regional to a national sales campaign or from a few key reference accounts to the broader market.

- The *Operations, Production, and Supply* section is represented by a supply chain icon. Here, your business model decisions can be so important. Will you be doing R&D in-house like most firms, or subcontract design and development? Will there be key technology or component suppliers? Also, will you do manufacturing in-house or, like many new firms producing physical products, use subcontract manufacturers? If you are running a Web services business, will you host your own services or use a secure third party (as do most startups)? If you have storefronts, this part of the business plan deals with location and store operations for the first several years of the venture. Or if you are shipping products to customers, a logistics vendor needs to be identified. It is this part of the business plan that may take considerable research in addition to all that you have done in earlier chapters—for you will need to investigate certain approaches and understand the fixed and variable costs of these approaches. For storyboarding, set forth your preferred strategies for each of these areas. This will help identify the calls you have to make. For ventures with manufactured products, we prefer to have a section in this part of the business plan that defines production goals in terms of volume for products.

- The *Organization* section is represented by an organization chart icon. New venture teams are notoriously nonhierarchical. The CEO is chief executive and bottle washer. Nonetheless, professional investors will want to know who is the top decision maker and his or her key staff for R&D, sales and marketing, production/operations, and finance. A number of these may be cofounders. Others may be people with whom you have already spoken and who have the skills you require to balance the team but will not leave their current jobs until you secure funding. Others may be people you do not know yet but know you need to hire. Storyboarding a winning team is one of the most important things you can do up front. Getting the right people involved will help you write a much better plan. Thinking about good external advisers at this point is also important for the same reason: They can help make your plan better.

- The *Major Milestones With Funding* section is represented by a task list. For the written plan, your investors will want to know what you plan to do with their money across all major functions within the business. For storyboarding, we prefer that you consider pragmatic objectives for getting your product or service in test mode with a customer(s), often called the "beta version"; bringing your first product to market for commercial sale; bringing in your first dollars of revenue; and the time period when you achieve first operating profit. These four key milestones, plus a few select hires to fill major gaps in your management team, are the stakes in the ground that you need to set if you are going to have a real business.

- The *Financials and Exit Potential* section. Just bullet point the highlights: the revenue over five years, the operating margins, any unusual considerations for converting revenues into cash, and the money you need to get the business started. Also, to add some fire to the discussion, do a quick search on the Web to find out the exit valuations for similar types of companies over the past several years. Most of these exits will be acquisitions by a larger corporation. Try to find the multiple on revenues for those deals—then look at your own thoughts about revenue ramp and think to the future! You will need to paint this picture later on for investors.

- The *Business Model* section is a simple bulleted list. Even though this section is presented in the written plan right after the Executive Summary, for storyboarding we like to have it come last—as an ending scorecard for all the prior sections. Your revenue model is absolutely critical here. So are your approaches to do R&D (if necessary), production and fulfillment, and selling. Lastly, investors want to know "the time to first dollar" and "the time to first profit." These goals should be clear from your financial modeling in the prior chapter. State them in months from startup for your storyboard.

We suggest that you try to develop your own *war room* for storyboarding the plan. That might be your kitchen or a conference room. This is also a full-day work session—so you'd better plan on doing it over the weekend. Find a big whiteboard, buy some new dry-erase markers, grab some pizzas and beer (only after lunch!), and start mapping out your storyboard for your business plan. Have fun with it—it is your future.

As you fill in each section, step back, take a look, and see how the pieces fit together. Again, writing a good business plan is akin to writing a good story that will be sold to investors—tight, customer focused, pragmatic, and pointing to attractive financial outcomes. It takes a lot more thinking and elbow grease to write a powerful short business plan than to write one that is long and rambling.

When you are done completing the storyboard, take a moment to show it to your advisers and friends. It is the prototype of your business plan. You want your advisers to candidly tell you any elements that seem unclear or that don't make sense.

The Business Plan Sections and Format: Starting With the Title Page and Executive Summary_____

Now we transition from getting prepared to write the plan to the plan itself. In the pages to follow, we go through each section and tell you what investors expect and their chief concerns as they read each section.

The Title Page

The title page must have the name of your business or corporate venture and your contact information. We also prefer to see the amount of funds requested for startup or the corporate venture. *Do not forget to include your personal contact information!* One of our VC friends who runs a firm that receives several thousand plans a year (and invests in only a half dozen or so) once told us that he regularly discards new business plans because personal contact information was not on the front page.

Executive Summary

The Executive Summary must grab the reader. It might be the only page or two that he or she reads! As indicated earlier, most investors and executives will only read the Executive Summary, then go straight to the résumés, and then to the financials. If they like what they read, only then will they read the rest of the plan.

Remember, professional investors want to see (a) a solid, growing market, (b) well-defined customers who need what you have to sell, (c) an attractive business model that produces cash, and (d) a team suited to the task. The Executive Summary hits items a, b, and d all in a page or two; and the next section of the plan hits item c—the business model.

Therefore, the Executive Summary is a concise statement of the purpose of the proposed venture—its vision of greatness in the form of a distinctive market position that you hope to achieve.

The first thing you need to write is two or three sentences that present the vision of what you wish to create and the market position you wish to achieve. This is often referred to as "The Company" section. It is imperative that these first few sentences show the clear focus of your venture. This opening paragraph is so very important—it sets the stage for everything to follow. For starters, you can take a look at your Venture Concept Statement for the Reality Check in Chapter 7. Our guidelines for that were:

> ABC is our business that [solves *what problem*] for [*who–which target customers*]. It is different from the current competitors because of [*why customers buy*]. The benefits that we expect to provide [*name the major benefits*] will make ABC stand out from all competitors.

Now we recommend that you frontload it with key words that include "to be a market leader" in the well-defined "target market":

ABC is a [*startup, spinoff, internal corporate venture*] seeking to be a market leader in the target segment of [*name your target segment*]. The Company is focused on [*solves what problem*] for [*who–which target customers*] in that target segment. The [*products or services*] of the Company will provide [*name the major benefits*] that will make it unique in the marketplace.

Here are a few examples from business plans that received funding in years past, with company and product names disguised. The first contains the initial paragraph for a private placement memorandum for a financial services company that selected medical billing as its target. It raised $1 million from angel investors at a post-money valuation in excess of $12 million!

Company X is a Web-based health care software services company that provides health care providers solutions to efficiently recapture lost revenue due to missed charges without requiring either investments in new enterprise software or significant changes to the way providers conduct business. The Healthcare Financial Management Association estimates that health care providers fail to bill approximately 3% to 5% of all reimbursable charges. Our company brings immediate financial and administrative benefit to its health care provider clients, generating sales primarily from a revenue sharing arrangement with its clients based upon reimbursed missed charges. Our lead-users have already proven that this win-win business model leads to a quick sale and rapid business growth.

Here's another one for a "green" engine company that received a combination of equity and debt financing to produce a new type of engine with extremely low emissions needed to comply with the new federal law:

XYZ Engine Technologies' goal is to become a market leader in the OEM segment for small vehicle or craft production. The company is commercializing proprietary technologies for lightweight high-performance 4-stroke engines that dramatically reduce pollution emissions as will be mandated by future federal and state law. These clean engines are ideal for motorcycles, snowmobiles, watercraft, all-terrain vehicles, and microcars. The first engines are in the tooling stage and should be ready for production in 18 months, with several other engine designs soon to follow. With commitments for significant orders on hand, XYZ Company now needs capital to complete manufacturing engineering and tooling for production.

Then, following "The Company" section, write one short (very short) paragraph for each of the four topics:

- The *market opportunity* in terms of target industry niche, target customer, and the customer problems (or uses) to be solved. This is what some investors call "the addressable market." Summarize the size and growth characteristics of the addressable market in a way that demonstrates a fertile, promising area in which to start a venture.

- The *distinctive products, services,* or *distribution assets* you seek to provide and the extent to which they either create intellectual property (IP) or leverage current IP. The IP statement can be critically important for certain types of biotech, materials science, or information technology ventures.

- The startup/management team, hopefully with a combination of industry *experience* and a *balance of skills.* If you don't have a management team—that is, it is just you— use a few sentences to identify key management that you seek to recruit in the first few months of the venture. An investor is going to want to see that you have the right people involved from the start, or at least know what types of people you require so that the investor can help you build a powerful team.

- *The funds* requested for the venture at this stage of growth and *the uses of those funds in terms of achieving major milestones.* Those milestones are typically expressed as "alpha," "beta," and "launch." Put some target dates on the milestones that work for your business.

The entire Executive Summary can be single spaced within the paragraphs, but double or tripled spaced between paragraphs, making for a concise, one- or two-page presentation. Some professors might advise to save writing the Executive Summary for last—but from our own experience, we know that this is virtually impossible to resist. So give in to the urge. Write a first draft of your Executive Summary and let it serve as a follow-on to storyboarding to help guide all the more detailed business plan sections to follow. When the plan is completed, set aside a couple of quiet hours to revise and improve the Executive Summary. It needs to be concise and powerful.

The Business Model: A Summary of How You Make Money, as a Business

Start this section on a new page of the business plan.

In this day and age, investors (and sponsoring executives for corporate ventures) are getting back to basics. They want to know that the products and services are *real*, and that there is a solid business model generated from these products and services. They want to know that customers have the cash to pay for what you wish to sell. And they want to see that the business itself generates cash. Jeff McCarthy, the venture capitalist quoted earlier, noted further that:

> In this era, we see a lot of plans that promise to bring millions of users to a Website, without ever really answering what all those users are going to do and buy once they arrive. We need to see plans that show how to monetize on any given opportunity. Without a clear plan on how to make money, it is a nonstarter.

This requires prudent decisions on how best to structure the revenue model as well as how to structure operations in terms of R&D (if needed), production, and distribution.

The framework we learned earlier provides an excellent tool to guide you through writing this important section of the business plan. If you did the Reader Exercises in Chapter 5, all of the hard work is already done. Figure 5.7, completed for your venture, should already be sitting in a file folder on your hard-drive called "Business Model." Use it!

Revenue Model

Briefly describe the types of products or the types of services provided by the company. Then, within this "mix," create a few simple sentences that show, for each stream of revenue, the type of revenue (purchase, lease, rent, subscribe, freemium, etc.), the frequency of purchase, and the price level relative to competition (based on your positioning). This information comes straight out of Chapter 5. Very important: *Put in a sentence on what creates recurring revenue.* This is a hot button for any investor. Figure out what it means for your venture and put that into this paragraph.

Also, another important question that investors will have is if you understand the basic principles and costs of acquiring a customer in your business, and then, the lifetime value of that customer for your business.   Investors may also want to know how many customers you needs to acquire in order to achieve operating profitability.

R&D Strategy (If Appropriate for Your Business)

Not all ventures do or need R&D. If you do, however, these few sentences describe your make-or-buy approach for R&D. In most high-tech ventures, there is a combination of internal R&D

that is complemented by some external infusions of technology for various components or add-on features. For example, are you building a software application on top of open-source tools or the Microsoft Development Studio? If you have or need to have trusted partners or suppliers for parts of your products or services, say who they are and what stage of development that relationship exists. (IP was covered already in the Executive Summary, so no need to cover it here.) Most professional investors are suspicious if you decide to outsource every bit of R&D to a third party because that introduces a new type of risk (e.g., no control over the technology and hence, no barrier to entry on the technology front should the venture become wildly successful). We recommend that you try to determine a particular crown jewel of knowledge or technology in your business, create that in-house, and then build around it with logical partners. And if you are a software company, a robust third-party developer program is a must!

Production/Manufacturing Strategy

Keep this to just a sentence or two. This is the in-house versus supplier strategy. For startups, it is essential to stretch out your invested capital—and that means doing whatever you can to keep it from getting tied up in hard, physical assets. Later on, once you have proven your business and it is scaling in terms of customers and revenue, you can consider how to bring these capabilities in-house to improve operating margins. But for a startup, your focus needs to be on surviving to the point where the business is generating unencumbered cash. For software and Web services firms, if you need to accommodate large amounts of traffic or data, there are numerous hosting services available for both computational needs and storage or backup. If you need high-performance computing, look at Amazon's Cloud solutions—they are inexpensive.

Go-to-Market and Brand Development

Keep this to just a sentence or two as well.

This means channels and branding. Summarize the best route to (a) sell your products and services, and (b) provide support customers. One of our mentors, Al Lehnerd (the fellow who invented the Dustbuster), used to say, "Think of being the product yourself. How would you want to go to market, to get into the hands of the customer?" You then need to put in one or two sentences that state, "We will build a direct sales force," or "We will sell through independent distributors," or "We will sell through mass merchandisers," or "The Web is our preferred channel." Or your best channel may be other manufacturers or systems integrators. This is often called selling through OEMs or VARs (original equipment manufacturers or value-added resellers). Then provide a statement that indicates the cost of a sale given your channel strategy—a 5% sales commission to your own salesperson, a 30% margin to a retailer, or a 40% margin to a VAR, or a large volume discount to an OEM.

As for branding, recognize that the value developed by ventures for exit events is often based just as much on the power of the brands developed for their products or services as in the technology with those offerings. Chapter 6 focused on this. You should include a sentence or two stating the brand you wish to develop, and then the functional, emotional, and social benefits for customers associated with that brand. *This is very important but is often left as an afterthought by entrepreneurs.*

Summary Financial Goals

No business model is complete without providing goals derived primarily from the Pro Forma P&L. We recommend creating a simple table that shows:

1. The number of customers over each year (one to five years is typical, but your business horizon may be longer)

2. The revenue or bookings per customer

3. The total revenue

4. The operating profit (EBITDA—earnings before income taxes, depreciation, and amortization—is easiest) from the business

5. The potential exit valuation after five years. Investors will think of multiples of revenue and EBITDA in Years 5 and onward to get a sense of the value you can create. In fact, it might not be a bad idea to include a single sentence underneath the table stating the current multiples used for exits within your specific industry sector and apply these to your summary projections at the end of Year 5.

Professional investors pride themselves on asking a whole bunch of smart questions. Since our goal in the book is to help you succeed, part of that is making sure you do not get caught unawares. For each of these sections, we have listed the major types of questions that will be on the investor's mind when he or she reads each particular part of the plan. For the Business Model section, here are a few questions that are likely to be on the investor's mind:

Questions on the Investor's Mind:

1. Is there solid, recurring revenue in this business?

2. Is the team using an agile or lean approach to its operations, for example, for R&D, production, and logistics?

3. Does the team understand the importance and difficulty of distribution and brand development?

4. Does the financial performance table look over the top? Are the entrepreneurs naive? On the other hand, do those same revenue projections after the business scales up by Year 5 produce the type of exit that I, as an investor, want and need to achieve? It may be a good business, *but perhaps it is not the business for my type of investing.*

Market Analysis

Start this section on a new page of the business plan. It contains three parts: the Target Industry, the Customer, and Competitors.

The Target Industry

This section provides information on the total size of the industry, its major segments, the growth rate of those segments, and then, your specific target niche.

Here you describe your target customer group, the specific uses or applications you plan to address, and then place a revenue or current "spend" amount against that focused target. This becomes your addressable market. In fact, it does hurt to use the words *addressable market* in this section of the plan because many investors now use that term to have entrepreneurs indicate their specific piece of a much larger market.

This information needed to define and size your addressable market typically comes from Web or library sources, your own company studies, published government statistics, trade association data, business magazine articles, and your field research with potential customers. Footnote key sources as part of the credibility game. *You must have data!* You need to be able to prove your choice of target industry niche. You should have a lot of these data from your work in Chapter 1. Chapter 2 makes this even more specific through specific customer groups and their occasions of use or applications.

Also in this section, include a brief description of major trends that affect buyers and buying behaviors in the target segment. These trends might be regulatory in nature, political threats or concerns, disruptive technologies, new science, or the emergence of new channels to market.

This is *environmental scanning*. Entrepreneurs are wise to look for signs of turbulence or chaos in an established market—this presents opportunities for creative problem solving.

Questions on the Investor's Mind:

1. Is the venture placed in a robust, growing market? Does the entrepreneur have hard, current data to back up his/her assertions that this is a robust market?

2. Has the entrepreneur defined an "addressable" or target niche, customer, or use within a broader market in a manner that is clear and actionable?

3. Does the addressable market represent a sizable revenue opportunity if the venture succeeds?

4. Are there compelling societal, governmental, technology, or industrial trends that are causing turbulence in a market, creating a compelling need among customers for new solutions? Is the venture riding a "wave" of consumer or industry demand and need?

The Target Customer

Every entrepreneur needs a clearly defined customer. This section provides specific information about customers' needs and preferences relative to your product and service. You should provide an in-depth profile of the target customer's relative size in terms of the overall market, needs and frustrations, buying preferences, and needs for related products and services in addition to your own.

Also, is there a difference between the end-user and the buyer for your products or services? List their respective needs and requirements. State how these fundamental insights drive your proposed product or service offerings.

The most effective way to gather this information about customers is to observe and talk to them in their own environment. This is in Chapter 3. Go to their place of use, and go to their place of purchase. The Reality Check in Chapter 7 can be very powerful here. You can even show summarized responses in an appendix. This is your proof that you really know your target customer. Level of dissatisfaction with current solutions and purchase intent for your innovative solution are the two big questions for which you should already have answers.

If you are a representative customer (which is how many new companies begin), you must still go out into the field to understand the needs of other end-users and buyers. Your own insights will be shaped by what they have to say. A shortcut is to find other organizations or companies that have recently completed a customer requirements market research study. If you can find this, all the more power to you. It becomes part of your arsenal.

Questions on the Investor's Mind:

1. Does the entrepreneur have a crisp picture of the target customer and the target buyer in terms of what they need and how they buy? Is that based on reading what others have written or firsthand, intimate experience with customers? Has the entrepreneur invested time with customers or is it all just conjecture?

2. What customers can I visit myself to validate what I am being told? Professional investors will do due diligence by talking to a number of customers on their own as part of their recommendation to their fellow investors. Have ready a few customers or areas where customers shop or work where this can be done. A tradeshow attended by customers is also useful.

3. As the investor reads and extends to other parts of the business plan, how does that understanding of the target customer translate into a compelling product or service offering? Does the business model proposed by the entrepreneur align with these customer insights?

Competitors

Competitive assessment identifies either the flaws in your direct competitors or gaps in the market that they do not address. Make a list or table of competitors. Identify the functions, features, and pricing of your competitors. You should have done this type of work already in Chapter 6.

This research should be far more than a simple Web search. Go to both the place of sale as well as the place of use to see your competitors' products or services in action.

One of the primary reasons why investors often shun business plans is that entrepreneurs think that they are the only show in town and simply have not spent the time to understand the strategies and activities of companies already in the market—large as well as small.

Use the competitor information table to summarize your competitors' marketing concepts and strategies—and their vulnerability. Where are the gaps? How will your venture differentiate? Is it in the area of product or service, in pricing, or in channel? Once again, *you must have data* from competitors, or more generally, about existing solutions to the problem you are trying to solve. Your Reality Check can also be used to prove that your idea is competitively different or *differentiated*.

Competition doesn't always have to be direct. The real competition for a business-to-business (B2B) venture might be the customer's own internal R&D or IT development teams. This needs to be factored into the competitive assessment as well. Write a sentence or two about the do-it-yourself or not-invented-here issue if it applies to your target customers.

Questions on the Investor's Mind:

1. Who are the primary competitors? What are the "big boys" in the mainstream market doing in this area? If they aren't working on it, why not?

2. How is the entrepreneur's appreciation of the customers' needs special or different than current competitors? Is the entrepreneur addressing problems that no one else is addressing that are or will be a priority within the target industry niche?

3. What other funded startups are working in this space? Who are the investors, and do I know them? Whom can I call to find out the action that is happening in this space?

4. What are the clear points of competitive differentiation that the entrepreneur is proposing? How is that achieved: by feature, cost, or sales capability?

5. How do actual target customers perceive the proposed products or services? What do they think about current competitors? Are customers so loyal to current competition that it will be extremely hard to unseat current suppliers? Once again, what live customer can I check this out with?

6. If this team is successful, are any of the large, established players in the market potential buyers for an exit strategy?

Final Checklist for the Market Analysis Section

The bottom line for the Market Analysis section of the business plan is that anyone listening to you and who reads this section must see that:

- The target industry and the addressable market within that industry are healthy and growing
- You deeply know customers' needs
- You know your competition and have a strategy for being better than them

This section is incredibly important for both a startup and a corporate venture. *In many ways, this entire project hinges on the quality of your insight into customers and competitors.* Part Web research and part field research in the place of use and the place of sale, your work here is the foundation for everything to follow. If you do not have a team member with experience in the industry in which you would like to start the company, forget it. Look somewhere else!

We typically like to see a few charts or graphs showing size and trend of demand and an exhibit showing competitive offerings.

Solutions: Technology, Products, and Services _____

Start this section on a new page of the business plan.

The purpose of this section is to describe the product and service portfolio, the staging of that portfolio, and the development effort and time needed to get the first product or service in the market. If your venture is strictly to be a reseller, then use this section to define those products and services you hope to distribute to the target market. This section should at most be three or four pages long, including an exhibit or two. If you are doing a high-tech venture, you must try to explain your technology in the clearest of terms (which are not necessarily the simplest of terms) so that the professional investor can learn and understand how your product or service works at a basic level.

Product or Service Design

This is Chapter 3—its thinking and your application of those frameworks. Write it up! Describe how your design meets the customer's needs and is differentiated from current competitors. How is it special? In what ways does it bring unique value to customers? An illustration or sketch of your product or service concept is important to include as an exhibit in this section.

> *Questions on the Investor's Mind:*
>
> 1. Are the insights discovered and presented in the Market Analysis section driven into a compelling base-level product, system, or service design? Does that design "sing"? Or do we need to get some professional product designers on the case? That's okay, but it will cost me more money.
>
> 2. Is this entrepreneur trying to do too much in terms of product or service development during the first two years? Can we get an initial offering out to market faster and see if it actually appeals to customers?

Product Line or Service Suite Strategy

Here you need to describe your product/systems/service portfolio. Terms such as *good, better, best* often work well here. Also, showing how your portfolio maps out against the segments of an industry can also be a powerful addition to the plan. *Professional investors do not invest in "onesies."* They need to see a product line, or a base-level service that can be customized to particular customer group needs. This is also a good opportunity to describe your "follow-on" or "add-in" strategy for driving recurring revenue.

Don't propose a strategy to conquer the entire world. Start off highly focused. Hand-waving doesn't work here. Understand what you know and what you don't know. Don't make stuff up. If you don't have the answer, be honest about that and get back with an answer later.

Another important part of a product strategy is evolution of the portfolio over the first three years of the business. Who is your first target customer in the first year, and what are you selling to that customer? Once you have established this "beachhead," what additional products or services do you wish to bring to market in the second year? What do you propose to add in the third year? Also, are you going to expand from your initial customer group to an adjacent set of customers after several years in business? All these are important in driving a product strategy that has "legs"—that fuels the growth of a dynamic enterprise.

Here again, the work you did earlier in the book should be all that you need to write this section of the plan. Chapter 4 focused on this. The Reality Check should have also validated your product or service ideas and identified other types of products or services customers want to use along with yours.

Don't forget to stage the evolution of your product or service portfolio. Do not try to create a richly diverse product line or service suite all in the first year. It's best to get an initial set of commercial offerings out as soon as possible, learn as much as you can from the in-market experience, and grow from there.

Questions on the Investor's Mind:

1. Is this entrepreneur trying to do too much in the first two years? Is he or she sufficiently focused? You would be surprised how the well-intentioned enthusiasm of "youth" can produce anxiety in an investor who relishes innovation but also wants to mitigate and manage risk. Yes, go conquer the world, but let's first start by creating a highly focused business providing X to customers Y. Then expand.

2. After the beachhead is secured, does the entrepreneur have a dynamic product or service strategy that can create a niche or segment leader that can provide the investor with a home run?

Proprietary Technology and Intellectual Property

For biotech, medical device, materials, and energy ventures, and to some extent even software ventures, you would be surprised how the IP issue can be a show-stopper for professional investors. This is often an essential component in technology-focused businesses because *IP can create an "unfair" winning advantage*. If you haven't figured out an IP strategy, the investor may walk away. Your work in Chapter 4 on considering the intellectual property in your venture fits right here. Also, remember the importance of branding—brand names in particular—as an important IP component of your venture (see Chapter 6).

Questions on the Investor's Mind:

1. Is there any IP in this venture? Does the entrepreneur appreciate the importance of it for the value of the company?

2. Who do I know that can punch holes in the IP strategy?

3. Is the entrepreneur working with a law firm that has a good reputation in the IP field? Or do I have to find a better one for them?

Development Plan and Key Milestones

You actually prefer to put this information in toward the back of the business plan under the section titled "Milestones With Funding." But this can also be a brief written section, accompanied by a short milestone table for developing your product or service. For most technology-intensive ventures, the typical flight plan is:

- Complete the "alpha" version and show it to key prospective customers.
- Complete the "beta" version and provide it to a few select customers for actual use. If you have done your work well, there shouldn't be much difference between the beta and the final commercial release.

- Complete and launch Version 1.0 to customers.
- Develop and release follow-on features and improvements for the next version.

In a software company, typical time periods are three months to get to alpha, and an additional three to six months to get to beta and commercial release, respectively. The terms also apply to a new retail concept, where there is a design of the store layout and merchandizing (alpha/beta depending on your point of view), and the opening of the first store (the "beta" or Version 1.0, again depending on whether your plan, from the start, is to open a multi-store operation). Designing and opening a new store, with all the various commercial contracts that such a process requires, tends to be a six-month journey. For a consumer packaged goods venture, a year's effort from concept to commercial release is also not unrealistic, particularly if you use outside subcontracted manufacturers for production. And the "alpha" is used for customer research, the "beta" for a local or regional test market with select retailers, and "commercial release" the beginning of national distribution. However, if you are working in the biotech space, there is an entirely different set of terms and time cycle calculus—FDA-mandated milestones take years for each major step!

Beyond your strategy for getting the work done, investors also want to see someone on the team who has had the experience of successfully bringing a new product or service from the idea stage to commercialization, someone with judgment, maturity, and strong organizational skills to run new product or systems development—even if the original "insight" comes from younger, brilliant engineers or scientists!

There are also many other things that a venture must do to launch a product—such as developing marketing collateral, tradeshow attendance, and promotion. Incorporate these, however, in the Sales section of the business plan.

Questions on the Investor's Mind:

1. Does the team have a sense of urgency? Do the members understand "agile development"—develop, test, and develop some more?

2. Can they get the work done? Do I need to make the founding technologist a CTO and bring on an experienced product development or IT manager?

3. Do they know who their beta customers are going to be? (Note: For a consumer packaged product, it's the first retailer; for a B2B software or service, the first large account; for a medical device/product, the test or clinical trial partner.)

Development Costs

Investors often want to see a short section on the costs associated with R&D for your major milestones—if your business is the type that needs R&D. These costs then tie into the Financial Projections section of your business plan, first as part of the Assumptions and next, as part of the Pro Forma P&L (e.g., the projected income statement for the venture). You need to think about in-house engineers or programmers, testers, fees to partner developers, and any sort of licensing costs incurred in developing the product, system, or service. It is easy to scare investors away without a good manager of projects on a team. It is also easy to scare investors by being totally unrealistic about how much it will really cost to get a functional product to market. Investors want realism, good R&D management, and a bunch of doers who are hungry to create new products.

Questions on the Investor's Mind:

1. Does the team have an engineer who knows what is at stake? Can they make a deadline? Do they know that "the Perfect gets in the way of the Good"? My money is at risk here, and I need a product in the market as soon as possible.

2. Do they have a solid core team driving development (be it for a product or a system or to design a new store)? Do they already know who they want to bring on board for key positions? Are they doers or just managers of process?

3. Is this venture going to cost twice as much as they think it is going to cost to get product ready for market?

Final Checklist for the Solutions Section

The reader needs to walk away with the impression of:

- A distinct product or service concept that matches up to compelling customer needs and frustrations and that is clearly different than solutions currently offered by competitors.

- A robust product and service strategy that will offer choice as well as value to the target customer.

- An understanding of what it takes to develop commercially viable products or services. If you don't have a member of your team with engineering (for products) or domain (for services) expertise, you had better find someone with that experience to be a part of your team or at least to advise you.

- If your venture is a technology venture, the reader wants to see an IP strategy and understand why your IP is potentially valuable to other companies in the industry. And, for any venture, the reader wants to see a powerful and unique brand.

In this section of the business plan, it is also customary to see diagrams or higher-level schematics of the product or systems architecture. If you are solving a workflow problem, a diagram of the "before" and "after" workflow would make for an excellent exhibit. You can also include a diagram that shows how your product family or services roll out over the first three or so years of the business. Also, if you have prototypes, include product prototype pictures in an appendix. *Definitely bring these prototypes to your investor presentations.*

Sales Plan: Customer Targets, Distribution, Pricing, and Branding _____

Start this section on a new page of the business plan.

Executives and investors are going to want to see four basic things in the Sales Plan:

- That you understand *the importance of selling*—and will not short-change investment in building sales capability in the first years of the business.

- That your go-to-market strategy is spot-on with the target buyer for your venture. This requires a tight "fit" between your *channels* (reach in your target market), your products and services (complexity of sale, price level, and service required), and your customers (where they like to shop or buy).

- That you have a strategy for building *a strong brand* in your industry.

- That you have a good strategy for *scaling distribution* once a successful launch is achieved.

Chapters 5 and 6 have all the meat needed to craft this section of the business plan. You learned about different types of distribution channels and what it takes to build a strong brand. Write up the results of your Reader Exercises. This section should be no more than two or three pages long.

Selling Strategy

In many businesses, the primary user is not the primary buyer; the grocer versus the consumer; the pet owner versus the pet; the IT department versus the office worker; the logistics department manager versus the truck driver. In this section of the business plan, you need to be specific about this difference if it exists for your product, system, or service. Then, if there is a difference, you need to get very specific about the needs and wants of these buyers. Approaches used in the Market Analysis section for customers should apply here to buyers: industry description, size, growth rate, buyer needs and concerns, and the best way to reach these buyers.

B2B enterprise selling is complex. One of the first things an investor is going to want to know are the key stakeholders in a company who are part of the purchase decision—and how long that extends the sales cycle. In tough economic climates, the sales cycle extends even longer.

Questions on the Investor's Mind:

1. If the buyer is not the end-user, does the team have as deep and clear of an understanding of the buyer as they do about the end-user? Is there any sort of seasonal or calendar type of buying cycle? How and where do these buyers become informed about new products? Does the team also know about the buyer's preferred buying amounts/volumes and financing methods for purchases?

2. Is "the sale" a lot more complex than the team is presenting in its plan? If this is a B2B venture, who are other key stakeholders in a business customer that need to be influenced in favor of the venture's products or services?

3. Is this something that has to be sold face to face, or can they use telemarketing? Face to face is going to be very expensive—but if it is necessary, so be it.

Trade/Channel Strategy and Targeted Channel Partners

In this part of the plan, you need to describe the channel structure—that is, if it is direct to the customer or through intermediaries. If you will use middlemen, describe who they are, their location, and importantly, their standard margins. If you are going to pursue multiple channels, how will they be synchronized and how will you avoid channel conflict? Perhaps most important, if you are going to use channel partners, who are the best ones for the launch of your venture and then, as your business grows, who might be the next logical partners? Provide names. Also indicate if you have already reached out to these launch partners.

As many an entrepreneur has learned (the hard way), the biggest channel partners are not necessarily the best because they may be carrying a thousand other products in addition to yours. For example, you will find new food products appearing in Whole Foods Market, but not necessarily in traditional, large grocers such as Kroger or Walmart. The same might go for targeting the True Value hardware stores as opposed to The Home Depot. The larger outfits have a tendency not to want to work with small firms who have limited resources to promote their new brands and a limited number of SKUs (stock-keeping units) to create on-shelf brand awareness—in other words, a lot of bother for not a lot of money. If working with a Home Depot or Walmart is part of your launch strategy, you had better show that you understand what it takes to reach an agreement with a large channel partner and demonstrate some type of access to that partner. When working with any large, established retailer, the details of developing marketing collateral, a sampling program, and a cooperative marketing program can be overwhelming for the inexperienced entrepreneur. Here, too, there is no substitute for experience. If you plan to sell products through a major retailer, get either a direct team member or a gray-haired adviser who has successfully launched products "to trade" in a prior job. This will make your work proceed much faster.

Perhaps more important, an initial set of conversations with buying decision makers in large channel partners of any sort, or store owners in small independent chains, is an essential part of doing your homework prior to pitching investors. How else is an investor going to know that you can deliver the channel in your plan as well as the revenue associated with that channel?

Another important element in this section of the business plan is to describe your activities regarding supporting the channel, be it for your own direct sales force or a channel partner, and to determine what it takes to make the seller successful. This might include training and product samples.

It goes almost without saying that for whatever channel strategy you choose, you must understand the margins and incentives needed to motivate your sales force and channel partners.

For those of you selling through your own direct sales force, do not be cheap with commissions. Consider *increasing* the sales commission percentages for superstar salespeople. That might mean 5% plus base for the first $1 million, 7% for the next $500,000, 9% for the next $500,000, and so forth. If these superstars end up making more salary than you (as the CEO), you should be delighted. Every extra dollar they bring into the company increases the value of your company and your owner's equity. In fact, show a good salesperson how they can make more cash salary than you and challenge them to do it! Also, any good B2B or channel salesperson is going to want you to go on the road with them to meet customers and help drive revenue. Do it! An understanding of the sales pipeline is critical. For many technology industries, the typical ratio is to have 3:1, three times the number revenue opportunities in the pipeline compared to monthly revenue goal. The VC is going to ask you this—and you need to know the answer for your industry sector. And salespeople have got to be closers—that means seeing their performance against quota for the past three years. Then you must do your own due diligence to make sure that candidate hit his or her numbers.

Questions on the Investor's Mind:

1. Is there anyone on board who has "carried a bag" for a living? (That means sold products or services for a living.) If there isn't, would the founders ever listen to what a salesperson might tell them about what it takes to sell effectively? This is where many small companies fail.

2. Success in a venture is all about revenue—at least in the first couple of years. Do these folks understand how to "engineer" revenue as much as they understand how to engineer their product or service?

3. Do they understand what it takes to prime a channel—to get the sellers in that channel competent in demonstrating and selling the venture's wares?

Pricing Strategy and Repeat Purchases/Recurring Revenue

This is where you bring to bear your research on competitors and the positioning of your products or services. Using the words *premium* or *parity* or *discount* are important signals for investors. Even though we are fans of the low initial volume, premium pricing revenue model, it is okay to have predatory pricing to gain share. Just look at Twitter or the early years of Google. However, you are going to have to prove to the reader in the Financials section of the business plan that you have a strategy for making money, typically within a one- or two-year period from startup. Chapter 5 (business model), Chapter 6 (competitive positioning), and Chapter 7 (the actual Reality Check) provide input into this section.

This is also where you should reiterate recurring revenue. If you are providing a physical product of one form or another, can you charge for accessories or services along with the core product? If it is software, will you be selling plug-ins and/or charging maintenance fees? If it is a service, will you be providing a "good, better, best" suite of value-added services? Does bundling mean anything for your business—such as combining different products together at a price break for customers?

Questions on the Investor's Mind:

1. Does the entrepreneur's price support the positioning of the venture relative to competitors?

2. Is the entrepreneur giving stuff away just to get customers, and what type of precedent will that set for the company's brand? A reference account or two based on a "freebie" is okay, but how does that translate into hard revenue soon afterward?

3. Has he or she thought cleverly about how to make additional money from hard-won customers? Is that thinking also part of the R&D plan?

Layout and Merchandizing (for Retail Ventures or Retailed Product Ventures Only)

A diagram of your proposed store layout or on-shelf/in-store display would be a very useful exhibit here. The investor wants to see that you appreciate key principles of merchandizing—where to place things in a store and how to place them for your target customer. If you are providing products to sit on retailers' shelves, how will you draw attention to SKUs in a crowded retail environment? Will it be with in-store sampling and displays or posters? Will it be through a point of sale "shipper" or rack? Here, too, an experienced hand on the team or a trusted adviser can make all the difference for a successful launch. You can also learn a lot by calling local vendors who are in the business of creating these materials.

The Question on the Investor's Mind:

1. Do the entrepreneurs really know what they are talking about? Let's go to a store together and see. It will also be a great opportunity to do a quick competitive check.

Branding, Advertising, and Promotion

Building a brand—for low-tech or high-tech products or services—is critically important for any venture. It is how you get customers to try your offerings; it is also how you get large companies to begin to think about an acquisition.

For this section, describe your company's brand architecture: the company name, the name of its product or service lines, and then, the specific product names. Also describe the messaging around this branding—the functional, emotional, and social benefits to target customers. Explain why this branding is relevant and truly meaningful to your target customers. Do you have any data—such as data from your Reality Check—that proves this? And how does your branding differentiate your venture from current competitors?

Then you need to briefly describe the venture's promotional efforts to build and support the branding strategy. These include media advertising, tradeshows, etc. Investors will also want you to have done your homework on the cost of these different venues and work that go into your Pro Forma P&L. These are expensive and important investments.

Questions on the Investor's Mind:

1. How much work are these folks going to need to make a first-rate impression in their target market?

2. Do they have an attractive Website right now? If not, is that because they are working in stealth mode or don't really care about marketing? And if they have a Website, what is the messaging conveyed? Solutions? Reliability? Customer value? Or just a tech or services shop?

3. Do I like what they are going to call their product or service? Does it make any sense to the target customer?

4. Are their approaches for generating awareness and demand appropriate for a startup venture? Are they being clever about how they want to spend money? Have they thought about how to get free publicity?

Final Checklist for the Sales Section

Should you receive funding for your venture, a lot of money and effort over the next five years is going to be allocated to building a powerful go-to-market capability and, hopefully, a significant brand. More than any other section in the business plan, these four (and if your venture is a retail product, five) elements must fit together in a cohesive, pragmatic, and affordable fashion. This is a great opportunity to apply everything that you should have learned in your marketing classes—and even better, work experience—into creating a dynamic market strategy for your own business. Perhaps more important, the investor must come away convinced that you have sales experience on your team and that you have truly listened to those team members. If you don't have a person with selling and channel experience, find that person and include him or her on your team or as a trusted adviser.

Operations, Production, and Supply _____

Also start this section on a new page.

This section typically describes the "back end" of your company—all the important activities that happen outside of R&D and sales or distribution. For most businesses, this section is critical because the management of production and manufacturing, and of the suppliers that come before manufacturing, is the key to achieving operating profit. The buzzwords are easy to say—low-cost, high-quality suppliers or low-cost, high-quality manufacturing—but hard to achieve. At this point in your business planning, what you need to do most is to show readers that you understand the importance of these matters and have developed some excellent if not world-class options for your venture.

Figure 11.3 shows the key elements that you need to consider in writing this section. All you really need for the purposes of a business plan are *strategies* for each of these

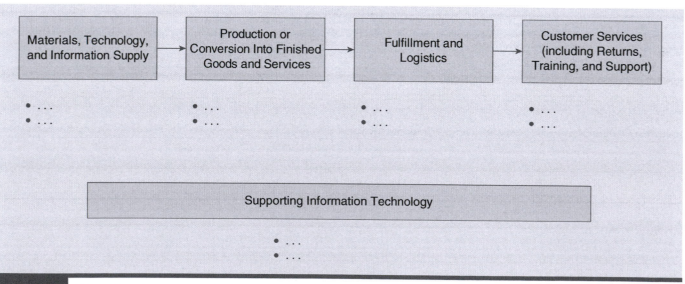

Figure 11.3 Strategies and Implementation Approaches for Operations, Production, and Supply

elements—suppliers, production, logistics/fulfillment, and customer service—that fit together in a cohesive and coherent manner and are then carried forward as base-level assumptions in your financial projections to drive cost of goods, operating expenses, and investments in "plant and equipment." Keep it simple, and keep it real.

The thinking behind each of these operational components is to make smart decisions about *what you do in-house, what you do outside the company,* and, for those areas that are external, being very careful about the external partners with whom you are going to entrust a major chunk of your operations. As noted in earlier, this is *lean or agile thinking* applied to startup operations. It is very important to get products to market quickly and optimize the right amount of fixed overhead and internal expenses for your type of business.

For example, if you are going to be shipping physical products directly to consumers or businesses, use UPS or FedEx, not some other fly-by-night operation that might cost a little less. This holds true for all other expects of the supply chain. What you put into your product, how it is put together, how it is delivered, and how it is serviced *all matter*. And a poor choice of partner in any one of these areas can lead to a tarnished image in the eyes of the customer—just like an ineffective salesperson or channel partner.

Managing Suppliers

The world is your oyster here. A simple Web search will quickly reveal all the major suppliers of components that might go into your product. That might be food ingredients, electronic components, entire computers, or chemicals. Select one or two well-known suppliers that match your venture's needs and then call their sales offices to find unit prices based on volumes. Use the most sensible of these choices in your financial projections. Or, if your company is making a software product, what are the toolkits that you or your engineers want to use, and what is the cost of these toolkits? (This might be somewhat redundant to the text in the R&D section of your business plan—but that is okay.) Here, you need to talk about ongoing licensing or "run-time" costs for deploying these tools in volume. Most entrepreneurs are looking to Red Hat, MySQL (now owned by Oracle), or Microsoft for low-cost tools solutions—that are, nonetheless, extremely powerful. If your venture focuses on technology-intensive services, these days that means getting your hands on streams of data, crunching those data, and incorporating the results into services for target customers.

Managing Production

In the "old days," entrepreneurs would carefully design and install their own production equipment and processes and then gradually ramp up production to meet growing demand. Today, however, just as products have become modular, companies have as well. Many entrepreneurs now find larger, well-established manufacturers who will cut, shape, extrude, and otherwise assemble finished products on a subcontract per unit basis. The good ones have extensive quality control systems that would take years and considerable sums for an entrepreneur to develop on his or her own.

At the same time, there is also risk in externalizing production. You need to invest considerable time and effort specifying materials to be used for both the product and packaging and do systematic sampling of outputs to make sure that finished products meet your quality standards. If you can get a patent on some aspect of design, this provides you with some measure of protection against deceitful contract manufacturers. But vendors need to be carefully investigated and contracts written carefully to provide penalties for late delivery and poor quality. And of course, the availability of subcontract manufacturers is industry-specific. The bottom line, however, is that this is an option that every entrepreneur should explore before writing a business plan that requires millions of dollars to buy, install, test, and operate dedicated machines. This transforms "fixed costs" into variable costs—a good working principle for entrepreneurs.

If you work for a large corporation and are planning an internal corporate venture, there will be considerable pressure for you to use existing plant and equipment. Executives reading your plan might say, "Let's give them a shift on one of our lines." Be careful, however. The overheads on those manufacturing lines might be totally acceptable per unit when there are thousands of units being produced each and every shift. However, for your small initial volumes, the overheads can be crushing—so much so, that the resulting COGS may kill your business altogether. Run the numbers, talk to people, and if you need to use a less expensive subcontractor to get started, be sure to support your strategy with numbers. You will need them.

Even businesses that do not make physical products can benefit from the same approach. For example, companies making complex software can "rent" machines from Amazon's Cloud computing business unit at a truly fractional cost for extra computing power. Or a service business that needs to crunch huge amounts of data in the delivery of its service can contract with any one of thousands of infrastructure service providers who will host your key applications. And most entrepreneurs go to a service provider to build and host their Websites—particularly those requiring e-commerce capabilities.

This is another area where getting that gray-haired adviser who has manufacturing and supply management experience in your target industry can be of tremendous help. When it comes to manufacturing, or using subcontract manufacturers, there is no replacement for field experience. There are just too many details and too many potholes where an inexperienced entrepreneur can make a critical error without knowing it. This is particularly true for entrepreneurs seeking low-cost manufacturing partners abroad. Knowing the lay of the land in an offshore business environment is essential for successfully negotiating business agreements and nurturing a productive working relationship with offshore partners.

Managing Logistics/Fulfillment

This one is getting easier and easier. For small packages, there is UPS and FedEx. For larger shipments, there are dozens of well-established third-party logistics firms that will organize the shipment of your containers around the world, handling customs and other regulatory affairs that would take the typical entrepreneur years to learn. For ventures providing software, the Web is the logistics channel. Simply go to Symantec or salesforce.com (www.salesforce.com) to see how online subscription management and software/services delivery should be done.

Stepping back, the message here is *do not* buy your own trucks, or do not print manuals or CDs unless your business or customers absolutely demand it. It is better to invest your capital into R&D to create new innovations and into sales programs to generate revenue from those innovations.

Managing Customer Service

Making sure that your customers feel well treated—particularly when they have problems or concerns, is the key to establishing long-term repeat customers. In this part of the business plan, you need to present a simple, effective process for providing customer service—whatever that means for your type of business. For some companies, that might mean training customers; for others, fixing bugs or problems with software; and for others, handling billing and account management questions. You cannot underestimate the importance of establishing good customer service for a fledging business. It is not the small problem here or there that will lose you a potentially lifelong customer; rather, it is the failure to respond to such problems with clarity and speed. You need to think of your customers as an extension of your sales force—and that means eating the cost of whatever it takes to "make things right."

Designing customer service can't be left to chance. We remember as young software entrepreneurs ourselves how customer support calls would be channeled through our little company. First, a call would go to our front desk receptionist. Then the call would be sent back among the programming staff, many of whom took great delight in speaking to live customers. However, after a few months, it became all too apparent that the programmers were enjoying their new friendships a little too much. The mornings were increasingly consumed responding to issues that came in the day before. Not only did we have to hire a customer support person, soon followed by others, but also a manager. We also had to implement a "bug reporting" system to keep track of issues and resolutions, and to serve as a valuable input to R&D.

Increasingly, computer systems can help you manage these different functions—and some of these are being provided on a Web services basis—which means rather than an expensive upfront license, a pay-as-you-go option in terms of usage. Investigate these and work subscribing to such services into your financials when your company begins to scale in Years 2 and 3.

At a more mundane level, you can also use this part of the business plan to specify the office space and location of your "headquarter" facilities to take you through the first several years of the business.

Questions on the Investor's Mind:

1. Do the team's operations plans show an analytical approach to assessing suppliers, subcontractors, and shippers? Has anyone worked the numbers?

2. Are they wasting money on a fancy office and furnishings?

3. Is there anyone on the team who has managed a business operation before? If not, can I find them one? And how much time do I have to do that? How far away are they from needing to scale up their operations?

Final Checklist for the Operations Section

This can be a crucial part of your business plan if you are presenting to investors with actual, hands-on operational experience. Strategy is important for them, but they have probably seen dozens if not hundreds of cool venture ideas that failed because of poor operational execution. This is also an area of the business where such investors will want to help you improve your thinking. So keep it simple and clean. Show that you have done your homework on production, logistics, and customer services, and have considered interested options for "make or buy" in terms of experienced suppliers. Investors want to see "lean operations," but at the same time, they want to see informed decisions on suppliers that you expect to become trusted partners as your business scales.

Organization Plan

Start this section on a new page and keep it to one or two pages.

The organization plan first provides a description of the management team and your key advisers. Write up your Reader Exercises in Chapter 10. You require experience, a balance of skills, and individuals who have a track record of success in prior jobs. Even better, a successful serial entrepreneur on your team or Advisory Board adds tremendous assurance to investors that *someone on the team has gone through the process before and made investors money.*

This part of the plan has three sections: the management team, a staffing plan for ramp-up, and the Board of Advisers (or Directors if you are seeking growth capital).

The Management Team

The two templates at the end of Chapter 10 are the meat for this part of the plan. Write a brief description of the current founders, their responsibilities in the venture, and their backgrounds. Then identify key roles where you feel there is a gap and where you need to recruit someone.

Let's talk about you. These days, startups that raise institutional venture capital always seem to have an experienced hand at the tiller. If you don't have experience and have proposed a business that needs more than $1 million for startup, you might have to find yourself a new partner with a track record of success. But as we also learned, only a small percentage of startups are actually funded by institutional sources. Most are funded by angel investors or by the founders' friends and family—where a little bit of money is used to quickly begin to produce cash from customers to fund further growth. Angel investors actually enjoy the enthusiasm of youth, and the energy and excitement of young entrepreneurs, as long as there is a solid, pragmatic plan behind them. Most angel investors are themselves prior business executives and entrepreneurs with extensive operating experience. Of all the angel investors we have met, the vast majority are just the type of people who you want as advisers as well as investors.

The Staffing Plan

This section briefly describes the types of functions you need to fill in the company during the first year or two of the business. Go to the textbook Website and look at the Headcount tab in the Health Monitoring Venture for an example of a detailed, carefully staged hiring plan. You can see that it is very specific about job titles, salaries, and when these expenses are brought on board to match development requirements and sales revenue. As a company grows, entrepreneurs must add staff across key functions to augment the amount of R&D, production, and selling that the business can accomplish.

Even if you are outsourcing key functions, you still require qualified personnel to manage these external relationships. In the financial projections, it is not uncommon to see fairly detailed breakdowns of human resources requirements and the salaries and overhead for particular types of individuals that are then summed up and carried forward into the appropriate areas of an aggregated P&L.

Board of Advisers/Directors

As described in Chapter 10, there are highly experienced individuals who can provide your team with the mentor capital it needs to deal at both the strategic and tactical levels of startup and growth. You should have someone who is an expert at sales in your industry; another in technology (if appropriate for your type of business); and another who is an expert across a broad spectrum of finance, be it raising money or establishing banking relationships for working capital. This would translate into a current or former VP of Sales, a CTO, and a CFO, respectively. It is also strongly advisable to consider your attorney a close adviser as well as the person who will prepare your business taxes. *Both* serve the role of keeping you out of trouble, *so listen to them!*

The difference between a Board of Advisers and a Board of Directors is that the former has no fiduciary responsibility to shareholders, including investors. The norm is to provide advisers some stock options in a startup. A Board of Directors is typically comprised of just one or two founders and two or three investors. The fact is that if you take investment capital from venture capitalists, you are not going to have any real choice in terms of who sits on your official Board. It is their money and if you mess up, they will be in the position to remove you as part of the original financing agreement.

Even if you have an official Board of Directors (which you must have for certain types of corporate organizations such as a C-Corporation or Subchapter S-Corporation), we still advise you to form a Board of Advisers and use them frequently as well.

Final Checklist for the Organization Section

The bottom line of this section is that you must not give short shrift to thinking about both your immediate and extended team. It may be the deciding factor for investors or executives in your corporation (if you are planning an internal corporate venture). Include brief résumés of key management in an appendix. If you are doing a biotech venture, forget the word *brief*. If you have a scientist on the team with page after page of journal publications, put them all in!

Questions on the Investor's Mind:

1. Can I see myself working with this team and its advisers?

2. Does the team have substantial experience and talent? If not, do they realize that? How hard will it be to convince them to "beef up"? If they don't have anyone who has been a CEO before, are they ready to take one that I supply?

Major Milestones With Funding

Start this section on a new page, too. And keep it to a single page of text and a figure.

This section of the business plan is critically important in your selling effort to prospective investors. It presents the major milestones that your business is committed to achieving with the specific round of financing. This needs only be a page featuring a task list with key dates. We also like to see a sentence or two on how to mitigate the risk of these key milestones at the bottom of the page. And even though it is only a page in length, you can be assured that if you have truly interested investors, you will spend hours working with them to sharpen these milestones and determine the people, partners, and resources needed to meet, if not accelerate, achieving them.

As noted earlier, there tend to be specific types of "development" milestones for startups:

- *Alpha.* This is the "alpha" version or prototype of your product, system, or service. In reality, most investors want to see that prototype with the business plan. However, in some cases, developing that "alpha" will be your first order of business. If it's more than two or three months in time, most investors will shy away. "Come back when you have a prototype, and then we will talk about investing," they will say.

- *Beta.* This is the "beta" version, a much more complete and working version of an alpha that is actually placed into the hands of lead users for test, feedback, and improvement. The time duration for achieving a beta varies widely on the type of venture; a consulting service can start providing services to clients right away, a software company might get to beta in three to six months, or a new pet food company such as that described in the first part of this book can get product for test marketing within several months with the use of contract manufacturers.

- *First commercial release.* This is the "Version 1.0" of your product, system, or service, together with a full marketing plan for launch and initial customer support. Sometimes this is referred to as the "first dollar" milestone. In most types of startups, investors expect to see a fairly quick follow-up to the beta test for full-scale commercial release. Unless you are working in the biotech or medical device space, try your best to get a first product or service to market within six to nine months from startup.

- *First operating profit.* This fourth milestone is derived from your Pro Forma P&L. Wouldn't it be great to achieve an operating profitability with the release of the first product or service? Unfortunately, there is often a lag. Investors want to see a path to profitability that falls within 18 to 24 months. Any longer will scare away most.

Of course, these time frames may well change for a particular type of venture. A retail concept will have its first test store that is both beta and first commercial release in the same shot. At the other extreme is a drug discovery venture. Your authors have invested in such a firm and don't expect to see a penny of return for eight years after startup, unless a large pharmaceutical firm buys the startup for its technology before it enters into full human clinical trials. However, a far shorter time horizon is expected for discovering new science and the filing of patents. Compared to all the other examples used in the book, *biotech is such a long haul.* But we know that even a single successful drug will generate hundreds of millions of dollars or potentially much more on an annual basis once brought to market.

Other types of milestones can also often be found in the planning of new ventures. The three most prominent are:

- *Key hires.* Certain investors will also see the hiring of managers in your firm as important milestones. Often, this is a VP of Sales.

- *Market tests.* This can be a local launch of your new product or service. This might also be a trial launch with a major new channel partner, such as a retailer or a computer company.

- *Next round of financing.* The next round is best planned well in advance and should match the needs of the growing business to achieve the next set of major milestones.

That might be $1 million to build the next-generation product or service, $2 million to build a professional direct sales force, $3 million to expand manufacturing to support major channel partners, or some combination of these and other company milestones.

You also need to state why your milestones are critically important for moving your venture forward. Your investors will want to be assured that you are using funds in the most cost effective manner possible. Have you considered ways to achieve your milestones at less cost; conversely, are you asking, for example, for $10,000 to create a proof of concept that will realistically cost $20,000, that is going to be picked up by smart investors. Regardless, for all major cost items, you need justification. Such justification may include quotes from service suppliers or contractors, prices of airlines tickets or attending trade shows, and so forth. This additional information should be placed in an Appendix in your business plan.

Questions on the Investor's Mind:

1. Are the venture's milestones well considered and appropriately staged?

2. Are these milestones sufficiently aggressive? What can we do to speed things up?

3. How long will the money last before we have to raise the next round? Does the current money give the venture enough time and evidence to prove that this is a viable market and good business opportunity? In other words, is it enough for me to get an uptick on my valuation?

Financial Projections

Also start this section on a new page. Chapter 9 provides the ammunition for this part of the plan. It contains your financial projections for:

- The key assumptions driving your revenue model, the P&L, and the Cash Flow Statement
- Your projection of revenue, hopefully detailed and "bottoms-up"; if it's all based on grabbing incremental market share in a large market, good luck!
- The Pro Forma P&L
- The Pro Forma Cash Flow Statement
- The funding request with detailed milestones and startup costs
- The exit strategy (potential exit valuation after five to seven years, or considerably longer if your venture is biotech)

Including a Balance Sheet is also a good idea just to round things off for investors. Not many actually look at it, however, for a startup.

Assumptions

As important as any of the specific projections in this part of the business plan are *the assumptions* behind the numbers. We covered this material in the prior chapter. Your assumptions should include:

- Unit prices for products, systems, and services and any discounting of those prices for volume procurements
- The number of customers by time period, and if need be, broken down by channel

- Any materials, direct labor, and subcontracting costs that drive COGS for the business, also on a per unit basis
- Officer salaries. Only pay the management team what the business can afford. Unpaid salaries placed on the Balance Sheet as debt are the first things wiped out in subsequent-stage financing. The founding team in a startup typically receives salaries of about $100,000. If it is a venture capital–backed business, they will hold between 10% and 20% equity after the first two rounds of financing. Angel-backed firms tend to leave the founders with substantially greater equity.
- Any specific difference between "sales," revenue recognition, and cash. Investors will want to understand these differences with an eye on appropriate revenue recognition and incentives that can be provided to customers to shorten the cash conversion cycle. Bottom line: Investors will want to know if there is a significant lag between sales and cash.

In general, any set of factors that have a major impact on your revenue model, the Pro Forma P&L, and the Cash Flow Statement should be noted in the financial assumptions. Same for any investments into hard assets of any sort, such as a machine, truck, or large computer. *Do not* short-change these assumptions. One way or another, these will come up as questions from discerning investors.

Format of Financial Statements

We have financial templates available on the textbook Website that you can download and adapt to your own specific venture. Some of these are for ventures making physical products, others software or systems, and yet others for pure services plays. You might find that they save you lots of time!

But what we don't want you to do is use any of these templates blindly. Even worse is to buy one of the popular commercial business-planning packages that ask you to answer 50 questions and then generate a dozen pages of detailed, small-font financial statements. You need to think through your financial projections as carefully as anything else in your business. Unfortunately, the human tendency is to let computers do the thinking for us. For venture finance, that simply doesn't work. It is far better for you to take the first pass at your P&L by hand—preferably on a large whiteboard surrounded by teammates to bat around the assumptions and the numbers. Start with a granular "bottoms-up" projection of revenues. Then, when it is time to start adding expenses, turn on the computer and use a spreadsheet.

The standard format that we observe in most funded business plans is to have a monthly breakdown of revenues and expenses for the first two years of operations and then annual projections for Years 3, 4, and 5. As noted in the prior chapter, your professor may ask for a different time period breakdown for financial information, such as quarterly projections instead of monthly ones. And we have rarely seen financial projections for internal corporate ventures that are anything but annual projections, even for the first year or two of the venture. However, we feel that the monthly projections reveal a much more precise analysis of cash burn before initial sales, and then, the path to achieving operating profit once sales commence. The monthly breakdown of revenue, operating profit, and actual cash flow is also the best way to assess the financing requirements at the current stage of growth. You simply add up the operating losses over the first set of months or year—and *voilà*, this aggregated amount should roughly match your capital request with some extra cushion built in to be safe.

If someone only wants to see quarterlies or annuals, you can simply roll up your more detailed projections as needed. You will have to do so regardless because in the first section of the business plan, we ask you to show the number of customers or units, annual revenue, and operating profit over the course of five years as a summary of the financial performance of the venture.

Even though the annual projections for Years 3, 4, and 5 are totally speculative, they do paint a picture of the size of the business and the value it can achieve in an ideal scenario. Plus, investors tend to look at industry sector multiples of sales and profits in those outlying years to get a notion of what your business *might be worth* if successfully implemented.

For those of you doing internal corporate ventures, you need to understand the financial metrics used by your company to evaluate new proposals. Measures such as ROA (return on assets) or FATR (fixed asset turnover ratio, or sales divided by invested capital for fixed assets) are common among large manufacturers. And nearly all major corporations now use the net present value of discounted cash flows to evaluate new business proposals. Bottom line: Take the time to learn how executives in your company measure business success and plan accordingly.

We need to reiterate: It is easy to print out 20 pages of spreadsheet projections that have little value and that are virtually impossible to defend. Your financial statements must be concise and realistic. Don't make your investors work too hard to understand your numbers. And be prepared to defend your numbers again and again—particularly your projections of revenue over the first three years of the business.

The Funding Request, Major Milestones, and Detailed Startup Costs

The funding request comes directly from your work in Chapter 8 (the stage and purpose of financing) and Chapter 9 (your financial projections). For most of you, your "ask" will be for either a "seed" or "Series A" financing. Once again, "seed" is typically to do initial product or service prototype development, run an "alpha" test, and then a more advanced "beta" test. Series A then kicks in from $250,000 to $1 million or more to get you to a full launch of your new product or service. As we described, this money typically comes from angel investors or early-stage VCs. If, on the one hand, your venture is in super-hot market space, a larger VC will enter the picture and put in much more for a Series A to launch and achieve scale in a much more rapid manner. The SilverRail case on the textbook Website, for example, got a $6 million Series A investment from a large VC. On the other hand, when a founder raises that much money for such an early-stage company, he or she will certainly end up with a minority percentage of the stock. Again, this is a game of balance: Get the money you need to achieve immediate milestones, which in turn make your company's valuation higher, so that when you raise the next round of capital, you give up less equity for each new dollar of investment. At the end of the day, you want to own as much stock as possible at the point of exit, or have majority control so you can have a major say on the timing and nature of that exit.

Each venture situation is different. Many entrepreneurs raise seed capital, develop and test their product or service, and launch it to market—and never have to raise a Series A investment. This is particularly true of services companies. The seed round is enough to get them to initial operations, which themselves are designed and priced to be profit-generating. Again, as we discussed in Chapter 8, the more milestones you can achieve with initial investment, the less stock you have to forfeit to external investors. Yet, if you need money to grow rapidly, it is a mistake not to try to find the money and put it to productive use. External equity financing is a balancing act between startup and successive-stage growth requirements, founder equity, and retaining control over major decisions.

The actual funding request made by an entrepreneur is often thought of as startup expenses. These come directly off the Pro Forma P&L in those first set of months where you are driving to alpha and beta. These will include your own modest salaries and office or facilities expenses, equipment expenses, Website costs, and so forth. Make these as detailed as possible, and include them as a separate spreadsheet for separate review. And be mindful that these are not just the expenses for the first number of months, but rather, the entire length of time needed to get to your first dollar of actual revenue. For most businesses, it is the gamut of work needed to get to alpha, beta, and launch.

Exit Strategy

No one can predict with complete certainty what is going to happen five to seven years down the road in terms of company growth and exit potential. But investors want to know that at least the entrepreneur is thinking about an exit strategy as he or she is in the process of starting and growing a company.

For investors, this is their hard-earned money, not a gift. There must be a return at some planned date down the road. Of course, events always conspire to make company growth better or worse. But at least you need to show that after a period of five to seven years, if the company meets its target level of sales and profitability, you and your Board can have the option of selling the company or doing an IPO at a certain market capitalization. This option to exit is not only good for them but also good for you. And you will find that after that time period, professional investors will get itchy for some type of exit. You will win as well, as long as you have been smart enough not to give a lot of stock needlessly to cofounders who never did much for the company or to investors at poorly negotiated terms and valuations.

As we saw in Chapter 8, the majority of exits occur by acquisition: 468 mergers and acquisitions compared to 53 IPOs in 2011 according to the National Venture Capital Association. So you had better count on an acquisition-type exit and build a promise of a healthy return for the investor's capital based on that premise.

This is done with a two-step process. First, take the revenue and operating profit amounts projected for Year 5 (or later) for your venture. Second, by multiples reported on revenue and operating profit for companies in your line of work in your industry niche. Multiply your projected revenue by the industry standard revenue multiple, your projected EBITDA by the operating profit multiple, see how close the results are, and if need be, take the average. It's a simple, reasonable way to determine the exit potential for a promising venture. And you will find that most investors will concentrate on revenue and apply an industry standard multiple to that revenue to derive a possible exit valuation.

How do you find an industry standard multiple? Well, this too can take a bit of research. Published financial databases from Thomson Reuters provide M&A information. Your university's academic finance department probably has authorized access to these databases for the professors' own research. Also, search the Web and ask friends about recent deals done in your industry. All you need is a couple of benchmarks for acquisition amounts at very general levels of current revenue to get the multiple you need.

Figure 11.4 shows a real example, a spreadsheet that one of our former students used to answer this question for several venture capitalists anxious to invest in his information services venture. Note that the figure was developed for a deal executed in 2005. *The numbers are not relevant for anything that you might be doing today.* However, the thinking and format fit the purpose for getting to a multiple needed for developing an exit strategy.

On the top part of the spreadsheet are publicly available stock prices, number of shares, market caps, and an adjusted "enterprise value" upon which multiples are created. Comparables are typically based on enterprise value rather than market capitalization. The reason is that in the event of an acquisition, the buyer would (a) have to take on the company's debt and (b) pocket its cash. Enterprise value is simply the market cap adjusted by the amount of "net" cash in the business—that is, subtract the debt and add the cash on hand. It can differ significantly from the market capitalization, and that is why it is often used in exit valuation analysis.

On the bottom of the spreadsheet are acquisitions of private venture–funded companies that our former students were able to dig up through their friends and published sources. Those ventures that are acquired five to seven or eight years down the road are typically valued as a multiple of revenue, and some, on next year's projected revenue. Operating profit sweetens the deal, but unlike the price/earnings ratios of publicly traded companies, it is not typically the foundation for the acquisition valuation. But pay attention to those gross margins! When a business scales, it needs to achieve similar gross margins because these ultimately drive the bottom-line profitability of the business.

You can see in the figure that the multiples on revenue and earnings for private company deals are lower than the comp's on publicly traded (and arguably more commercially successful) public companies. It is then a matter of arguing for a middle ground between these two averages. You will also find yourself arguing about the companies included in the comparables basket. Nonetheless, doing the work needed to complete this template for your

Company X (Information Services) (Created for an investment valuation in February 2005)

Public Comps		Stock price Feb 2	Equity market cap $m	Cash $m	Enterprise value $m	Revenue estimates $m		Enterprise value/ revenue		Gross Margin
						CY05	CY06	CY05	CY06	
Salesforce.com	CRM	13.30	1,370	110	1,260	174	283	7.2x	4.5x	80.00%
InfoUSA	IUSA	11.32	605	6	599	395	415	1.5x	1.4x	68.89%
ChoicePoint	CPS	47.22	4,190	23	4,167	1,000	1,150	4.2x	3.6x	45.00%
Equifax	EFX	28.80	3,750	39	3,711	1,270	1,330	2.9x	2.8x	58.12%
Dunn & Bradstreet	DNB	57.85	4,002	275	3,727	1,440	1,530	2.6x	2.4x	68.76%
Thomson	TOC	34.97	23,130	483	22,647	8,000	8,640	2.8x	2.6x	
Monster	MNST	29.11	3,470	142	3,328	853	1,000	3.9x	3.3x	52.43%
Factset	FDS	52.27	1670	67	1,603	309	332	5.2x	4.8x	70.27%
CoStar	CSGP	41.64	761	113	648	112	135	5.8x	4.8x	67.37%
McGraw Hill	MHP	93.58	17,770	423	17,347	5,650	6,000	3.1x	2.9x	59.92%
United Business Media	UNEWY	10.34	3,540	1000	2,540	1,000	1,001	2.5x	2.5x	38.93%
SAP	SAP	38.61	47,970	2640	45,330	10,480	11,590	4.3x	3.9x	
ProQuest	PQE	33.44	955	8	947	462	494	2.0x	1.9x	51.17%

	CY05	CY06
Max	7.2x	4.8x
Min	1.5x	1.4x
Median	3.1x	2.9x
Mean	3.7x	3.2x
Mean (Ex. Max/Min)	3.6x	3.2x

Gross Margin: 60.08%

Private Comps: Precedent Acquisitions

Date	Target	Acquirer	Revenues (million)	Transaction Value (million)	Multiple
Jan-05	SRD	IBM	$8	$40	4.7x
Jul-04	Seisint	Reed Elsevier	$119	$775	6.5x
Dec-04	BitPipe	TechTarget	$10	$40	4x
Dec-04	Prime Assoc	Metavante	$5.2	$28	5.4x
Oct-04	Pinacor	MarketWatch	$7.0	$18	2.5x
Jun-05	IHI	Thomson	$88	$441	5.1x
Sep-04	CCBN	Thomson	$50	$188	3.8x

Figure 11.4 Developing Comparables for Exit Valuation Potential

From personal contacts and published sources.

own venture will impress the investor with the fact that you are thinking about making both of you a lot of money! This type of detailed analysis should clearly be kept in an appendix of the business plan. All you need to do in the body of the plan is write a few sentences stating several recent deals, the multiples achieved, and what that might mean for an exit strategy for your venture.

If you cannot find a standard industry multiple on sales or operating profit, use the following until you do: for product ventures, 2–3 times revenue; for software ventures, 4–5 times revenue; and for pure services, 1.5–2 times revenue. And for social networking Web ventures—those with super-cool technologies, lots of eyeballs, and virtually no revenue—just get a printout of the latest mega-deal, and let your investor know that this could be him or her, too! It's as good a benchmark as anything else.

Questions and Expectations on the Investor's Mind:

Investors want to see that your financial projections reflect an understanding of certain key principles:

- *Produce a robust stream of revenue:* a clear structure and nature of revenue, the time to first dollar, and how revenues scale.
- *Turn that revenue into cash:* incentives for customer payments and how you manage your accounts receivables.
- *Produce strong operating profits:* Unless you are doing a biotech startup, the bottom line is that operating three years in the red while revenue ramps up is no longer feasible. You need to show a clear path to profitability in 12 to 24 months—and the sooner the better. This is known as the path to profitability. Anything that you can do to reduce cash outflows should be strongly considered. Deferring paying up front for supplies, software, or services is essential. Office overhead, including computers, should be considered with extreme care. You might be able to sublet space at attractive rates, and avoid longer-term leases, from a larger corporation in the process of cost cutting.
- *Return on investment:* Most venture investors are looking for a 10X return on their invested capital upon exit, preferably within five to seven years, even with dilution based on later rounds of financing. The way that investors tend to calculate this type of return is not on the book value of your Balance Sheet but rather as a multiple on the sales and profitability in your P&L in the out-years. Multiples on sales and profitability for recent "exits" are simply applied to your own projected revenues in Year 5 on your Pro Forma P&L to get a feel for the potential exit valuation of your venture.

Each one of these expectations can be turned into specific questions:

a. Is there a solid revenue stream with recurring revenue from existing customers as well as new revenue from new customers?

b. What is the product–service mix? Am I comfortable with that mix?

c. Is there a structural cash conversion problem in the business? What can be done to shorten that cycle?

d. When does the company achieve operating profitability? Has the entrepreneur really asked for sufficient investment capital to reach that point?

e. Does the entrepreneur have the details to back up his or her "ask" for this round of financing? Are the startup costs realistic? Has the team underestimated the cost of getting to alpha, beta, and launch? Do they have the right expectations for their own salaries and office space, or do they hope to be "living large" on my money?

f. Taken all together, do the business plan and the financials lead to a world-class global company that can achieve an IPO, or is it really a niche company that would be the candidate for an acquisition by a larger corporation down the road? And is that acquisition likely to be a $30 million, $50 million, or $100 million plus type deal? How does that scenario fit with my own investment objectives and priorities? Is the entrepreneur thinking clearly about how investors are all going to make money from the venture?

Closing Thoughts on Constructing Effective Written Business Plans

A potential investor will do his or her own due diligence on your business plan. If your information is inaccurate or you omit a critical detail, good investors will find the error and hold you accountable. Every element of the plan needs to be considered carefully. The same holds true for missing information—such as failing to identify important competitors in the Market Analysis section.

The most important questions your business plan must answer to the satisfaction of the investor are:

1. Is the venture situated in a robust, growing industry?

2. Does the entrepreneur have a clearly focused "addressable market"—those target customers and uses within a specific industry niche—that is sufficiently large to generate a substantial revenue stream?

3. Is there something clearly different and distinctive in what the venture proposes to make and sell that differentiates it from competitors? (For some tech ventures, is there clear IP potential?)

4. Is there any proof that target customers actually want to purchase these new products or services, or is it all just speculation?

5. Is there a strong, balanced team, with some members who have successfully developed new companies before, and others who have strong operating experience? For some investors, this is often the very first question.

6. Does the business plan clearly show how the opportunity can be monetized—how the business can make money?

7. Are the revenue and expenses realistic? And are the revenues and profits sufficiently large to warrant the type of return on investment required by the type of investor to whom you are pitching?

It is also important to remember that investors are ideally looking for 20- to 25-page business plans, clearly written, nicely formatted, with a few selected diagrams or illustrations at key sections, and equally clear, reasonable financials. Many professional investors take new plans on business trips or to their home offices. Guess what tends to happen to a 100-page "heavy" binder? It gets left behind!

Reader Exercises

Step 1: Storyboard Your Plan

Creating a compelling, seamless story about the focus and promise of a new venture is your objective here. Planning the different parts of that story and how they connect is the purpose of storyboarding. Use Figure 11.2 as a template. Convene at a large whiteboard if possible and fill out with just a few bullet points each part of that chart. Sit back and assess. Do the parts fit? Does the story flow? Can you give a two-minute elevator pitch that captures the essence of the storyboard for each section?

Step 2: Write the First Draft of the Sections and Assemble

Assemble all of your materials from the prior chapters and write the first draft according to team roles and responsibilities. Each section should be no more than two to four pages, single-spaced, with several lines as paragraph breaks. The financial statements are attached at the end of the plan.

Step 3: Review and Critique

We have provided typical questions that investors will raise at the end of most of the sections of the business plan. Organize a team meeting and work through these questions, section by section. Role play if that is helpful. Having a "devil's advocate" is a tried and true method for improving projects. Remember that it often takes more work to make a section of text shorter and more powerful than it typically takes to write it. Leave sufficient time for such editing.

Step 4: Get Even More Specific on the Assumptions for the Financial Section

For the financial section, pay particular attention to the list of key assumptions for revenue, expenses, cash flow adjustments, and capital expenditures. Assume that the investor or an analyst working for the investor will pore over your financial statements back at the office. This part of the business plan must be self-explanatory.

Step 5: Review "Funding Request With Details, Milestones, and Startup Costs" as a Team

Assess with team members and trusted advisers the strategies for reducing the time to achieve major milestones and the amount of money needed to accomplish these goals. The quicker you get to market, the quicker you not only produce revenue but also begin the essential process of learning from customers and sellers how to make a better product or service. Also, the less money you need to raise, the more equity you get to keep.

Step 6: Polish—Formatting and Graphics

We recommend single-spacing, with several blank lines between paragraphs. Font size should be either 11 or 12, depending on the font selected. We also recommend that you start each major section on a new page. For example, the Business Model, Market Analysis, and so on should each start on a new page.

Financial statements should probably be no smaller a font size than 10 because anything smaller becomes hard to read. Landscape printing for the projections is totally acceptable. Please make sure that the numbers add up, and that the different financials integrate correctly for items such as operating profit, working capital adjustments, and longer-term investments. These come at the end of the plan.

Traditionally, documents of this sort have a Table of Contents. However, if your plan is short and focused, we don't think that a Table of Contents lends anything to the plan. In fact, for some investors, it might make the document feel "academic." Most investors know what to expect in each part of the plan and where those parts fit within the overall plan.

You might wish to include résumés of key team members in the back of the plan in an appendix. For biotech or other scientific ventures, this is mandatory because investors will want to see the backgrounds and research publications of technical leaders. Your authors vividly recall reviewing a business plan where the "plan" itself—calling for the development of a new generation of antibiotics by two brilliant professors at our university—was about 20 pages. However, the résumés in the back of the plan went on for over 100 pages! There were two key principles, and each had hundreds of publications and dozens of research grants. A patent was also included, as was the reprint of a seminal article in a leading journal.

We also strongly recommend that you incorporate a few choice graphs or charts into the business plan. Break up the text with some eye-candy. The Market Analysis section could use some type of industry analysis or competitive positioning chart, just as the Solutions section might benefit from a product/service architecture illustration or a development milestones chart.

Last, don't forget to put your name and contact information on the front page! Also, put in a very small font, a correctly formatted copyright notice on the bottom of the pages in the text.

After this chapter and all the work you have done leading up to it, there should be no question about what to write. *Go for it!*

The next chapter—our last—turns to the PowerPoint presentation needed for investor pitches and that accompanies the business plan. As in this chapter, we will also share our thoughts on what to expect from investors in such presentations.

Visit the Student Study Site at **www.sagepub.com/meyer2e** to access the following resources:

- Web Resources
- Video Resources
- General Resources in Entrepreneurship

12

Making the Pitch

The Purpose of the Chapter

You've come a long way to the point of launching your enterprise. You have defined and tested both a venture strategy and a business model for it. You have created a powerful, focused business plan with financial projections that hopefully show attractive and growing streams of revenue and operating profit. Your Cash Flow Statement should also give a good approximation of the funding tranches that you require to achieve alpha-beta launch, and then to scale the business to achieve operating profit. For most of you, that capital can be clearly segmented into "seed," "Series A," and perhaps even "Series B" financing. If you were able to do some of the Reader Exercises in Chapter 8 in which you searched for angels, venture capitalists, and strategic investors in your local area that are in some way connected to your university or part of your business or social network, then you might even know *who* you wish to target for a capital raise.

Now it's "show time." In the parlance of American football, you are now within ten yards of the goal line—within scoring distance. Everything you've done to this point has fortified your understanding of the opportunity, the market niche and users you aim to serve, and how the venture will make money. Your confidence has grown apace with that understanding and with your mastery of the Venture Concept.

Just one more push—one more task for most of you—and you will be ready to cross the goal line.

That last task is to pitch your venture to investors with the money you need first for startup and then for growth. As we noted in Chapter 8, that capital may come from friends and family, business "angels," or in rare cases, from venture capitalists or strategic corporate investors. If yours is an internal corporate venture, your "ask" will be to one or several executives who control the purse strings for new product, service, and business development.

No matter the source of capital, you will be obliged to make a *presentation*. The quality and persuasiveness of that presentation must be first rate. Helping you achieve that end—to get your money—is the purpose of this chapter.

There Are Presentations, and Then There Are Investor Presentations

Contrary to your inclination after all the hard work in this book, and the numerous templates you have completed—the shorter the presentation, the better. All the other detail will come into play in the questions and answers during and after your presentations, including the extensive *due diligence* that professional investors will undertake in the weeks to follow.

Guy Kawasaki, the noted observer of technology industries and a successful venture investor in his own right, stated this so very well in a blog post that he titled "The 10/20/30 Rule of PowerPoint":[1]

> Most of these pitches are crap: sixty slides about a "patent pending," "first mover advantage," "all we have to do is get 1% of the people in China to buy our product." These pitches are so lousy that I'm losing my hearing, there's a constant ringing in my ear, and every once in a while the world starts spinning.
>
> I am evangelizing the 10/20/30 Rule of PowerPoint. It's quite simple: a PowerPoint presentation should have ten slides, last no more than 20 minutes, and contain no font smaller than 30 points. While I'm in the venture capital business, this rule is applicable for any presentation to reach agreement: for example, raising capital, making a sale, forming a partnership, etc.
>
> - *Ten slides.* Ten is the optimal number of slides in a PowerPoint presentation because a normal human being cannot comprehend more than ten concepts in a meeting—and venture capitalists are very normal. (The only difference between you and your venture capitalist is that he is getting paid to gamble with someone else's money.) If you must use more than ten slides to explain your business, you probably don't have a business.
> - *Twenty minutes.* You should give your ten slides in 20 minutes. Sure, you have an hour time slot, but you're using a Windows laptop, so it will take 40 minutes to make it work with the projector. Even if setup goes perfectly, people will arrive late and have to leave early. In a perfect world, you give your pitch in 20 minutes, and you have 40 minutes left for discussion.
> - *Thirty-point font.* The majority of the presentations that I see have text in a ten-point font. As much text as possible is jammed into the slide, and then the presenter reads it. However, as soon as the audience figures out that you're reading the text, it reads ahead of you because it can read faster than you can speak. The result is that you and the audience are out of sync. The reason people use a small font is twofold: First, they don't know their material well enough; second, they think that more text is more convincing. Total bozosity.

---

[1]http://blog.guykawasaki.com/2005/12/the_102030_rule.html.

Guy goes on to suggest that the entrepreneur take the oldest person in the investor meeting, divide his or her age by two, and use that number as the average font size for the text in the presentation. Most professional investors will be between 50 and 60 years old, and for angel investors, older by a decade or more. In our experience, anything less than a font size of 20 is probably not a good idea. As for the ten slides, we might extend that to a dozen—but no more! And if you have been able to create a prototype of your product, system, or service, at the end of your presentation definitely ask the investor if he or she would like to take a look!

You must also realize that most professional investors are, by nature, skeptical. They listen to so many venture proposals, often several or more a week. The sheer volume of these presentations, the repetitive nature of the pitch-criticize-decide process, puts a hard shell on the active investor and makes the entrepreneur's task all the more difficult. Interesting ideas can become "so-so" in comparison to so many others.

With so many interesting ideas circulating in the entrepreneurial milieu, it is that presentation that translates an interesting idea into a dynamic venture strategy that shows a clear path to generating revenue, and then profit, that stands apart and gets the investment capital. Often, it is the passion and conviction of the entrepreneur for his or her venture that makes the difference above and beyond anything else, particularly for the angel investor.

The Foundations of a Great Investor Presentation

Throughout this book, we have explored the most important features of any new venture, the same sought by prudent investors. These boil down to:

1. A well-defined, attractive addressable or target market—with the size of demand and growth over the next five years that can support a well-conceived venture

2. Solutions—be they products, systems, services, or some combination of the three—for which target customers have a compelling need, and sufficient evidence that your solutions can actually solve the identified problem or need

3. A pragmatic, cash-generating business model—one that can be well tested as a startup, improved, and scaled into a major force in the target market niche

4. Perhaps most important, a strong, committed team behind the venture, with the knowledge and experience needed to make the idea a working reality

Put these points on the wall next to your desk, front and center, as you work on each slide and assemble the presentation.

An Outline for the Presentation

The goal here is to create a short, powerful pitch for investors. We recommend the following format as a guideline for the investor presentation:

1. *The team.* The background, experience, and motivations of the founders (no need for a slide here—address this in your opening statement; investors want to know who they are talking to).

2. *The customer and the problem.* The target customer, the customer's problem to be solved, and the cost or importance of that problem for the customer.

3. *The market opportunity.* The size and characteristics of the addressable market that this target customer and the problem to be solved for the customer represent.

4. *The solution.* The new product, system, or service that solves the customer's problem, and how this translates into a product or suite of services. Also include the "secret sauce" (if any) lying at the heart of the solution.

5. *The competitive positioning.* Not only the competitors, but the venture's positioning of the venture against them in classic price/performance terms as well as emotional and social positioning—the open opportunity space from the customer's perspective.

6. *The business model.* This includes the structure and nature of revenue (sale, license, subscription, service, etc.), and your approach to R&D, production, and sales that leads to gross and operating margins and profit. The goal is to show a cash-generating business model within a reasonable time period from startup.

7. *Summary financial projections.* This is a high-level P&L for five years, plus key revenue drivers such as number of customers and unit prices.

8. *The go-to-market strategy.* The route to market, key channel partners, and promotional and branding factors that will power growth in sales. Strategies to reduce the sales cycle or secure major channel agreements are described.

9. *The funding request, major milestones, and startup costs.* This is your "ask." You must show how you intend to use the money to achieve specific milestones to which you will be held accountable. Terms such as *alpha, beta, first dollar sale,* and *first operating profit* are used as appropriate. The funding requested should be staged with a clear purpose. Within this, you should also reveal the startup costs for the business.

10. *The exit strategy.* This is your vision for the value of the business five to seven years down the road, once the business has scaled and taken a leadership position in your target industry niche. Your investor will already be thinking about a post-money valuation for the current round, and how his or her stock will dilute over two or three successive rounds, leading to a value and return on the investment should things go reasonably well.

Adapt this outline for your own venture. In addition to covering these essential elements of information, you must be comfortable with the flow of the presentation. If you wish to shift elements to a different order, try it! Chances are that you will have multiple opportunities to give your pitch and will soon come to the order that works best for you. Now we will get into a few details.

Create a Set of Compelling Stories

There is much more to the presentation than simply covering these elements.

Audiences of just about any kind, including investors, don't care to listen to a rote presentation of facts, detached from the excitement you wish to create in the marketplace. Instead, you want to capture the investor's interest—and to do this, you want to craft a story that is both interesting and compelling, first from the point of view of the target customer, and then from the perspective of creating a money-making business.

There are excellent books on preventing "Death by PowerPoint." We prefer those that recommend a story-telling approach, using pictures as much as text, and creating simplicity in layout and design. *Presentation Zen*, written by Garr Reynolds, is a worthwhile read.[2] The goal is to deliver a short, powerful story that leaves a crisp image in the listener's mind.

For the entrepreneur, there are four stories to be told within a dozen slides in the investment presentation:

1. *Story A: The story of the target customers and the attractiveness of the market they represent.* Focus on the target customers and the problem that you wish to solve for them. Then, state the clear value of solving that problem in terms of saving the customer time or money or bringing unparalleled levels of convenience or pleasure in a leisure activity. Lastly, provide your assessment of the opportunity solving these problems for those customers represents.

[2]Reynolds, G. (2008). *Presentation Zen: Simple Ideas on Presentation Design and Delivery.* Berkeley, CA: New Riders.

2. *Story B: The story of your business.* This means how your business can become a leader in its target market, and how your business model will generate the type of revenue flow and cash needed for hungry investors, and an exit strategy that will make both you and them more than pleased.

3. *Story C: The story of* you *and your team; the backgrounds, experience, and motivations for starting the venture.* As noted above, this doesn't necessarily even have to be a separate slide. It could best be a 30-second introduction in which you make direct eye contact with the investors sitting at the table. Show your passion and conviction for the Venture Concept.

4. *Story D: The story of your milestones.* How will the funding that you seek lead to the makings of a working, growing business.

Tell Story A first, Story B next, then to Story C, and only then, Story D.

The Story of Serving the Customer _____

The approach we recommend here is to create a "tension" in the form of an important problem or unexploited opportunity on the part of the target customer. This requires intimacy with that customer. If you've worked through the first part of this book, you are now the master of customer knowledge. Now is the time to show it.

There is no doubt that investors enjoy a crisp identification of the target customer, the target buyer (if different), and the needs not yet filled by competitors currently in the marketplace. Show these insights and you are off to a good start.

Define the Customer and the Customer's Problem

First, clearly define the customer, its role, position, stage of life, or economic level depending on the nature of your business. Then explain the customer's problems and frustrations associated with the current situation. In the case of our three running examples in this part of the book, this would be the lack of healthy pet snacks for pet owners, the fear of the elderly falling and dying unattended in their own homes, or the difficulty of keeping up with the latest in cost-effective networking and telecommunications equipment for building owners. In earlier chapters, we dug deeper into these customer situations in the form of developing "use case scenarios," and these were featured in your Venture Concept diagrams. Showing your insight into the "world" and needs of the target customer should take, at most, a slide or two. Remember, prudent investors will want to see for themselves through customer visits before making an investment. At this point, your goal is to provide customer insight. Figure 12.1 provides the

- "Problem" captures the attention of the investor
- The specific user scenario is compelling
- The customer's current "negative" outcome creates tension
- Your solution to the customer problem relieves the "tension"

Figure 12.1 The Springboard "Problem" Story From the Perspective of the Target Customer

Source: Image, Digital Vision/Thinkstock.

essence of a "springboard story" that creates a tension around the problems of the customer that your venture exists to solve.

The next part of the story of your customer is to dimensionalize the customer problem into an economic or opportunity cost. In other words, for the specific use case scenario, what is the cost or penalty of doing business or performing an activity under the current situation? How significant or large is this cost for the user? Is this a little problem, or one that is truly compelling? This might be included as just a bullet point on one of your first two charts.

Define the Addressable Market, the Size of the Opportunity

The next essential step in the presentation is to describe how your target customer represents a substantial market opportunity. That opportunity represents the "spend" or economic activity for your target application or problem area. You have the data from the first part of the book—and in the business plan—so use it. The addressable market is simply the combination of the target customer group and the target use or application within your industry niche.

For example, "the market for pet snacks in the United States is . . . ," or "the money spent on emergency admissions for the elderly is . . . ," or "the design and implementation services niche within the telecommunication network infrastructure market in North America is. . . ." This is where you create a single slide that shows the size, growth rate, and competitive dynamics of the target market. A graph here that shows the current size and growth rate of that target market is a good addition, with a bullet point or two describing additional salient trends.

That addressable market should be substantial if you are seeking investment from an angel, a VC, or a strategic corporate investor. In their minds, these investors will be thinking, "If those folks can capture 5% of that defined market, it translates into a $50 million a year business, or 10%, a $100 million a year business." Many will then quickly work the multiples for acquisitions in your industry sector on revenues, and start thinking about the potential value of owning 20% of the equity five years down the road as part of a larger syndicated investment group. This sizing up not only of your customer knowledge but of the business opportunity it represents happens surprisingly quickly. In five minutes, you want to get the investor thinking about his or her own possible financial returns in large, unsolved problem spaces.

Describe the Solution, the "Secret Sauce," and the Competitive Positioning

This is where your creativity, customer insight, and nose for the competition have to really shine.

Some of our friends, experienced entrepreneurs and now angel investors, actually think that this Solutions section should come right after the Customer Problem slide in the presentation. Your choice. We have chosen here to first define the customer, the problem, and the size of the business opportunity represented by that problem space—and then the Solution. This is your pitch, and you can even try it both ways and see which works best for you.

Regardless of the order, when you get to the Solutions section of your pitch, we recommend that you first have a single slide that presents your new product, system, or service—its key features, functions, and performance. If it is a consumer product, a good photograph is useful here. If it is a piece of software, leave the imagery for a demonstration of your prototype—reprints of computer screens never look as good as what appears on a live screen. On the other hand, graphics showing the context of use can help bring a new technology to life. If you are enabling a new business process, a very simple process diagram that shows the improved process is good, again highlighting the benefits for the customer.

As you are talking to this slide, it is also very important that you address the following four points:

- First, describe the compelling, distinctive aspects of the product, system, or service in the eyes of the customer; not what you think is "cool," but what the customer perceives is a compelling benefit based on the results of your Reality Check. (Those data make a good set of additional slides to have in your back pocket.) Place a few large bullet points next to your images on this slide that convey these customer benefits. Remember, often the benefit of an innovation is cost savings or productivity gains for the customer. Try to be specific here and dimensionalize the scope of these benefits.

- Second, describe the product line or suite of services that emerge from your product, system, or service idea. Remember to use the words *good, better, best* here if appropriate. They mean a lot to certain types of investors who have pragmatic operational experience; these investors know that customers want choice.

- Third, describe the proprietary technology or process lying with your offerings. If you have such a "secret sauce," this too deserves a separate slide, with high-level bullet points presenting the points of unique intellectual property. If your secret sauce is in a nonpatentable process, such as a method for integrating different systems in a customer's facility or for interpreting the results of particular types of data or analytics, then you should address these as well. All investors are looking for some type of special "know-how" to give a venture competitive advantage.

- Fourth, share your insights regarding the competitive positioning of your solution. This also deserves a separate slide focused on the competition—but much more than just a list. The perceptual map is an interesting and powerful idea that professional investors will appreciate. They are searching for solutions that occupy some sort of "white space" relative to competitors, and solutions that customers will be emotionally attached with as well as solutions that have a socially responsible element.

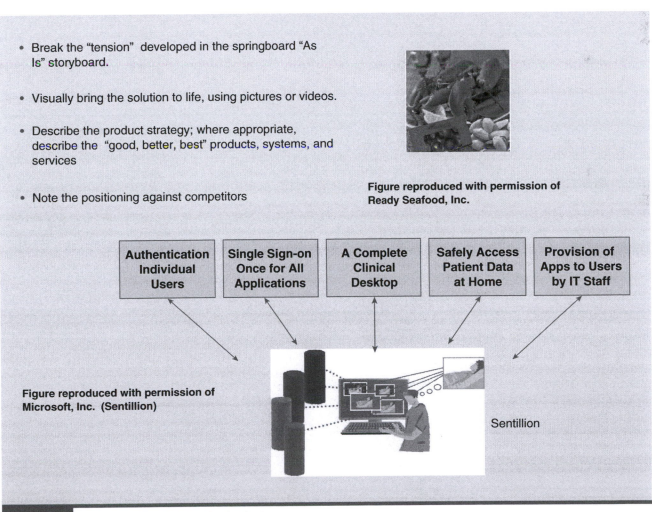

- Break the "tension" developed in the springboard "As Is" storyboard.

- Visually bring the solution to life, using pictures or videos.

- Describe the product strategy; where appropriate, describe the "good, better, best" products, systems, and services

- Note the positioning against competitors

Figure reproduced with permission of Ready Seafood, Inc.

Figure reproduced with permission of Microsoft, Inc. (Sentillion)

| Authentication Individual Users | Single Sign-on Once for All Applications | A Complete Clinical Desktop | Safely Access Patient Data at Home | Provision of Apps to Users by IT Staff |

Sentillion

Figure 12.2 Your Compelling Solution for the Customer

Sources: Portions reproduced with permission of Ready Seafood, Inc.; Portions reproduced with the permission of Microsoft, Inc.

If you feel that you need a slide or two more to cover these points, that's okay. Be mindful that if they like your pitch, they will want to dig in to your business plan.

Don't forget customer and product/service pictures! Figure 12.2 shows examples of visual aids for a product and system solution that come from two of the teaching cases on the textbook Website: catch a piece of Maine's seafood gifting service and Sentillion's single sign-on security and provisioning software for healthcare. Illustrations such as these bring the Venture Concept to life. (Don't forget to check out the videos for these two entrepreneurs on the Website. We think these videos provide great examples of entrepreneurial focus and drive in two completely different types of ventures.)

Put your images or sketches of your solution together into a single slide along with bullet point statements of customer benefits. Also, try to include the positioning of your venture and its solutions against competitors. Show differentiation! This is certainly a foundation for a great company.

Students have asked, "Some of your templates summarize the target market, the customer need, the solution, and positioning all in one page. [The Venture Concept Template, Figures 7.1 or 7.10.] Why not show it to investors?" The answer is that it's simply too much information on a single page. Investors will get lost in all the detail. It is best to partition the information into two or three slides.

The Story of the Business

Describe the Business Model

This story—the "story of the business"—focuses on creating a business that not only produces revenue but one that generates operating profit once the business achieves reasonable scale. In this part of your investor pitch, you need to provide the impression of a clean, powerful business model.

In Chapter 5, we had you develop the business model for your venture, and in Chapter 7, you tested it. Then we had you develop a set of financial projections based on that model in Chapter 9. This work is the platform for this part of your investor pitch.

You can simply describe the business model to the investor. Then again, a simple bullet-point slide wouldn't hurt, either. The slide will also help you organize your story and keep to the straight and narrow—even if you decide not to use the slide in the presentation. Investors will want to understand your business model. We also want to reiterate that reasonable sales projections are absolutely essential.

Use your planning in Chapter 5 to create a set of bullet points that focus on:

- *The revenue model.* This includes the type, frequency, and price level relative to competition for each major stream of revenue, product, or service. The Reality Check and your competitive research should give you a good handle on the pricing for your products and services. Also, try to include the magic words *recurring revenue* in this part of the presentation.

- *How revenue scales over time.* This means how you expect to realize your very first revenue, and then, how you expect it to grow over the course of at least five years.

- *Your approaches to R&D, manufacturing, and distribution.* If you don't have a high-tech R&D business, skip that part. But the other areas may have significant impacts on your startup capital requirements and ongoing operating margins. Seasoned business investors will want to hear about your approaches for a lean, agile venture.

- *The profit model and when operating profit will be achieved.* Your comments should be directed at the gross and net margins that you expect to achieve and how these compare to the margins of businesses like yours operating generally in your industry. If it is a software business, investors will expect to see gross margins approximating 90% or more, for example, but high R&D expenses, leading to a net margin before tax of, say, 25%. Check the Web for comparative margin benchmarks in your industry sector. In a manufacturing business, gross margins tend to come in between 40% and 50%, and net margins before tax at 15% to 20%. These benchmarks are for scaled-up businesses, like yours will be in three to four years.

- *The cash conversion cycle for revenue.* This must also be addressed as part of the business model if there is any particularly long delay—beyond, say, 45 days. You will find that experienced investors view this as a critical issue.

- *The exit potential after five years to seven years.* This is the potential business value based on the revenues and profitability once the business "scales" or becomes significantly large. As you may recall from earlier chapters, relatively easy-to-explain slides can take your P&L projections and infer an exit valuation from the five-year targets. This is based largely on the multiples of sales based on recent M&A events in your industry. In fact, take a moment now to look at the figures for the SilverRail case and the Generate case used in prior chapters of this book. These are Figures 9.2 (Chapter 9) and 11.4 (Chapter 11). The first focuses on an overall view of the exit valuation itself, and the second on building an argument for a particular multiple. Given the dominance of M&A exits over IPOs over the past decade, you should focus your exit strategy on the valuations and sales/profit multiples of the acquisition route. Most investors expect this.

We want to emphasize to use the Business Model Template in Chapter 5 (Figure 5.7) to help you think—*but not to show* in an investor presentation. Simple, large-font bullet points work best!

As part of the material in this section, you should include a very high-level Pro Forma P&L for five years. You should also include other key data, such as revenue drivers (the number of new customers and repeat customers, and/or the unit volumes and price per unit), which come as rows above the revenues. The challenge here is to create a summary in a reasonably large font from the detail you developed in the financial projections in Chapter 9. The numbers have to be shown on a projected screen, so keep the font rather large—say, size 16 or greater. Figure 12.3 provides an example, and even that figure verges on "too small" for an investor presentation. The figure is part of the Generate case on the textbook Website.

	Year 1	Year 2	Year 3	Year 4	Year 5
New customers	2	30	49	147	303
Recurring customers		2	34	83	147
Total customers	2	32	83	230	450
Average revenue per customer	17,000	50,000	50,000	50,000	50,000
Recurring bookings		28,900	1,066,831	3,020,568	7,350,000
New bookings	34,000	1,571,000	3,034,043	8,458,897	15,150,000
Total bookings	34,000	1,599,900	4,100,874	11,479,465	22,500,000
Revenue	4,250	1,001,844	3,401,870	10,102,559	20,925,000
COS	59,250	978,417	1,700,935	4,649,710	8,997,750
Gross margin		23,427	1,700,935	5,452,849	11,927,250
%		2%	50%	54%	57%
Operating expense	613,093	1,552,233	3,100,438	4,903,550	10,156,514
Operating income				549,299	1,770,736
%				5%	8%
FTE	5	27	55	81	105

Figure 12.3 Readable Financials: Large Font!

Bring printouts of your more detailed financial projections to the meeting. Should the investors start asking specific questions, reach for your bag and bring out the heavy ammunition!

Remember, no wild projections! In particular, the sales projections should be reasonable. However, there is a fine balance between being conservative and underselling the potential of your venture. If you undersell, no one will invest. If you oversell, investors will run the other way. It is a balance that you will have to learn to achieve.

One last word of advice—and perhaps this is truly a personal bias of your authors. *Do not present financial projects on a line chart!* Use a simple table or spreadsheet to show revenue growth over five years and the initiation and growth of operating profit. Why this aversion to line charts for financial projections? Investors are sick and tired of seeing the "hockey stick" curve; seeing yet another one in your pitch will most likely turn them off. Line charts hide all supporting detail; stick to your summary spreadsheets.

Describe the Go-to-Market Strategy

There are so many entrepreneurs with clever ideas, technology intensive or not. But few make the transition to an equally clever, aggressive sales strategy for their wonderful inventions. And it is those few who are far more likely to get funded.

The Go-to-Market Strategy deserves a separate slide. The bullet points on the slide need to include:

- *The primary route to market* (a direct sales force, a channel partner such as a major OEM or retailer, the Web, or one of the other alternatives described in the prior chapter). As part of your work in this book, you should know the best channel partners for your venture. If you are serious about starting a business, you should take the initiative to find out what it takes to do business with these partners and have begun that process. This will show investors that you really are serious about this side of the business.

- The cost of customer acquisition and the expected lifetime value or revenue of that customer for your business.

- *The branding activities you plan to pursue.* As IBM has shown, branding is not something left to consumer products companies alone. All companies need to design and implement a branding strategy. This includes the name of your company, the name of your products and/or services, and the messaging for these offerings that is consistent with how you have positioned them relative to competitors.

- Perhaps above all else, *the fact you like to sell.* Selling is something you look forward to doing and do not view as a necessary evil that every new company must undertake. Going into the market and busting it wide open is a challenge that you and your team relish. Remember this as you speak to this slide. Selling produces revenue, and revenue— for new ventures—makes the rest of the business tick with energy and excitement.

The Story of Your Milestones

You are there to make an "ask." Make it. You require a certain amount of money to achieve very specific development and marketing milestones over the coming six to nine months. For that time period, you have a breakdown of specific startup costs. You are not going to live rich, nor are you going to work in a fancy office space. In fact, you have already considered a bunch of ways to keep expenses to a minimum, including the use of subcontract programmers for Website development or Skype or WebEx for initial sales calls.

Feasibility, timeliness, and capital efficiency will be on investors' minds now that you have sold them on the stories of your customers and your business. Have a simple, clear slide showing your milestones to achieve the "alpha," "beta," first dollar sale, and first operating profit as these apply to your business. A horizontal timeline works well here. Then show the dollar amounts of funding indicated by your own financial projections, for example, the money needed to achieve each stage of growth. See Figure 12.4 for a general example.

Have another slide that details your startup costs for that period of time. That amount should be reflected directly in your projected P&L and Cash Flow Statements. Then make your "ask." Make the "ask" grounded in careful consideration of what needs to be done and the best way to achieve it.

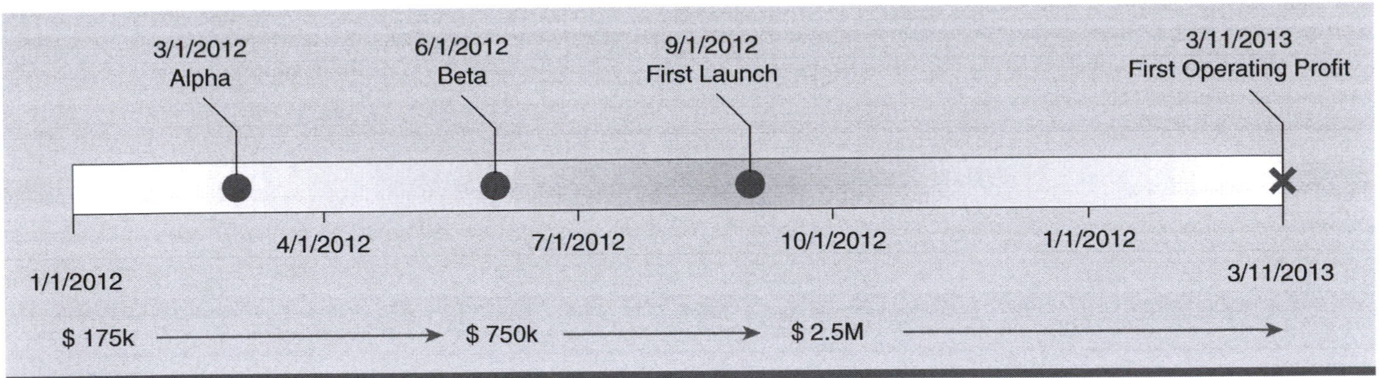

| 3/1/2012 | 6/1/2012 | 9/1/2012 | 3/11/2013 |
| Alpha | Beta | First Launch | First Operating Profit |

1/1/2012   4/1/2012   7/1/2012   10/1/2012   1/1/2012   3/11/2013

$ 175k → $ 750k → $ 2.5M →

Figure 12.4 Milestone Chart and Financing to Achieve Goals

A milestone chart sounds simple to create, but it takes a lot of careful planning to establish sufficient, reasonable levels of funding—as well as a conviction in your voice that you truly believe in the milestone dates with the funding proposed. Once again, keep it simple and direct. We prefer to see the milestones and funding displayed together in a single slide, to show that the money requested has a specific purpose and that the entrepreneur fully understands the successive stages of funding needed to achieve scale.

Presentation Style

Use Graphics and Illustrations, and Avoid Sensationalism

Good stories are complemented by interesting graphics and illustrations. For example, investors will expect to see a graph of the market demand, a picture of the target customer, and illustrations of the product concept.

By some estimates, people remember only 25% to 45% of what they hear, but a much greater percentage of what they *see*. Bring your slides to life. At the same time, a standard clip or word art in PowerPoint will come off as amateurish and silly. Animations also come off as "cute." Skip these. Same with garish colors.

Simplicity in the slides is essential. Keep the slides straightforward and unencumbered. Remember Guy Kawasaki's dictum on font sizes. Offering a slide that is so complex that its creator must read or interpret it to the audience is a no-no in the world of presentation arts. Slides should *highlight* your presentation; they shouldn't *be* your presentation. Whatever time and attention your audience devotes to viewing slides is time and attention diverted from you. And you should be the center of attention.

Focus on Your Listeners: Watch Their Body Language and Adjust

Don't read the slides! Speak to your audience. Let *them* read the slides. Point to trend lines on graphs if you have them, or to design points in a picture of your new product or the architecture diagram of your system; but otherwise, your eyes must be front and center whenever possible.

Once again, please *do not read the slides!* This is a classic mistake nervous entrepreneurs make during their investor presentations, and it is a fatal one. In fact, not reading slides is a good rule of thumb for any presentation.

Watch the reactions of the investors. If they seem engaged, great. If they seem bored or disengaged, try asking them for their thoughts or questions. Try to bring some energy into the room.

Naturally, repeated rehearsals before an audience of colleagues will help you uncover and repair the holes and the weak spots. Rehearsal will also increase your self-confidence—and you need to be the very image of self-confidence. Thorough preparation—just as you would for the most rigorous examination in your college or graduate career—is so important for a successful outcome. That preparation quickly becomes clear to investors. It really impresses them. Even if a particular investor finds that your venture is outside of his or her preferred investment focus, a strong showing will often motivate that investor to call friends who are interested in your field of work.

As you rehearse, experiment with the various techniques that speakers use to engage and maintain audience attention and involvement:

- If you've been given a lectern or podium, escape from its confines every so often. Even step in front of it occasionally, as if to remove a barrier between you and your listeners.

- If you feel disconnected from the investors listening to you, you can ask a question. For example, "Has anyone here had an elderly friend or family member who had to be taken into the hospital every week or so for monitoring that might have been done at home?" Getting responses from investors can help lighten up what is typically a tense atmosphere.

- Build hand-offs into the presentation. For example, if the technology wiz of the team is not the main presenter, shift the presenter role over to that person at appropriate times. These shifts and the variety they bring will give a little jolt to the crowd.

- For certain forums, you might have the opportunity to demonstrate a prototype. The prototype makes the venture all the more "real" for potential investors.

These proven tactics will help you convert part of your presentation from "talking *at*" to "talking *with*" the audience. Remember, preparation is so important. Go through the slides in a final edit to eliminate any words that are not really necessary. Remove the silly stuff, remove the "fat," and strive toward a lean and powerful presentation.

If you have captured the investors' attention and sincere interest in the slides leading up to this point, now is the time for "the close." The close in this case is a commitment to a rapid due diligence process on the way toward getting a check. If the investors are truly interested in your venture, they will begin a rapid-fire stream of questions—and it is for these questions that you must be prepared.

Prepare for a Grilling (Where You Are the Meat)

During investor presentations, most (if not all) entrepreneurs feel as if they are a tasty slice of rare roast beef sitting warming in front of hungry diners (the investors) who relish the opportunity to feast on any real or perceived weakness in the market insight, the solution, the business model, or the team. It's just the nature of the game.

Wear that thick skin—and even though it is difficult, try not to take criticisms personally. In fact, an investor may be deliberately trying to get under your skin just to see how you handle pressure. The pressures in the startup world are intense; those thinking about giving you their money are trying to make an assessment of your ability to think on your feet, to work under pressure, and to stick to your convictions. The same applies to internal corporate ventures—plus the heat of internal corporate politics!

Take confidence, however, in all the work you have done in this book! You have the data needed to make a robust defense. Bring these data the table. Take your time. Patiently show that you know as much about the market, customers, and competitors as anyone else. Reveal how you did deep dives with customers; ran your Reality Check; and obtained direct and specific feedback on the design of your product, system, and service, as well as guidance on the percentage uptake in the target market for the commercial offerings you wish to sell. The customer insight work and the Reality Check in the first part of the book comprise powerful stuff. Don't leave these at home. Take confidence in the insight you have gained! If a particular investor doesn't "get it," pack up your show and find one who does. All but the most successful serial entrepreneurs get dozens of *no's* before they get to a *yes*. And in the current economic climate, it is a rough ride for anyone seeking to raise startup capital.

Perhaps most important, be prepared to defend your numbers during investor presentations! As Aaron Gowell, an alumnus of our university and the subject of a teaching case for this book, said, "Be prepared to defend you numbers six ways from Sunday." This means having the numbers to back up your numbers: market size and growth, the size of the specific target niche or addressable market, the revenue model, the sales cycle and cash conversion cycle, and the margins in production and other operating expenses.

Our recommendation is to keep your PowerPoint presentation to 20 to 30 minutes in duration. If it hits the mark, the discussion afterward will probably continue for another 90 minutes or so—just in that first meeting. The really hard work—the money time—comes in the dialogue after the presentation.

In the prior chapter, we ended each major section of the business plan with the common questions and concerns of an investor reading the plan. You must prepare yourself to answer these same questions in an investor presentation. We constructed those questions based on our experiences as entrepreneurs and investors. We also reviewed those questions with friends who do angel investing or are venture capitalists. For better or worse, those questions are real, and you will encounter them in your search for startup or growth capital. Take confidence in the fact that you enter these meetings armed with all the work you have done in this book. Without being arrogant, wear that confidence on your sleeve.

So with the questions from the prior chapter in mind, assume that the following types of responses and questions are raised either during or after your presentation:

1. *"Let's run through those market numbers again."* Here, the investor is going to try his or her best to poke holes into how you have defined and sized your target market—for example, that specific addressable market from which you plan to get revenue.

2. *"How does it really work? And tell me again why the target customers really need it."* Expect a question of this sort. Walk the investor through the most common use case scenario for the customer. Explain what they use now and why they are still having problems. This is also the point where you can bring out the data from your Reality Check and work through indicators showing favorable response. Also remember that the best investors will want to go talk to some of those customers. You might jump ahead of this by saying, "Would you like to see this for yourself? Why don't we go visit some customers together next week?" In other words, you may be able to facilitate this part of the due diligence process.

3. *"Why isn't Company X already doing this?"* Experienced investors often find that young entrepreneurs "don't know what they don't know." This becomes particularly relevant when it comes to competition. Proposing a new product that is already in the portfolio or on the immediate radar screen of a current industry leader is not a recipe for success. Being in the pack with a bunch of startups all focused on the same general target is not a bad thing—if you know who else is in the race. Show the investor that you are not naive here. Demonstrate knowledge of the industry by responding with the activities of major corporations as well as other relatively new companies.

4. *"Walk me through the sales cycle and then tell me how long you think it takes until revenue gets converted into cash."* The investor wants to make sure that you fully understand the cash cycle in your business. Use a specific number of days here as opposed to general types of answers. The more specific, the better.

5. *"Who are you working with on IP? What do they think about your chances of getting a patent?"* For those readers with technological ventures that have the promise of proprietary intellectual property, the way to answer this question is with the name of an attorney in a reputable law firm. The investor will have his or her own personal network to get further insight into any claims made—but it is unlikely that you will have to go into significant details in the first meeting.

6. *"What's to keep a market leader such as Company X from learning about your idea and doing it themselves and then having a much larger sales force to capture the market?"* This is a tough but important question. There are three answers to it. First, owning some type of intellectual property is a barrier to entry by a large corporation. Second, developing a loyal customer following—"owning" your customer—is another powerful barrier to entry. And third, large companies seem to be slow going

after new technologies and new market opportunities. Using all three points in your answer with specific reference to the current market leaders in your industry sector should suffice. Of course, everyone knows that if a global leader wants to compete with you, it can do so. But generally, there are other large competitors who might then be even more motivated to acquire your venture to get to market first with a well-oiled, robust product or service.

7. *"You say that your primary channel is through Company Y. How real is that? What's to prevent it from owning the customer and shopping around for a substitute at a lower price in 18 months?"* Another important question. The first order of business here is actually to have had conversations with that channel partner and to be able to say that they are highly interested in helping to sell your products or services. Second, you should then describe your approach to make that channel partner successful in terms of training, samples, marketing collateral, and selling support in the field. Third, you should indicate that you, too, think it is important for startups not to rely 100% on a single channel partner and that you are already looking for other partners—be it an OEM or retailer, and so forth. Last, you should then describe your strategy for reaching directly to customers even though they are buying the product through someone else. This might be a Website for end-users to purchase additional products or services. Or it might be conference attendance where you interact directly with customers. These responses might not eliminate the risk of overreliance on a channel partner, but at least it shows that you are thinking about motivating and managing channel partners. Successful entrepreneurs know their customers; being totally shielded from customers by a large, controlling channel partner puts the venture in the backseat in terms of understanding what customers need and how best to serve them.

8. *"How much money are you looking for? Let's go through those key milestones again and see what you plan to spend it on."* Come through hard and clear in your response. Walk through the specific steps within your key milestones. Show how these lead to very detailed and reasonable startup expenses. Talk about the number and types of people needed to achieve alpha, beta, and commercial launch. Then share your insights on the number of people and financing needed to achieve substantial scale as a business and—with that—healthy operating profit. Stage the timing and cash needed to achieve these steps, digging a little deeper into the milestone chart you have in the presentation. Show that you know what needs to be done and can organize the work. While there are numerous stories about investors finding their own managers to run a new company, they would vastly prefer to have the entrepreneurial team be fully capable of getting a business through its first stage of growth.

Throughout all of this tough questioning, investors are looking for conviction and commitment. They want to make sure you've got the right stuff, the mettle and enthusiasm for this way of life. Investors need to walk away from the meeting with a strong impression of your passion, knowledge, and conviction. They know that you and your key team members will require all of these to get through the tough times ahead. Trial by fire is but a taste of the challenges that will occur after their investment.

What Tends to Happen After You Make the Pitch

One frequent outcome is that, for whatever reason, the investor is simply not interested. He or she will say they like you personally and wish you all the best. And perhaps provide a tip or two about where else to look for money.

Your job at this point is *not to get dejected*. Take out a pencil and pad of paper and ask the investor his or her reasons for not being interested. Learn from each and every pitch event. You will only get better with each new attempt if you learn from the last. As the founder of IBM was known to say to his salespeople, it is even more important to learn why a customer *does not buy* from you than to understand why they say "yes." Same with investors. You will call on many in your search from successive rounds of capital. Learn from "no's" so you will be more effective at getting to a "yes."

Professional investors know lots of other professional investors. Even if you are given a "no," the investor might give you a couple of names of peers who might be more suited for your type or stage of business. Show your appreciation, and then ask the investor if he or she can make a phone call as an introduction to those individuals. It does you little good if you have to cold call on those individuals. You need a qualified introduction. If you can't get that introduction, then at least you know where the investor stands with respect to your venture.

Discussion on Company Valuation and Exit Strategy

If you have a wonderful pitch session and survive the questions above and others like them, your investors might invite you to lunch to talk "business," code word for investment. Or it might come up right across the conference table, even though this is rare during the initial pitch. If an investor is truly interested, he or she will invest time in checking out your business and customer references. But if and when the discussion turns to equity and exit, expect the following two questions:

1. *"How much equity are you prepared to provide for my investment?"* Some investors will actually ask you for your thoughts on company valuation to see if you are in the same ballpark as they are. So you had better be ready to provide a simple, direct answer. Beating around the bush serves no purpose here. Learn the comparable valuations for seed or Series A financings in your industry sector. Perhaps suggest something higher (this is a negotiation!) and justify it. And conclude with the impression that you understand fully that this is a matter for further thought and consideration.

2. *"What is your vision for exit?"* Go back to the discussion toward the end of Chapter 11 on exit strategies, look at Figure 11.4, and see what you can put together—*in advance*—based on the revenue projections and industry multiples for your venture. These days, you will need *something*. A professional investor intrigued by your presentation will want to see your thinking on exit. Whether it is in the first meeting or the second, this question is going to come up. And if you have an answer prepared, it shows the VC that you are already aligned with his or her own priorities on creating value and providing a return for shareholders.

As noted earlier, as you pitch, many investors will already be thinking about a valuation for the current round and the percentage of company stock that will go along with their investment. The investors will also be thinking about how that stock holding will likely be diluted after two or three rounds of subsequent investment. If the investors have done deals likes yours before, they will be able to do this math quickly in their heads and get a sense of the return that you expect five to seven years down the road. They have lived "the power of equity" figure that we showed in Chapter 8—in fact, that is probably the reason why they have the money to invest in your company.

It's also a very good idea to be thinking about an exit strategy and valuation for yourself, *even as you are starting your business*. It provides a certain discipline and purpose that fuels all your hard work. It will help you say to yourself, "This is a business, not a hobby. Let's get serious and get things done! Go nail that development milestone. Let's close that sale!"

As we said in the first chapter, for the entrepreneur, starting a company is not all about making money. It's about the joy of building something substantial from scratch, of innovating to improve the lives and work of others, and about the autonomy in work enjoyed by the entrepreneur. But the money—the financial reward of owning a substantial amount of founder's stock in an exit event—certainly doesn't hurt! Having each been through such an event, as entrepreneur and angel investor, your authors can tell you that there is also a certain joy of rather suddenly being financially independent from something that you, your team, or your investees have created in a fiercely competitive world.

Due Diligence

Due diligence is the term investors use to cover all the various things done to investigate individuals and their companies. Our advice is to think ahead to make the due diligence process easy for interested, qualified investors. Professional investors will want to perform due diligence on a number of things, including:

1. *Customers' needs for your solution.* Is it really a big problem, a compelling need, and an equally powerful solution? This due diligence is performed by talking to colleagues experienced in your industry. Investors will also want to talk to customers themselves. Think ahead about providing opportunities for them to get exposure to target customers.

2. *Your competitors,* particularly those you did not mention in the presentation or your business plan. This due diligence is often best performed by talking to their current investees or other investors in their business network. And investors are also known to attend tradeshows focused on certain industry areas where major competitors are on full display. A comprehensive list of competitors in your business plan is the best way of helping the investor get through this aspect of due diligence. And a name or two of an independent authority in your area of work can prove useful as well.

3. *You and your team.* This due diligence tries to assess your personal and professional integrity. If there are any issues in the past, such as a failed prior company or a legal suit, be up front about the causes of the event and what you learned from that experience. Successful entrepreneurs get their learning from many different sources; an earlier failed venture is more common than you might think! But you've got to come off as an "A" player, and that means a record of commitment and proven accomplishment, be it at school, at work, or in some other aspect of your life. Be ready with a list of names of people who will testify to your character and hard work. If possible, include the name(s) of an individual who is a prospective customer or channel partner. Even with your own list, rest assured that professional investors will makes calls to their own networks of professionals for a full range of opinions.

Also, if yours is a technology-intensive venture, professional investors will ask other people in their professional network to assess the technology and your application of it.

What If the Investor Is Clearly Interested, but Shows Concern About Your Age and Experience?

The "experience factor" is obviously problematic for young entrepreneurs (say, below 27 years old). One of your own authors went into his first startup at the age of 21—and we did well. But that was with money from friends and family, incredibly tight-fisted operating expenses (we didn't pay ourselves much and rented the cheapest office space in town), and a hunger for good, old-fashioned customer revenue as soon as humanly possible. This is the best approach for young entrepreneurs.

There are other ways as well. Get a "salt-and-pepper"-haired entrepreneur to join your team or serve as an active venture adviser. The next time you meet an interested investor, try to get that senior adviser to attend the meeting. That individual will help ease investors' concerns about a young entrepreneurial team, and he or she should know angel investors and venture capitalists on his or her own. Just be careful with your stock and have good legal counsel to help you set up performance-based grants of stock (e.g., stock options). You just don't know if an individual who you have not worked with earlier is going to be a good fit for you and your company.

Understand That No Matter How Good the Pitch, It Just Might Be the Wrong Investor for Your Venture _____

Most professional investors have other parameters that serve as lenses through which they see any new proposal. An angel investor is often going to want to have some type of operating experience in the industry in which he or she is investing. That is the value-add that this person can bring. It is a good idea to do your homework beforehand. When you speak to an angel who is meeting you privately or who is introducing you to an angel investing group, ask that person about his or her background in a way that is interested, not pushy. In other words, try to find out how the investor made his or her money. That should tell you whether the meeting is worthwhile for you or not. You have to decide whether you want to restrict your meetings to individuals who are likely investors. Often, however, even if an angel investor is not interested in your type of venture, chances are that if the person likes you over breakfast or lunch, he or she will make the introduction to a peer who is experienced in your industry sector. The Web remains a powerful tool for doing a little research on angel investors and their present or prior companies.

Venture capitalists have areas of portfolio specialization. These focus points are provided directly on the VC firm's Website. They are highly unlikely to invest outside of those industry sectors. So do your homework once again. Find out the VC firms in your region. Visit their Websites. Look at their portfolio companies. Determine if there are companies in the same area as your venture. If not, keep looking for VC firms that do specialize in your field. The most common investment areas for VC firms are software; energy technology and services; networking equipment; biotech; Web-enabled health, financial, or entertainment services; and social networking ventures. But there are also boutique VC firms that specialize in consumer or industrial products. As noted in Chapter 8, the National Venture Capital Association's Website (www.nvca.org/) is a good place to study investment trends and get the names of specific VCs in your region of the United States.

Once you create a list of VC firms that work in your industry sector, find out the partner(s) in the VC firm who specialize in your area and the names of the companies on which they sit on Boards of Directors. Do a quick Web search on that individual(s). Learn their background—see if there is an educational connection for you or members of your team. Look at the companies where hopefully those VCs had operating experience before becoming VCs—for those are the VCs who we find are far and away the most valuable in helping to staff, structure, and scale a venture. Then find out the companies in which that partner has led the VC firm's investments. Do a quick Web search on those companies. Even better, see if you know anyone working in one of those companies, and if so, inquire about the interaction with the investor and see if your acquaintances know the partner in the VC firm who is working with their company. In other words, arm yourself with knowledge about the background, experience, and current activities of the individual you are going to meet. And don't forget to check out social networking Websites such as www.thefunded.com to gain insight into the level of knowledge and speed in specific investment firms. Most important, try to get some type of personal introduction or referral to that VC. It makes all the difference.

Strategic investors—corporations making direct investments into smaller firms—obviously need to have that company provide synergy to the larger company's business. So here, once again, you need to do your homework on the Web to try to find a match between the corporation's interests and yours. As we described in Chapter 8, on sources of financing, there are a number of major corporations with dedicated innovation programs geared to outside innovation. These programs will each have their own form of paperwork to complete, but we strongly advise you to first make a call. Sell yourself and your idea to someone working within the innovation program and seek their advice on suitability and the best way to approach the corporation for support. The person on the other end of the phone may become your internal champion for navigating the different business units and R&D groups within the corporation.

TIP: WATCH OUT FOR THOSE NDAS!

HELPFUL TIPS

If you get a chance to meet the R&D group of a major corporation, some caution is required. You will probably be asked to sign a nondisclosure agreement (NDA). Rather than being forced to sign that in the corporation's conference room, it is best to have the NDA e-mailed to you beforehand. Read it carefully and make sure you can live by its terms and conditions. If not, propose a few select changes (typically to the term or length of the agreement and the process by which a party can terminate the agreement). Some of the larger innovative companies have NDAs that are far too lopsided to the benefit of the large company and against the interests of the entrepreneur. For example, here is an actual clause from a corporate NDA that entrepreneurs (friends of the authors) received from a Fortune 100 company that would be the perfect go-to-market partner and strategic investor for the venture:

> Except for the obligations of the parties with respect to Confidential Information disclosed prior to expiration or termination, this Agreement shall (unless extended by mutual agreement) expire or terminate at the earliest of the following events:
>
> One (1) year after the Effective Date of this Agreement, or
>
> Thirty (30) days after written notice of termination provided by either party to the other.

Obviously, the Fortune 100 company could simply write a letter voiding the NDA, and even if it did not, a year's protection is nothing for a new firm that needs at least two to three years to enter the market and achieve some scale. An NDA with these types of clauses is analogous to throwing a drowning person an anchor!

The lesson is clear: Find legal counsel experienced in your domain of work. A good NDA and a provisional patent will provide a good degree of protection for the entrepreneur—and neither should cost you very much money. The last thing you want to do is to give your idea away to an R&D department in a major corporation that has trouble thinking for itself.

But remember, you won't have this problem with angel investors or VCs. They are not going to give you an NDA; nor should you force one upon them.

The Last Important Step: Go Get That Meeting!

Sending a business plan or presentation blindly through the mail or e-mail to an investor—any type of investor—is a fool's errand. No matter how good the idea or how well written the plan, the chances of getting a meeting through this approach are virtually zero. For example, VC firms receive numerous business plans "over the transom"—that is, blindly sent through the mail. These end up on the desks of "associates" or analysts working for these firms who will review the plans and forward them to the general partners. Our experience is that adds at least two to three months to your fund-raising process, and for some reason, plans forwarded by an associate to a general partner never seem to take priority.

As we have discussed earlier, professional investors such as VCs want a trusted referral first. And with that trusted referral, a solid venture concept, and a well-written business plan, the chances increase substantially for getting that meeting.

So the question becomes, What is the best way for you to get that trusted referral into an angel group, VC firm, or strategic investor? Here are some methods that our own students use to find that trusted source.

Getting a Meeting With Angels

Use your university's alumni network. Do not discount the utility of successful alumni wanting to help "the next generation" at their respective colleges and universities. Many have formal mentor networks where an administrator will connect you with an experienced business person who matches your particular interests. Forums and panel sessions geared toward entrepreneurship in different fields are also common in educational institutions. University business plan competitions are another common venue for meeting successful business people looking to fund new ventures. All of these are great networking opportunities for the young entrepreneur. Attend, dress smart, have a firm handshake, look people in the eye, and have a set of business cards printed beforehand with your contact information. Again, suggest a phone call or coffee/breakfast/lunch and show the courtesy of picking up the tab if the location is of your own choosing. You are asking your guest to do you a very big favor. If your guest is an experienced business person friendly to your university, there is a strong probability that he or she is either a private investor or knows other angel investors.

Getting a Meeting With VCs

There are four effective methods for getting a meeting with a top-flight venture capitalist:

1. Be a serial entrepreneur who has made money for VCs in a prior company. Unfortunately, this is a rare situation. You goal perhaps is to work yourself into that position over time!

2. Retain a first-rate law firm as the corporate counsel for your venture. Remember our earlier remarks about such firms offering a discounted billing rate as a startup in the hope of more, full-priced work in the future. With that in mind, prominent business attorneys are well connected into both the angel and "institutional" money (which means VCs and private equity funds). If you have the right attorney, you will probably get a meeting with the appropriate VC. Be prepared, however, to have to sell that attorney on the qualities of your venture.

3. Develop a relationship with another entrepreneur who has successfully raised money from a VC firm that invests in your area of interest. The basis of that relationship can be one of seeking advice or mentorship, appreciative of the fact that VC-funded entrepreneurs have barely a second during the work week to focus on anything other their own company. Nonetheless, a breakfast or lunch might just produce an e-mail or telephone call to the general partner of the VC firm that sits on that entrepreneur's Board. That's what you need.

4. Meet with alumni of your university, as described above, for coffee/breakfast/lunch. If these alumni are successful in business, chances are that they know a few partners at local VC firms as well as angel investors.

Another way to get access to a VC for the meeting is to retain a special boutique investment firm in your city or region. These firms are often run by former VCs. Their job is to help ventures find money, and they work on a sales commission on the money raised—typically 5% to 8%. Unfortunately, many if not most are small-time operations that can consume a lot of your time. Furthermore, most VCs do not take kindly to seeing 5% of their money going to pay a sales commission to an intermediary.

Getting a Meeting With Corporate Strategic Investors

The very best way to get investment meetings with strategic investors—large corporations—is first to develop a relationship with them as a customer or channel partner. In other words, do business with a manager in that corporation. Here, too, you will invariably share a meal at some point—and it is typically at such occasions that the manager will say, "And how are you folks doing for money? Maybe we should get involved." Again, a call to the investment arm from a senior business manager in the corporation is the best type of referral for this type of investor.

There is also another source of contacts into major corporations: your college or university. If your institution is well established, it will have many alumni who are executives in important companies. We have found that the "development" (fund-raising) officers in universities are the best source for this type of information. They manage events where successful alums come on campus to participate in Advisory Boards and related events. Ask for the opportunity to get a cup of coffee or tea with a visiting alumnus but remember, at this point you are only seeking advice—not money—from that alum on your venture idea. In fact, be sure not to bring up the word *money* to your development officer because this will surely make them feel threatened for obvious reasons.

Additionally, if your school has an executive MBA program, ask your professor to network for you into the students enrolled in that program. These will tend to be seasoned professionals—middle- to high-level operating managers already. Ask to see a class roster and identify those who work in the industry sector where you wish to venture. These are also very busy individuals—working and going to school at the same time. Perhaps you can meet for 30 minutes before their class. Or better yet, go out for a beer or two. See if there is synergy with that executive MBA student's company as a potential customer or channel partner. Again, the goal is to develop a business relationship with that company as a lead user or early adopter. From there, strategic investment can follow.

The Bottom Line for Making Investor Presentations

Your job is to infect the audience with your own enthusiasm for the opportunity. Remember that. This is definitely a sales process. And if the investor tells you that he or she is not interested, try not to get mad or frustrated. Ask "Why?" and dig a little deeper into those whys. Incorporate their thinking into your plans and presentations for the next group of investors. After each pitch, grab a cup of coffee or a beer and think about what you have learned.

If you have to speak to 15, or 20, or 30 investors before reaching the right one, simply know that *countless entrepreneurs have walked this road before you and have achieved success.* You are the next generation carrying the entrepreneurial torch. The opportunity is yours for the taking.

Be bold, be smart,

learn as much as you can whenever you can,

and above all else, remain true to your vision.

Visit the Student Study Site at **www.sagepub.com/meyer2e** to access the following resources:

- Web Resources
- Video Resources
- General Resources in Entrepreneurship

Appendix

SilverRail Technologies, Inc.

November 2009

Aaron Gowell sat at the desk in his home office. The laptop monitor illuminated the dimly lit room and the pile of papers in front of it. Peering into the screen, Aaron contemplated the rough outlines of a five-year financial forecast for the new venture he would be pitching to venture capitalists in less than two weeks' time. That venture, dubbed SilverRail, would be the first-ever aggregator of rail passenger seats for corporate and online travel agencies, with a focus on the booming market for high-speed train travel across Europe. With the glaring exception of rail, every mode of business and vacation travel booking—air, car rental, hotels, and cruises—had moved to the Web. This represented a huge hole that Aaron aimed to fill.

In Europe, train travel was the dominant form of intercity transportation and by 2009, an $80 billion industry—50 times the size of its U.S. counterpart. Aaron aimed to develop B2B e-commerce software that travel agencies could use to view schedules, prices, and availability, and make reservations—just as they currently did for other modes of travel. Aaron's company would aggregate the inventory from all the different European national railroad systems and make the combined result available to corporate travel agencies like Amex and online travel agencies like Expedia. His new company would receive a commission on all bookings through the system. Even with very conservative assumptions, net revenues and EBITDA could be huge within five years.

Aaron was no newcomer to the online travel business. He had worked the numbers and made successful investor pitches in prior ventures. Now he had to do it again. The question was, would the VCs share his confidence in the future of rail travel, and the opportunity for SilverRail as an inventory aggregator? What would they have to hear and see before they'd open their wallets? And, beyond the pitch, what deals would he have to strike along the way with European rail systems and online travel sites to validate the plan?

These thoughts were on his mind as he planned his fund-raising presentation. That presentation would include a Pro Forma P&L and a set of PowerPoint slides. To spark the interest of venture capitalists in the gloomy economic environment of late 2009, that presentation would have to be *very* powerful.

Aaron Gowell

Launching a new business was the furthest thing from Aaron Gowell's mind in the 1980s.

As a member of the U.S. Army's 82nd Airborne Division, Aaron was more concerned with launching himself with a parachute from the belly of a C-130 airplane. But after combat tours in Panama and Gulf War I, he returned to civilian life. Under the GI Bill, he completed college at Northeastern University with an MS in Finance. Graduating summa cum laude in 1996, he was one of the rare few "coops" who was hired by Bain & Company, a prestigious management consulting firm headquartered in Boston, where Gowell helped found Bain's highly successful private equity consulting practice that consulted to companies during acquisitions, such as when AOL acquired Compuserve.

Two years later Aaron was on the move, this time to General Catalyst Partners. General Catalyst was a private equity firm with major investments in the travel industry. One of the firms General Catalyst had acquired was a cruise business—National Leisure Group with the idea of turning it into the travel industry's first online cruise agency. The managing partners of General Catalyst dispatched Aaron to help build the business. He quickly became the chief operating executive. (See Appendix A for an article describing Aaron's work at NLG.) Aaron described his venture capital firm's activity:

GC decided to buy a small traditional travel company that understood cruises and built an Internet travel company around it. We called it National Leisure Group (NLG), and I was appointed as CEO. I wrote the business plan, raised money, and built a team and the technology—the whole thing.

NLG built the cruise industry's first online booking system, which aggregated all of the cruise suppliers into one e-commerce platform—and then provided white label Websites to online travel agencies like Expedia, Orbitz, Priceline, and Yahoo! Travel.

Under Aaron's leadership, NLG grew its business and made a series of strategic investments, increasing employees from 80 to 1,800. It eventually owned or operated 20 private-label vacation brands. The NLG cruise platform was similar to the airline industry's SABRE system. NLG's system made it possible for travel agents and online Web services to see all available cruise inventory and prices in real time, and then, book customers. As Aaron noted:

NLG specialized in complex travel and grew to be one of the largest travel agencies in the country. Expedia and Travelocity were focused on airlines, cars, and hotels, but they entirely ignored cruise vacations—a $16B market!

Over the course of six years, Gowell grew the business from $110M in sales to over $1B and successfully sold the business in 2006.

Mission accomplished, Aaron returned to General Catalyst as an "Entrepreneur In Residence." From this perch, he was exposed to all important developments in the travel and vacation space.

One opportunity that caught his eye was a small firm whose R&D unit had developed a beta version of online booking technology for rail travel. "That company had lots of problems," he recalls, "and General Catalyst withdrew its interest."

Aaron, however, was intrigued by the possibility of doing for rail travel what NLG had done for cruise vacations, and what Expedia and others had done for air, car, and hotel rentals. The little company might have problems as a money-making business in its present form, but Aaron thought the new technology within the company was outstanding.

Aaron started hitting the Web and making telephone calls. A little research made it clear that rail in auto-centric America was limited to the perennially money-losing Amtrak with no immediate prospects for significant growth. For the rest of the developed world, however, passenger rail travel was huge and growing, driven by new 250 mph trains, often at expense of air travel. Aaron sized the broader opportunity in rail travel this way:

Whenever rail connects two cities that are less than three hours apart, new high speed trains take most of the market away from air travel between them. Once the Chunnel was built between London and Paris, 80 percent of travel between those cities shifted from airplanes to trains—and that was the heaviest traveled air route in the world!

With more high-speed rail projects on the drawing boards in Europe and Asia, it was clear that rail's share of the travel market—already substantial—would grow even larger. Fueling the entrepreneurial opportunity was the European Union's push to increase train travel across the continent—because rail had a much lower carbon emissions footprint compared to both air and car travel. Aaron got his hands on the high-speed rail installation plan published by the European Union over the coming decade. It was clear that the Chunnel-type projects for intercity travel was a major investment priority for Union members. Other factors, such as the growth of European equivalent online travel sites similar to Expedia, Travelocity, and Orbitz, further wetted his appetite.

Aaron thought it was time to approach the owners of the troubled software company with an offer to buy their technology in return for cash and an ownership interest in his new venture. They agreed in principle to the transaction, realizing that their technology would only see the light of day with a person like Aaron behind the wheel. Now it was time to put together a business plan and a presentation to raise the capital to complete the software and create the operations needed to support the global rail marketplace.

Rail Industry Research

Numbers to substantiate the market opportunity and prove the addressable market were going to be crucial. Thanks to his Bain training in industry analysis, Aaron had a good idea about how to proceed:

> I learned at Bain to get as much information about an industry or company as I possibly could and then develop a story from it.
>
> At Bain we used to say that we could win every argument if we had enough data. If you're going to approach VCs, you'll have much more success if you're in command of all the facts and done all your homework. They have a hard time saying no to a fact-based case.

A self-described "research hound," Aaron worked hard to gather data on the market size, the forces that were driving more consumers to rail travel, and opportunity to make rail travel information and booking more accessible. Some of the information he needed was available online. He also relied on PhoCusWright, the leading source of data for the online travel industry.

Current Market Sizes

These industry data[1] revealed a large and growing market. In 2007, the worldwide market for rail travel was roughly $300 billion and projected to increase at a compound annual growth rate of 8%.

Aaron found great variations in the dollar size of national markets, with small geographic entities having disproportionately large rail travel expenditure in many cases. For example, the tiny Benelux countries accounted for $7.2 billion in annual passenger rail receipts in 2007, the UK stood at $12 billion, and Germany led the Euro league at $23 billion. In total, European spending on train travel was $80 billion. In contrast, U.S. travelers spent a mere $1.6 billion (Exhibit 1).

---

[1]"International Railway Statistics" International Union of Railways (UIC), Paris, 2007, and a "Ten Year Growth Report" made available by the Association of Train Operating Companies in June 2007.

51699

USA	$1.6
Canada	$0.3
Australia	$6.7
Japan	$7.9
Korea	$12.0
China	$18.0
Russia	$16.0
Europe	$80.9
India	$20.0

Exhibit 1 2007 Spending on Passenger Rail Travel (rounded, billions $)

Source: "International Railway Statistics," International Union of Railways (UIC), Paris, 2007.

Rail Versus Air Competition

With all the security in air terminals plus increased passenger volumes in the post-9/11 world, frequent travelers like Aaron were keenly aware of the pain and frustration associated with air travel. They had to arrive an hour before take-off, run a gauntlet of metal detectors and X-ray devices. Passenger volumes in Europe had increased substantially as well with the growth of budget carriers such as Ryan Air, and security had become increasingly tight.

The Europeans were also much further along in rail travel compared to the United States. Major cities were amply linked with rail service. Many of these were high speed and offered passenger amenities that airplanes lacked, such as Wi-Fi access, unrestricted usage of cell phones, laptop power sources, and so forth. And unlike airplanes, these trains traveled between city centers, making long, expensive taxi rides from outlying airports unnecessary. Except for Amtrak's operations in the Northeast Corridor, U.S. travelers had few alternatives to the annoyances of air travel for distance travel.

Given the expanding high-speed rail infrastructures of their respective countries, Europeans, Koreans, Japanese, and others were turning to rail travel in high numbers as the preferred alternative to intercity plane flight. Aaron's research revealed that rail's share of the travel market (versus air) was especially high along rail routes greater than one hour and less than four hours in duration. This became the sweet spot in his target market. His data sources showed the relationship between rail travel time and rail's market share (versus air) in the EU countries (Exhibit 2). Of the total European market for rail travel of $80 billion, the one- to four-hour travel focus still left him with a well-defined addressable market of approximately $48 billion a year.

Travel Time (hour)	Rail's Share
1.5	90%
2.0	80%
3.0	58%
4.0	40%
5.0	23%

Exhibit 2 Rail's Market Share Relative to Rail Travel Time

Sources: Thalys NBTA, May 2009; *Travel Weekly*, 4 December 2009.

Short-haul high-speed rail between major European cities would clearly disrupt the trend of low-cost air carriers that had emerged over the past decade. Europe had 3,700 kilometers of high-speed rail in 2009, but was projected to have 9,000 kilometers by 2020.[2] Aaron recalls:

> Based on these data, I estimated that high-speed rail would effectively eliminate air travel as a competitor between routes of 600 kilometers or less. All of that business would be captured by trains.

Supporting Factors Behind the Business Opportunity

A number of political and environmental factors pointed to a rosy future for passenger rail. Many governments were pushing their citizens toward rail travel as a solution to climate change, highway congestion, and to reduce their dependence on foreign oil.

As a centralizing decision-making authority, the European Union was moving strongly toward rail. It had made the bold decision to begin to deregulate the European rail industry in 2010, making it possible for carriers to compete across borders. The plan would allow a German carrier, for example, to take passengers all the way from Munich to London, competing directly with French or Dutch or Belgian or English carriers along the way.

This would be an enormous change from the two centuries of history where strong national governments established dominant national governmental organizations to build and operate rail travel for passengers and freight. Rail gauges were often deliberately built in different sizes to disrupt resupply by rail from invading forces. Booking systems were different, currencies were different, and in more recent decades, computer systems were different. Now, all of this was going to change.

The EU had stepped up and committed $250 billion to develop new high-speed rail infrastructure across the continent! That is compared to the meager $18 billion plan presented for high-speed rail in the United States. Globally, Aaron's research showed an expected four times increase in high-speed track over the next 15 years.

Using mostly freely available Web sources, Aaron found evidence of other factors that favored train travel:

- Rising fuel costs—rail was more fuel efficient per passenger miles than air or autos. Some researchers had found that rail moved people at *700 miles per gallon of fuel*—far better than all other modes of transport.

- Climate issues—*rail produced 89% less CO_2 than air travel* and 70% less than automobiles on a per passenger mile basis.

- Shorter travel times for consumers versus air on most routes of 300 miles or less due to no early security checks, and city center-to-city center routes.

- Greater passenger comfort and more on-board amenities provided in trains compared to no-frills budget air carriers that had emerged across Europe.

- New 250 mph trains allow travel times to compete with air travel.

These findings pointed to the simple, powerful conclusion that rail travel in Europe and Asia was already huge and growing. One study forecasted a growth rate of 8% per year over the next

---

[2]International Union of Railways data.

15 years.[3] This signaled a healthy and buoyant environment in which to launch a passenger rail-related venture.

Booking Rail Travel: Industry Research

Aaron's vision was to create a Global Distribution System (GDS) for booking rail travel. Here, thanks to his past experience as CEO of National Leisure Group, he had substantial working knowledge of the industry and well as existing relationships with many of the key players in the channel.

For the U.S. and Europe, Aaron's research showed that the travel booking market was estimated to be $600 billion per year. It included air travel, car rentals, hotels, and cruises as well as rail. Over 50% of that travel was booked through two competing channels: corporate travel agencies and online travel agencies.

Corporate Agencies

Corporate travel agencies are companies that sell travel products and services to business travelers on behalf of suppliers: airlines, car rentals, cruise lines, hotels, etc. Notable agency examples include American Express, Hogg Robinson, and Carlson Travel.

All of these travel agencies source the product info through the GDSs that included SABRE, Amadeus, and Galileo. These GDSs aggregate the inventory from suppliers and make it easily available for search and booking by the travel agents. The GDS's business model is to charge booking fees to the supplier equivalent to roughly 5% of sales on anything booked through their systems.

There were GDSs for air, hotels, rental cars, and so forth, *but none yet for rail travel.* While agencies could book rail by communicating directly with the individual rail supplier, there was no single source to see open seats from all rail carriers. Each customer inquiry required a separate phone call or online check with a particular rail service. If a customer needed to travel between different countries, that meant a number of phone calls or Web checks to different systems—and then, the skill and knowledge on how best to put forward an integrated itinerary for the customer. This was highly inefficient. The result is that in spite of the fact that travel agencies sold >50% of all travel, they sold less than 1% of rail travel! These agencies knew that they were missing out on a large and growing segment of the travel industry.

Online Booking

By 2009, online travel agencies (OTAs) such as Travelocity, Orbitz, Expedia, and Priceline had taken a huge chunk of commission business from traditional travel agencies. Increasingly, the consuming public was Internet savvy. In 2009, 60% of all U.S. travel was booked online; in Europe the percentage was 50%. And for the U.S., 71% of non-commuter trips were booked online through Amtrak's Website. All of these various percentages were climbing year-over-year.

Like their corporate agency rivals, online travel agencies relied on the same GDSs, and gave customers information and booking access to the same range of travel products and services. And, like their corporate rivals, the online travel portals lacked access to a rail travel GDS aggregator and booking broker.

In Europe specifically, only 13% of rail travel was booked online. The more Aaron thought about Europe as an initial target market, he saw a huge gap between actual rail travel and the

---

[3]Association of Train Operating Companies; Amadeus Rail Market Whitepaper.

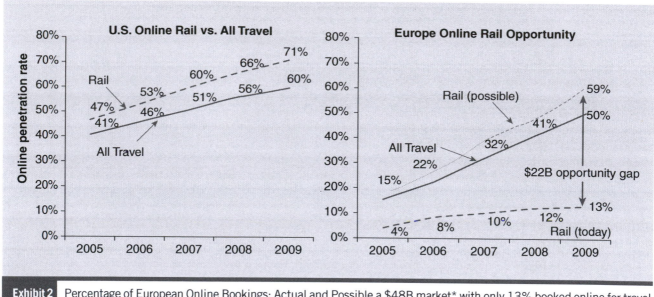

Exhibit 2 Percentage of European Online Bookings: Actual and Possible a $48B market* with only 13% booked online for travel between one to four hours

* Long distance leisure + business, excludes commuter and regional

Sources: PhoCusWright 2007 Travel Report, PhoCusWright 2007 EU OTA Travel Report.

percentage of that travel booked online, particularly in his sweet spot of travel between one to four hours in duration (Exhibit 2).

The only way to bring online rail books in line with other travel—and with its potential—was through a GDS such as the one Aaron wanted to create. Without it, rail bookings would remain complex and frustrating for agents and consumers doing it on their own.

To prove his point, Aaron developed a range of use case scenarios for booking travel between cities within and between different European countries, counting the number of steps required to book each trip using various national rail and travel agency Websites. He found that to travel from London to Brussels, for example, required seven steps, and from Brussels to Cologne, nine steps! Even going from Manchester, England, to London England, required seven specific steps. So, if a passenger wanted to travel from Manchester, England, to Cologne, Germany, 23 separate steps were needed. That included three separate rail bookings, using three different Websites, and two currencies. Aaron noted:

> That includes three credit card transactions. You have to buy UK tickets in pounds and other tickets in Euros.

One of Aaron's industry sources indicated that two-thirds of attempted rail books in Europe *failed* due to a combination of booking and financial transaction complexity. He remarked:

> That's as clear a customer need as you will ever find. The rail supplier sites present information on travel in ways that are not uniform or easy to understand. There's no Expedia to clean it up and make it easy. The result is a terrible consumer shopping experience.

This situation reminded Aaron of one of entrepreneurship's Golden Rules: Opportunity lurks wherever you can save a customer time or money, eliminate pain, and remove frustration.

Going after the $48 billion addressable market in Europe, Aaron figured that if his venture could capture, and apply the 5% fees charged by other GDSs, he could realize a whopping

$3.5 billion in annual revenues! Even if he could only get a third of the booking, his business could still become another NLG.

The SilverRail Solution

With the U.S.-based technology he knew he could purchase as the software GDS engine, Aaron set out to build an "aggregator" that would contain all seats on all routes offered by European rail lines—a rail version of the SABRE GDS that every travel agency and every online ticket service used to serve their air travel customers.

Though train companies in the UK, Germany, France, and other nations maintained separate databases, Aaron knew that his software had the flexibility and power to bring all these data together, store them in a standard, accessible format, and present easy-to-use screens for users. With this integrated system, a customer taking Aaron's hypothetical trip from Manchester to London to Brussels to Cologne could book the trip with one search and four steps—not three searches and 23 steps required previously! (Exhibit 3) Customers would see a booking page very similar to those used by Expedia and other online systems (Exhibit 4).

Would the travel agencies and online ticketing services be interested? His inquires through old NLG contacts returned nothing but enthusiasm. The travel agents knew they were not participating in Europe's hottest travel segment. The online travel portals were seeking to simplify complexity, reduce cost, and increase their business in cross-national rail travel. Aaron's venture would put money on each of their respective tables.[4]

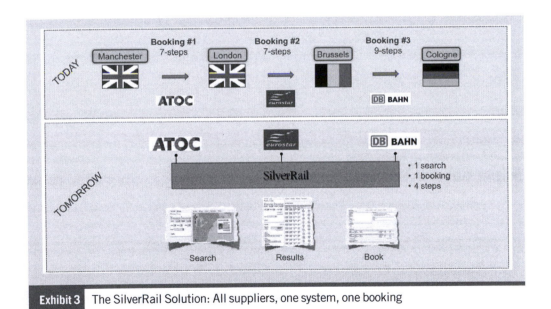

| **Exhibit 3** | The SilverRail Solution: All suppliers, one system, one booking |

ATOC, Eurostar, and Bahn are current national rail travel booking Websites, each with different formats, and representing two different currencies.

---

[4]While Aaron's focus was to be a B2B GDS travel services provider, he learned that if he wanted to be licensed as a GDS doing business in Britain, he would also have to create a B2C direct consumer site. This raised the potential of competing with his channel partners and he had to make sure that they knew that his consumer site was a regulatory requirement. This B2C rail travel site, Quno, was launched in the first year of business.

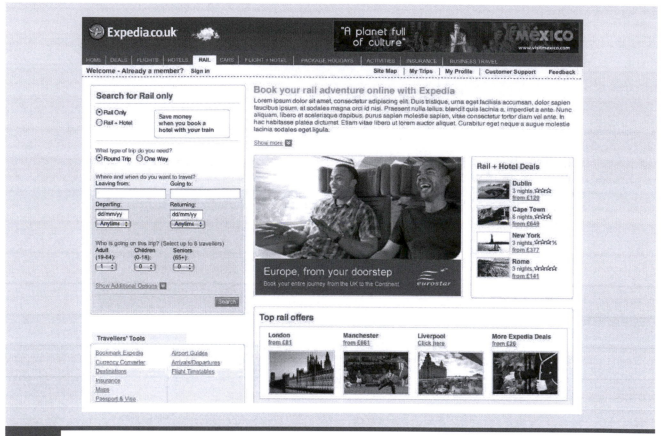

Exhibit 4   Booking Page With a SilverRail Channel Partner

The Financial Forecast

Aaron now had to create a compelling story around the data he had assembled. He could image how his VC audience would respond even to such compelling market data: "That's interesting Aaron, but how will you make money from all this—and how much?"

To answer that question convincingly, he would have to build and refine a financial forecast that was reasonably conservative, *yet* contained the expectation of a very high return.

The Revenue Model

Aaron had the data to show that the worldwide market for rail travel was about $300 billion. As a startup, he was also in no position to address the world market right away. As he saw it, the best initial opportunity was Europe. This represented $80 billion in annual rail bookings. The one-to four-hour sweet spot gave him 60% of that number, or $48 billion. Next, the "opportunity gap" he had discovered between possible and current online rail bookings was about $22 billion (47% of the $48 billion, as shown in Exhibit 2). That $22 billion was what he would use for his initial addressable market. Then, he would expand to other regions of the world. Aaron noted,

> When pitching VCs, it's very important not to talk about tackling the whole market, but to segment the market down into something more believable and achievable—it builds credibility with the VCs who are tired of companies pitching them on how they're going to "capture just 2% of the total market," which is simply not a believable approach. If you talk about tackling the whole market, you're going to get kicked out of the room. The more detailed you are in your segmentation, the more credibility you gain.

Industry practice in air, rail, and cruises awarded GDS operators 5% of booking, and Aaron had assurd himself through contacts with rail companies that they would pay him the same percentage if he could create a system that would make online bookings easier for travelers and agencies.

With the 5% standard industry commission for GDS providers in other travel segments, Aaron had his annual revenue target: $1.1 billion in annual revenue for his new venture.[5]

Next, Aaron knew that VCs tend to think in five-year windows for exit valuations. Based on this, Aaron figured that:

> If I estimate capturing more than 10% of the $1.1 billion by the end of Year 5, they won't believe me. If I estimate less than 10%, they'll think I'm not sufficiently aggressive. $110 million in revenue seems a very achievable target. If we knock it out of the park, we might even get to $300 million.

Aaron then ran detailed projections on the revenues possible from selling rail through the major European corporate and online travel agencies. This more granular revenue projection also got him into the hundreds of millions of dollars by the end of Year 5.

He also knew that his percentage of market capture would have to ramp up to that 10% by Year 5. It wouldn't happen overnight. Starting at 1% in Year 1 seemed reasonable. Assumptions would have to be made for Years 2 through 4. He further assumed that software development would take yet another six months from the point of Series A financing to create a better user interface as well as greater scalability in the database design. When revenues did begin, the ramp would be slow for the next three months as the first customers went live with a few kinks to be resolved. Aggressive ramp up of sales would then start in the last three months of the first year and continue forward.

Looking at the end of the five-year planning horizon, Aaron figured that 10% of the $22 billion market in Year 5 would give SilverRail *gross* bookings of $2.2 billion. And if suppliers would pay him 5% of that amount, the new venture would be looking at *net* revenues of $110 million. This calculation, however, did not account for the anticipate 8% annual growth in rail bookings indicated by his research. Aaron went back and recalculated his total and addressable market figures to reflect that growth.

Aaron also found out that wholesalers/brokers in the travel business could expect a 40-day average receivables period from agents. Not ideal, but still, manageable in terms of preserving working capital in the business with appropriate funding.

The Path to Profitability

Aaron continued with his five-year financial forecast, estimating anticipated costs for scaling up SilverRail's technology systems and the venture's general and administrative expenses. He developed detailed monthly forecasts for systems operating costs (which were integrating data from the various national railroad systems and hosting the GDS with trusted third parties), programming and customer support staff, as well as other types of GS&A expenses. The results of this planning are provided in Exhibit 5.

Within the GS&A were extraordinary year-one costs for setting up business in Europe. This included:

- $200K in legal expenses
- $80K in travel costs
- $120K in recruiting costs
- $200K in computer hardware
- $100K to set up a UK office

---

[5]One would think that over a billion dollars of annual, recurring revenue would be enough to whet any VCs appetite, but Aaron had to make 36 different presentations to VCs before he got his Series A financing—from presentation #37! "Raising $6 million for a startup during the economic downturn since the Depression was incredibly hard," he noted. "My combat experience came in handy."

	Year 1	Year 2	Year 3	Year 4	Year 5
Systems operating costs	$283,000	$7,053,000	$22,323,000	30,913,000	$40,374,00
GS&A expenses	$2,148,000	$5,184,000	$5,836,000	$5,848,000	$5,941,000

Exhibit 5 Estimated Costs and Expenses

Subtracting these expenses from projected net revenues would give him annual EBITDA figures, from which a valuation could be estimated, using a travel industry multiple. Based on his research of comparable ventures, Aaron determined that multiple to be eight times EBITDA.

The Series A Capital Structure

Aaron needed to raise money to complete the purchase of the booking software, create an R&D team to scale and otherwise improve it, and build a marketing and operations capability in Europe. Looking at his cashflow projections, he thought that $5 million should be sufficient for the first round, which should last him 18 months before a second round was needed—hopefully at a much higher valuation than the first round. Being an experienced entrepreneur, Aaron also wanted to leave himself a cash cushion for unexpected expenses during those first 18 months. He thought that an additional $1 million would be sufficient for that purpose. He knew that in the present economy, raising a $6 million Series A would be no small feat, even for an individual with a track record such as his own. He was prepared to visit dozens of venture capital firms over the next two months.

As part of this financing, Aaron had agreed to give the former owners of the technology a 10% equity position in the business, post Series A financing. In addition, Aaron researched the market average for employee ownership in new ventures such as the one he wished to start, and found that 30% ownership for the team was reasonable. The result was that he was prepared to provide 60% of the business to investors for $6M, giving him a post-money Series A valuation of $10 million.

It was time to get to work preparing the investor pitch. Now that he had thought through the various elements of his presentation, Aaron was ready and eager to put everything together in a compelling and convincing package. "If I have enough data," he reminded himself, "I can win any argument."

Student Assignment

Put yourself in Aaron's shoes. Using the information provided in the case, do the following:

1. Develop an outline of Aaron's verbal presentation to venture capitalists (less than one page). What should be his major points?

2. Create a set of presentation slides for his pitch.

3. Prepare a five-year financial forecast in the form of a P&L. Be sure to account for the 8% CAGR estimated for passenger rail travel over the planning period.

4. Determine the year in which the venture will be cash positive.

5. Calculate the SilverRail's value at the end of Year 5, using a multiple of eight times EBITDA. Assume two rounds of investment: a Series A from one VC at the start for $6 million and 60% of the stock, and a Series B in Year 2 for $15 million for another 25% of the stock ($5 million from the first VC, and two $5 million tranches from two additional VCs for expansion of services beyond Europe). What would the founders' and investor's stock be worth if your Year 5 company valuation became an actual exit point?

Appendix 1

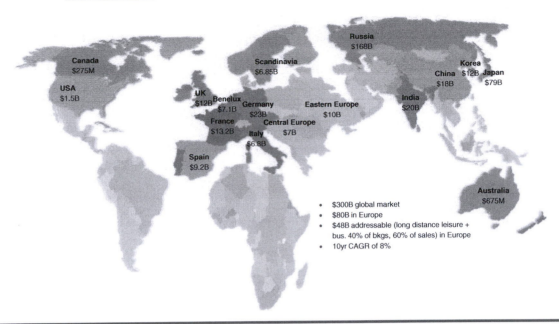

Rail travel in major national markets (2007)

Sources: UIC "International Railway Statistics" (2007); TOC "Ten Year Growth Report" (6/07).

Appendix 2

High-Speed Rail is transforming the travel landscape. In ten years, European air travel on routes <600km will be virtually eliminated>.

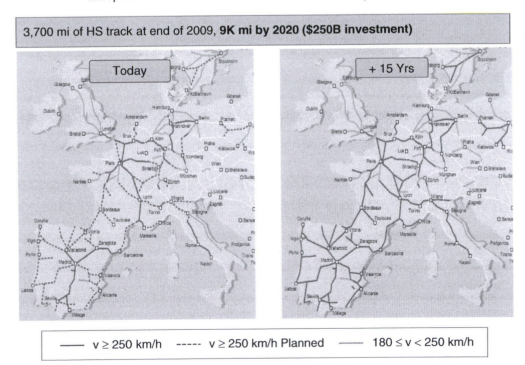

The Growth in European High-Speed Rail

Sources: UIC "International Railway Statistics" (2007); TOC "Ten Year Growth Report" (6/07).

HomeMedTech

A Business Model for Home Healthcare[1]

January 1, 2010

Jeff sat in his home office faced with the task of developing a Pro Forma P&L as a key part of his business plan to raise startup funds for a new venture focused on medical monitoring for the elderly. He was well experienced in assisted-living operations and management. Rather than bring medical monitoring to the mass residential market, he thought it best to start at the top of the market pyramid—working with large assisted-living center companies first and home healthcare agencies next. These would be his selling channels and delivery partners to the elderly. He had talked to a number of venture capitalists who seemed skeptical only because other companies had tried to provide automated alerting before, and failed. Yet one seemed keenly interested in Jeff's ideas and his team. "Get me a business plan, and most of all, show me how this is more than good technology. Show me how it makes money," the VC said. Doing precisely that was Jeff's intention. An anticipated $5 million in Series A financing hung in the balance.

The Market Opportunity: Monitoring for the Elderly

The growth in the elderly at-risk medical population is extraordinary. This growth is being fueled by the pending annual retirement of Baby Boomers, which will begin in about five years and continue to accelerate over the next ten. The 65+ segment will likely double over the next 20 to 25 years. According to Forrester Research, the personal health monitoring market sales are expected to reach $34 billion by 2015.

According to the Administration on Aging (part of the U.S. Department of Health and Human Services), persons aged 65 or older numbered 39.6 million in 2009 (the latest year for which data are available). They represented 12.9% of the U.S. population, about one in every eight Americans. By 2030 there will be about 72.1 million older persons, more than twice their number in 2000. People 65+ represented 12.4% of the population in the year 2000 but are expected to grow to 19% of the population by 2030. This demographic trend is also occurring in Western Europe, Japan, and, increasingly, in China. The aging of the population is also happening faster than it ever has before.[2]

---

[2] Kinsella, K., and W. He. (2009). *An Aging World: 2008.* Washington, DC: National Institute on Aging and U.S. Census Bureau.

The majority of this growing elder population requires some degree of formal and/or informal care either due to loss of function or failing health as a result of aging. According to findings of the Centers for Disease Control, nearly three quarters of elders over the age of 65 suffer from one or more chronic diseases. The cost and burden of caring for elders is steadily increasing. As a source of medical expense, the chronically ill represent over 80% of hospital inpatient stays and 90% of prescription drug usage (from studies done in 2004 and 2005 in the *New England Journal of Medicine*).

By 2010 there were roughly 23 million people caring for about 45 million elders (aged 65 and over) in the United States, which is expected to increase to 78 million by 2020. There are approximately 20,000 home healthcare agencies and over 11,000 senior housing communities. Such healthcare providers focused on the elderly are already at a shortage today, and this problem will only be exacerbated by the dramatic demographic trends underway in the United States. The elder care industry is growing rapidly, and is attempting to keep pace with demand for new facilities and in-home care networks. At the same time, however, shortages in care providers and employees, along with rising costs of providing such care, are driving demand for efficiencies and new revenue opportunities in the elder care industry.

The Specific Business Opportunity

Jeff had run into a brilliant, university-based scientist who had developed noninvasive, passive monitoring devices that could be used to measure heart rate, breathing, and movement in someone's bed. These devices could be tuned to an individual's medical conditions by downloading instruction sets from a central server. With proper funding, Jeff had friends in a third-party software development shop who could build the software that would send medical alerts back up the network to be handled by a rules-based, workflow engine. That engine would notify care providers and families of an impending disaster. Having managed assisted-living centers himself, Jeff knew exactly what was needed—not only for the residents, but for their families, nursing staff, and center managers. This system would be proprietary, wireless, and smart. The scientist, who would become the CTO of the venture if funded, had also developed proprietary fall detectors that could identify the sound of a human body, as opposed to a book or chair, falling and hitting the ground. These, too, would be part of the solution.

Jeff segmented the market into acute-care nursing homes, assisted-living companies, and the at-home elderly. As an initial thrust, he was focused on the assisted-living companies because of direct channels to individual residents (there were a half dozen-major assisted-living management companies reaching several hundred thousand individuals), noninsurance-based revenue potential direct from residents (as opposed to nursing homes), and a controlled environment (unlike the elderly at home applications).

Discussions with executives at these assisted-living companies showed a number of benefits to wellness automation solutions:

- *More revenue per resident.* A system would provide information required to upgrade residents to a higher level of care.
- *Improved healthcare to support pricing.* More timely alerts on either emergency conditions or emergencies in the making, which directly improves quality of care and supports premium pricing for assisted-living services. Detecting, alerting, and responding to heart and breathing issues, falls, and impeded activities of daily living are powerful drivers for improved care.
- *Operational efficiency.* Additional data that will help the healthcare coordinator assess the timeliness and effectiveness of staff interventions. These data will also help the coordinator prioritize nursing staff workloads and physician visits.
- *Organizational effectiveness.* Aggregated activity and outcomes data that will help facility managers to design and implement policies and programs to improve wellness.

Figure 1 places these benefits into the actual context of the different users of medical automation:

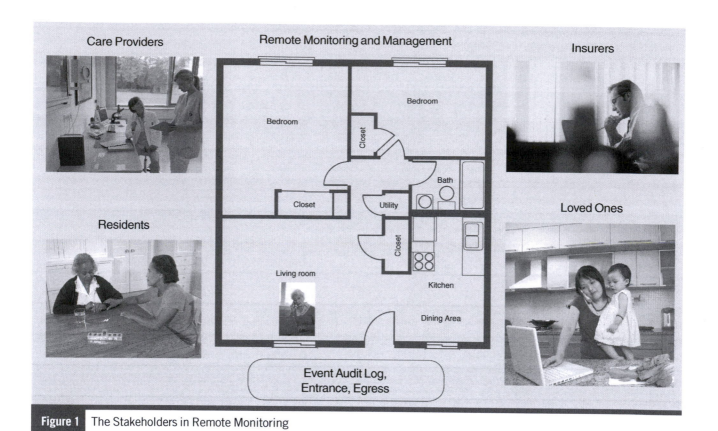

Figure 1 The Stakeholders in Remote Monitoring

Sources: Care Providers, Jochen Sands/Digital Vision/Thinkstock; Insurers, David De Lossy/Digital Vision/Thinkstock; Residents, D. Anschutz/Photodisc/Thinkstock; Loved Ones, Creatas Images/Creatas/Thinkstock; Elderly person on computer, Jupiterimages/Brand X Pictures/Thinkstock.

The actual design of the solution was a system that included:

- A variety of sensors, placed at points of interest throughout the residence, including beds, chairs, hallways, bathrooms, and doors. These sensors measured pulse/heart rate, movement, and falls. The sensor technology was appropriately licensed from a major university known for its research in medical and computer technology.

- A wireless communication linking the sensors to a central router.

- A central server, containing a patient database and a proprietary workflow engine that customized alerts to particular individuals based on their medical conditions and individual preferences.

- Communications and collaboration technology to coordinate response among the patient, caregivers, and family members.

Importantly, the venture team conducted several multi-month controlled studies on 100-person populations, on-site with two large (each close to $1 billion in annual revenue) assisted-living companies. They showed clear benefits:

- Passive monitoring (without use of cameras) was acceptable to older adult populations and gave their family members peace of mind.

- Professional caregivers at monitored sites attained significantly higher levels of efficiency in care delivery than their control site counterparts.

- Cost of care for monitored patients was nearly 75% less than the cost of care for unmonitored subjects (where cost includes hospital and emergency room visits, doctor visits, and other billable events).

The results were presented to various governmental organizations and published in a peer-reviewed journal.

The Pro Forma P&L

Jeff had substantial interest from the venture capital community. He needed to build an initial Pro Forma P&L for the business based on a monitoring services model.. As he started to build his model, he realized all the assumptions that he had to make in order to project revenue, expenses, and operating profit. He made a list of the following major assumptions.

Users and Uses for the Technology

- Residents, for monitoring and alerts—residents' falls, heart rate, breathing, weight loss, and falls.
- Healthcare coordinators/providers, to help them prioritize and track care across residents.
- Loved ones, who have a need to communicate and understand the care being provided to their parents. Nursing staff need help knowing the who, where, what, and when for effective response. Management needs the same data for quality improvement.

Product Revenue "Swags"

- The cost of goods for a PC, a router, and medical monitoring devices comes to about $500. If Jeff were to seek to make money on selling the equipment and sensors, he might double that cost to get a list price to consumers.

Service Revenue "Swags"

- What would you pay for a monitoring/alert service per resident per month? What benchmark makes sense? Do a Web search on GE's QuiteCare for a medical monitoring comparable. ADT for traditional home security is another benchmark. Jeff was thinking of a monthly service fee in the range of $99 per month.
- Should there be an installation fee for putting in a bedstrip and provisioning the user for monitoring? Or should it be bundled into the monthly charges?
- Should you charge more for aggregated reporting for healthcare coordinators, or bundle it into the monitoring service wherever it is adopted?
- Should there be a loved ones' portal—and how should it be priced?

Market Data for the Assisted-Living Market

The market for assisting-living centers is highly fragmented. However, there are four industry leaders that are gaining share. Which one should you go after first, and then next?

- Sunset*, with 50,000 resident units in about 500 very large facilities, and which is expected to add 5,000 units per year over the next five years. This company has been known as the aggressive moneymaker in the industry.
- Erick, with only 15,000 units, but which is known as the technology leader and which plans to add 5,000 units per year over the next five years.
- SingingBrook, which is the same size and has the same growth rate as Sunset: 50,000 units growing at 3,000 units per year over the next five years. Large and growing, SingingBrook has been investing in new administrative systems.

- GoodFellas, which has 35,000 units, and which is expected to add 2,000 new units per year over the next five years. This organization, a nonprofit, has an outstanding reputation for trying new ways to improve the quality of care.
- VCare, which has 30,000 units, and which is expected to add 1,000 new units per year over the next five years. This is also an exceptional organization in terms of its focus on the needs of the elderly.

Other Factors and Constraints

- *R&D Budget.* The R&D budget for the resident health automation/alert suite is $2 million (a number of robust tools already exist, but the applications are all new) in the first year, growing to $3 million as a fixed cost of doing business every year.
- *Test case.* The first year will be the test case, covering installation and monitoring for 50 residents and working out the kinks. The estimated cost of running that test is $200,000 for the first tested assisted living center chain. Jeff thought that the first trial would run nine months, after which marketing into the first partner assisted-living center resident would commence full scale. Subsequent trials for additional assisted-living partners would begin every year thereafter. He thought that each of these would run only $100,000 for each successful assisted-living center chain for a similar number of residents.
- *Management Budget.* The management team budget for this venture is set at $1 million, covering key functions and support staff and growing at 50% a year for the first five years, which will include additional marketing, financial, and administrative staff.
- *Applications hosting.* The venture team has a choice of building its own server environment to host the application, or to outsourcing that to a firm such as IBM or HP. A cost estimate for outsourcing charges is 7% of revenue, scaling down to 5% over five years. With that hosting comes Tier 1 support for facilities managers and staff in the assisted-living centers.
- *Field support.* The company also needs to develop a technical field service capability to do the installations and check any problems that might arise with the sensors and wireless communications system. Jeff planned to hire three technicians a year for the foreseeable future at a cost of about $60,000 a year for each person and $25,000 to lease and stock vans with replacement sensors. These technicians would support the facilities managers in assisted-living centers.
- *COGS.* Sensors for vibration analysis, heart rate, and weight, plus a PC and wireless router come to about $500 per residence.
- *COGS.* Installation, $250 per unit, based on 30 minutes to install devices and perform a quick check between the sensors and the wireless routers. A major telecom has offered to serve as a strategic partner, and will provide network installation, routing, and networking services. The resident pays for basic telecom services already.
- *Five-year rollout.* Each major assisted-living center requires a five-year rollout to achieve national coverage. Jeff thought that, given the size of these organizations, his company could start deployment in just one major assisted-living network a year, reaching all five major assisted-living companies over the course of six years. The uptake rate is anyone's guess, but Jeff thought that 35% or more of all residents in each channel partner would ultimately be users, leading to 7% of all current residents being installed each year over the course of five years. His hope was that these institutions would make these systems a requirement for new residents, but he could not count on that.
- *Commission.* As an incentive, Jeff built into his model a 10% sales commission back to the nursing home chain as an incentive for recommending the system and training its own nursing staff on the new software.
- *Vacancies.* Residents do vacate. This can be due to death or simply moving to a new living situation. For planning purposes, Jeff thought that these empty units would be sold to residents who were purchasing in part due to working medical monitoring. Therefore, current units would remain in operation and continue to produce revenue.

*These company names are disguised.

Street Furniture

Business Model Design

Boston, Massachusetts, is one of North America's most historic and vibrant cities. The cradle of the American Revolution, it is also a center of science, finance, technical innovation, culture, and higher education. In a typical year it hosts more than 250 thousand college students and 12 million visitors from around the world.

Beginning in the early 2000s the city began to take on a new look, thanks to an enterprising corporate venture with a European firm called Street Furniture.[1] That company had won a contract to install hundreds of pieces of "street furniture": lighted bus shelters, telephone/information pillars, self-cleaning public toilets, information panels, and newsstands. These were not cheap products cranked out of a low-rent metal shop, but utilitarian architecture that combined world-class design with strong engineering. (See Exhibit 1 for an illustration of these distinctively styled bus shelters.) The company maintained several distinct product lines, each the brainchild of a recognized designer, and these were periodically upgraded and/or supplemented with new designs.

The product line that won the Boston bid was the creation of a world-renowned designer. A city panel of architects—as well as the mayor—thought that the Bauhaus style was well suited to Boston's traditional architecture, with dark green to match cast iron fittings.

Exhibit 1   After: Bus Shelter, Boston

Source: Marc H. Meyer.

[1]The names of the individuals and company in this case, with the exception of Mayor Menino of Boston, are disguised. Forthcoming in *The Journal of the Academy of Business Education*, Volume 14, Spring, 2013.

The inspiration for the project came from Boston Mayor Tom Menino, who had seen automatic street toilets while attending a national conference of mayors in San Francisco. Elegant in appearance and ingenious in design, these toilets eliminated an annoyance experienced by pedestrians and city managers everywhere, and improved the civic infrastructure. When he returned from his conference, Menino directed his staff to contract for toilets and a coordinate infrastructure of bus shelters and other items. The mayor reflected back on his vision for the city:

> In Boston, we wanted to make sure that our "street furniture" added to instead of detracting from our city's wonderful natural beauty. We are very meticulous in every aspect of how we design our city from the architecture of new developments to the meticulous care of our parks, so it would only make sense that we were interested in improving these very necessary yet often times bland and boring pieces of furniture.

By early 2010 Street Furniture had installed 4 high-tech, self-cleaning toilets, 293 bus shelters, and dozens of other items throughout the city at a cost of over $8 million. Furthermore, its 12-person maintenance unit was providing weekly cleaning and 24-hour repairs at an annual cost to Street Furniture of almost $1 million.

No other U.S. city had had a single vendor provide such a coordinated and intensive addition to its street-level infrastructure. The project provided amenities for visitors, pedestrians, and bus riders, and gave Boston's streetscapes a unified, elegant look rivaling those of other great cities. And more was on the way.

A remarkable feature of the Boston installation was that it cost the city *nothing*. Under the terms of its 20-year contract, Street Furniture was obliged to manufacture, install, and maintain its installations at its own expense. In return, it would have the right to sell advertising space on those products. The city would receive 10% of annual ad revenues during the first ten years of the contract, and 15% during the final ten years.

Street Furniture: The Company

The founder of Street Furniture, a mechanical engineer, went into the "street furniture"/outdoor advertising business in Europe in 1976. One part of his company designed products and built relationships with municipal governments, while another sold space on those structures to advertisers.

A major milestone was achieved in 1984, when Street Furniture received a contract from a large European city to build, install, and maintain 1,000 high-design bus shelters throughout the city in return for the right to sell space on them to local advertisers. This model worked well for both parties, and the company expanded its operations within Europe, where cash-strapped municipalities were eager to upgrade their streetscapes without having to pay for construction and maintenance. Street Furniture opened a new manufacturing facility. From there it expanded operations throughout Europe, into Turkey, and eventually to the United States. By 2008 the company had grown to be a large outdoor advertiser in Europe, and was harvesting advertising revenues from more than 56,000 ad panels, many backlit (Exhibit 2).

Europe	42,185
Turkey	10,359
United States	1,593
Bulgaria	531
Total	54,668

Exhibit 2 Street Furniture's Advertising Panels, by Location (2008)

Despite its success, Street Furniture faced stiff competition in Europe and North America. Michael, the entrepreneur managing this street furniture venture, had to determine a fast, effective way to get started in Boston.

Michael

When the City of Boston put out its RFP (request for proposals) for public toilets and street furniture in 2000, the company decided to respond with a strong bid. At the time Street Furniture had a three-person office in New York City and a fledgling operation in St. Louis. The New York people put together the bid; a 20-year lease to manage the advertising contract within the city was the prize.

Winning the bid seemed a long shot, since the competing bidders—including Clear Channel Communication—were larger companies with greater resources and experience in the United States. Nevertheless, the company got the word that it was the leading contender. What it needed now was a person who could implement the bid once the competition was over and the contract signed. Enter Michael.

Michael, a Boston native with an undergraduate mechanical engineering degree and an MBA from local universities, went to work after his MBA with a leading manufacturer of pressure-sensitive, adhesive-coated films for labels and labeling. The label company drafted Michael to start up and operate a manufacturing facility in Scotland during the late 1990s. After several years in that position, Michael recalled:

> An executive search firm called to ask if I'd be interested in speaking with an executive who was in town and looking for someone with my background. I said, "Sure." Later that day I got a phone call from the then CFO. "I'm at the Four Seasons Hotel," he said. "Can you be here in ten minutes?"

The CFO thought Michael might be the right person for the job. While he had no experience in the advertising business, Michael had a solid track record in building and running an operation, and—a big plus—he understood business-to-business selling. The job was offered, and Michael took it with relish:

> I spent most of the next several months between Boston, New York, and Europe, learning Street Furniture's business model and operations. The assumption from the beginning was that both would be directly transferable to the U.S. market. Once we got the contract, we would work out a plan with the city on where our street furniture would be located, install the products, and then start selling ad space to media buyers—just the way Street Furniture did things in Europe.

Finalizing Contract Terms

Street Furniture executives had a business plan for the Boston project, with anticipated capital expenditures, and projections of cash flows and return on investment. Michael knew that the assumptions for many factors in that plan would be revised over the coming year as he worked with the city and various consultants and contractors on final contract terms.

Once the contract was signed, a comprehensive site and implementation plan was due within 90 days. Moreover, the contract required the installation and operation of 4 automatic public toilets and 175 bus shelters with 9 months. All remaining structures were required to be installed by a year later. This would be a challenging task.

Bid proposal development. One of the costs that Michael had to include in his plan was the significant cost of developing the bid proposal to the city. This included the research and writing of the proposal itself, urban planning with various state and local agencies and with community groups, the creation of glossy brochures, and building demonstration units for the city. The bid proposal would be complex, involving hundreds of pages showing detailed aspects of furniture and toilet placements, and so forth. Michael estimated the cost of proposal development alone at $500,000.[2]

While he would spend the next three months working days and nights on the proposal, Michael needed the help of attorneys, engineers, landscape architects, and urban planners. Demonstration street furniture was another expense in the bid process: Boston's decision makers wanted to see these things in the flesh. Thus, Street Furniture would have to ship over a bus shelter, information display panels, and later, an urban toilet. The cost of these units delivered to Boston and assembled there had to be calculated. Altogether, Michael estimated the cost of consulting service, the architect/planner, and the demo units at $750,000.

Other bid costs include the development and printing of various brochures and marketing materials, small-scale street furniture mock-ups, and other items, which would cost an estimated $100,000.

Revenues. Michael thought that Street Furniture USA would be able to follow the revenue model of its European parent with few alterations. It would receive recurring revenues from its advertising panels and share a percentage of them with the city. However, many unknowns had to be better understood, and some well-reasoned estimates had to be made in developing cash flow projections:

- *The number and types of units to be installed.* There was an opportunity to install 250 bus shelters and above-ground streetcar stops, 9 information kiosks, 4 newsstands, up to 200 ad pillars with city information displays, and 8 automatic toilets.

- *Advertising rates.* Since the concept of street furniture advertising was new in the United States, there was no competitive "rate card" to guide the U.S. subsidiary's price negotiations with Boston media buyers. Consequently, initial rates were determined by comparing street furniture ad formats to traditional billboards. By working with major advertising agencies, media buying agencies, and media clients, Michael and his sales team (two account reps and a sales manager) learned that they could command higher monthly rates than those charged in European cities. In Europe, the company sold large networks of "faces" at lower monthly rates, while the U.S. market encompassed smaller networks but higher rates. Michael's plan was to price each advertising face at $1,000 per month, which was somewhat more expensive than the European advertising rate.

- *Ad panels per unit.* Each of Street Furniture's bus shelters had two ad panels, or "faces." The concept of wrapping the shelter with advertising on both the side and back "faces" became a strong moneymaker for the company. (See Exhibit 1 for an illustration.) In addition, Street Furniture offered city information panels with advertising on one side and a city map on the other. (See Exhibit 3.) Ad pillars were similar but taller, and had two double-sized, 4-by-12-foot posters. Automatic public toilets had four posters per unit but were not a key part of the media mix.

- *Installation rate.* Initial revenues would depend on how quickly the company could obtain ad permits and manufacture and install its street units. Experts were brought over from Europe to ramp up manufacturing. Permits were dependent on city and state approvals. Product maintenance and poster installation, a core element of the business, would be undertaken by Street Furniture's newly hired Boston crew. After talking with a local utility construction company that had worked for years on other transportation-related city projects, Michael figured that each unit could be installed over the course of a week. For everything except the toilets, the construction company committed to installing 4 units per week, or about 200 per year. Because toilets required plumbing and electrical grid connections, one every two months seemed a reasonable estimate. He knew, however, that the process of the installations was more than just engineering and construction; there would be numerous hurdles and issues to overcome, with each potentially causing delays in revenue and increases in costs.

---

[2]The numbers in this case are approximates of the actual numbers the company used in its plan.

Exhibit 3 An Information Panel

Source: Marc H. Meyer.

Cost of materials. Street Furniture had centralized its design and R&D activities in Europe, saving its U.S. subsidiary any expense in that category. However, Michael estimated that it would cost $15,000 for each bus shelter delivered to Boston; $5,000 for each information display; and $160,000 for each automated toilet.

Assembly, installation, and maintenance. Once the project was launched, manufacturing would be handled in Europe, with assembly and installation in Boston. An operations manager was hired, along with a shop foreman and manufacturing and maintenance technicians (at $60,000 and $40,000, respectively); all worked in concert with staff in Europe to scale up the Boston operation. Michael estimated an additional cost of $1,000 per unit to assemble and test.

Installation was another matter. Street Furniture USA had neither the time nor the money to do its own installation. And there were too many written and unwritten rules about doing civil engineering in the different parts of the city. Consequently, the company decided to subcontract installation to an experienced local construction firm, which quoted a price of $10,000 for the installation of shelters and information displays, and $50,000 for the toilets.

Lastly, Michael thought it best to hire his own maintenance crew, which would be responsible for rotating advertising posters, sometimes on a weekly basis, as well as cleaning and repair. An in-house crew would ensure consumer-visible quality. Michael figured that a one-person crew with a van could service 100 installed units. The cost of that person, the van, and materials and travel came to about $150,000 a year, or $1,500 per unit.

Poster production. Street Furniture's ad panels accommodated large, multicolored posters. The advertising agencies wanted to keep control over poster printing, and agreed to ship them to Street Furniture USA as needed. In most cases, these posters would have to be switched every two weeks as one ad campaign ended and another began.

Marketing to advertisers. Selling space to ad agencies would take time. Being new to the business, Michael had to hire a sales team to identify target customers (media buyers), and then sell them on the concept of street furniture advertising—a relatively new concept in Boston. They soon discovered that a small universe of advertising agencies (roughly ten firms) dominated the national outdoor advertising market. All were looking for new ways to gain exposure for their clients' consumer products and services, primarily financial services (e.g., credit cards), electronics (e.g., the Apple iPod), cell phone, cable wireless services (e.g., Comcast and Verizon), and food services (e.g., Starbucks). Roughly 80 percent of advertisements sold involved national brands, with the remainder representing local retailers and universities.

Based on conversations with his contacts, Michael figured the base salary with benefits for each salesperson could be kept to $55,000 a year, plus a 5% sales commission. His goal was to create a business in which each salesperson could earn an additional $50,000 a year on top of base salary through the commission structure.

G&A expenses. Michael figured three salary components to G&A: his own salary and those of two other managers—an operations VP to oversee assembly, installation, and maintenance, and an urban planner. He estimated that $600,000 would cover all three.

There was also rent to consider. Michael found a bright and spacious second-floor location with an expansive view of Boston Harbor. He wanted to present an upbeat agency image to advertisers as well as to city officials. Fortunately, beneath the office was a bottom-floor assembly area with a loading dock. The street furniture could be assembled downstairs and visitors could take a look at various finished products. The building owner quoted Michael annual rent of $400,000.

Secretaries, equipment, supplies, office furniture, and various marketing materials would also be needed. And there would be utility bills. Together, these general administrative expenses were estimated to be about $50,000 per month.

*** *** ***

Michael entered all these anticipated revenues and costs into a spreadsheet and emailed it to the people in Europe. These were more realistic numbers than those developed earlier, in the business-planning stage.

Getting Started: Unforeseen Problems _____

In April 2001 Michael was pleased to report back to Europe the good news that they had won the Boston contract bid.

However, there were unanticipated challenges. In Europe, Street Furniture and its competitors sold citywide ad plans to their customers. Advertisers who purchased space paid one rate and had their signage posted throughout the city—in the downtown business districts, the theatre districts, upscale and downscale neighborhoods alike—wherever bus shelters and other street furniture were located. They bought into a "network plan," taking optimal locations with the suboptimal. U.S. media buyers, however, resisted the European practice of the "network" purchase contract with citywide rates, insisting instead on buying ad space in particular locations. "They wanted to cherry-pick their locations," recalled Michael. In response, Michael broke with the traditional way and offered customers prime and nonprime network plans, with rates commensurate with location attractiveness.

The company also ran into various forms of civic resistance. While Michael and his team thought they could simply develop and implement a site plan and run it through City Hall, some locations required permits from state agencies, property owners, and federal authorities. To complicate matters further, Boston had historical districts with fiercely protective residents and legal constraints on everything built within them. Those districts were off limits to Street Furniture's modern designs and slick advertising panels. So too were sites where advertising would be visible from parks and cemeteries. And some members of the community objected loudly to the entire concept of advertising on city streets. "It's not an appropriate role for the City of Boston to assault its citizens with ads," said one opponent. "Some things should not be for sale." It seemed that nearly every installation had some issues that increased costs and created delays.

Bringing power for lighting to hundreds of installations proved to be another unanticipated impediment. "The contract required us to connect directly to power company manholes for our electricity source. However, we soon found ourselves digging trenches across city intersections at $100 per linear foot, which was not cost effective and resulted in huge construction delays—sometimes 6 to 12 months," recalled Michael. "That wasn't feasible from either a time or cost perspective."

Michael also heard from prospective advertisers that it was important that the units always be working. Many agencies would have personnel drive around a city to confirm that the "lights were on" at the units and that the advertising was displayed in clean and attractive units. Given the importance of the units always being functional with lighting, he began to wonder if his initial budgeting for maintenance, specifically electrical service upkeep, would be accurate. As an alternative he began to consider the added cost of having an in-house electrician who could get to units with electrical problems quickly instead of using third-party independent electrical contractors. While the cost was clearly higher, he thought, the overall value to the company would be justified.

Another consideration on Michael's mind was the possible use of solar-powered units. These units would cost about $3,000 more in initial capital costs, but would be less expensive in installation with the elimination of the trenching and other on-site electrical installations. Plus, the units would be less expensive to operate. Unfortunately, the solar-powered units would not produce enough energy to support advertising signage, but Michael thought they would be good for bus shelters and other units located in areas where the company could not get continual advertising. This would most likely be in the outlying neighborhoods of Boston.

Even the project's crown jewel, the handicap-accessible, self-cleaning public toilet, met unexpected resistance. An advocacy group for the disabled claimed that Street Furniture's amazing product failed to meet the requirements of the Americans With Disabilities Act, a federal law. Unless design changes were made, it insisted, toilets could not be installed. With a thousand other chores to do, this was the last thing Michael needed to hear.

Truly, Michael had entered the job thinking that he could apply Street Furniture's European operating blueprint directly to Boston. After all, the European company had been doing this work for years, and it must have worked through all the traps. This had proved to be only partially correct. Clearly, some aspects of Street Furniture's business model could be directly transferable to the Boston setting, while others could not. Some features of the model could be executed without delays or surprises; others would challenge the company and its manager. He had to understand the ecosystem for his project—the various suppliers, partners, and customers—showing the flow of product and services, as well as the flow of money. He also had to develop cash flow projections for the Boston project, based on the quarterly format preferred by his own European managers. In preparation for his meeting with the Mayor's Office, Michael also had to show a projection of how much money the city would make over the 20-year term of the contract.

Much was at stake. The company's foray into the North American market would hinge heavily on its success in Boston.

Ready Seafood

Business Model Innovation and Venturing in a Mature Industry

Introduction

It's a perfect September day in Portland, Maine. Crisp and clear. And the harbor side location of Ready Seafood is already busy. A lobster boat has pulled up alongside the wharf and is unloading its morning's catch. The boat's skipper, who has been on the water since before sunup, relaxes on the pier, regaining his land legs as a Ready employee examines and weighs the lobsters, then puts

A lobster boat at the Ready Seafood dock.

Source: Catch a Piece of Maine, with permission.

Originally published as: Meyer, M.H., Allen, M., and Crane, F.G., (2011). "Ready Seafood," *International Review of Entrepreneurship*, 8:3.

them into a holding tank with dozens of their crustacean kin. Within a few minutes the lobsterman has been issued a check and is casting off, heading seaward to check his other traps.

Meanwhile, inside a 5,000 square feet leased building, several young men are busily pulling lobsters out of super-cooled holding tanks and packing them into specially designed cartons for a journey that will speed them by truck to Logan airport, then on by air express to distributors in Europe and Japan. Others lobsters will be taken to the loading dock for local and regional distribution. The holding tanks in the backrooms could contain 45,000 pounds of lobster at any given time.

The Ready operation just described is quality-oriented and highly efficient. With the exception of its overseas sales, however, its business model differs little from the model followed by other lobster and seafood distributors on the same wharf and up and down the Atlantic coast. That model is simple and straightforward: take in freshly caught product from boats on one side of the wharf and sell it at a modest markup out the other side to local restaurants, supermarket chains, and other buyers. If a distributor can manage its cost, he or she can earn a 3% to 5% operating margin.

While Ready has the appearance of a standard seafood distributor, a small, cramped office with two employees on the building's second floor is creating something new and different—and immensely more profitable: catchapieceofmaine.com. This small but growing operation has established a direct supply link between ruggedly independent Maine lobstermen and the far flung individuals who purchase and consume their harvest. That link is tight and personal: the customer owns an interest in a lobster trap, and knows the fisherman who regularly baits and checks it. And she'll hear from him often. "Hello," says a voice on the phone as a customer is preparing a special meal for her guests. "This is Captain John from the Port of Cape Elizabeth, Maine. I'm on the boat and just calling to see if your lobsters arrived today in good condition. I caught them yesterday."

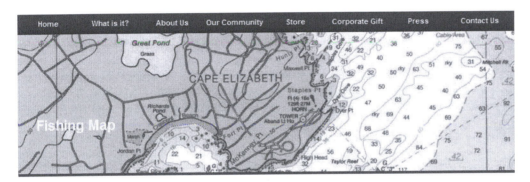

John and Brendan Ready grew up in Cape Elizabeth, just south of Portland, Maine. Their uncle Ted, like many other local men, was a commercial lobsterman, and through him they learned the trade. The business is dangerous and physically demanding to the point of breaking strong men before their time. But the two young men couldn't get their fill of being out on the water, baiting and hauling traps. Before either was ten they owned their own boat and gear and were earning modest incomes. "Lobstering was our passion," says John Ready, "and the older lobstermen were our heroes."

Off the Water and Onto the Dock

The brothers continued lobstering through elementary and high school. Then Brendan went off to Stonehill College, where he majored in marketing. John enrolled in Northeastern University's "coop" business program, a five-year undergraduate curriculum characterized by alternating periods of work internships and classroom study. While there, John took a "venturing" course, which, among other things, required him to develop a plan for a new business. His choice of business, with Brendan's participation, was a lobster distributorship. "We realized that the working lifestyle we so admired could not be sustained as we got older," says John. "We could see that in the older men we had looked up to as kids. Being out in rough weather day and night, lifting traps and heavy equipment, and so forth, takes a huge toll on your back, your knees, your whole body."

There was also a clear economic reason for moving a step up the supply chain from harvester to distributor. Lobstermen are stuck selling a commodity product at a price dictated by supply/demand forces over which they have no control. They also feel the full force of bad harvest seasons and rising fuel costs. One or two years of low prices or bad harvests can force even the hardest working lobsterman to sell his boat and quit the business. And because a license holder can work no more than 800 traps, a lobsterman's potential income has a ceiling. Says, John:

> There are some five thousand full-time licensed lobstermen in Maine. Because of the trap limit, and other dynamics such as the amount of fierce competion amoung harvesters, it is difficult for a lobsterman to catch more than 50,000 pounds each year. At the current $2.50 per pound dock price, that means $125,000 in revenue—tops! After boat payments, insurance, fuel, equipment, and so forth, it's hard to net more than $50,000 in a year of very hard work.

A distributor, in contrast, works "out of the weather." He can ride the spread between harvester and retailer and may squeeze out a bit more profit margin through operational innovations and efficiencies. And if he has good marketing sense, he can scale up volume by generating more or larger accounts.

When they finished college in 2004, the Ready brothers began implementing John's business plan which, coincidentally, won Northeastern's undergrad business plan competition that year. With the financial support of friends and family and an SBA-guarantee bank loan, they leased a building on Hobson's Wharf just off Portland's bustling Commercial Street, purchased holding tanks and other necessary equipment, and used their contacts to generate initial customers. "It was a grind," John confesses.

> During the first 18 months I spent most nights here in the building, sleeping on a cot. You never knew when a lobster boat would pull up wanting to sell its catch. Someone had to be here at night, but we didn't have the cash to hire anyone.

To preserve cash, the brothers took turns running the shop while the other was out catching lobsters. That catch was distributed without payment to the business.

Distribution is a simple and straightforward business. As described by the brothers, "We buy lobsters from one side of the building [dockside] and sell them out the other side [the loading dock where vans and trucks make pickups]. For the many lobster distributors in Portland and elsewhere along the New England coast, this business model produces low margins: about 5 percent. "It's an easy business to enter," according to John. "All you need is a building with boat access, a winch and scale, and a tank system."

The Ready's built their small distributorship buying lobsters from their local Maine lobstermen and selling their lobsters to restaurants and fish markets in Maine and its surrounding states. Although finances were extremely tight, they reached $2 million in sales within two years, and the profits from that allowed both to "get off the water."

From Local to Global Distribution

Once they had their feet on the ground, the Readys turned their attention to optimizing the three key factors that affect margins in their industry: buying, holding, and selling lobsters.

- *Buying*. Eager to assure a reliable supply of product, the Readys adopted a strategy of buying both direct from lobstermen as well as indirect from dealers. Dealers who would work as middlemen to accumulate lobsters from the lobstermen and then sell to the Ready brothers. They located and signed deals with different buying stations/middlemen up and down the Maine Coast to secure supply. The Readys also adopted a COD, "fast pay" buying plan. This practice aimed to make them a *preferred* buyer among local lobstermen. By their estimate, 90% of rival distributors make both harvesters and middlemen wait weeks for payment.

- *Holding*. Ready Seafood has a number of seawater holding tanks where live lobsters are held until they are packed for shipment. The brothers invested in cooling apparatus that keeps water temperature in two of these tanks at a very low 38° F, a technique that reduced mortality among lobsters shipped long distances from an industry average of 5% to 1%. The brothers also developed low cost packing materials that further enhances survivability over long shipping routes. By their calculation, that one improvement has reduced costs by $40,000 per year.

- *Selling*. Most of the Maine distributors that cater to the Eastern seaboard market fight intensely for sales to supermarket chains, fish retailers, restaurants, and individual customers. Their success depends on quality, reliablity, and price—but mostly price. Brendan and John managed to carve out a modest niche in this traditional market; but unhappy with low margins, they decided to seek out more profitable opportunities. By means of persistent phone calls and personal visits, they established a number of accounts with major seafood dealers in California and other distant states. Following a suggestion by the Maine International Trade Center, the Ready brothers traveled to Europe where they met with and forged relationships with distributors in Italy, France, and Spain. These customers put greater stock in product quality and less on price. France and Spain also represented volume markets that provide large bulk orders for fresh seafood, making them highly attractive to a growing company like Ready Seafood.

Within four years, Brendan and John were shipping almost 2 million pounds of Maine lobster each year from a facility that could hold 20,000 pounds of lobster at any given moment. They had their eyes on expanding on the same dock, renting additional warehouse space to double capacity. This was generating domestic and international sales of approximately $10 million. Margins were roughly 5%, somewhat better than those of their local competitors. As revenues grew, however, overhead costs also increased. It became more important than ever for the Readys to examine all aspects of their operations—from customer order processing, to transporting lobsters from harbors up and down the coast, to the backroom lobster holding tanks, to shipping product to customers—to make these as efficient as possible to preserve their margins. The operation had become a lot bigger and more complex than the typical Maine distributorship. It had leased two trucks, had banking relationships, was paying workers compensation and interstate licensing fees. "We were much much bigger, but not proportionally more profitable."

Left to right: John and Brendan Ready.

Source: Catch a Piece of Maine, with permission.

Connecting With End-Users

The brothers viewed entry to the distribution business as a means to more profitable end. Their intention was to use it as a financially reliable base from which to seek out higher-margin ventures within the lobster business. Once that base was secure, John and Brendan began thinking about those other ventures.

During his senior year at Northeastern University's business school, John Ready learned from an entrepreneur professor how Mars, the largest U.S. confectionary company, had successfully carved out a direct connection to the people who consumed its candies, generating higher profit margins in the process. Mars is a master at mass-producing M&M'S, Snickers, and many other candies and selling them by the truckload to mass market retailers, supermarkets, convenience store chains, and other intermediaries. Like Ready Seafood distribution, Mars is a high-volume, low-margin business. But thanks to a technical innovation that made it possible to print short personalized messages on individual M&M'S candies, a development team at Mars created a profitable and growing business selling small volumes of custom-printed candies to individual customers for weddings, retirement parties, birthdays, and other special occasions. They successfully bypassed layers of middlemen and sold direct at higher prices to end-users who appreciated—and were willing to pay for—the personalized aspect of the product. That professor, Marc Meyer, had helped the internal Mars venture team organize and launch "MyM&Ms" to market.

Two years after the brothers launched Ready Seafood, John recollected the M&M'S story. His old professor had challenged him to consider what the MyM&Ms business model might mean for Ready Seafood. John wondered if he and Brendan could do something similar to break out of their high-volume, low-margin business. Could they premiumize a commodity product and position it as a service for special occasions?

The Aha! Moment

One day in the fall of 2006, the Readys were visited by a New York banker for whom John had worked briefly as part of his Northeastern co-op program. The brothers thought it would be nice to give their visitor some live lobsters to take home for dinner. So when a boat pulled up to the dock, they took their guest onboard, introduced him to the skipper, and invited him to pick out the lobsters he wanted. "He thought this was so cool," John recollects. "Being on the boat and meeting the guy who had caught his dinner really made his day. That experience meant more to him than his lobster dinner."

Bingo! That episode on the dock got John and Brendan thinking that many customers, like their banker friend, would value and pay for a piece of the lobstering *experience*.

> Our gut feeling was that we had more to sell than a commodity seafood product. We tested that idea through focus groups of affluent summer visitors to Maine—people who loved Maine and loved lobsters but didn't see all the people and all the work that brought food to their tables. We also talked with friends and acquaintances in different parts of the country. What we learned was that most of them valued and would pay a premium for something that connected them to life here in Maine—call it the Maine mystic.

Despite lots of positive feedback, the brothers recognized that this would be a risky venture. "But we had a solid and profitable business [Ready Seafood] as a safety net if our idea failed."

Developing the Concept _____

Over the course of 12 months, the Ready brothers fleshed out their concept and processes for marketing and delivering it to customers throughout the United States. "It had to be more than simply selling lobsters online," says John. "Other people were already doing that. We wanted to sell a piece of the Maine experience."

As initially conceived and offered, the "product" was the annual catch of a single lobster trap, along with other dinner items. For $2,995, the customer would receive a *minimum* of 13 gourmet lobster dinners delivered anywhere in the country with free shipping: at least fifty-two 1–1/2 pound lobsters, clams, mussels, and Maine-made desserts. A "partner" customer would be assigned a lobsterman who would fish the partner's trap over the course of the season. Partners would capture some of the excitement of the lobstering experience by monitoring their traps online. They would also get to know their assigned lobstermen via online video clips and DVDs. And as an added personalized touch, they would receive a phone call from their lobsterman on the day of shipment.

Each customer would also receive literature about the Maine lobster culture, and how their participation helped support lobstering families, a sustainable fishery, and working waterfronts on the coast of Maine. For their part, participating lobstermen would receive a premium price for their catch. In this sense, the Ready's concept was analogous to the "community farm share" and "buy locally grown food" movements then sweeping the country. Both aimed to help the small family producers who were doing the hard but poorly rewarded work at the very beginning of the food supply chain. The Ready's tactic of connecting customers with their assigned harvesters via Internet and telephony put a human face on this concept.

The brothers had to engineer every piece of the process that made their offer possible and financially viable, from recruiting seven Portland area lobstermen, to creating and staffing an e-commerce site, and dozens of logistical arrangements. They also set up Catch a Piece of Maine as a limited liability company, with Brendan and John as shareholders.

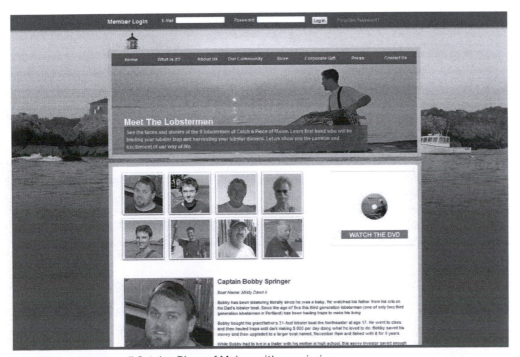

"Meet the Lobstermen." Catch a Piece of Maine, with permission.

Making a Wave

In November 2007, a year after conceptualizing the new business, the brothers launched Catch a Piece of Maine, with John as manager. For his part, Brendan would tend primarily to the ongoing distribution business.

Their launch immediately caught the attention of the Associated Press, thanks to a personal call from John. The uniqueness of the offer and its beneficial intentions for struggling lobstermen presented a good story opportunity. *USA Today,* a huge nationwide daily, ran a feature on Catch a Piece of Maine. The next day, 30 people purchased full-trap partnerships, producing roughly $90,000 in sales in the first few hours—until the Website crashed. "This was a great start," says John, "and we didn't spend a bundle on advertising and, unlike the distribution side of the business, we didn't have to wait 30 to 60 days for our money. With credit card purchases we were paid in a few days."

More Ready-generated publicity followed on Fox News and other media outlets with the result that November and December 2007 brought in $200,000 in revenues. John and Brendan were amazed. Media coverage continued into 2008, with some reporters traveling to Portland to film the company's lobstermen at work. When the *CBS Sunday Morning* television show ran a segment on Catch a Piece of Maine, the company's Website crashed under the weight of incoming orders—but not before booking $60,000 in 10 minutes. Revenues for that year totaled $375,000 with profit margins five times higher than the core business. And despite a terrible economy, the company appeared on its way to $500,000 in sales for 2009.

While recognizing the beneficial impact of media news stories, John Ready attributes much of the company's revenue growth to "viral" marketing "an infectious message spread by happy users of a brand or product. . . ."

> Many of our customers are businesses. They'll buy a full trap for $2,995 then gift each of its 13 shares to a key client or outstanding employee. Each of those 13 recipients receives a great meal for four people, gets a personal call from a lobsterman, and a piece of the Maine experience. The next thing you know, those gift recipients are calling us to order shares for *their* friends or *their* business associates. And so far they keep coming back. Eighty percent of share purchasers have renewed their shares for the coming year.

The benefits of viral marketing were not immediately apparent. As a result, the company spent several hundred thousand on traditional advertising before it realized that traditional ads were not cost effective.

Tweaking the Offer

Despite good initial results, market research by the company confirmed that the initial product offer at $2,995 left too many potential customers on the sidelines. So the company created an alternative. It subdivided every trap into thirteen "shares," each priced at $249. One share consists of four 1–1/2 pound hardshell lobsters, along with four servings of mussels and Maine-made desserts (e.g., whoopy pies), a map showing where the lobsters were caught, a DVD, and a personal phone call from a lobsterman timed to correspond with their package's delivery. "For many customers, this is the perfect gift for a friend, family member, or business client," says John Ready. "And the personal phone call makes a huge difference. It separates us from anyone selling lobsters online."

The "share a trap" program was launched for the holiday season in 2008. With economic times becoming even harder and luxury spending dropping, the "share program" began to exceed "total trap" purchases. Most customers were now looking for lower price points. Even very highly influential customers were stressing that they wanted a lower to entry price point making the "share a trap" an attractive option.

Sales hovered around the same level but the brothers decided to limit their spending for the time being on costly outward bound marketing programs. Their focus was to keep existing customers happy and using them to recommend new people.

The brothers launched promotions following certain gift-giving cycles such as the Christmas holidays, Valentine's Day, and other special occasions. They found that promotions created secondary spikes in demand following those holidays.

Managing Growth

Sales continued to increase into late 2009, and the fact that 80 percent of share and trap partners were renewing for a second year inspire much confidence in the future. Participating lobstermen were also doing well, receiving a year-end bonus equal to 40 cents per pound of the catch they sold to the new enterprise. This could potentially increase their annual revenue by 20 percent.

All of this good news, however, brought John face-to-face with an unanticipated problem: building an infrastructure capable of handling current and future business. He had his eyes on a 15,000 square foot facility on the other side of the harbor that would triple his holding tank capacity to 150,000 pounds of lobster and offer the potential of tripling his revenue if marketing efforts were successful. Finding employees was also a challenge. They needed to be personable and effective on the telephone and this was proving difficult. "We can't grab just anyone off the street for this type of work. I had to go through four people before I found the two effective employees I have today. Competent people are proving to be an important constraint."

And he did not consider his e-commerce site (www.catchapieceofmaine.com) capable of handling much more in the way of new business. "It simply isn't up to the demands of a much larger business," John complained out loud.

We'd like to be able to put Webcams in waterproof housings in the traps, so that our customers can tune in anytime to see what is going on. Can you imagine the excitement they and their friends will feel watching lobsters coming in for the bait? We'll need a better system for that.

Discussion Questions

1. Apply the Figure below to identify and discuss the four distinct business models that the Ready brothers have journeyed on their path to success. Are the Ready brothers selling just lobsters in their direct-to-consumer business?

Business Strategy

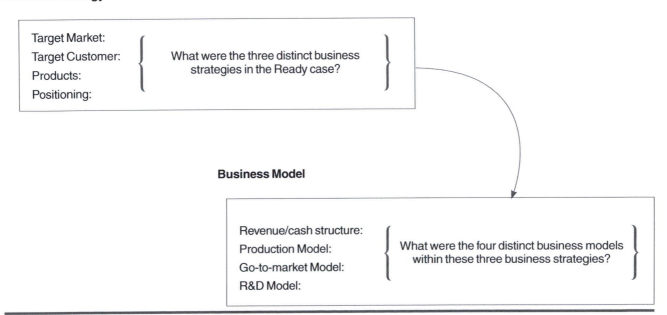

2. Why did the Ready brothers shift their entrepreneurial efforts from harvesting lobsters to distribution, and then, to expand from distribution to a direct-to-consumer business?

3. The company is presently operating under two different business models. Is managing two different business models too much to handle? What are the benefits and drawbacks of staying in both businesses?

4. What are some things the Readys will have to do to in terms of operations to double or triple the size of Catch a Piece of Maine? Please consider the marketing skills and capabilities that the Readys need to bring into the company. Also consider the limitation of its current facility (a 10,000 square foot facility on the docks, filled with holding tanks that could contain 50,000 pounds of lobster at any given time).

My M&M'S®

An Internal Corporate Venture

MY M&M'S® is a customizable version of the familiar M&M'S® product found at almost every supermarket checkout counter and convenience store. It emerged from innovations in process technology that enabled the printing of personalized images or expressions on every tiny candy piece. These customized candies are now a popular item at birthday parties, weddings, and other special occasions. The case underscores the challenges faced by managers innovating within companies whose success has been built on a very different business model.

Hackettstown, New Jersey. USA. June, 2003.

When Neil Willcocks moved from Britain to the United States to work as director of Mars, Inc.'s Advanced Development Group, he was fascinated by the success of the company's M&M'S® candies. "It had become part of Americana—like Coca Cola." He found it on store shelves and display racks wherever he went. And when the company experimented with selling individual orders of the tiny candy pieces in a customer's choice of color, the market response was enthusiastic. People ordered pounds of orange and black candies for Halloween, green ones for St. Patrick's Day parties, and red, white, and blue mixes for July 4, U.S. Independence Day.

Wondering about other possibilities, Willcocks engaged an artist to create images that might be printed on each candy piece. Mars had been printing the letter "m" on M&M'S® candies for years using a 1950s engraved rolling drum technology (offset rotogravure). Why not print something else and sell it as a special occasion, customizable product?

The process development group Willcocks directed was behind the idea and began thinking broadly about how more effective printing technology could be developed and applied. But when Willcocks shared the artist's images and the new business idea with other managers, the response was lukewarm. He was told, in effect, not to waste too much time on personalization.

Indeed, the idea of making and selling a customized product flew in the face of Mars' operating philosophy that had made it the world's largest candy and snack food company: high volume, low cost. "But my process engineering people," he recalls, "wouldn't take no for an answer. They wanted to keep working on the concept." Willcocks agreed to support them. Together, they would handle it as an underground project.

Though Willcocks's initial concept had encountered resistance, top management's concerns with market saturation and anemic growth would give him a second chance.

Written by Marc H. Meyer and Richard Luecke. Copyright © 2011, Marc H. Meyer.

The Company and Its Culture[1]

Mars, Incorporated, is among America's ten largest privately held enterprises, and a consumer products powerhouse with more than fifty business units operating in 65 countries around the world. With some 64,000 employees (in 2009) and an estimated US$27 billion in annual revenues, the company owns some of the world's most popular snack food and confectionary brands, including M&M's®, Snickers®, Milky Way®, 3 Musketeers®, Dove® chocolate and ice cream bars, Kudos® snacks, and Skittles® candies. It is not only the world's largest confectionary maker, but it is also the largest manufacturer of pet food, with brands such as Pedigree®, Whiskas®, and Royal Canin®.[2] Mars' experience in snack food retailing had also led it to develop the Klix® electronic vending equipment business and, in Europe, Flavia® packet-based coffee and teas. Its 2008 acquisition of Wrigley Company added that enterprise's brands to its list.

Frank Mars founded the company around the turn of the last century in Tacoma, Washington, where he produced a small line of locally marketed gift chocolates. In 1920, he moved to Minneapolis to grow the business. There, after visiting a local drugstore, Mars got the idea for a chocolate and malted milk snack that could be enjoyed anywhere. The result was the Milky Way bar—an immediate success. Snickers, a peanut-filled bar, followed, as did 3 Musketeers. All have been enduring successes. Frank's son, Forrest Mars, joined the family business in the 1930s and established the enterprise in Europe with a manufacturing plant outside of London. He also used an acquisition to enter the pet food business.

As Forrest Mars traveled through Europe in the 1930s, he observed a Spanish company producing panned candies, coated in chocolate, with sugar providing both a barrier and special taste. That encounter inspired his development of the now ubiquitous M&M'S®, which was introduced in 1941 as a chocolate candy that would not melt in a person's hands during hot weather.

Through the years, the company developed an egalitarian culture and relatively flat organizational structures. Those characteristics remain in place today. There are no private offices in any of the company's plants or offices. And despite Mars' size, people still know other people around the globe to a remarkable extent. Every employee, including the President, punches a time clock, and the company offers a "punctuality" bonus to people who show up on time. There are no executive parking spaces. Whoever arrives at work first is entitled to the best spaces.

Volume and Efficiency Rule

Efficiency is a key operating principle at Mars and has led to sophisticated process engineering and careful management of supply chains. Though product R&D has always been important, high volume, low prices, and distribution to grocery, mass merchants, and convenience channels are king. "Tons R Us" is an expression commonly bandied around by Mars people. Cost of goods and conversion costs, measured by the tonne, are important metrics for any business plan seeking senior management approval.

By the late 1990s Mars had begun feeling the effects of market saturation. As one Mars executive put it:

We already owned a huge percentage of available retail shelf space, leaving little room for growth. A big sales effort would increase revenues somewhat, but not enough to move the needle in a major way. Marketing and R&D would periodically come up with extensions or different package sizes of our successful brands, but introducing them was

---

[1]To learn more about Mars and its culture, see Chapter 10 in *The Fast Path to Corporate Growth*, by Marc H. Meyer, Oxford University Press, 2007.

[2]M&M's®, Snickers®, Milky Way®, 3 Musketeers®, Mars Bar®, Dove®, Kudos®, Skittles®, Pedigree®, Whiskas®, and Royal Canin® are registered trademarks of Mars, Incorporated.

costly, and many would experience sales slips once we let up on the initial promotional effort. In some cases these new products simply cannibalized sales of our other brands. It was like pushing water up hill.

Experimentation

Given the maturity of its current market categories, senior management in Mars knew that it had to break out into new food occasions to achieve meaningful organic growth. Mars already had specialty M&M'S® shops located in four key cities and a high-end chocolate store (Ethel M's) in Las Vegas. These were not dramatically moving the sales "needle" but they were useful test beds for new business model approaches. For instance, the four M&M'S® shops allowed customers to create their own color blends, using stock M&M'S® colors—an offer that proved fairly popular.

The idea of customization caught John Helferich's attention. As Vice President of R&D, Helferich was Neil Willcocks' boss. "I was scanning the horizon, looking for some way for us to build confidence in our ability to work outside Mars' core model." He recalled Willcocks' idea and asked him to develop it further. Tapping his R&D budget, Helfrerich gave Willcocks' team $250,000 to work with. Their goal was to experiment with different ways to print—both words and pictures—on flat chocolate surfaces using ink-jet technology and edible ink. And before long they had a working model.

Willcocks found himself in an uncomfortable position. He had an idea and a functional ink-jet printer, but no real interest from marketing or top management, who viewed the idea of customization as interesting, but "not a big idea" capable of supporting a serious new business outside Mars' core. The only interested party was a manager in the UK, who wanted to use the new ink-jet printer for a local product promotion. Feeling that he had come to a dead end, Willcocks agreed to ship the equipment straight away.

Hours before the printed equipment was scheduled for air shipment across the Atlantic, Willcocks received a call from, Paul Michaels, general manager of Mars USA. Michaels, who had guided the M&M'S® brand growth years earlier, had gotten wind of events and told Willcocks that *no way* would the equipment leave the building. "I wondered if I was in deep trouble," Willcocks recalls. Instead, his project was about to get a new lease on life. Michaels talked to him and Helferich about the concept of customized M&M'S® and their market possibilities, and he gave them the green light to pursue it aggressively.

The team pushed the customization concept forward using fellow employees as an initial test market. Using the old rotogravure technology, they began making up small batches of personalized candies for company events: employee birthdays, retirements, and weddings. These were a big hit with employees, and the team received more requests as word of personalized M&M's traveled around the Hackettstown facility. "Each event required us to engrave a special rotogravure printing drum at about $1,500 apiece. That wasn't a major expense," Helferich recalls, "but it certainly wasn't the path to cost-effective customization."

The team redoubled its efforts to master ink-jet printing on the curved surfaces of M&M'S®, and it soon had a working prototype. This opened new commercial possibilities. With ink-jet technology, order lead times for internal event candies dropped from five weeks to a matter of hours, and the $1,500 cost of each order set up disappeared. "We seemed to have the basis for a real business—one for which we could charge a lot of money."

Getting Serious

Within a few months, a landmark event appeared on the Mars calendar. Caught by a case of innovation fever, Mars' senior management asked product line and R&D managers to make a case for their latest and most promising new ideas. An off-site "Pioneer Week" was planned two months in the future as the setting for this show-and-tell event. John Helferich didn't have to think twice about his unit's best and brightest idea. But could they put together a plan for a real business in just 60 days? Neither he nor anyone else on the team had any business start-up experience. No one had given any thought to the operation elements of this potential new business:

pricing the product, communicating with individual customers, taking and fulfilling orders, safeguarding peoples' credit card numbers, and so forth. Every team member was acculturated to a giant firm that produced 100 million M&M'S® candies every day, loaded them onto 18-wheel trucks, and sent them off to Walmarts and similar distributors. Could they model a profitable business that produced one or two thousand candy pieces for a small number of individual customers? Would the company's marketing, finance, and manufacturing people embrace their idea or try to kill it?

The venture team had just sixty days to answer those questions and to create a business model and a business plan for what they dubbed "My M&M's ." (See Figure 1)

Figure 1 Custom-printed candies: the earliest versions

Learning the Business

Since no one on the team had ever planned or operated a new venture, a consultant was brought in to help. With his coaching, they developed a segmentation strategy, a Web channel plan, and a business model that included estimates of capital and financial projections. The market segmentation strategy (Figure 2) shows a sharp contrast between the segment focus of standard M&M'S® (a commodity candy) and the many possible usage occasions for customized MY M&M'S®.

Launch and Learn

Everyone knew that their estimates and plans were unlikely to survive initial contact with real customers. Consequently, the team decided to develop and launch an internal version of the business to test out its concepts and systems. Mars employees in this experiment would represent the market. An intranet site would be used as an order taking link to "customers." And a small scale printing/packaging line would handle manufacturing. The reasoning behind this internal prototype was simple: use customer feedback to better calibrate pricing and minimum order sizes, improve and perfect all systems of the business prior to a public launch of the My M&M'S® enterprise, and do it all within 60 days.

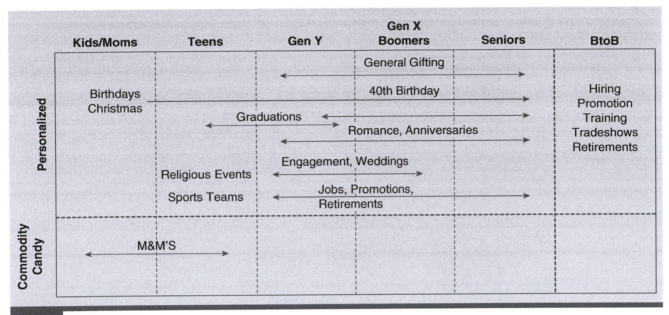

Figure 2 Initial market segmentation

Source: Adapted from Marc H. Meyer (2007). *The Fast Path to Corporate Growth.* Oxford University Press, N.Y.

Pricing was an initial point of contention. The team felt strongly that personalized candies should command a substantial price premium over standard M&M'S®. Willcocks felt that a unique, one-of-its-kind product, supported with the tremendous branding of core M&M'S®, justified premium pricing, plus he knew that there would be substantial R&D expense to refine and improve the product in the years ahead. The company's marketing department was more cautious, however, and requested a low test price. The team bowed to their wishes and set the price at about twice the retail price of standard M&M'S®.

The Website launched with no advertizing or public relations other than word of mouth amongst M&M enthusiasts working with Mars itself who wanted customized candies for their own personal occasions. At the launch price per pound, these "customers" buried the Website with orders. After being "live" for just 4 hours, the My M&M'S® team had enough orders for the entire month, given its single production machine. The team decided on the spot to double the price, hoping to keep orders in check. When the Website was turned on again the following week, just the opposite happened. The team had to turn off the Website after just two hours. *The more they raised the price, the more consumers wanted to buy!* Higher price conveyed the special nature of customizing the world's most popular candy brand.

Marketing staff in the company, however, remained cautious on pricing. They were fearful that this early high-demand experience might be an unsustainable aberration. Unable to reach a consensus, the parties initiated a consumer research study.[3] Respondents in the study were asked to make trade-offs between product features, packaging features, and price. One finding was that $20 per pound before shipping costs was about right. Another finding was that male respondents were substantially less price sensitive than women and professed that they would continue to buy even as the price continued to increase. (See Figure 3.) After further discussion and analysis, the team tried to choose a middle-ground price point between the female and male segments. And, shipping was made an additional charge. The team also reduced the minimum order size to 2 pounds. (Since launch, the MY M&M'S® team has supported its premium pricing relative to traditional M&M'S® with a range of new features, including the ability to print jpegs on the candies! See Figure 4.)

---

[3]The study was conducted by students in the High Technology MBA Program at Northeastern University.

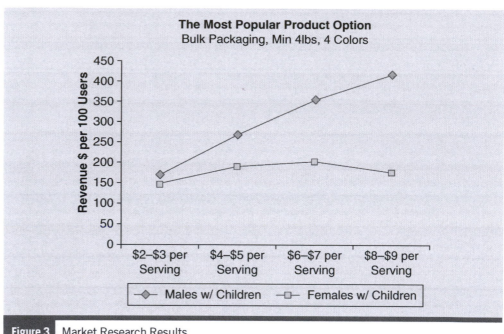

Figure 3 Market Research Results

Source: Adapted from Marc H. Meyer (2007). *The Fast Path to Corporate Growth.* Oxford University Press, N.Y.

Figure 4 The Next Generation of My M&M'S®

Source: Image used with permission of Mars, Inc.

Creating Financial Projections to Make the Business Case for Senior Management

Based on its experience with internal sales and pricing changes, the team put together financial projections for the business showing sales, cost of goods, shipping costs, and other expenses. It also estimated the cost of adding new printing machines and the number of new machines needed as volumes grew. The major assumptions that the team used for its financial planning were as follows:

- The price per pound: $25, which did not include shipping and handling.

- Shipping and handling: Since special insulated cardboard boxes were involved, delivered by UPS, an average price of $12 was added to shipping and handling. Large order amounts over 10 pounds would be charged twice as much for shipping and handling. Given the labor-intensive process for packaging goods and the special box materials, the team did not expect to make any profit on these shipping and handling fees—at least not in the beginning.

- Minimum order size: 2 pounds. The majority of consumers would order between 2 and 4 pounds of candy. Business customers would order less frequently, but in much greater volumes, with an average order size of about 10 pounds of custom printed candies.

- Orders per day: The team thought that 300 orders per day in the first year was reasonable (based on the test launch of the MY M&M'S® Website internally). The team thought that this amount could easily double year over year over the course of the first five years. The team also segmented its buyers into consumers and businesses. In the beginning, it thought that only 5% of the orders would come from businesses—but that over time, the B2B part of the business would grow to 20% of the business by the fifth year of operations. Within these segments, the team also saw three quarters of the demand coming from first time users, and the other quarter coming from repeat purchases by existing customers for other family occasions. These percentages were just the opposite for business customers who would purchase the candy for hiring, promotion, retirement, product announcement, and educational events.

- Cost of goods: in the range of $3 per pound, including labor and the use of clear cellophane bags as the packaging for the product. The team expected that over time, it could add all sorts of value-added packaging that would be supplied by third parties. As noted above, the cost of the insulated shipping cartons was born by a "breakeven" shipping charge—separate from this cost of goods.

- Capital invested into printing machines. Willcocks' process engineers had done a marvelous job designing high-speed printing equipment for the round M&M candies. Conveyor belts load within the candies (blank side up) would zip by and special purpose piezo electric printheads would add the customized messages. (Several years later, this technology would be enhanced to print high-quality images on the same surface area!) The team performed calculations on the throughput rate for improved versions of its prototype machine and determined that each one could produce 200,000 pounds of printed candies a year. And it estimated that each machine, loaded up with multiple printheads, a conveyor system, and control technology would cost about $500,000 fully loaded with equipment, installation, and maintenance.

- Advertising to grow revenue. The team had been amazed by the explosive demand for the product just in its internal trials. Word of mouth had capped out production capacity on the prototype machine in under four hours! However, the team knew that it would have to advertise to generate the hundred plus million dollars in revenue that it wanted to achieve in the future. Speaking with the company's advertising agencies, the team determined that for this type of business planning, $1 in advertising could be expected to generate $10 in revenue.

Show and Tell

The Pro Forma P&L developed from these estimates and assumptions prompted the first executive to see it to remark, "You are in the ballpark. That would be a very nice business." This was encouraging, and specific line items in the P&L were refined over the next month in consultation with experts from different parts of the company.

Getting approval from top management, however, would not be easy. Many aspects of the nascent venture were troublesome. Order taking, fulfillment, and logistics were going to be entirely different than those used to support conventional M&M'S® and Mars' other snack food products. My M&M'S® would involve small, discrete orders shipped directly to thousands of customers—the opposite of traditional M&M'S® transactions, which were characterized by large quantities shipped in bulk to a handful of retailers and distributors. Indeed, the company was totally geared for mass production, not small batches. "Ton R Us" was baked into the DNA of company decision makers. Could a small order business earn enough to make the venture worthy of attention?

As they prepared for "Pioneer Week," Helferich and Willcocks wondered how they should make their presentation. With all the excitement generated by the internal trials, this was still not going to be a walk in the park. Not even close. They knew that there would be challenges such as, "How do you know that personalization is just not some new fad?" Or, "What do we know about making print heads or developing specialized inks?" Or, "I like it, but it can't be a pet project in R&D anymore. It's time to place it under the core M&M'S® team." What could Helferich and Willcocks say to the executive committee to get behind My M&M'S® as a new business?

Discussion Questions

1. Define a business model for this venture and explain how it would differ from the model followed by traditional M&M'S® candy. What parts of the core business does My M&M's® leverage?

2. Create a simple P&L using the estimates and assumptions provided in the case. Then, develop a capital plan for buying the machines that scales with your revenue projections. Calculate a return on these assets.

3. If you were the team leader, how would you sell the venture to senior executives schooled in "Tons R Us"?

Generate, Inc.

Partnering With a Strategic Investor

Concord, Massachusetts

On a cold winter day, Tom and Darr Aley, twin brothers in their mid-forties, were busy working in a spacious office above Tom's attached garage. Shafts of midday sunlight warmed the room. Tom's dog, Billje, slept in the corner.

Having successfully sold their company, Generate, Inc., Tom and Darr now had the financial wherewithal and the leisure to choose their next opportunity. As serial entrepreneurs, the brothers would not be idle for long. "We're both ADD types," they liked to joke. In fact, Darr was at that moment creating a Webpage for their newest opportunity, a social venture project that aims to help single mothers re-enter the workforce.

As Darr was working, Tom thought back to their experience in starting, developing, and eventually selling Generate, Inc. "What a journey that was." And their relationship with a strategic corporate investor had helped bring the journey to a happy conclusion.

Tom worked for his father for two years following college, and then went on to work for several technology ventures, including a speech recognition software developer. He would add an MBA from Northeastern University's High Tech MBA program to his résumé. While in that program, Tom took a product management job with ZDNet, the Web arm of the Ziff Davis computer publications empire, where he rose to found and lead its e-commerce business, creating a number of new services, including one of the first successful PC e-tailing sites: ComputerShopper.com.

Tom, however, had the entrepreneurial bug and left ZDNet to help found OneZero Media, which created a CBS-backed nationally broadcast TV show called "The Wild Wild Web." The show featured the lifestyles and sports of the young and wild, and drove viewers to a Website where they could purchase products featured on the show. It was one of the first true "convergence plays," attempting to marry traditional media with an e-commerce back-end. After several years of national syndication, the company was acquired for over $20 million by GT Interactive Software, game software company most well known at the time for "Doom." GT Interactive Software had gone public the prior year with one of the largest public offerings of the time.

Moving on, and working with Darr, he helped to create Net Value Holdings, a multi-city business incubator that went public during the halcyon days of the Web bubble.

> Using about $5 million of investor capital, we began funding promising companies in many cities around the country. Shortly after going public, our market value approached $50 million. Analysts were telling us that we were the next CMGI [at one time, a hugely successful publically traded venture investment company.] However, most of that value evaporated when the market bubble burst in 2000.

Tom knew it was time to move on and to try his hand at another side of the venture finance business.

Between 2000 and late 2004, Tom worked in the corporate venture capital wing of Reed Elsevier, the $8 billion leading global publisher and information provider with prowess in legal (LexisNexis) science and technology domains. In that position, he worked with an interval venture capital team, sniffing out investment opportunities for Reed Elsevier. During this time, Reed Elsevier made a number of successful investments in software and information products companies that in one way or another leveraged its own formidable information assets.

This was good preparation for Tom's next venture, Generate. He had learned how to evaluate the merits of different opportunities and, equally important, to understand the mix of market opportunity and management talent that made venture capitalists sit up and take notice. He had also learned the ins and outs of the different types of venture financing: angel investing, "institutional" venture capital (typically, VC firms), and corporate or "strategic" investing.

While Tom was building his finance and deal-making skills, brother Darr was also working in several successful startups. One of these was Lycos, one of the top search engines of the 1990s. Subsequently he co-founded an "e-procurement" company that was acquired by Accenture, and was recruited from there to run Amazon's entry into the procurement market. He later helped run corporate development and strategy, helping Amazon identify and make several acquisitions.

Experience in marketing and finance for information intensive industries, and their combined networks of software and computer infrastructure development, prepared the twin brothers for a new, bolder venture.

The Seed of an Idea called Generate, Inc.

While at Reed Elsevier, Tom marveled at the success of one of that company's business units, a $2 billion legal data service called LexisNexis. Lexis offered subscribers searchable data bases from newspapers, periodicals, legal documents, and other printed sources. This provided real value to users—the legal research community—allowing them to slice and dice a wealth of information with a few simple keystrokes. For Reed Elsevier, LexisNexis became a source of continually recurring revenues as subscribers came to rely on it in doing their work.

Lexis's combination of real value delivery and recurring subscription revenue got Tom to thinking about other information services for the corporate world. Several already existed in an industry estimated at $200 billion per year. These included Dun & Bradstreet, Bloomberg, ThomsonReuters, Hoovers, Experian, Equifax, MarketWatch, and InfoUSA. Yahoo!Finance provided a wealth of free information, choosing to make its money off advertising. These information services provided mountains of financial, credit, and transactional data (e.g., on mergers and acquisitions), and also listed corporate executives.

Other ventures had tried to gather detailed information about public and private companies, such as product information and the names of executives in charge of different parts of a company. These included Individual, Inc. and Corptech, both started in the Boston area. While neither of the ventures was particularly successful, the idea of allowing individual users to set filters to screen real-time events and announcements for specific companies was an important building block in Tom's thinking.

Something new entered the game in the early 2000s. By 2004, Web-based social networking had taken hold. Tom looked at LinkedIn and liked what he saw. That Website allowed users to develop personal networks of business contacts, and then, through the magic of database cross referencing, provided a modest ability to find out "who knew who," making it possible to bridge across personal networks.

By November 2004, Tom was eager to make a move. He had learned a great deal at Reed Elsevier but did not want a big company career. He wanted to do a startup instead—and with his brother. For his part, Darr had enjoyed great success as an Amazon executive, but he too wanted to get back into a startup. Together, they had enough money saved to provide seed funding for a new information products/services business. And the more they talked, the more they were convinced that combining social networking capabilities with the real-time news feeds and data aggregation represented solid opportunity. Their vision was to create an information service for the business-to-business space that would harness a world of information and put it at the finger tips of B2B sales people, wealth managers, investment bankers, and many others. "Our vision," said Darr, "was to provide people like us with all the *who, what, where* in real-time about executives and their companies, and then provide them with a path on how to reach an executive through a personal social network. There was nothing like it and people needed it." He continued:

> For example, if a computer systems salesperson were to open the *Wall Street Journal* and read that XYZ Inc. had just taken in $250 million through an IPO, he'd immediately think, 'XYZ is growing and probably needs to buy more computing power—and it has $250 million in the bank.' The sales person would now have a prospect company. The next step would then be to arrange a sales call. Everyone knows that cold calls are tough and will do whatever is possible to avoid making them. So, the salesperson would ask, who is the executive in charge of IT? Who do I know that might introduce me to that executive? When I get a chance to talk to that person, how can I break the ice and develop a relationship? What can I learn about the executive's background, his or her prior jobs, or whether he sits on company boards?

The Aley brothers played through this and a number of other use case scenarios—such as the sales triggers created from real estate transactions, new product announcements, and legal proceedings. And the more they did this the more they were convinced that such a service would deliver concrete value to corporate sales forces around the world.

A Company is Born

At the beginning of 2005 each of the brothers decided to put up $100,000 as seed capital for their new company, and would have to double this amount over the course of the year. "We were fortunate to be our own seed investors," said Tom, "because we didn't have to give up half our company just to get started." Having their own skin in the game would also mean a lot for the next round of investors.

The brothers left their respective corporate jobs "on good terms." And Darr, to the chagrin of his warm-weather loving wife, moved his family from the Seattle, Washington, area to Concord, Massachusetts, to work out of Tom's home office. Tom had just built a house near the banks of the Concord River, upstream from the Old North Bridge, scene of the celebrated battle that touched off the American Revolutionary War. After being there four years, however, Tom and his wife would sell that house and invest some of the capital in the new company. The family then moved into a smaller house on the other side of town. Tom had three young kids; Darr, two. Both families were putting a lot on the line to make this venture successful.

The number one job at this point was to capture company and executive information in real-time and make it accessible to the B2B sales community via a front-end portal on a subscription basis.

GENERATE'S BUSINESS MODEL

Most enterprise subscriptions to Generate's service were sold "per seat" (initially $3,000) with volume discounts. Generate also licensed it's content and functionality to News and information publishers (OEMs) who used it to provide more compelling services to their end-users, and in turn derived ad revenue and incremental subscription revenue.

OEM's such as Dow Jones and Dun & Bradstreet came onboard as customers in 2006, when the company was very needy of cash. Revenues in that year were $500,000, thanks largely to these information providers.

"Our plan was to license-in corporate data through one of the current services—data was a commodity," Tom recalls. "But that was only half of the puzzle. Information on executives was thin and there was nothing available to tie those people to the companies." Convergence had been an important element in Tom's career—be it at ZDNet, in the television show, or overseeing Reed Elsevier's venture investments. "We wanted to do a convergence play between information about executives and information about their companies, and then personalize it to the individual salesperson via our relationship mapping services." The brothers decided on a strategy of performing extensive Web searches on people's names and then building their own proprietary extraction and indexing scheme to not only link individual with corporate information, but do so within a social networking framework.

For the first piece of the puzzle—information supply, such as company news and events—Tom and Darr talked with a number of established information suppliers and, over the next six months, came to terms with several major players. One of these was Thomson Financial—which held a massive amount of financial data on companies around the world. (Thomson subsequently merged with Reuters to become an even larger, global powerhouse.) Another important information supplier was American City Business Journals (ACBJ)—publisher of 44 regional business journals across the United States. Within a year or so, Thomson was not only a supplier, but also a major OEM customer, private labeling Generate's service as part of its own offerings. ACBJ evolved from information supplier into a potential equity investor in the business.

For the second piece of the puzzle—gathering information about the lives and events surrounding business executives—Tom and Darr knew that they needed a specialized Web search crawler. From his Reed Elsevier days, Tom knew of a small private firm in Montreal called NetVention. NetVention had a Web-crawler that gathered and aggregated company information from designated Web pages; Tom and Darr, along with Howard Schneider, the CTO of Generate, felt the technology could be re-engineered to also crawl and extract data about individuals, a very compelling, non-commoditized market opportunity. Tom and Darr thought they could rent the same capability from companies like ZoomInfo, but figured that the cost would be prohibitive and that they would sacrifice control over a key part of their business. Acquiring NetVention's technology outright might be another possibility. Said Tom Aley:

> Our vision was to capture and aggregate company and executive data from the Web and then map the relationships between the people and the organizations we found. Using LinkedIn-like software, we aimed to reveal connections between those executives and our users, up to three degrees of separation. In effect, we'd have LinkedIn meets Hoover meets Dun & Bradstreet on steroids—with the ability to filter out information that individual subscriber didn't need. They would also have a key ability to show subscribers corporate hierarchy and governance—something LinkedIn was not chasing.

Thus, if a Generate subscriber needed information on Jeff Bezos, Darr's old boss at Amazon, he would get whatever biographical information existed on the Web, along with data and news stories about Bezos and his company. The service would also reveal how the subscriber was related to Bezos through other people (relationship mapping). For salespeople and others looking for clients, this capability would save huge amounts of time, create new selling opportunities, and provide personal information on prospective clients that the sales person could use to initiate an interesting, meaningful conversation. The Aley brothers saw this as the essence of relationship-based selling.

The third piece of the puzzle was how to tie everything together within a scalable computer system. That meant building databases, connecting people with companies, creating user-defined filtering mechanisms on the raw data, and a portal for users to access everything. Infrastructure! Tom and Darr knew that they couldn't outsource this part of the business—it was the core engine. A large part of their invested capital would be used to hire the people needed to build that engine. The first of these was Howard Schneider, whom Tom had known at ZDNet. The information repository that Howard had built at ZDNet could slice and dice the information from thousands of articles across Ziff's various computer publications and make it available for individual search. The brothers made Howard an offer to join the company with a salary plus some stock, and he accepted in February 2005.

Going for the Money—The First Try _____

While Howard was designing an "alpha" version of the system, Tom and Darr further developed their concept, better defined the target market, and created what they believed to be a powerful business plan and presentation. Being a VC himself, Tom knew what VC investors were looking for. "I thought that getting funding would be a fairly easy. I knew these companies and their partners knew me." The plan was to show them a business plan and an alpha version of the software in three months, raise between $1 million and $2 million in a Series A financing, and release a beta version four months later. They planned on having paying customers within 12 months.

Tom's first stop was Union Square Ventures, where he knew one of the partners. That acquaintance, Fred, seemed receptive. He liked the concept and had confidence in Tom and Darr because of their successful startup experience. Fred made a soft verbal offer of $3 million on a pre-money valuation of $4 million. That would leave Tom, Darr, and Howard with about 57% of the company. In the next round of financing, a Series B presumably to build a sales force, Tom knew that the outside investors would have majority control.

Fred wasn't the only interested party. "By the end of Q1 2005," says Tom, "I thought that I had three big New England VCs who were very interested." The brothers twice left meetings with one of these financiers thinking that the deal was a *fait accompli.*

But funding would not be completed that easily. "We love the team," said one VC, "but it's a little early." Others had questions about the market: Was it large enough to support a knock out venture? "How can you prove demand?" said another. Tom thought these questions were ironic since Generate would provide a first of its kind service, and VCs were supposed to relish first of its kind technologies.

There were also concerns about the product itself: "You're adding too many bells and whistles and I'm getting distracted," said another VC. Tom's plan to acquire two or three small tech companies (including NetVention) to power Howard's system architecture also raised a red flag for some VCs: agreement on the valuation of these companies was not obtainable. Nor did most funding prospects fully understand the technology: "It feels like you're doing too much sausage-making," one complained.

By this time, Howard had identified four programmers he wanted to hire immediately to begin building out the system. Tom and Darr gave the okay, and before long Howard and his crew were busily working in Howard's basement. Tom and Darr now had to buy some computers and begin paying five monthly salaries. Their initial $200,000 contribution was now gradually moving from their personal bank accounts into those of the new employees.

"We had a two-stage plan at this point," recalls Tom.

Stage 1 was to build an alpha version of the front end of the product, which we hoped to wrap up in three to four months. A beta version would occupy stage 2, with an end date of November 2005. In completing these, we'd have something to show potential customers and gain their commitment.

Tom and Darr were unconcerned about potential rivals stealing the march on them. In their view, the big B2B information providers (Dow Jones, Dun & Bradstreet, etc.) needed what Generate was building, but were not sufficiently tech-savvy or entrepreneurial to build it themselves.

Even as he kept up communication with interested VCs, Tom continued to make contact with other potential investors. "You have to turn over every rock. Placing all your bets on one VC is like putting a gun to your head. You have to talk to as many as possible while giving the impression that they are the only one you're courting."

Beyond Institutional VCs

The VCs approached by the brothers Aley were in the business of taking money from large institutions, such as pension funds, and investing it through limited partnerships in technology-focused companies. Most, however, had been badly burned during the crash of 2000–2001 and were gun-shy of new startups. At this point in time, their preference was for second-or third-stage equity investments. For these, "venture capital" and "venture startup" had become oxymoronic.

Frustrated by their reticence, Tom began turning over rocks elsewhere. During July and August 2005, he began talking to "mega-angels," investors capable of putting a million dollars or more into a venture. Unfortunately, while Tom valued the operating experience of these private investors, and recognized how much they could help him grow the business, $1 million was simply insufficient. Consequently, he began courting potential strategic investors: large corporations that might wish to invest in a startup that would add to their own product or service portfolio. A corporate strategic investor might also increase the value of its equity holdings in the venture by being a sales channel for the start-up's product or service. A corporate investor might also want to acquire Generate outright at some point further down the road.

Knowing in his bones that Generate's product would have real value for any purveyor of business-related information, he cold-called American City Business Journals (ACBJ) the largest U.S. publisher of metropolitan business news weeklies, with 44 business journals across the country. ACBJ was owned by the $8 billion Advance Publications Inc., which also operated Conde Nast Magazines, *Parade* magazine, the Golf Digest companies, Newhouse Newspapers, and cable television interests.

Though its parent company focused on consumer products, Tom knew that ACBJ understood the market for B2B information and seemed a logical beneficiary of Generate's innovation—as either an outright owner or investor. Moreover, Generate would benefit greatly from access to the publisher's deep information sources. Perhaps a deal could be arranged.

Tom connected to an executive with ACBJ, Tim Bradbury, senior vice president of ACBJ's Interactive business. More than his colleagues on the print side of the business, Tim understood information technology and its value to the enterprise. Though his company didn't normally invest in new ventures, Tim was intrigued by Tom's idea and offered to visit him when the alpha version was available. In the meantime, curious as to how Generate might handle ACBJ's data, Bradberry offered Tom a free data "feed."

In the meantime, Tom kept knocking on the doors of VCs, all of whom remained non-committal:

"That's interesting. Come back and see us when you have customers."

Or, "Let's talk again when you have a CEO—preferably a guy who has delivered for us before. You lack operating experience."

Even the initial group of interested financiers, people who knew Tom well, were reluctant to move forward—at least on their own. Most proposed syndicating the deal as a way of hedging their bets.

"Where's the 'venture' in venture capital," Tom asked himself. His frustrations continued until September 2005, when Howard and his tech team unveiled the alpha version of the product. By that time, the venture was scraping the bottom of the cash barrel, forcing each brother to put another $100,000 of his own savings into the enterprise. This was the point at which Tom and his wife sold their big house and moved to more modest quarters across town.

Three Potential Series A Deals _____

In September 2005, Howard unveiled his alpha version of the system's front end. Tom and Darr had their business plan worked out. (See financial projections in Exhibit 1.)

True to his word, Tim Bradbury traveled to Boston to see the system in action, using his company's data feed as one key input. Tim was impressed. He invited the brothers to visit ACBJ's Charlotte, North Carolina, headquarters in the next month and meet with the CEO Ray Shaw, a former Dow Jones executive, was an old school newspaper man who, Bradbury warned, would be more interested in Generate's people and concept than in the details of its technology.

Meanwhile, two of the VCs Tom had been courting came through with term sheets. VC #1 (called Great Capital for this case) and VC#2 (Ocean Capital) both had their fears allayed when Howard finished the alpha version and felt comfortable that beta was only three to four months off with proper funding. Great Capital put a pre-money valuation on the deal of $4 million. Ocean Capital's pre-money valuation was a little bit better at $4.5 million. The term sheets from both VCs were remarkably similar—and equally painful for Tom and Darr. Tom remarked:

> You have to be very careful about terms. A VC offer to buy 40% of the company typically leaves you with majority ownership but don't confuse ownership with control. There are always "protective provisions" in the term sheet—usually 5 to 15—that many uninitiated entrepreneurs fail to consider. Typically, these say that even though you own majority ownership, you can't sell the company, can't raise more capital, can't spend more than X dollars, and can't add a board member without their approval. Effectively, they can block any big decision the company faces. Additionally, the money that *you* put in vests over a number of years. So much for control. And if they don't like you, out you go!

He then shared another frustration: "participating preferred" shares. This was one of the provisions in the term sheets received from both Great Capital and Ocean Capital. Tom and Darr were aware that this type of structure was typical, especially in New England and in Series A-C term sheets.

> Here's how those work. If the VC puts in $3 million for a 30% ownership stake, and the company eventually sells for $30 million, the VC will take back its $3 million, before anyone else gets a dime, and then have a right to 30% of the remaining $27 million. In the industry it's called 'double-dipping.' The VC is first in line for a payout and then enjoys its pro-rata ownership of what's leftover. This can be very painful the more money a company raises. The only place this is legal is in the world of venture capital!

Tom Aley's reflections on those term sheets continued:

> They insisted that we create an incentive pool for future employees, which we wanted to do anyway. One firm proposed setting aside 10% of all equity, and the other, 20%. Fair enough. We want to incentivize our employees. But the problem was that the 10% or 20% option pool had to be taken out our own founders shares first, *before the VCs put in their money*. They want the entrepreneurs to take all the dilution. Again, Tom and Darr weren't strangers to these types of terms—they're the very ones that Tom had negotiated with entrepreneurs during his 6 years of being a VC himself. "That didn't mean it tasted good."

Darr reflected further on these VC deals:

> Here's the worst of the provisions. One of the VCs, Great Capital as I recall, wanted us to reconstitute all of our founders' shares as options that would vest over three years. This

is called reverse vesting—and it is a lousy deal, but it's pretty standard with VCs. This doesn't sit real well—I mean we invested the same hard cash as the VCs and they want us to vest into *our* shares?! We bought those shares just like the VCs are buying theirs. We're not asking *them* to vest into their ownership!

This meant that if the company needed another round of capital in 12 months—a certainty if the enterprise were to grow—the founders would face an impossible dilemma. First stage investors are expected to participate in later rounds. If they don't, that sends a bad message to other potential investors. Thus, a VC sitting on a startup board who doesn't think the entrepreneur is the right person for the job might then say, "Listen, you've done a pretty good job so far, but we don't think you are the right person to run the business moving forward. You need to go start another company and let us build this one. For all your work, you can keep the first year's vested stock, but you need to forgo the rest. We are going to need it to bring on a professional management team. If you don't agree, your company will probably be dead and all of your stock won't be worth a dime."

Tom and Darr had seen a number of VC deals from both sides of the table. Tom had a special caution for the legal profession:

You need a good lawyer to wade through all these provisions. And the rub of it is that your own lawyer—the person who you trust to represent you and tough it out in final negotiations—may not be entirely on your side. He wants the deal to get done so that he can get paid—usually $20,000 to $30,000, which comes out of the proceeds. The attorney has an incentive to urge you to sign. He'll say, 'These are standard terms,' which is true enough, but they're all in the VC's favor.

Also during October, Tom and Darr flew down to Charlotte to meet Ray Shaw. The meeting went well. Tom, who later described Shaw as one of the smartest, warmest, most genuine business people he'd ever met, was full of confidence.

With Tim Bradbury's endorsement, the CEO asked them, "What's the deal?" Generate had just signed three paying customers for its forthcoming beta version—one of them being ACBJ![1] Tom told him that he needed to raise $3 million. Shaw was agreeable and deferred to the Aley's request to eliminate most of the protective terms that Tom and Darr found so painful to swallow in the VC deals. Further, the investment would be structured without participating preferred shares. An incentive pool was set up, but with all owners contributing to it on a pro-rata basis.

As important as anything else was the valuation of Generate. Tom proposed a $9 million pre-money valuation on Generate, which for $3 million would leave the founders with 75% of the equity. Ray did not immediately say no, but as an experienced executive running a cash-generating business, he said:

"Tom, I like your team a lot. Tim says your system is going work just fine. But please explain to me now, why is a company with no revenue worth $12 million?"

Discussion Questions _____

1. What are the pros and cons of each deal? Which deal should Tom and Darr take?

2. How can the brothers justify their valuation to Ray?

---

[1]ACBJ signed a three-year subscriber agreement at $60,000 per year paid up front. The other two were T-Mobile, which has a large enterprise sales force, and Deloitte & Touche.

Appendix A:
Generate Pro Forma Financials _____

	Beta–2005	2006	2007	2008
New customers	2	30	49	147
Recurring customers		2	34	83
Total customers	2	32	83	230
Average revenue per customer	17,000	50,000	50,000	50,000
Recurring Bookings		28,900	1,066,831	3,020,568
New Bookings	34,000	1,571,000	3,034,043	8,458,897
Total Bookings	34,000	1,599,900	4,100,874	11,479,465
Revenue	4,250	1,001,844	3,401,870	10,102,559
COS	59,250	978,417	1,185,000	4,649,710
GM	(55,000)	23,427	2,216,870	5,452,849
%	−1294%	2%	65%	54%
OpEx	613,093	1,552,233	3,100,438	4,903,550
Op Inc +/−	(668,093)	(1,528,806)	(883,568)	549,299
Adjustments for Working Capital		(30,055)	(102,056)	(303,077)
Ending Cash	3,774,144	2,215,283	1,229,659	1,475,881
Headcount	11	33	73	91
FTE	5	27	55	81

Appendix B:
Explaining the Term Sheet Provisions _____

The offers that Tom and Darr Aley received from VCs were loaded with restrictive covenants. We will take one of these offers and examine the key terms and provisions.

Pre-money valuation: $5 million. This is the valuation set by one of the VCs on Generate before investment. The VC offered to invest $3 million at this valuation. The post-money valuation would therefore be $8 million, and the VC would therefore receive 37.5% of the company stock in this Series A financing.

Participating Preferred Stock

Tom, Darr, and Howard all owned common shares, which represented ownership in the venture and carried full voting rights. These were founder's shares. The VC didn't want common stock. It demanded preferred stock. This type of security has numerous protections that a VC can use to limit its loss in the event of company failure or poor performance. The preferred stock had full voting rights in its pro-rata participation in all equity issued by the company (e.g., 37.5%). It also comes with liquidation preferences that are described next. It was also structured as "participating preferred stock," which means that upon any liquidation event, the preferred stock would convert immediately to common stock to participate pro-rata in the distribution of the company assets.

Liquidation Preferences

The participating preferred stock came with liquidation preferences. VCs usually have a broad definition of "liquidation," which includes an acquisition, bankruptcy, and the sale of company's assets. The purpose is that the VC wants to get its money *ahead* of the founders. This is usually structured as a 1X liquidation preference with terms attached. In the Generate case, Great Capital put a 1 times liquidation preference into the term sheet. Consider the following two scenarios:

1. If Generate was liquidated (acquired or went into bankruptcy) for only $4.5 million dollars, then even though Great Capital owned only 37.5% of the stock, it would still get all of its original $3 million dollars back plus another $1.5 million before the founders.

2. If Generate was acquired for $30 million, Great Capital would still get its $4.5 million right off the top before the common shareholders, and then 37.5% of the remaining $25.5 million, or $9.5 million, making for a total of $14 million or close to five times its original investment.

Dividends

Great Capital also insisted on dividends on its preferred stock in the amount of 5% or $150,000 on its $3 million investment. If the company wasn't cash flow positive, then that amount would be paid in additional preferred shares.

Reverse Vesting. Great Capital insisted that Tom, Darr, and Howard put all their shares into the employee option pool, and then have their pro-rata amounts vest over a period of three years, losing effective control of the company even though the Series A investors owned only 37.5% of the venture! Even if Tom and Darr could negotiate the first third to vest immediately, that would still leave the founders with only 20% voting rights. In other words, Great Capital could decide as a Board Member to replace the founders and get a new management team at any time, in which case 40% of the founding stock would go back into the kitty for whatever purposes the VCs thought best.

Reserved Stock

Great Capital requested that an employee stock option pool of 10% of all outstanding shares be set aside pre-money. For Tom, Darr, and Howard, that meant that they would have to give up 10% of their collective stock—for example, dilute themselves by 10%—before Great Capital put in its money. That meant that Great Capital would still own 37.5% of participating preferred stock with a 1.5 times liquidation preference, and that Tom, Darr, and Howard's collective 62.5% ownership would drop to 52.5% ownership.

Great Capital's term sheet contained other significant clauses. These included:

- A "take me along" clause. If the founders wished to sell some of their stock to another party, they had to also sell the same percentage of the VC's at the same time unless the VC approved otherwise. This would prevent Tom, Darr, and Howard from using their stock to bring in another investor to effectively run the company.
- Preemptive rights. Great Capital also put clauses into the term sheet stating a right of first refusal to preserve any portion of its 37.5% equity stake in subsequent rounds of financing.
- A rachet clause. If the price of the stock dropped below the Series A price per share in any subsequent round of financing, Great Capital would first be issued additional participatory preferred shares in the amount that would preserve its 37.5% ownership. This was effectively an anti-dilution clause. For example, if the Series A price was $10 a share, and the next round was only $5 a share, Great Capital would be issued the same amount of shares that it already held to preserve its ownership stake. New investors coming in at the lower $5 per share price would effectively be diluting the common shareholders, for example, the founders.
- Regardless of Board Membership, Great Capital inserted approval rights on any expenditure of cash over $100,000.

Taken together, these provisions meant that even though Great Capital would be a minority shareholder after its Series A investment, it would still effectively control the company.

Sentillion, Inc.

The Anatomy of a Corporate Spin-off

> *"Do you think it's really possible to start a company to do this type of thing?"*
>
> —Robert Seliger, Co-Founder and CEO, asking a friend
> about spinning off technology from HP into a
> new company April, 1999, Winchester, Massachusetts

Rob Seliger was sitting across from John Douglass at his kitchen table. Rob Seliger had been an R&D manager in Hewlett Packard's Medical Products Group. John had been a marketing manager in the same division. Together, the two men were now partners in a new healthcare IT venture and had just raised $2.7 million in Series A financing. The process of spinning out their new company from HP had been a year-long journey. And with the funding, their work had just begun.

Origins in HP

The Medical Products Group was located in Andover, Massachusetts, an entire continent away from HP's Silicon Valley headquarters. The Group at that time accounted for roughly $1.5 billion of HP's $40 billion annual revenues. Seliger had arrived at HP 18 years earlier, at the very beginning of his career. An electrical engineering graduate from Cornell, he had added an MIT masters in computer science to his resume, thanks to a fellowship from his new employer.

Over the course of those 18 years, Seliger had risen to become the senior software technologist in the Medical Products Group. Being on the opposite side of the country from HP headquarters, and serving the specialized market of healthcare systems, had given the Group a fair amount of operating independence. It handled nearly all of its own business functions— ranging from R&D, to sales, manufacturing, finance, and customer service. This relative independence had made the Medical Products Group a training ground for up and coming HP executives. Lewis Platt, for example, a prominent CEO of HP during the 1990s had first been the General Manager of the Medical Products Group.

The 1990s had been a decade of transition for HP. Historically the company was a creator and manufacturer of high margin, sophisticated electronics, measuring instruments, and software for niche applications in industrial, scientific, and medical markets. With the advent of client server and home computing, however, management redirected the business to

Published as: Meyer, M.H., Adomzda, G., and Crane, F.G., (2011). "Sentillion," *The Journal of the Academy of Business Education,* 12, pp. 163-175.

lower-margin, high-volume businesses such as servers, PCs, ink-jet and laser printers, scanners, and so forth. And management wanted more of the same.

The Medical Products Group was not "more of the same." It was the market leader in patient monitors for adults and infants, and in ultrasound machines for cardiology applications—all complex systems. The Andover facility also had its own automated surface mount manufacturing machines to fabricate the unique, multi-layered printed circuit boards for its various products. These products departed sharply from the new path that corporate HP was pursuing, and top management was finding it harder to keep these different businesses under the same roof.

Hospital managers at this time were urging their vendors to integrate diverse data sets into electronic medical record systems. Care providers were convinced that such integration would improve the quality of care, reduce medical errors, and lower administrative costs by eliminating redundant processes and databases. As a gifted software architect, Seliger understood their need and believed that well designed software could bridge different types of systems with different specific purposes. His customer visits convinced him that this was what users wanted.

At the time, Seliger was an architect working on a highly advanced clinical information system that gathered data from a patient monitor and displayed computerized flowsheets and reports that in most hospitals were still documented manually by physicians and nursing staff. He wanted to connect the data in his system with other systems produced by the Group but he found no resources to develop such connections. In fact, he saw that different units within the Group were doing just the opposite of what customers wanted. Everything was decentralized. Each product line had its own R&D team building its own applications software to its own self-defined standards, using the tools of their own choice.

Seliger's R&D executive, Mark Halloran, also recognized the problem but was struggling for ways to get the division business managers to allocate resources to the development of common "software platforms." He knew that such platforms—common databases and application programming interfaces—would allow for seamless interconnectivity between the Group's different product lines. The same platform could also be opened to HP's partners. However, division managers were so focused on near term improvements to feature and functions in their own systems that common software for the common good was not an issue of interest. The impact on customers was predictable. Said Seliger:

> There was no connectivity. Cardiology had its computers and ran cardiology applications. Obstetrics had its computers, which ran applications for it alone. This did not bode well, for example, for treating pregnant women with mitro valve prolapse, a common heart condition among pregnant women. Customers would complain to us that they had bought a system for the intensive care unit, another for radiology, and another for the OR, but they didn't work together. And they were right. Different departments were using different operating systems, had different standards, and so forth. You couldn't have made these systems less integrated if you had tried.

Doctors and nurses who wanted to use these information systems to get a complete picture of their patients and patient care were frustrated at every turn.

> They would first have to find the application of interest—say radiology—then log on and enter their password. But if they were in the radiology application and wanted to check a lab report, they'd have to log into the lab's system, which required a different id and password. Want to order a medication for the patient? Then the doctor would have to log into yet another system. This was so frustrating and time consuming that most care providers stuck to their paper records and manual systems. Using the computer system was just too painful. At best, they would log into the single application most pertinent to their discipiline and ignore patient information available elsewhere.

"A company should organize the way it wants it products to operate," Halloran would say. He believed that the Group needed a small centralized R&D unit to build common components to be used across all divisions.

In 1996, Halloran hired a consultant to size up opportunities to create common parts and pieces across both hardware and software in the Group. Working with senior technologists such as Seliger, the consultant—known as "The Professor" because of his affiliation with a local university—found numerous opportunities for platforming. In software alone, there were different database management systems, programming languages, and even operating systems across the five different divisions. It was during this time that Seliger and Halloran kindled a friendship based on their shared interest in the power of product platforms. Halloran built support among Group executives for the creation of a new, central R&D team to create common software components to connect the five different product lines. He asked Seliger to lead the team.

At the time, being a formal leader at HP was not what most people would expect. HP culture was to give managers lots of responsibility but no real authority, as Seliger quickly discovered. He was charged with bringing the divisions together to build common software components. However, he was given few resources to get the job done. Nor did he have much leverage over the other R&D managers. They all had tight deadlines to meet in their other jobs and these had priority.

Forming an Industry Consortium to Create a New Standard

The opportunity to create common software existed at two primary levels. The first was at the database level, as common formats for identifying and storing information about patients, medications, or clinical procedures. By 1997, various industry standard groups had created fairly well-defined database standards to address these needs, and most medical device and software developers had adopted them. Even HP's medical divisions had begun to incorporate these industry standards.[1]

The second opportunity to create common software was at the user interface level. Nothing existed within HP or any other medical systems vendor that standardized how physicians and nurses interacted with clinical software.

- Patient information resided in multiple clinical IT systems
- Doctors, nurses, and other caregivers required access to many applications
- Navigating among those applications was cumbersome and time-consuming
- Even if a "single sign-on" for caregivers existed, it would not, by itself, get them into the specific applications they needed to see.
- There was no working technology to synchronize applications to present a single patient's data across the multiple applications used by caregivers.

As a result, each physician had to maintain a separate log-in and password for each software application used over the course of the day—up to a dozen or more in many situations. There was also no way that a single patient's information could be populated across these myriad applications once the doctor logged on. For each application, he or she would have to look up the

[1]HL/7 (which stands for Health Level 7) is an important set of standards for the electronic interchange of clinical, financial, and administrative information among healthcare-oriented computer systems. It specifies a number of flexible standards, guidelines, and methodologies by which various healthcare systems can communicate with each other. Within HL/7, document, data, and messaging formats have been proposed and adopted by the industry. DICOM was a major database standard. It stands for the Digital Imaging and Communications in Medicine (DICOM) standard for distributing and viewing any kind of medical image regardless of the origin.

patient's ID and wait for the system to access that information. When the doctor changed or added information (which is the whole point of providing care assisted by computers), s/he would have to update each clinical application separately. If the doctor had to race off to answer a page, for example, those systems might never have the correct information. Or, the results of a laboratory analysis shown in one system were not carried over into ordering drugs into another system. Incorrect or missing information could lead to suboptimal care, causing further illness, and sometimes, worse! For example, it was well known that in the United States alone, giving people the incorrect medications in the hospital was the cause of over 100,000 deaths each year!

These were the problems—for physicians, nurses, and other care providers—that Seliger wanted to try to solve. In his new position as the head of the Medical Product Group's central R&D team, that became his responsibility. But, as noted earlier, he had no authority to make any of the R&D managers in the five HP divisions help design and use common software infrastructure. None. Frustrated, he began asking for advice—of the political sort. Wes Rishel, a personal friend and industry consultant, offered a potential solution:

> Rob, why don't you create an industry standard? Focus on your ideas about patient and user context management. If you get people outside the company to embrace that standard, that might compel HP developers to fall into line with everyone else.

Going outside to encourage collaboration inside seemed a strange way to reach the goal, but at this point, Seliger was willing to try any good idea. He invited companies that worked in the healthcare IT space to come to Boston and form a consortium to create tools to identify care providers and synchronize patients across their respective systems. In March 1997, 20 companies showed up for the first meeting of what became the Clinical Context Object Work Group, or CCOW. Of those, a number were HP's archrivals. Yet, everyone realized that these standards, if well designed and implemented as a new type of healthcare IT "middleware," would significantly improve the productivity of care providers using computers and eliminate a wide range of errors.

Seliger's middleware initiative had, until now, gathered little attention from top HP management. The fact that archrivals were participating in CCOW, however, gave his work greater visibility, and he was given a staff of programmers to get the job done.

Taking the lead within the consortium, the HP team developed an application programming interface (API) that any vendor could use to enable caregivers to sign on only once in order to use any application they are allowed to use. They also began work on a second set of software that would allow different systems to synchronize on a patient across different applications. By the end of 1997, Seliger's team had created the first version a software toolkit that offered the promise of being an industry-wide platform.

What to Do with the New Technology?

For Seliger, success bred both more success, and then new challenges.

The HP Medical Products Groups was always one of the major exhibitors at medical device and information systems tradeshows. As word spread about CCOW and HP's implementation of it emerging standards into a working toolkit, competitors quickly began to seek him out at trade shows, asking if they could license HP's new software to enable their own applications.

HP management took notice, and in early spring 1998 asked Seliger to continue his work in Andover *and* take over R&D responsibility for managing the software development of all of Medical Products Group, which had recently been combined into a single business unit. Now, with the top R&D job in the business unit, as well as increasing demand for his new software toolkit, things appeared to be looking up. Nevertheless, there were so many pressing priorities that transforming MPG's clinical information products into a suite of interoperable solutions continued to be elusive.

Seliger was getting increasingly concerned. He was the top R&D person in the Clinical Information Systems Business Unit and he had never been more on top of his game in terms of architecting software and leading people to build it. Still, he wondered if there was a different way to ignite the interoperability opportunity, especially in the form of clinical context management. During a quiet, reflective moment following a weekend of hiking with his family, he contemplated this challenge—and had an epiphany: maybe the new technology needed a new company to fully develop it and bring it to market. Perhaps he should start his own company! "Once that idea infected me," Seliger recalls, "I had trouble concentrating on anything else."

On Monday morning, he called The Professor. Seliger's friend had been a cofounder of a venture capital backed software company several years earlier and been involved in other start-ups. Seliger asked, "Do you think it's really possible to start a company to do this type of thing? Could we spin the technology out of HP and build it in a separate company?"

Over the next 30 minutes, The Professor fanned the flames, describing how other software entrepreneurs had created corporate spin-offs with the blessing of their former employers. He described what had to be done and ways of doing it. He talked to the software engineer about product strategy, writing a business plan, developing realistic projections of revenue and startup expenses, and the level of financing that might be necessary. He sent his friend various planning templates and financial boilerplates. "But one of the first things you have to do, Rob," the Professor said, "is have a heart to heart with your boss, Cynthia. You need to sell her on your vision for the technology."

Cynthia Danaher was the senior executive of the Medical Product Group. Cynthia had risen quickly to become the head of marketing for the company's industry leading ultrasound system division, and then, its General Manager. She had exceptional insight into HP as a company and the Medical Products Group's role within it. She had been a strong supporter of developing the CCOW standard, but knew the company well enough to know that HP corporate had a limited appetite for Seliger's type of project—at least at that time. In fact, corporate was probably in the process of spinning out its entire sensor and industrial systems businesses (which became Agilent), although this was certainly not known to Seliger at the time. The Medical Products Group would be packaged into that new business. Given that the Group's patient monitors, ultrasound machines, and clinical information systems were so different than industrial systems, it was only a matter of time before decision-makers in what would become Agilent would also seek a buyer for the Medical Products Group.[2]

When Seliger spoke to her about spinning out the CCOW technology into a new venture, Danaher quickly agreed. To her, the idea made sense because it would be good for HP, as the technology would help HP address the interoperability requirements that the market was increasingly demanding. And to Seliger's surprise, she offered to get HP Board approval for it and introduce Seliger to her friends in the venture capital industry. Seliger even wondered if seed funding for the venture might come in the form of licensing payments from HP to use the initial software products from the venture for its own "next generation" clinical information systems.

High Anxiety

Word of the possible spin-out quickly leaked out within the Medical Products Group. Some of Seliger's peers resented the idea of HP's technology working to his personal advantage and went out of their ways to create stumbling blocks. One individual even circulated misinformation about an outsider's interest in purchasing the technology from HP—which would have left Seliger high and dry! None of the rumors were true, but the turmoil they caused left Seliger anxious and somewhat disoriented. The idea of leaving HP was also disconcerting.

---

[2]Phillips acquired the Group a few years later.

I had only had one job interview in my entire career—with HP. I'd been with the company at that point for 18 years. It had been my whole world. I was well-known within the company and had access to people and resources. I knew nothing about the world outside of HP, and even less about starting a company or about venture financing. And here I was about to take this huge leap.

During the period when the spin out was being negotiated (May through November 1998), Seliger experienced a level of anxiety he'd never felt before. "I'd wake up in the morning with shortness of breath—hyperventilating. I'd tell my wife that I couldn't get out of bed and go to work." Seliger had climbed every rung on the technical career ladder within HP Medical and had a big, talented team working for him. He was earning a very good income and had a company car and stock options.

All that was about to go away because of my crazy idea. I'd ask my wife, 'What will I do if this doesn't work out?' and she'd tell me 'Don't worry—you can get another job.' But I didn't want another job. I liked working at HP.

It wasn't until several months into this period that he realized that leaving HP wasn't the source of his anxiety—it was the fear of his spin-out plan falling through and *not* getting to create this company. "I was so excited about the idea and fixated on starting the company that every rumor and stumbling block triggered anxiety. Once I recognized that, my anxiety evaporated, and I never looked back."

Writing the Business Plan

Seliger called his friend The Professor, inquiring about the form and structure of a business plan. They reviewed some templates and Seliger went to work. With coaching from his friends and advisors, Seliger wrote the plan over the course of a month. A dozen improved iterations would follow over the next six months as the entrepreneur sharpened his strategy and secured funding

The first question that Seliger confronted was "What products am I going to sell?" The CCOW software he had developed in HP was a toolkit to implement the CCOW standard. As good as this new "platform" was technically, Seliger was skeptical that his new company could produce substantial revenue by selling a software toolkit kit to other medical software companies. "People don't buy platforms; they buy solutions. Good solutions, however, need to be built on strong platforms," he remarked. "We had the platform, but now we needed to create solutions that could be sold as products."

He focused on an initial product for end-users and on a software developer's kit (SDK) for software developers. The initial end-user product, *Vergence,* provided a single sign-on product that would allow care providers to sign-on just once, and be securely logged onto all the applications to which they were entitled. Vergence also provided patient context sharing, so that a user need only select the patient of interest once in order for every open application to "tune" to and display that patient's data. The software toolkit was comprised on a set of reusable components and an API that other medical software developers would use to simply if the process of "CCOW enabling" their applications for single sign-on and patient context management.

Armed with this basic product strategy, Seliger turned his attention to building a projection of revenue over the first three years that he could defend with confidence. Countless hours were spent in discussion with his advisors on the assumptions behind the revenue projections. These included:

- The number of hospitals buying these software products over the first five years
- The number of users in each hospital

- The price per user per year for the various software products
- The number or medical software companies buying the SDK a year, and what if anything, he should charge them for it

Given the pressing need among healthcare providers for this capability and strong interest by the dozens of companies who had attended the CCOW meetings, Seliger felt confident in the following assumptions:

- A dozen hospitals would adopt the single sign-on product during the first year of its release, with several dozen following in the year after.

- There were over 5,000 hospitals in the United States alone. The new venture's primary target market would be large healthcare providers that had, on average, approximately 1,000 physicians and 4,000 nursing and related support staff. Also, certain key accounts represented dozens and dozens of facilities in different geographic locations, the Veterans Administration and Kaiser Permente being two prime examples. Getting those accounts would anchor Seliger's position in the medical IT market.

- Seliger knew that pricing was a great challenge for new products. However, he had now spent several years talking to hospital administrators, doctors, and nursing staff. Hospitals were already buying identity management products from vendors such as RSA on a per user license model. And many were spending millions on enterprise software for electronic medical records and clinical information systems. Based on all this, Seliger felt that he could charge a per user fee for the single sign-on, and an additional fee for the patient context management.

- To seed the market, Seliger also felt early on his new company was probably going to have to give the CCOW software development kit away for just a nominal fee. He also suspected that he would have to allocate his own programming staff to help other medical software companies enable their own applications. This came to be called the "immersion program" in which Seliger's team helped vendors perform "software surgery" on their applications.

Working Toward the Spin-out _____

Once he had a business plan, Seliger began pitching it to venture capitalists, some of whom were acquaintances of Danaher. In this process, he had a phone conversation with Bruce Bauer, a Silicon Valley financier with Newbury Ventures. Bauer had been tipped off by a key HP R&D executive that Seliger was working on something important. This piqued Bauer's interest, as he had wanted to do a deal with HP for a long time. The two agreed to meet at an industry tradeshow at which HP would profile CCOW to the medical technology community.

The two met and got into deep conversation. At the end of it, Bauer gave Seliger some advice: Rob had too many jobs to do. If he wanted to launch a company, he had to make it his only priority. Seliger reflected, "That was the best advice I could have received. Besides being an early investor, Bruce and I became and remain close personal friends."

Two days later he was in Cynthia's office, explaining what Bruce had told him. As he recalls. "She was in total agreement, and to my amazement, gave me the next four months to work on nothing but the spin off." Moreover, Danaher teamed Seliger up with one of her staff who was experienced in structuring agreements with VCs. Her one caveat was that if Seliger couldn't make the deal work—that is, failed to gain external financing—he had to reassume his operating responsibilities as a full time head of R&D.

It took three months, but by November 1998, the HP Board or Directors approved the spin out and agreed to an intellectual property agreement with the venture.

Building a Team

Seliger knew that he had to quickly assemble a skilled and knowledgeable team, a task that proved easier than anticipated. As word of the spin-out leaked, he was approached by a senior product manager for one of the large medical device divisions, John Douglass. Douglass came up to Seliger in the cafeteria line and said a bit too loudly, "Tell me all about this!" Seliger quickly shuttled Douglass off to a vacant section of the cafeteria where he could talk about the project without being overheard. Douglass listened and liked what he heard. He joined as co-founder, and later took a lead role in defining and launching the company's first wave of products.[3]

Staff on the technical side of the business was also needed. Once the HP Board approved the spin-out in November, things could be out in the open. A standard exit agreement restricted Seliger from soliciting HP personnel for the new business. However, MPG was considering a downsizing due to challenging business conditions. To his surprise, the Group's HR manager presented Seliger with a list of people he could hire without violating the "non-solicit" agreement. "I couldn't believe the names I saw on that list—these were some of the very best," he said later. Several people were hired directly from that list, and others later joined on their own volition, including a brilliant software engineer from Germany—Ralf—who later became Seliger's head of R&D in the new company and led many of its most important projects. When the spin-out became a live company, in March 1999, Seliger had a total staff of ten employees, six of whom were former HP colleagues.

Series A Funding, Key Milestones, and Important Decisions!

Bauer became the lead investor and brought along two other VC firms in a syndicated Series A financing. The $2.7 million round closed in March 1999, almost a year to the day after Seliger had returned from his fateful hiking trip. (Subsequent B and C rounds are also provided in Exhibit 1.) His exit from HP was a *fait accompli*. In February, after considering many potential names, Seliger decided to call his new company Sentillion. The name satisfied Seliger's desire for a "cool" and unique name for which the Web domain name was also available.

With help from Bauer and other investors, he and John Douglass had to establish key milestones for:

- R&D, including the beta test and first commercial release for the Vergence, the single sign-on service
- A program to get third-party software companies to incorporate Vergence into their own software according to the CCOW standard
- First key hospital accounts
- Intellectual property, including a patent and clarity on ownership of the IP relative to HP
- Key hires for major functions inside the new company

Driving all this planning was the question of the ongoing relationship to be formed with HP now that startup funding was secure. Should HP own Sentillion stock? What would that mean for Sentillion's position as the "Switzerland" in the industry? How else might HP gain from Sentillion's success? Seliger knew that this question was the elephant in the room.

---

[3]Douglass left the company in 2003 to sail around the world with his wife and two children.

The race was on. The team needed to achieve these goals in order to raise the next round of financing. Bauer and other advisors thought two to three times the Series A financing should get the company to operating profitability.

Questions _____

1. What is a corporate spin-out?

2. How should Seliger try to structure the deal with Hewlett Packard, including the handling of equity and intellectual property?

3. What is the market opportunity facing Seliger and his team?

4. What is Sentillion's core IP and what types of products do you see based on that IP?

5. What should be Seliger's key milestones with the Series A funding?

Series A:	March	1999	$2.7 million
Series B:	March	2000	$9 million
Series C:	August	2001	$18 million

Exhibit 1 Sentillion's Equity Financing

The Applications

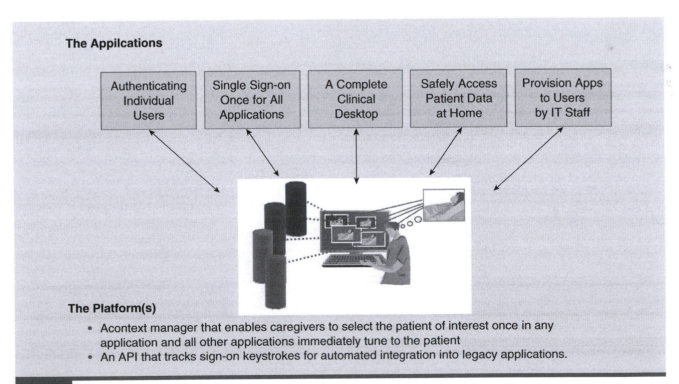

| Authenticating Individual Users | Single Sign-on Once for All Applications | A Complete Clinical Desktop | Safely Access Patient Data at Home | Provision Apps to Users by IT Staff |

The Platform(s)

- A context manager that enables caregivers to select the patient of interest once in any application and all other applications immediately tune to the patient
- An API that tracks sign-on keystrokes for automated integration into legacy applications.

Exhibit 2 Developing a Product Strategy Focused on Major Use Cases

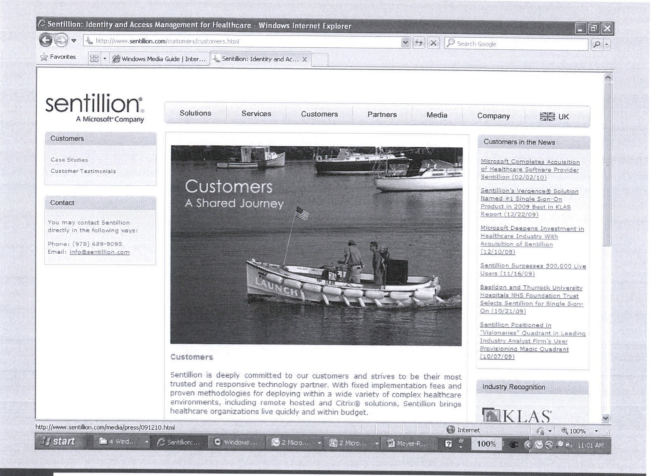

Exhibit 3 Sentillion's Website 12 Years After Startup

mInfo

SHANGHAI, CHINA. SEPTEMBER, 2010. CEO Alvin Huang Graylin and CTO Derrick had come a long way in a very short time. From the launch of their mobile Internet search company in early 2005 until now, they had built a company of 100 employees with a user base of tens of millions of mobile subscribers. And the company's performance had reached cash flow breakeven since Q4 of 2009. This had not been easy. Though born in China, Graylin had been raised and educated in the United States; thus, he had to learn the ins and outs of Chinese business culture, and was generally perceived as a foreigner by regulators and telecom company clients. Threading a course through government officialdom had also been a challenge. Entrepreneurs in the Peoples Republic of China—both foreign and domestic— had to master an opaque regulatory system and patiently build relationships with bureaucrats.

China was very different than the hi-tech entrepreneurial environment in which Graylin had forged his career. He had spent five years after graduate school helping Intel in its Shanghai Office, doing business development in the PC industry. Now, with five years of mInfo under his belt, with mInfo, and the help of his Chinese co-founder, he had learned how to get things done.

The Company and its Service _____

mInfo was initially founded as an SMS mobile (text messaging) search service. Within six months, and after using their own savings, the two founders had developed a working proto- type. With the backing of US and domestic investment capital[1], the company was soon able to address the search needs of the large and growing Chinese market of mobile Internet users, and had become that country's leading English and Chinese language mobile search service. mInfo was also China's only "natural language"[2] search provider. "We've only raised about $6 million in financing," says the CEO, "but here in China, where operating costs are much lower, that kind of money can take you a long way."

For Graylin and CTO Huang, mobile Internet computing represented the next big wave in an industry cycle that began with mainframe computing in the 1950s (Figure 1). Mobile Internet technology made it possible for people to use "smartphones" such as the iPhone and Droid to send and receive email, access the Web, and conduct online searches for news, weather, phone numbers and addresses, restaurant reviews, and other information. Because smart- phone screens were small and their bandwidths are narrower than those of desktop and lap- tops machines, mobile online searches were limited in the volume of information they could

---

[1]From its inception through mid-2010, mInfo raised $6 million in capital through a seed round and two A financing rounds. Roughly 70% of that capital had come from US investors, with bal- ance put forward by Chinese financiers.

[2]Natural language processing refers to the interaction of computers and human, or natural, languages.

deliver. These constraints represented challenges to search service companies such as mInfo. Since these companies cannot deliver page after page of search results, they must assure that the results they provide to subscribers are on target and the best available. "It has to be fast, and it has to be right," said founder Graylin.

mInfo's initial technology strategy was to provide mobile SMS. Over time, that strategy migrated to mobile search on the Internet, and then to a hybrid "automatic/operator" model. The latter delivered some 90% of search responses automatically; the remaining hard-to-find subscriber queries were addressed through a combination of search engines and human operators. This use of human operators raised the cost to mInfo, but it assured higher quality service to subscribers.

China's mobile telecom market was the world's largest. Dominated by China Mobile, China Unicom and China Telecom, it had grown from 400 million subscribers in 2004 to over 800 million in the U.S. 2010. In contrast, the number of mobile subscribers in 2010 was only about 270 million.[3] Subscribership in China was forecasted to continue at a rate of more than 7 million *per month* over the next several years. The rate of penetration of this technology (though less than half the penetration rate of the US) had far surpassed those of fixed-line telephone and PC-based Internet communication (see Figure 2).

Not all telecom subscribers, however, owned devices capable of mobile Internet search. Smartphones (3G +) were more costly in China than in the West, often running to $500–700— easily twice the monthly salary of a worker in China's urban commercial centers. Consequently, only 15% to 20% of mobile phone users subscribed in 2010 to Internet services. Rising incomes and the relative decline in smartphone costs, however, were likely to increase that percentage. With China's GDP growing at 8% to 10% per year, rising household incomes and buying power would increase demand for smartphones—a highly prized personal luxury item in China's modern cities and a symbol of personal success. And the number of mobile Internet searches would escalate in step. One industry analysis forecasted 52% compound annual growth in the number of those searches between 2007 and 2012.

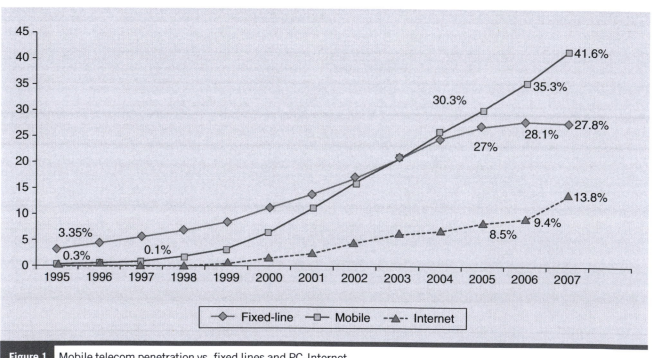

Figure 1 Mobile telecom penetration vs. fixed lines and PC-Internet

Source: Information from the Ministry of Information Industries, the People's Republic of China.

---

[3]World Bank, "World Development Indicators," updated 27 July 2010.

WHAT ARE MOBILE INTERNET USERS SEARCHING FOR?

According to the company, in 2010, 65% of mobile subscribers searched for news, 59% use it to "chat", 42% read novels on their mobile devices, and 39% searched community forums for information. Others searched for stock prices, directions, phone numbers, weather forecasts, and so forth.

Business Model

By 2010, mInfo had successfully negotiated service contracts with several telecom companies, including the country's two giants: China Telecom and China Mobile. During the Beijing Olympics, it won the contract to be the Games' official search provider.

Under the terms of its agreement with provider clients, mInfo received a fixed annual fee plus incremental revenues once the number of subscriber searches exceeded a particular annual level. The company also generated revenues by placing ads on its pages. It has agreements with many ad companies. As of 2010, Graylin believed that it has only scratched the surface of this potentially huge revenue source. Much more was anticipated as 3G mobile technology and broader bandwidth continued to gain a broader foothold in the Chinese market.

An Entrepreneurial Journey

Graylin was born in China in 1971. His Chinese father was a Western art professor of over 20 years at the Guangdong Art Academy; his mother—half Chinese and half American—was a dancer with the BJ ballet troop who had studied for a time in the United States. Eager to give Alvin and his siblings an opportunity to experience life in the West, the parents moved their family in 1980 to Seattle, Washington. They were among the first Chinese families to do so as their homeland emerged from decades of isolation.

The move to Seattle was economically difficult. "My parents came to the US with only $500 in their pockets," Graylin recalled. "My father couldn't find work in his field immediately and had to take two jobs painting ad signs and whatever else he could find. My brothers and I were expected to help the family by taking odd jobs after school."

After completing high school, Graylin attended the University of Washington, where he majored in electrical engineering. Midway through that program, he took a nine-month internship with IBM in Minnesota. Inspired by that first taste of real-world technology development, he returned to Seattle and finished his degree, graduating at the top of his class.

During those final years at UW, Graylin and four classmates launched and ran an enterprise that provided systems integration and custom programming to local educational institutions and small businesses. At its peak, the venture generated about $500,000 per year, half of which was profit.

Intel

Upon graduation in 1993, Graylin took a chip design and system architecture job with Intel, which would employ him in many capacities over the next seven years. One of his early assignments (1994) took him to Shanghai, where he and two other US expats set up a new office and he led a team of 25 employees focused on growing the Chinese consumer PC business. Its goal was to develop and bundle hardware and software, and find a business model that would break through the then-sluggish pace of Home PC adoption in China. This was a large order for a 23-year old with limited experience, but Graylin rose to the challenge. As he recalled, "It gave me a chance to hone my management skills, and it kindled my interest in business." Within three years, his Shanghai unit was able to reduce the retail price of consumer PCs from roughly $2,000 to a more affordable $600. This greatly expanded the sales of PCs to consumers in China, many of which had "Intel Inside."

MIT and iCompass

His assignment completed in 1997, Graylin rotated back to the US, and to life in the corridors of Intel. The pay was good, and he enjoyed being back where he would spend more time with his relatives and friends. But missing the independence and responsibility he had enjoyed in Shanghai, he began looking for another situation. He found it at MIT in 1998, where, with Intel's support, he enrolled in a dual masters degree program in business management and computer science, in the University's renowned "Leaders in Manufacturing" program.[4]

While at MIT, Graylin entered two business plan competitions with a team of classmates. One of them was for an Internet marketing analytics company called iCompass. The company's proprietary technology was capable of discerning the search patterns and profitability potential of online shoppers—something that direct and online retailers were eager to know.

The iCompass concept and technology attracted attention from both investors and potential customers, enough so that Graylin and his colleague were able to raise $1 million in a first round of financing. Shortly thereafter, however, in March 2000, the "dot-com" bubble burst, share prices fell off a cliff, and investor interest in technology companies evaporated. Like many comparable start-ups, iCompass folded in 2001. But for Graylin, "Getting customers, raising money, and hiring a team had been a great learning experience," which he would carry forward to subsequent ventures.

Back to China

Between 2001 and late 2004, Graylin worked for two security software companies, the first in Taiwan, the second in the United States. In each case he was given business unit responsibility and opportunities to deal with people in North America, Europe, and Asia.

Frustrated by the internal politics of the last of these firms ("We had three CEOs in one year"), Graylin was ready for self-employment. So, in late 2004, he quit his job and spent the next several months looking for a promising new opportunity. Among his first contacts was Derek Huang, a Chinese electrical engineer he had hired years earlier, during his days with Intel in Shanghai. Huang was familiar with the mobile messaging business in China and shared Graylin's entrepreneurial spirit. Huang had been the CTO of two VC funded startups after leaving Intel in 1999. After a lunch meeting discussing opportunities, the two identified a potential opportunity that was still unfilled in China. Mobile Search. Graylin had been working on search-related projects with a VC firm since leaving his last job and Huang was an expert in mobile technologies and had access to a qualified technical team in Shanghai. On the next day, they both wrote emails to each other, saying there could be a billion-dollar market for this space long term. Working together, they planned and launched mInfo in mid-2005.

Graylin's initial investments came from wireless/tech industry angels in the Seattle area and they provided a lot of support and advice for getting the project off the ground. Graylin was also able to recruit former WA governor, Gary Locke, to serve on his board for over three years until he was picked by President Obama to be the US Commerce Secretary. Locke was viewed as a rock star in China, being the highest ranking Chinese American in the US government at that time. He helped open many doors during his term with mInfo.

Graylin's earlier experience in mainland China had been useful, but much had changed in that country over the past decade. Besides the usual startup challenges of business development and connecting with customers, he and his partner had to overcome difficulties in several other important areas: special if not unique to the Chinese business and consumer environment.

Human Resources

By the mid-2000s, China's blistering GDP growth (typically 9% to 10% per year) had created wage inflation, particularly at mid- and upper-levels of the technology and managerial labor markets. Further, demand for individuals with proven skills had grown so strong that that

---

[4]Later named the "MIT Leaders for Global Operations."

recruiting and retention were very difficult. Many talented employees could pull up stakes one week and begin work with a competitor the next—often at a higher salary.[5]

Graylin and Huang had to cope with this situation as they began recruiting programmers in 2005–2007. As Graylin recounted later, "Hiring was and remains one of our most difficult issues." He discovered that only a minority of experienced technical people in China were attracted to small, unknown entities, and very few had entrepreneurial experience. In general, both seasoned and newly minted engineers and programmers preferred employment at large, stable, "brand name" firms. Many experienced people were working for state-owned companies; Graylin found most of these skilled workers unsuited by temperament and work ethic to the requirements of a startup entrepreneurial firm.

In the end, the two entrepreneurs found that the most productive approach to their human talent needs was to recruit directly from the best technical universities. New people were brought on as interns, giving the company an opportunity to assess their abilities and work ethics as a prelude for formal employment. Graylin explained his HR strategy further: "We provided a combination of industry average cash compensation, stocks and generous social/welfare benefits. Our cash comp wasn't the best, be we were generous with stock and had many fun activities for the team. Even still, finding and keeping staff was not easy. And most people didn't know the value or potential value of Stock Options."

Graylin continued: "In terms of salary, the cost of low-level employees is very inexpensive. The salaries of mid- and upper-level people are lower than their counterparts in the States, but not dramatically lower."

The mobility of technical workers was a large concern for Graylin and Huang because it jeopardized mInfo's emerging intellectual property. This was in a computing culture where, at the time, the majority of software used on desktops was unlicensed or pirated. mInfo decided to take specific steps to assure that no individual employee had access to the entire code base. Huang designed and controlled the architecture and then assigned specific teams to program certain pieces. Only a small and highly trusted team under Huang's direct supervision assembled these components for the final build and test.

Government Bureaucracy

Regulators presented another hurdle for the founders. mInfo needed a special telecommunications operations license. To obtain that license, Graylin had to have a specified level of capital in the bank. And as a company with foreign backers, mInfo needed a three-tier structure: it had to be under the umbrella of a foreign holding company; it had to register as a wholly owned foreign entity; and it had to give evidence that it had contractual relationships with local Chinese partners. The company's US legal counsel handled these details, setting up the holding company in the Cayman Islands at a cost of roughly $50,000. The lawyers deferred payment of that bill until such time as the company had completed its first financing round.

To meet the capital requirements of the law, Graylin and Huang borrowed the requisite amount of money and put it in their company bank account.

Adherence to regulatory requirements was the easy part. Getting approvals from an inscrutable bureaucracy was another matter. In contrast to the US, where licenses and other approvals can often be obtained in straightforward ways, often online, Chinese regulators must be appealed to with personal visits and, in many cases, gifts.

As a Westerner, Graylin found these requirements both frustrating and time consuming. "Sometimes an official would make us wait four hours or more for a five-minute meeting. In other cases, scheduled meetings would be canceled at the last minute for no apparent reason. They'd say, 'Sorry. Reschedule next month.'" Many officials did not return phone calls. Patience and persistence were the entrepreneur's only recourse in dealing with this system.

He also discovered the importance of gifts. Gift giving is part of Chinese culture and extends into the world of government. The tradition is to bring a gift when visiting an official. "And

---

[5]The Economist Intelligence Unit/Mercer HR Consulting, 2009.

during holiday periods, the expectation is that gifts will be more valuable—for example, you might bring a $700 smartphone as a gift." Graylin also noted that officials where much more open to visits during holiday periods, when the expectation of a fine gift was highest.

Contracts

In the West, any contract that does not violate the law or public policy is enforceable in court. In China, contracts are less than "iron clad."

mInfo successfully negotiated contracts with several mobile telecom providers and advertisers—and it depended on those contracts for its success. In several cases, however, and mid-way through the life of their contracts, customers would ask to renegotiate contract terms. "They'd figure," says Graylin, "Well, those guys [at mInfo] are making lots of money. Let's cut them back'." mInfo had very little power to oppose these requests from valued customers. In the end, mutual self-interest, and not the language of contracts, ruled.

Interpersonal Protocols

Graylin also discovered the importance of properly matching hierarchical "levels" when conducting business with customers, suppliers, and regulators. In contrast to the informal and egalitarian culture of the US, Chinese culture expected that CEOs meet with CEOs, that mInfo sales representatives meet with mid-level customer officials, and so forth. Mismatching levels during sales calls and negotiations were deemed breaches of protocol.

RELATIONSHIPS COME FIRST

It's often said that "relationships" are an essential part of business life in China—and in Asia in general. Research by Edward Hall and Mildred Hall[6] has identified "low- and high-context" cultures. In the former (e.g., northern European countries and North American), business people like to get right to the point with little ceremony and a minimum of perfunctory small talk. In contrast, business in high-context cultures (which include Korea, Japan, China, and Arab countries) is preceded by more extensive formalities and relationship building. For example, a prospective Asian customer will ask to know about the visitor's company and about the visitor's personal background. A luncheon or dinner may be a necessary prelude to any substantive discussions. According to Hall, these preliminaries may take substantial time, but time is less important to people in high-context cultures. For low-context Westerners, who are eager to get down to business, the value of these formalities and relationship-building activities are not always appreciated.

[6]Edward T. Hall, *Silent Language* (Garden City, NY: Doubleday, 1959) and Edward T. Hall and Mildred R. Hall, *Hidden Differences: Doing Business with the Japanese* (Garden City, NY: Doubleday, 1987).

Discussion Questions _____

1. Alvin Wang Graylin is a highly skilled and energetic businessperson, with experience in many parts of the world. Why do you think he was so attracted to China?

2. Put yourself in Graylin's shoes as he began his venture in Shanghai. As you organize and develop your business, what would you describe as "different" from the US or other non-Chinese environment? What would be the same?

3. If you found an irresistible high-tech venture prospect in China tomorrow, what preparations would you make for handling that country's unique labor market and its business and regulatory cultures?

4. What are the lessons learned by this entrepreneur operating in a foreign country?

Evergreen Memories

A Green Business With a Greater Purpose

Introduction _____

Margot Woodworth sat in her office overlooking a beautiful lake and surrounding forests in Northwest Ontario. Her small company had achieved success in Canada creating and delivering Earth-friendly favors and gifts directly to consumers. Now she had achieved the size and credibility as a business to expand into the United States—a much larger market. Margot had a real passion for the planet and had brought this forward into her business, making her products and services special in the eyes of her customers.

She had two burning questions as she considered scaling up the business. The first was personal: Would she be able to preserve the nature and integrity of her social venture as it grew larger? The second was strategic: What should be the focus of her market expansion? There were three clear opportunities based on her current business and some preliminary market research she had done over the past month: (a) wedding favors for environmentally sensitive couples, (b) "green gifts" for the corporate market, and (c) "thank you" items for fund-raising campaigns for environmentally focused nonprofits. Should she pick just one of these niches to launch into the United States, or try all at once? And what would be a good way to test each idea before committing a lot of money for further expansion? All told, she had only $50,000 in hard-earned cash to launch her U.S. expansion campaign.

Background _____

The original business, or forerunner to Evergreen Memories, was called Tamarac Nursery. The company had a single-minded focus: to grow tree seedlings for reforestation purposes only. However, this market was basically commodity based, where price was often the key determinant for the customer. Moreover, demand for forestry seedlings was also declining. It doesn't take a genius to figure out that under these conditions this company's future was likely to be truncated. So the company set out to determine how to sustain and grow the business. A review of other possible markets for its existing product resulted in some possible options. After much discussion, the idea of entering the "wedding favor" market emerged. However, the wedding favor market would be a big change for the company. It would be a business-to-consumer (B2C) play and not the current business-to-business (B2B) play, which was the original focus of the business. But the company decided to give it a try. With very little marketing and promotion of this new idea, the company had three requests from "brides to be" for tree seedlings that could be given out as favors to their wedding guests.

In addition to limited marketing and promotion, the company was also not well prepared to execute in this new market. The presentation of the wedding favors, according to the company, was not well executed in the beginning. So the company began to experiment with how best to prepare and present the wedding favors. The company also began to further study the wedding favor market and began experimenting with different decorating techniques. One day the company experienced an "Aha!" moment. It sent some personnel to attend a major wedding show in Toronto, Canada. There the company finally found some insight into its competitive set of offerings and how those offerings were being presented and merchandised. The company also made contact with personnel from several wedding magazines. These contacts provided some insightful assistance and encouraged the company to advertise its new wedding favor offerings in their magazines. Within a few months orders began pouring in. At the same time, the company made continual improvements in its product presentations. It also began listening to customers' feedback in order to make further refinements.

The New Concept, the New Vision, the New Mission

Tamarac Nursery was evolving from a commodity-based business to a new value-added enterprise. Enter the new owner of Tamarac Nursery, Margot Woodworth. She would be the perfect fit for the company's new focus. Margot was always very conscious of the importance of preserving and protecting the natural environment. That love and respect for nature was something that was ingrained in her growing up in her native Germany, which had been a leader in promoting green behavior for many years. Yet when Margot arrived in Canada 20 years ago, the emphasis on "green" was in its infant stage. In contrast to Germany, Canada appeared to be a "throw-away culture" to the detriment of the natural environment. Margot believed that every product came from the Earth and would inevitably return to it in one form or another. Her hope was that Canadians would soon realize the importance of preserving the planet for future generations.

So, with her nursery background, Margot began the task of really building this green business. She knew, for example, that billions of dollars annually were being spent on weddings in North America. Margot believed some of those expenditures could be turned into ones that would support a green business—a business committed to the environment and to social responsibility. Margot believed that the company's new Earth-friendly wedding favors (the tree seedlings) focus was a good one. But she also felt the company needed a broader product portfolio. So she began to design seed packages for an alternative favor to give during the winter months and also developed other green options suited for giving on every occasion. She undertook the design of a professional Website that would enable the company to accept customer orders from all across North America. And, importantly, she believed that the company needed a new brand name, one more consistent with its new focus. She renamed it Evergreen Memories.

Business Growth

Margot was extremely passionate about and committed to her new business. She considered her green favors "gifts of oxygen," since trees clean our air as well as fight global warming and prevent soil erosion. Margot believed that by the time her customers celebrated their silver wedding anniversaries, their wedding guests would have nurtured small forests that both beautified and protected the planet. In addition to her tree seedling product line, Margot included her packaged seed line for special occasions. She also discovered that many large eco-friendly companies were interested in using "green favors" as part of their promotional efforts. So she decided to embark on a marketing effort to gain some customers in this corporate space, a B2B play.

Margot also believed that entrepreneurs had an obligation to be good citizens and to give back to their communities. Therefore, Evergreen Memories became a sponsor of school projects, as well as other charity and fund-raising events. Margot said that starting and growing a successful business was very similar to growing a tree from seeds: Both endeavors required much care and nurturing. She saw her business success as inextricably linked to her love and passion for nature and the planet. Ultimately, she demonstrated in a very tangible way that a green business could be a success, both in terms of profitability and in preservation of the planet.

Under her stewardship, the company doubled its sales in its first year. Since then, sales had increased 30% per year. These results were impressive considering the business only operated six months a year, from April through October.

Now 60% of total sales came from tree seedlings/seed favors sold as wedding favors. The other 35% were derived from corporate sales to companies such as Xerox, Honda, Jamieson Vitamins, Bell Canada, and TD Bank, which provided "green gifts" to their clients. The remaining 5% came from school districts where tree seedlings were sold as part of school fund-raisers.

The company also saw major growth potential in the United States. Now about 30% of total sales were derived from U.S.-based customers. Margot believed the wedding favor market in the United States was ten times bigger than in Canada. There were over two million weddings per year in the United States. The average cost of a wedding was close to $20,000, making the market size over $40 billion. The average wedding size was about 100 guests. Margot roughly calculated that the average expenditure per wedding favor per wedding guest was five dollars. Thus, she figured that the wedding favor market in the United States was approximately $1 billion.

As part of her plan for U.S. expansion, Margot planned to advertise online as well in bridal magazines in the United States. She planned to attend both wedding trade shows and corporate trade shows. She purchased the Web domain name evergreenmemories.com to complement her evergreenmemories.ca Website. And she discovered that some gift-giving occasions in the United States were much different and much bigger than in Canada. For example, she felt that there was a major opportunity to market green gifts during the U.S. Thanksgiving holiday—something that did not exist in Canada.

Enter *Dragon's Den*

The company underwent a further transformation when Margot entered the *Dragon's Den* competition in 2011. *Dragon's Den* was a Canadian television show that featured entrepreneurs meeting with potential investors in the hopes of securing venture financing for their enterprises. Margot actually won the competition and received angel financing. A well-known Canadian entrepreneur and investor, Jim Treliving (owner of Boston Pizza International), provided equity financing to Evergreen Memories in return for a 20% stake in the company. In addition, Margot's exposure on *Dragon's Den* led to a 50% sales growth increase! Margot remarked, "Each time the episode runs and re-runs on television, sales spike." She added, "It would have cost $500,000 in national advertising dollars to get the exposure we gained from just being on one episode of *Dragon's Den*. Entrepreneurs have to take advantage of such opportunities."

While the company focused on the wedding favors market in Canada and the United States, another unexpected opportunity emerged as a result of *Dragon's Den*. Shortly after Margot won the *Dragon's Den* competition she was contacted by Bob Graham, of Northbrook Sports, who asked Margot to partner with him in his various community fund-raising and marketing programs. The interesting twist was that Bob, who had extensive NCAA university soccer connections, wanted to partner with Evergreen Memories to sell its tree seedlings as part of fund-raising activities for university soccer programs in the United States. This would provide Margot with another entry point into the lucrative U.S. market beyond the wedding favors segment. And perhaps the selling of tree seedlings as part of fund-raising efforts would open up an additional revenue stream for the company in the United States. She knew the company needed to find customers and new uses for her products. She found some research to indicate that there were more than 1.5 million nonprofit organizations in the United States that attempted to raise funds for their organizations every year, and that overall this market was estimated at $100 billion. She thought that this market was 100 times larger than the wedding favor market (see above, where she valued the wedding favor market at $1 billion). Typical examples of nonprofits involved in this space included educational, healthcare, religious, human rights, wildlife, environmental, alumni, and fraternal organizations. Moreover, this endeavor would be consistent with her social responsibility commitment—in other words, creating win-win situations where Evergreen Memories won but so did its partners and customers.

Another unique opportunity emerged for Margot and Evergreen Memories as a result of the *Dragon's Den:* She was asked to be a partner in the "Tree of Hope Campaign" with the Unity of Hope Foundation. The goal of this campaign was to sell ten million trees over the next ten years to raise money for children in need in Canada. In this case, this program would provide funds for college education for needy children. This endeavor would help scale up Evergreen Memories in terms of its production and its outreach.

Questions

1. What does the evolution of Tamarac Nursery to Evergreen Memories tell you about the entrepreneurial journey?

2. What other opportunities do you see for Evergreen Memories in terms of sustaining the growth of its enterprise? Be specific. In Canada, what market segments and product offerings do you recommend? Why?

3. What advice can you offer Margot as she makes her move to expand into the United States from her home-base in Ontario, Canada? For example, should she focus on the wedding favors market? The corporate green gifts market? Or the fund-raising for nonprofits market? Why?

4. What do you think of Margot's approach for calculating the market size for wedding favors in the United States?

Index

About the Authors

Marc H. Meyer is Robert J. Shillman Professor of Entrepreneurship at Northeastern University as well as a Matthews Distinguished University Professor. Northeastern is a leading Cooperative Education academic institution where student work experience is closely integrated with academic programs. Dr. Meyer is the founder of Northeastern's Entrepreneurship and Innovation Group in the D'Amore-McKim School of Business, where he has helped numerous students and alumni start their own companies. In addition, Dr. Meyer currently leads Northeastern's executive education programs in innovation and corporate venturing. In 2012, he was named a director of Northeastern's Center of Entrepreneurship Education, an interdisciplinary, experiential "system of entrepreneurship" to help undergraduates, graduate students, faculty, and alumni launch new ventures.

In research, Dr. Meyer is an internationally recognized scholar in the field of innovation. *The Power of Product Platforms* (written with Alvin P. Lehnerd) continues to be a leading work in the management of architecture for products, systems, and services. *The Fast Path to Corporate Growth: Leveraging Knowledge and Technologies to New Market Applications* provides methods to link innovation with enterprise growth, the focus of Dr. Meyer's work throughout the industry over the past several decades. He is the recipient of the Maurice Holland Award from the Industrial Research Institute for this work.

In this book, Dr. Meyer returns to his roots as a technology entrepreneur. He has been part of the startup teams of companies that include VenturCom (acquired by Citrix), Intervista Software (acquired by Platinum Technology–Computer Associates), Sentillion (acquired by Microsoft), and AcuStream, and is an "angel investor" in a number of startups in New England. He has also helped corporate innovators design next-generation products and launch new businesses across a broad range of industries, including consumer products, industrial equipment, healthcare systems, and new financial products. It is the richness of these diverse work experiences that Dr. Meyer brings to his teaching, research, and mentoring.

Dr. Meyer is a graduate of Harvard College and holds his masters and doctoral degrees from MIT. While a student in his mid-20s, he left MIT for five years to build his first software company before returning to complete his PhD. Having been one himself, Dr. Meyer relishes teaching the next generation of entrepreneurs.

Frederick G. Crane is an Executive Professor of Entrepreneurship and Innovation at the D'Amore-McKim School of Business at Northeastern University and editor of the *Journal of the Academy of Business Education*. He was formerly a professor of marketing and entrepreneurship at the University of New Hampshire and a chair and full professor at Dalhousie University. He currently teaches courses in entrepreneurship, innovation, and entrepreneurial marketing.

Dr. Crane grew up in a family business and also founded and operated several of his own businesses. In addition to being a serial entrepreneur, he has also been an investor in several startups, served on the advisory boards of entrepreneurial firms, and worked as a consultant for angel investors, venture capitalists, and government agencies on venture funding projects. In addition, he has developed and delivered numerous training programs and workshops for entrepreneurs and small-business owners.

His academic research activities have resulted in more than 100 publications, including 11 books, and he currently sits on the editorial boards of several academic journals. His current research stream intersects the domains of marketing, entrepreneurship, corporate venturing, and innovation, and he is conducting ongoing research on the psychology of entrepreneurship, entrepreneurial education, entrepreneurial branding, and innovation readiness. Dr. Crane has received numerous honors for teaching excellence over the past 20 years.

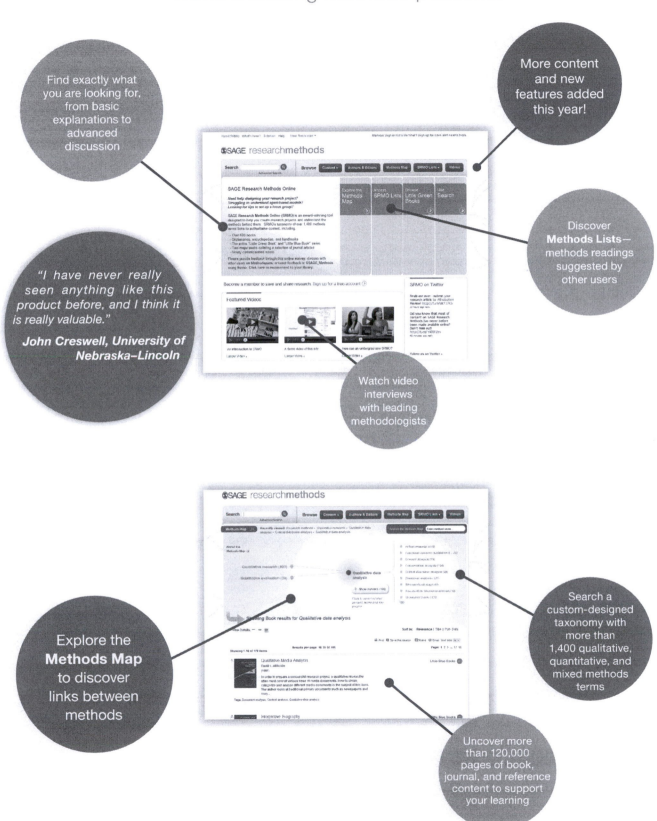

SAGE researchmethods

The essential online tool for researchers from the world's leading methods publisher

Find exactly what you are looking for, from basic explanations to advanced discussion

More content and new features added this year!

"I have never really seen anything like this product before, and I think it is really valuable."

John Creswell, University of Nebraska–Lincoln

Discover **Methods Lists**— methods readings suggested by other users

Watch video interviews with leading methodologists

Explore the **Methods Map** to discover links between methods

Search a custom-designed taxonomy with more than 1,400 qualitative, quantitative, and mixed methods terms

Uncover more than 120,000 pages of book, journal, and reference content to support your learning

Find out more at
www.sageresearchmethods.com

Printed in Poland
by Amazon Fulfillment
Poland Sp. z o.o., Wrocław